Dale Fisher

WASHTENAW COUNTY

Visions of the Eagle

An Eagle's Eye View of Ann Arbor, Chelsea, Dexter, Manchester, Milan, Saline & Ypsilanti

Photography by
DALE FISHER
& JOANNE ACKERMAN

This book is dedicated to
Joanne Ackerman
Doug Fisher
&
Bene Fusilier
Thank you for your constant support with all my endeavors.

Special thank you to the following,
without whom this book would not have been possible:
Joanne Ackerman, Design FX by Joanne, partner
Douglas Fisher, photographer
Heide Otto-communications director, writer, editor
Julia Zaher-writer, editor
Tom Putters-graphic design
Lisa Murphy-graphic design
Alan Bradstreet, Magnum Helicopters
Chuck Blaylock, Magnum Helicopters

Graphic Design: Joanne Ackerman,
Design FX by Joanne

Printed in China
Printed by TOPPAN Leefung Printing
www.kingstimeprinting.com
ISBN: 978-0-9615623-7-3 $65.00 retail

All images in this book are available as framed photographic art, for use in printed materials or on websites. Many open and limited edition photographs from Arizona, Florida, Hawaii, Michigan and New York are also available. Contact the Dale Fisher Galleries for current prices and additional information, or visit www.DaleFisherGalleries.com

Address all inquiries to:
Eyry of the Eagle Publishing
Dale Fisher Galleries
1916 Norvell Road
Grass Lake, Michigan 49240
517-522-3705
DaleFisherPhotography@gmail.com
www.DaleFisherGalleries.com

Other Books by Dale Fisher:
Jackson County: Visions of the Eagle (Published in 2015)
Ann Arbor: Visions of the Eagle III (Published in 2011)
Ann Arbor: Visions of the Eagle II (Published in 2008)
Ann Arbor: Visions of the Eagle (Published in 1995)
Southeast Michigan: Horizons of Growth (Published in 2005)
Building Michigan: A Tribute to the Construction Industry (Published in 2003)
Detroit (Published in 1985)
Michigan: From the Eyry of the Eagle (Published in 1986; out of print)

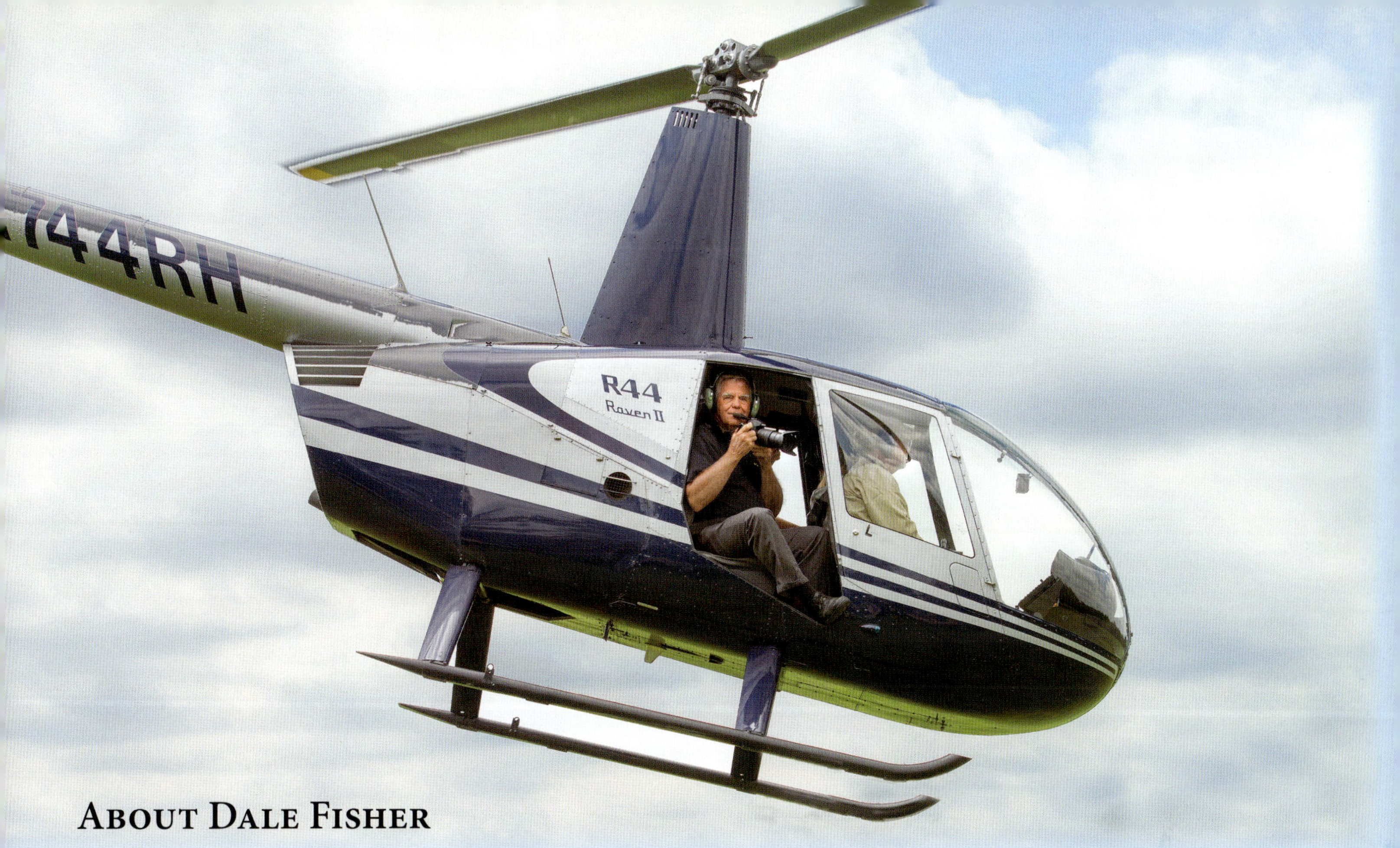

About Dale Fisher

"Flying photographer" Dale Fisher has lived his entire life in Michigan. Born in Ann Arbor in 1933, Fisher found his calling at an early age. He started taking pictures as a youngster in elementary school and continued his training working as a photographer for the school newspaper at Pioneer High School. While in high school, he apprenticed with Master Portrait Photographer, Clifton Dey, and spent weekends photographing weddings.

At 17, Fisher enlisted in the U.S. Navy. During his service during the Korean War, Fisher trained as an aerial reconnaissance photographer. In 1954, after completing his military service, Fisher founded his Dale Fisher HeliPhoto business while also working as a photographer with the Ann Arbor News. Most of his work is done from a helicopter: "Helicopter photography gives a distinctive perspective unmatched by photographs taken from airplanes, drones or on the ground," says Fisher.

Fisher has published more than a dozen books of his work including photographs of Detroit, the State of Michigan, the University of Michigan, Jackson County, Southeast Michigan, as well as New York City, the former World Trade Center twin towers, and the Statue of Liberty. His photographs of the U of M's Michigan Stadium and football, and other athletic events are famous among Wolverines fans.

Fisher relocated to Grass Lake in Jackson County in 1985. His Grass Lake farm is home to galleries of his works, a state-of-the-art digital photography laboratory, and framing center. Also located on the farm is the Michigan's Center for the Photographic Arts, a 501(c)3 non-profit mentorship program for children which Fisher founded.

Pilot, Alan Bradstreet, and Photographers, Leon Halip and Dale Fisher wait for permission to take off to photograph the Winter Classic on 1-1-2014.

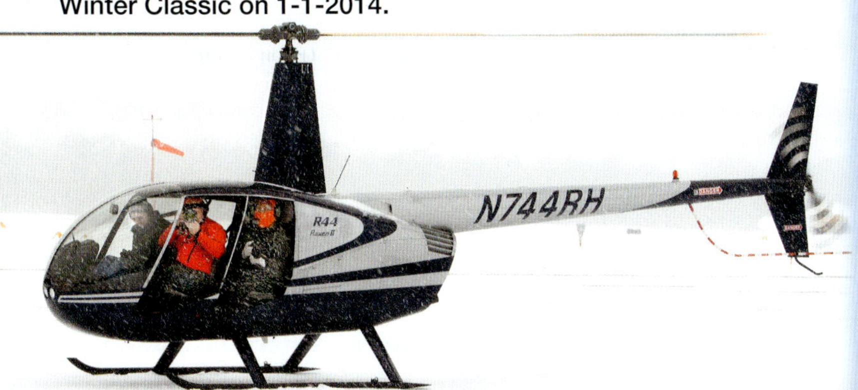

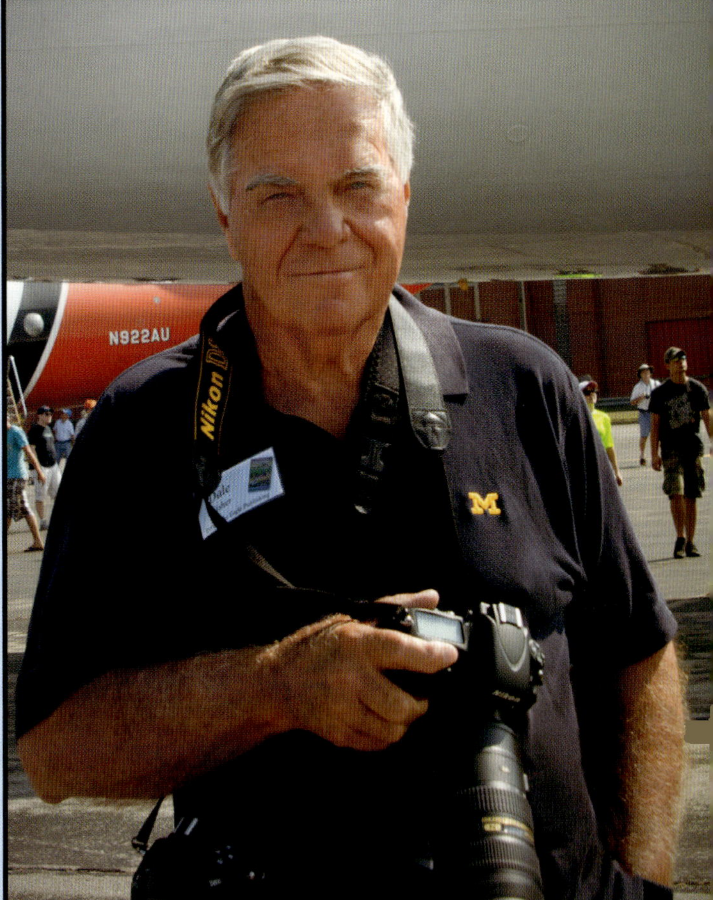

Welcome to Washtenaw County

Washtenaw County has gone through substantial changes in the last 87 years. I am privileged to have had a front-row seat to its development and capturing those changes from a flying artists' perspective. Looking back, I realize I have created an aerial photographic history of our county.

According to the 1930 US Census, Washtenaw County had 65,530 residents. There were two cities, Ann Arbor and Ypsilanti. Saint Joseph Hospital was on North Ingalls in Ann Arbor, and Michigan Stadium held 85,000 fans. The University of Michigan, Michigan State Normal College (now known as Eastern Michigan University), and Cleary College were the only higher education institutions.

My interest in photography started as a child after my father gave me a camera. By high school, I was working as an apprentice with Clifton Dey, master portrait photographer in the Nichols Arcade. On weekends, I was photographing weddings alone. At 17, during the Korean War, I enlisted in the Navy. The Navy spent a fortune training me in aerial photography and filmmaking, introducing me to the latest technology and techniques. It set the bar high. After my military service, I made it a point to keep current with the changes in visual media.

My first job after being honorably discharged was at the Ann Arbor News as a photographer/reporter. During my time at the News, I did aerial photography from a J-3 Piper Cub. Since leaving the Ann Arbor News, I have been an entrepreneur and had several portrait and commercial studios in different locations around Ann Arbor and in Detroit. I am proud to have established the first 24-hour color film processing service in the Ann Arbor area, serving more than a dozen locations.

I have witnessed history-in-the-making. Starting this journey over 60 years ago, I have a pictorial history of Washtenaw County. "The news is the first rough draft of history," Philip Graham publisher of the Washington Post once said. It is incredible to see the changes.

Washtenaw County has grown to a population of almost 371,000. There are six cities and six chartered townships. Saint Joseph Mercy Hospital has relocated to a complex between Ypsilanti and Ann Arbor on a 340-acre parcel. Michigan Stadium now seats 109,901 fans, making it the third-largest stadium in the world. Higher learning is available with three universities and Washtenaw Community College. The City of Ann Arbor is recognized as the most educated city in the nation.

I have spent my lifetime capturing those changes on film and digitally. Even though this book is my biggest (and best) book published, it is impossible to showcase everything in Washtenaw County. We have thousands of beautiful photographs that we couldn't make fit. I hope you enjoy the photographs I selected for you in my final book.

You are welcome to schedule a tour of the Dale Fisher Galleries located on the Eyre of the Eagle farm in Grass Lake, Michigan. The galleries are open by appointment. I hope to see you soon.

Best regards,

Dale Fisher

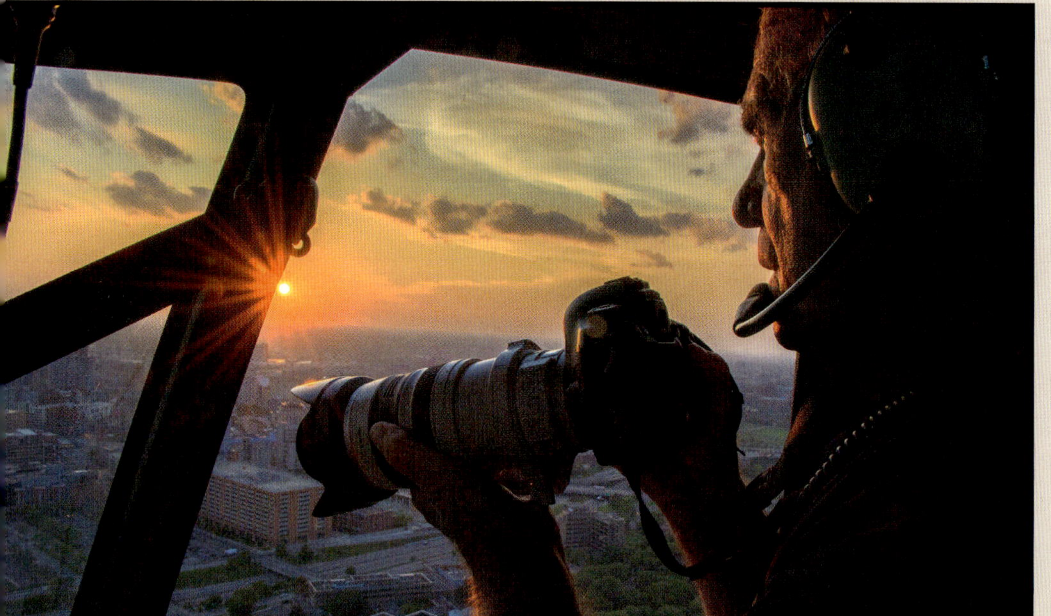

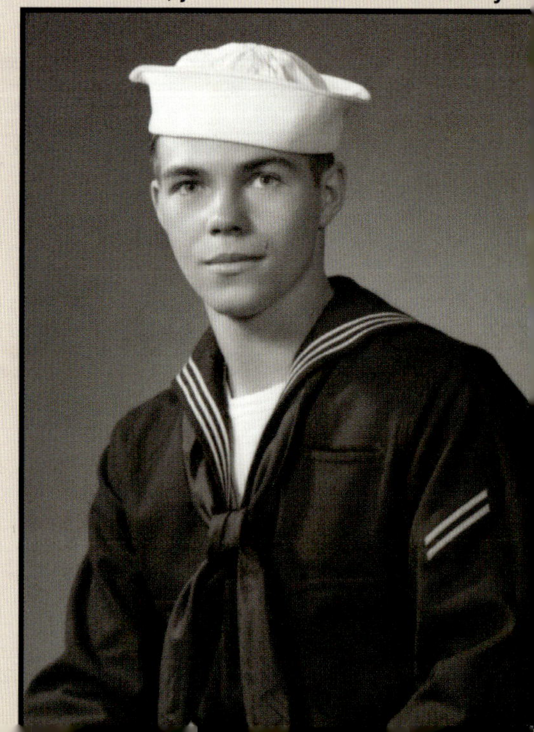

Dale Fisher, just before his 18th birthday.

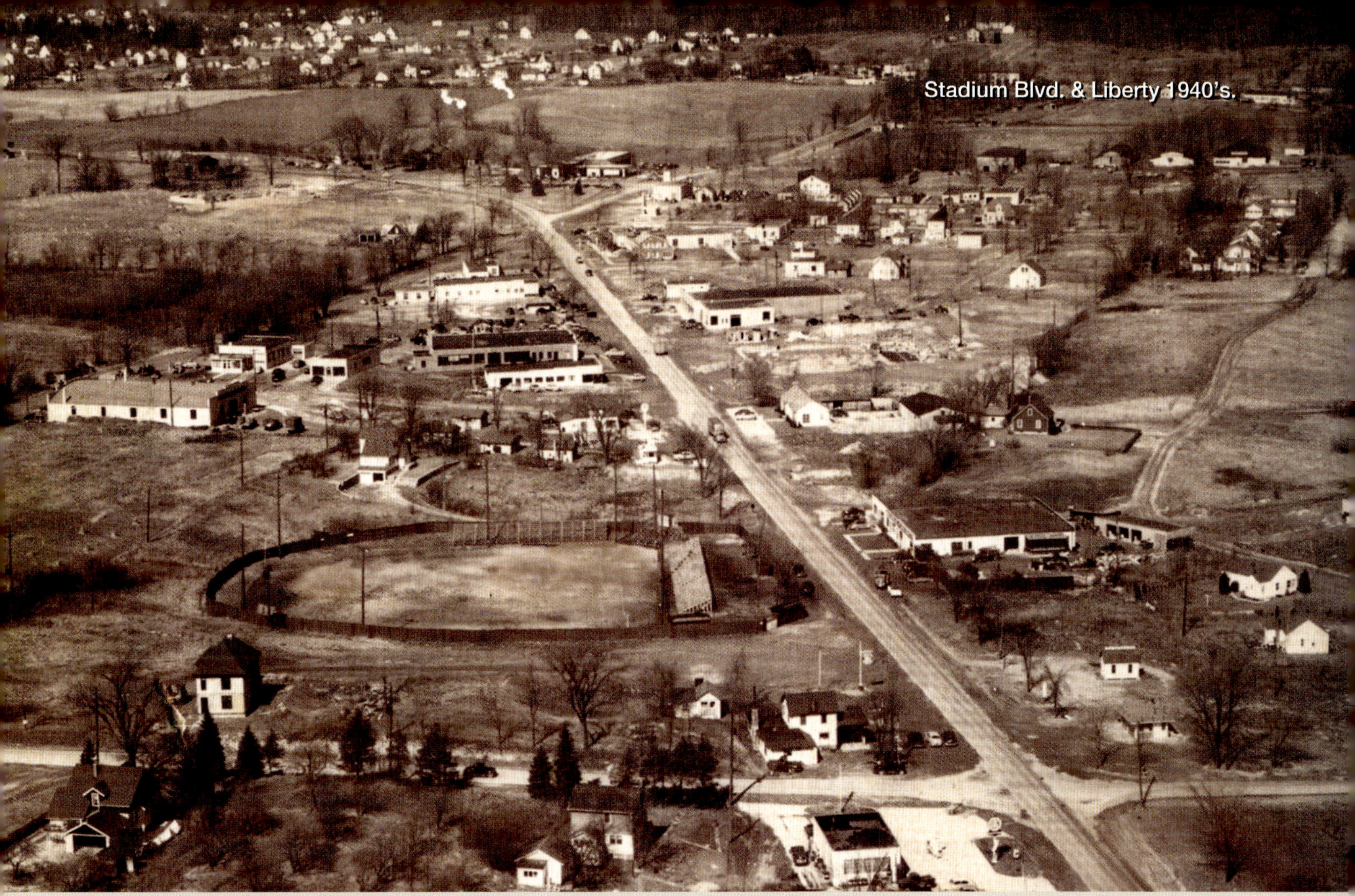

Stadium Blvd. & Liberty 1940's.

The above photograph was taken more than 80 years ago. Sportman's Park is in the center and hosted ball games, rodeos and many other events. Stadium Blvd and Liberty roads were both Dirt Roads.

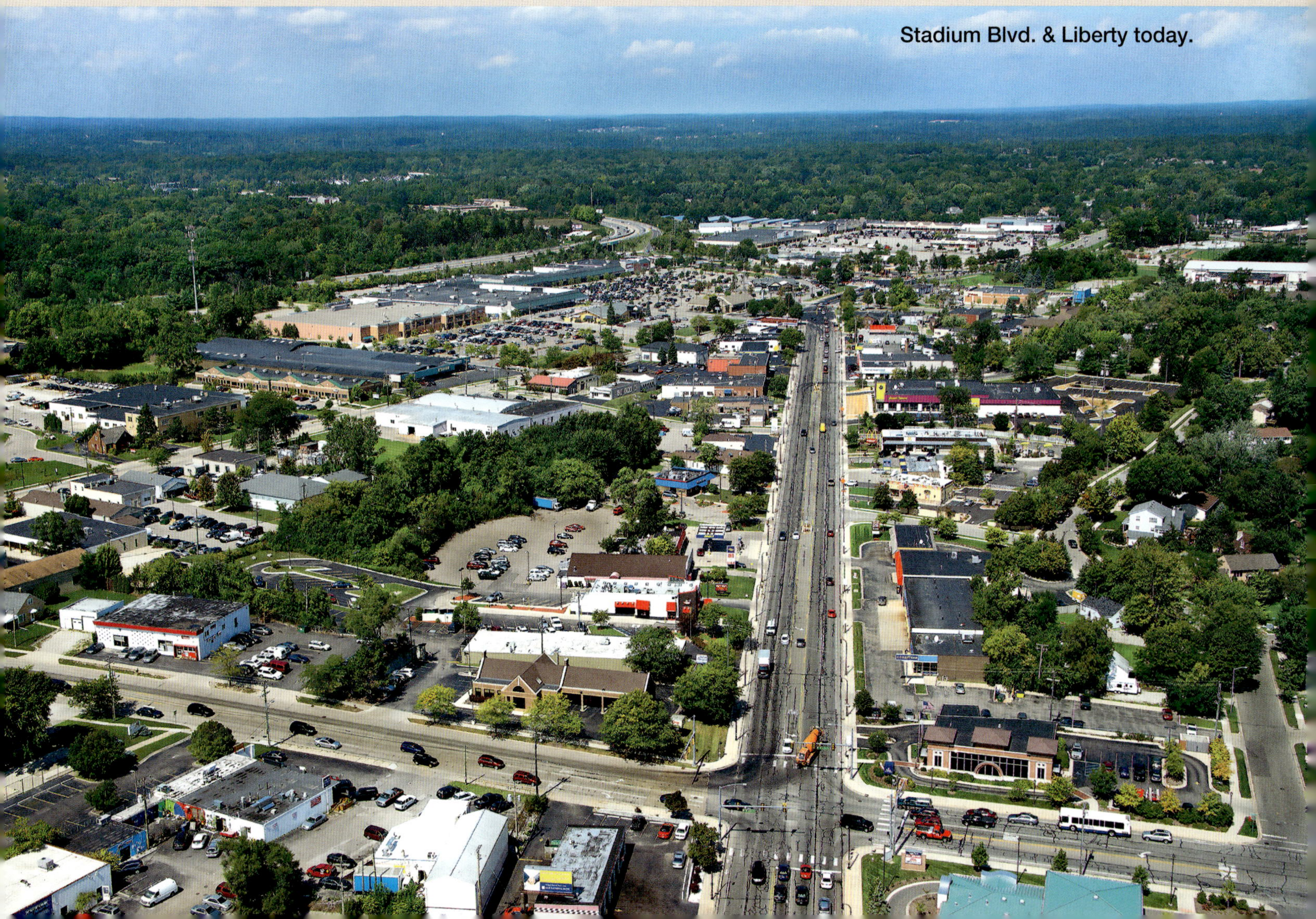

Stadium Blvd. & Liberty today.

From the visions of the eagle & by the grace of God...

When I first met Dale in the winter of 2013, he was working on his fourth book on Ann Arbor and had started a new book, ***Jackson County: Visions of the Eagle***. The Jackson County book, which published in 2015, inspired us to expand the Ann Arbor book to include all of Washtenaw County.

In order to capture the beauty and uniqueness of Washtenaw County, we took countless flights covering the entire county. Low-level helicopter photography captures everything from a different perspective – the Air! We also photographed Washtenaw County in action at an incredible number of events.

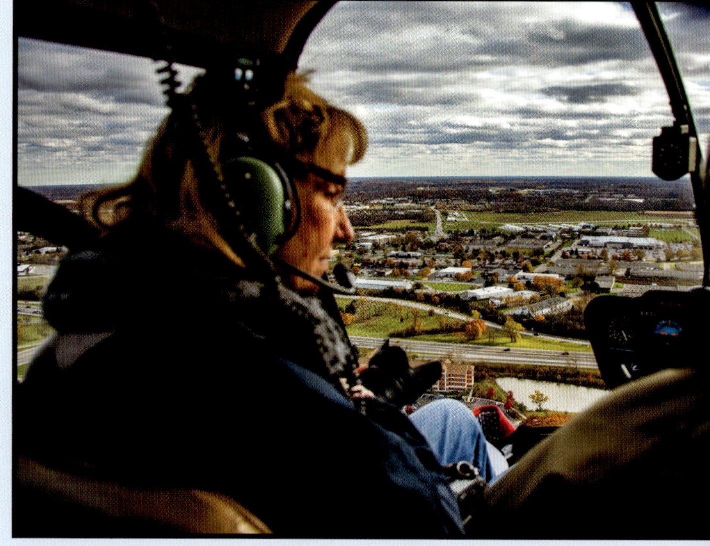

In addition to graphic design and photography, I support the creation of this book by coordinating the photo shoots, determining flight plans, and serving as navigator. I spend more time planning our flights than time spent in the air. Using the GPS on my smartphone, I can view the exact photo shoot location and capture the beautiful landscapes of Washtenaw County.

During the creation of this book, I was blindsided by blood cancer (Multiple Myeloma). I am grateful to my doctors and care team at Michigan Medical. Dale has been my rock during this journey. Although I needed to enlist help to finish this project, I appreciate the creative outlet that was afforded to me in the creation of this book.

There are too many family and friends to mention to thank who have helped me through this journey. Their prayers, kind words, well wishes, and acts of kindness give me strength, and are appreciated. This past year has been the most challenging time of my life. I am still learning to accept my limitations and embrace my new normal. Although I am still healing, I am getting stronger every day. Cancer may have started the fight, but God and I will finish it.

This book is the largest, most time-intensive project I have worked on in my 30+ year graphic design and marketing career. I never dreamed that I would ever be working with Dale, my mentor, friend, and partner. It has been an honor and a privilege to be included in such a fabulous communication piece. I am humbled and blessed.

From the visions of the eagle, by the grace of God and on the wings of an angel, this dream has become a reality.

Thank you to everyone who has helped us on our journey,

Joanne Ackerman

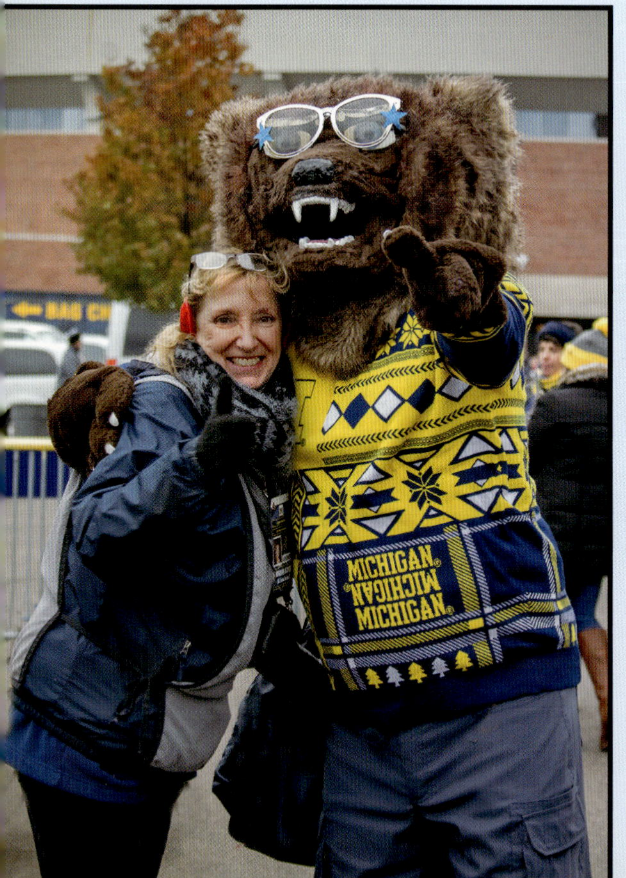

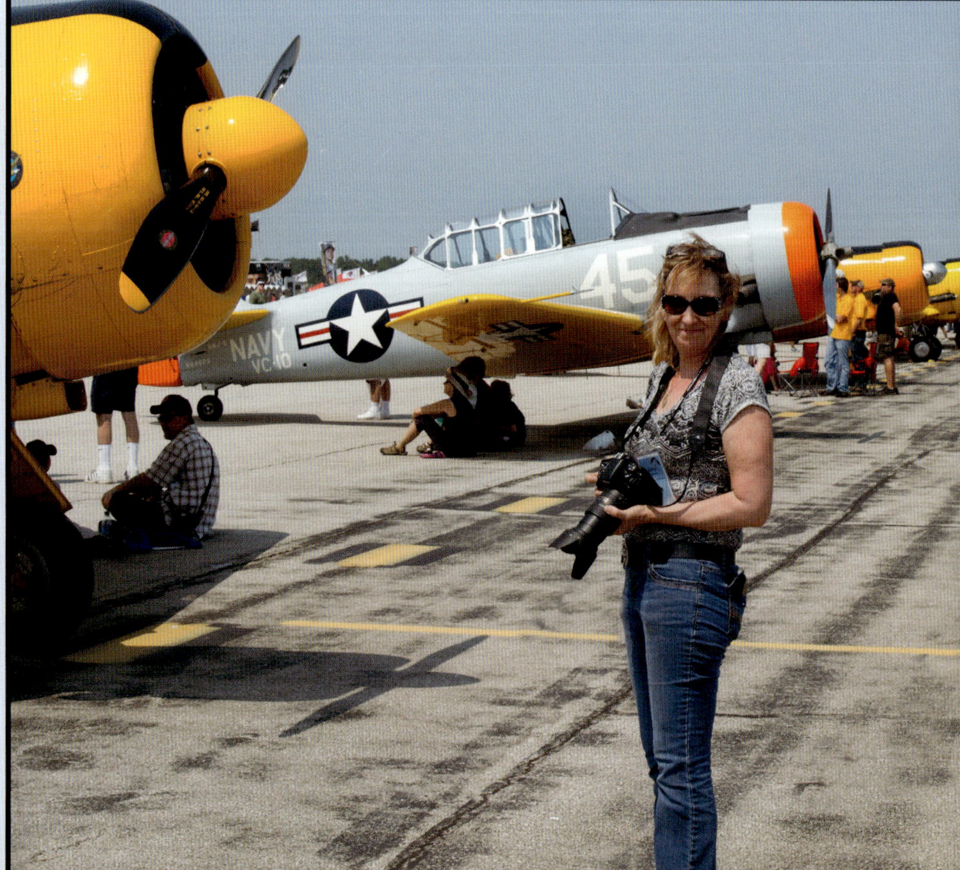

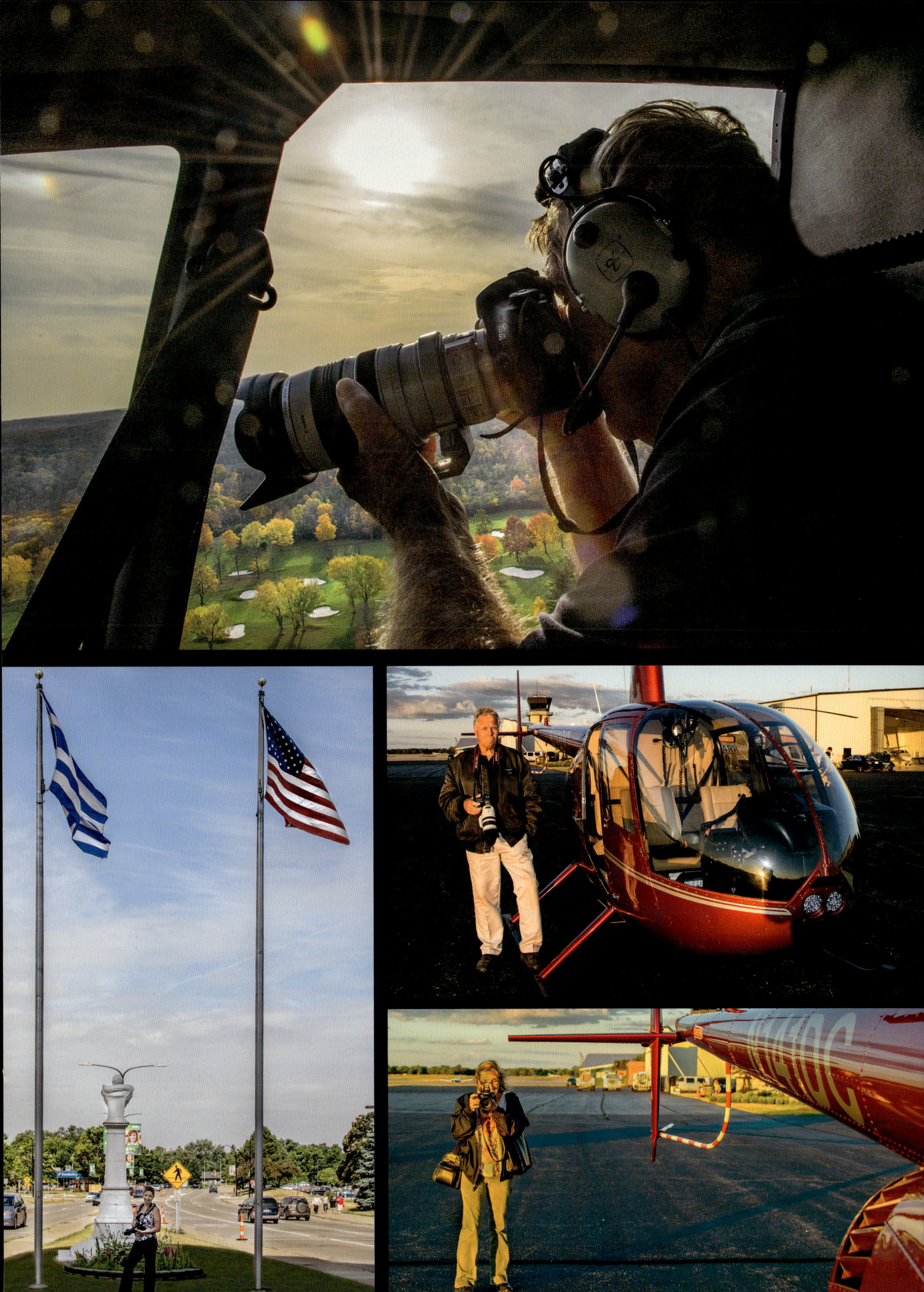

Dale Fisher
Galleries of Fine Art Photography

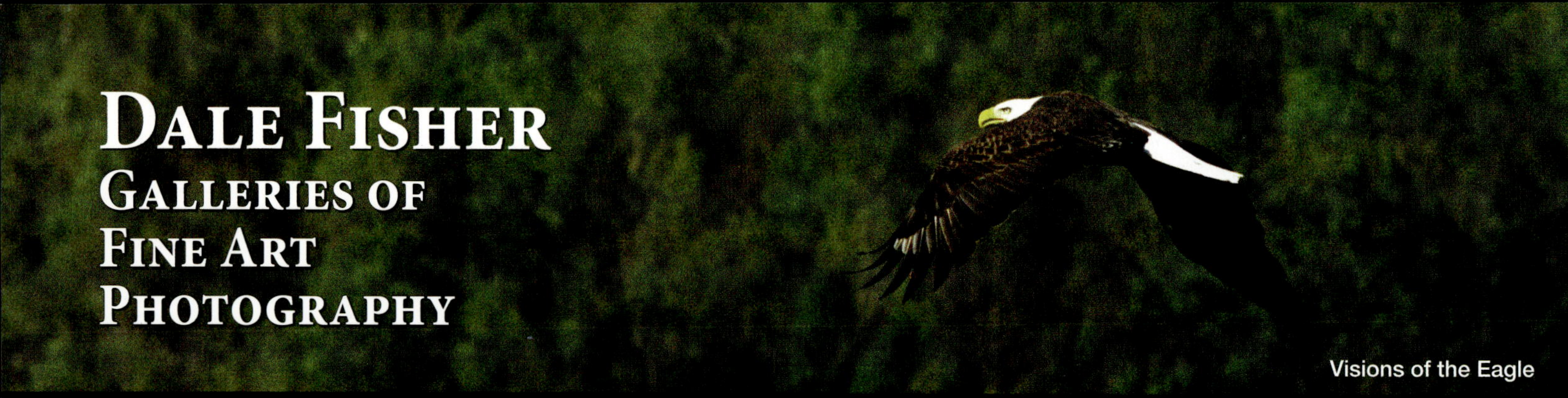

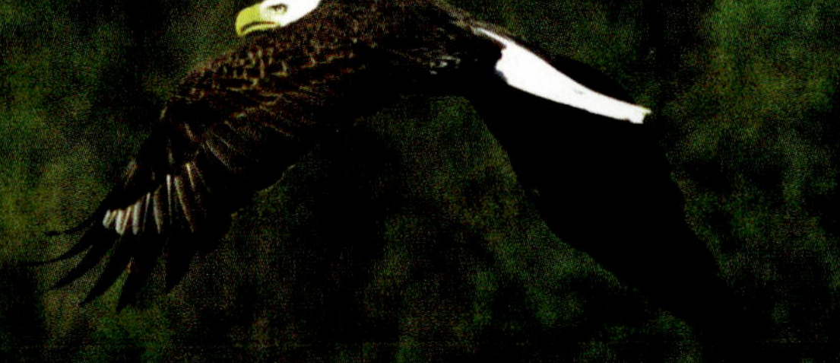

Visions of the Eagle

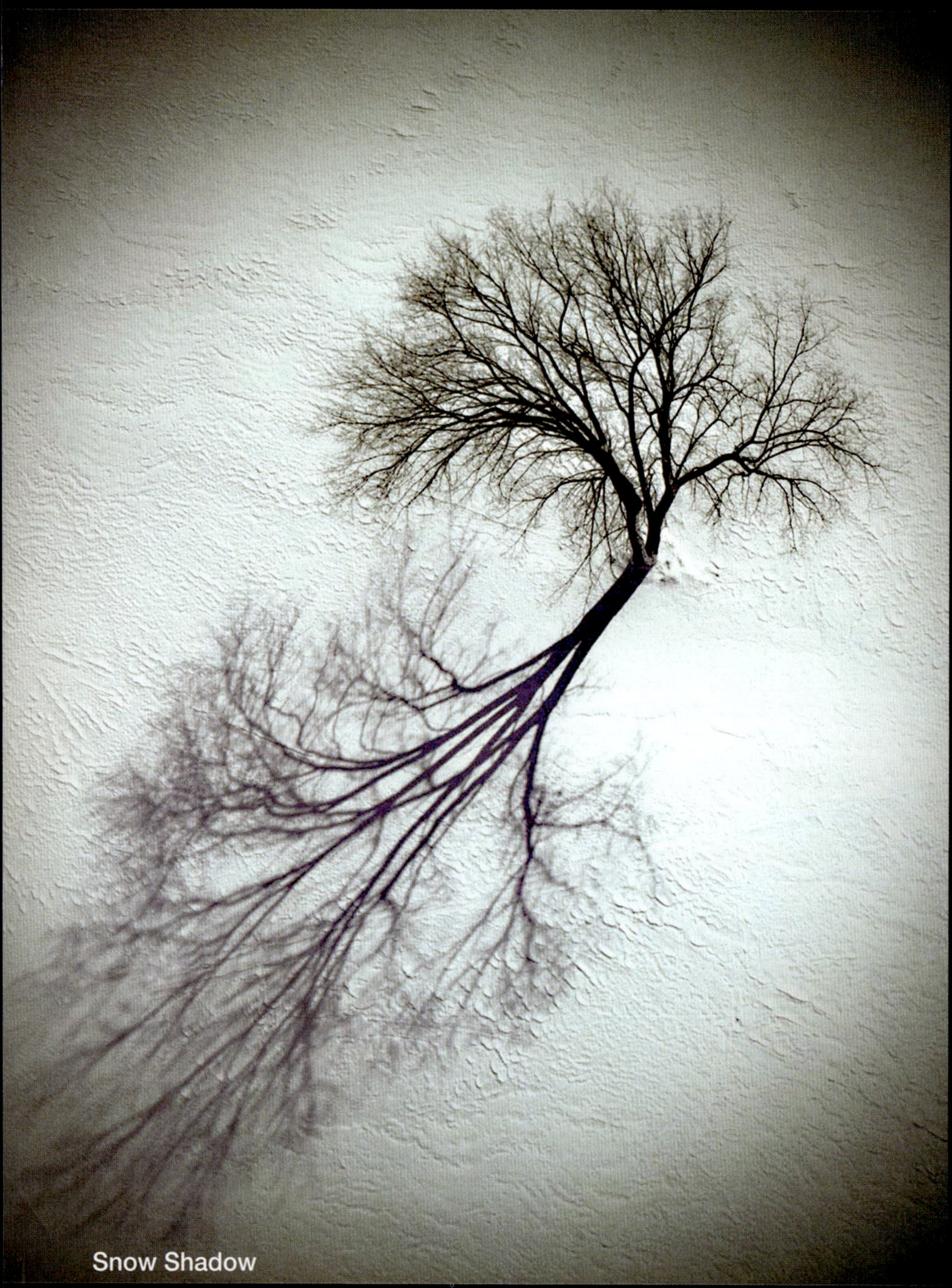

Snow Shadow

The Photographic Art of Dale Fisher

Few people will ever have the opportunity to fly eyeball to eyeball with a bald eagle.

For more than 60 years, Dale Fisher has been creating photographic art from a helicopter flown at low levels. Fisher's unique "eagle's eye" perspective allows his audience to share with him the thrill of seeing what life looks like when you fly like an eagle, and you capture split-second visions with a camera.

As perhaps the world's only artist-photographer who works almost exclusively from a helicopter, Fisher sees the world as few others do. Combining artistic vision with his unique perspective from above, he creates extraordinary art. By working with color, light, and shadows—all while skimming over his subjects at ground speeds of up to 120 miles per hour—Fisher optimizes the perfect setting of each subject.

The Dale Fisher Galleries are nestled inside the Eyry of the Eagle Farm's Retreat and Reception Centers and houses a lifetime collection of open and limited-edition photographic art from around the country. The farm includes a wedding venue, reception center, and gallery. The galleries are open by appointment.

Dale Fisher Galleries
of Fine Art Photography
1916 Norvell Road
Grass Lake, MI
517-522-3705

Guenther Pond Swans

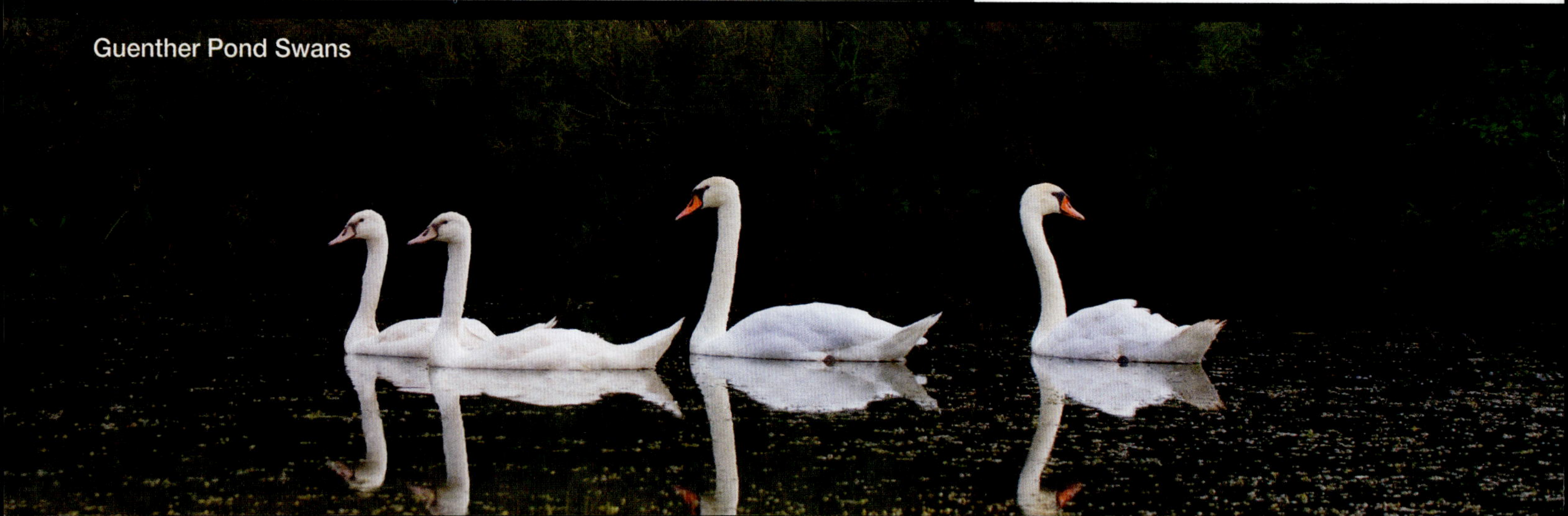

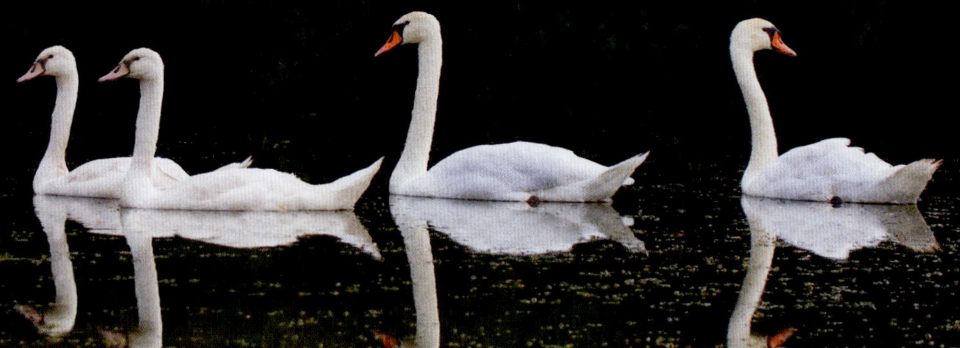

Visions of the Eagle—Welcome to the domain of the eagle. Limited edition photograph of a bald eagle flying over lake Superior. Photographed from a helicopter just as he came over a forest from the lake. This single image was created just as the eagle dropped his right wing and left the scene.

Snow Shadow—Monochromatic aerial helicopter photograph of a single tree casting a shadow in the snow. Corners are darkened, causing a vignette effect. Taken east of Ann Arbor on Sarah Gill's Farm.

Guenther Pond Swans—Part of a nature series and is an image of a family of four swans swimming on Guenther Pond.

Color Fall Beautiful—Barn and farmhouse nestled in green pasture, surrounded by trees boasting bright fall colors; Taken northwest of Traverse City, featuring large bright red tree in foreground.

The 900th game at the Big House—Majestic view of the Big House on a beautiful fall day. The sun is brightly shining on the city of Ann Arbor in the background.

Willow Bridge—This photograph of an old footbridge on an abandoned farm was taken near Dexter, Michigan.

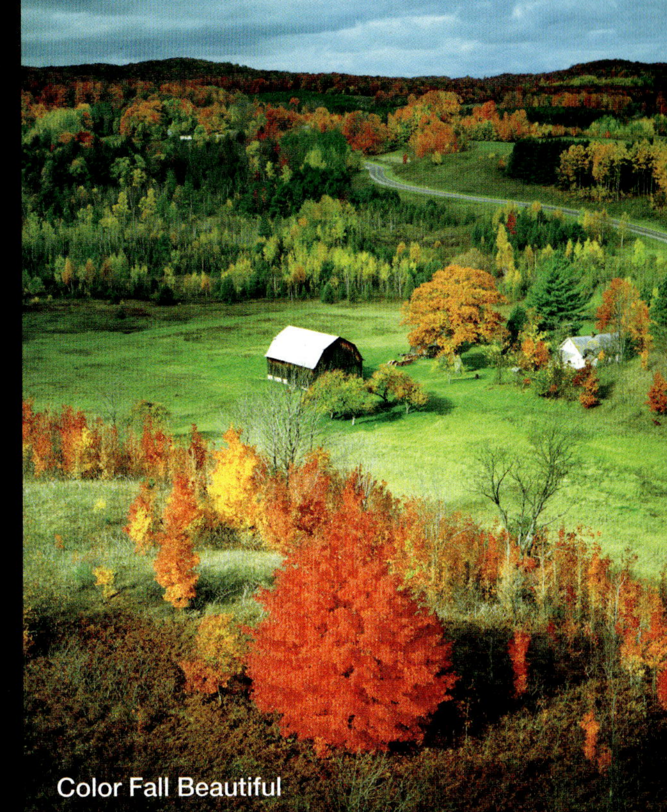

Color Fall Beautiful

In the Ann Arbor area, most people recognize Dale Fisher for his University of Michigan sports & stadium photographs.

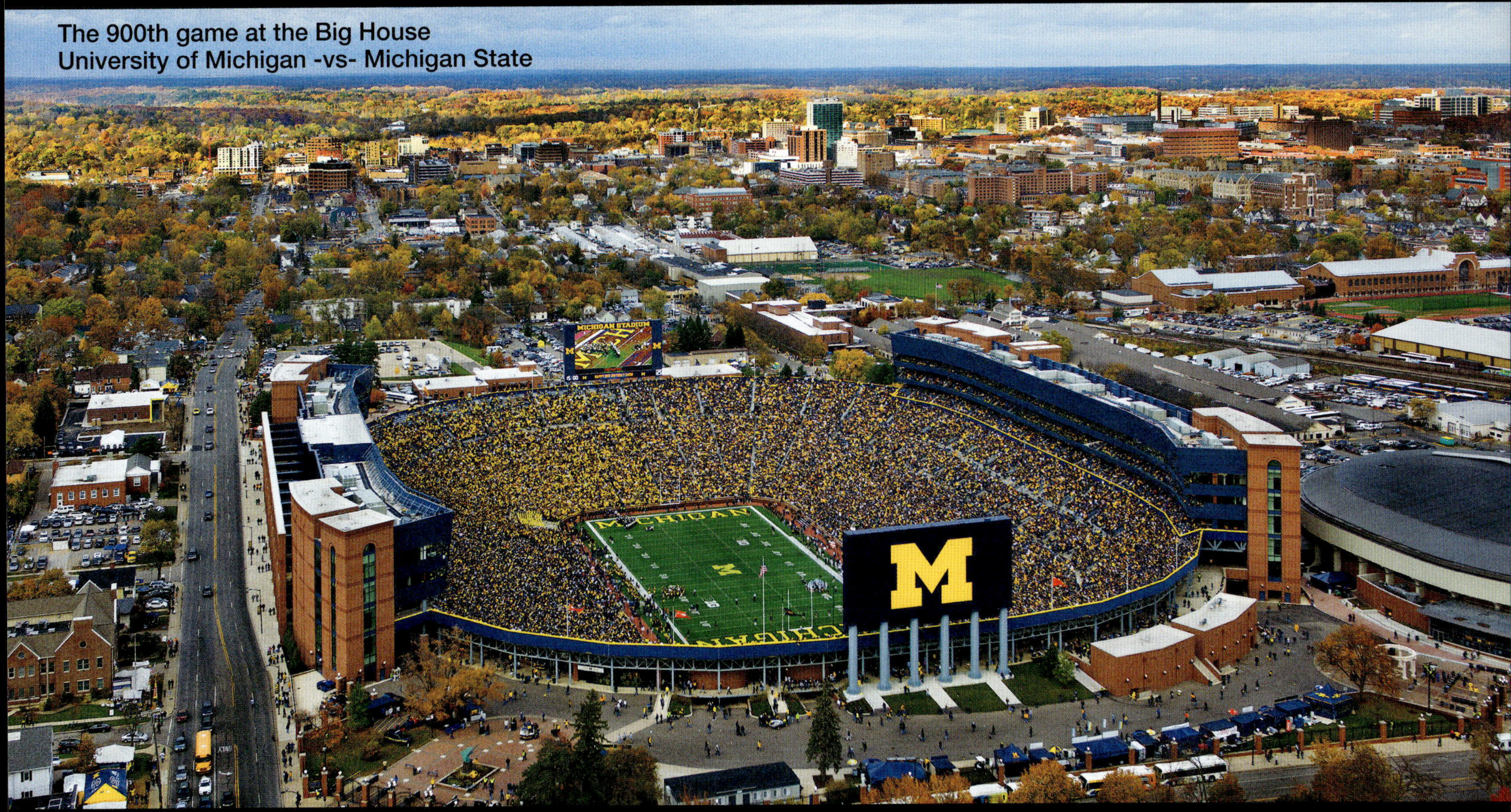

The 900th game at the Big House
University of Michigan -vs- Michigan State

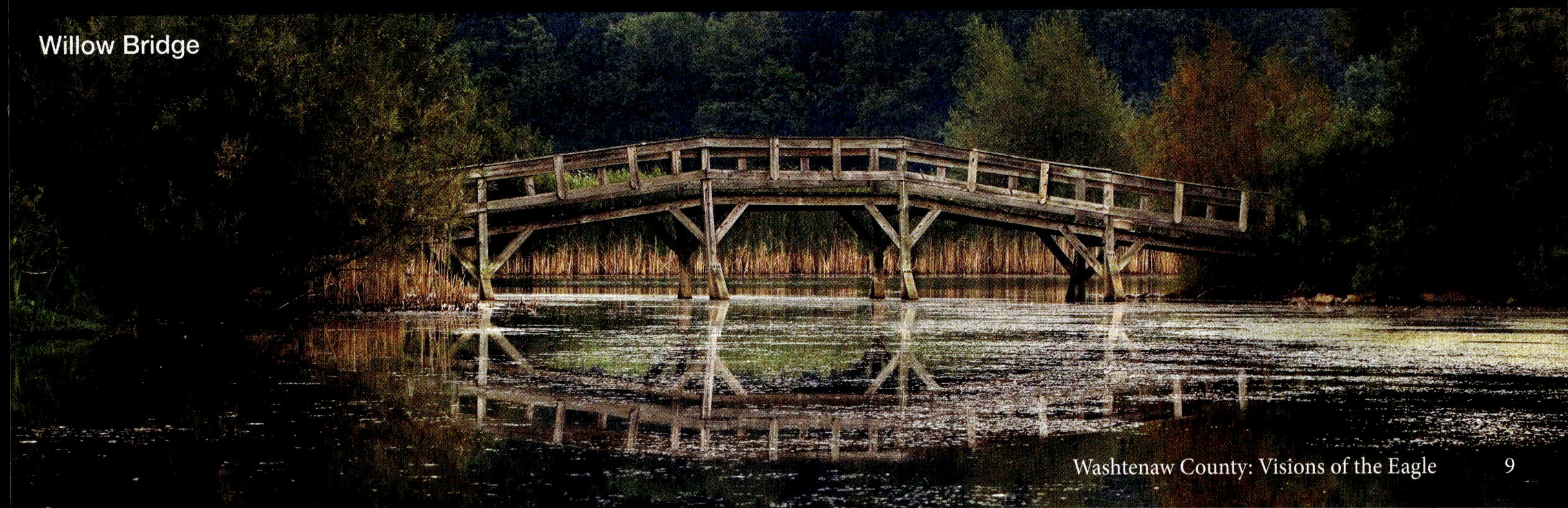

Willow Bridge

ANN ARBOR

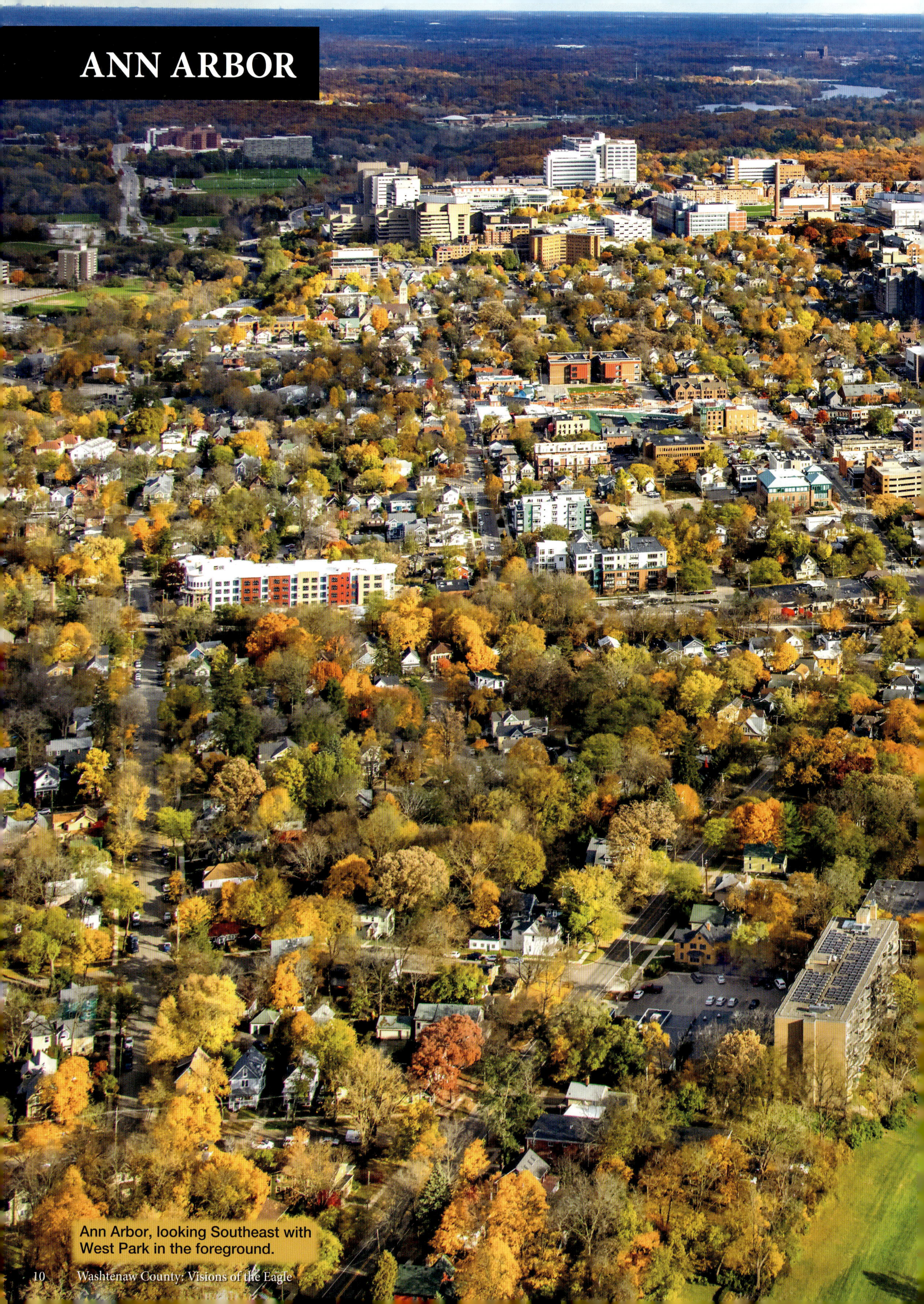

Ann Arbor, looking Southeast with West Park in the foreground.

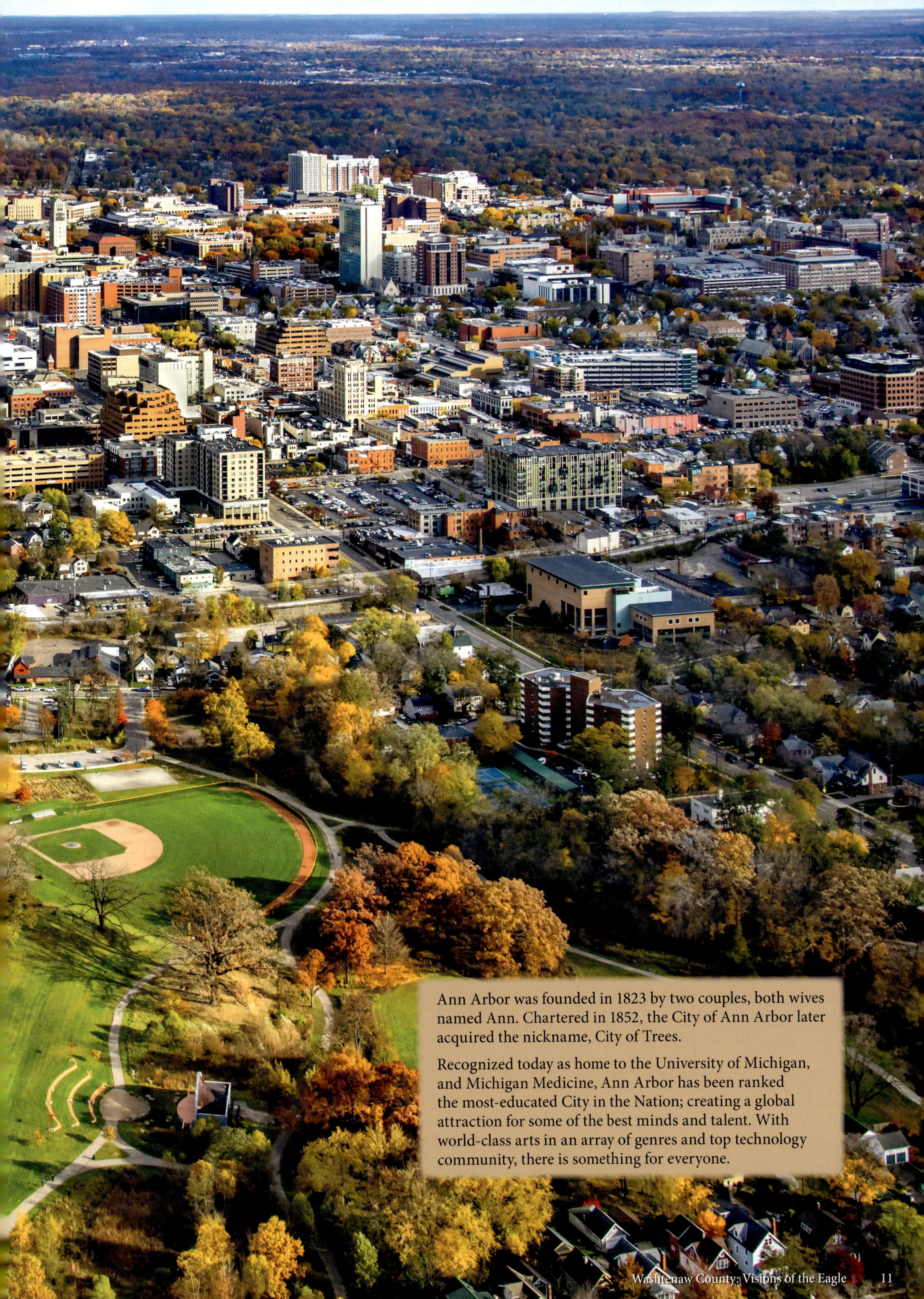

Ann Arbor was founded in 1823 by two couples, both wives named Ann. Chartered in 1852, the City of Ann Arbor later acquired the nickname, City of Trees.

Recognized today as home to the University of Michigan, and Michigan Medicine, Ann Arbor has been ranked the most-educated City in the Nation; creating a global attraction for some of the best minds and talent. With world-class arts in an array of genres and top technology community, there is something for everyone.

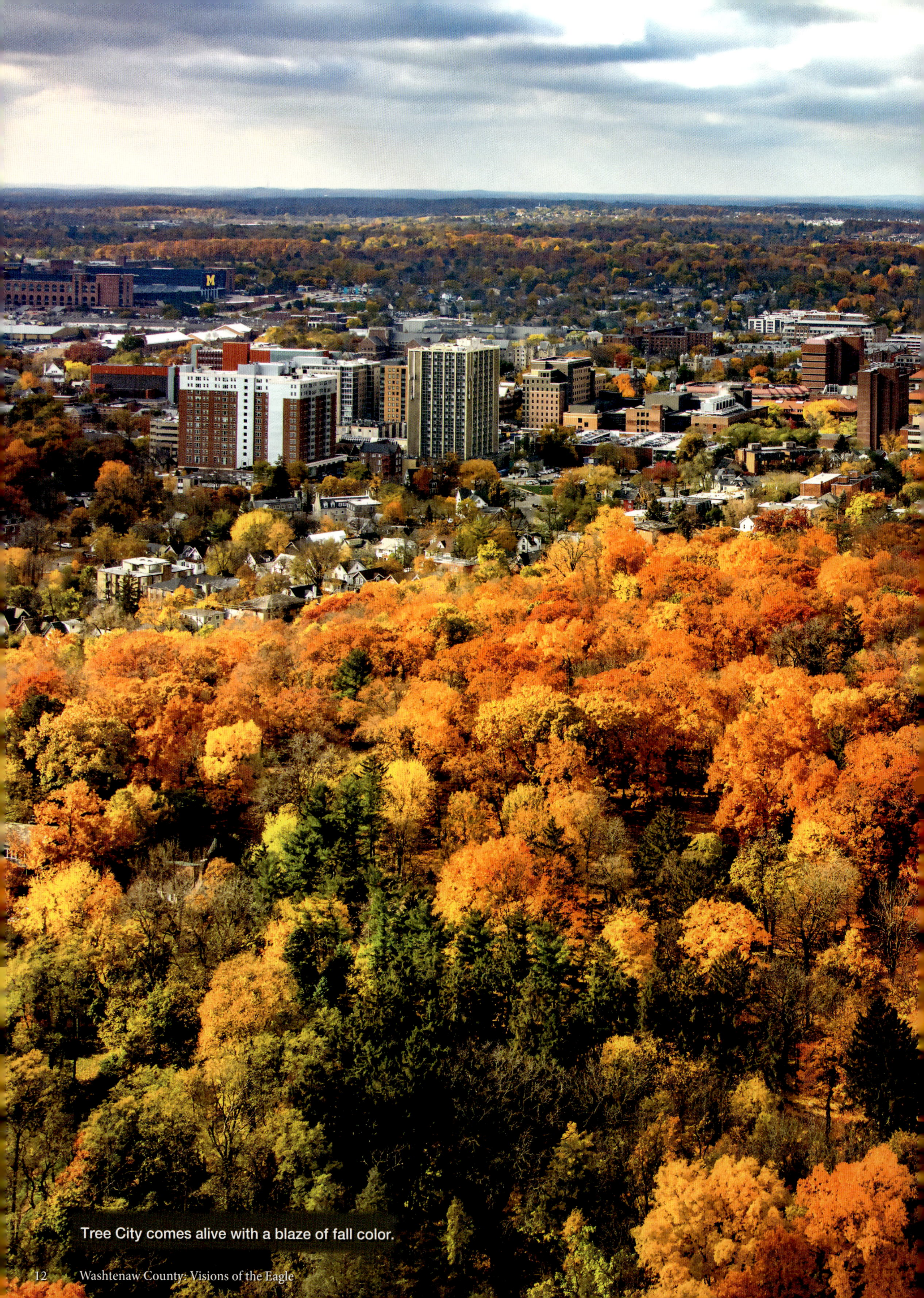

Tree City comes alive with a blaze of fall color.

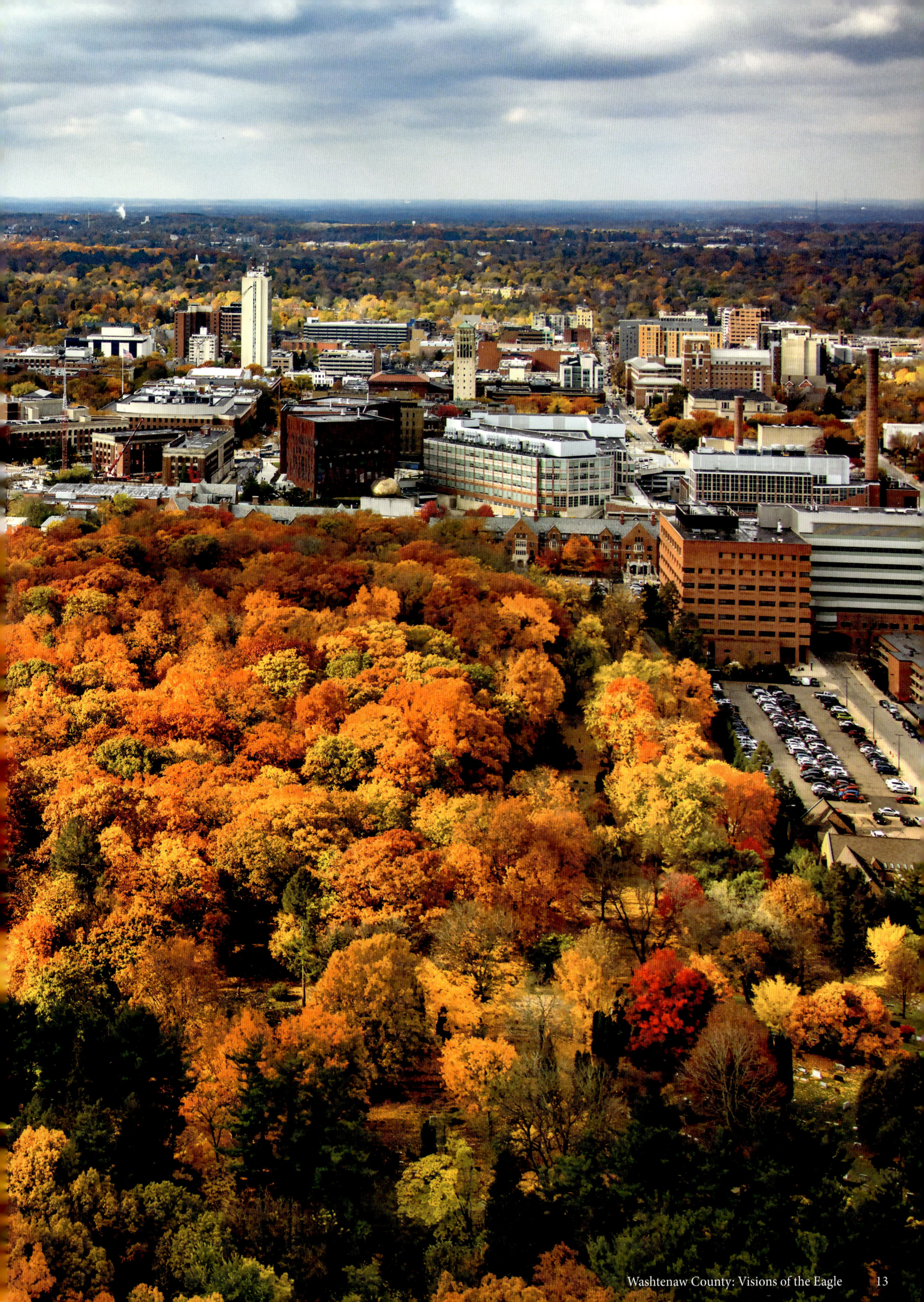

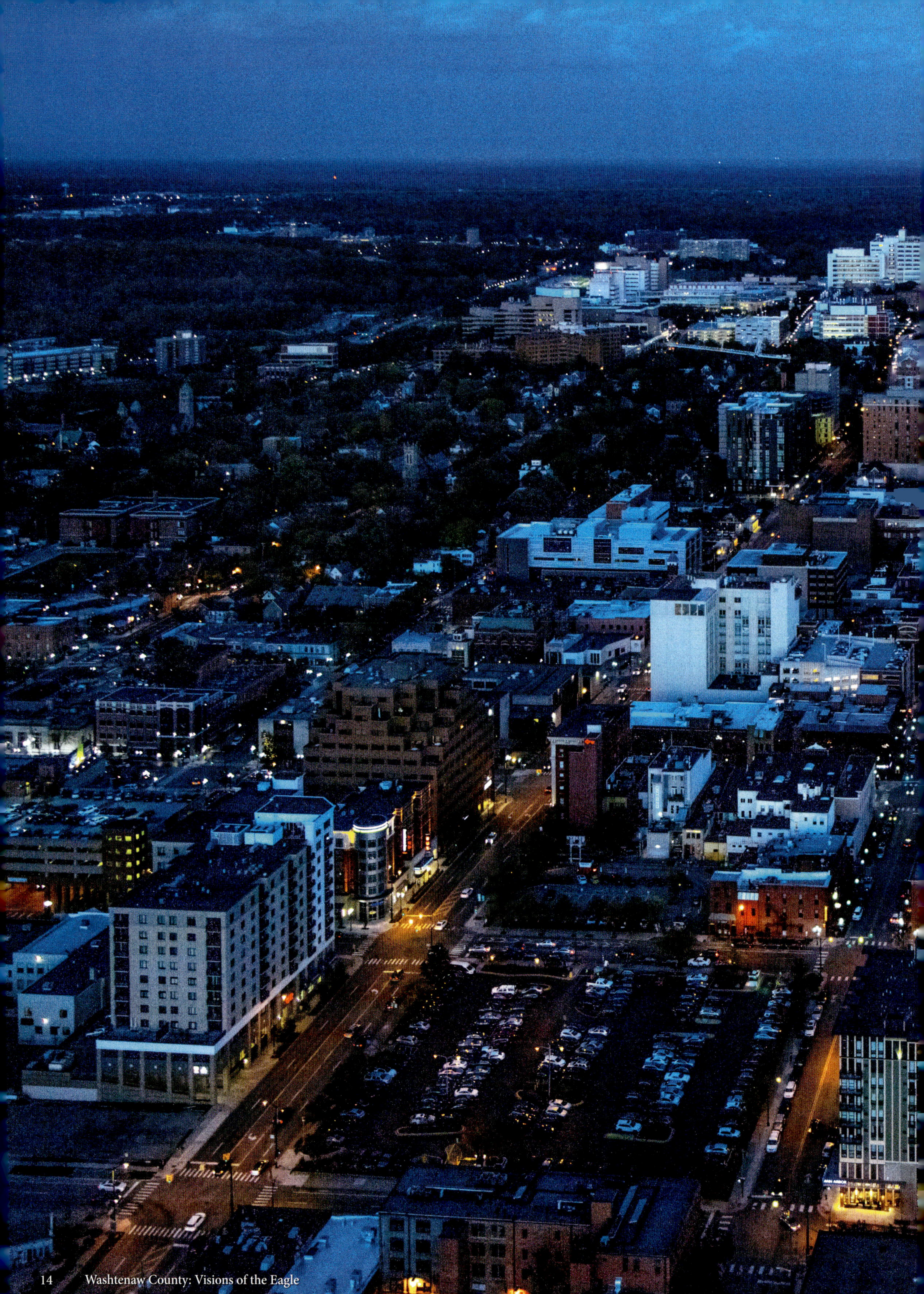

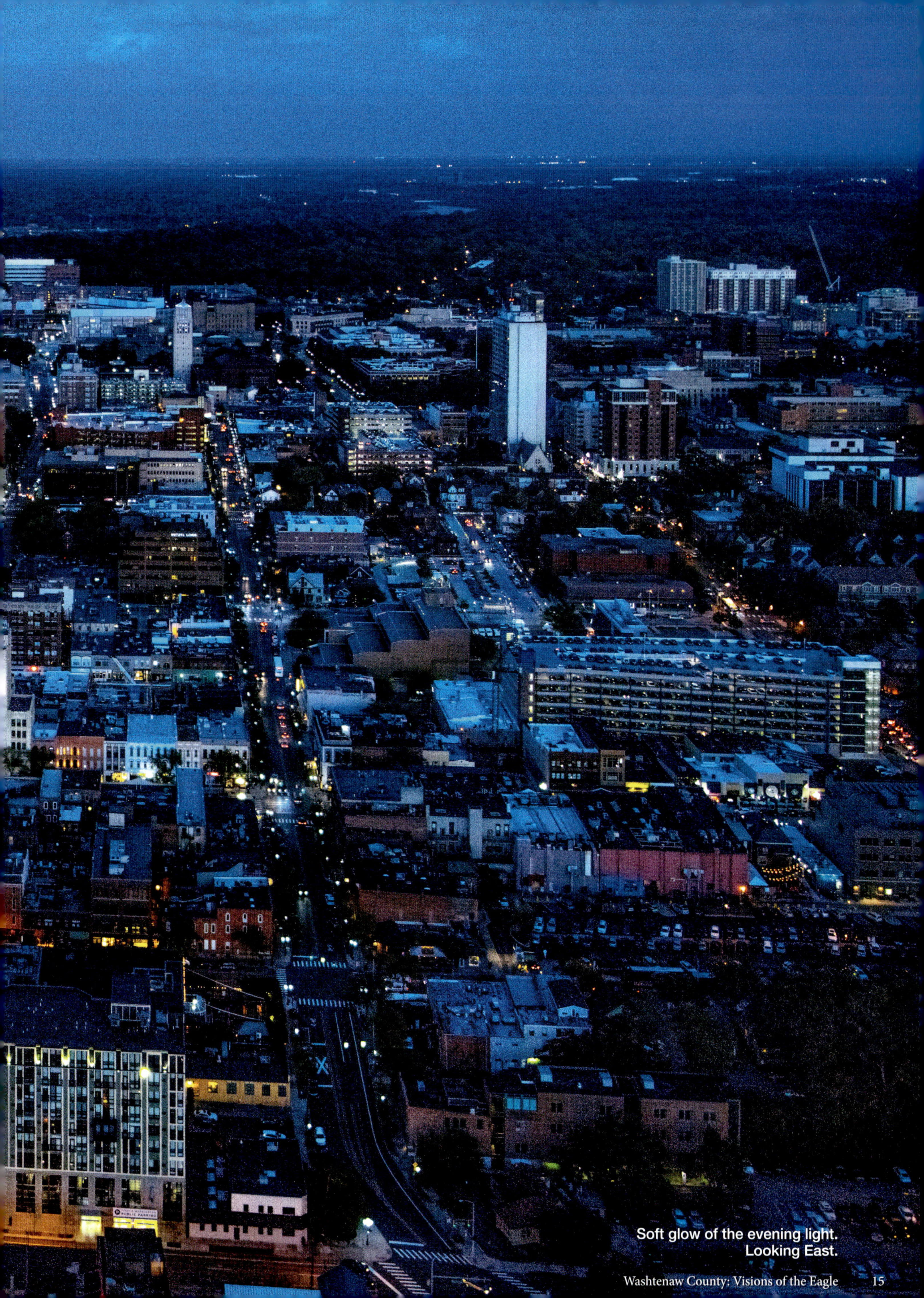

Soft glow of the evening light.
Looking East.

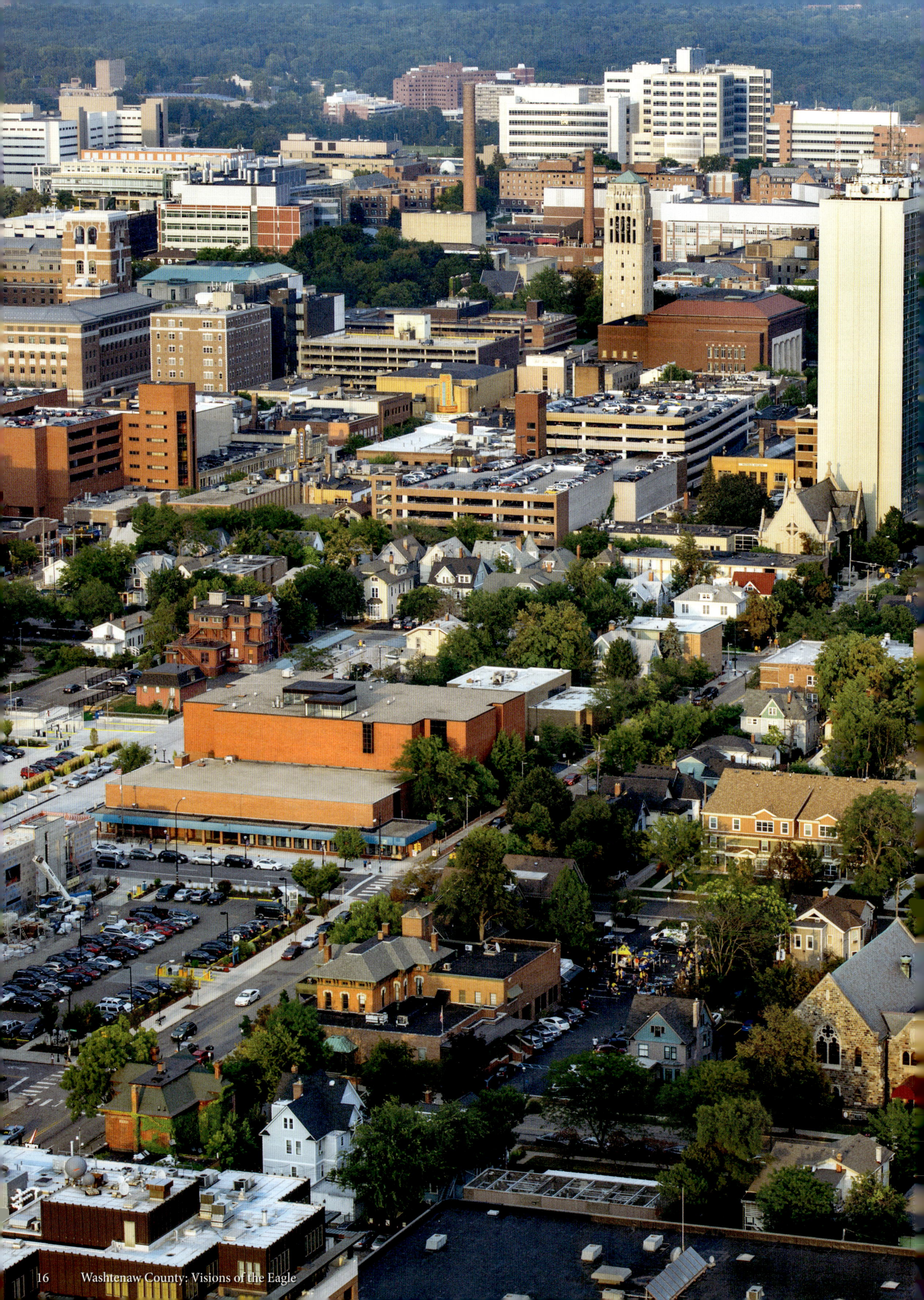

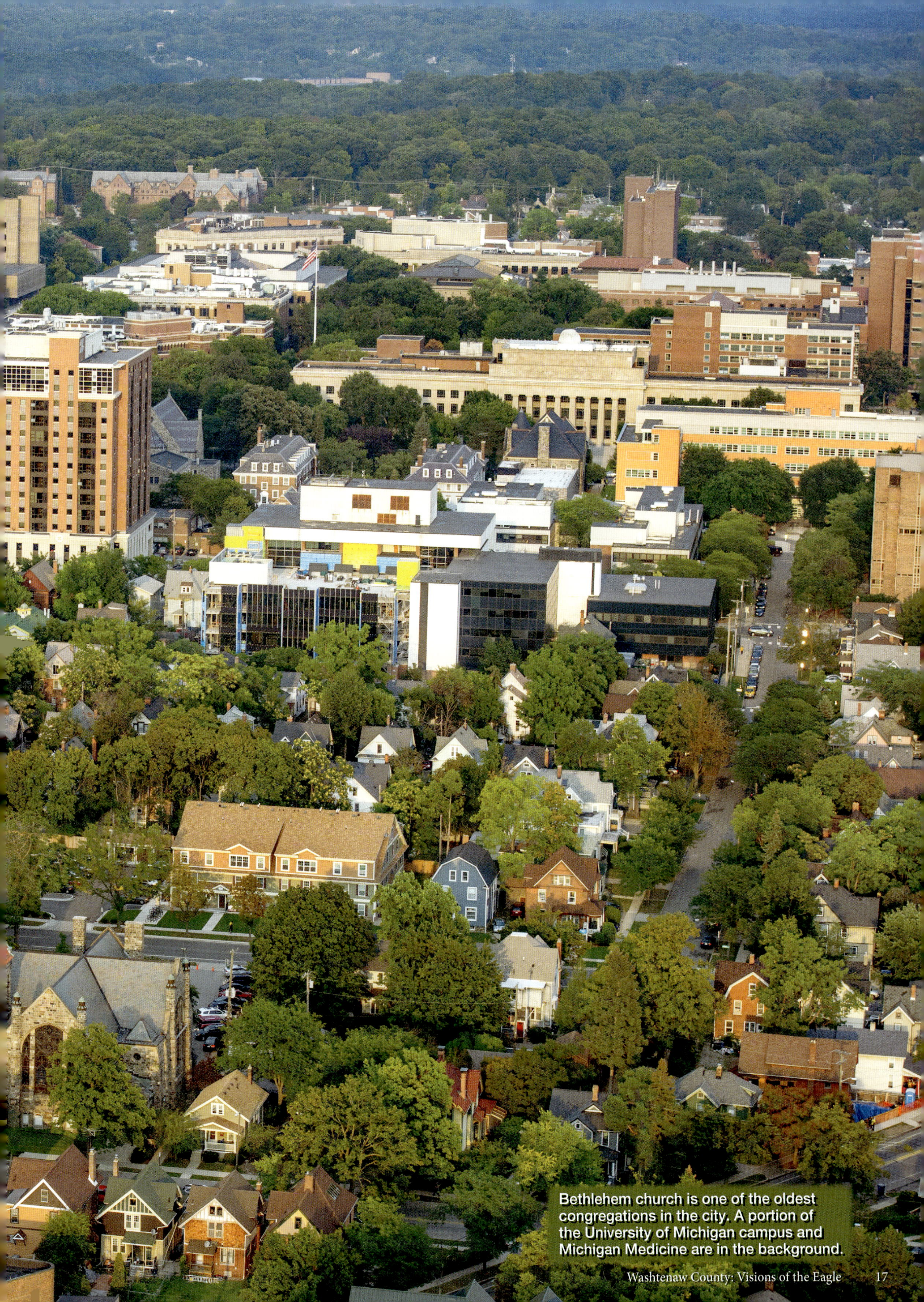

Bethlehem church is one of the oldest congregations in the city. A portion of the University of Michigan campus and Michigan Medicine are in the background.

Bethlehem United Church of Christ

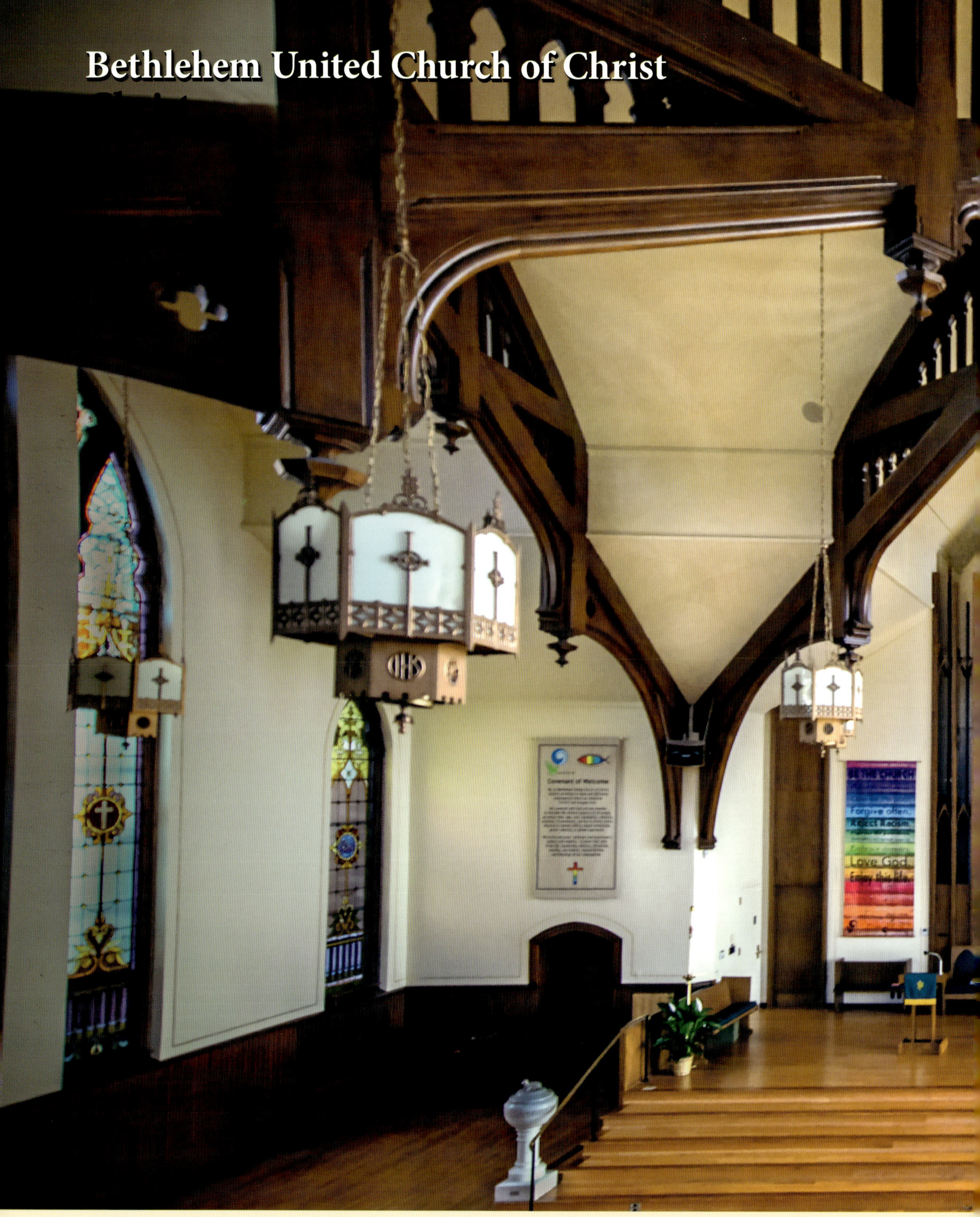

Bethlehem United Church of Christ's iconic stone structure, designated as a Historic Site by the State of Michigan, is a landmark in downtown Ann Arbor where the faith community put down roots in 1833.

Bethlehem UCC's emphasis is on encountering the sacred through meaningful worship. It is committed to service and social justice, alleviating poverty, hunger, and environmental devastation, living as a community with mutual care, and relevant Christian education.

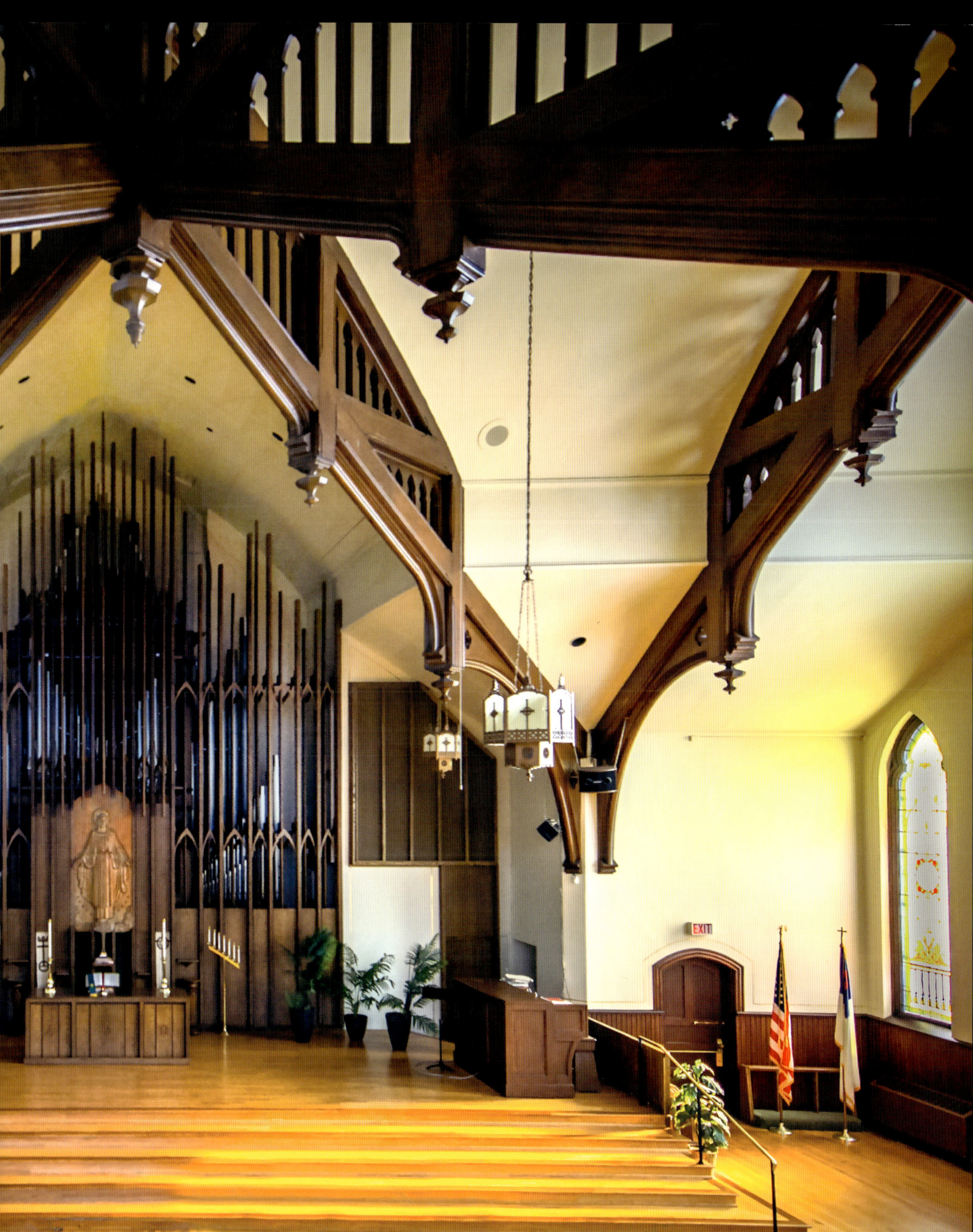

There is great joy in the love of God and a shared vision of inclusiveness, which brings worshippers together as one people. Bethlehem UCC is a caring community excited to share God's love and celebrate all of God's children. It believes, preaches, and teaches that no matter who you are or where you are on life's journey, you are welcome.

BETHLEHEM UNITED CHURCH OF CHRIST

423 South 4th Ave.
Ann Arbor, MI
734-665-6149

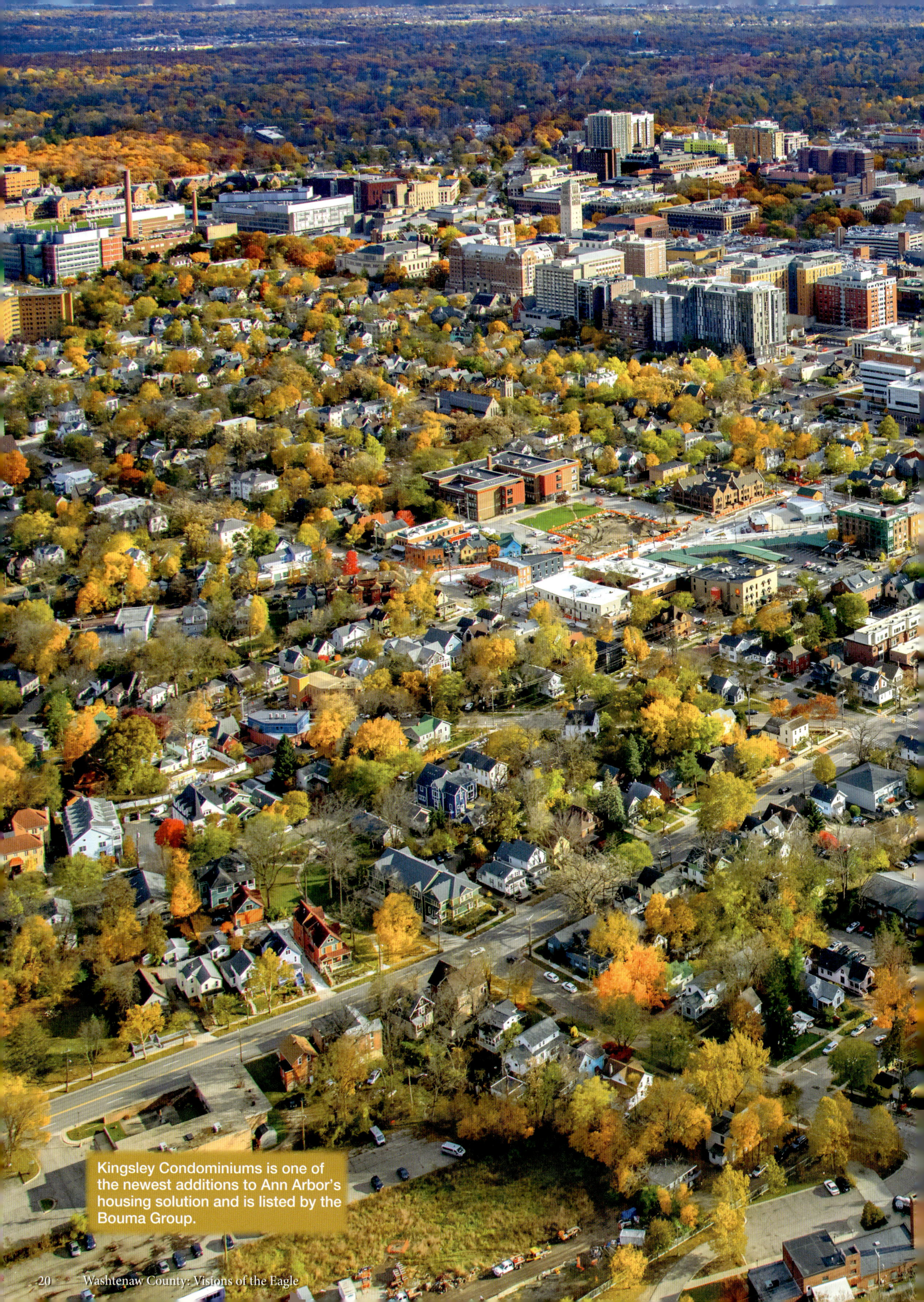

Kingsley Condominiums is one of the newest additions to Ann Arbor's housing solution and is listed by the Bouma Group.

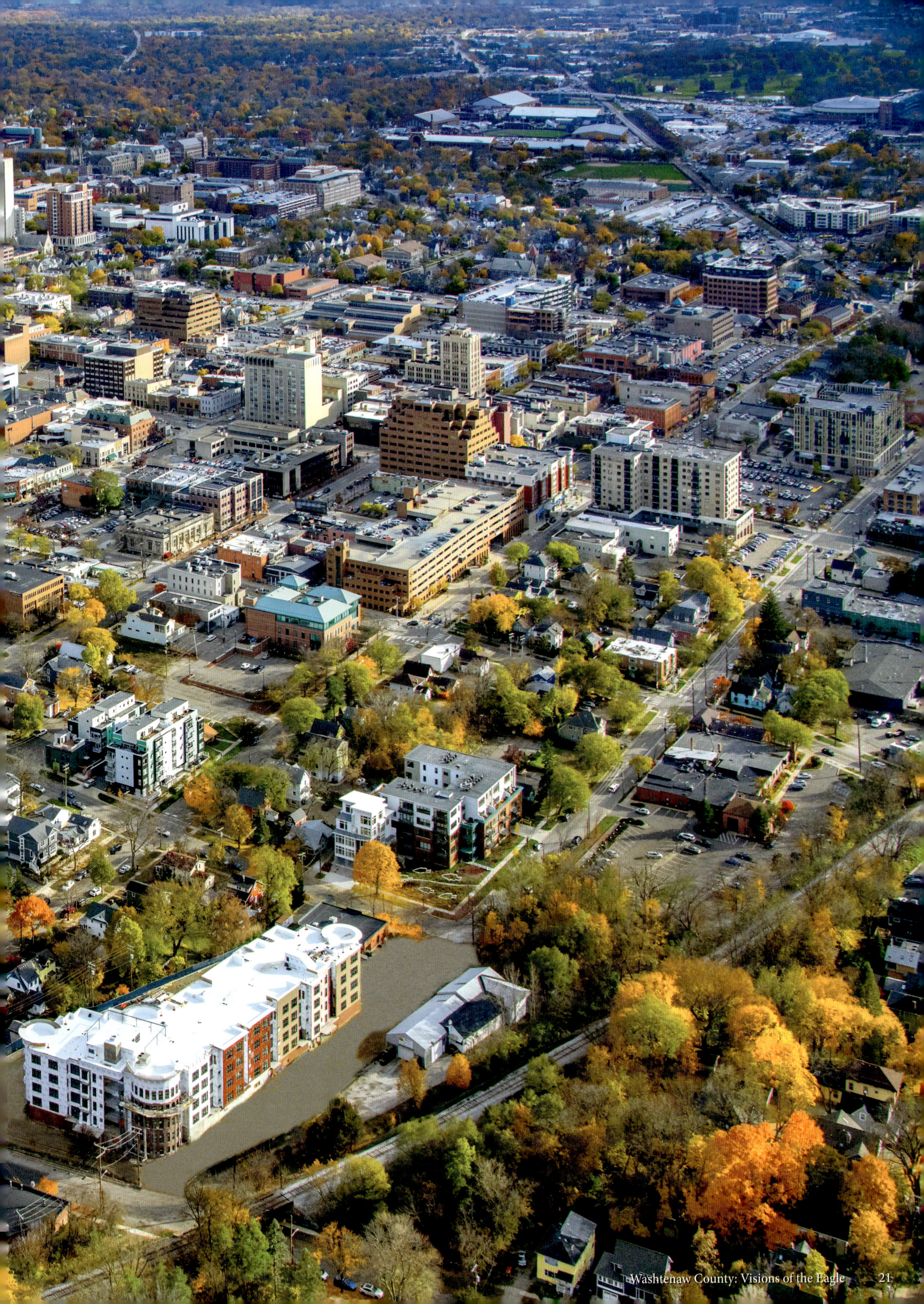

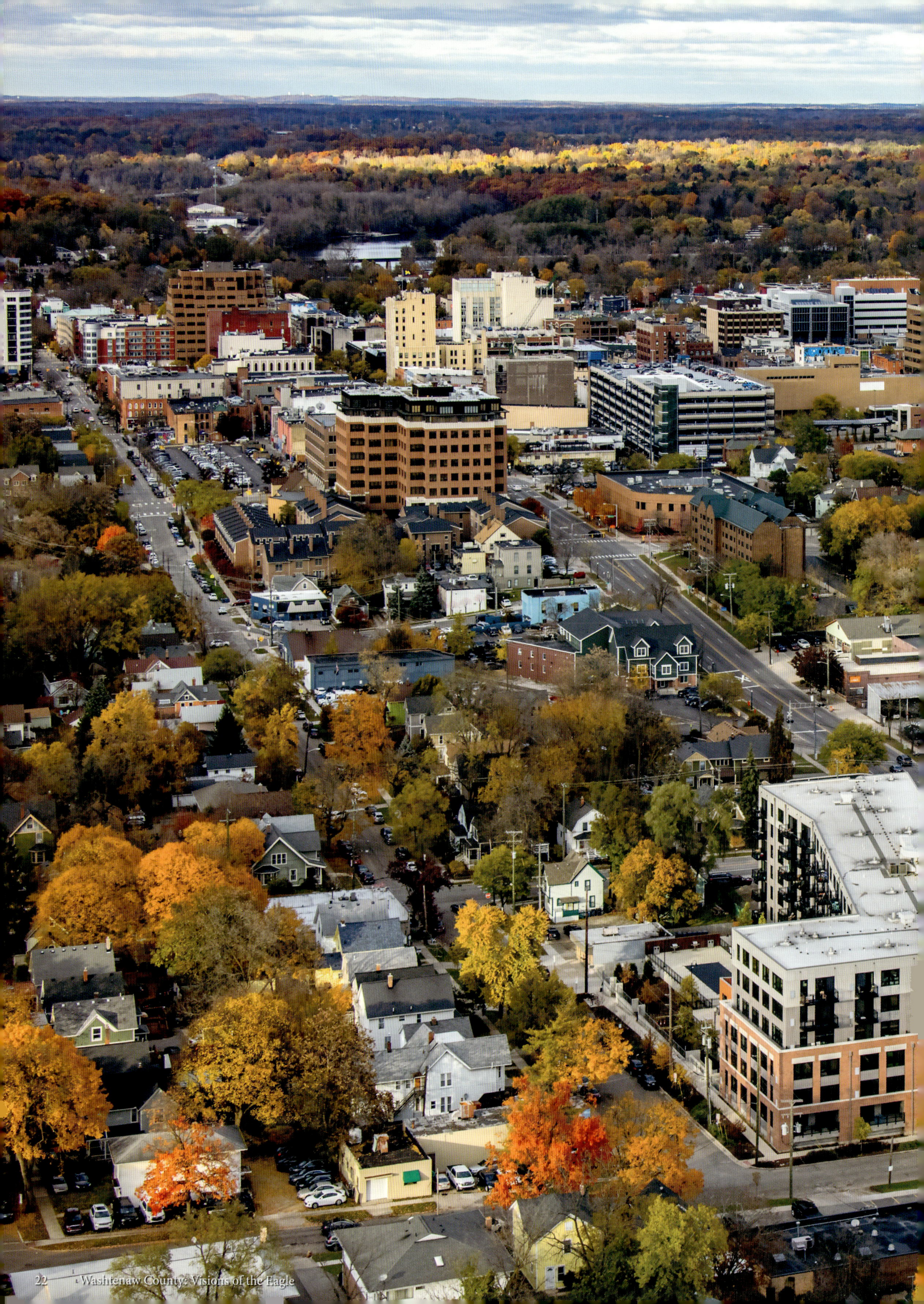

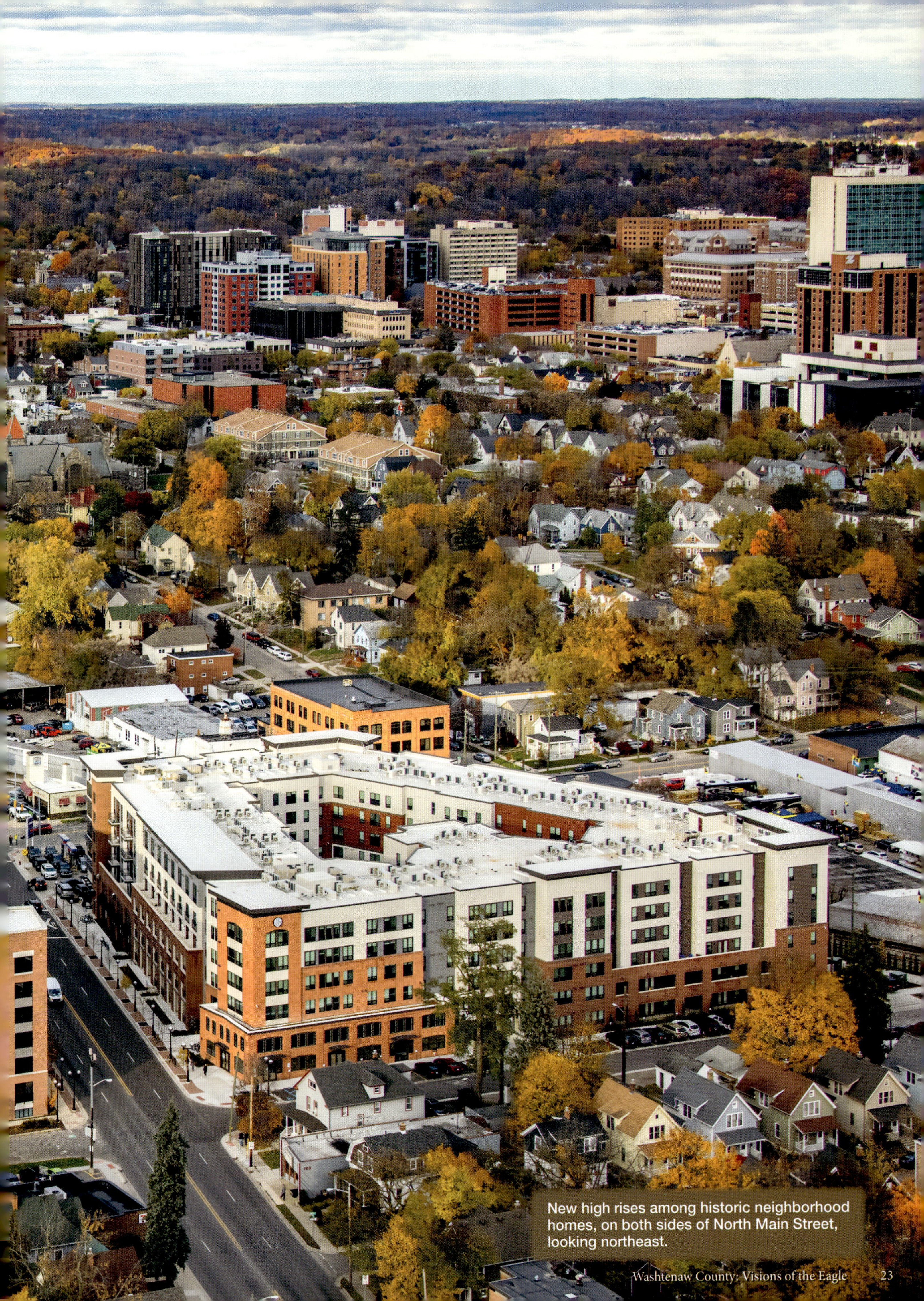

New high rises among historic neighborhood homes, on both sides of North Main Street, looking northeast.

IBEW

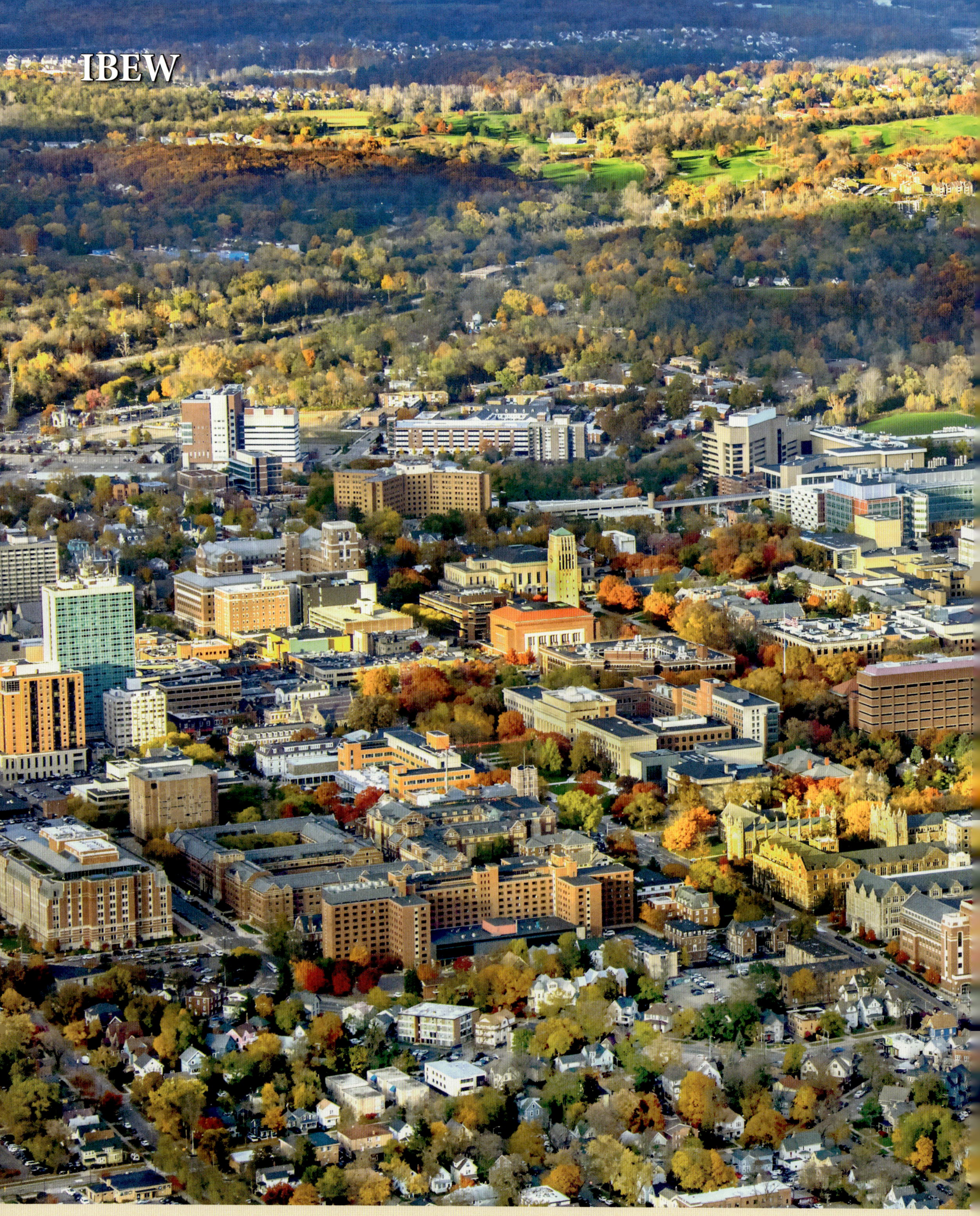

International Brotherhood of Electrical Workers Local 252, established in 1916, is affiliated with the National Electrical Contractors Association. Offices in Ann Arbor and Jackson serve Washtenaw, Jackson, parts of Ingham and Livingston counties. With 850 members and growing, we provide voice/data/video in addition to electrical service to our residential neighbors, area businesses, organizations, and schools. We pride ourselves on building a brighter Michigan.

IBEW
7920 Jackson Rd.
Suite A
Ann Arbor, MI
734-424-0978

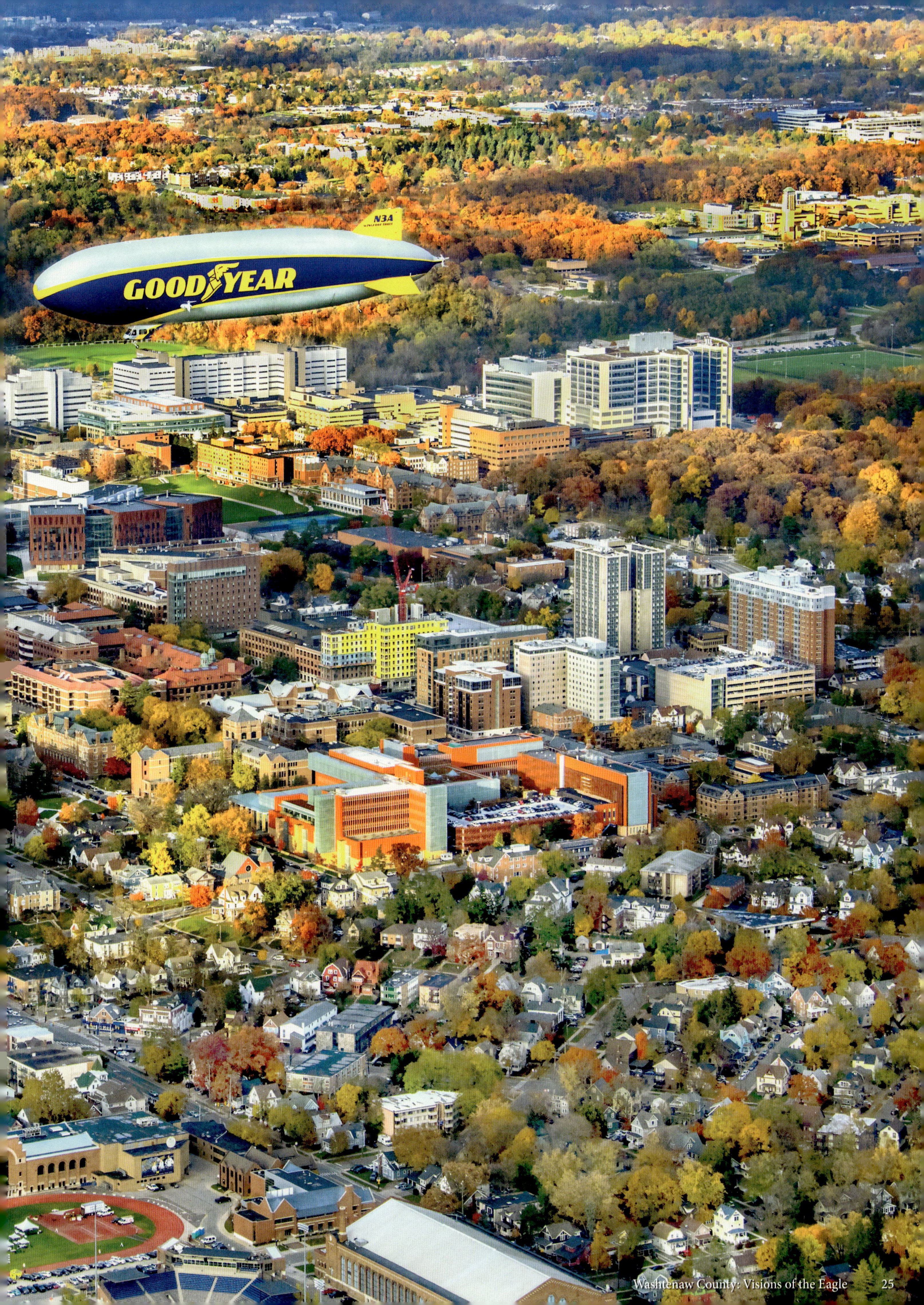
N3A
GOODYEAR

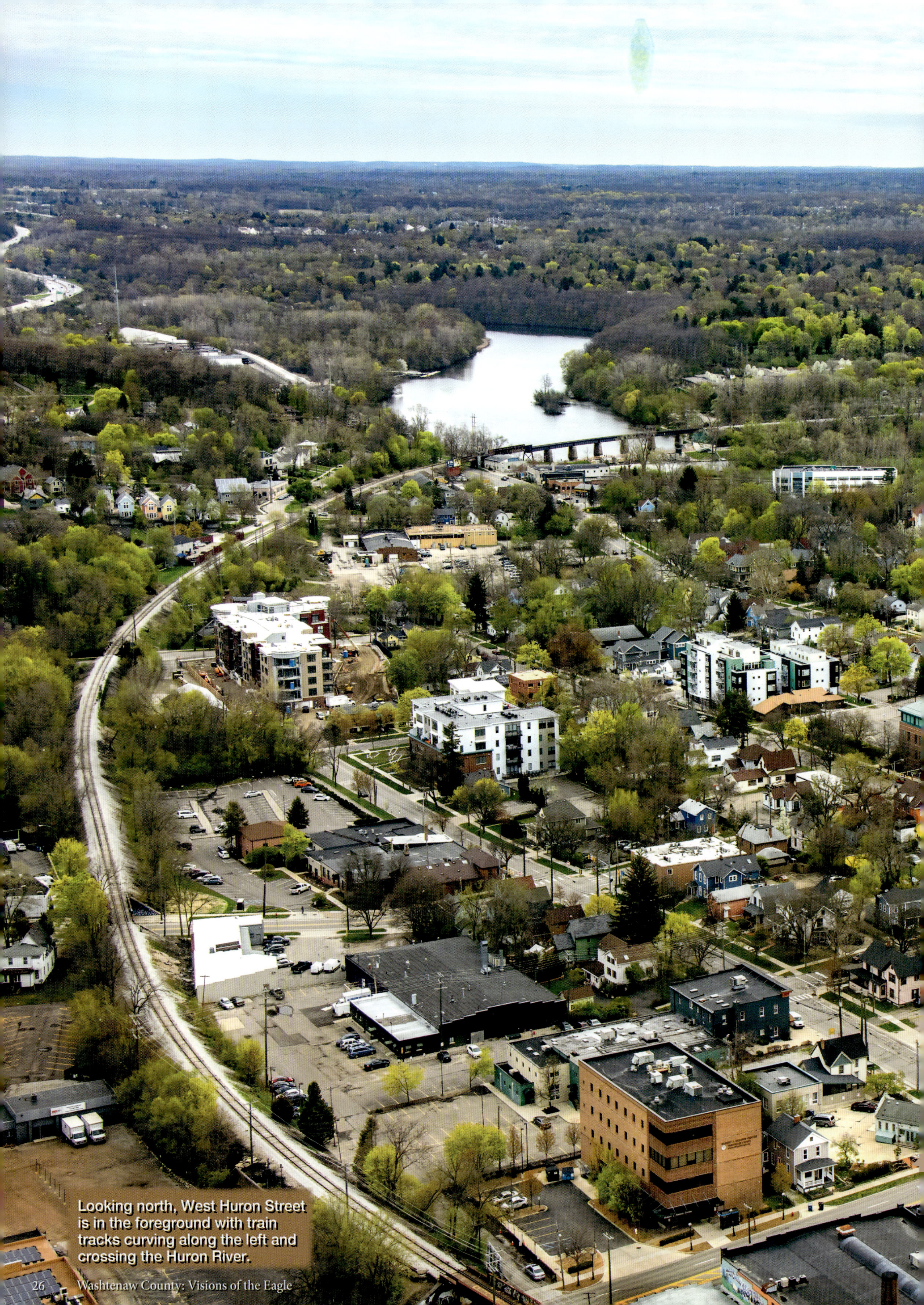

Looking north, West Huron Street is in the foreground with train tracks curving along the left and crossing the Huron River.

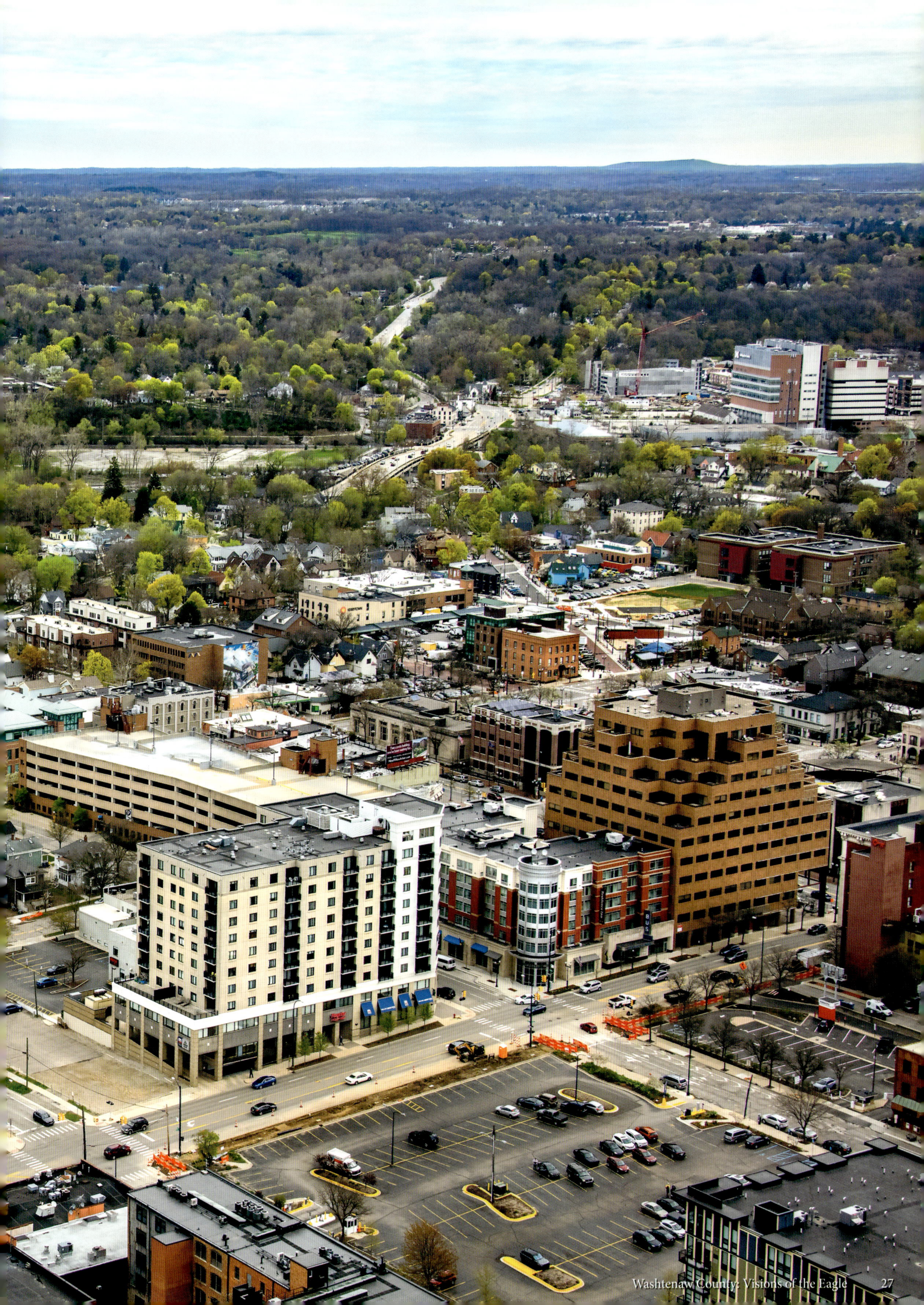

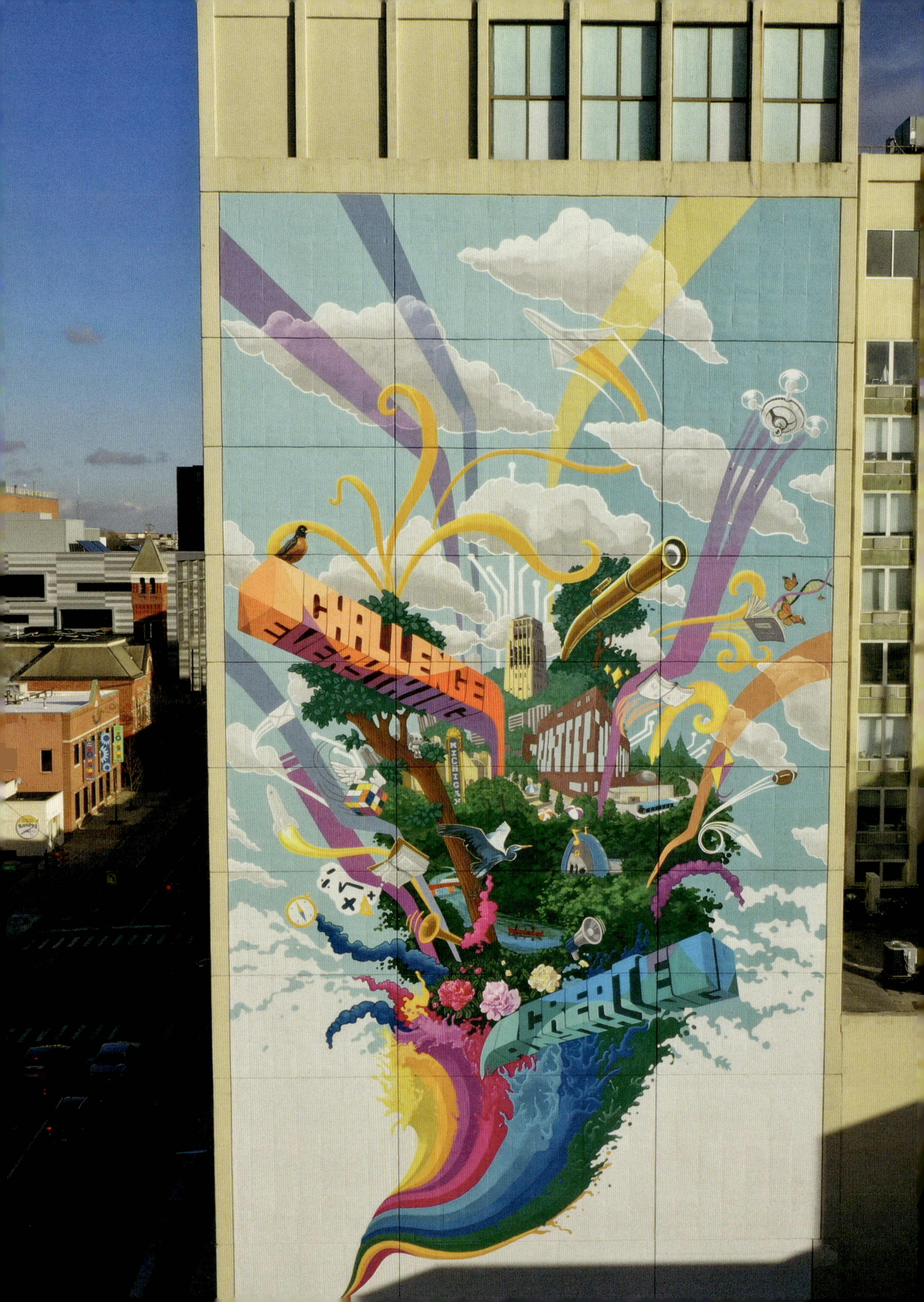
CHALLENGE
EVERYTHING
CREATE

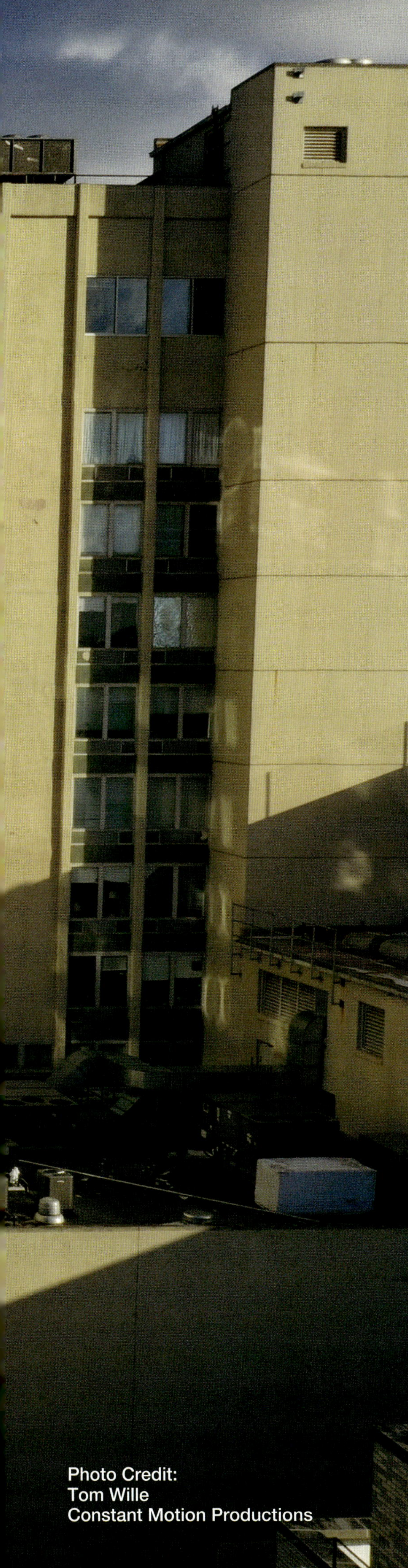

Photo Credit:
Tom Wille
Constant Motion Productions

Destination Ann Arbor

The 10-story wall of Courthouse Square at 100 S. 4th Avenue in downtown Ann Arbor serves as the canvas for a mural titled "Challenge Everything. Create Anything." In 2019, Destination Ann Arbor commissioned renowned local husband and wife artists, Mary Thiefels and Danijel Matanic, to create the work as a celebration of the creativity, ingenuity, and curiosity that imbue Ann Arbor with its vibrant energy and strong community spirit.

"We wanted to celebrate our local arts community, inspire our residents, create something beautiful for our community, and motivate travelers to visit the Ann Arbor area," said Mary Kerr, President & CEO of Destination Ann Arbor.

Destination Ann Arbor is a non-profit organization that elevates the economic vitality and quality of life in Ann Arbor and Washtenaw County by promoting the area as a destination of choice for visitors. The mural is part of a larger initiative to showcase area artists that think and dream bigger. The initiative includes a mini-documentary series that highlights local artists and what inspires them about Ann Arbor and Washtenaw County.

Ann Arbor is a place for the bold and independent among us, a catalyst for creativity, a vibrant community of passion, purpose, and ingenuity. It inspired muralists Mary Thiefels and Danijel Matanic to transform ordinary walls into works of art. See the story and get inspired at AnnArbor.org/CreateAnything.

DESTINATION ANN ARBOR

315 W. Huron St.
Suite 340
Ann Arbor, MI
734-995-7281

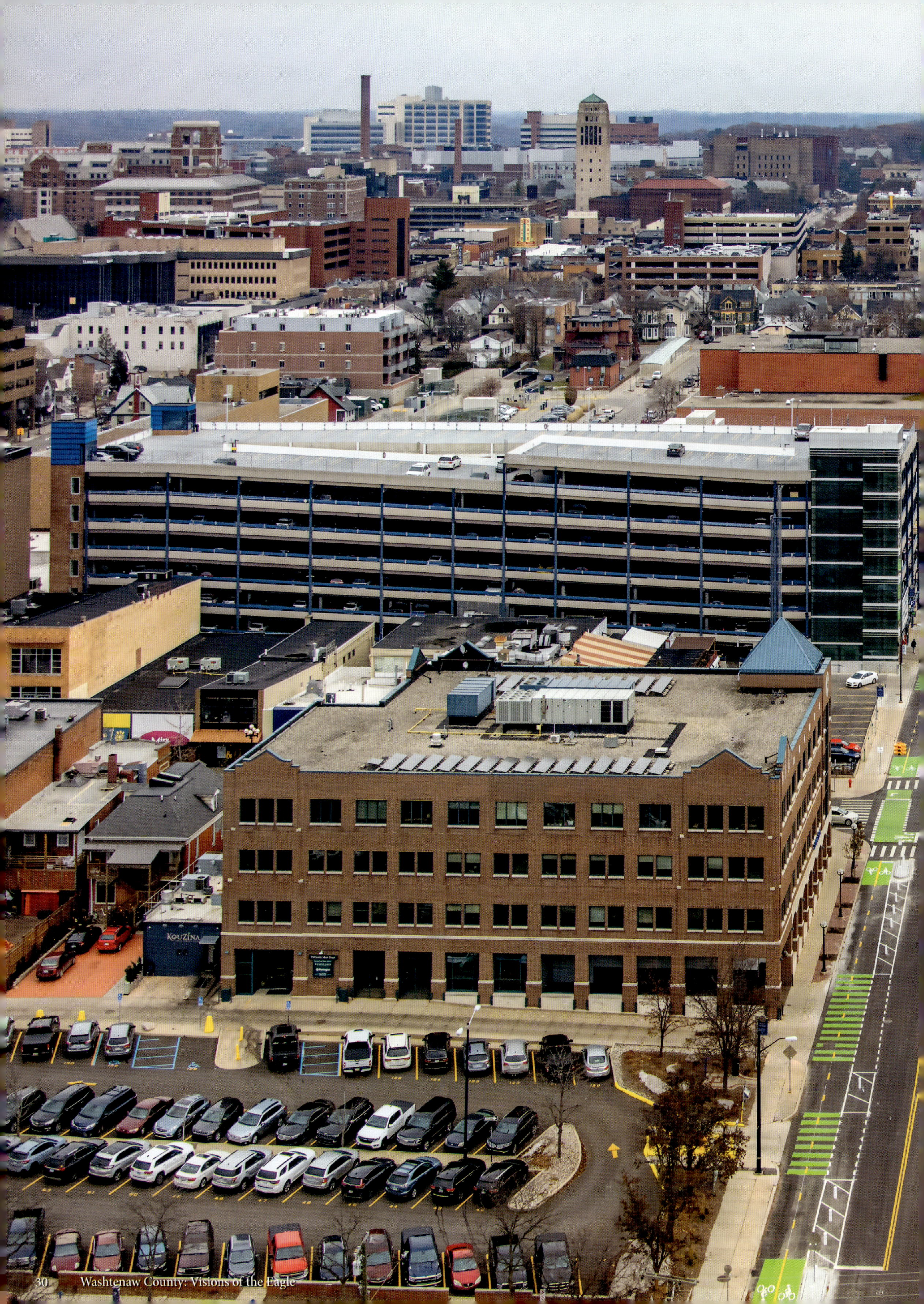
KOUZINA

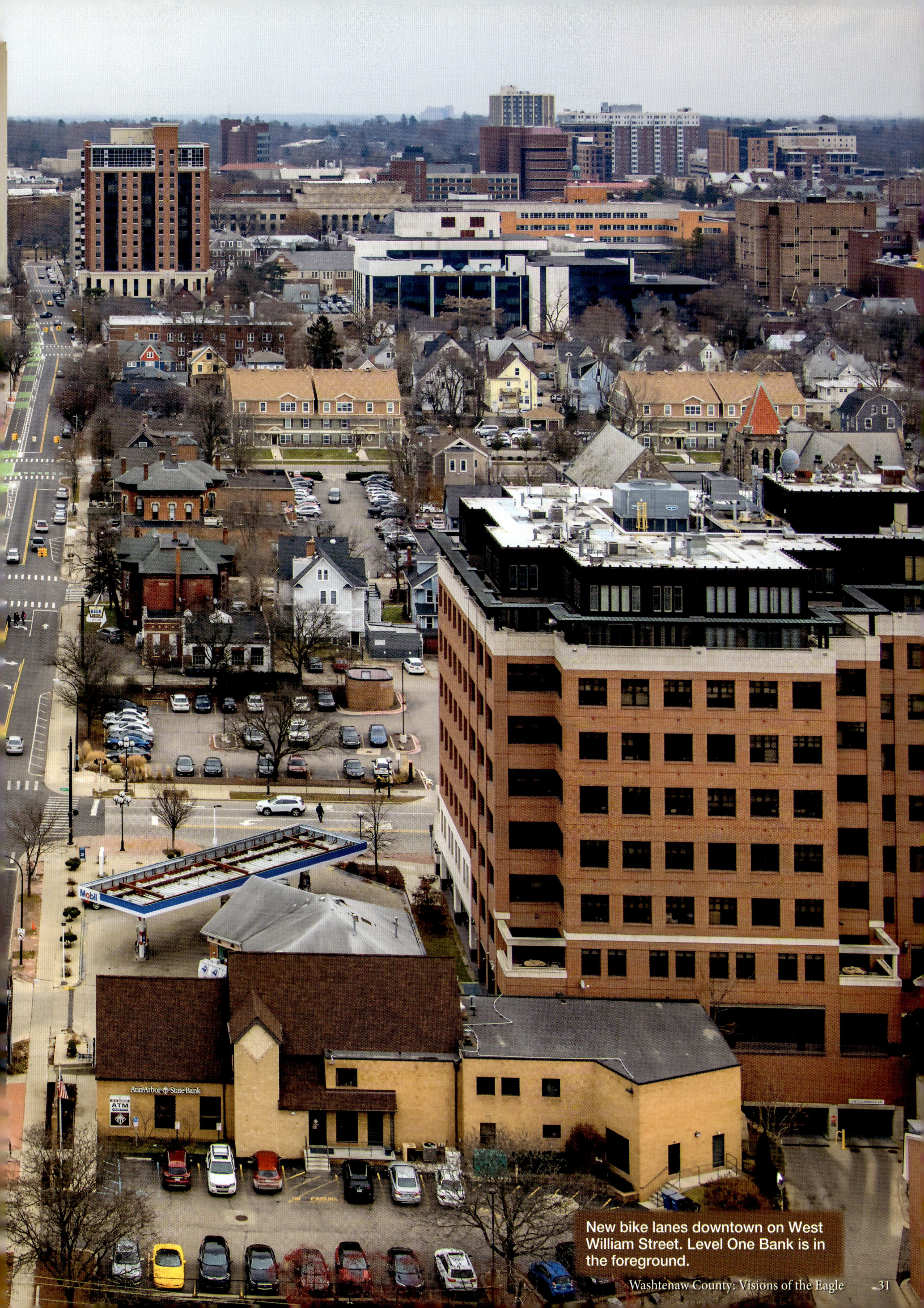

New bike lanes downtown on West William Street. Level One Bank is in the foreground.

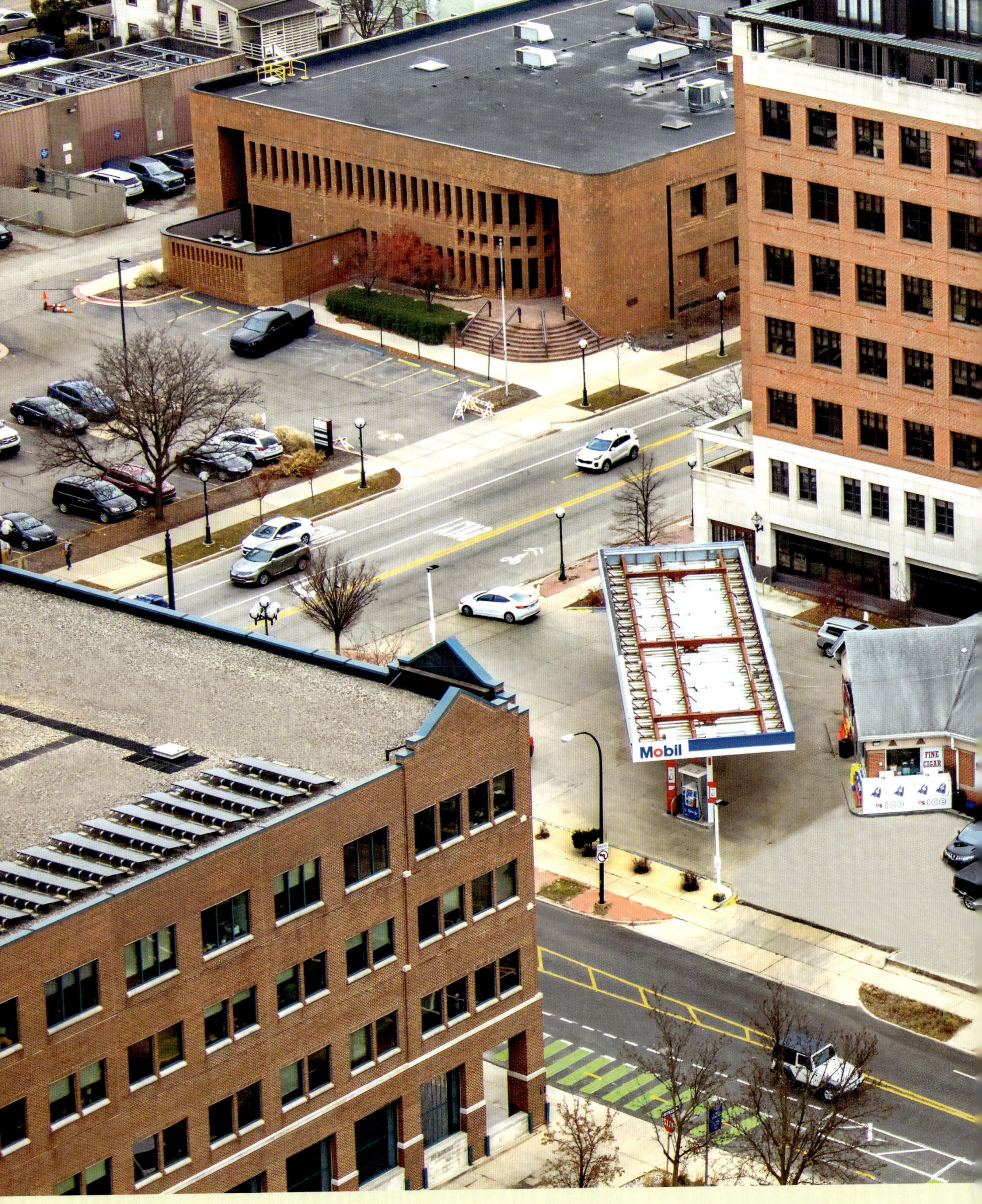

In 2020, Ann Arbor State Bank merged with Michigan-based Level One Bank. The combined organization currently has 16 banking centers located throughout Ann Arbor, Metro Detroit, Jackson and Grand Rapids.

With a focus on local community banking and superior customer service, Level One Bank and Ann Arbor State Bank shared similar banking philosophies which made the merger a natural fit for both companies.

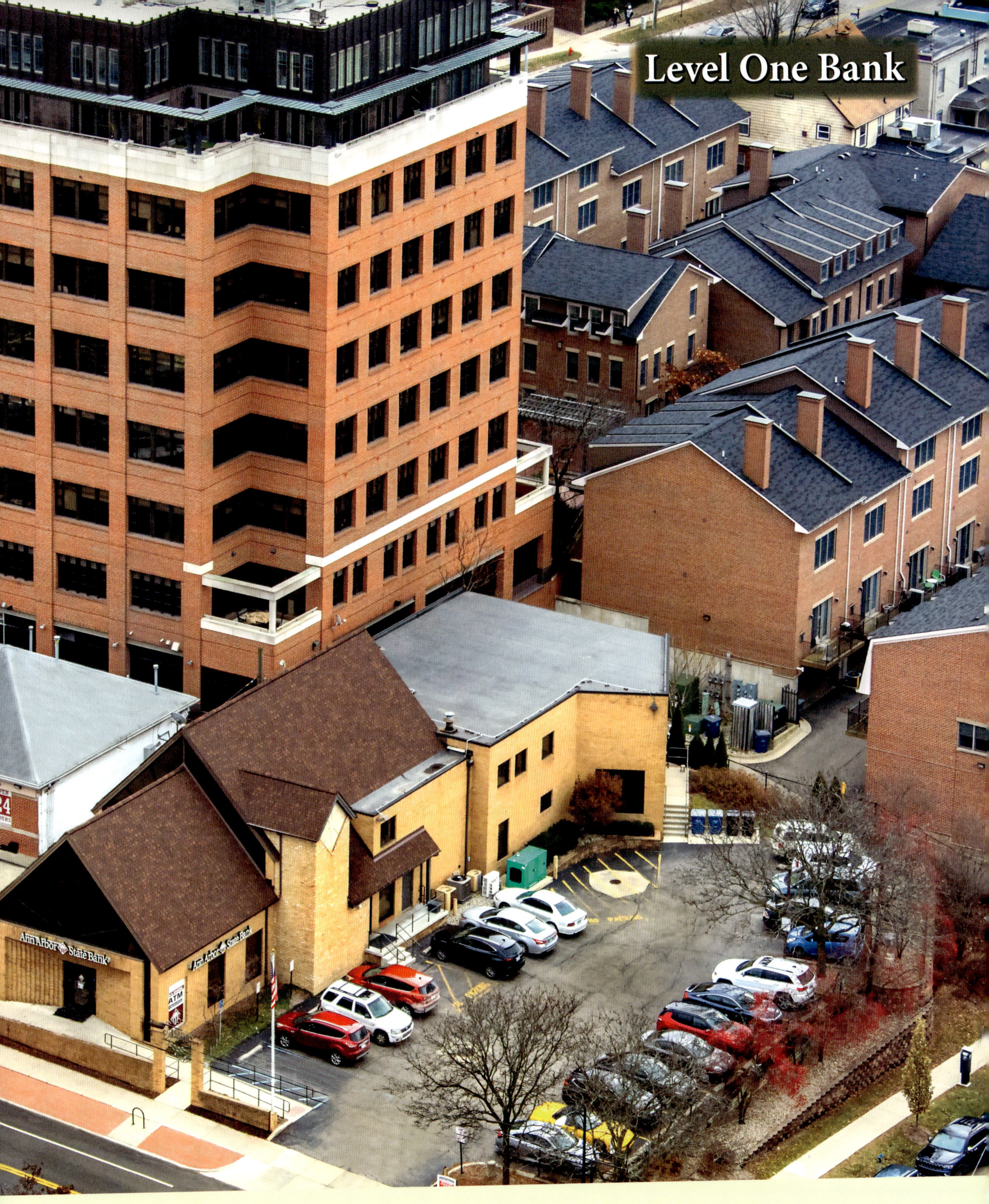

Level One Bank was founded in 2007 in Farmington Hills by a group of local entrepreneurs and community leaders who believed in the importance of personal service, local decision making, and strong community values. Level One Bank was thrilled to expand its footprint in Ann Arbor with Ann Arbor State Bank and looks forward to becoming an even bigger presence in this vibrant community. You can learn more about Level One Bank at www.LevelOneBank.com.

LEVEL ONE BANK
Formerly
ANN ARBOR STATE BANK

125 West William St.
Ann Arbor, MI
734-761-1475

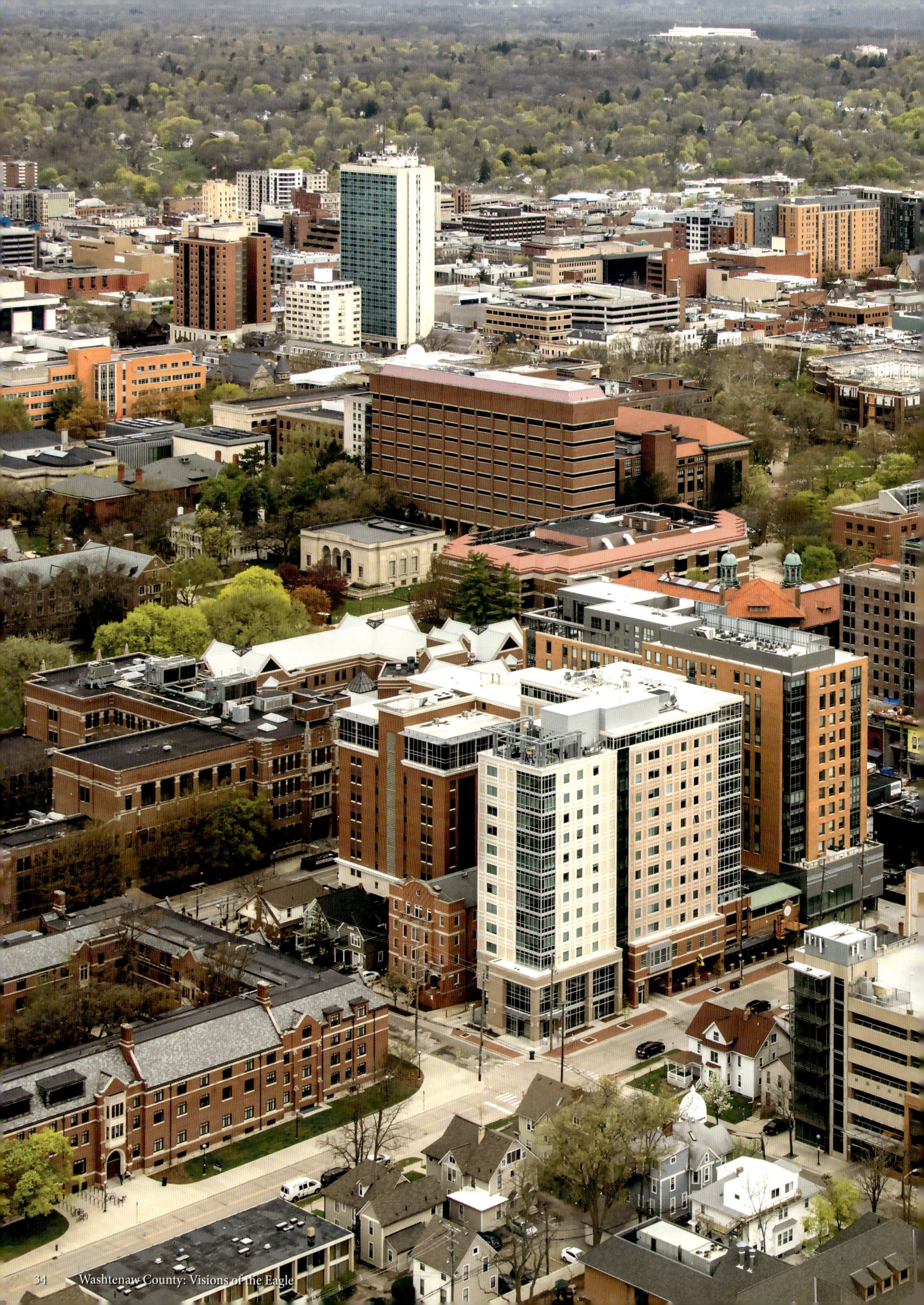

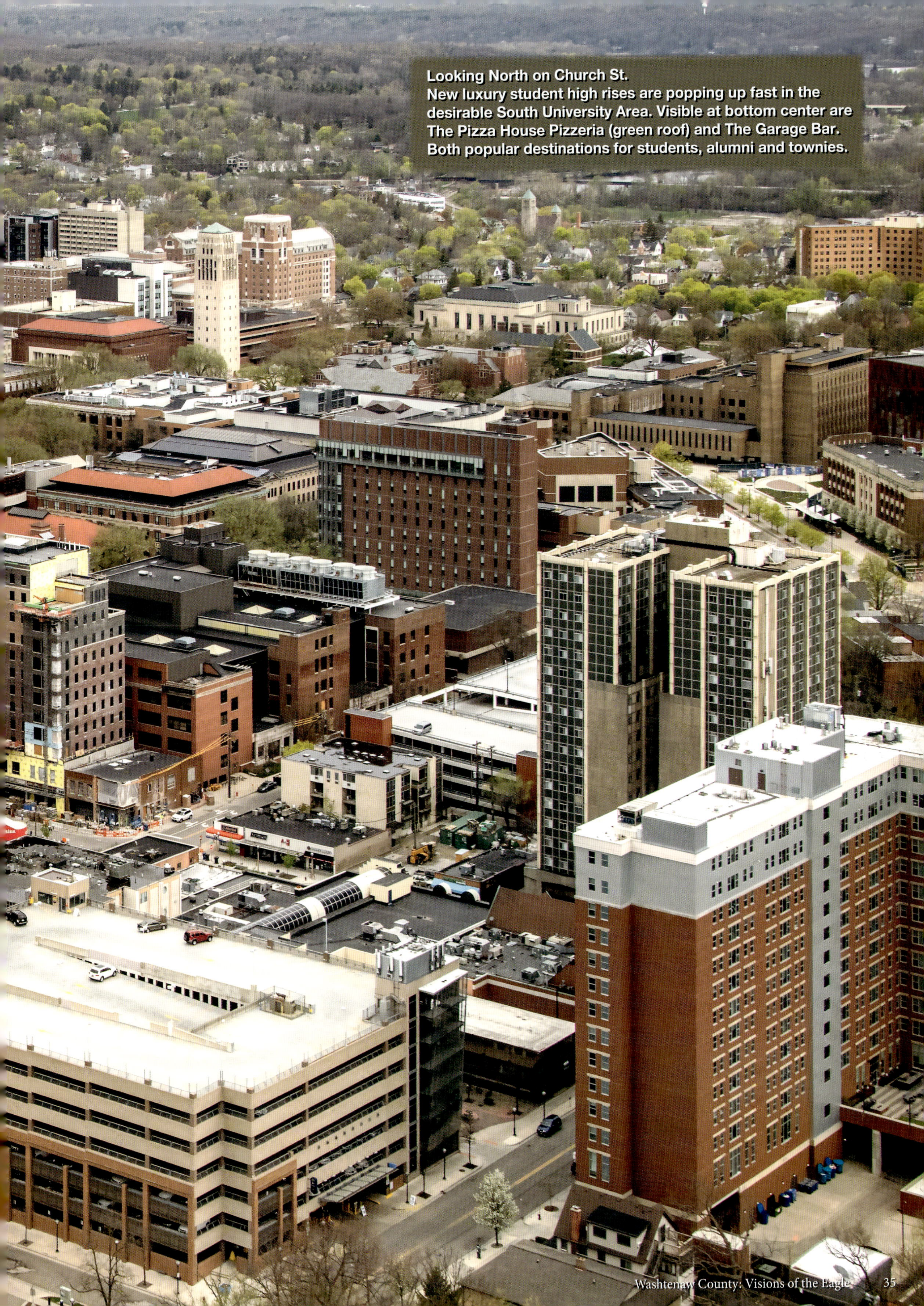

Looking North on Church St.
New luxury student high rises are popping up fast in the desirable South University Area. Visible at bottom center are The Pizza House Pizzeria (green roof) and The Garage Bar. Both popular destinations for students, alumni and townies.

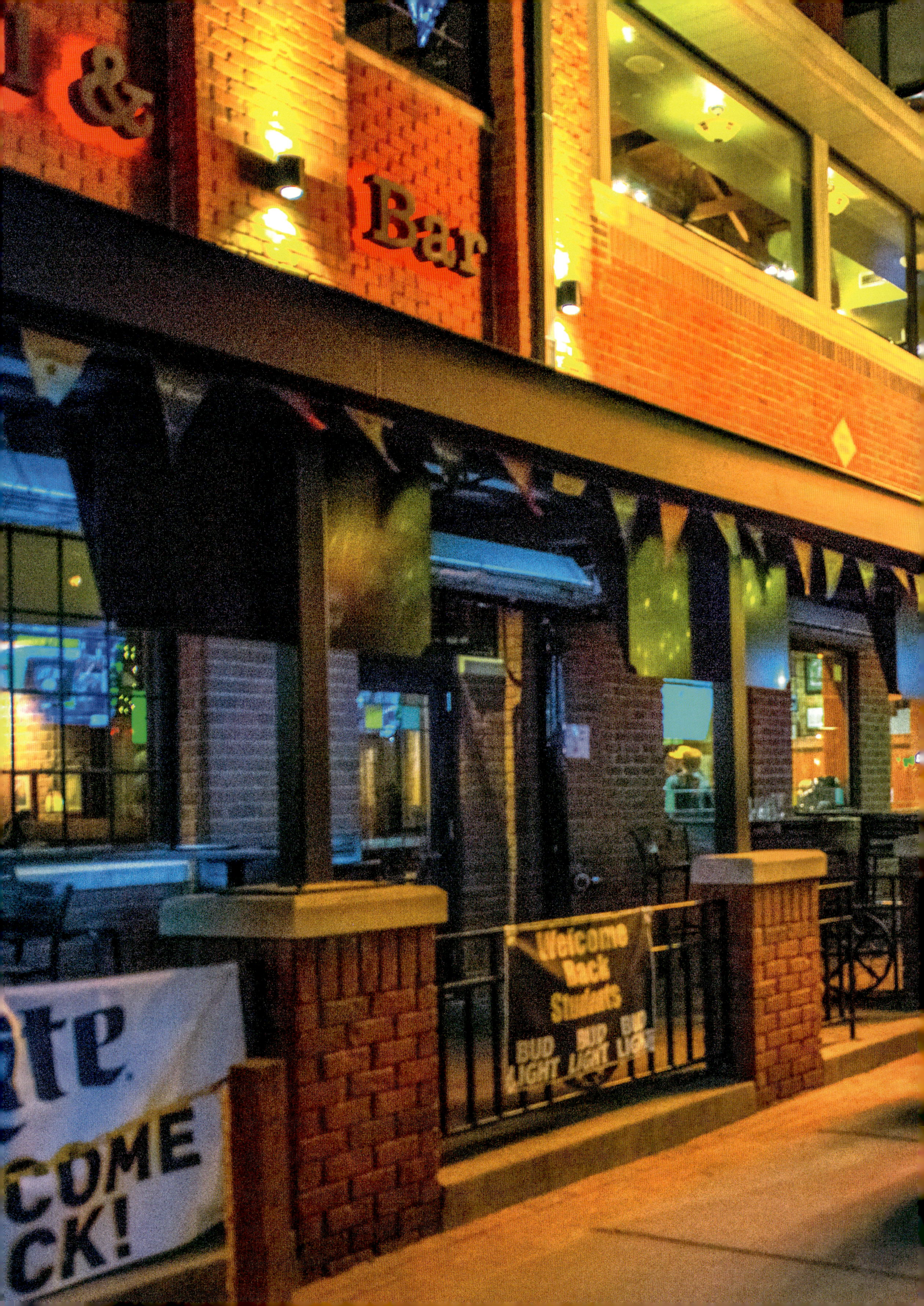
Bar
Welcome Back Students
BUD LIGHT BUD LIGHT

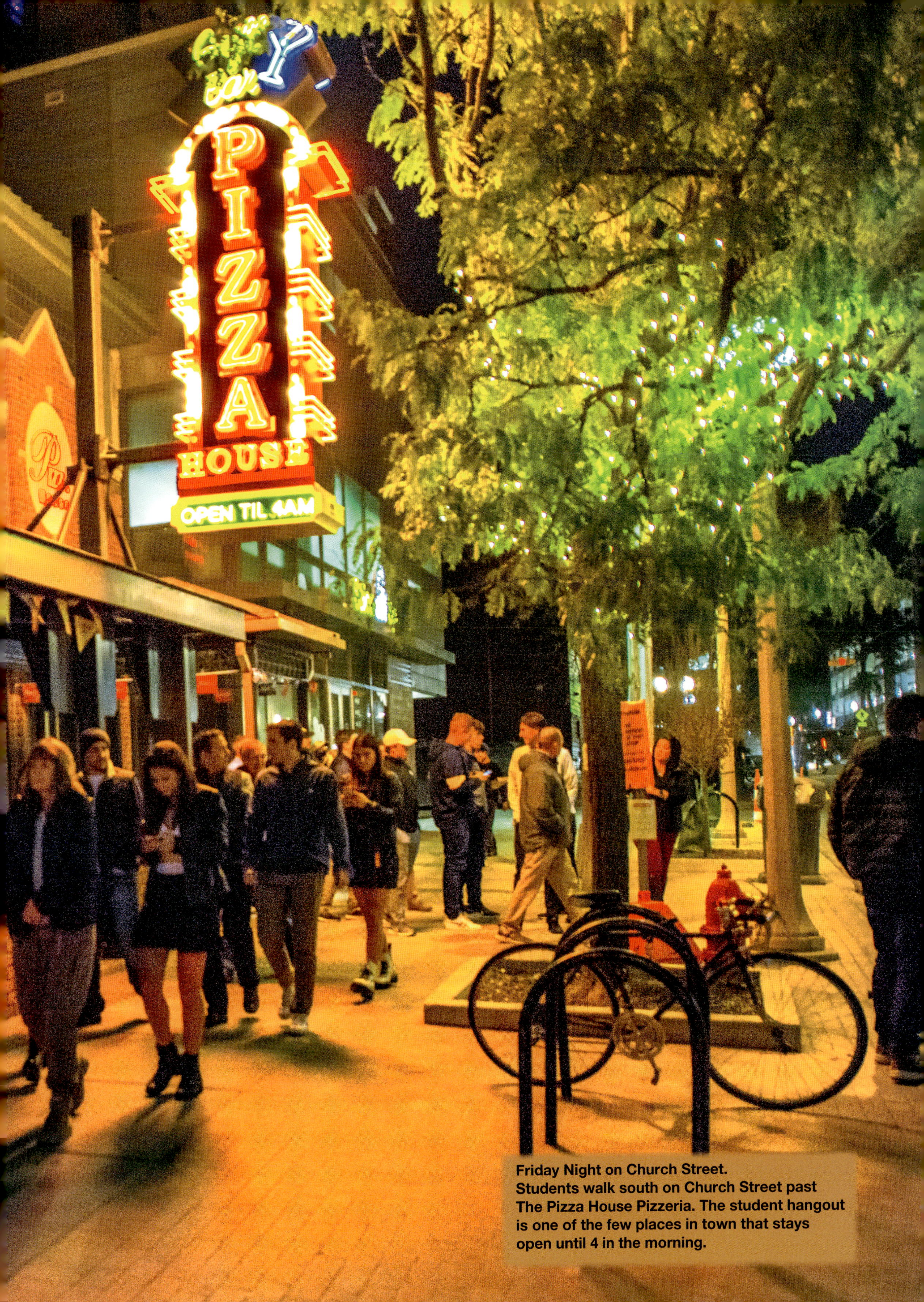

Friday Night on Church Street.
Students walk south on Church Street past The Pizza House Pizzeria. The student hangout is one of the few places in town that stays open until 4 in the morning.

Pizza House

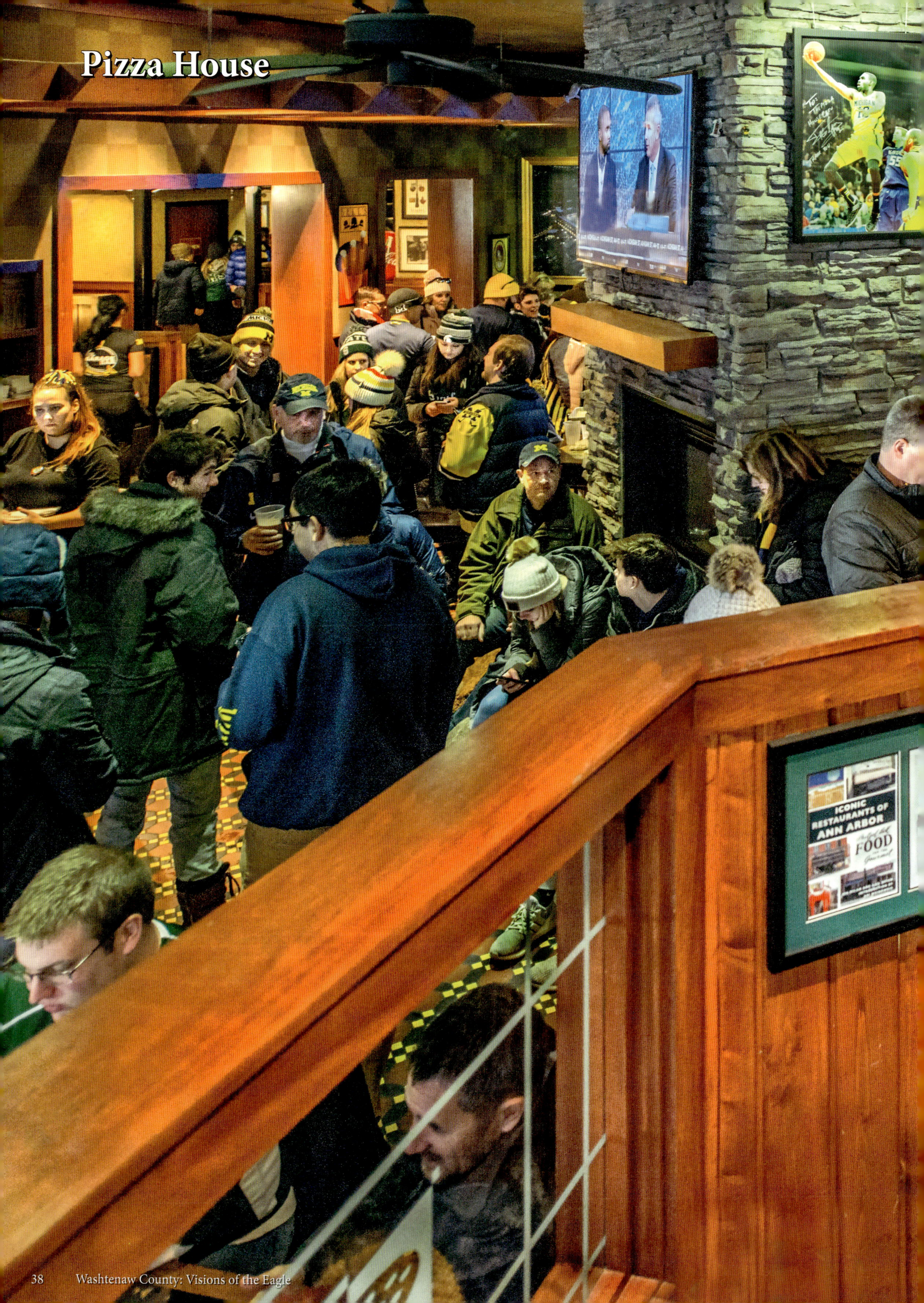

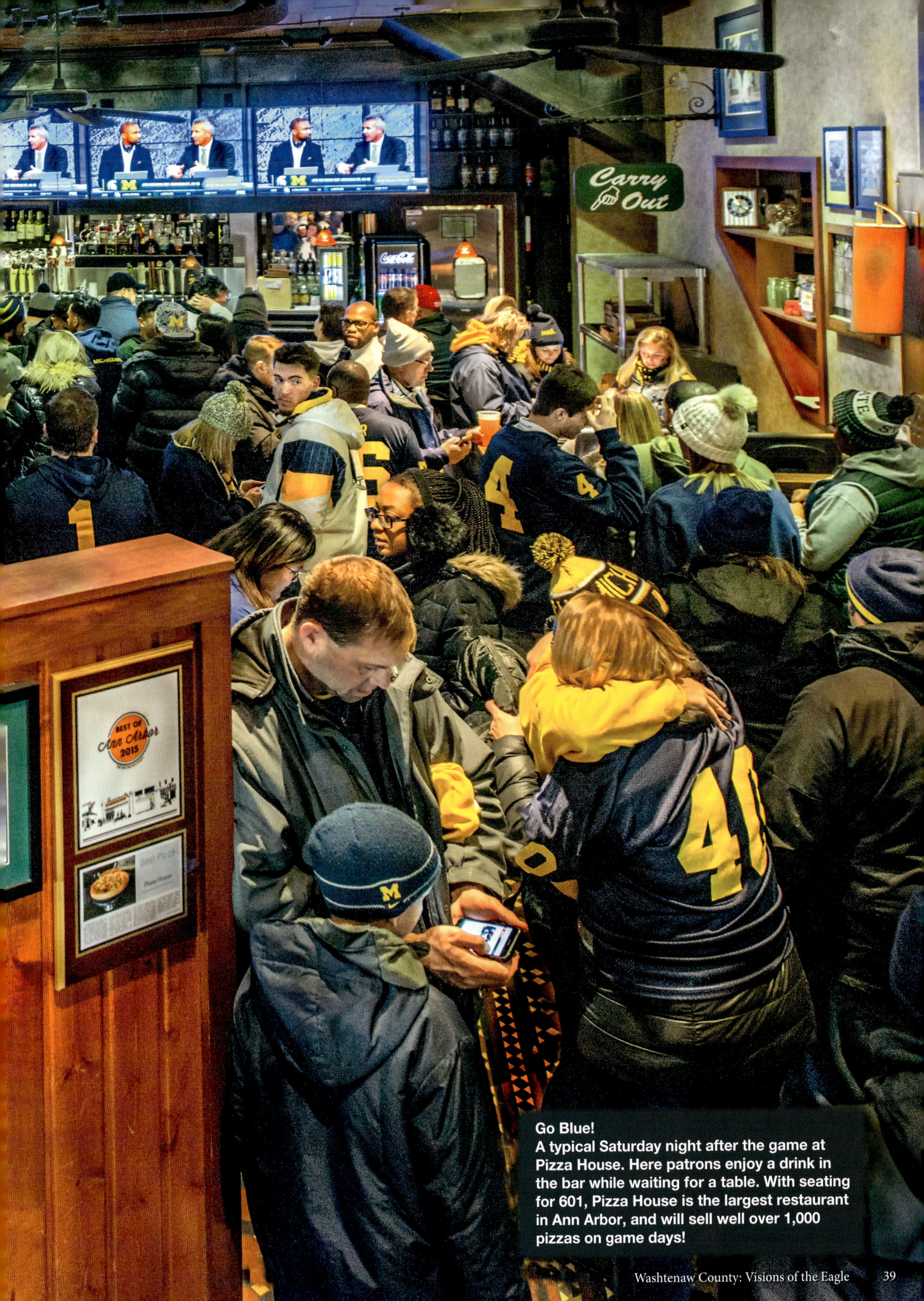

Go Blue!
A typical Saturday night after the game at Pizza House. Here patrons enjoy a drink in the bar while waiting for a table. With seating for 601, Pizza House is the largest restaurant in Ann Arbor, and will sell well over 1,000 pizzas on game days!

Hobbs+Black Architects

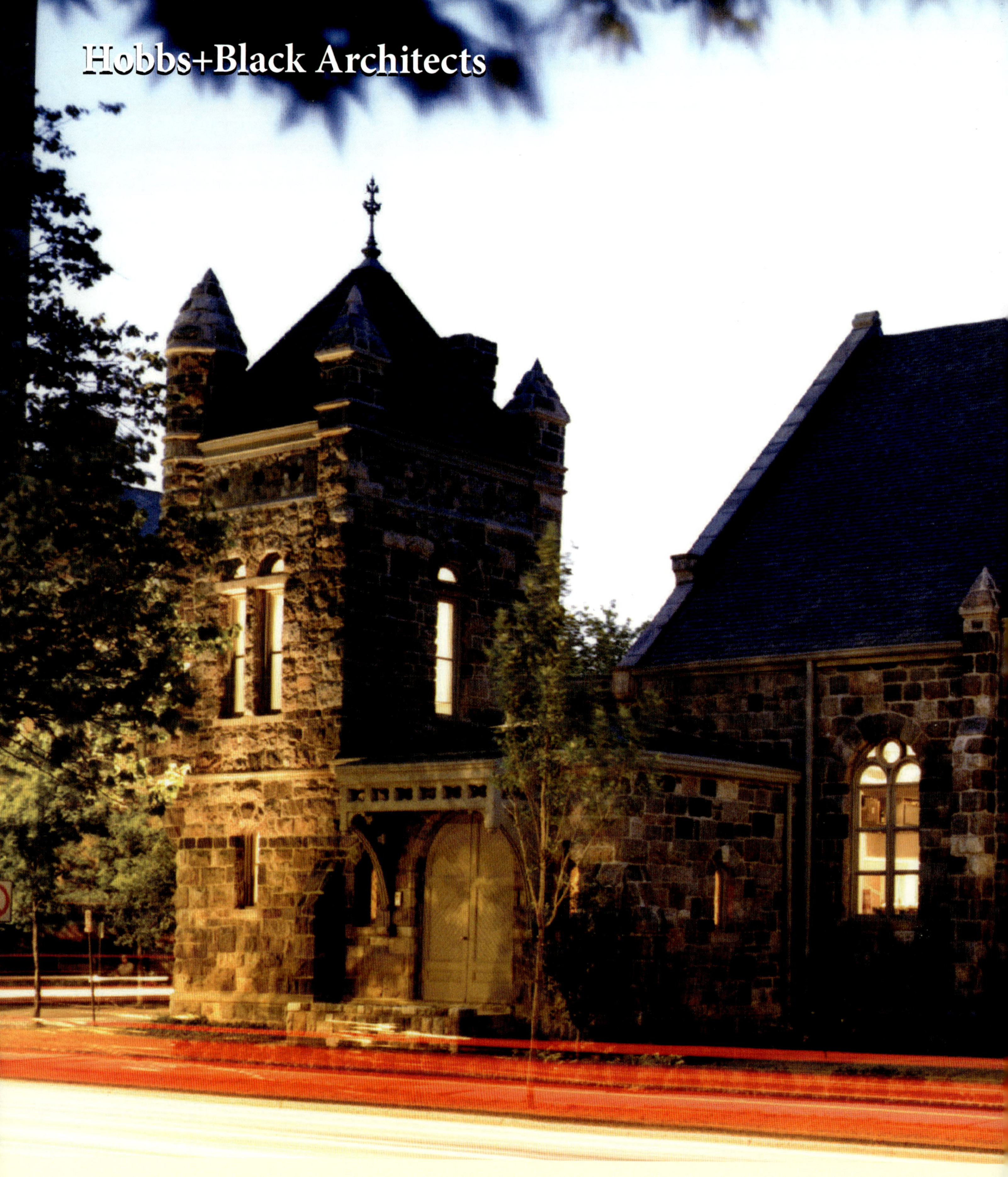

Ann Arbor has been the home of Hobbs+Black Architects since 1965 when William Hobbs and Richard Black founded the firm. It has since grown to become Ann Arbor's largest architectural firm and is proud to be part of the Ann Arbor community. In its 55 years, Hobbs+Black has earned a solid reputation for design nationwide.

Dedicated to helping shape and preserve the unique character of Ann Arbor, Hobbs+Black engages in design projects ranging from new building construction to historic renovation, rehabilitation, and adaptive re-use plans.

Many projects by the firm have become city landmarks, such as Sloan Plaza, One North Main, Brauer Building, Vic Village, University Commons, and the University of Michigan Lurie Engineering Center.

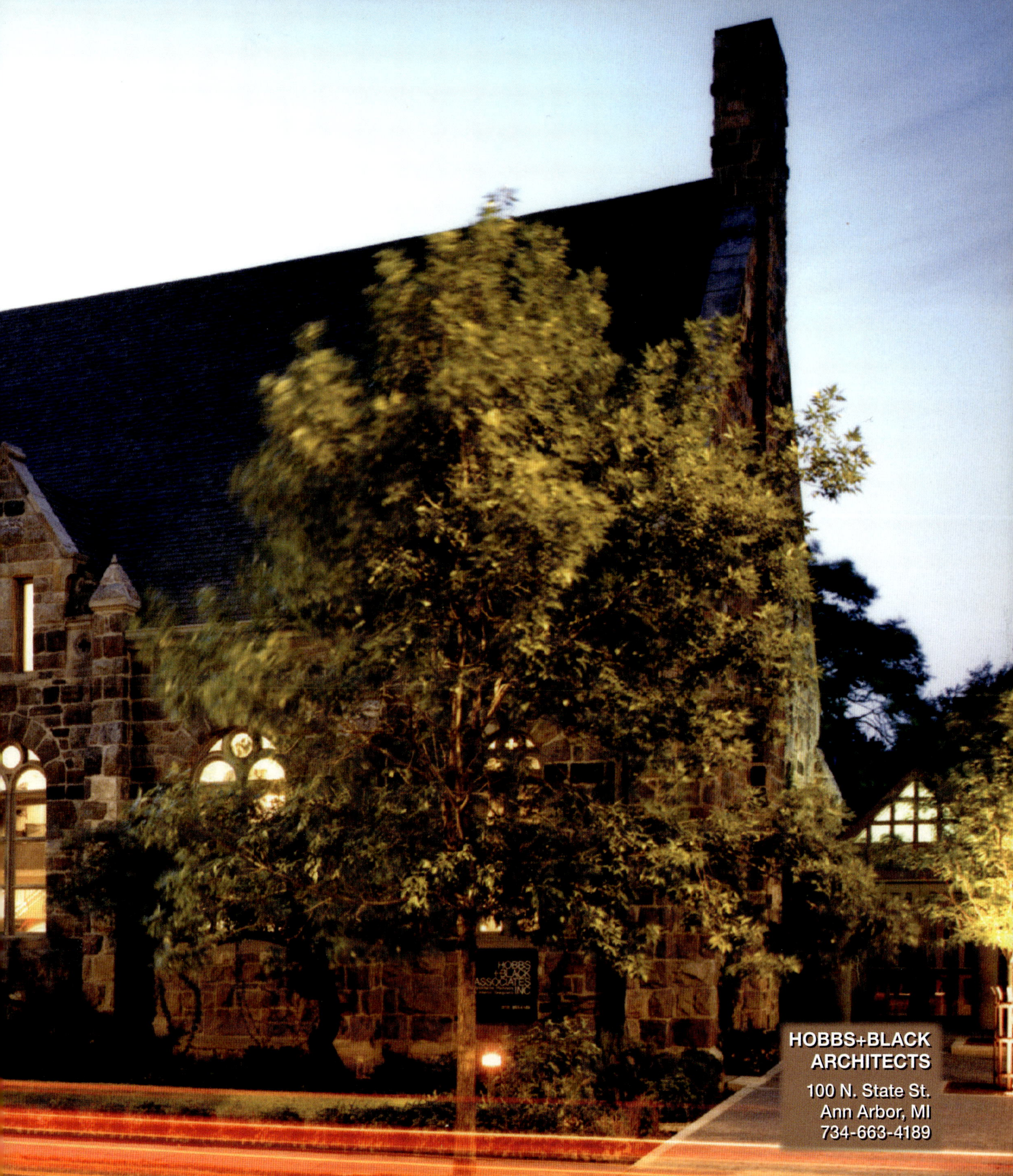

Hobbs+Black brings new life to older buildings while honoring the character and integrity of their original design. Its adaptive re-use and rehabilitation projects include Liberty Lofts, Kerrytown Shops, and the Gandy Dancer.

The firm's corporate headquarters, a church built in 1882 in Ann Arbor's historic Old Fourth Ward, is one of Hobbs+Black's notable endeavors. In the 1980s, the firm needed more office space. Instead of moving to new buildings on the city's perimeter, the trend at the time, Hobbs+Black rescued the historic church, renovated and adapted it into offices, and stayed in the heart of downtown.

In addition to its corporate headquarters in Ann Arbor, Hobbs+Black has full-service regional offices in Lansing, Michigan and Scottsdale, Arizona.

Ann Arbor/Ypsilanti Regional Chamber

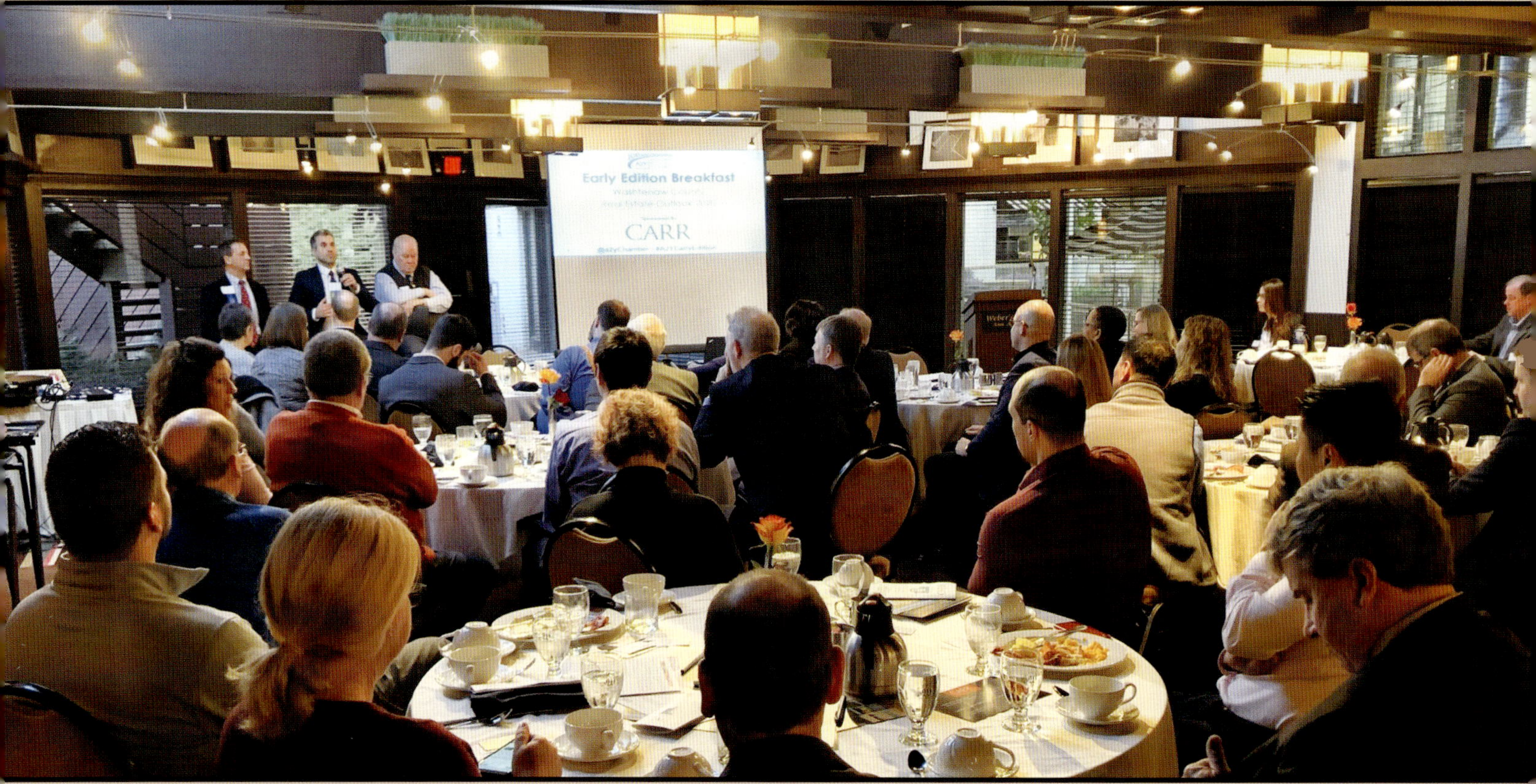

A2Y Early Edition Breakfast, covering new topics each month impacting our local business community.

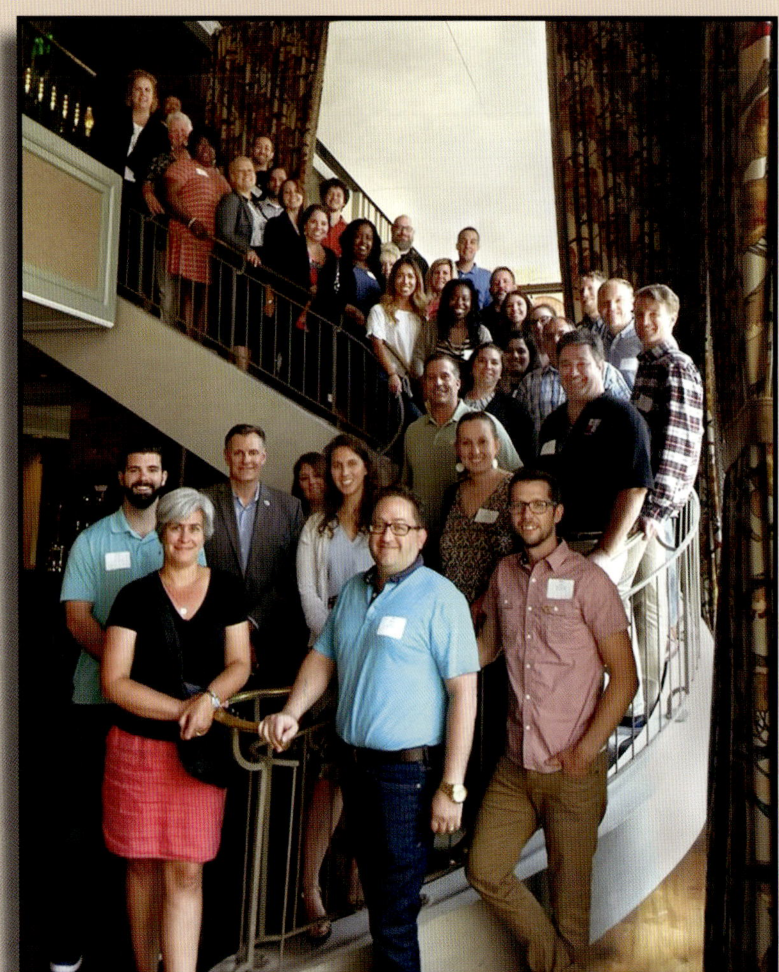

Leadership A2Y Class.

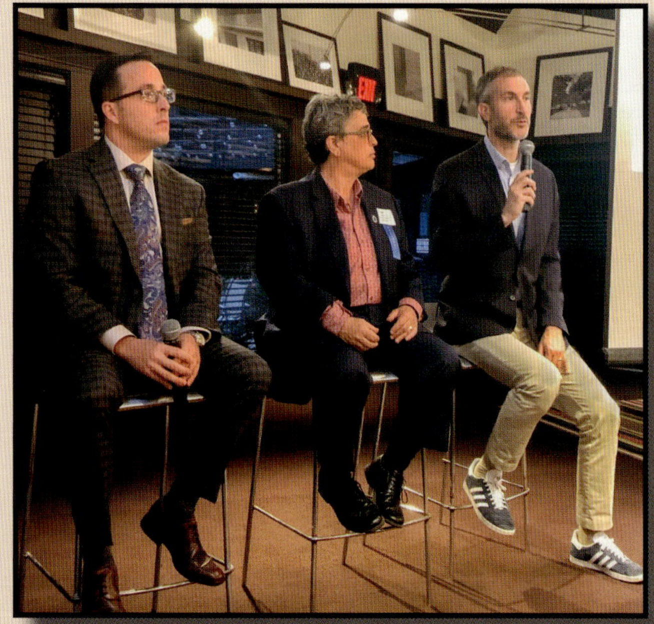

Presentation by the Mayor of Ann Arbor, Christopher Taylor, the Mayor of Ypsilanti, Beth Bashert, and the Mayor of Saline, Brian Marl.

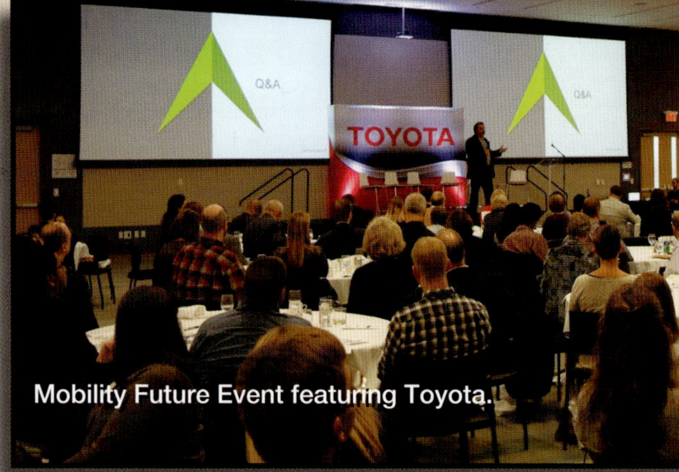

Mobility Future Event featuring Toyota.

For more information on chamber activities visit A2Ychamber.org

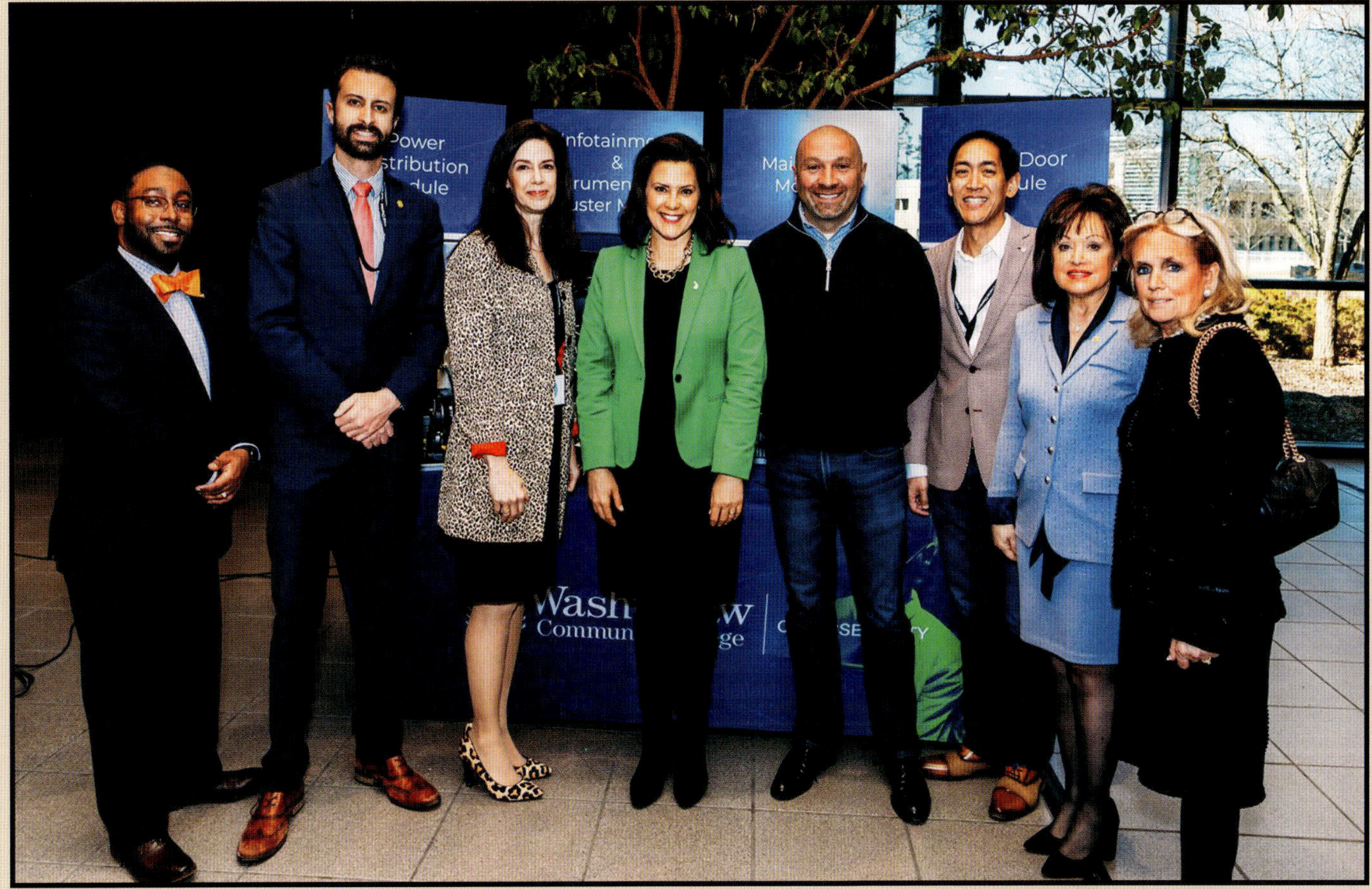

Workforce Pipeline Summit, (L to R) Brandon Tucker-Dean of Advanced Technologies and Public Service Careers at Washtenaw Community College, Yousef Rabhi-State Representative, Diane Keller-Ann Arbor/ Ypsilanti Regional Chamber CEO, Gretchen Whitmer-Governor, Raffaele Mautone-Duo Security, Rich Chang-CEO, NewFoundry, Rose B. Bellanca-CEO of Washtenaw Community College, and Debbie Dingell-Congresswoman.

Representing 1000 businesses, the Ann Arbor/Ypsilanti Regional Chamber is a non-profit organization committed to fostering regional economic success, community prosperity, and improved quality of life by advocating for, and supporting, their local business community.

The Ann Arbor/Ypsilanti Regional Chamber proudly celebrates 100 years of success. In the new century, the A2Y Chamber continues to develop programs that meet the business needs of the future workforce. Expanded programs include monthly networking events, Early Edition breakfasts, Workforce Pipeline Initiatives, and mobility, diversity, equity & inclusion topics. Additionally, kicking off Creative Chamber collaborations, including the development of the new Creative Spotlight App.

The Ann Arbor/Ypsilanti Regional Chamber has a vision for the future and will continue to develop impactful programming for the next generation of entrepreneurs, creatives, and business professionals in our community.

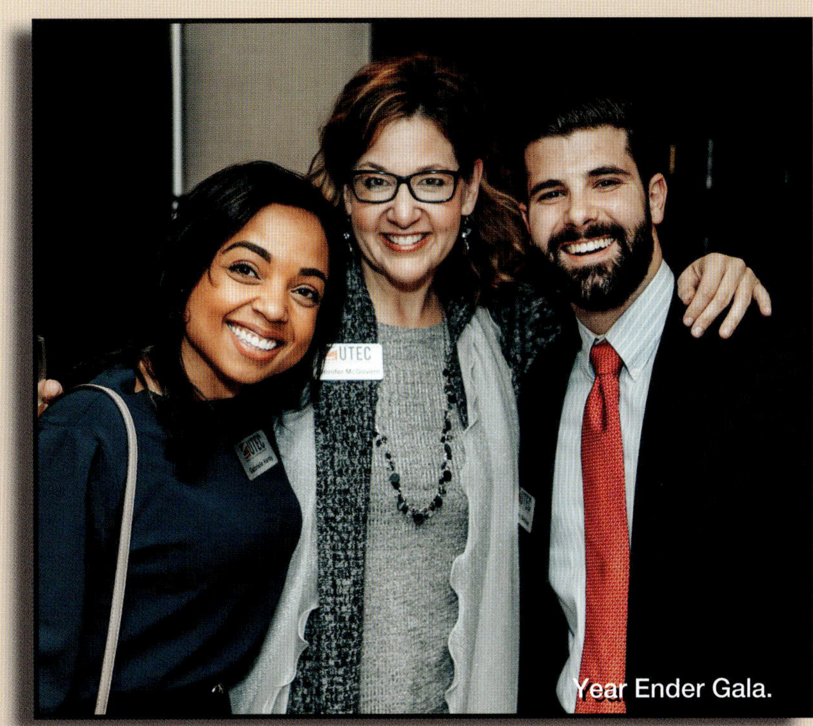

Year Ender Gala.

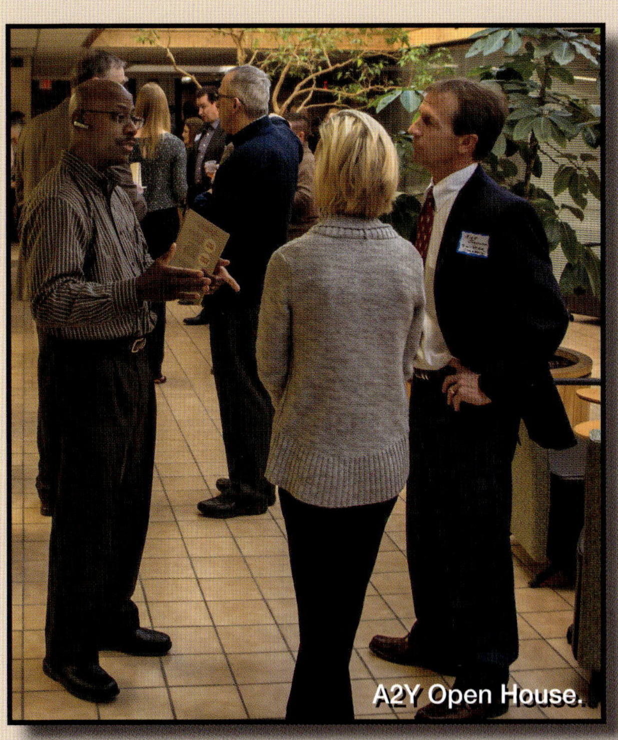

A2Y Open House.

The Bouma Group

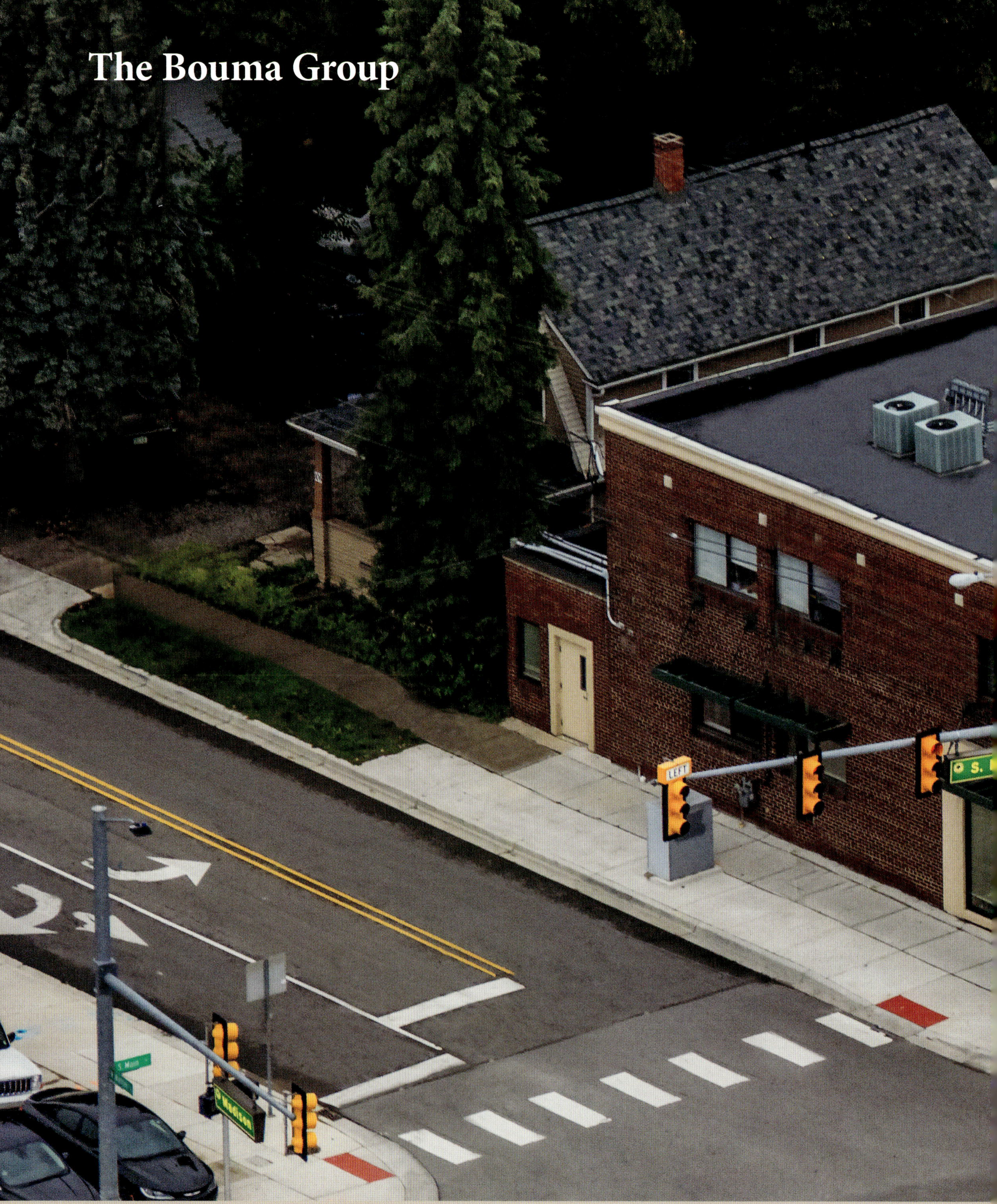

Founder and visionary of The Bouma Group Realtors, Martin Bouma has built a team of experts who consistently rank #1 out of 800 Realtors for total volume and units sold in Washtenaw County. Since 2000, The Bouma Group has ranked in the top 100 nationally of more than 180,000 Keller Williams agents. Martin's unique business model which utilizes specialists in key areas such as listing, closing and marketing, are among the key ingredients of delivering world-class customer service. Martin's 34+years have yielded an in-depth knowledge of the Ann Arbor area real estate market. In addition, his extensive marketing and social networking have been integral to his broad reach and influence. He has shared his real estate expertise and spoken to audiences of more than 8,000 people.

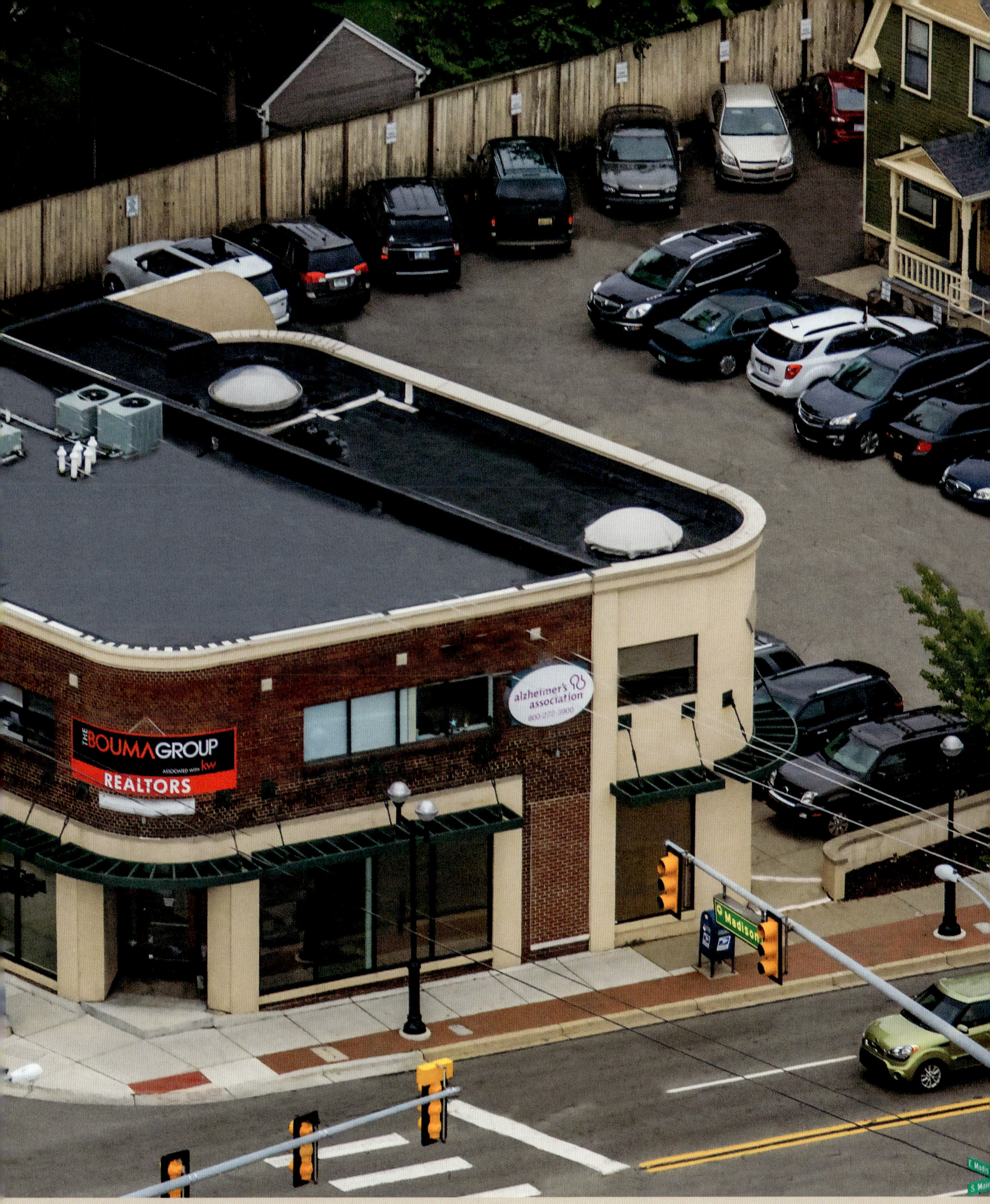

The Bouma Group Realtors support many community organizations, including Ele's Place, ChadTough, the Humane Society of Huron Valley, to mention a few. To celebrate its 100th home sale each year, the community nominates and votes on non-profit organizations. Those ranked in the top five receive cash awards each in varying amounts for a grand total of $13,000. This annual event is one of the ways Martin and The Bouma Group have chosen to serve the community which has been such a wonderful source of business over the last three decades.

THE BOUMA GROUP REALTORS

564 S. Main St.
Suite 100
Ann Arbor, MI
734-761-3060

UA Local 190

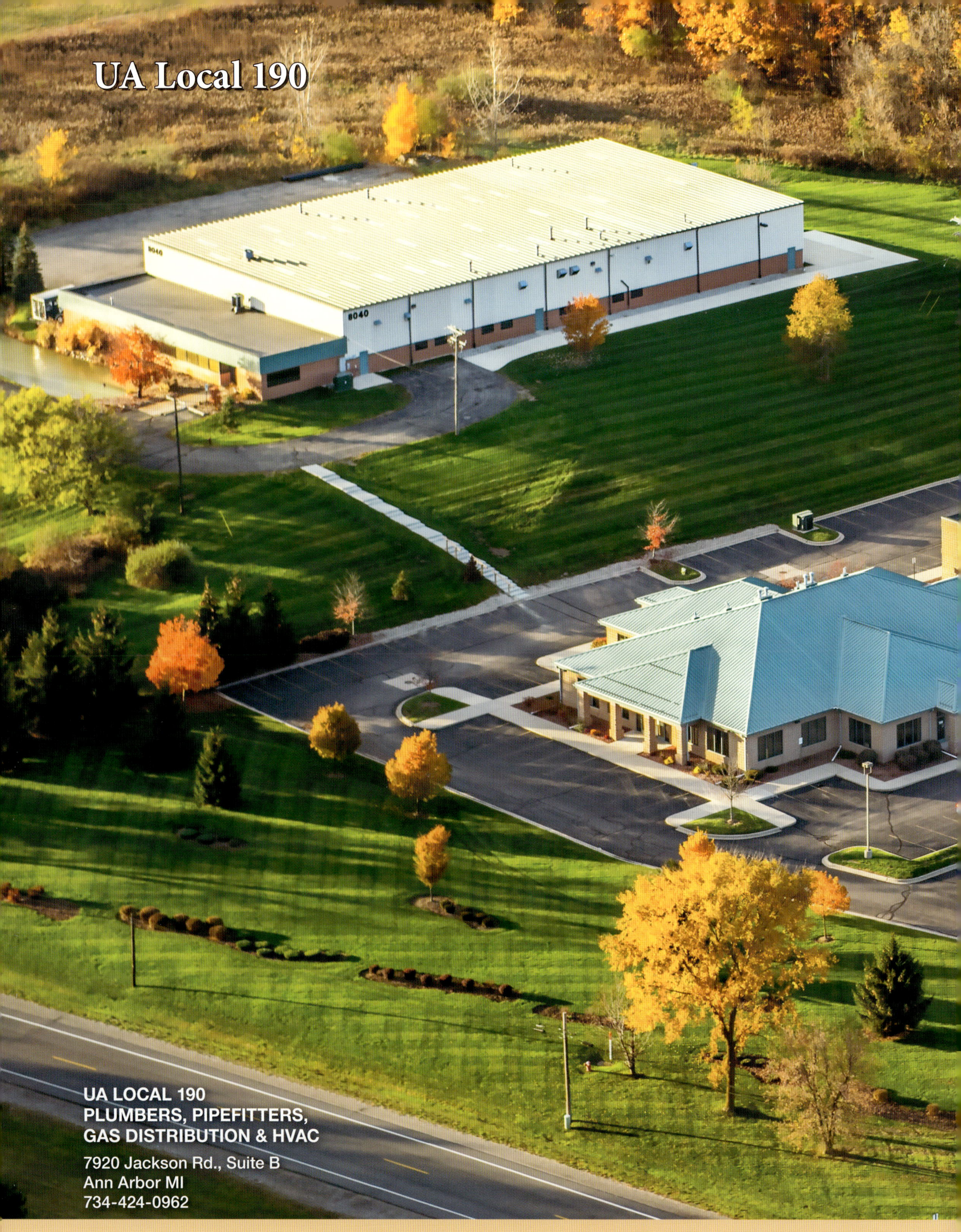

UA LOCAL 190
PLUMBERS, PIPEFITTERS,
GAS DISTRIBUTION & HVAC

7920 Jackson Rd., Suite B
Ann Arbor MI
734-424-0962

U.A. Local 190 is an affiliate of the United Association, an international organization. Serving Washtenaw County since 1900. Growing from 15 members to over 1,500 today, our professionals work on residential and commercial projects. They are Plumbers, Pipefitters, Service Technicians, and Gas Distribution workers. Gas line installation includes Michigan and Ohio.

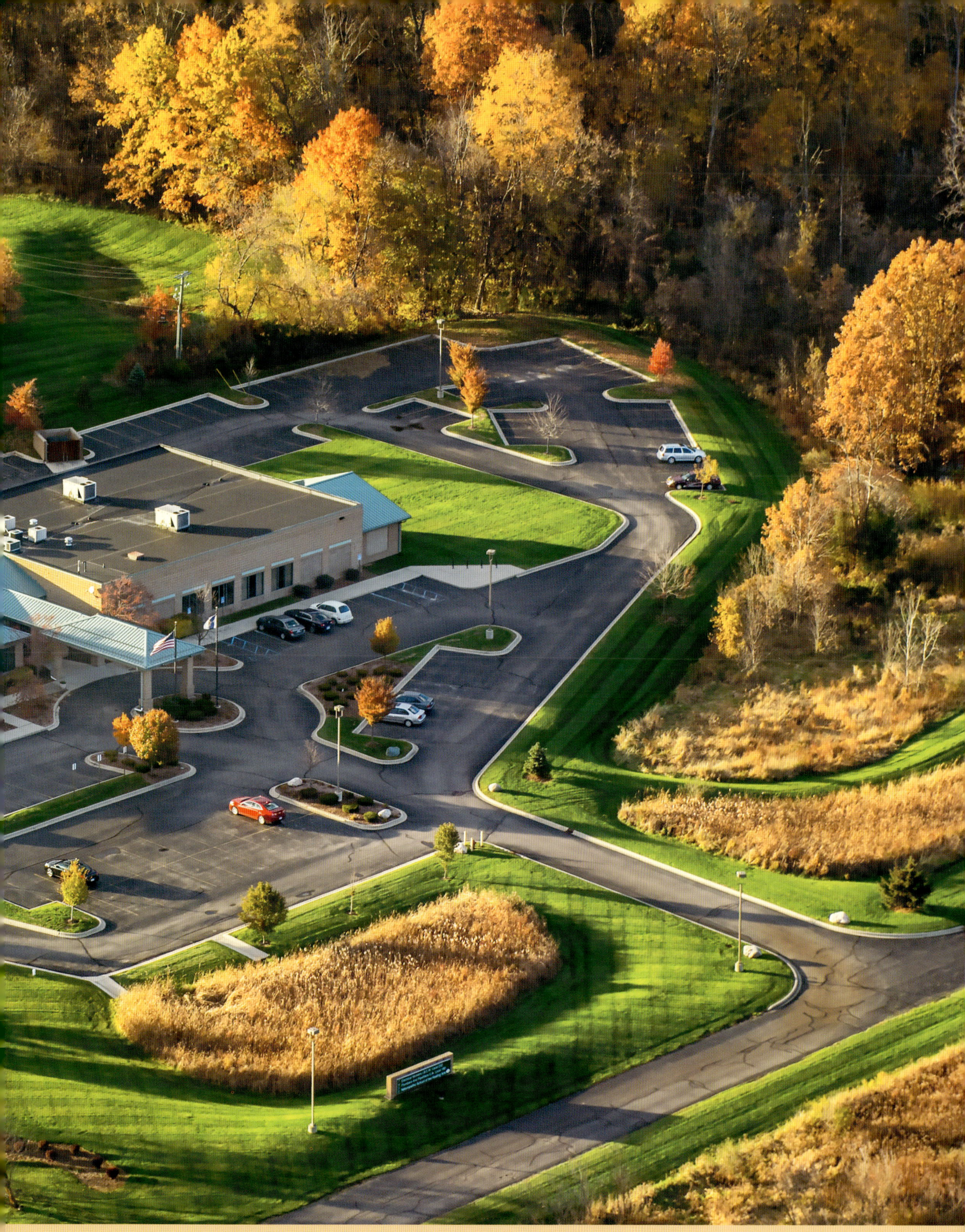

Training is a top priority. No other organization matches its financial investment in workers. The reason is simple; they know the importance of providing the highest skilled labor to contractors. The apprenticeship program and journeymen upgrade classes are offered through a partnership with Greater Michigan Plumbing and Mechanical Contractors Association. This allows workers to stay ahead of the curve on safety, installation methods, new products and materials.

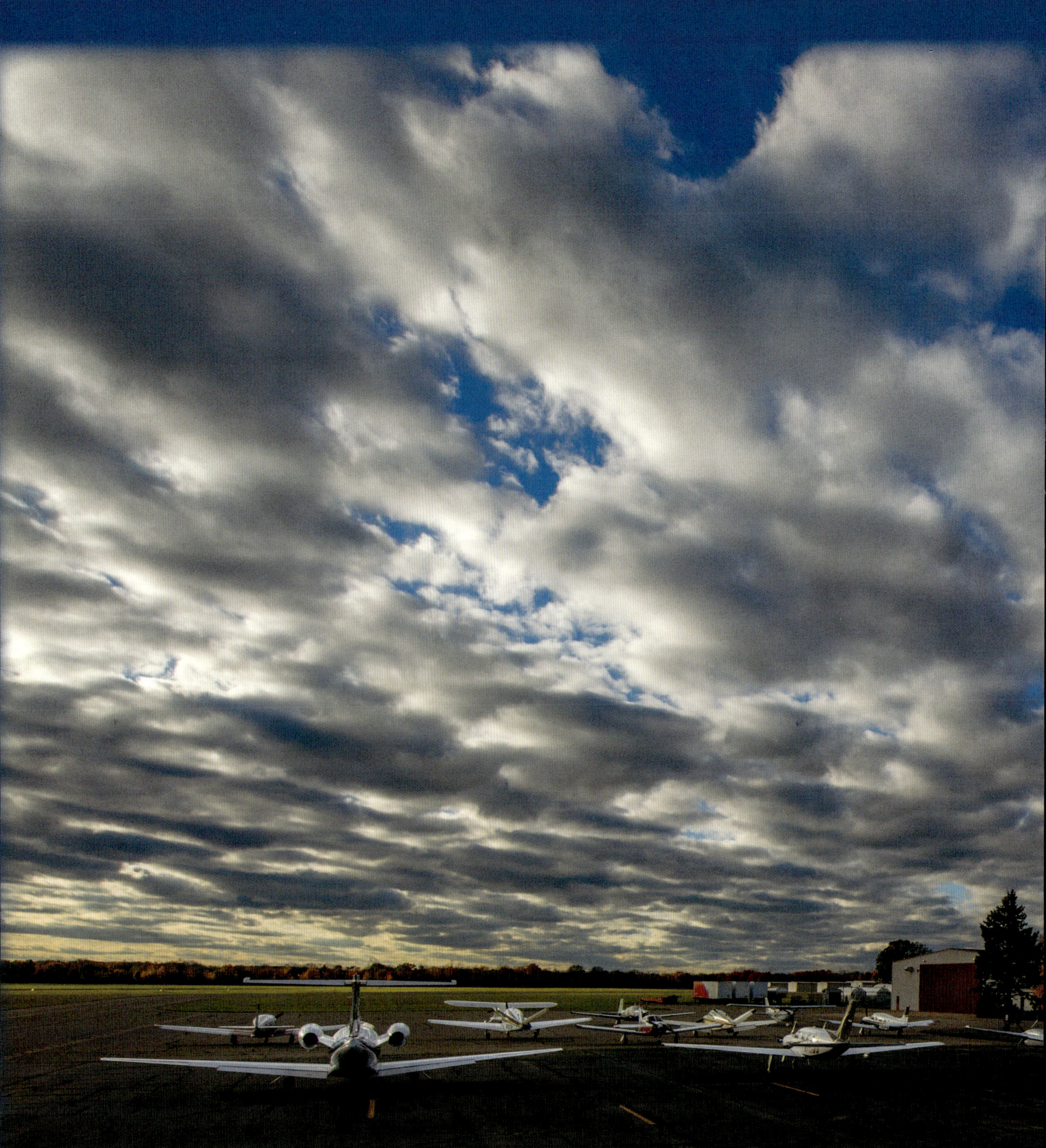

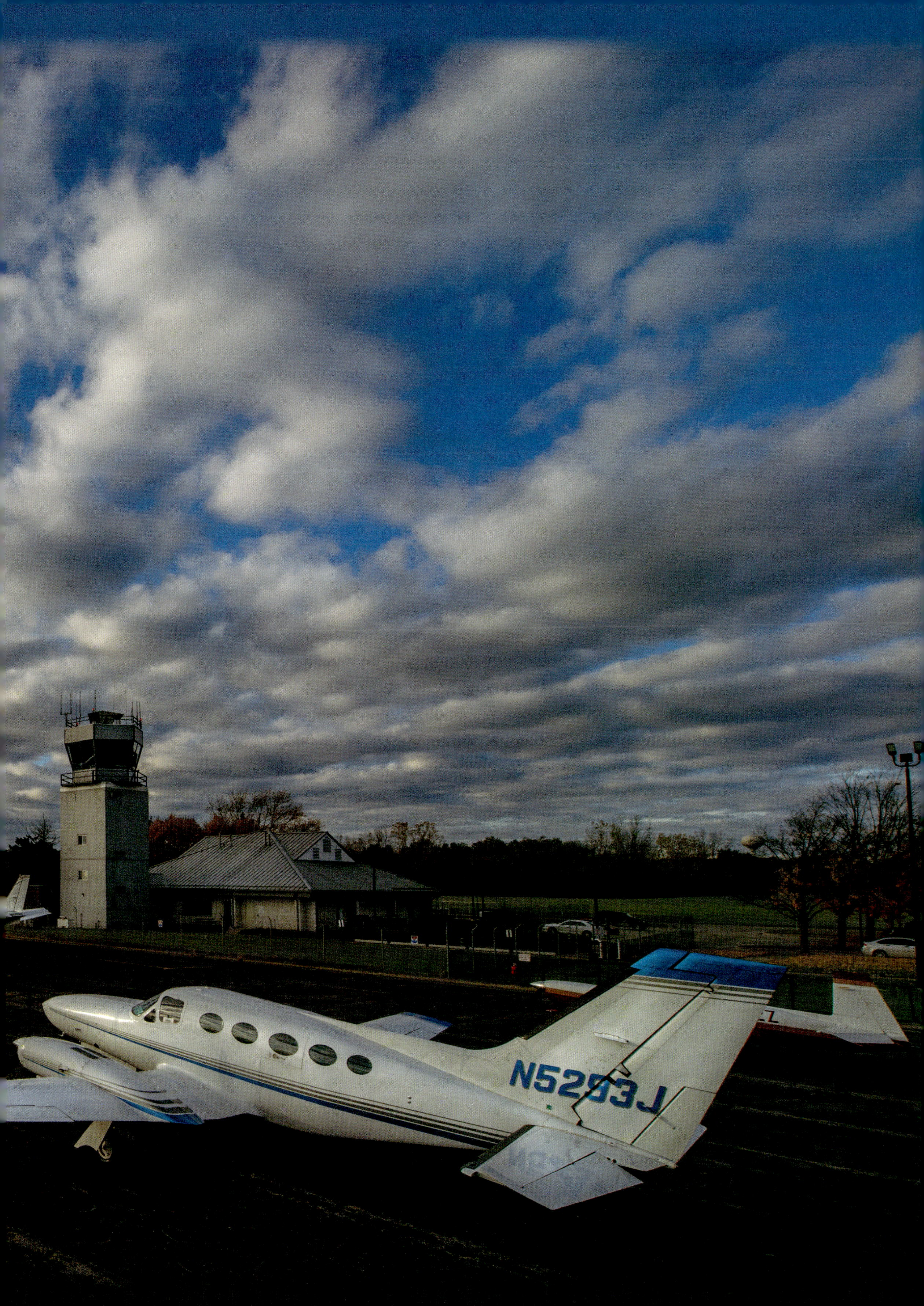
N5293J

IMRA America, Inc.

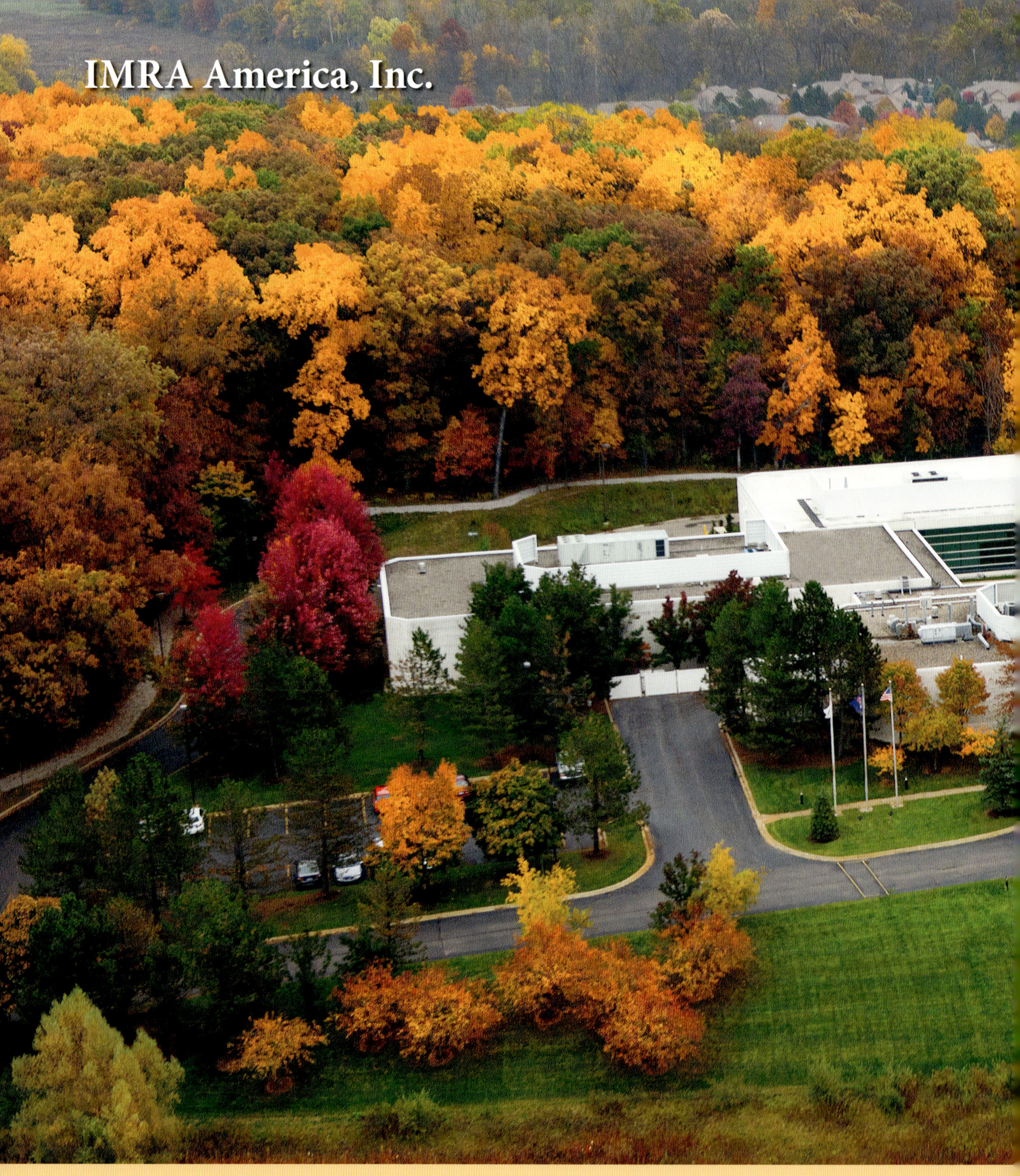

IMRA America (Institut Minoru de Recherche Avancé) was founded in 1990 in Ann Arbor and has become a leading member of a global set of companies anchored by AISIN of Japan, one of the world's largest manufacturer of automotive components.

IMRA America, Inc. was established following the philosophy of Mr. Minoru Toyoda, an honorary advisor to the All AISIN Group: "World harmony through the development and sharing of science and technology."

It is the world's largest leader in the research, development, manufacture, and application of ultrafast lasers. Its first commercial product, Femtolite, was developed in 1995. IMRA's lasers are at the forefront of metrology and sensing, offering new functionalities in instrumentation and systems. As the oldest and most experienced femtosecond fiber laser company, IMRA's history reflects the successful implementation of breakthrough technologies into everyday life.

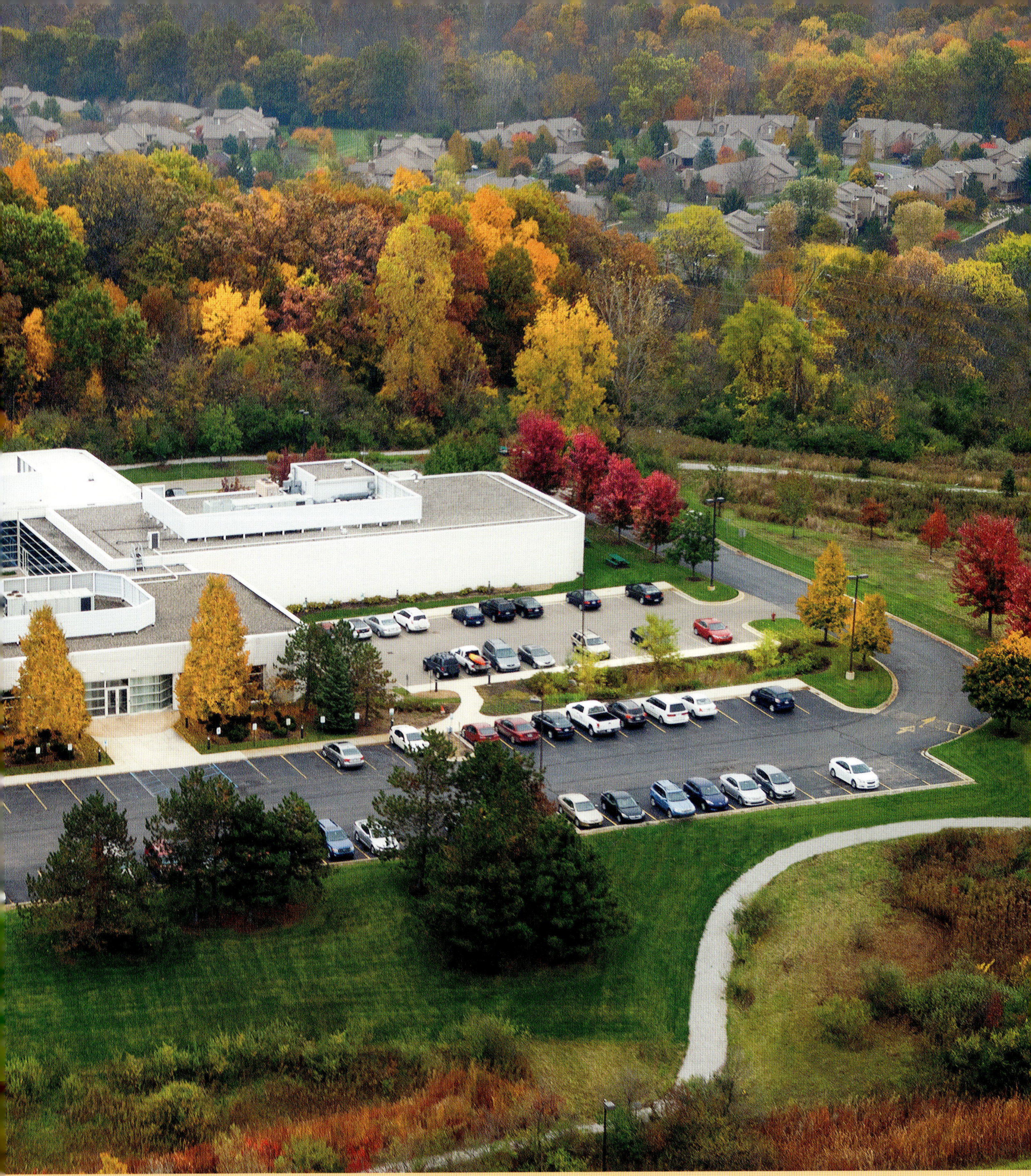

The Application Development Center (ADC), located in Fremont, California, creates process solutions. IMRA's research facility, Boulder Research Lab (BRL), resides in the burgeoning scientific community of Boulder, Colorado.

IMRA has endorsed the University of Michigan's Solar Car Team, winners of national and international competitions. It also supports U-M's College of Engineering and its impressive work in research of alternative energy technology. IMRA has supported the Ann Arbor Public Schools Educational Foundation. Most notably, it saved the Pioneer High School Planetarium from pending closure. It is now called the Argus IMRA Planetarium. The company helped develop the Skyline High School computer lab.

IMRA AMERICA, INC.

Headquarters and Manufacturing
1044 Woodridge Ave.
Ann Arbor, MI
734-930-2560

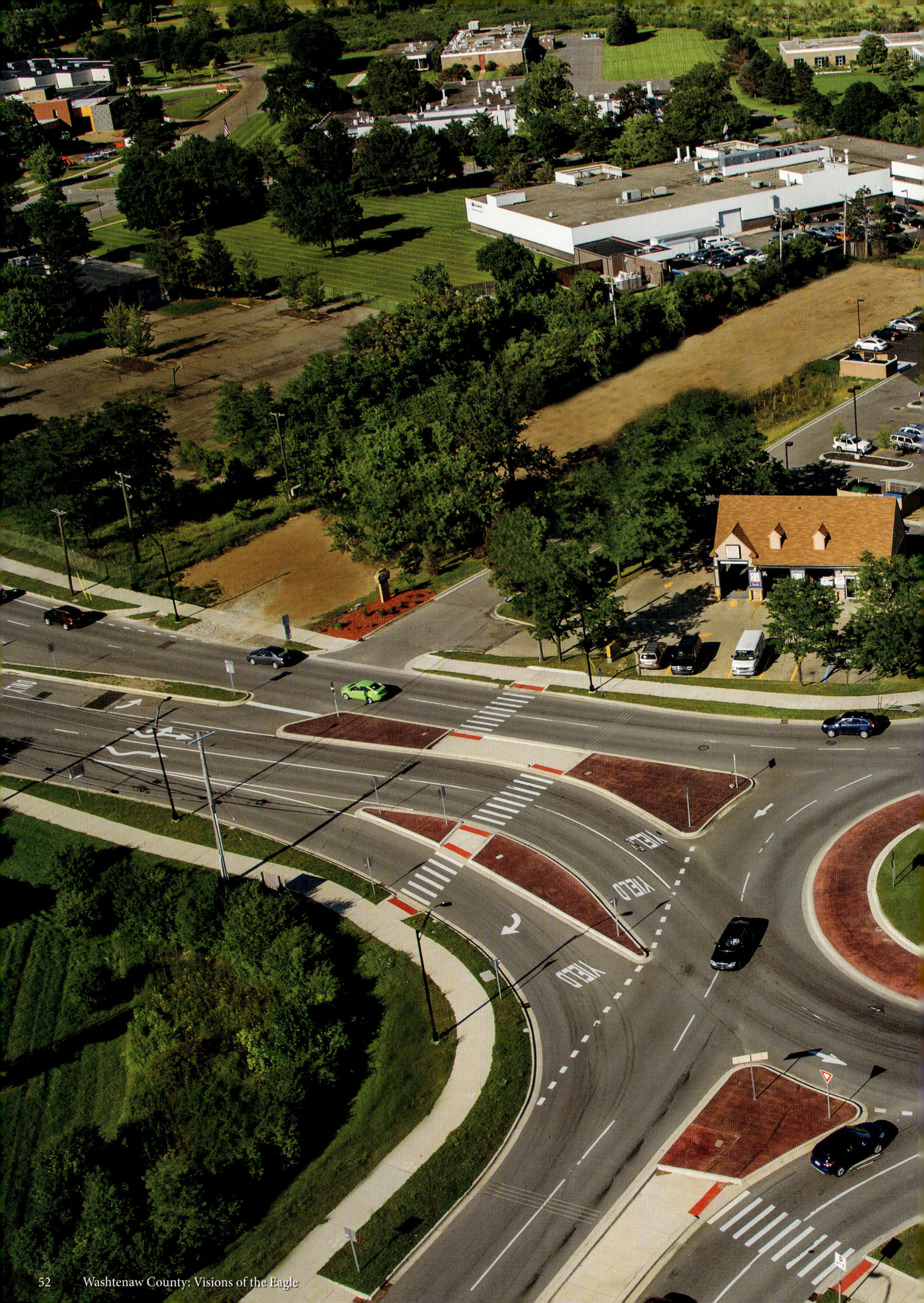

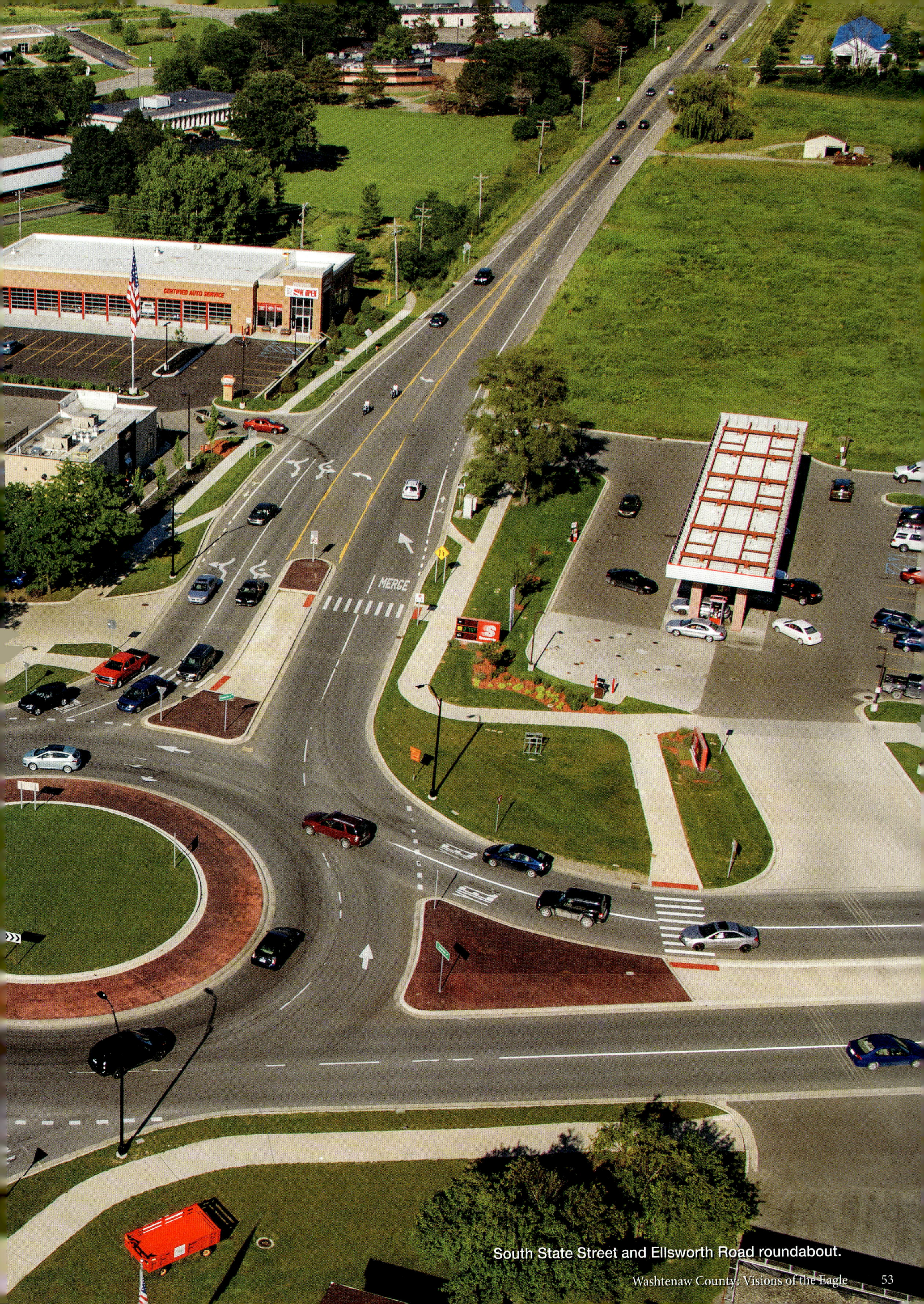

South State Street and Ellsworth Road roundabout.

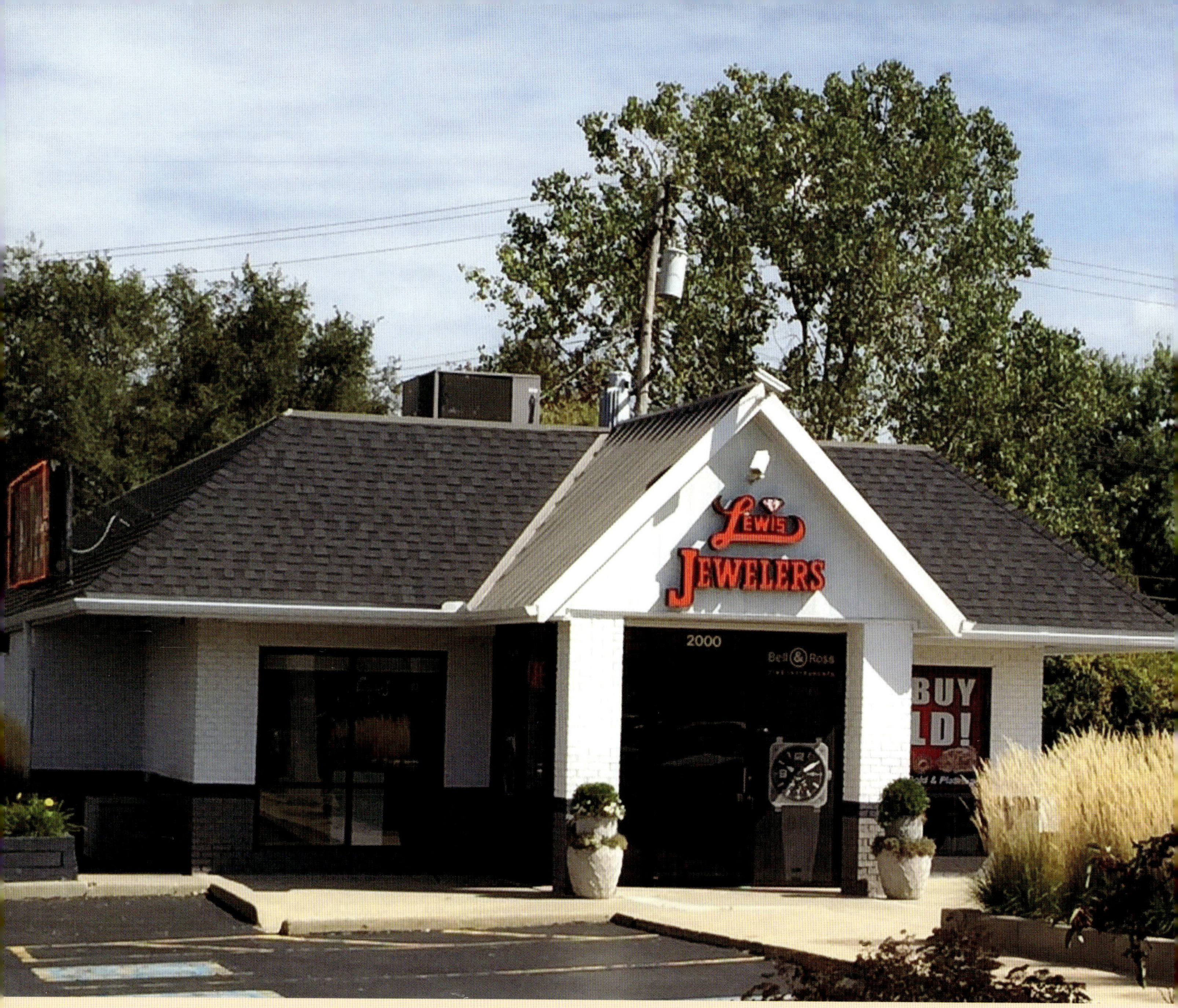

Since 1921, Lewis Jewelers has served Ann Arbor and the greater Detroit area with excellence as a full-service jewelry store. A team of master jewelers with more than 100 combined years of expertise surpasses expectations with custom designs, repairs, restorations and engravings.

Lewis Jewelers' reputation and success come from a commitment to integrity, quality customer service, and exceptional product lines. Its team of trusted advisors puts their expertise to work for every client who walks through the doors. Sales advisors do not work on commission so there's never any pressure to buy. Clients take their time and find the perfect piece.

"Our focus is to help our customers celebrate the moment with the best jewelry to represent that expression," said Keith A. Largin DG, GIA, custom design specialist.

LEWIS JEWELERS

Current location:
2000 W. Stadium
Ann Arbor, MI

New location:
(Fall 2020)
300 S. Maple
Ann Arbor, MI
734-994-5111

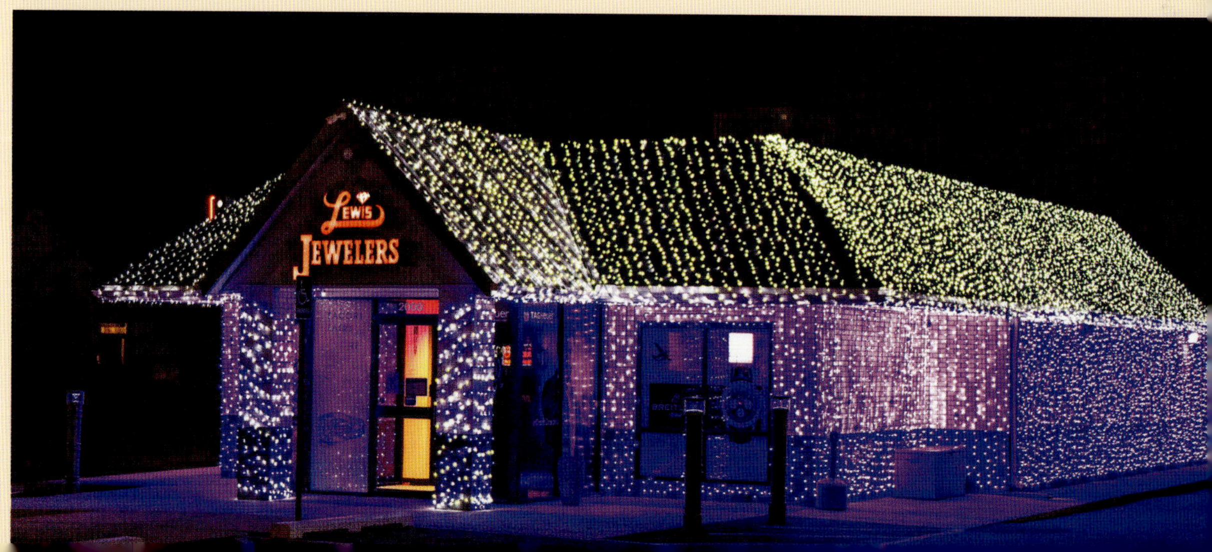

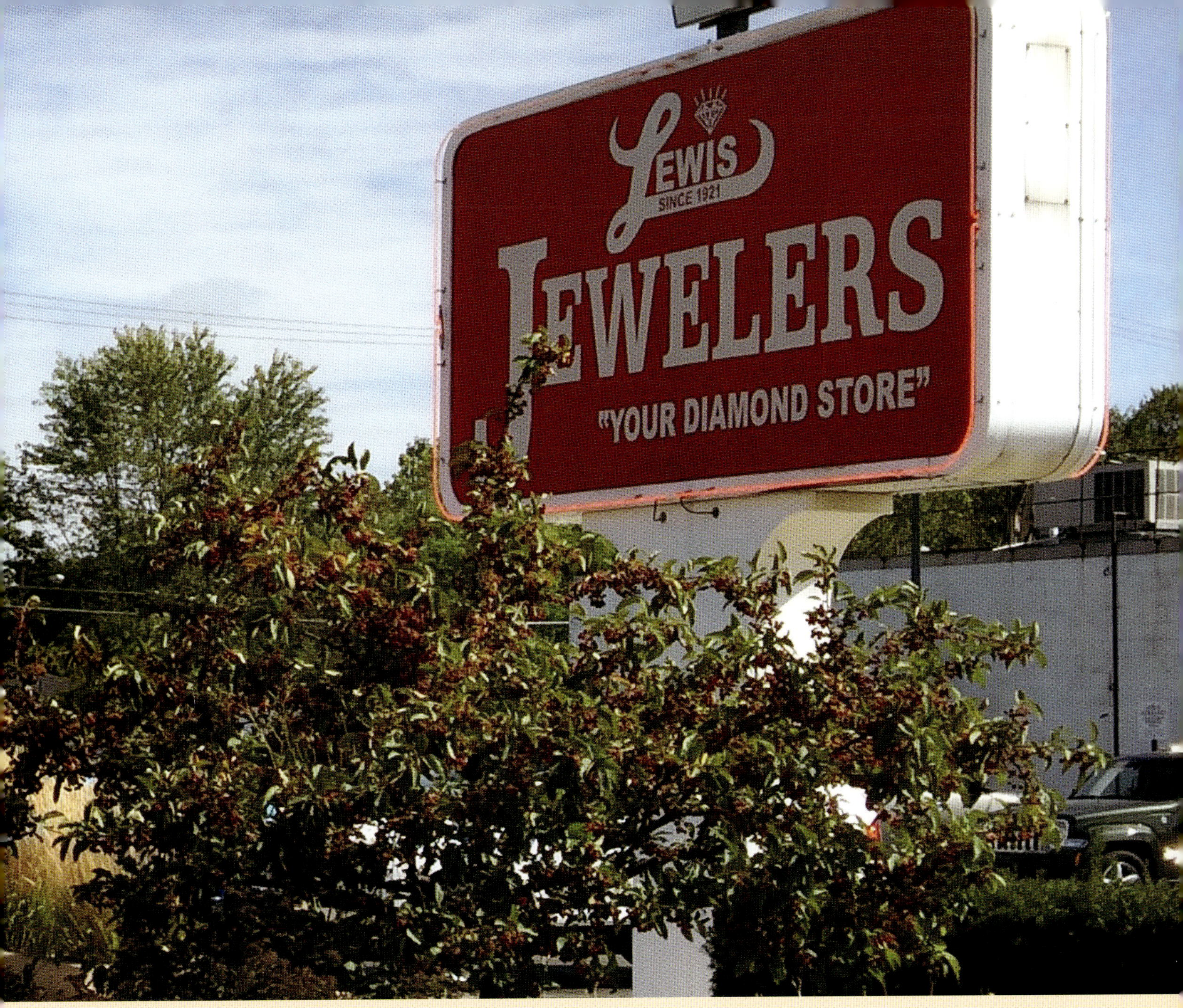

Family-owned, Lewis Jewelers treats its customers like family and is known for providing service after the sale, including inspection, cleaning and polishing, and repairs. More than 500 happy customers have provided positive online reviews making Lewis one of the top reviewed jewelry stores in Michigan.

Ann Arbor has been good to the Lewis family. In turn, they focus on giving back.

"Our friends Doug and Julie Stotlar founded The Kite Network after the sudden and tragic loss of their six-year-old daughter Lauren in 2000," Largin said. Now known as GrieveWell, the organization helps others rebuild their lives after a devastating loss.

ChadTough, the Alzheimer's Association, and the Ann Arbor Hospice Diamond Giveaway event are among of the many charities Lewis Jewelers has supported.

In 2020, Lewis Jewelers created a state-of-the-art mega jewelry store and its new home at 300 South Maple Road near the Westgate Shopping Center. They look forward to another hundred years of serving Ann Arbor and Washtenaw County!

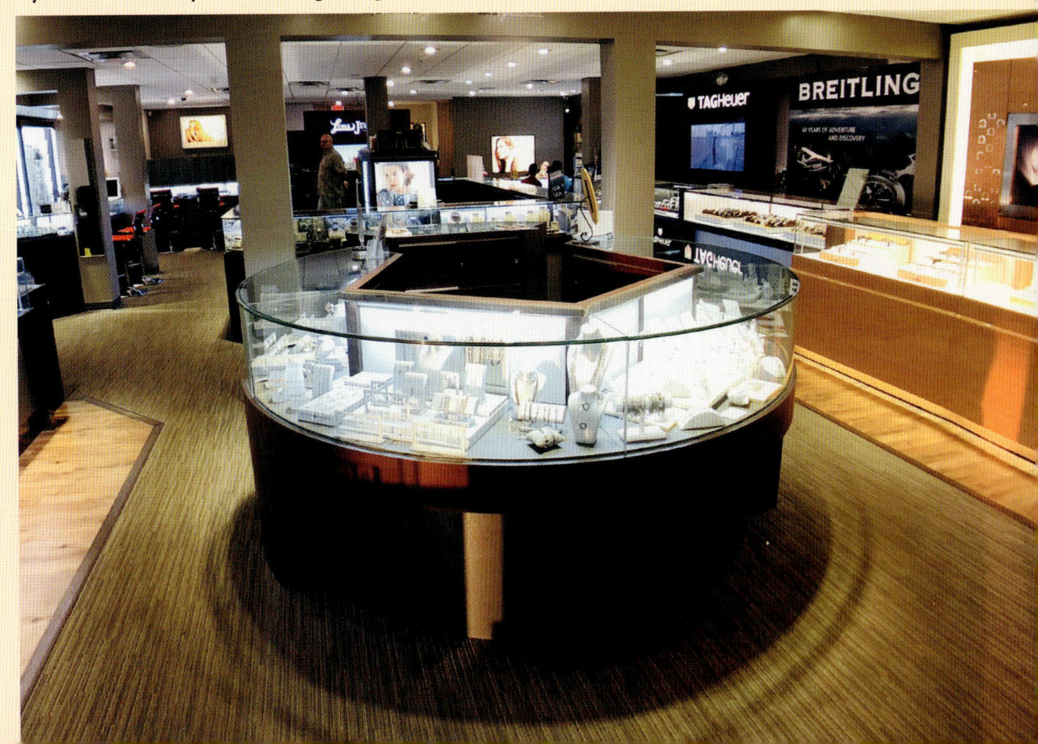

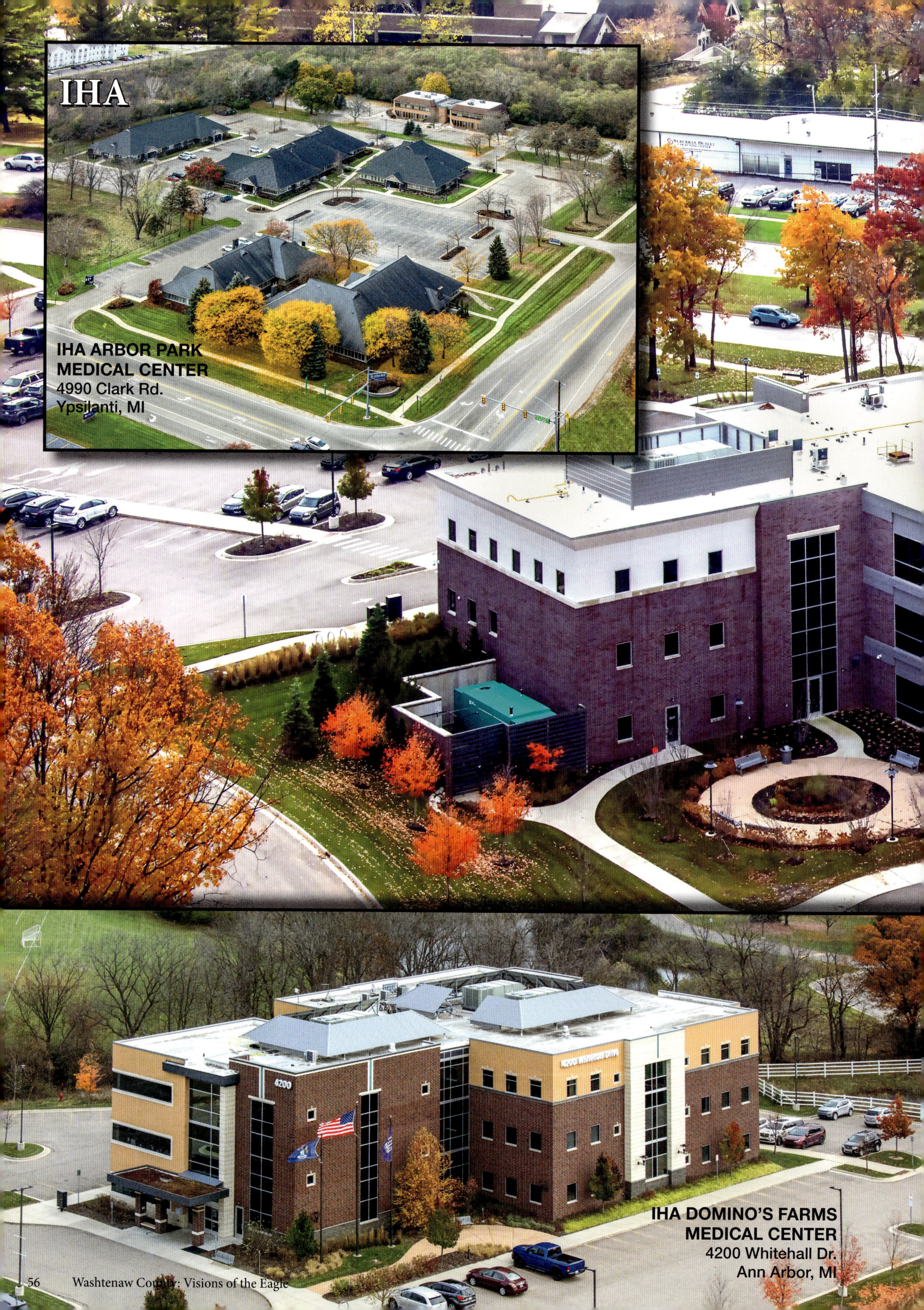

IHA
IHA ARBOR PARK
MEDICAL CENTER
4990 Clark Rd.
Ypsilanti, MI
4200
IHA DOMINO'S FARMS
MEDICAL CENTER
4200 Whitehall Dr.
Ann Arbor, MI

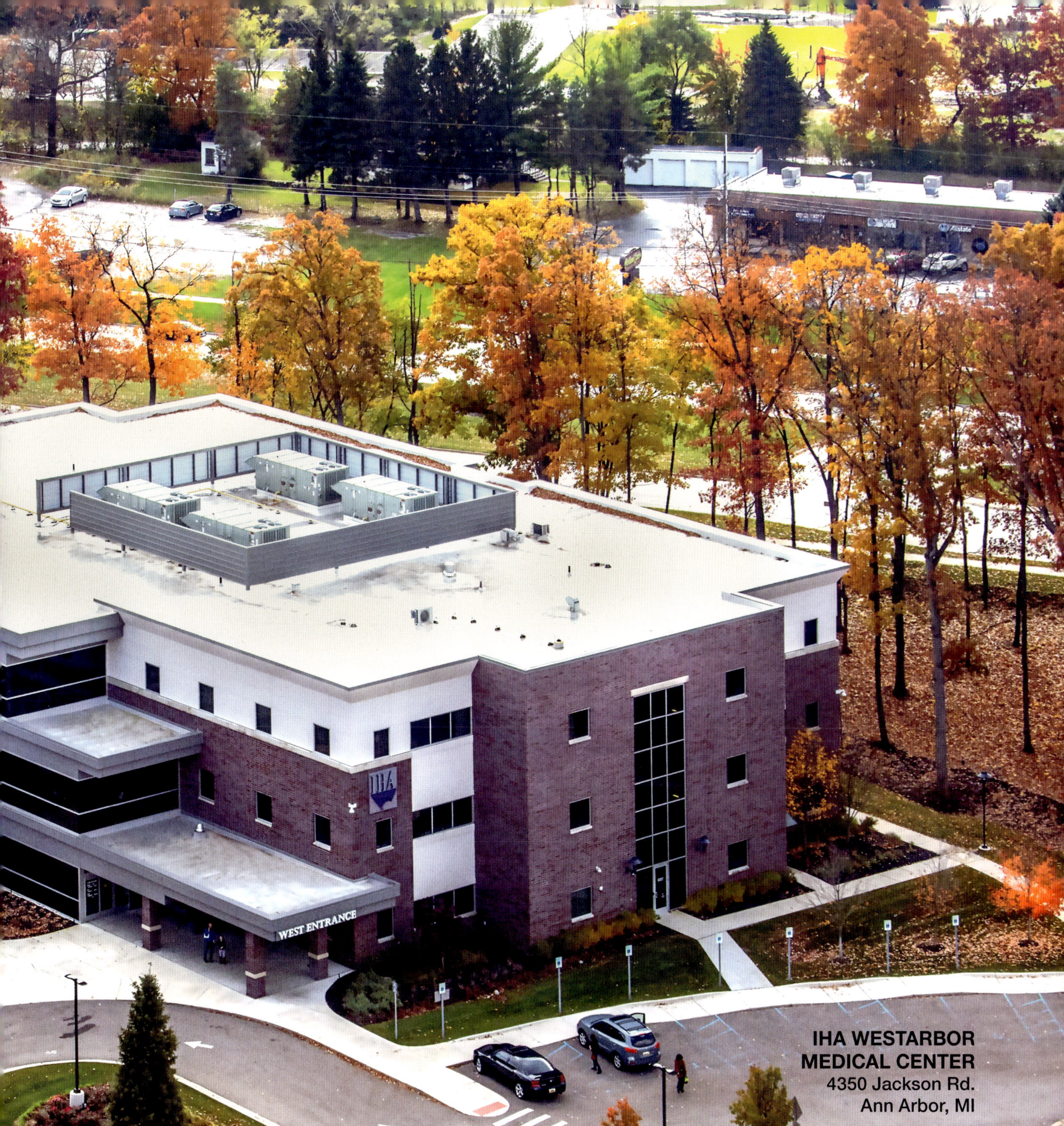

IHA WESTARBOR MEDICAL CENTER
4350 Jackson Rd.
Ann Arbor, MI

A little more than a quarter-century ago, a handful of physicians came together to form IHA. This multi-specialty medical group, headquartered in Ann Arbor, Michigan has grown into one of Southeast Michigan's largest groups. With more than 750 providers in nearly 80 locations around the area, the providers and staff currently care for more than 400,000 patients. As one of Washtenaw county's premier healthcare organizations, IHA's singular focus is to provide patients with the best care possible while treating them as a member of the IHA family. A majority of IHA's locations can be found in Washtenaw county, including three of the group's largest medical complexes.

IHA Domino's Farms Medical Center, built on the east side of Ann Arbor in 2014, sits on nearly eight acres of land and consists of more than 44,000 square feet. Home to IHA's first, seven-day a week urgent care.

IHA Arbor Park Medical Center, a series of single-story buildings encompassing 6.5 tree-filled acres, was acquired in 2002 and is home to several of IHA's founding practices.

IHA WestArbor Medical Center is the largest facility currently operated by the medical group. Built in 2016, this three-story 76,460 square foot facility brought together many of IHA's primary care and specialty practices into one convenient location. For additional information visit IHAcares.com or call 844.IHA.DOCS.

The ChadTough Foundation

About Chad Carr

Chad was a precious, beautiful, fun-loving boy who — on September 23, 2014 — was diagnosed with an inoperable brain tumor called Diffuse Intrinsic Pontine Glioma (DIPG). Three days later, he spent his 4th birthday in the Coach Carr Unit of Mott Children's Hospital in Ann Arbor, Michigan. (The unit named for Chad's grandfather, former University of Michigan football coach Lloyd Carr).

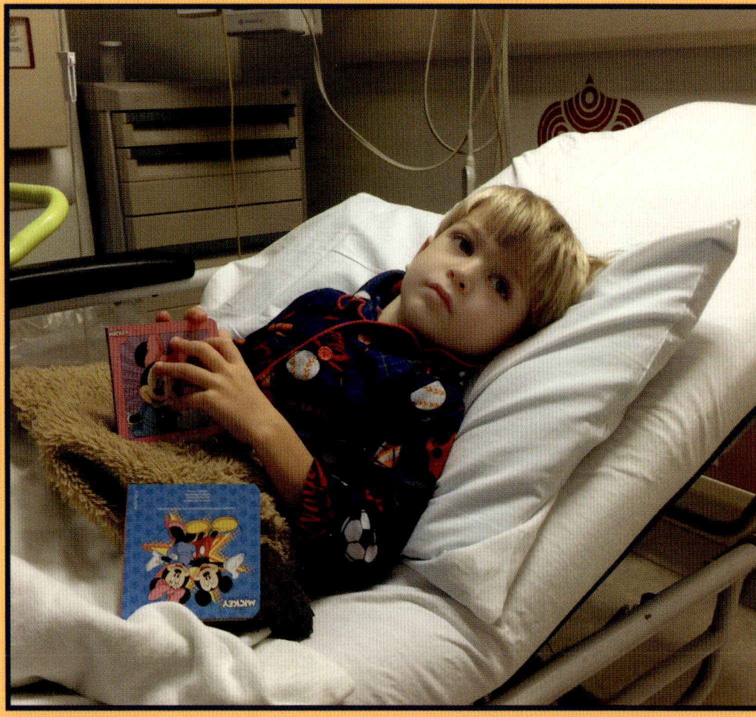

Chad underwent 30 rounds of radiation at Mott. Afterward, he participated in a Memorial Sloan Kettering Cancer Center clinical trial in New York. On November 23, 2015, after a brave 14-month fight, he earned his angel wings.

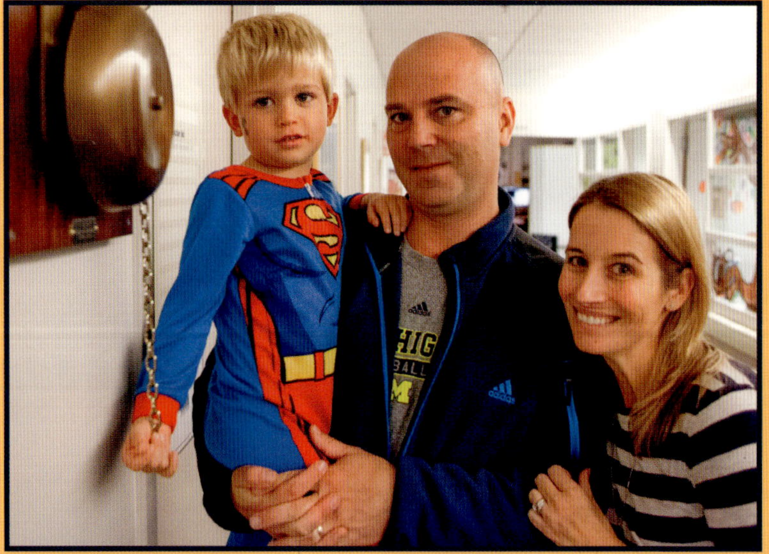

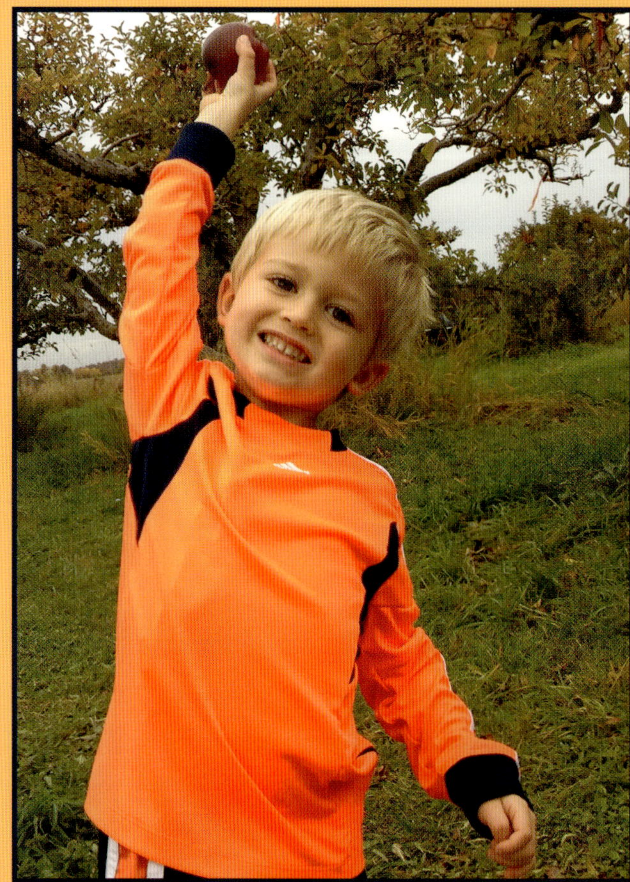

About DIPG

DIPG is a brain tumor found in the pons of the brain stem. Children are typically diagnosed between the ages of 5-7, with around 300-350 new cases per year in the United States. The median survival rate is 9 months from diagnosis. Only 10% of patients survive 2 years from diagnosis. Long-term survivors total less than 1%.

What makes DIPG difficult treating is not only its location (a very small area of the brain stem responsible for many critical bodily functions, including breathing, swallowing, respiration, equilibrium, and eye movement), but also the fact that it is "diffuse" (as opposed to looking like a solid mass or ball, it spreads out and mixes with healthy cells and is sometimes described as looking "marbled").

One of our doctors called it "the worst kind of tumor in the worst possible place." The only standard of care to treat DIPG is radiation. Used to shrink the tumor, giving temporary relief of symptoms, but after a period of time, the tumor typically grows back. As it grows, it cuts off those critical bodily functions until the child can no longer swallow or breathe and eventually succumbs. DIPG cannot be surgically removed, and until very recently, it was considered dangerous to even biopsy. This has resulted in very little DIPG tissue being available for researchers to study.

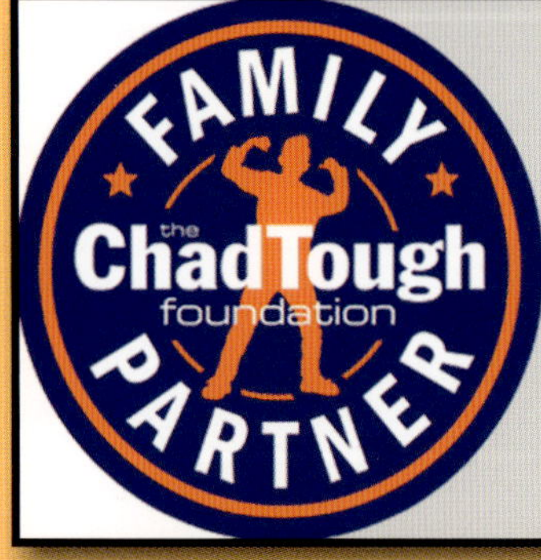

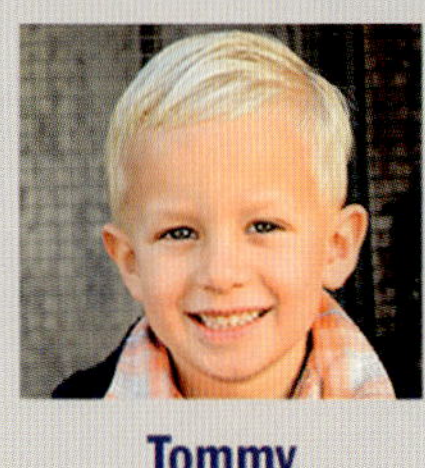

Tommy
The Ruddy Family

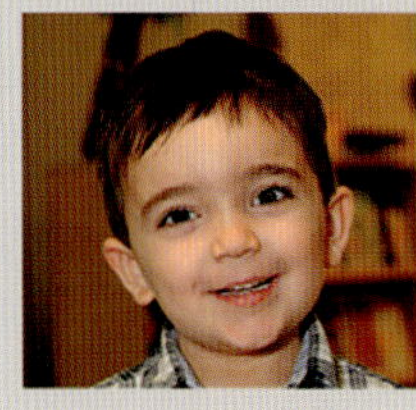

Julian
The Boivin Family

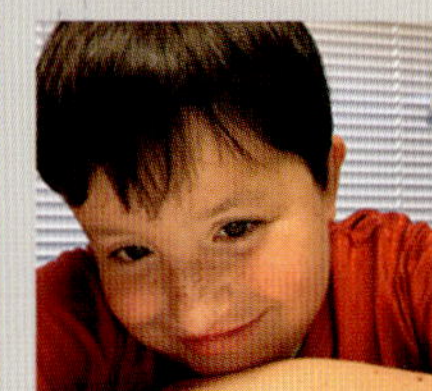

Colt
The DelVerne Family

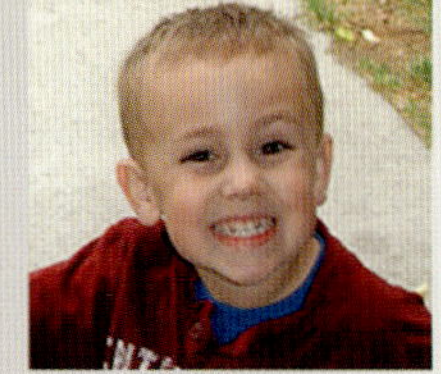

Carter
The Jones Family

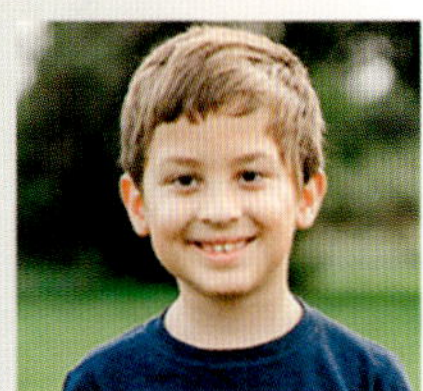

Benjamin
The Reinhold Family

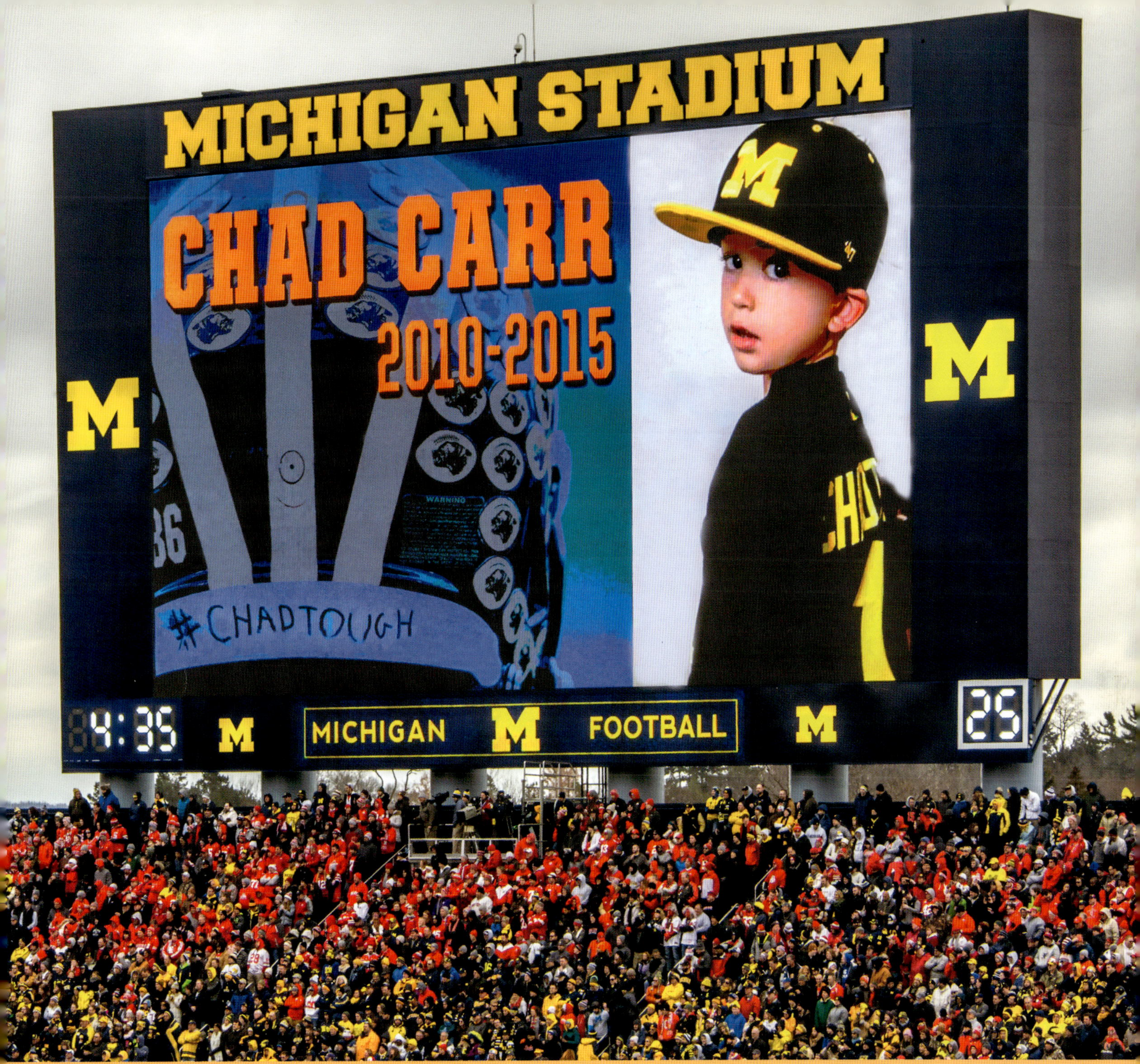

The most hated word in the world of pediatric brain tumors is “rare.” “Rare” is the reason there is not enough research being done. “Rare” is the reason there aren’t drugs being developed. “Rare” is the reason there is so little funding. “Rare” is why our kids don’t have more options.

These three facts negate the claim of DIPG being “Rare”

Cancer is the number one disease killer of children in America.

Brain tumors are the leading cause of cancer-related deaths in children.

DIPG is the leading cause of death from brain tumors in children.

Our vision is for DIPG to no longer be a death sentence.

www.ChadTough.org

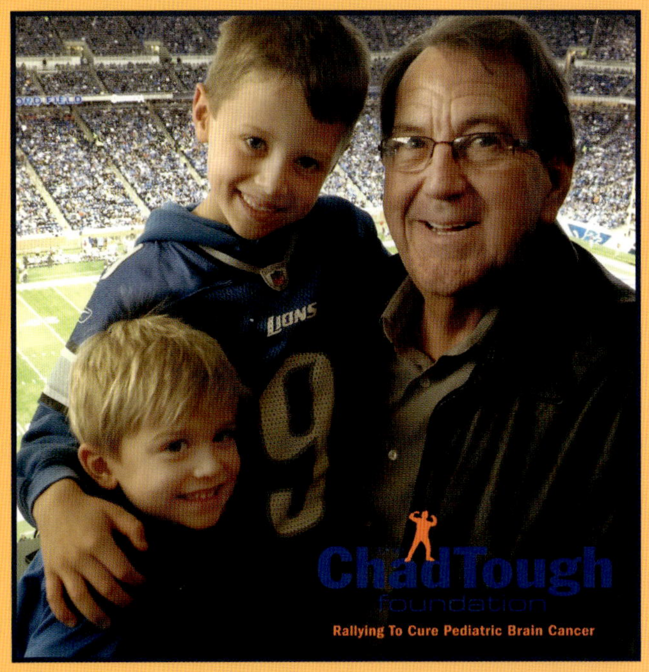

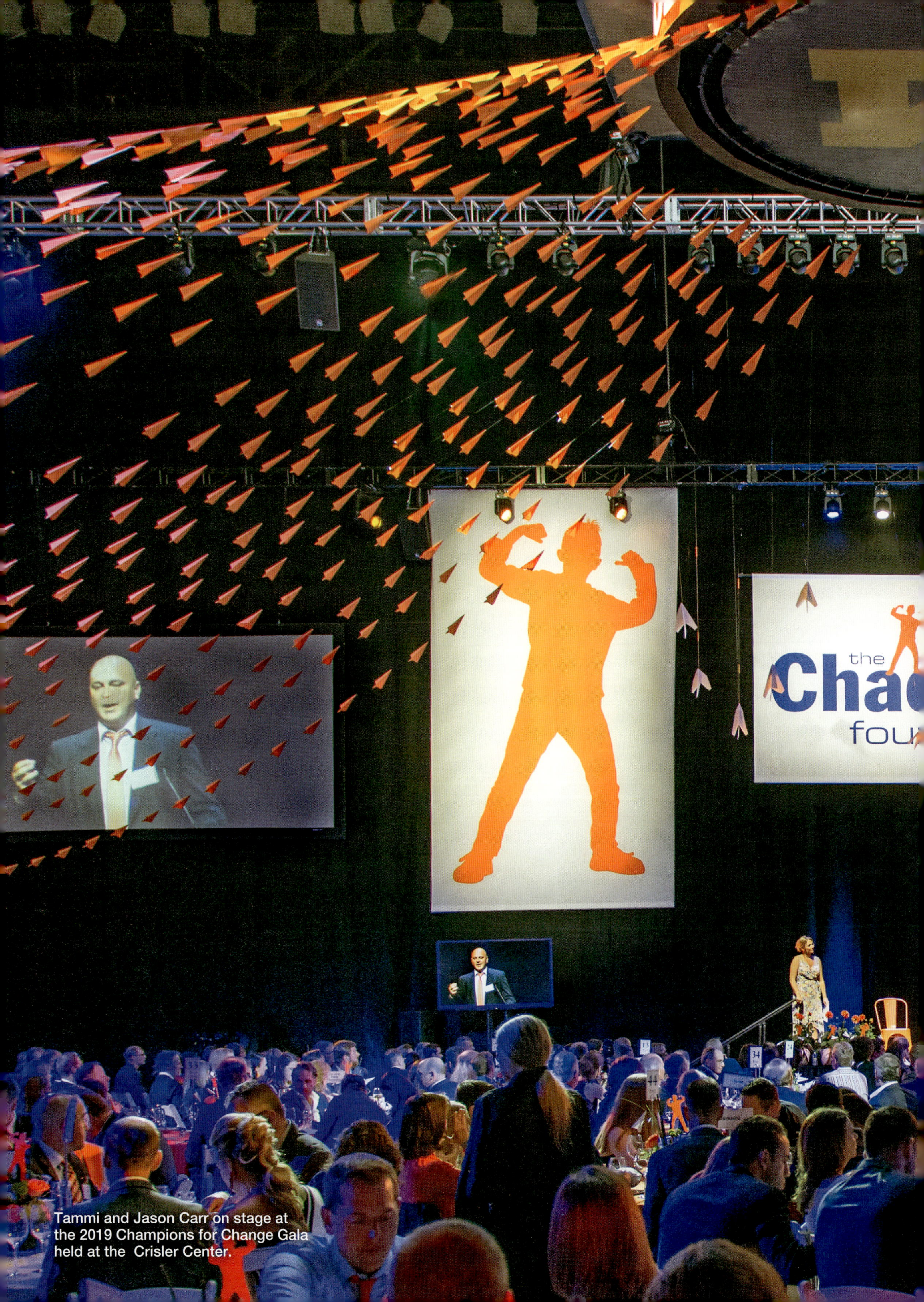

Tammi and Jason Carr on stage at the 2019 Champions for Change Gala held at the Crisler Center.

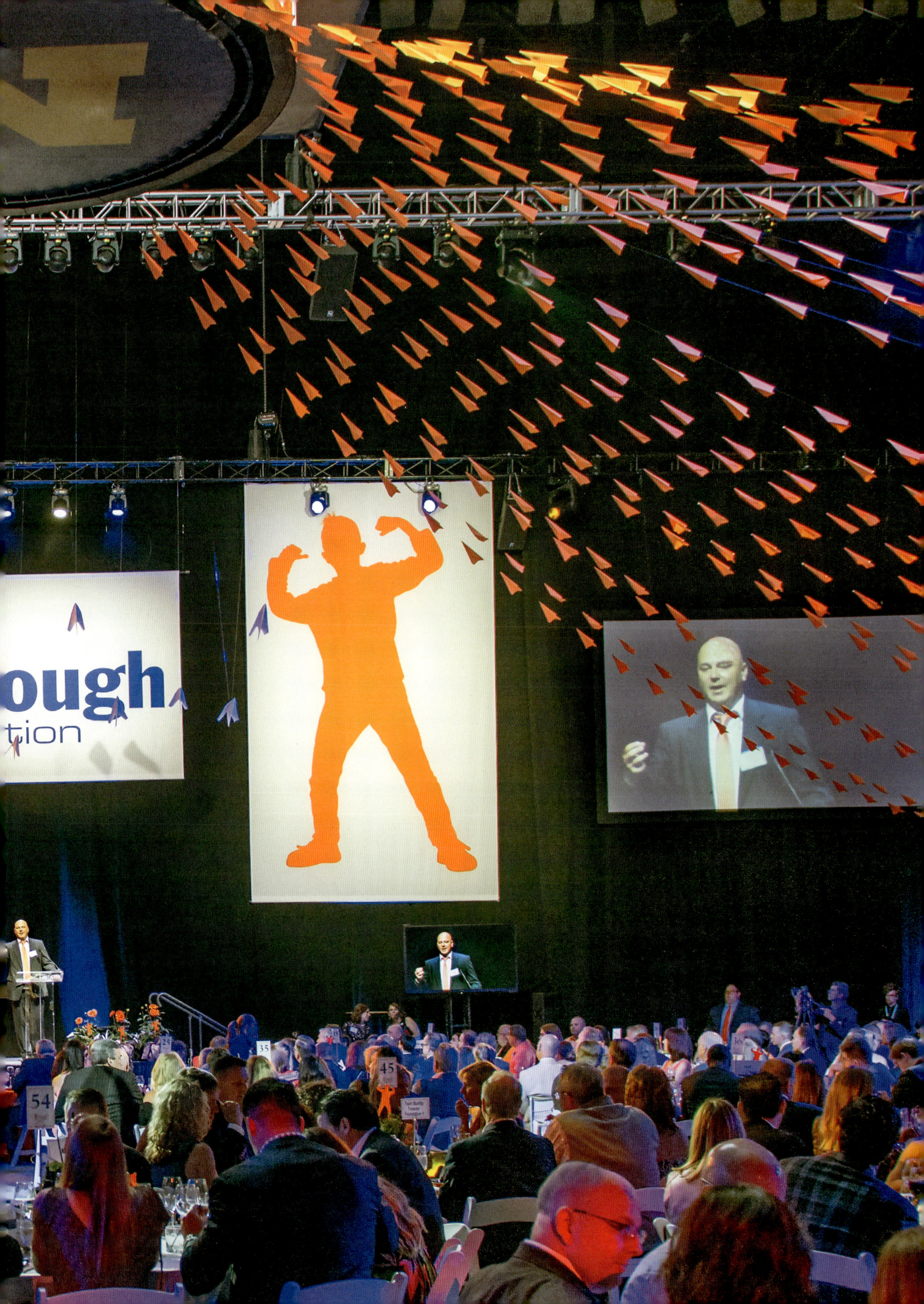
ough
tion
54

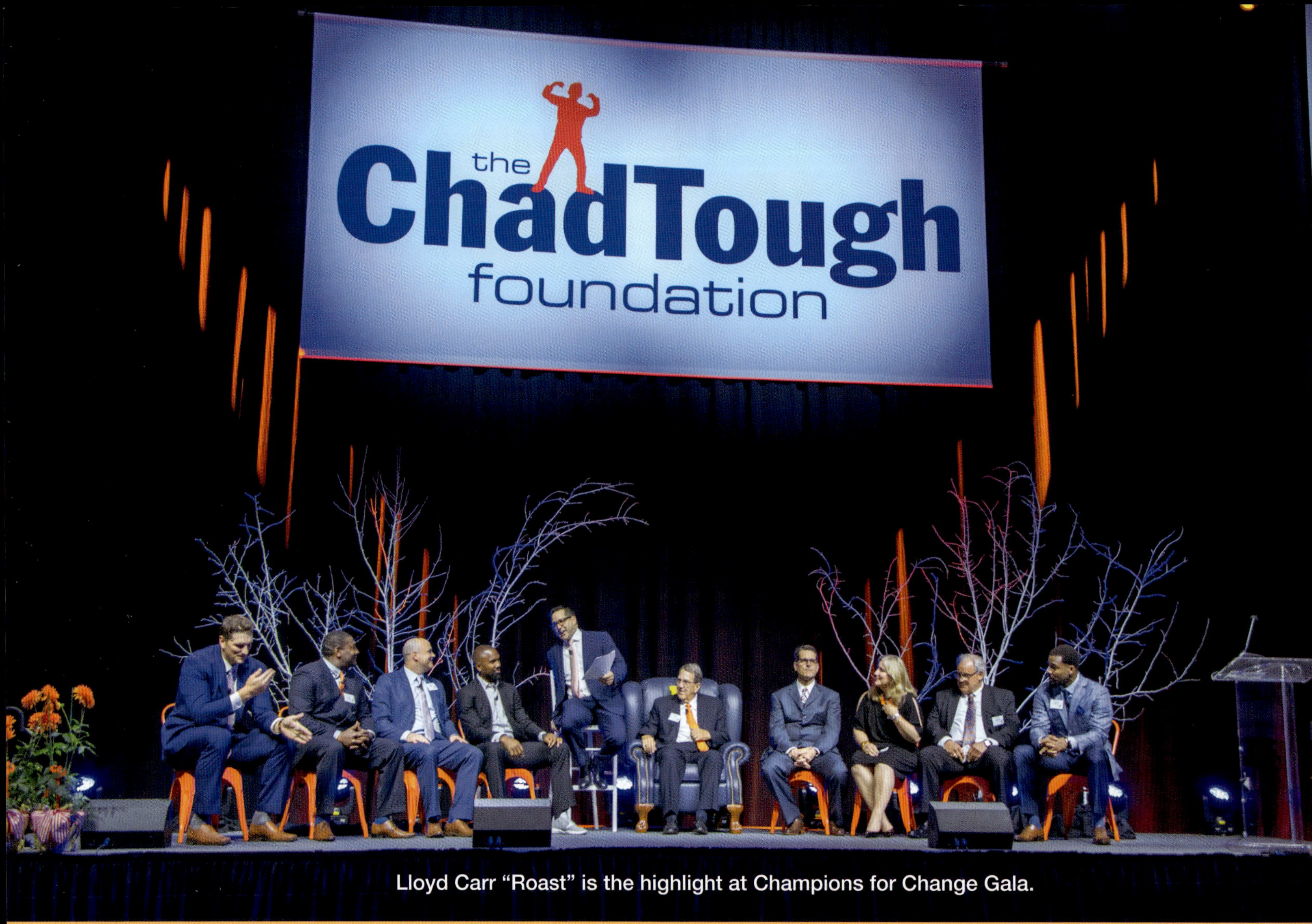

Lloyd Carr "Roast" is the highlight at Champions for Change Gala.

About the ChadTough Foundation

The mission of The ChadTough Foundation is to inspire and fund game-changing research to discover effective treatments for pediatric brain cancer, with an emphasis on Diffuse Intrinsic Pontine Glioma (DIPG).

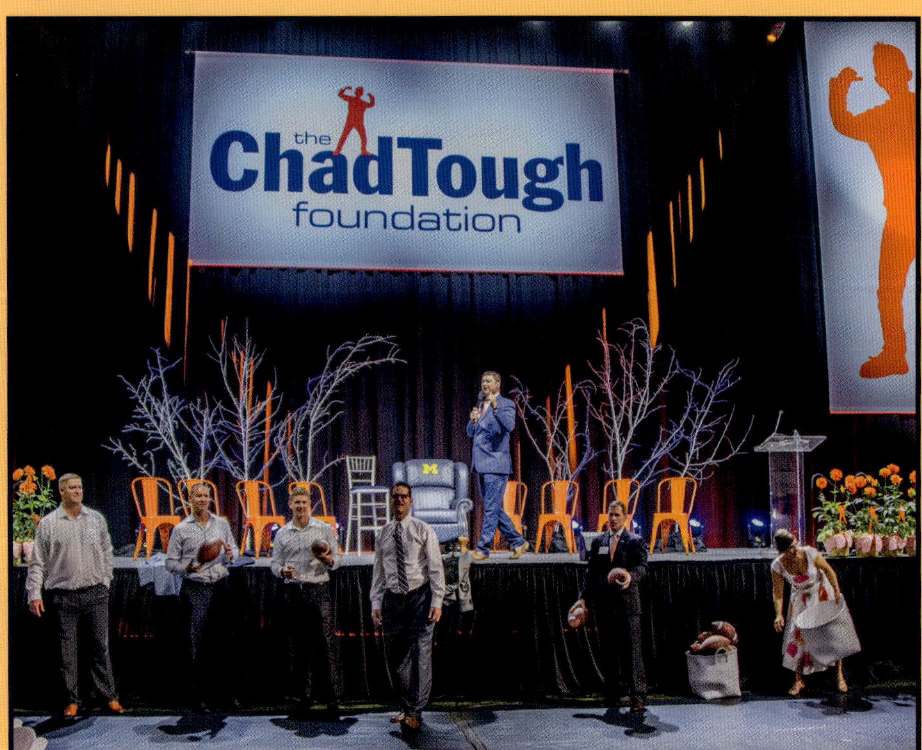

Football Toss at the Champions for Change Gala.
John Navarre, Scot Loeffler, Jake Rudock, Jim Harbaugh, Dave Ablauf, Tammi Carr.

Our Guiding Values

Family –
We believe in prioritizing family, and acting like a family. Life is too short to miss opportunities to be with our families. We value relationships and informality.

Collaboration~
We work collaboratively internally and externally, funding only researchers who fully collaborate with other researchers. Collaboration leads to the best results and most efficient use of funds.

Integrity~
We adhere to moral and ethical principles.

Transparency~
We operate openly and candidly providing full disclosure on issues around conflict of interest, operations, and funding practices.

Toughness~
We are resilient, and fund resilient researchers. This battle against DIPG will present frustrations, disappointments, and setbacks, but our Chad inspired toughness ensures our eventual victory.

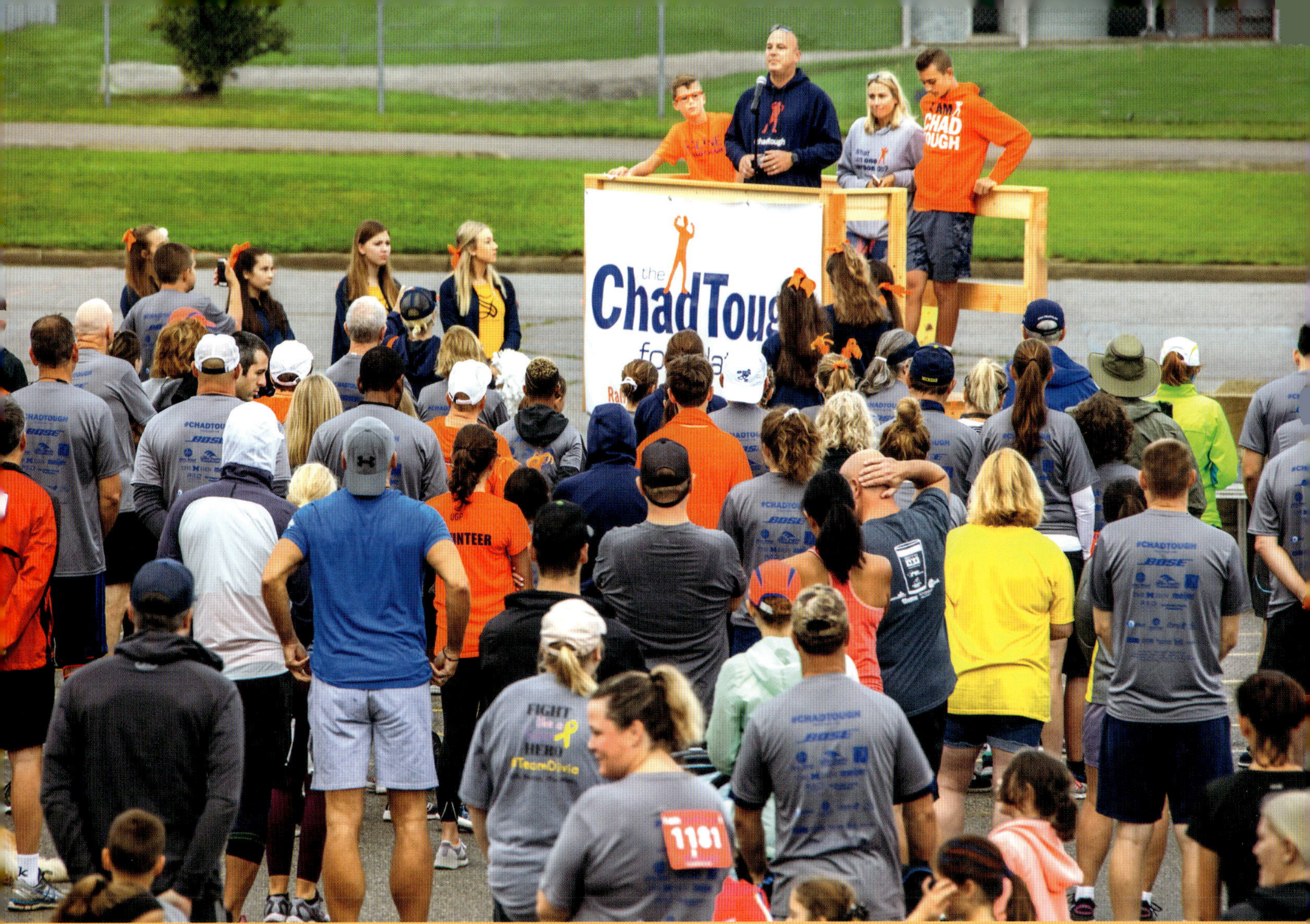

The Carr family speaks to the crowd about how much the RunTough event means in the race to cure pediatric brain cancer.

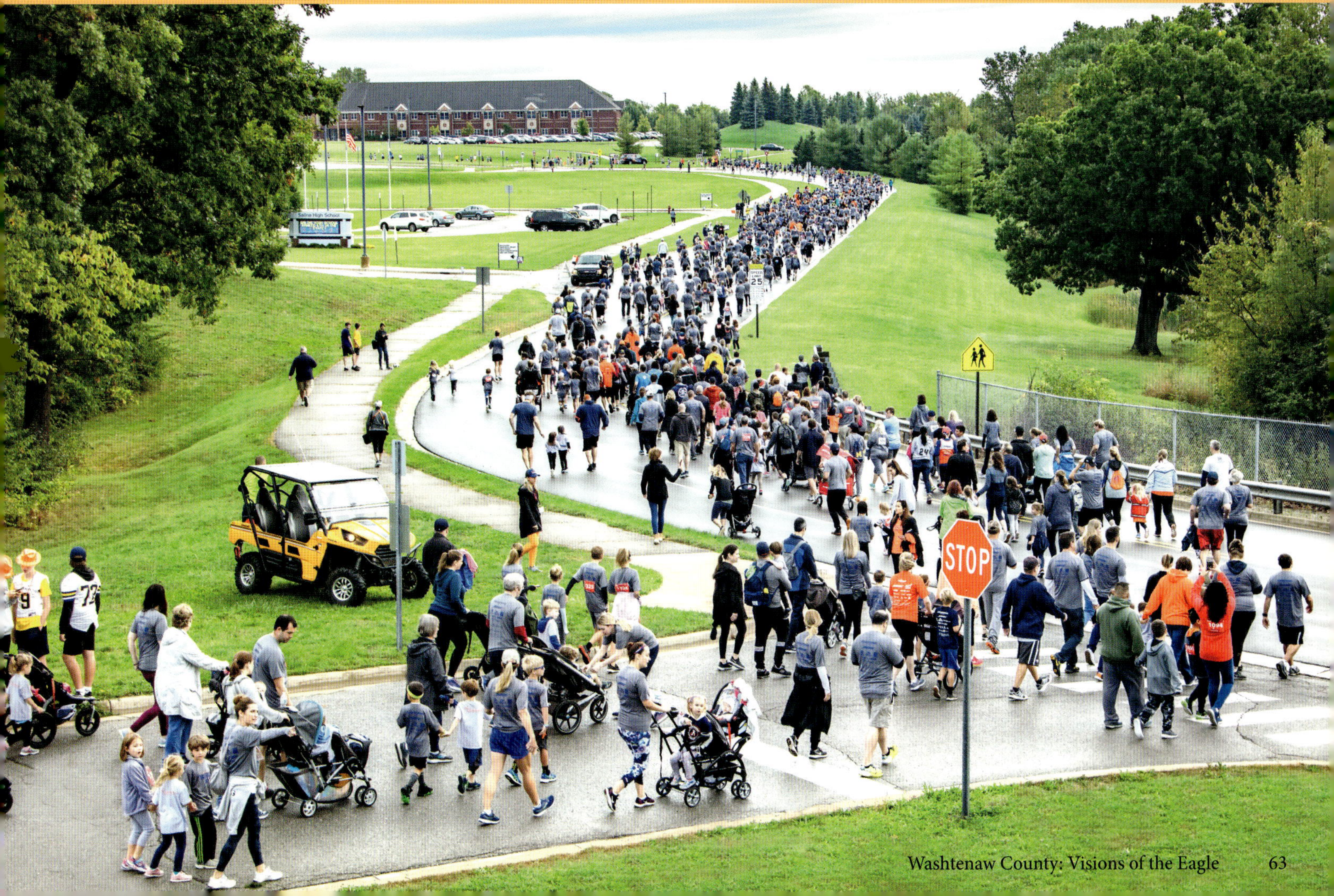

THE M DEN is the Official Merchandise Retailer of Michigan Athletics

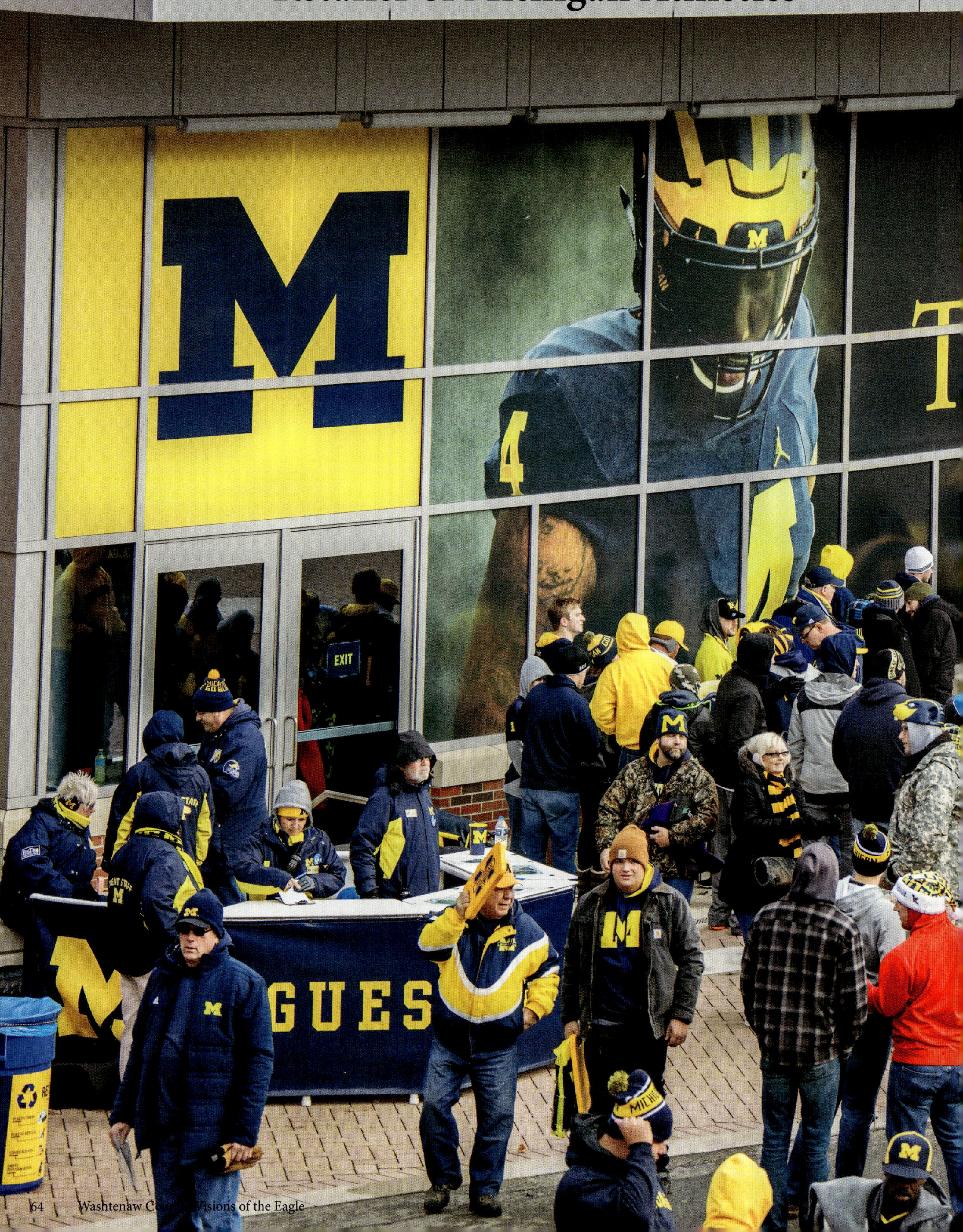

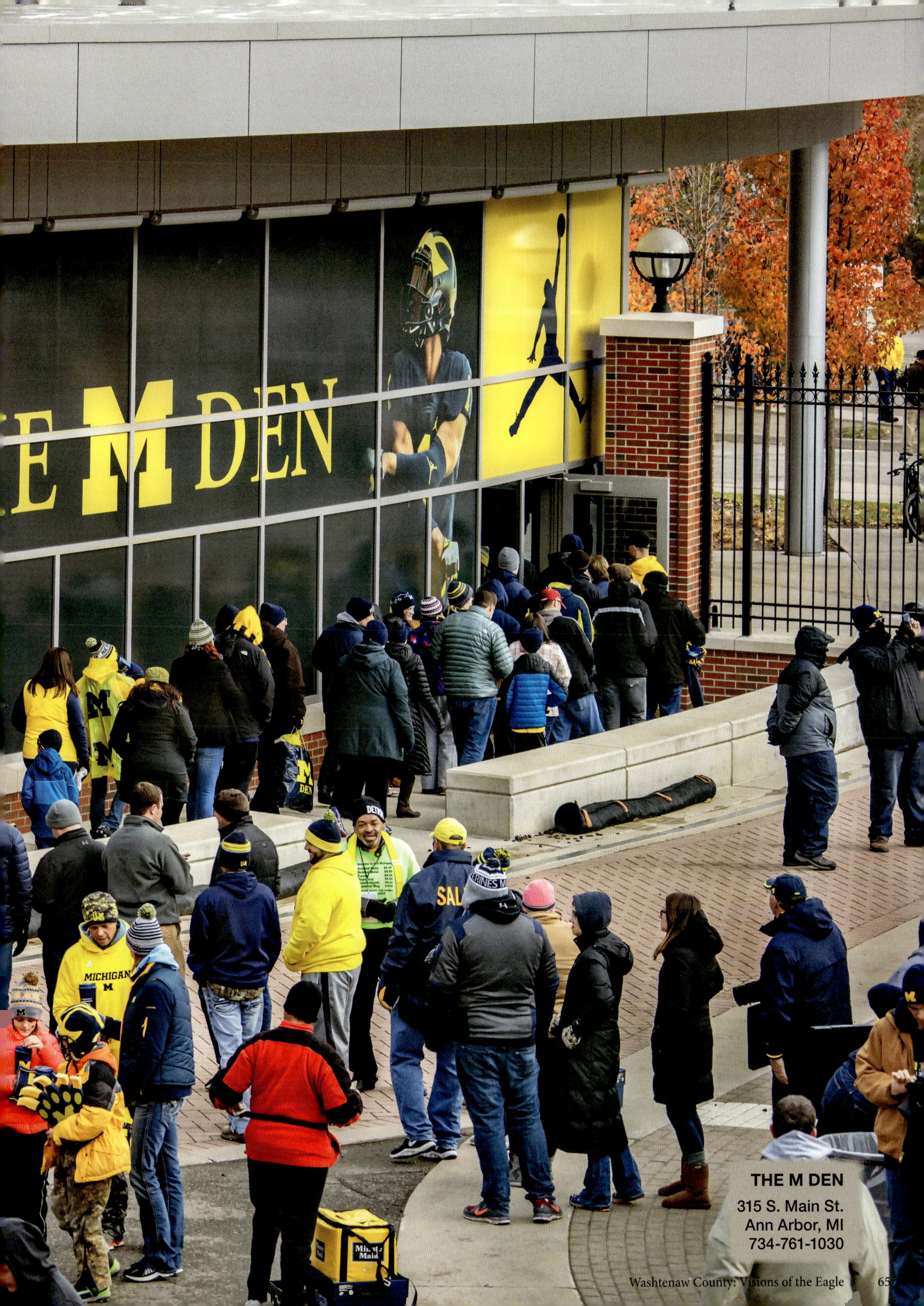

THE M DEN
315 S. Main St.
Ann Arbor, MI
734-761-1030

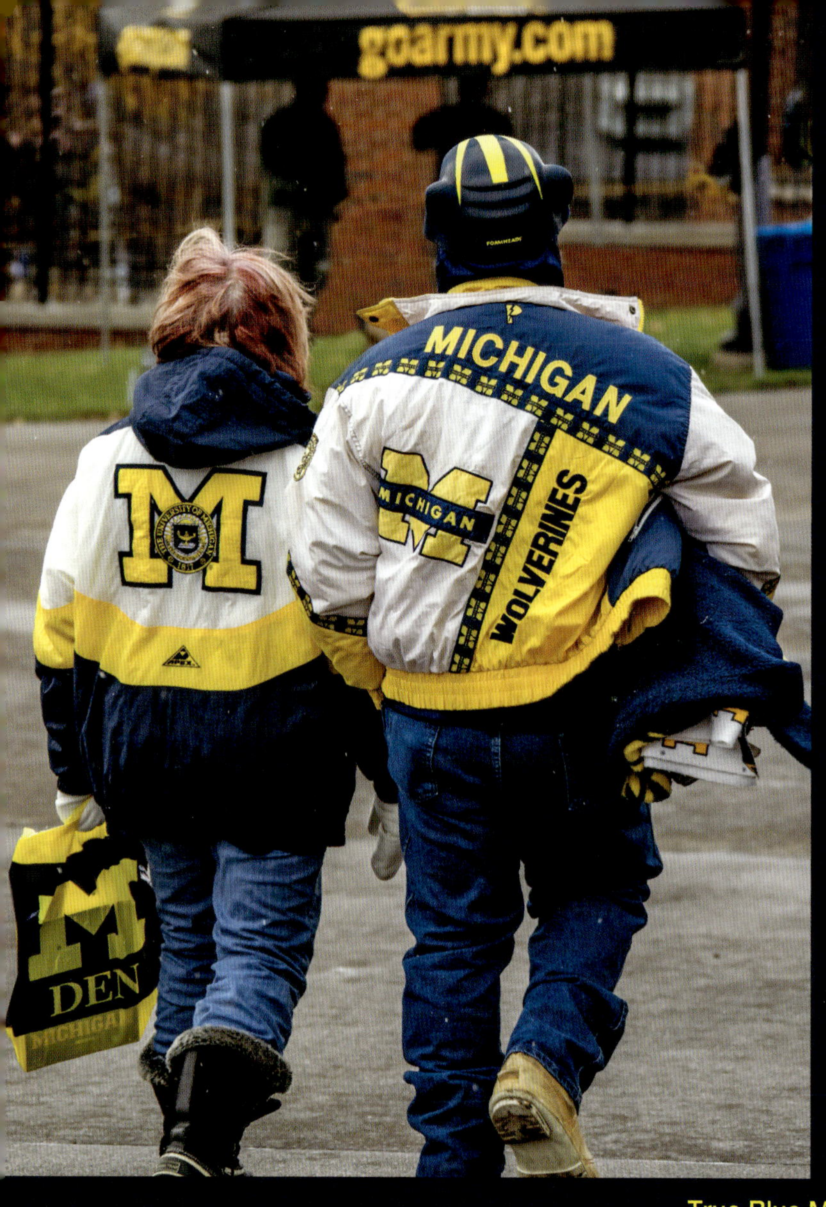

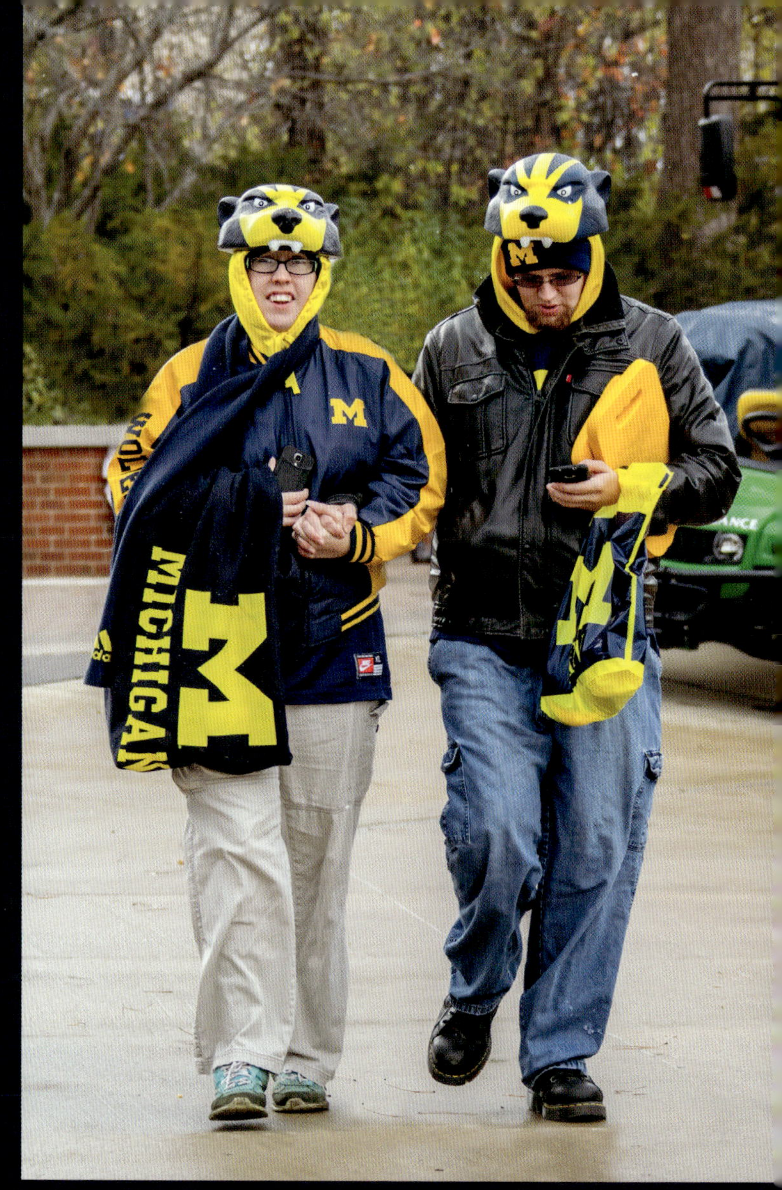

True Blue Michigan Fans!

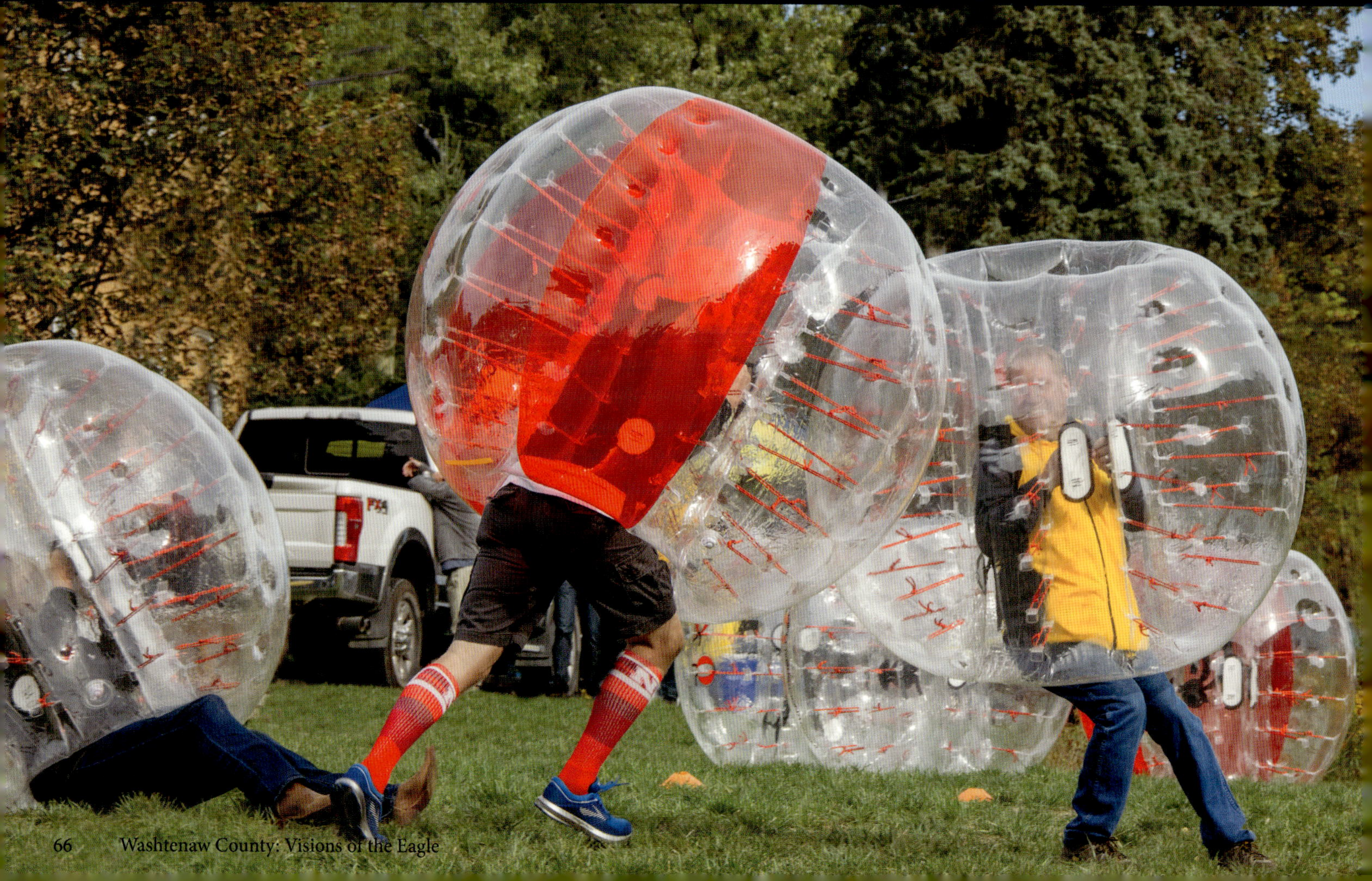

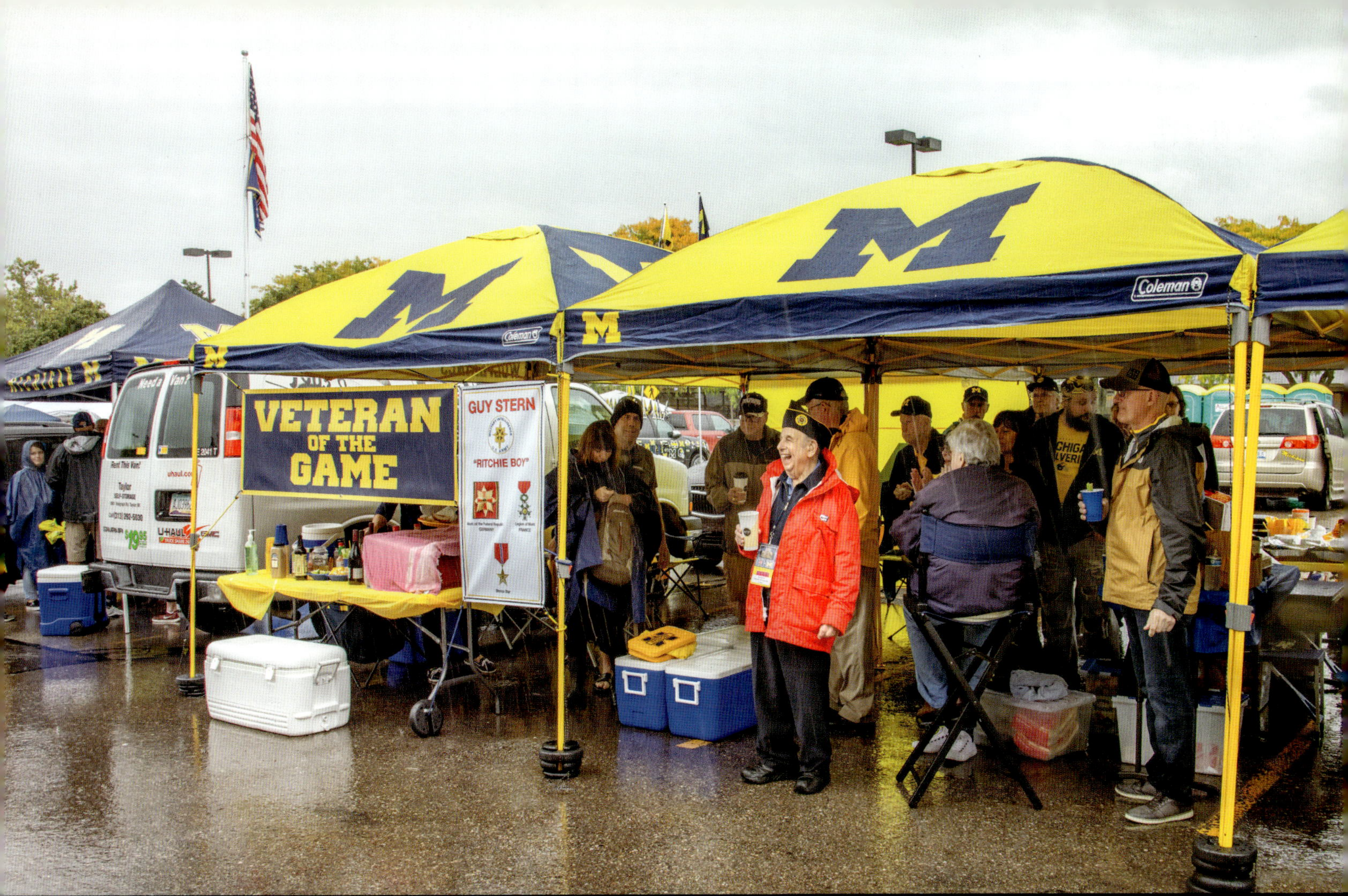

Game Day Fun.

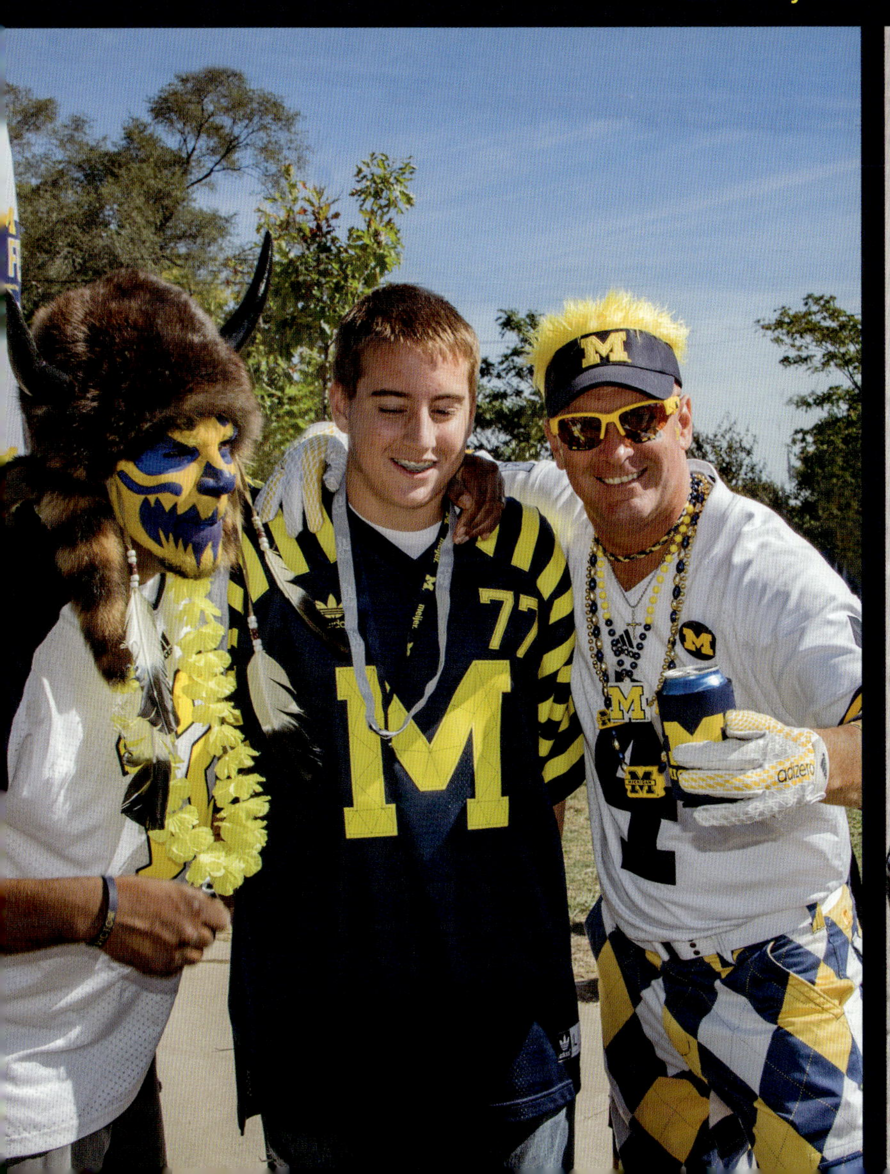

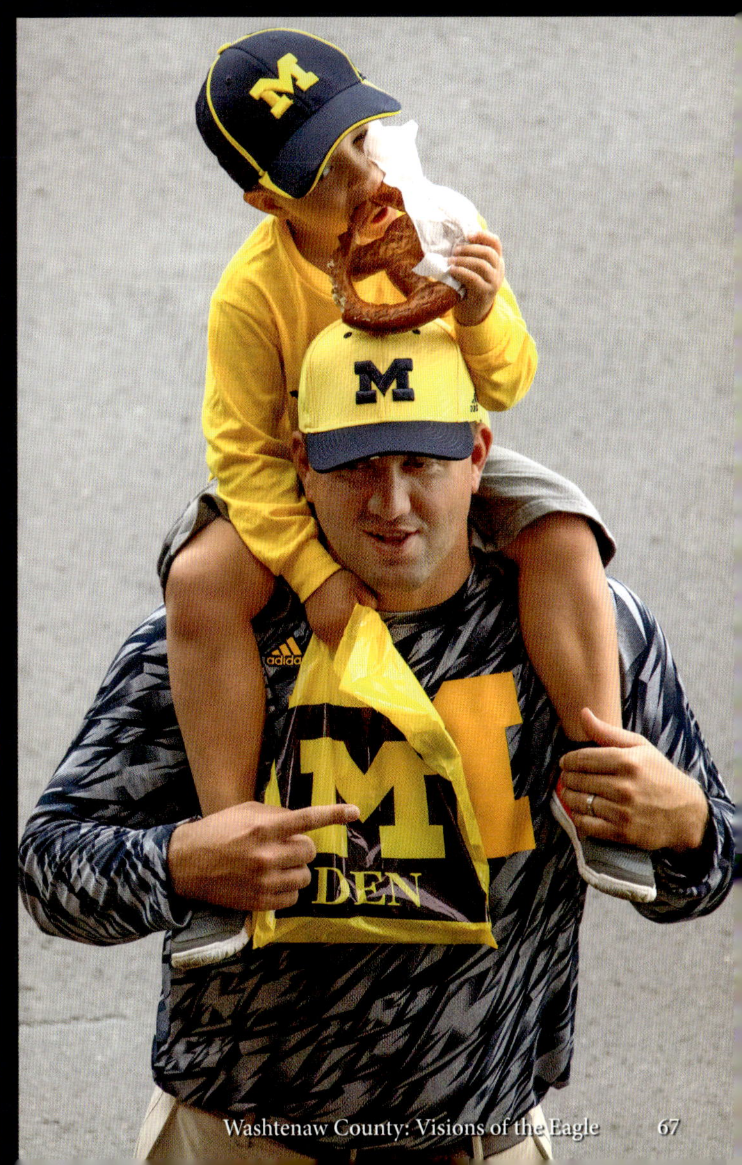

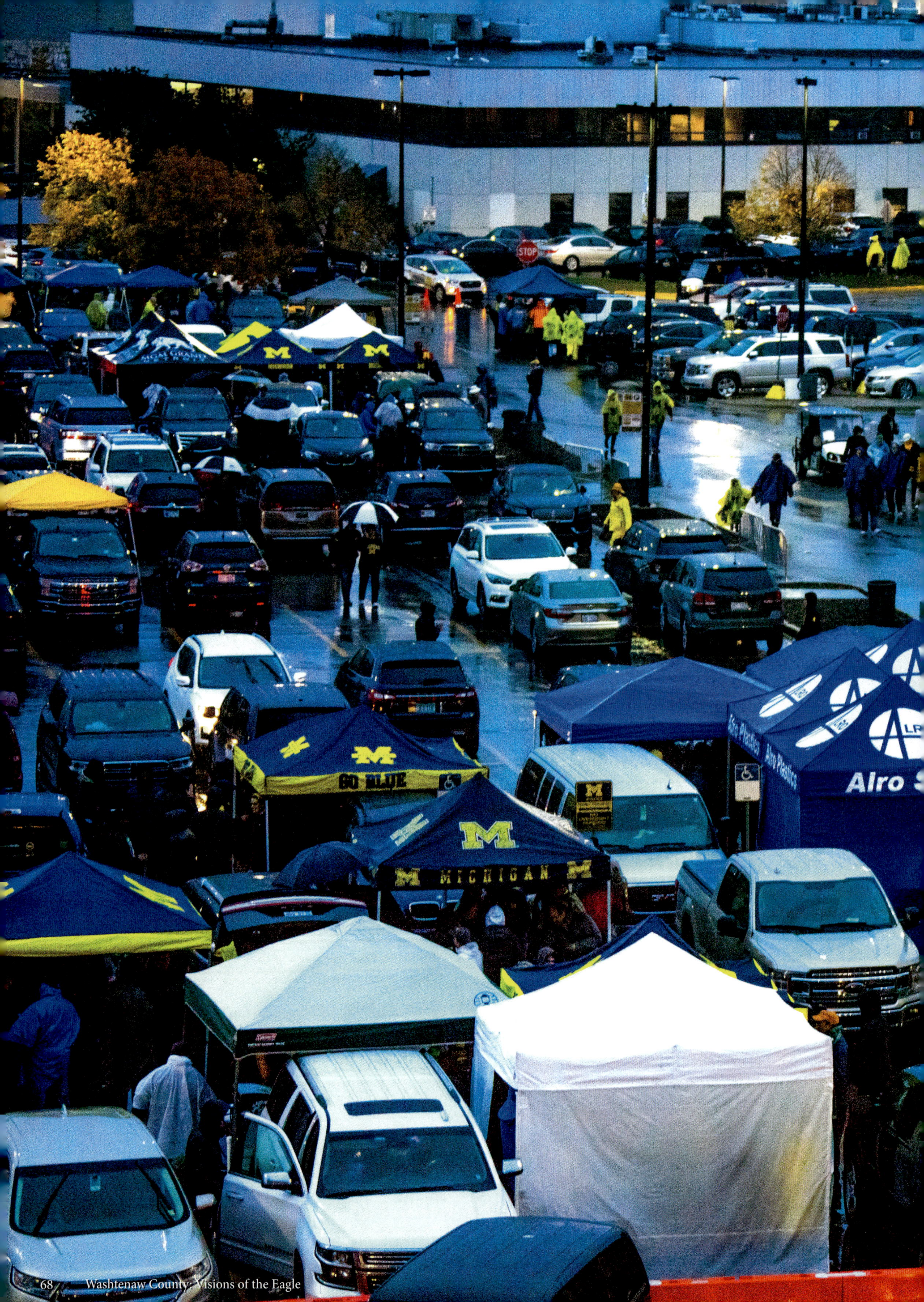
STOP
GO BLUE
MICHIGAN
Alro Plastics

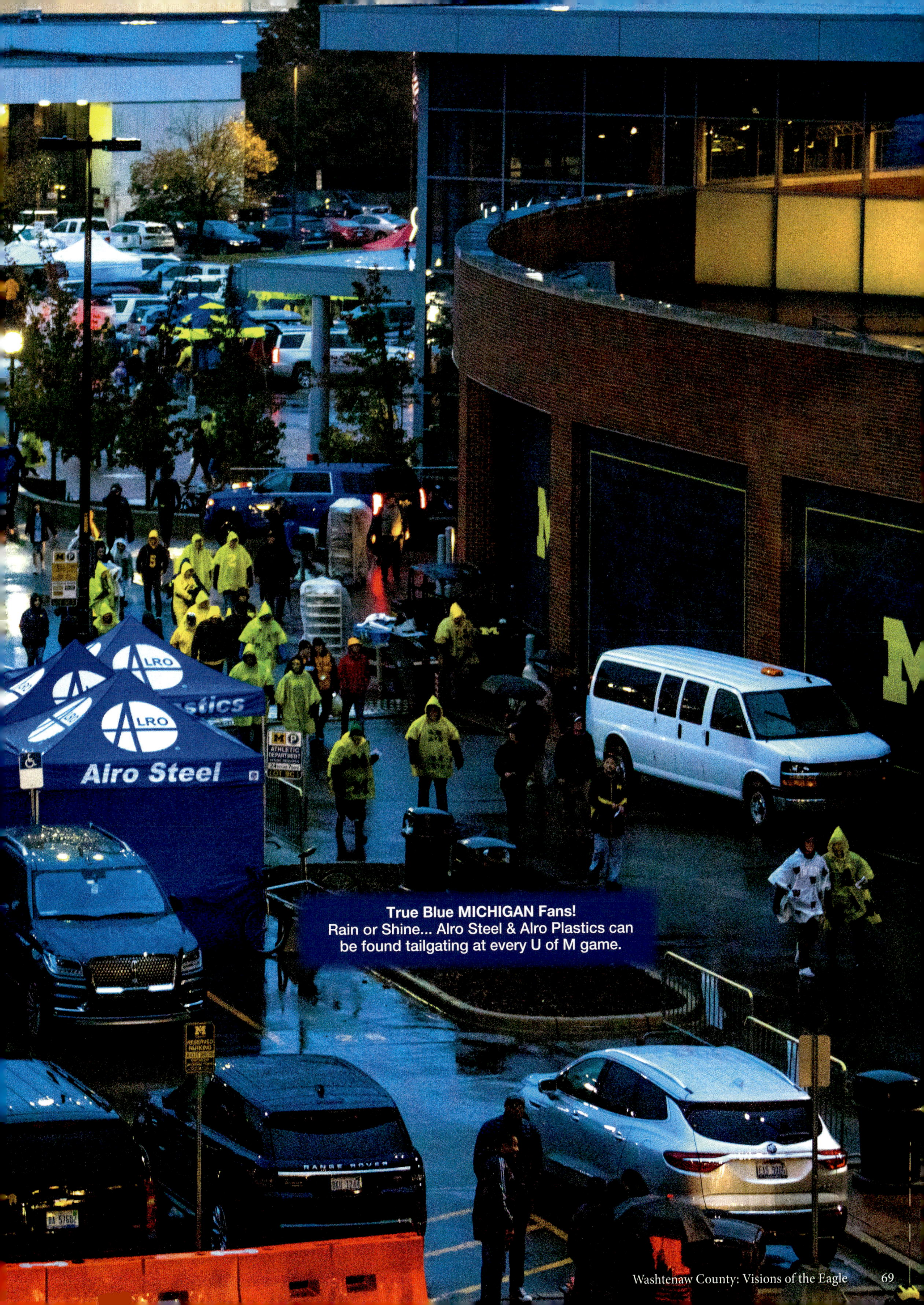

True Blue MICHIGAN Fans!
Rain or Shine... Alro Steel & Alro Plastics can be found tailgating at every U of M game.

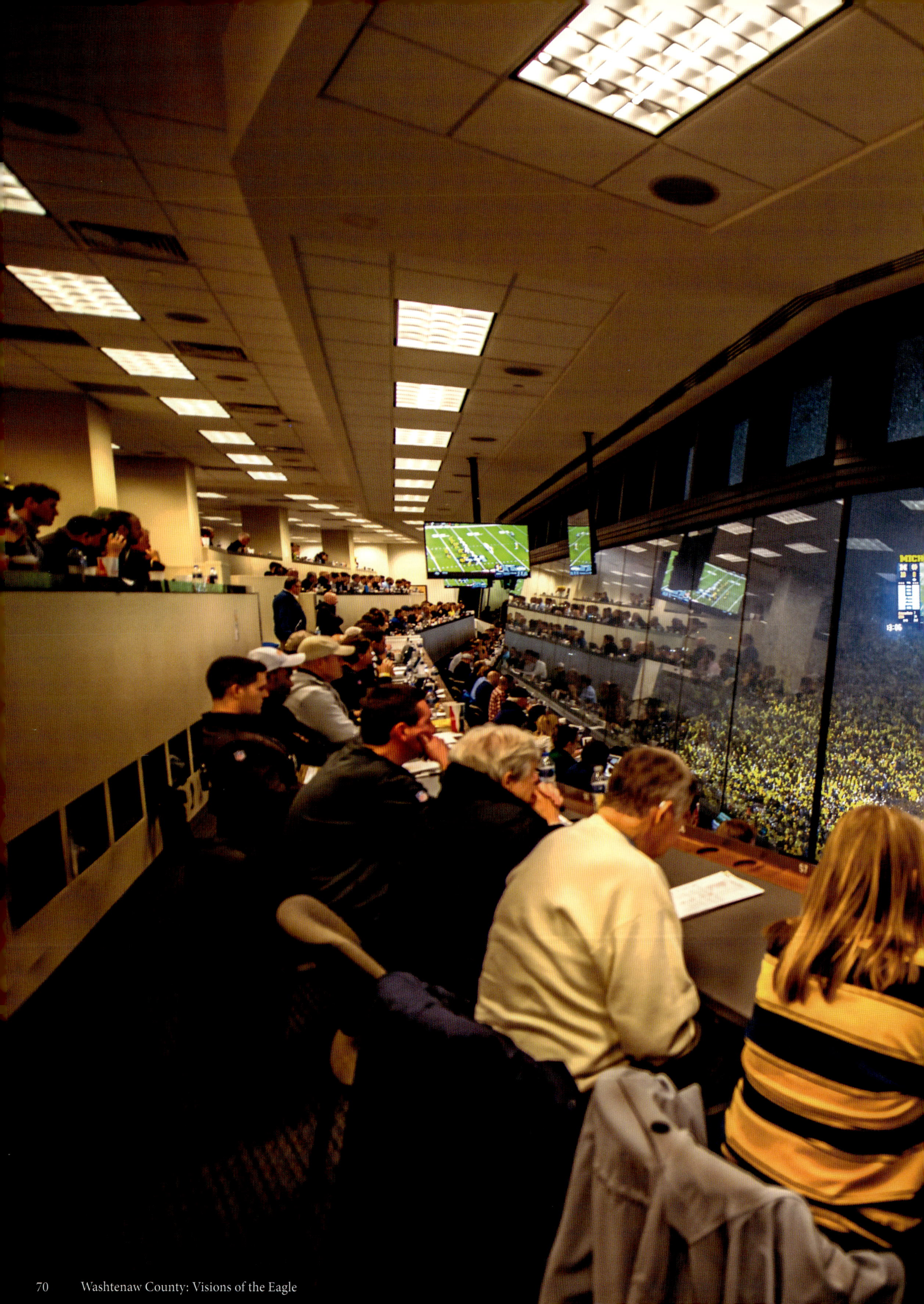

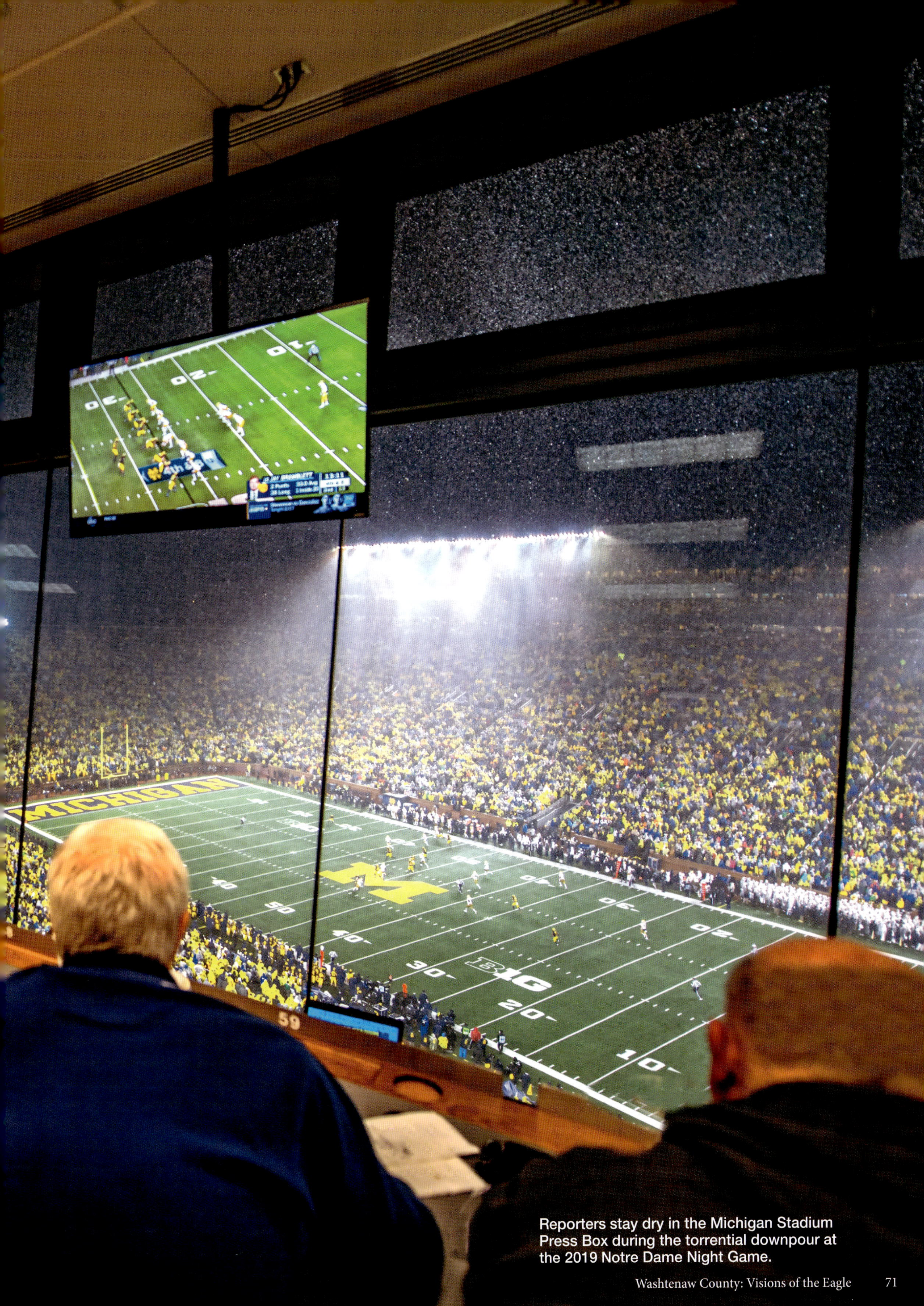

Reporters stay dry in the Michigan Stadium Press Box during the torrential downpour at the 2019 Notre Dame Night Game.

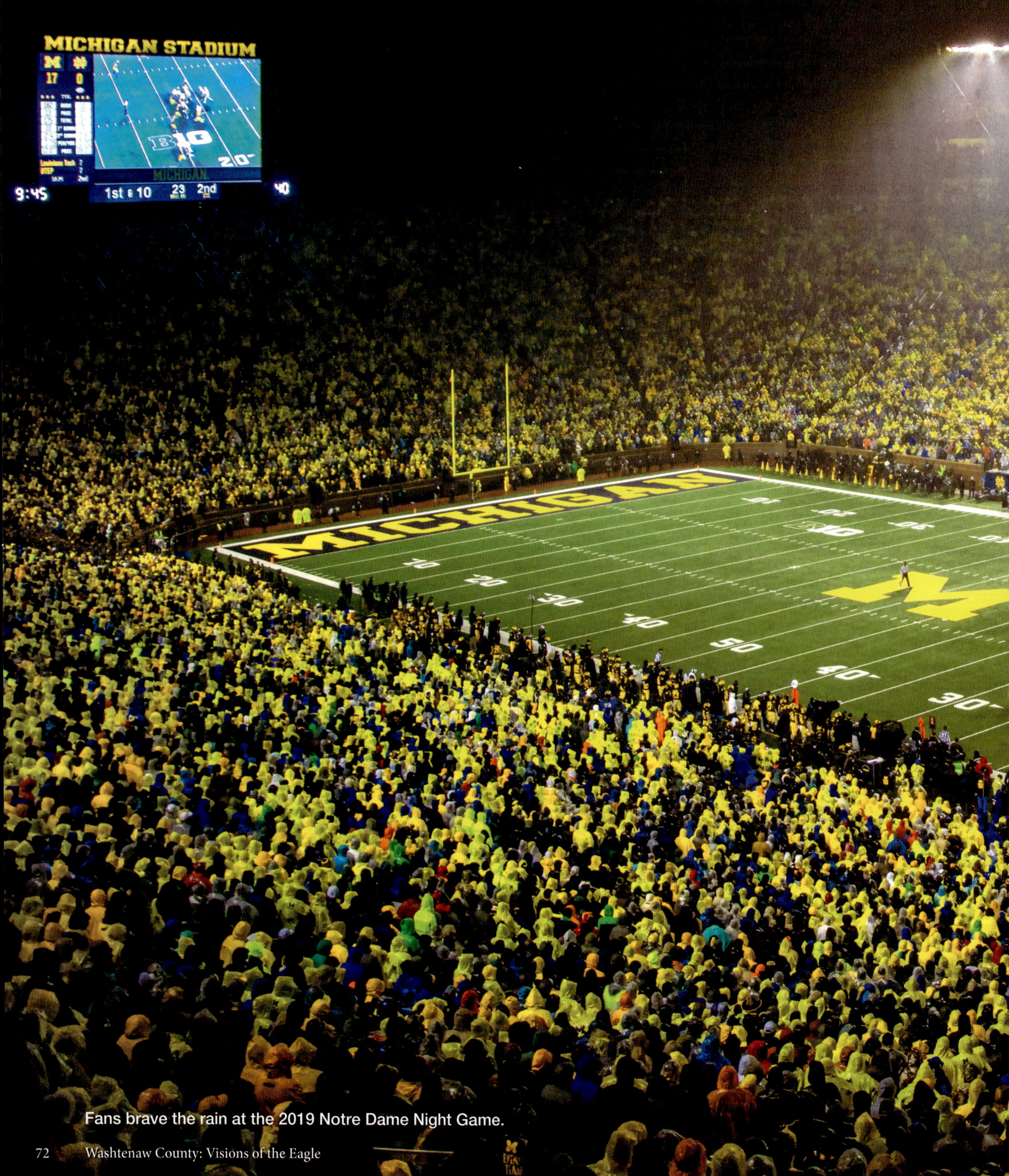

Fans brave the rain at the 2019 Notre Dame Night Game.

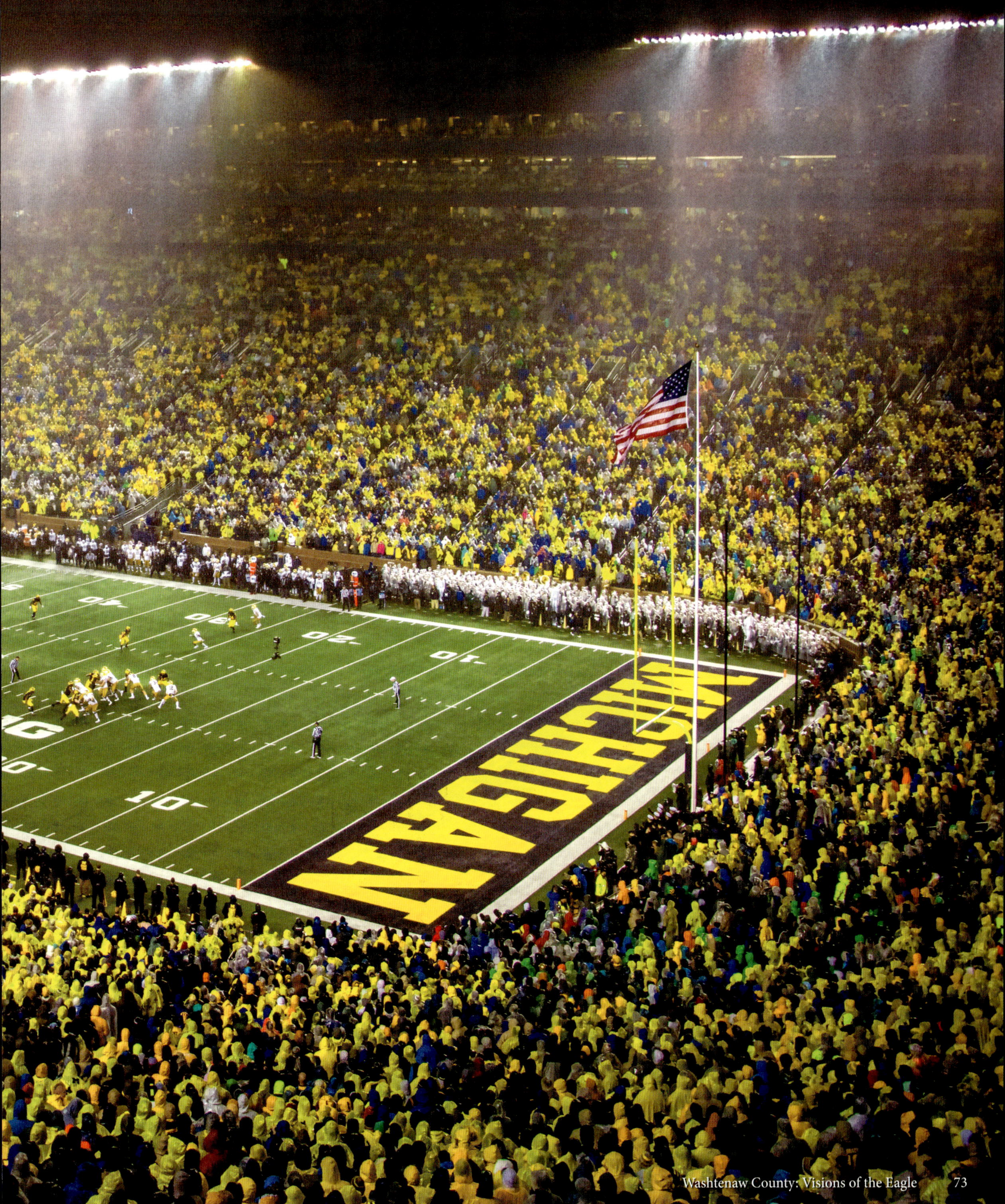
MICHIGAN

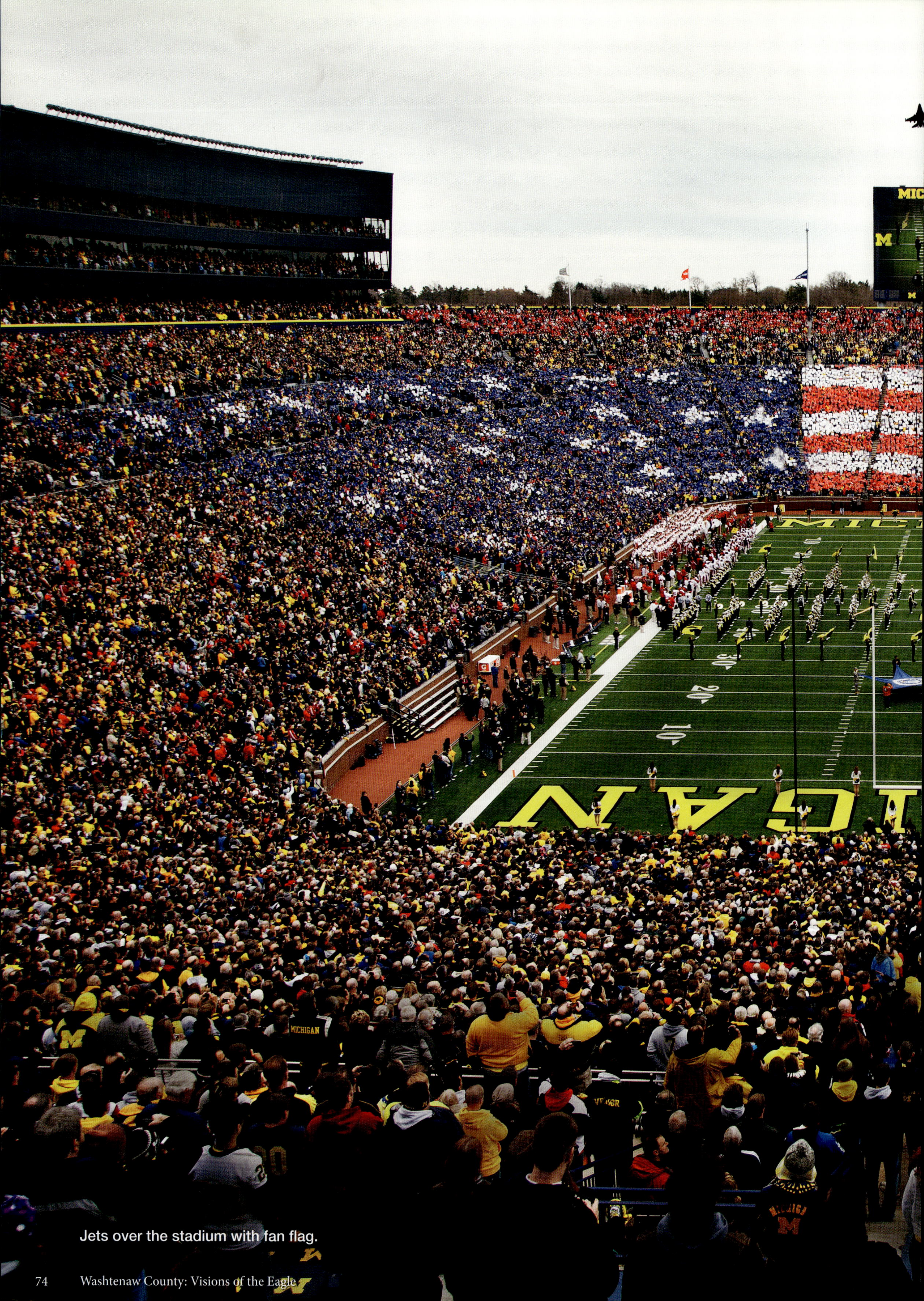

Jets over the stadium with fan flag.

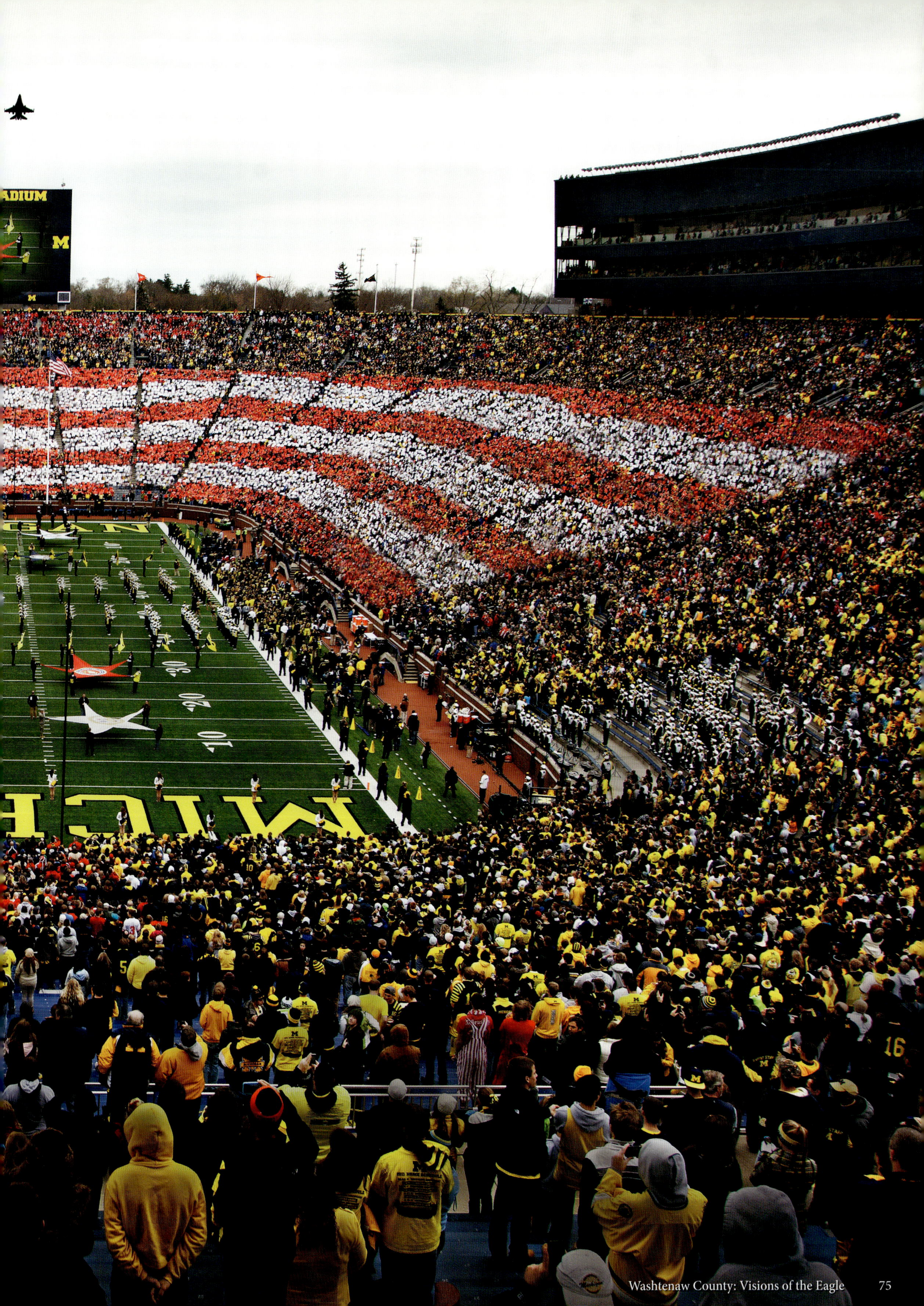

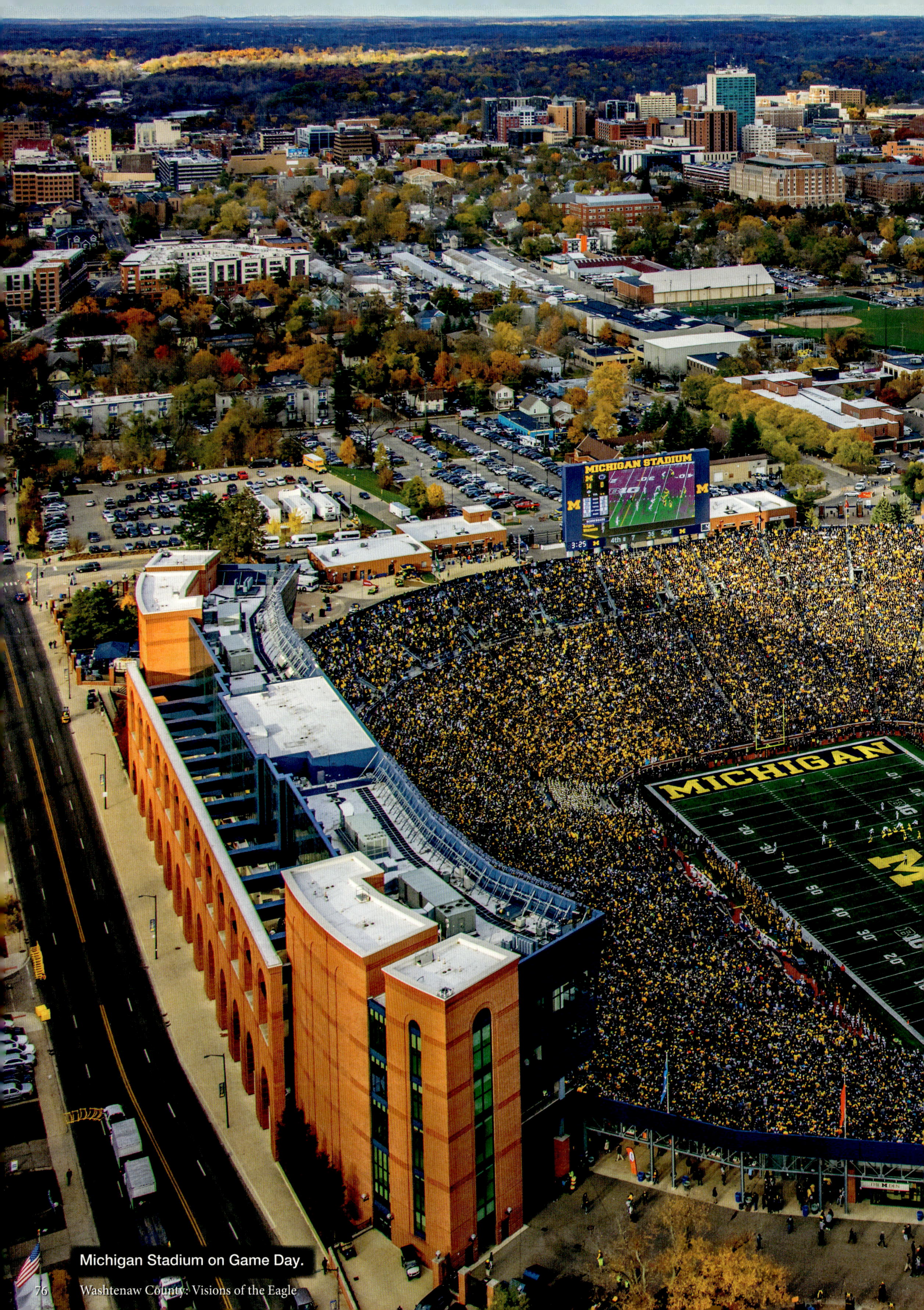

Michigan Stadium on Game Day.

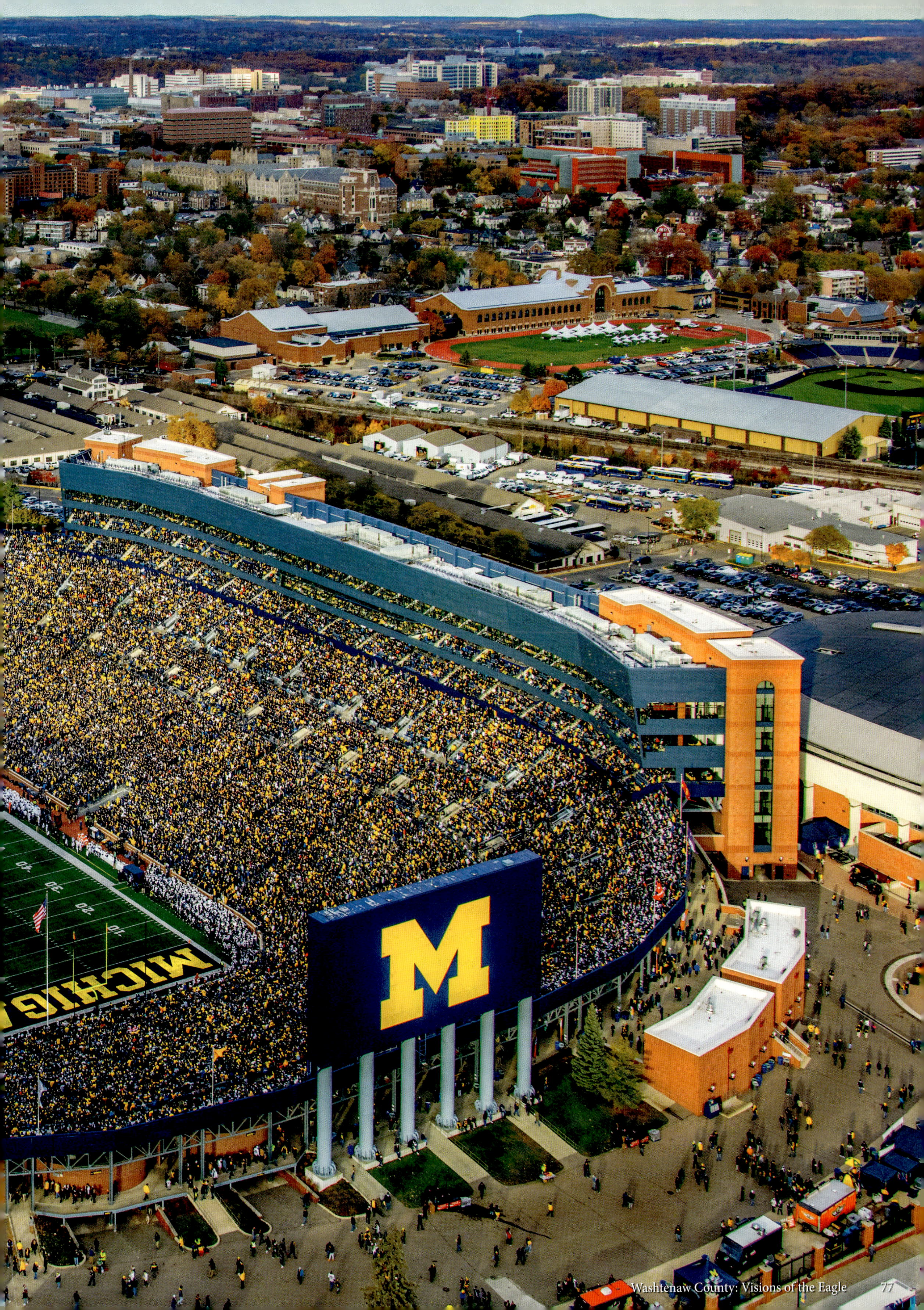
M

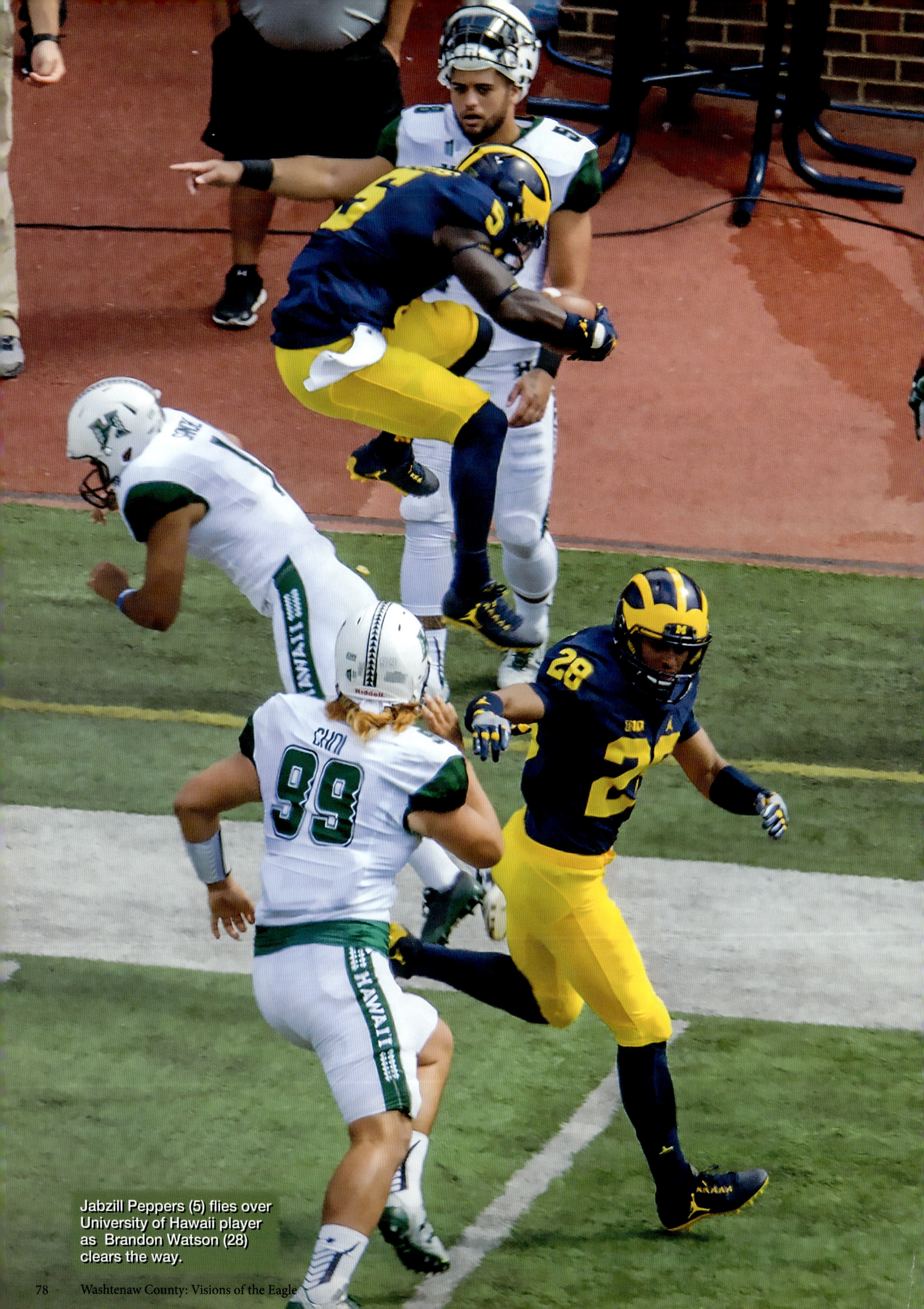

Jabzill Peppers (5) flies over University of Hawaii player as Brandon Watson (28) clears the way.

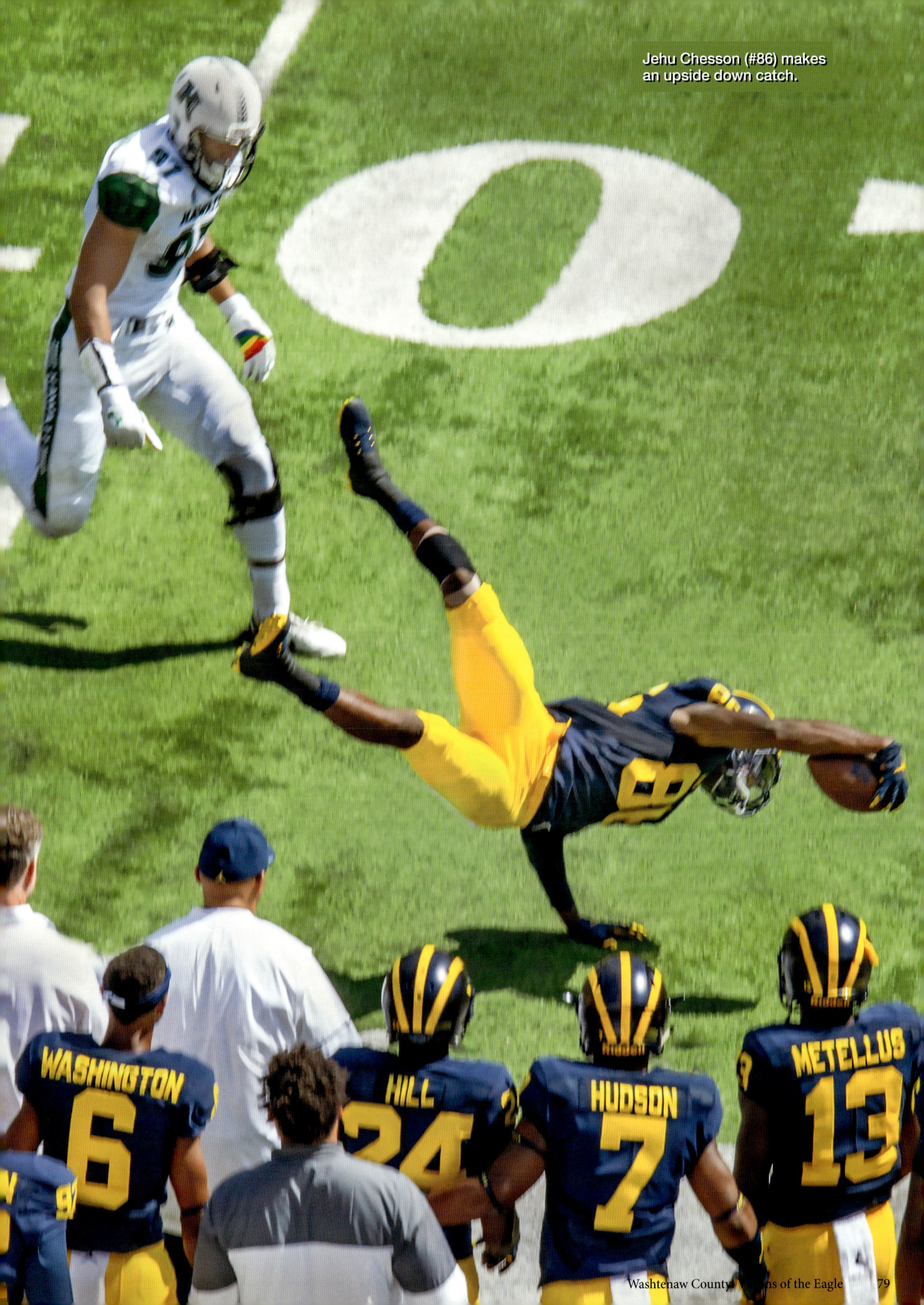

Jehu Chesson (#86) makes an upside down catch.

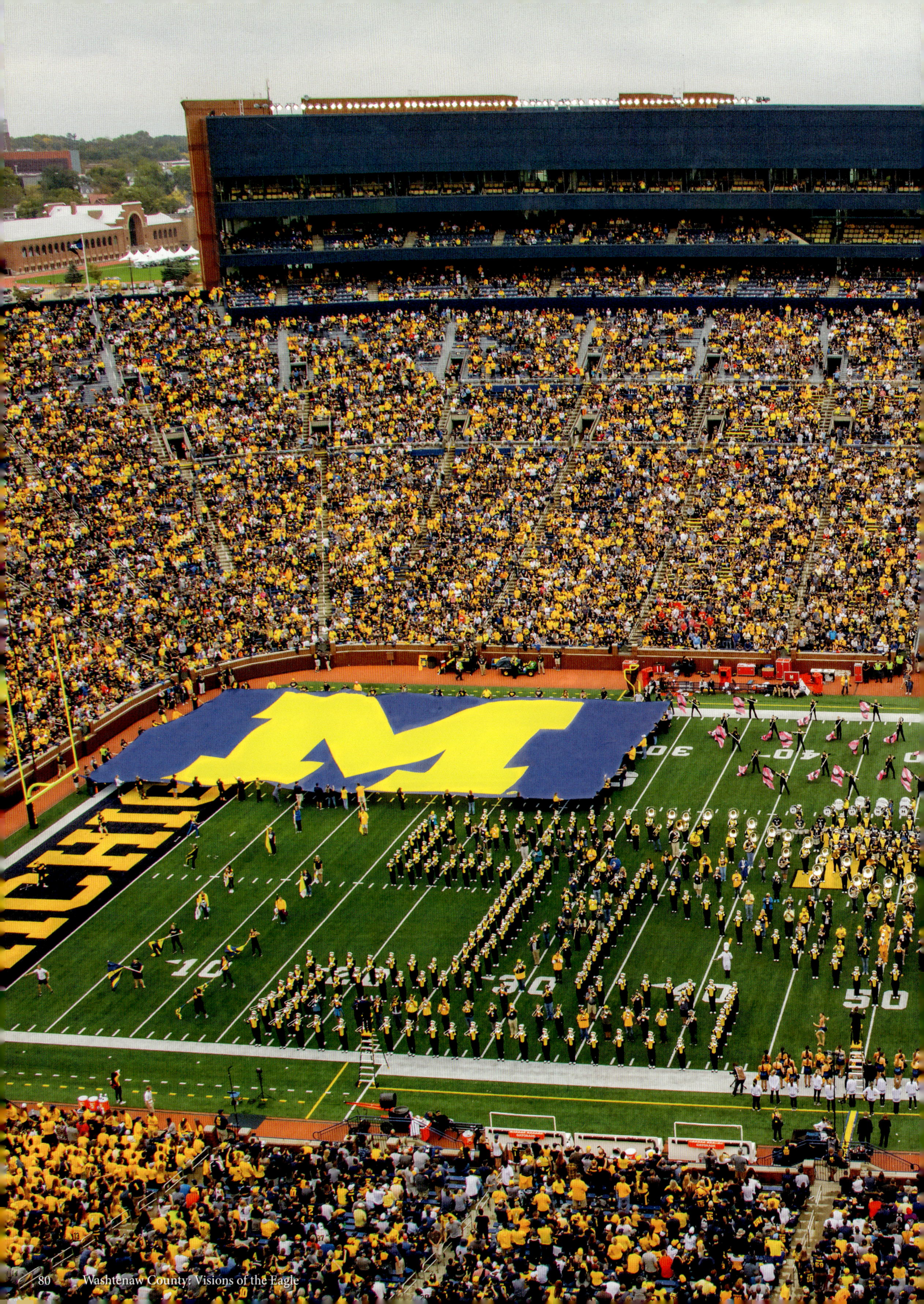

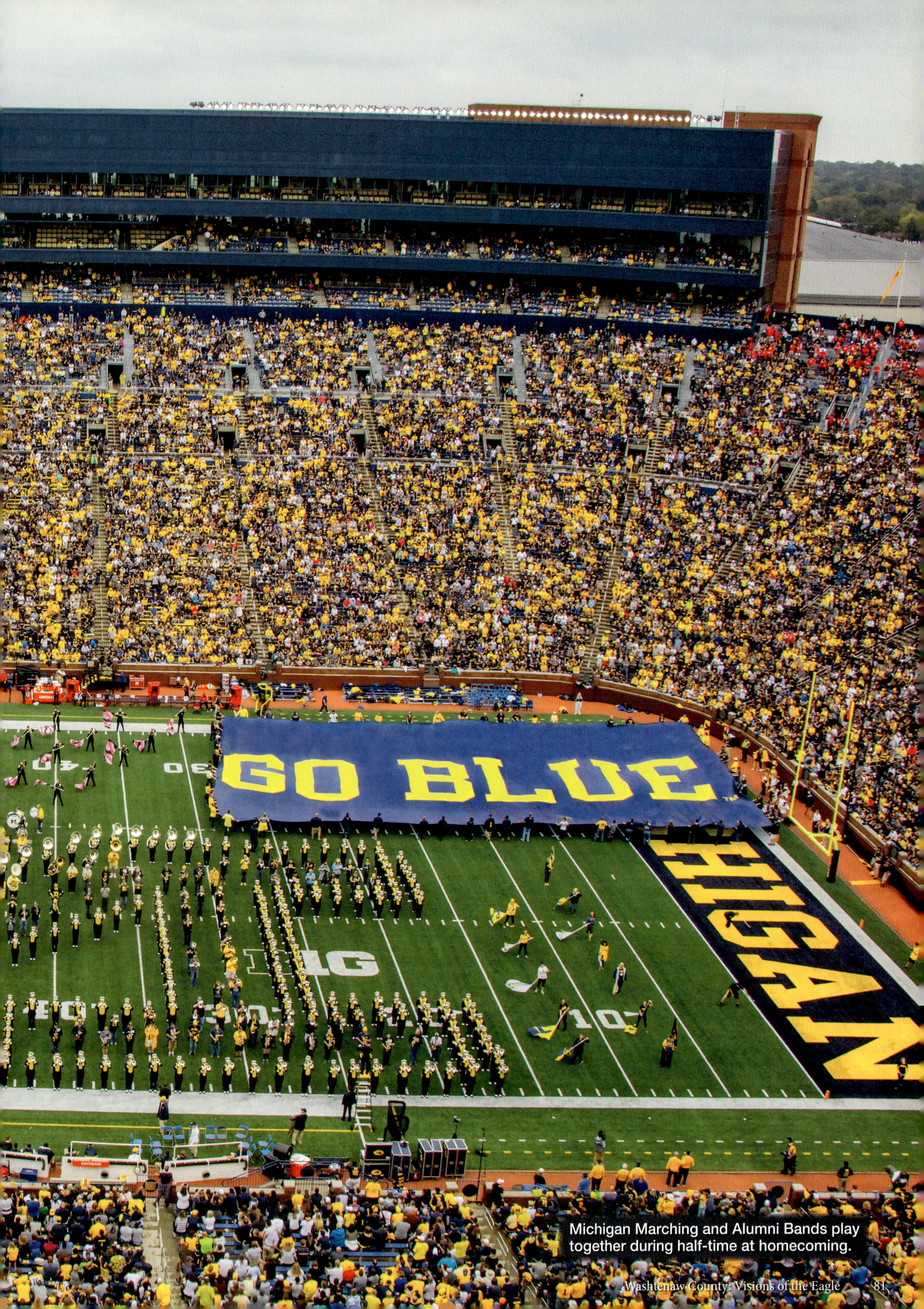

Michigan Marching and Alumni Bands play together during half-time at homecoming.

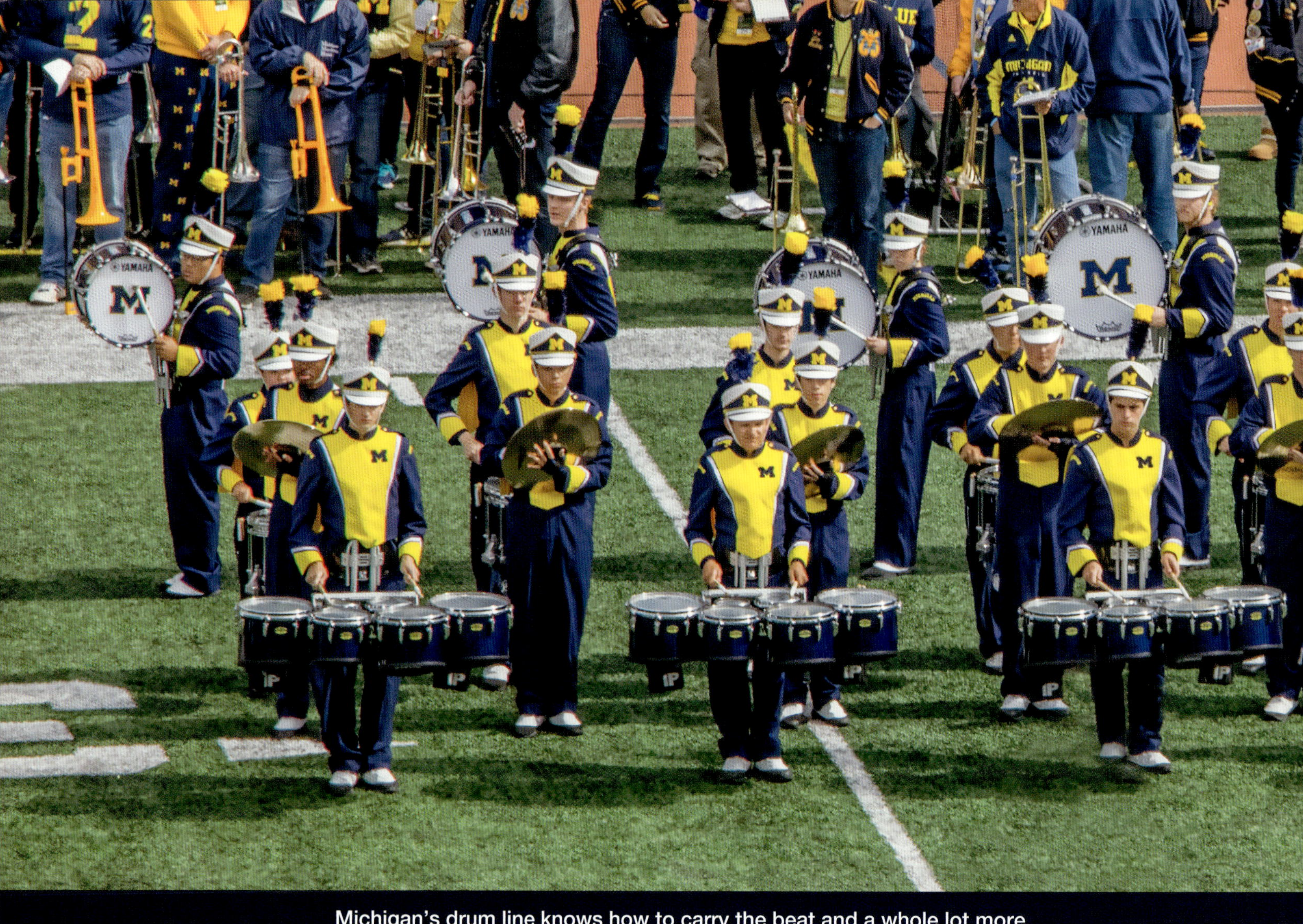

Michigan's drum line knows how to carry the beat and a whole lot more.

Kelly Bertoni from Chelsea, is the university's third female drum major.

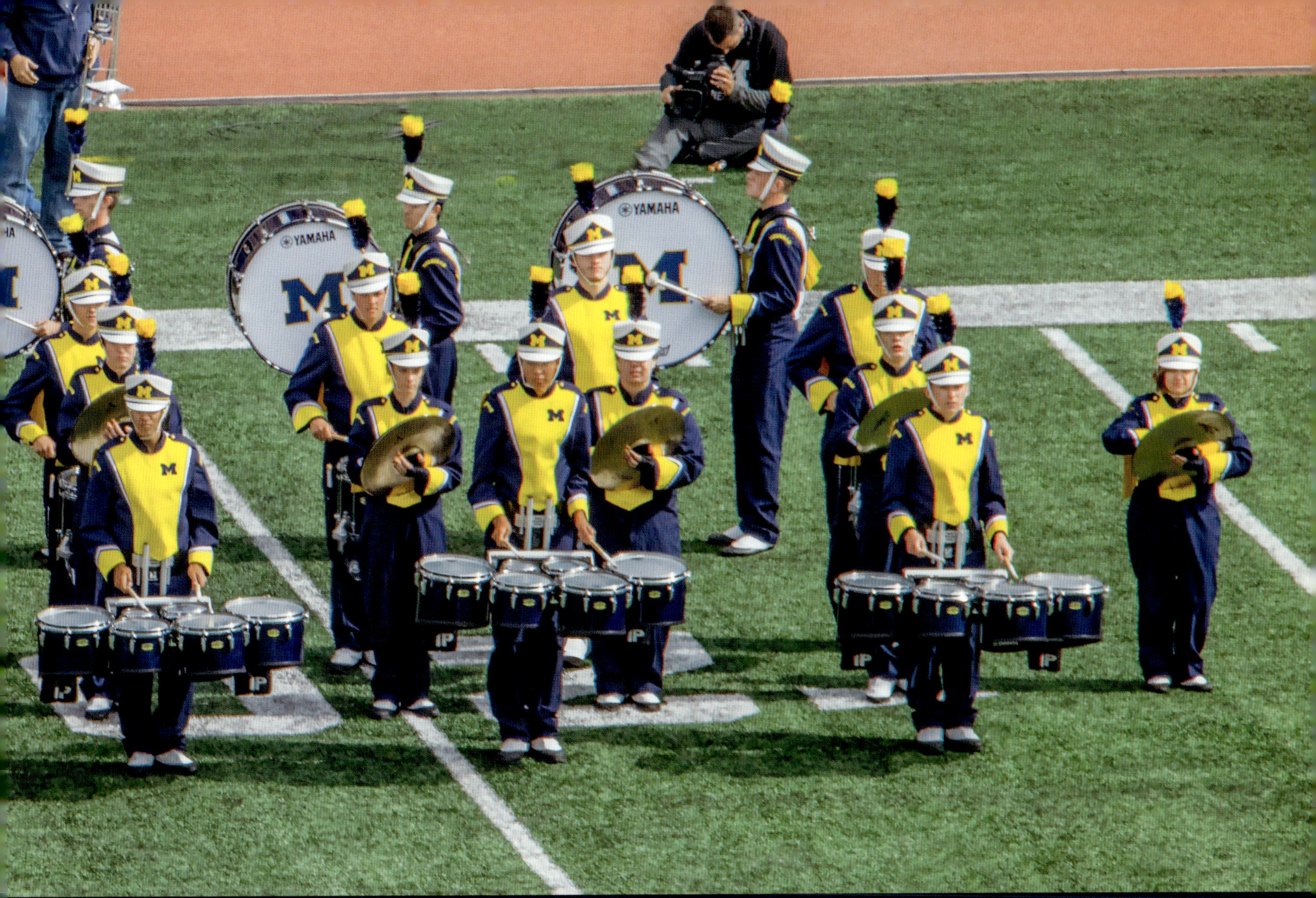

Marching to the Big House on Green Street.

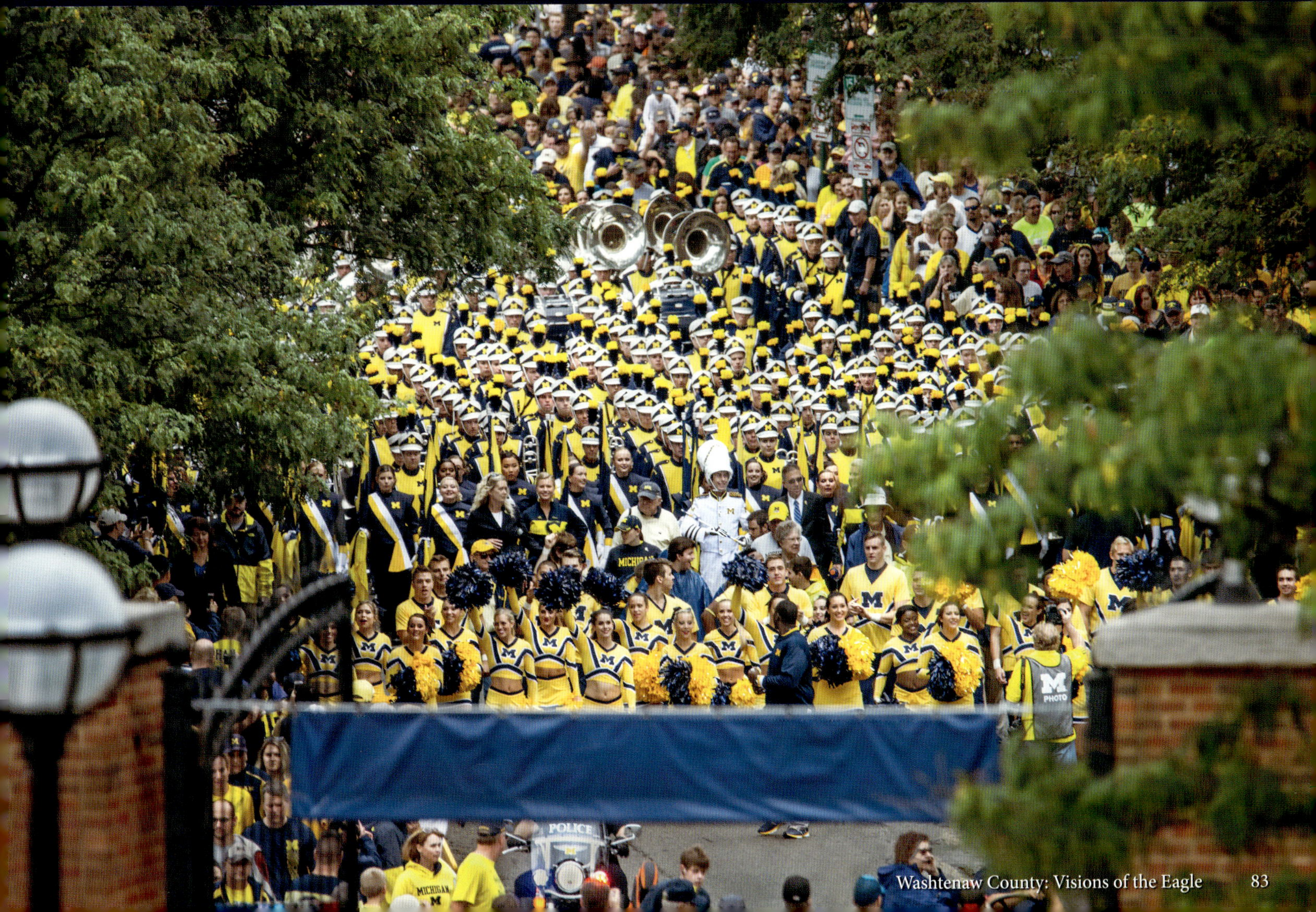

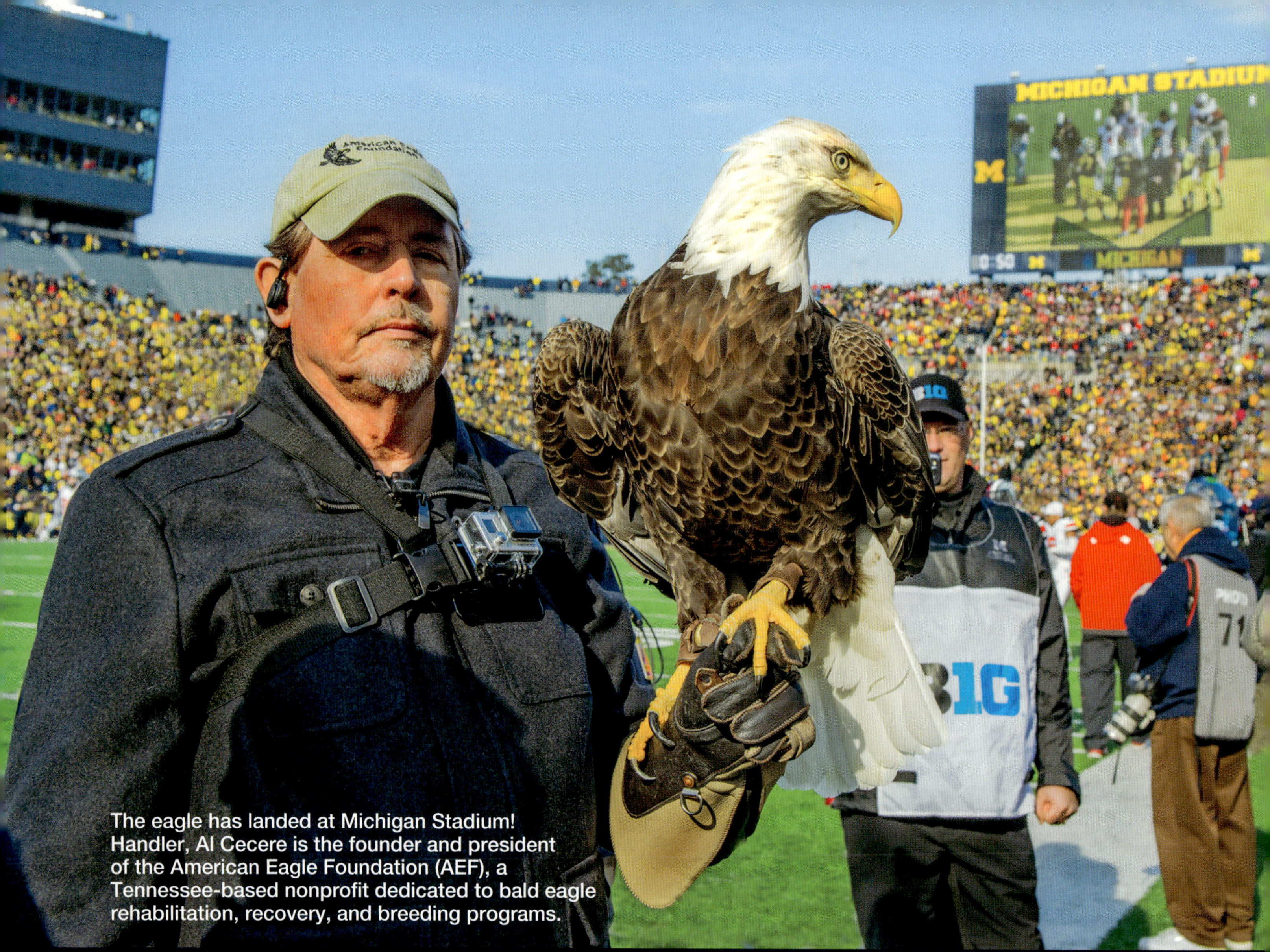

The eagle has landed at Michigan Stadium! Handler, Al Cecere is the founder and president of the American Eagle Foundation (AEF), a Tennessee-based nonprofit dedicated to bald eagle rehabilitation, recovery, and breeding programs.

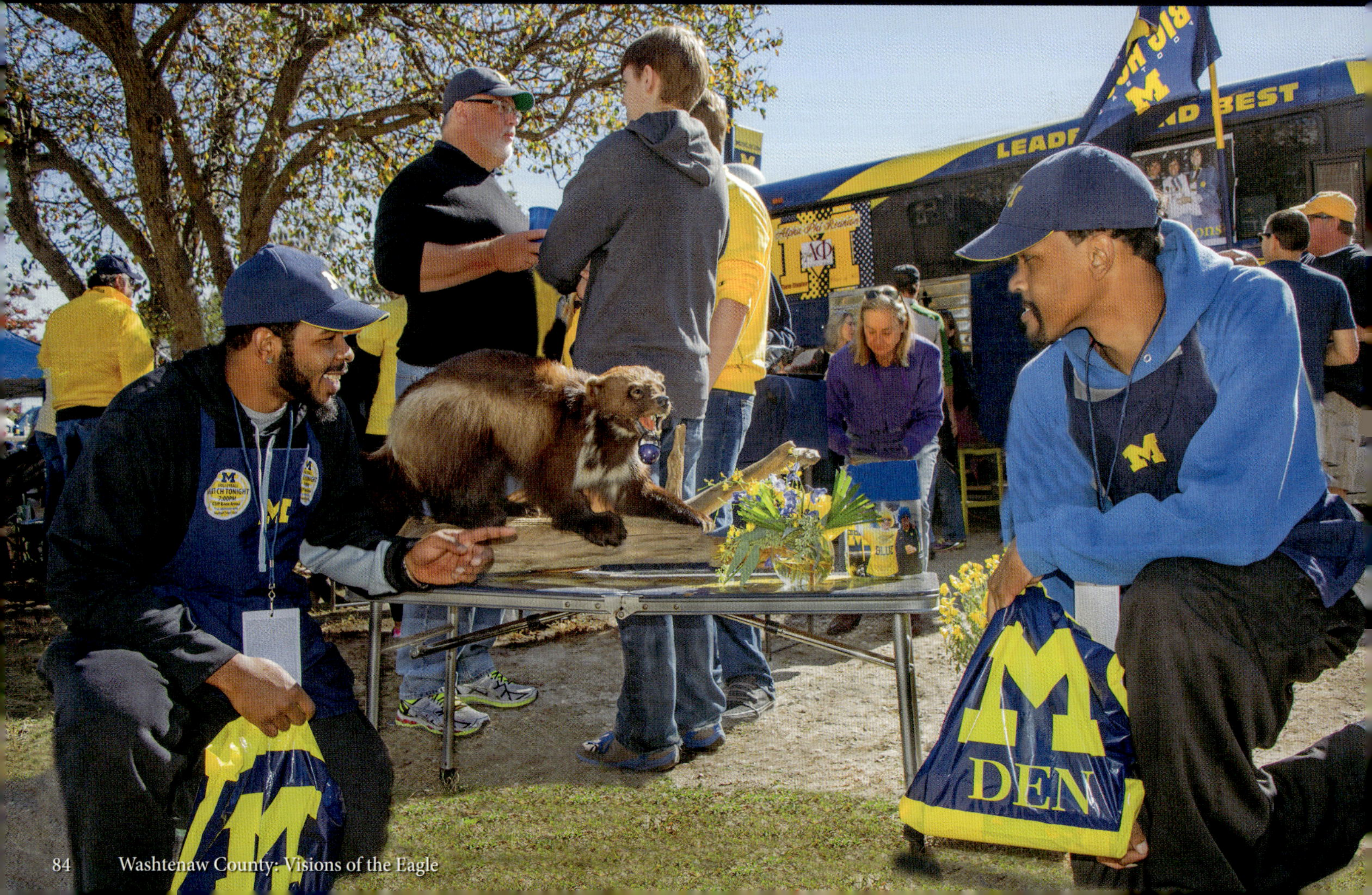

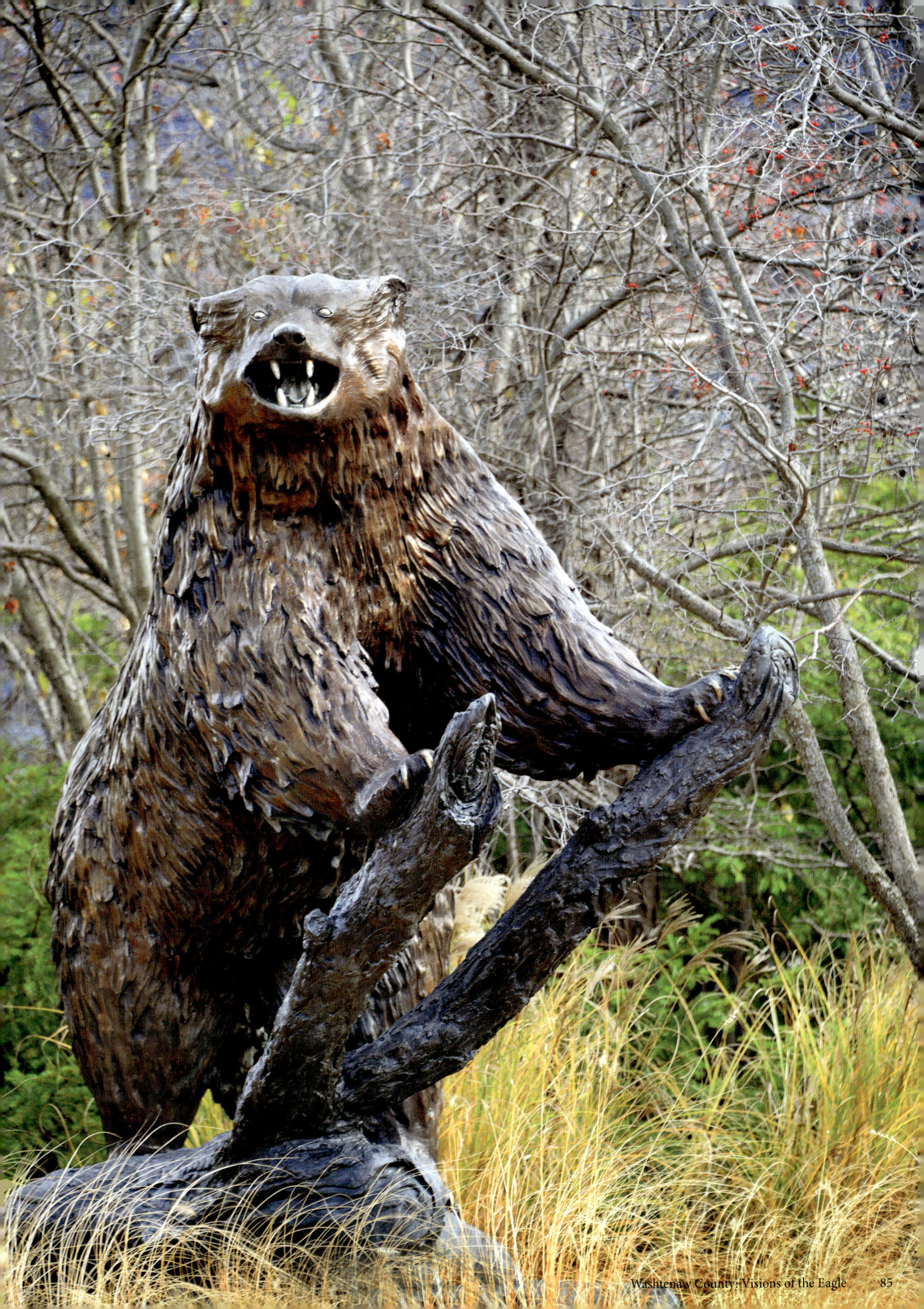

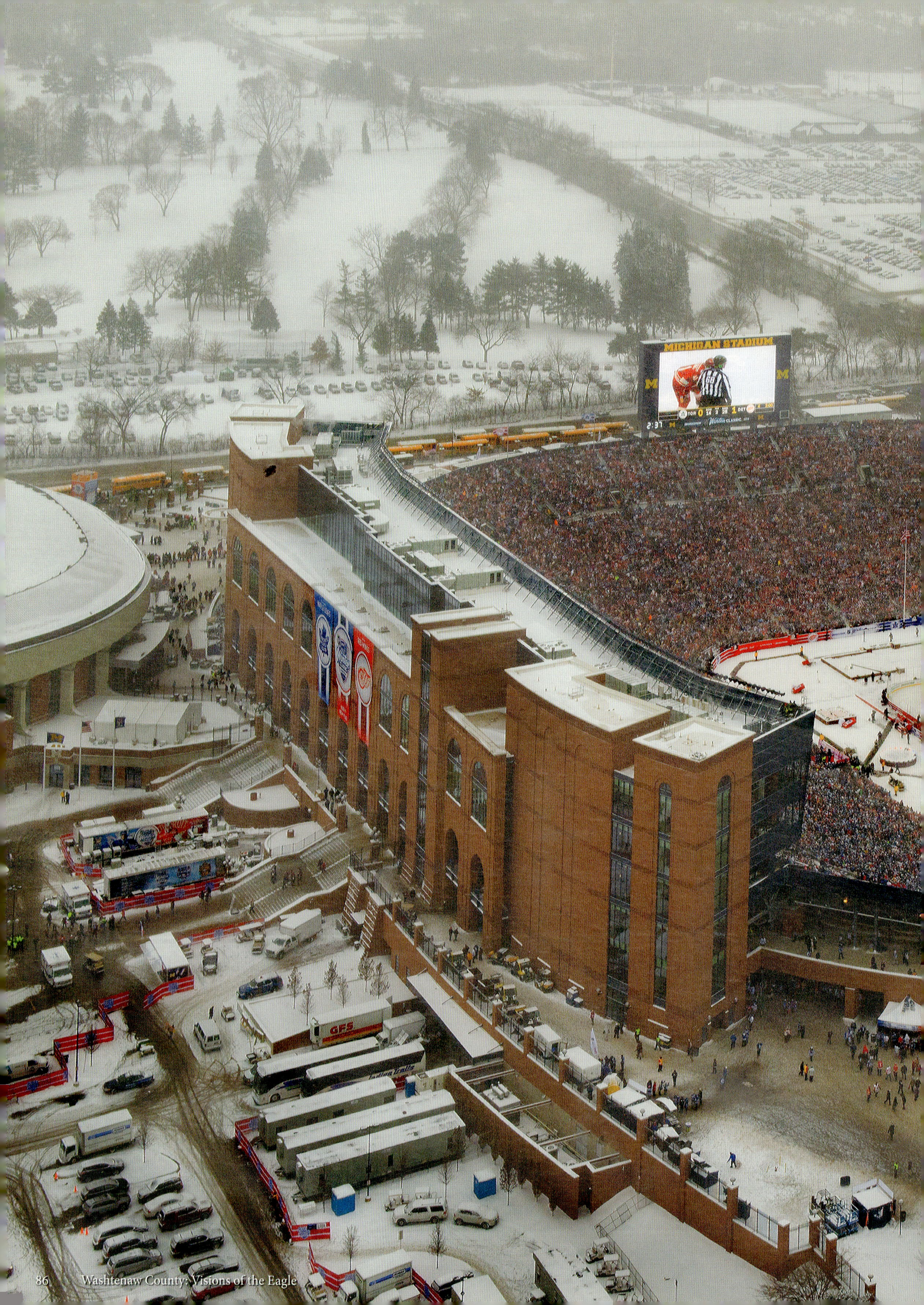
MICHIGAN STADIUM
GFS

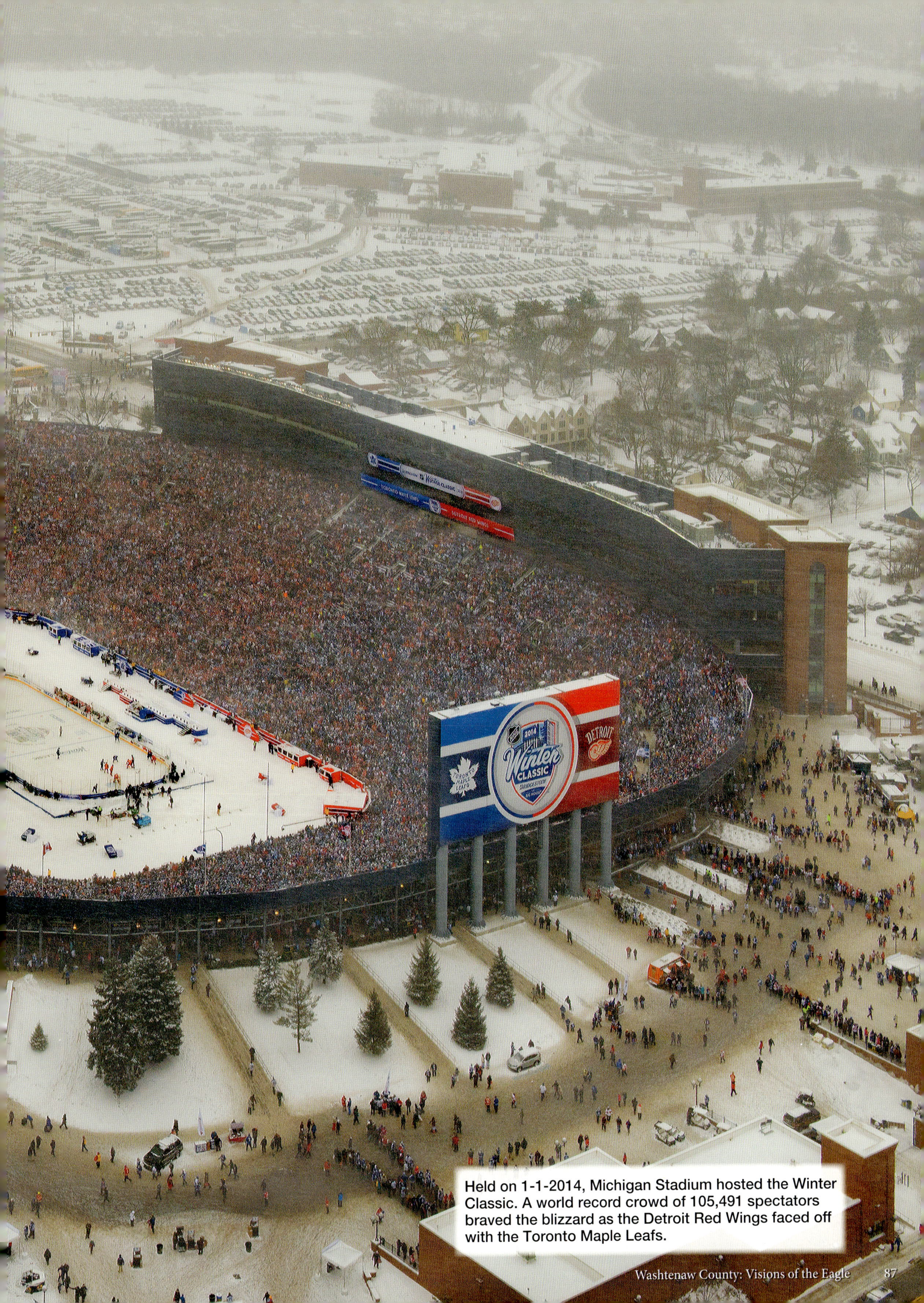

Held on 1-1-2014, Michigan Stadium hosted the Winter Classic. A world record crowd of 105,491 spectators braved the blizzard as the Detroit Red Wings faced off with the Toronto Maple Leafs.

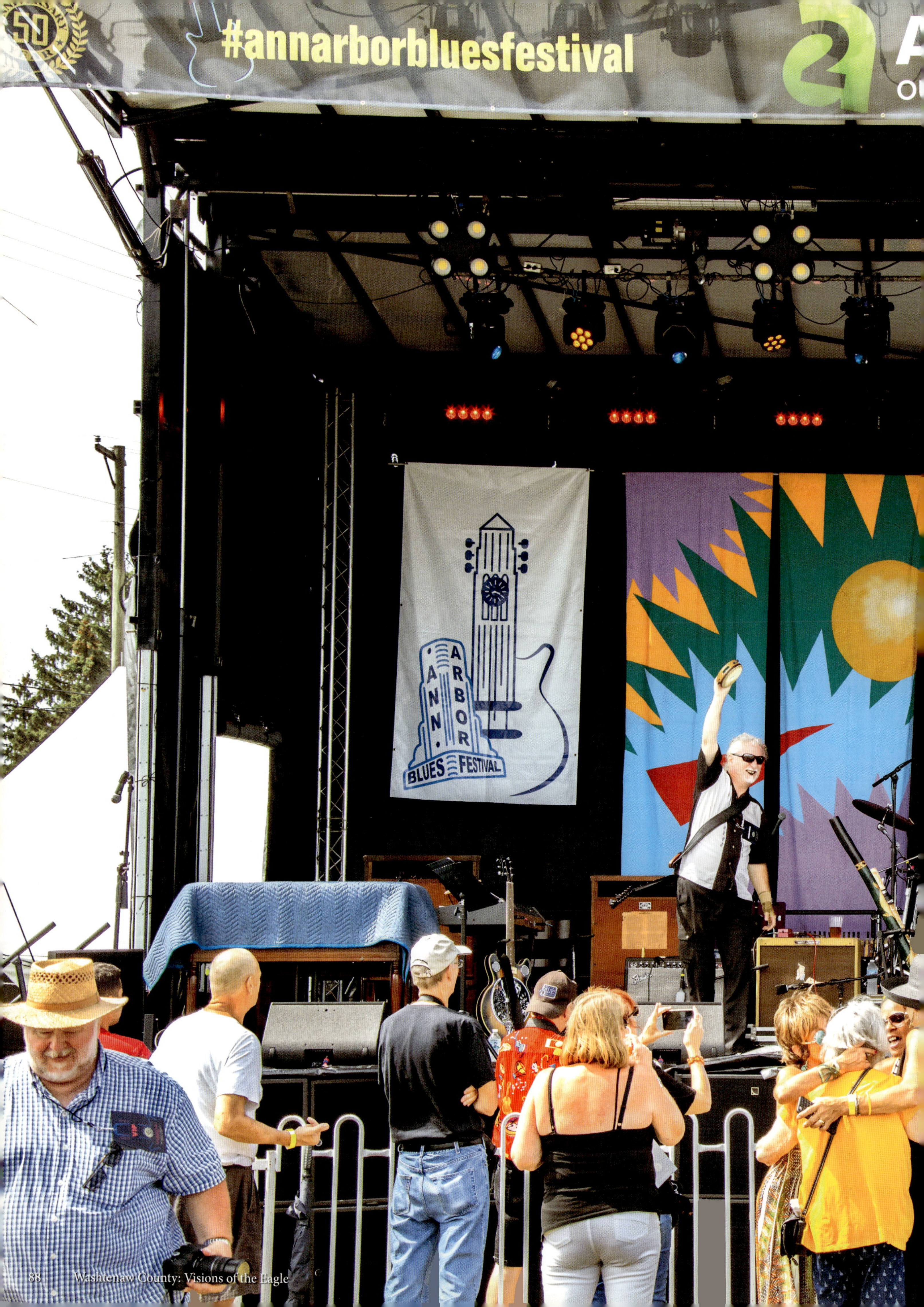
#annarborbluesfestival
50
ANN ARBOR
BLUES FESTIVAL

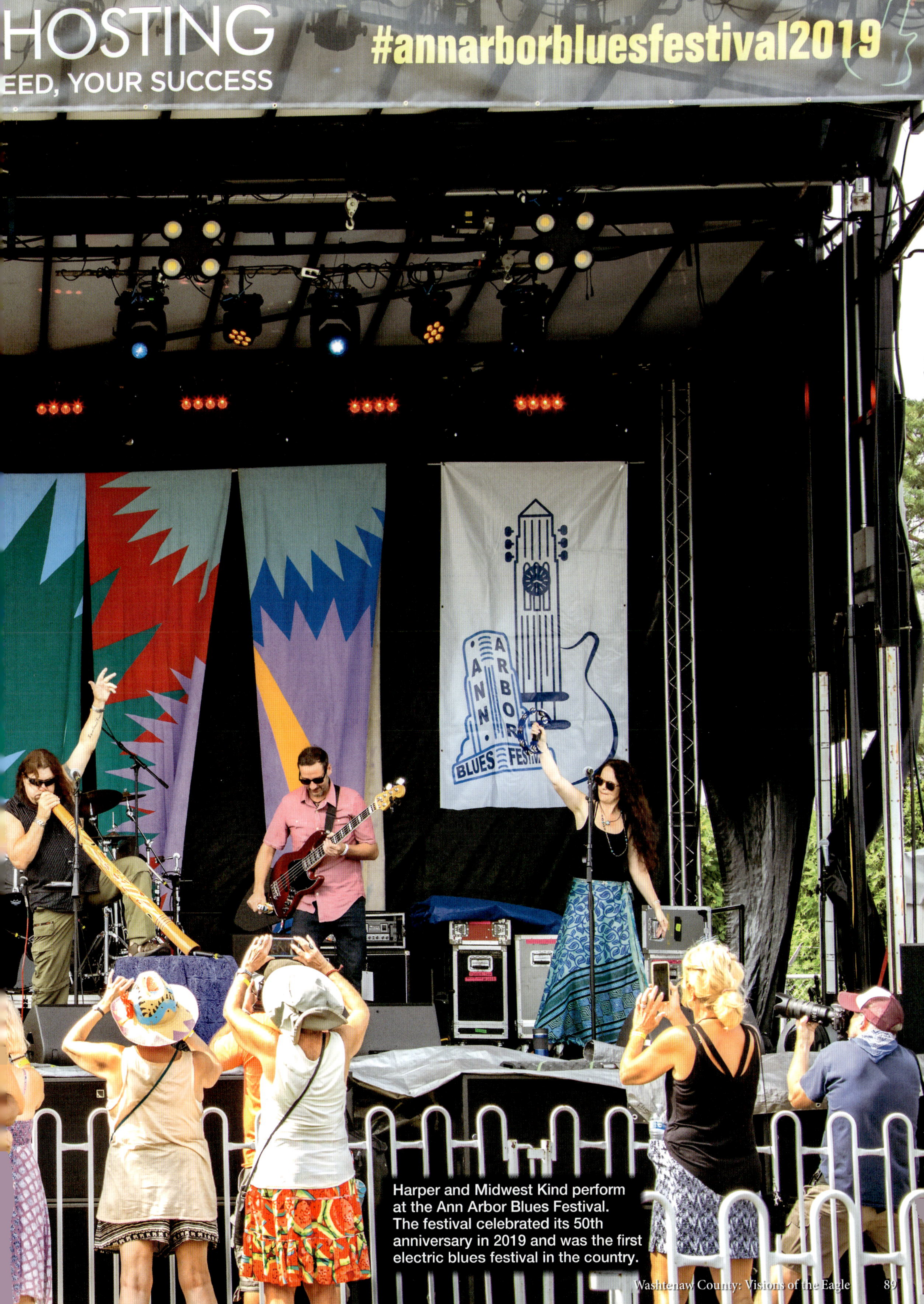

Harper and Midwest Kind perform at the Ann Arbor Blues Festival. The festival celebrated its 50th anniversary in 2019 and was the first electric blues festival in the country.

Varsity Ford

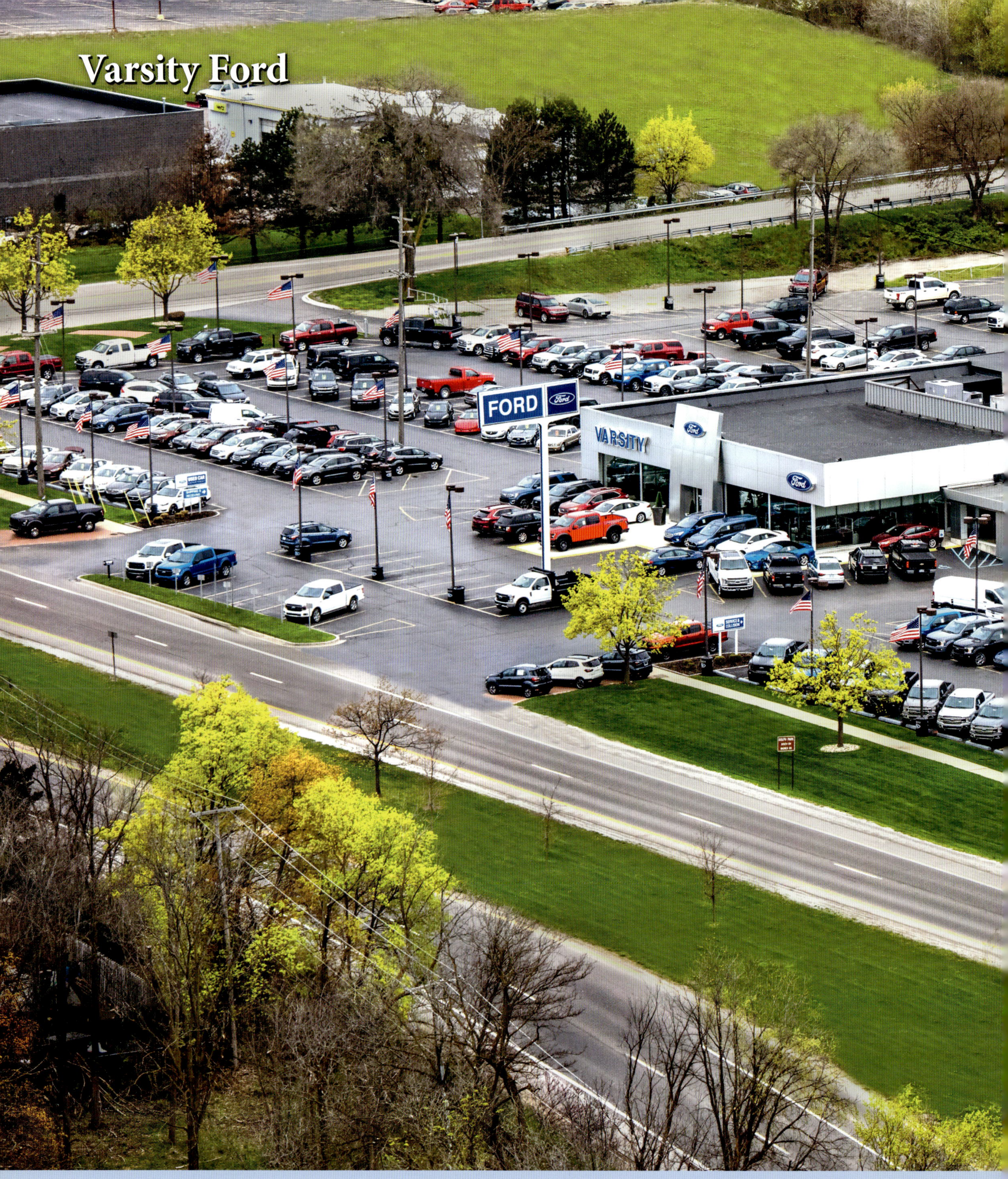

Varsity Ford, located at the corner Jackson Road and Wagner in Ann Arbor, was founded by Lou and Hank Stanford in 1981. The Stanford family grew the dealership into one of the highest volume Ford stores in the U.S., by always putting customers first. Varsity Ford has led the nation in sales 14 times throughout its history. The dealership also offers one of the largest inventories of Ford vehicles anywhere in the country.

Nearly 40 years later, the second generation of Stanfords – Matt, Joe and Maxwell – continue to care for Varsity Ford customers with the same family tradition of dedication to excellent service. Their dedication is shared by the entire Varsity staff, many of whom have been with the team for decades, earning repeat business from customers and numerous national awards for sales and customer service.

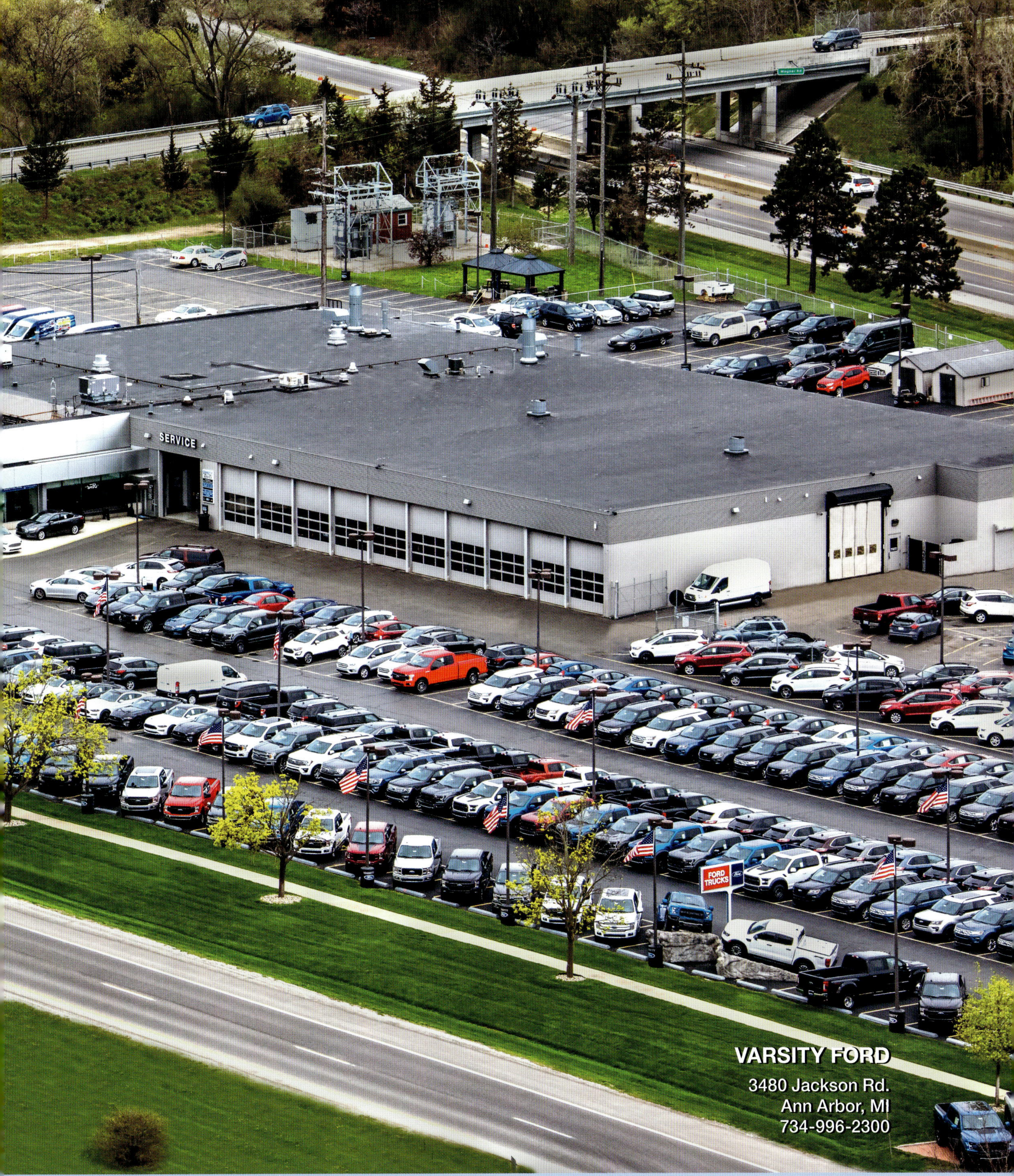

In fact, Varsity Automotive Group is the only dealer in the U.S. whose Ford and Lincoln dealerships have both received the President's Award from Ford Motor Company. The President's Award is only given to the top one percent of Ford dealers for their outstanding excellence in customer satisfaction. Ford Motor Company also awarded Varsity Ford its highest honor - the Triple Crown.

Varsity Ford's commitment to its customers is evident in countless ways, from its friendly service and frequent national awards, to its extensive involvement in the community. Not only does Varsity sponsor and support several local charities and fundraising events each year, but also its employees regularly serve as volunteers in the communities where they work and live.

St. Joseph Mercy Ann Arbor

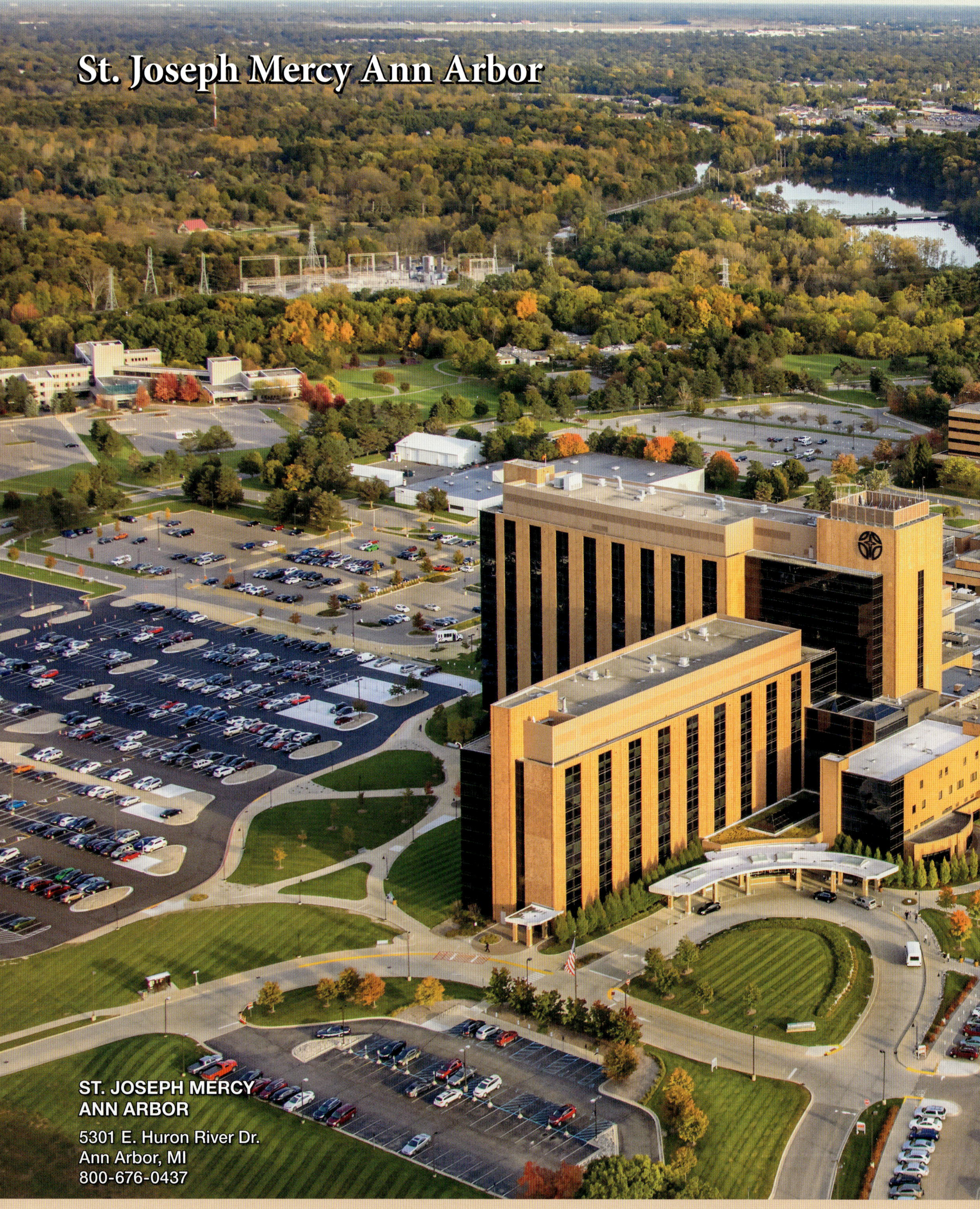

ST. JOSEPH MERCY ANN ARBOR
5301 E. Huron River Dr.
Ann Arbor, MI
800-676-0437

St. Joseph Mercy Ann Arbor is a 548-bed teaching hospital that sits on a serene 340-acre campus, nestled between Ann Arbor and Ypsilanti since 1977. It was founded in 1911 by the Sisters of Mercy in downtown Ann Arbor and is a member of the five-hospital, Saint Joseph Mercy Health System, a subsidiary of national Catholic health care system, Trinity Health.

St. Joe's has regularly been listed among the nation's 100 Top Hospitals and 50 Top Cardiovascular Hospitals by IBM Watson Health™. The hospital currently employs over 6,000 individuals and has a medical staff of more than 1,100 physicians. Services include Michigan's first Senior ER and Intensive Cardiac Rehab program, 24-hour Emergency Center,

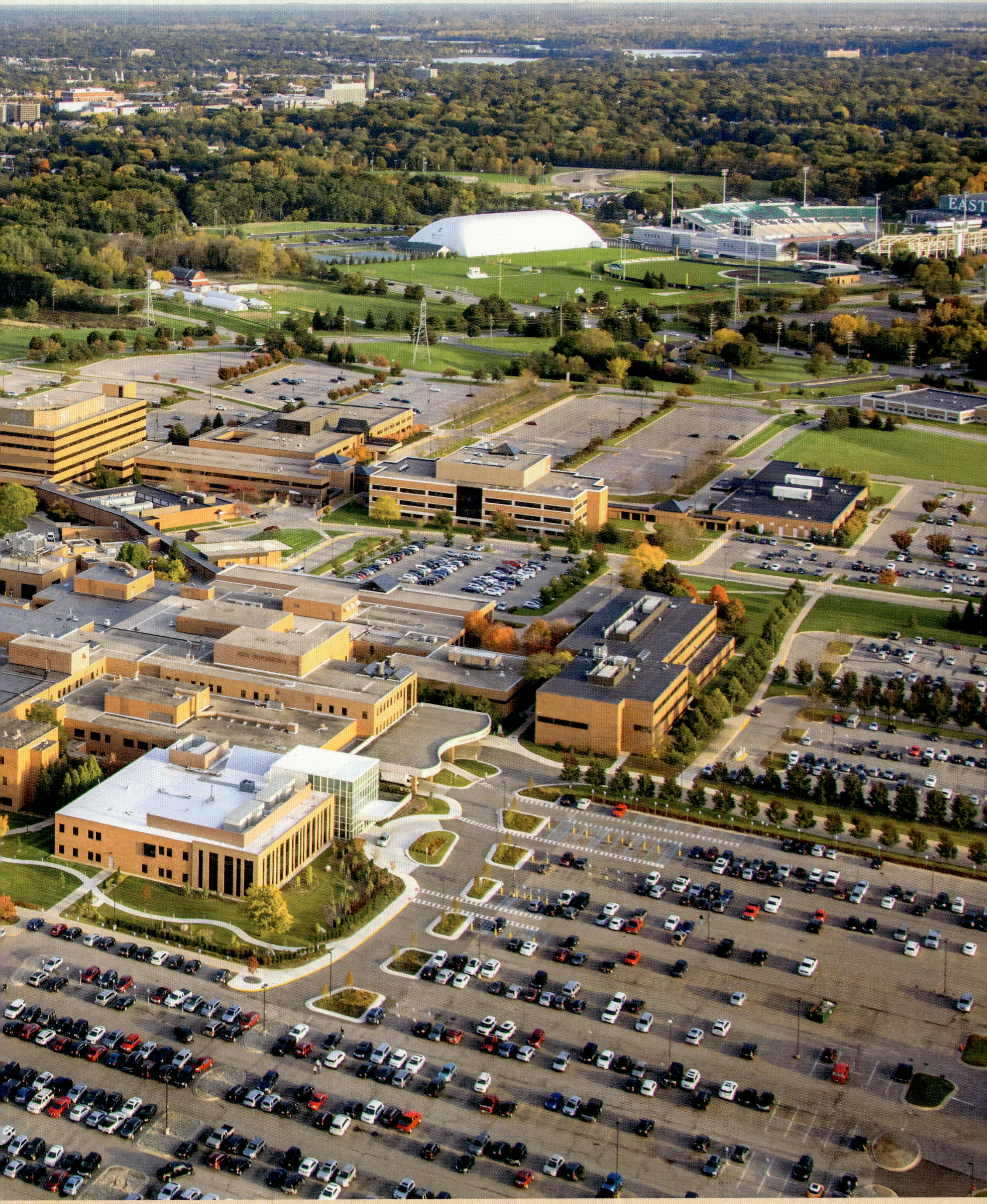

Level I Adult Trauma Center, Pediatric Emergency Services, Robotic Surgery, Family Birth Center and a Level III Neonatal Intensive Care Unit.

In the recent years, the Cancer Center underwent a $24 million transformation that added 66,000 square feet of space including a 2-story glass atrium. St. Joe's has been awarded a $19.3 million grant as part of the National Cancer Institute's Community Oncology Research Program (NCORP), allowing access to leading-edge clinical trials and the nation's most advanced cancer treatments.

Washtenaw Community College

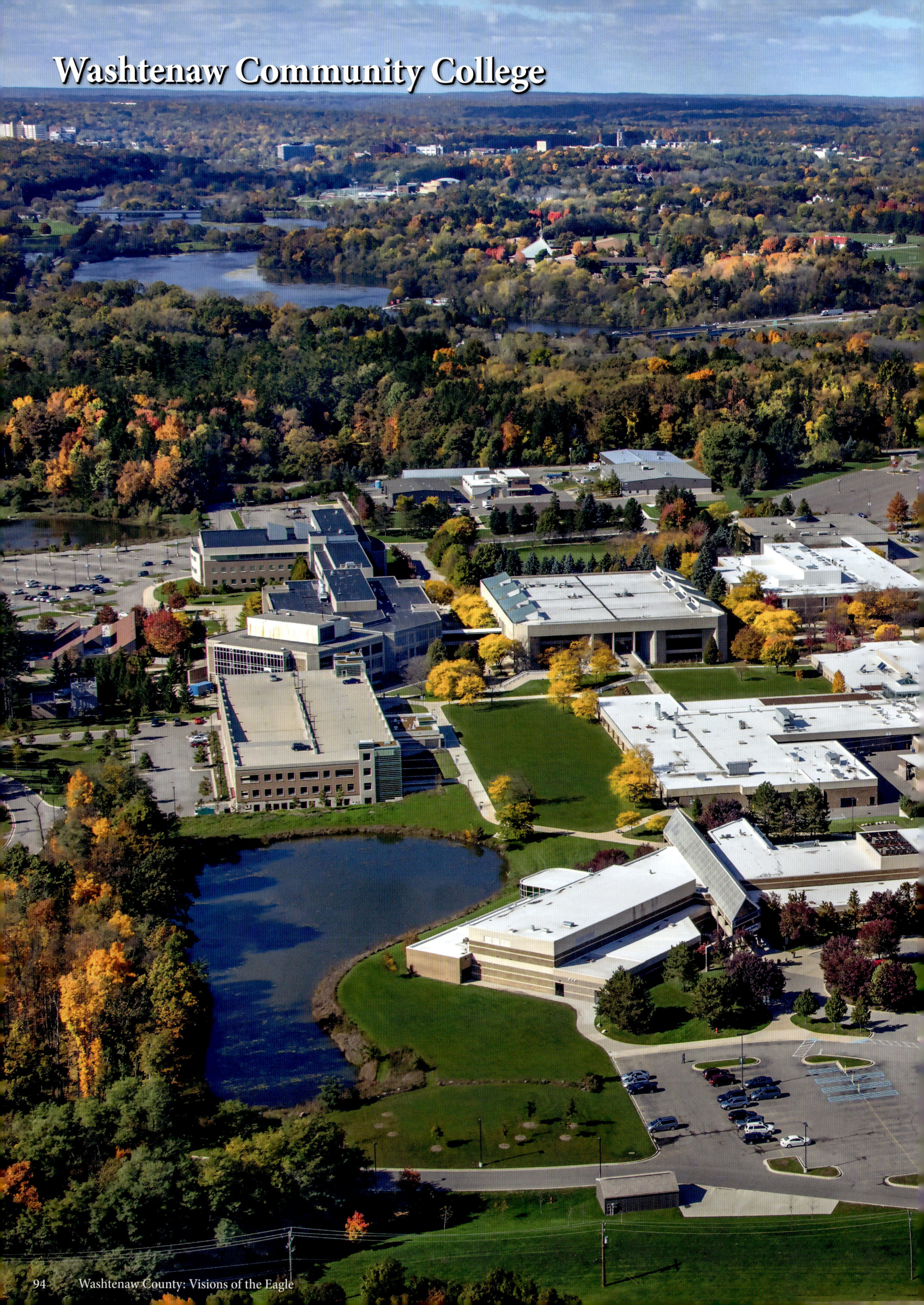

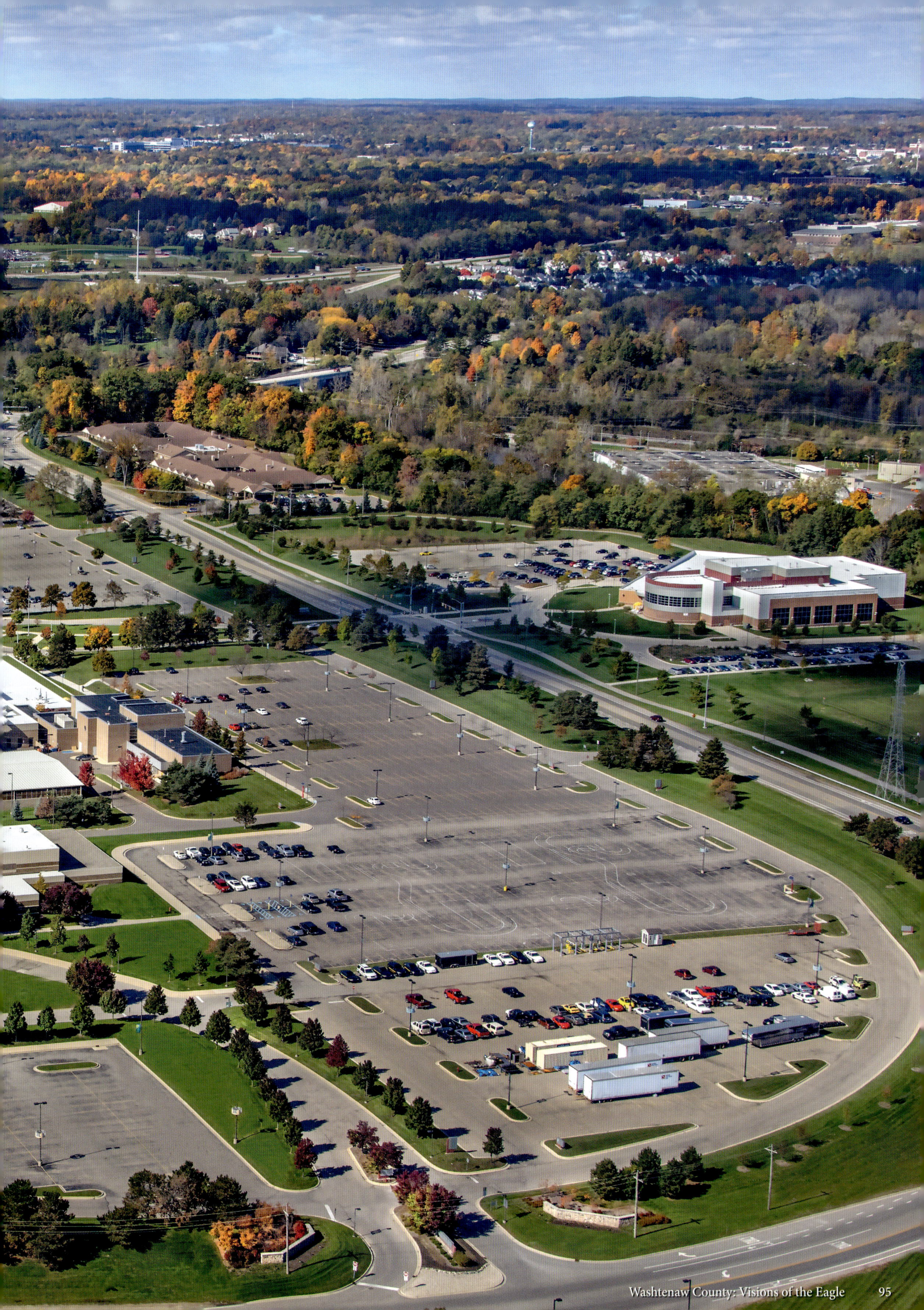

Washtenaw Community College

Higher Education in the Heart of Ann Arbor

Since 1965, Washtenaw Community College in Ann Arbor has opened doors and made a difference in people's lives through accessible and excellent educational programs and services. With its 285-acre campus, strategically located extension centers, operating resources, technology-enabled facilities, and instructional quality make WCC a top choice in the area.

With an average student age of 28, more than 20,000 students mix, mingle, and exchange ideas across generational lines. A diverse student body includes more than 1,000 students from over 100 countries who contribute to a rich cultural experience for all.

Washtenaw Community College is, by design, local, affordable, and accessible. Tuition at WCC is a fraction of that at most four-year public colleges in Michigan. WCC offers financial aid and scholarships to those who qualify. Students can complete their first two years of college without amassing significant debt.

Nearly one-third of all WCC students transfer to another college or university within three years of enrolling. In the 2015-2016 academic year, 176 WCC students – more than any other community college – transferred to the University of Michigan.

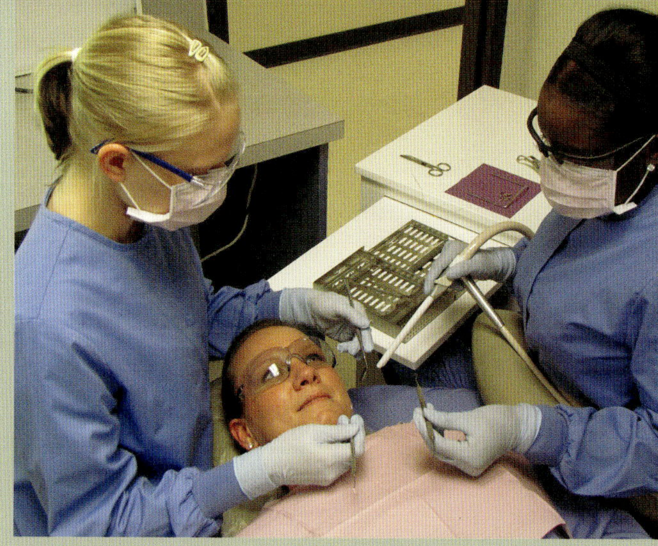

Students in WCC's accredited Dental Assisting program practice technique in a chairside course.

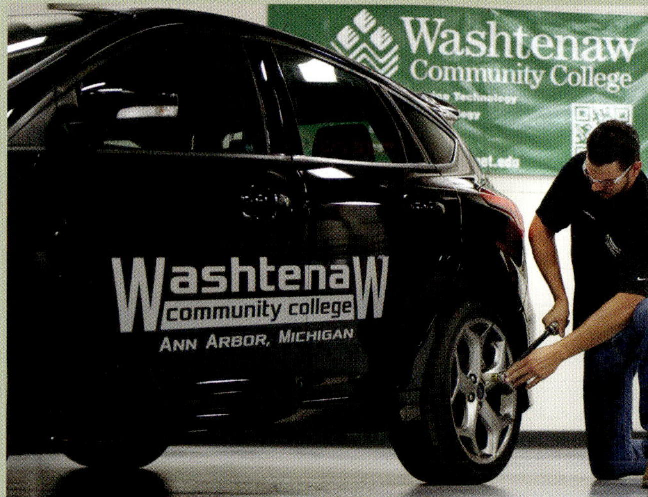

A faculty member demonstrates how to properly tighten a lug nut on a vehicle inside Washtenaw Community College's automotive lab.

WCC students enjoy an autumn walk across campus.

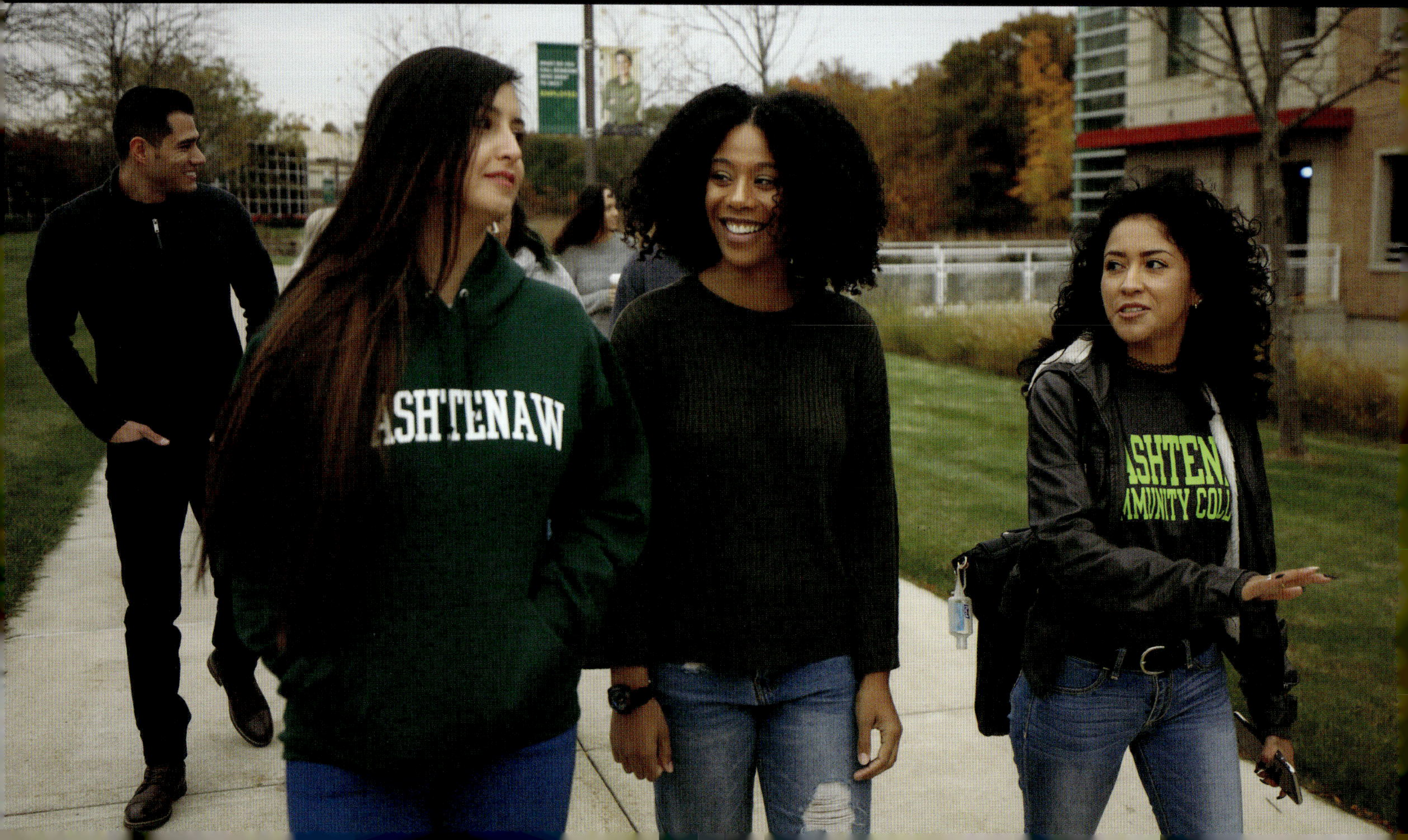

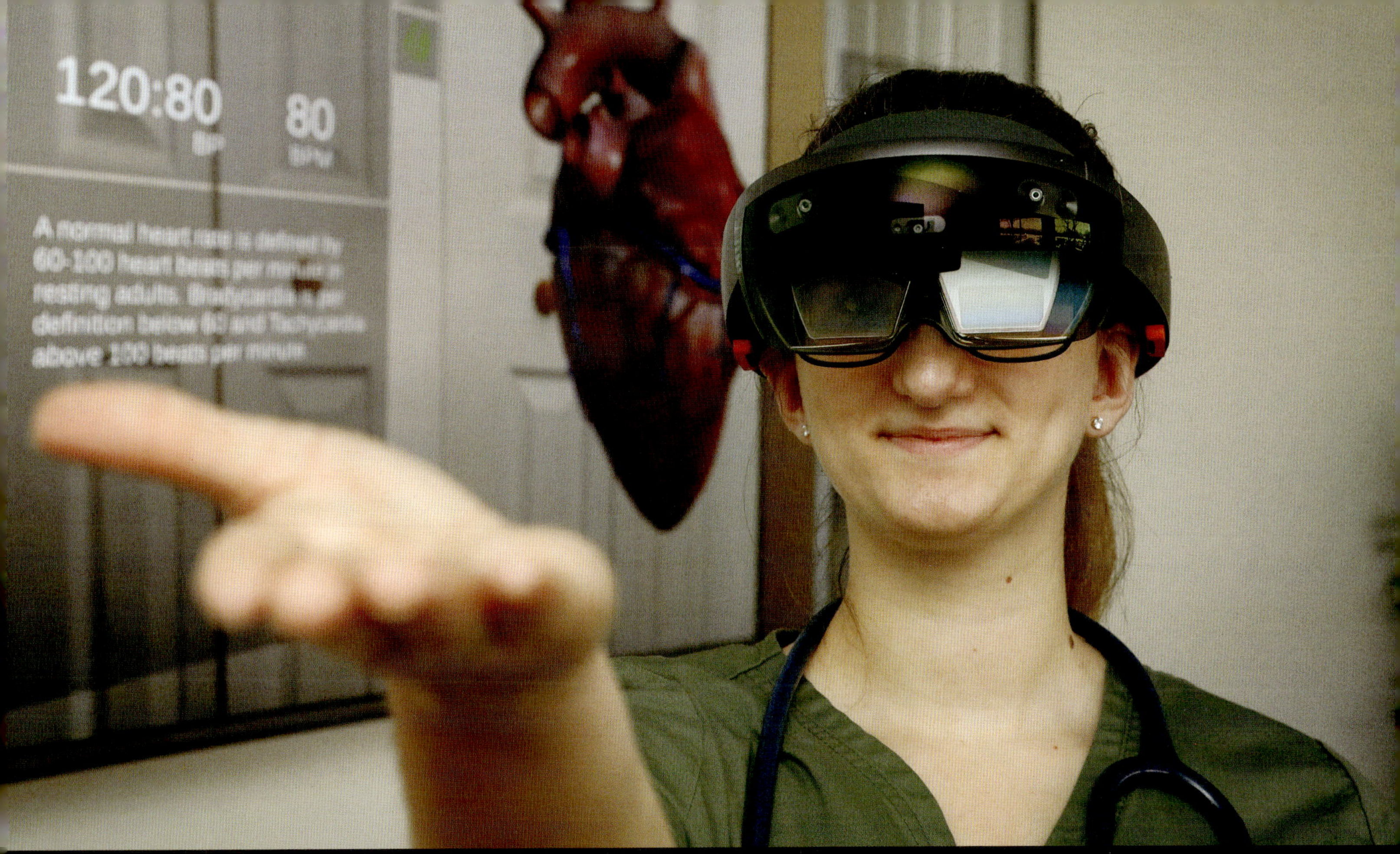

A WCC nursing student demonstrates virtual reality goggles, allowing her to view the workings of the heart.

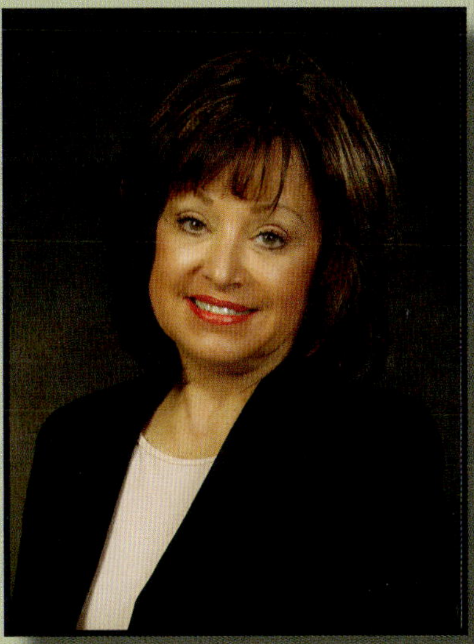

From its founding more than 52 years ago, Washtenaw Community College has blossomed into one of the top-rated community colleges in Michigan. "Blossomed" is the appropriate word because the college occupies nearly 300 acres on what once was a family-owned apple orchard located three miles east of the University of Michigan and three miles from Eastern Michigan University.

WCC proudly stands alongside its higher education neighbors by providing first-rate academic programs, professional and community enrichment classes and a robust workforce development program. Every year, 21,000 students take classes at WCC and an additional 5,600 people enroll in non-credit professional development, workforce training and continuing education classes.

The quality of education at WCC is reflected in the number of our students who transfer to the University of Michigan. For the 2018-2019 academic year, 201 WCC students were accepted at the U-M. No other college or university comes close to that number.

The college has long received strong support from the community, enabling it to provide a top-notch yet affordable education for our students.

And it's a busy place, serving not just students but the entire Washtenaw community as well. More than 90,000 guests visit the campus each year to attend one or more of the 4,500 community events we host.

As times change so does the college. Working with business and industry partners, WCC has responded to their employment needs with first-rate technical classes and programs. Strategic initiatives like the Advanced Transportation Center, Center of Excellence in Nursing Education, Automotive Cybersecurity Education Workbench and the STEM Scholars program all grew out of needs expressed by our partners.

Another way the college gives back is through its support for seniors. WCC's Emeritus Scholarship program allows county residents 65 and older to take credit and non-credit classes tuition free.

WCC is proud of the role it plays as an important and irreplaceable part of the community.

Our mission never changes—meeting the educational needs of our current students as well as the needs of the students who follow in their footsteps.

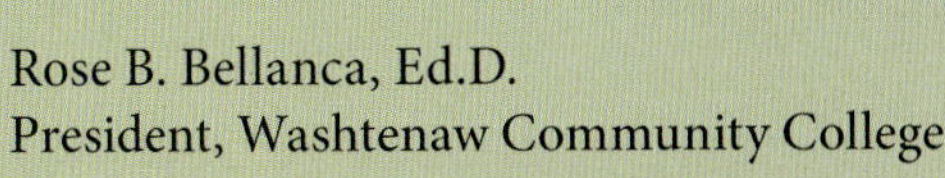

Rose B. Bellanca, Ed.D.
President, Washtenaw Community College

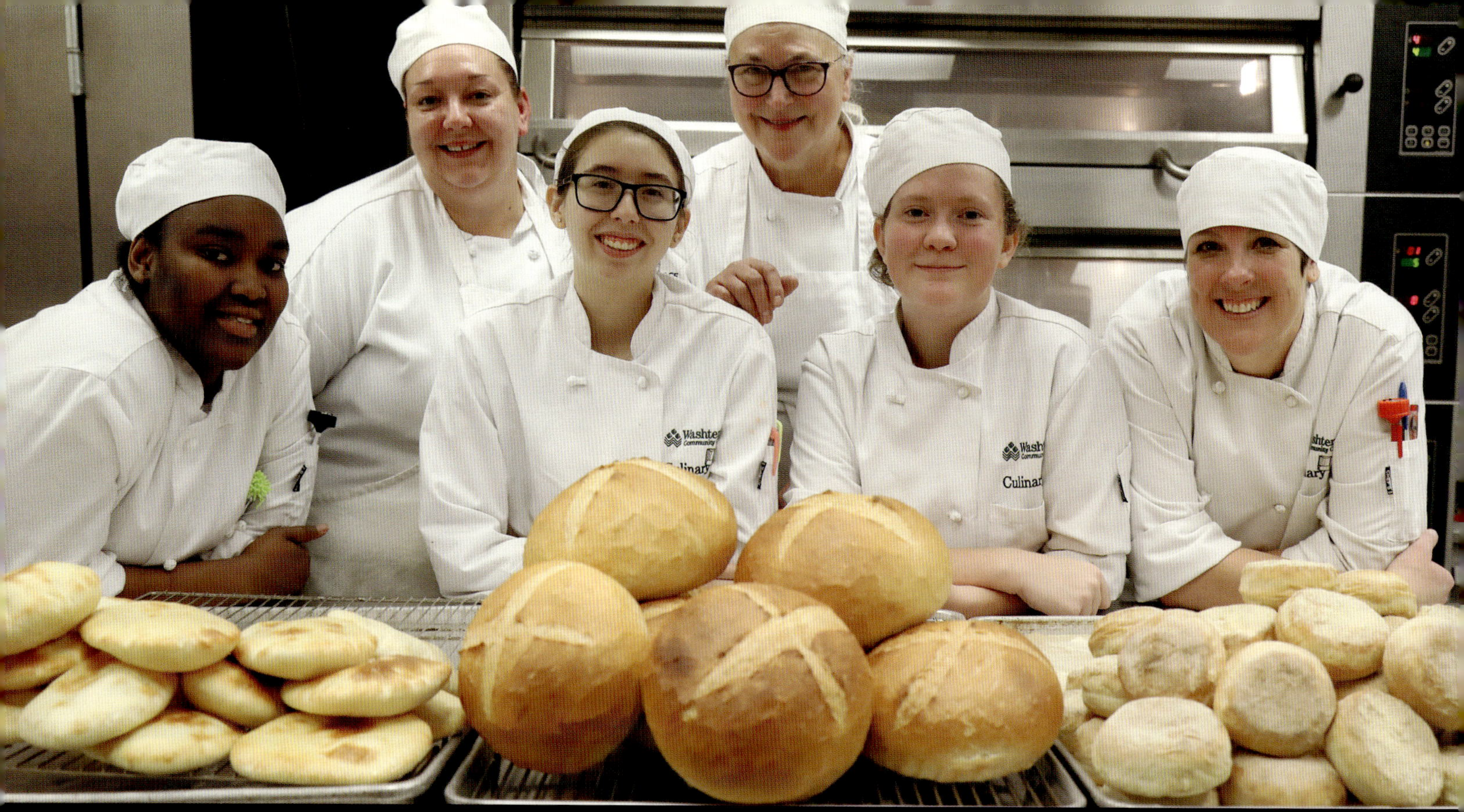

Students in the Artisan Bread Baking class display a variety of their fresh baked breads.

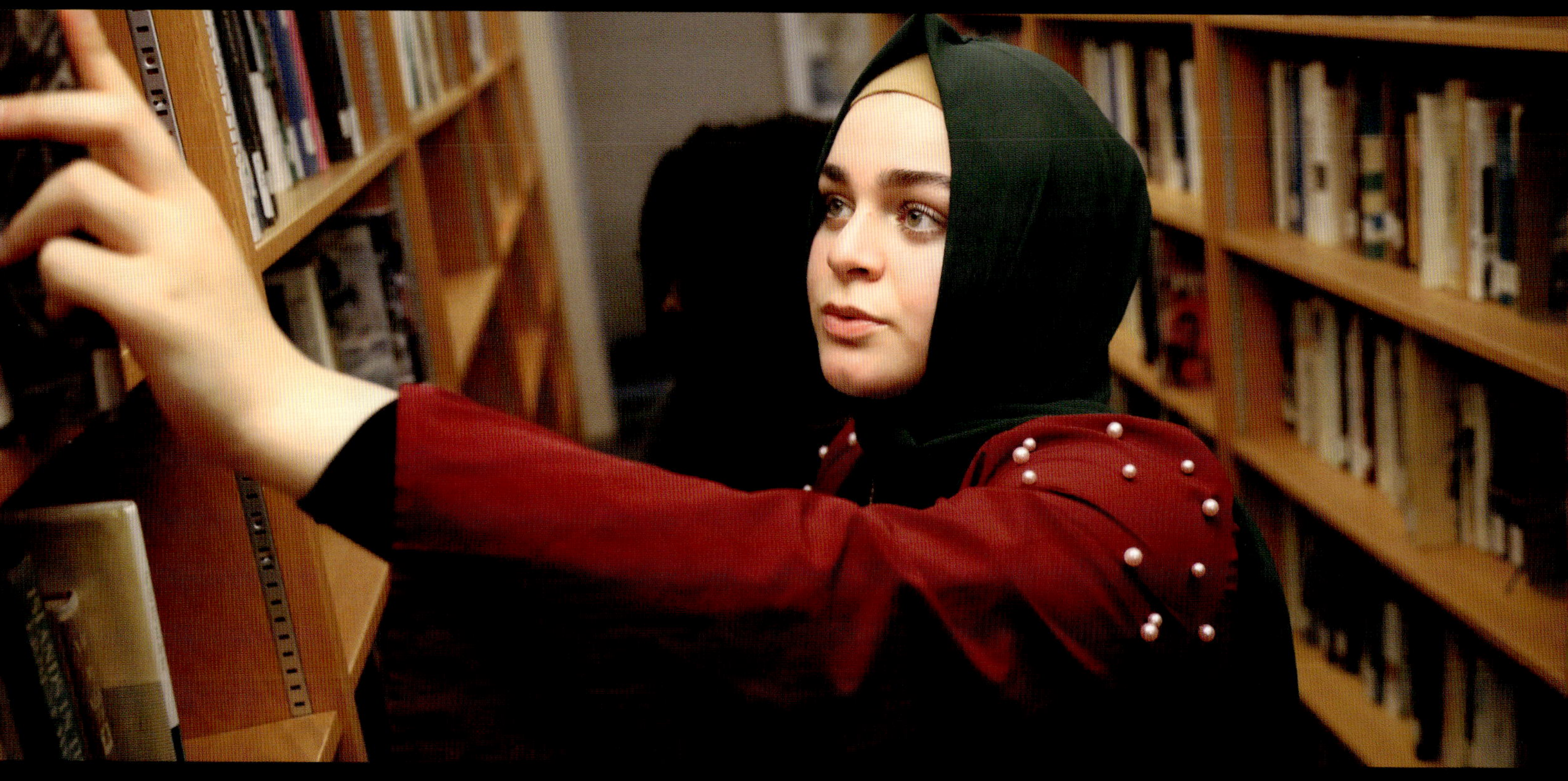

A student finds reference materials in the library.

Washtenaw Community College offers day, evening, and weekend classes, as well as online classes, including 23 degree and certificate programs available entirely online. The college also provides onsite childcare for busy parents, as well as credit for prior learnings such as on-the-job training, apprenticeships, or military training.

With a veteran center onsite, the Michigan Veteran Affairs Agency recognizes WCC as a Gold-Level veteran friendly school. It also follows the "Principles of Excellence Institution" guidelines outlined by the U.S. Department of Veteran Affairs, and meets the "8 Keys to Veteran's Success" criteria outlined by the U.S. Department of Education.

Its slogan is, "What do you call someone who went to Washtenaw Community College? Employed." WCC is the first step toward success for people from every walk of life.

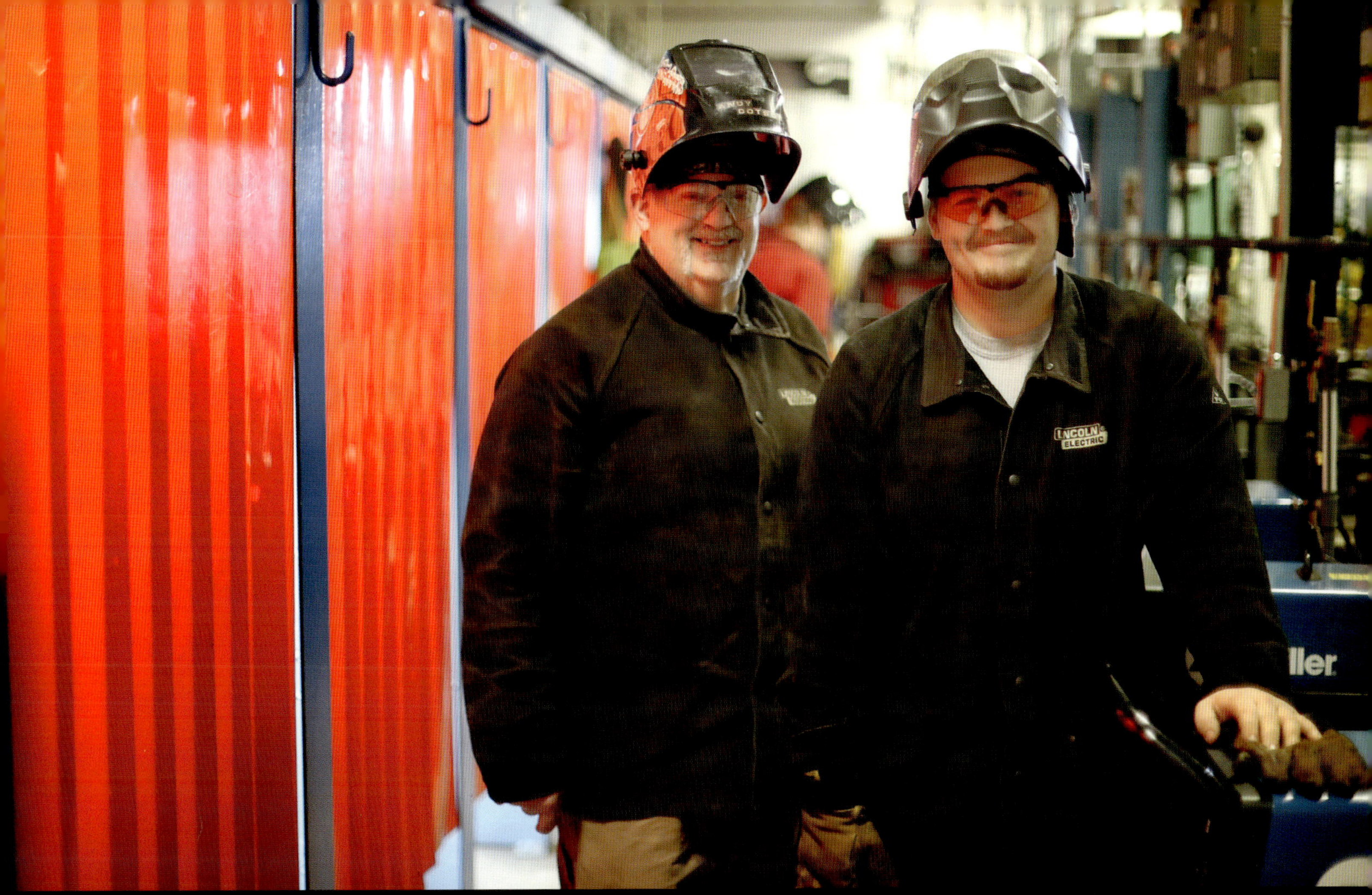

Father and son welding students working toward Welding Technology associate degrees.

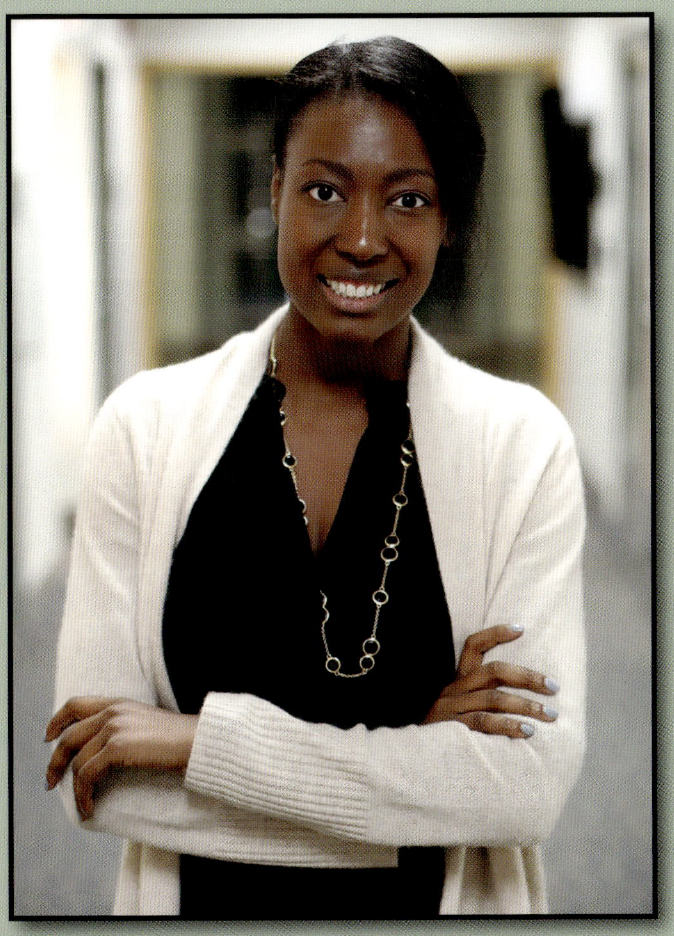

WCC alumna Aisha Bowe on campus during STEM week to share how she started at the College and ended up earning her Aerospace Engineer Degree and working for NASA.

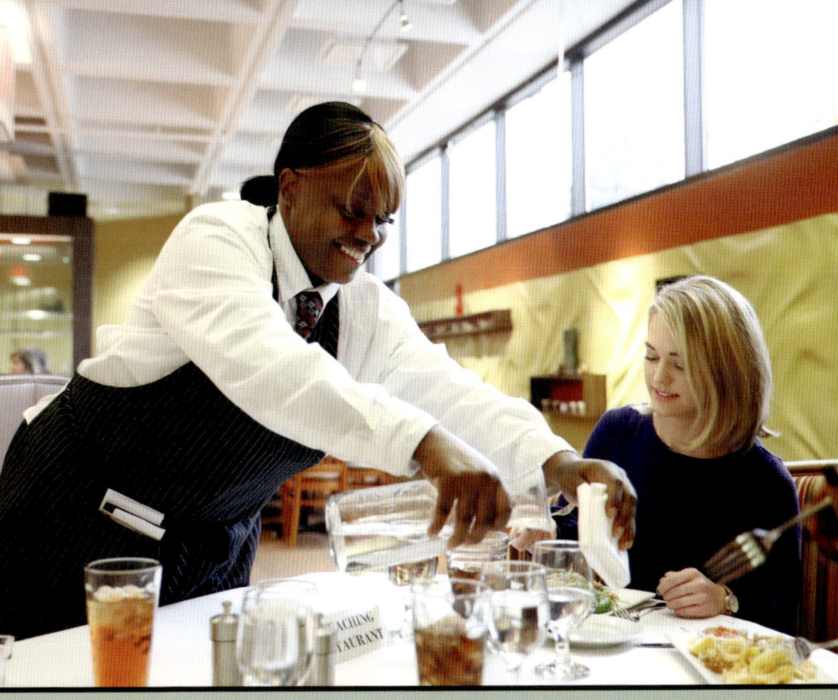

Garrett's Restaurant offers hands-on restaurant experience to culinary and hospitality students on the WCC campus.

Washtenaw Community College
4800 E. Huron River Dr.
Ann Arbor, MI
734-973-3300
www.wccnet.edu

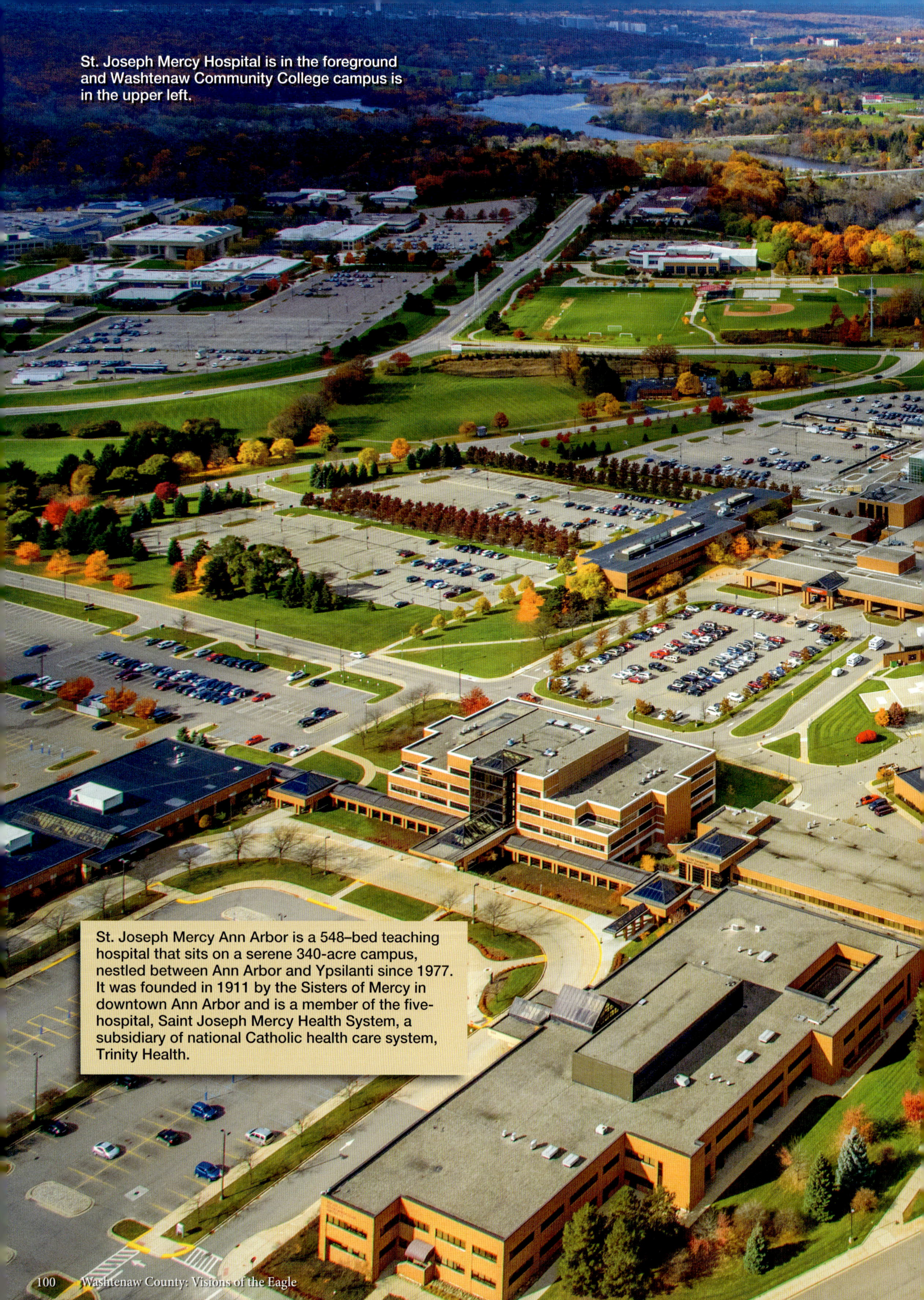

St. Joseph Mercy Hospital is in the foreground and Washtenaw Community College campus is in the upper left.

St. Joseph Mercy Ann Arbor is a 548–bed teaching hospital that sits on a serene 340-acre campus, nestled between Ann Arbor and Ypsilanti since 1977. It was founded in 1911 by the Sisters of Mercy in downtown Ann Arbor and is a member of the five-hospital, Saint Joseph Mercy Health System, a subsidiary of national Catholic health care system, Trinity Health.

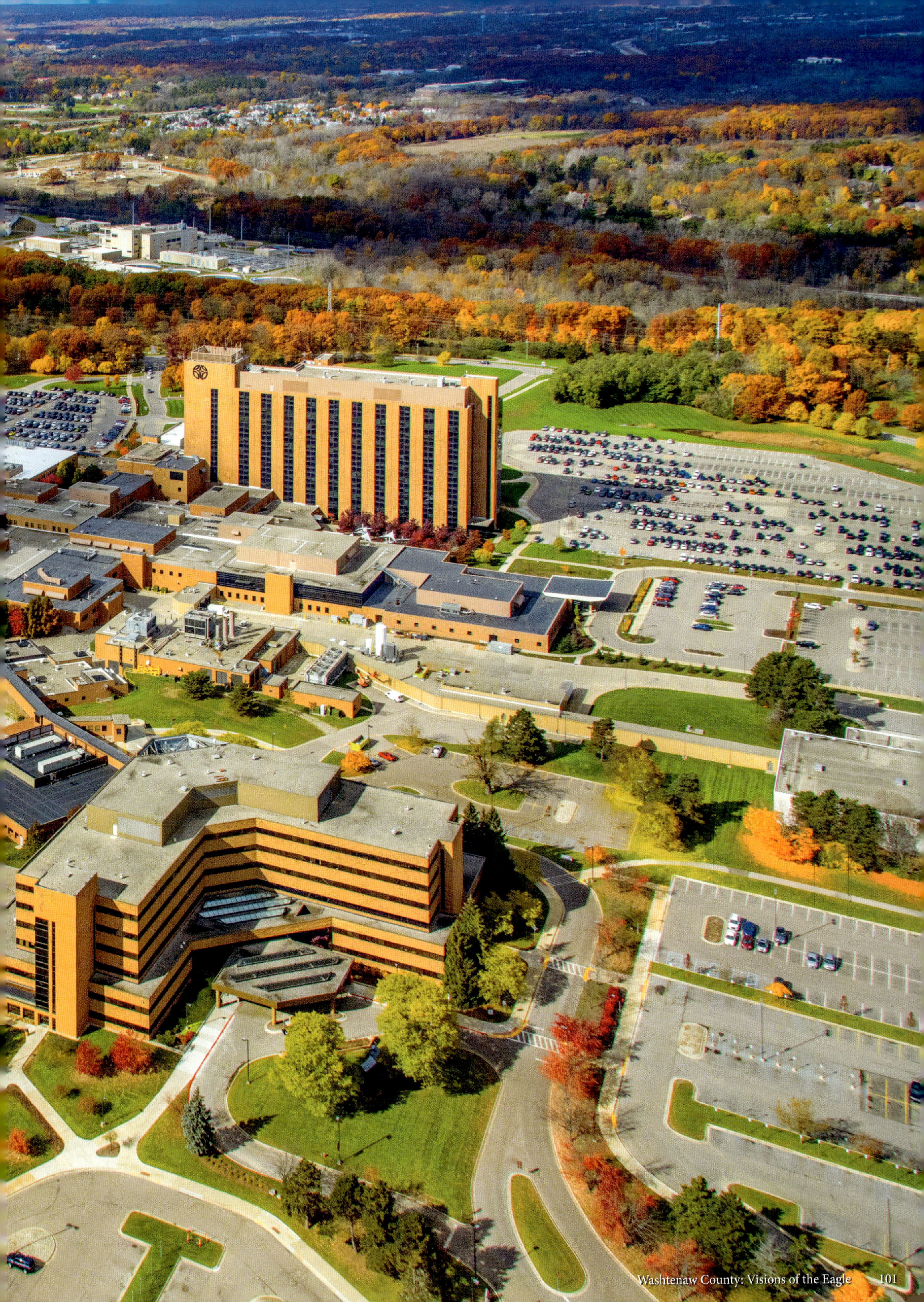

Washtenaw Intermediate School District

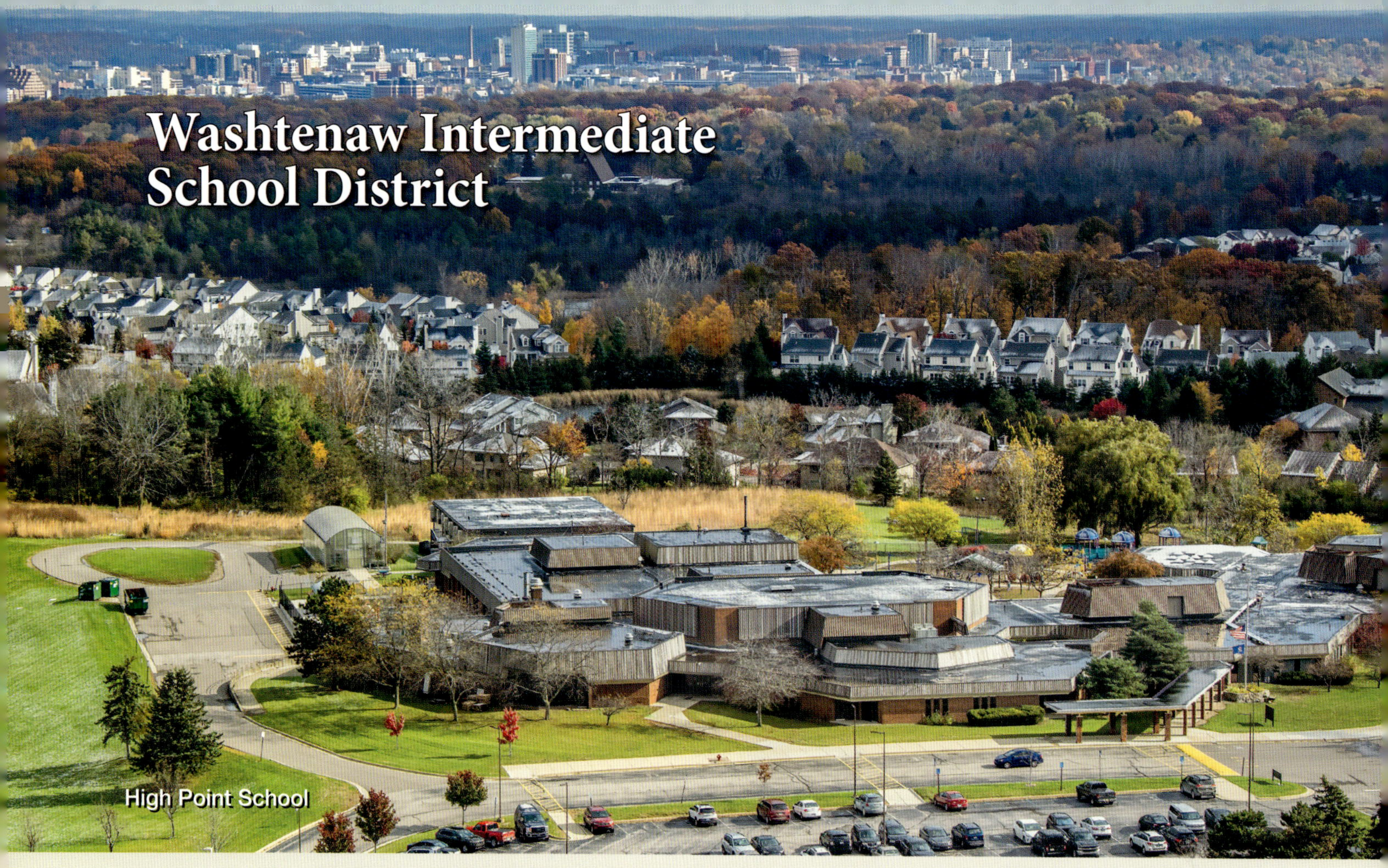

High Point School

Washtenaw Intermediate School District (WISD) is the educational service agency for Washtenaw County, Michigan, serving nine public school districts and the public school academies in the greater Ann Arbor region. Collectively, more than 46,000 students attend public schools across the county. The WISD provides a wide array of services to the community and local schools, including special education coordination, early childhood services, technology support, business and human resource assistance, Cradle-to-Career community partnerships, and teacher and staff professional development.

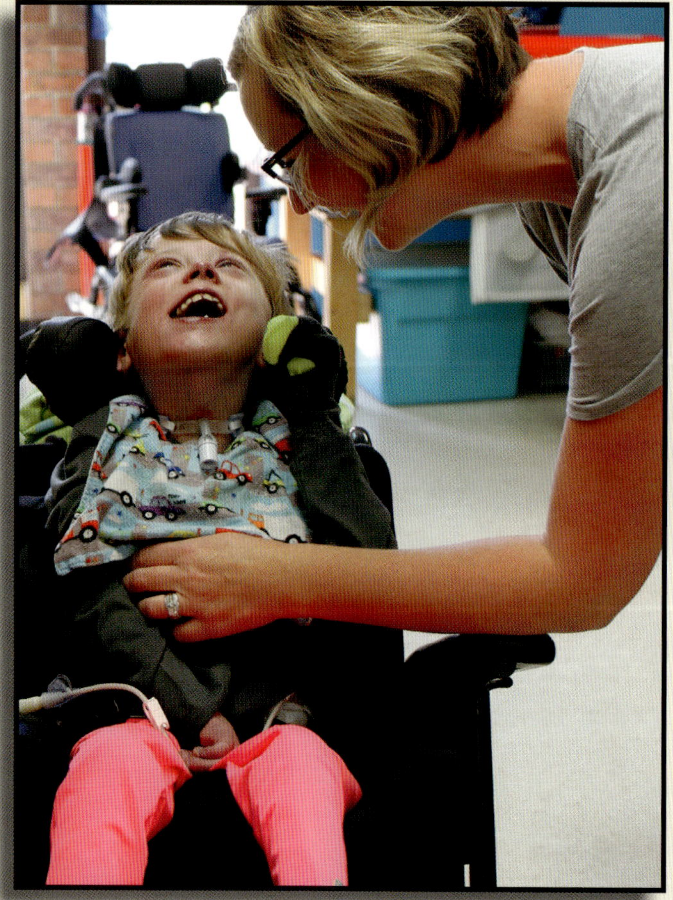

Because the WISD puts students first, the WISD Board of Education is committed to ensuring that resource allocation, policy, and practice is designed to close the opportunity gap to ensure equitable educational access for all students, with a focus on achieving an equitable system for students in poverty, students with disabilities, and students of color.

Opened in 1975, High Point School (pictured above) serves students with severe cognitive and multiple disabilities, many of whom are medically fragile, and require specialized learning environments, equipment, and support. Students ages 3 through 26 years old attend High Point School and represent all nine public school districts in Washtenaw County.

The High Point program is co-located with Honey Creek Community School and Gretchen's House to create an integrated learning environment so students with disabilities learn alongside their general education peers. In August 2019, Washtenaw County voters approved a $53 million bond proposal allowing for significant renovation and reconstruction of High Point.

WASHTENAW INTERMEDIATE SCHOOL DISTRICT

1819 S. Wagner Rd.
Ann Arbor, MI
(734) 994-8100

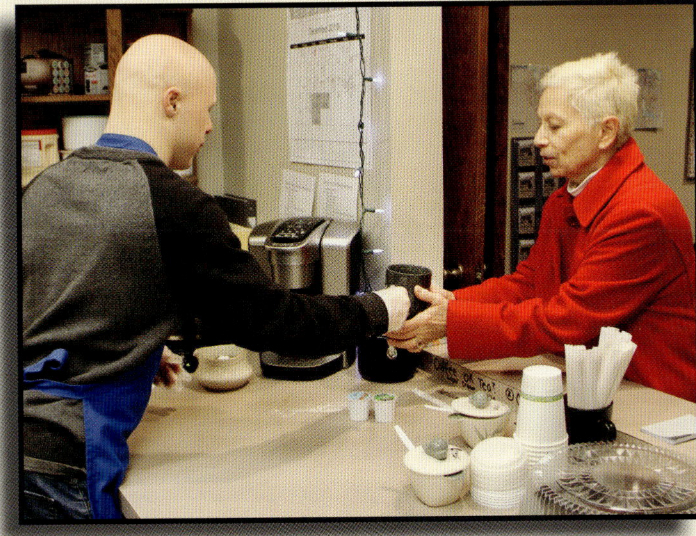

Young Adult students host "Café Liberty" weekly to provide coffee and fresh baked goods to local businesses and community members. Café Liberty helps students develop positive social skills and learn how to manage job responsibilities.

The WISD Young Adult program assists students with disabilities ages 18 through 26 as they transition to adulthood. Students in the Young Adult program work toward gaining independence. Young Adult students strive to earn and maintain a job, develop positive social skills, contribute to their communities by volunteering, and establish important routines such as navigating public transportation, grocery shopping, and cooking.

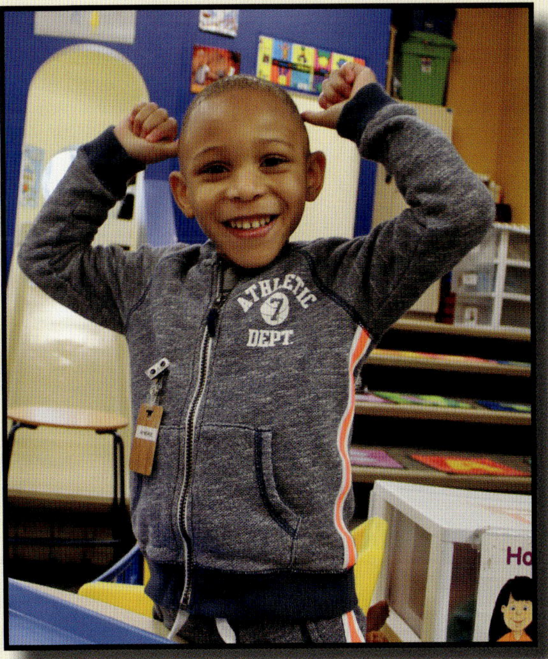

This Head Start student in Ann Arbor is excited for a full day of learning!

WISD's Early Childhood department coordinates state and federal grants to provide free early childhood education to children across Washtenaw. Each year, more than 1,100 children enroll in Early Head Start, Head Start, and the Great Start Readiness Program, providing greater access to high-quality early educational opportunities.

Trusted Parent Advisors regularly convene over lunch to plan community outreach activities, learn about new community resources, and support each other in reaching goals for themselves and their families.

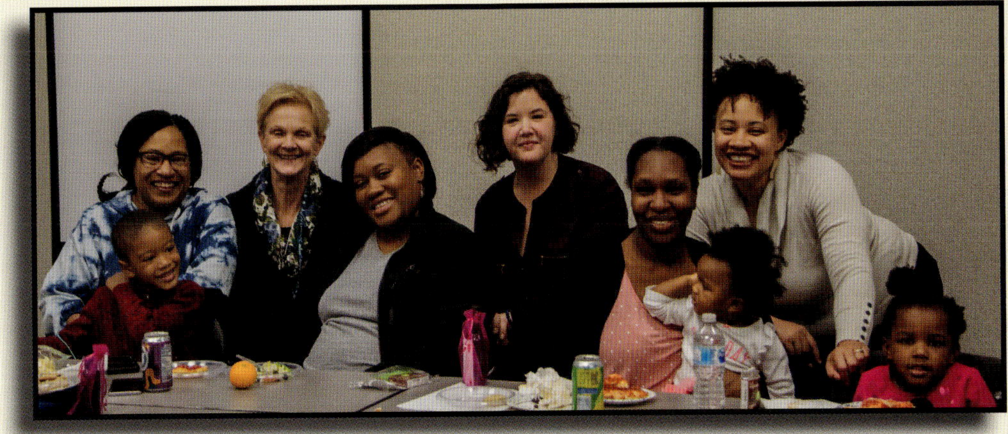

The Trusted Parent Advisor initiative trains parents to support families who are isolated from community services and education programs by leveraging the power of parents helping parents. The Trusted Parent Advisors go door-to-door in low-income neighborhoods to talk about the importance of early childhood programs and assist families in connecting to early education programs and community resources. In addition, they help families with elementary-age children reduce barriers that cause chronic absenteeism. The Trusted Parent Advisors make a difference in their community one family at a time.

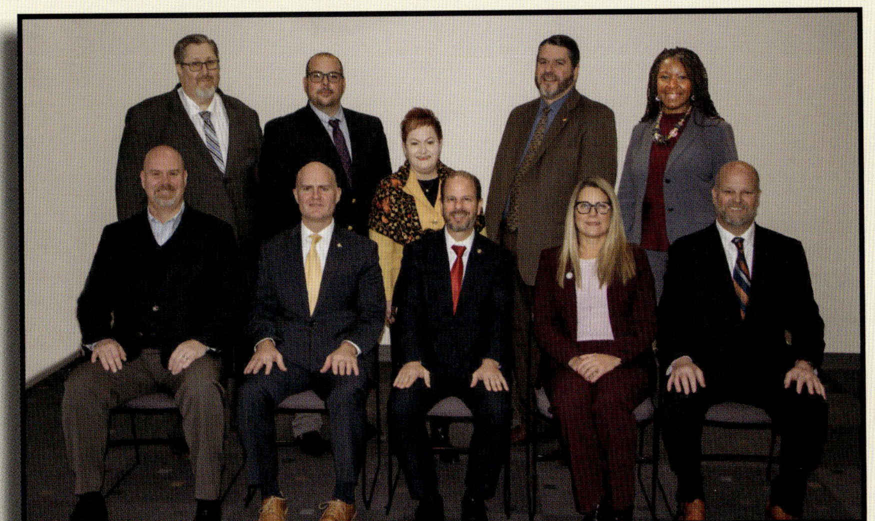

WASHTENAW SUPERINTENDENTS' ASSOCIATION
Back row left to right:
Sean McNatt (Lincoln Consolidated Schools),
Nick Steinmetz (Manchester Community Schools),
Jeanice Swift (Ann Arbor Public Schools),
Bryan Girbach (Milan Area Schools), and
Alena Zachery-Ross (Ypsilanti Community Schools)

Front row left to right:
Chris Timmis (Dexter Community Schools),
Scot Graden (Saline Area Schools), Scott Menzel (Washtenaw Intermediate School District),
Julie Helber (Chelsea Schools) and
Tom DeKeyser (Whitmore Lake Public Schools)

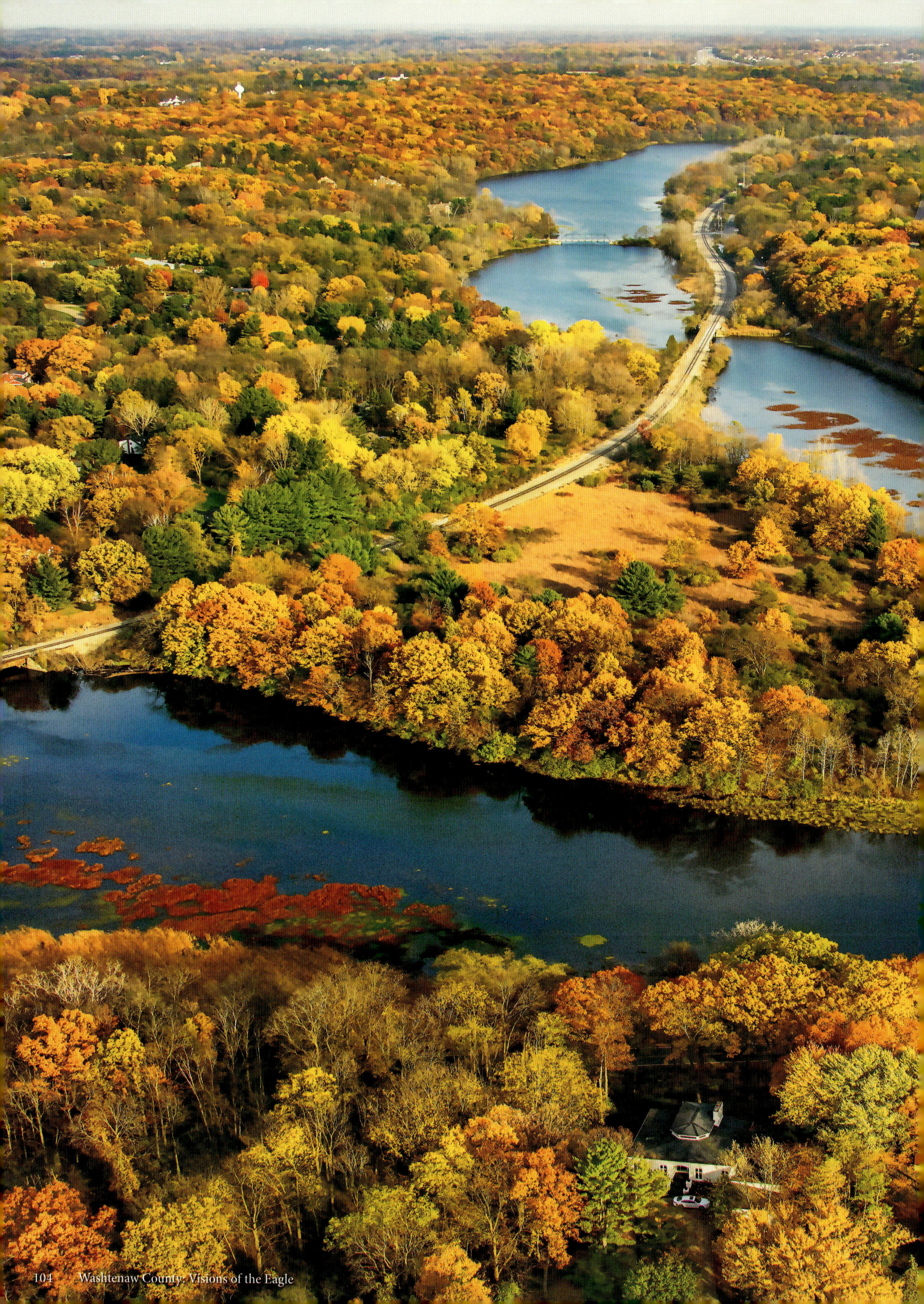

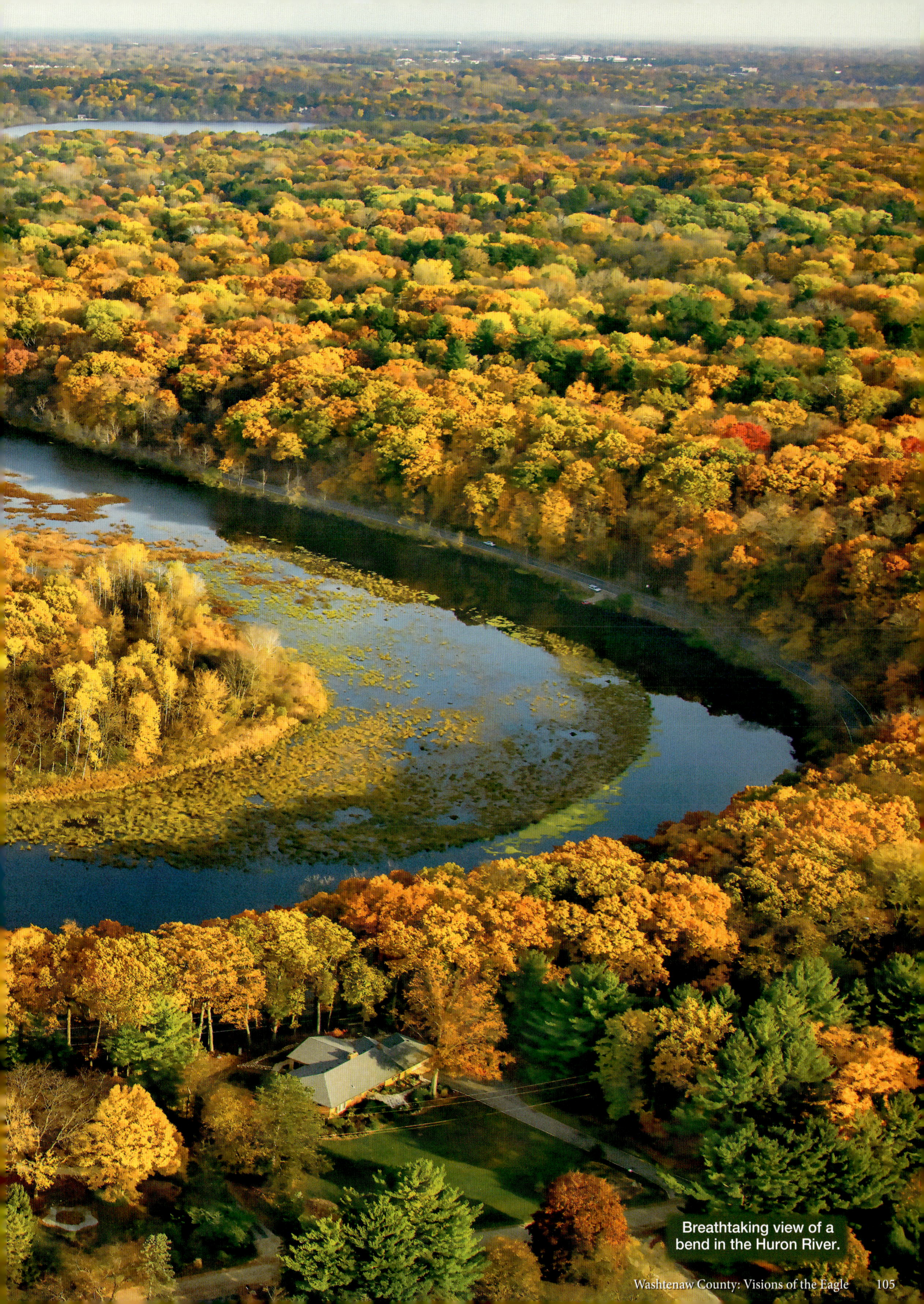

Breathtaking view of a bend in the Huron River.

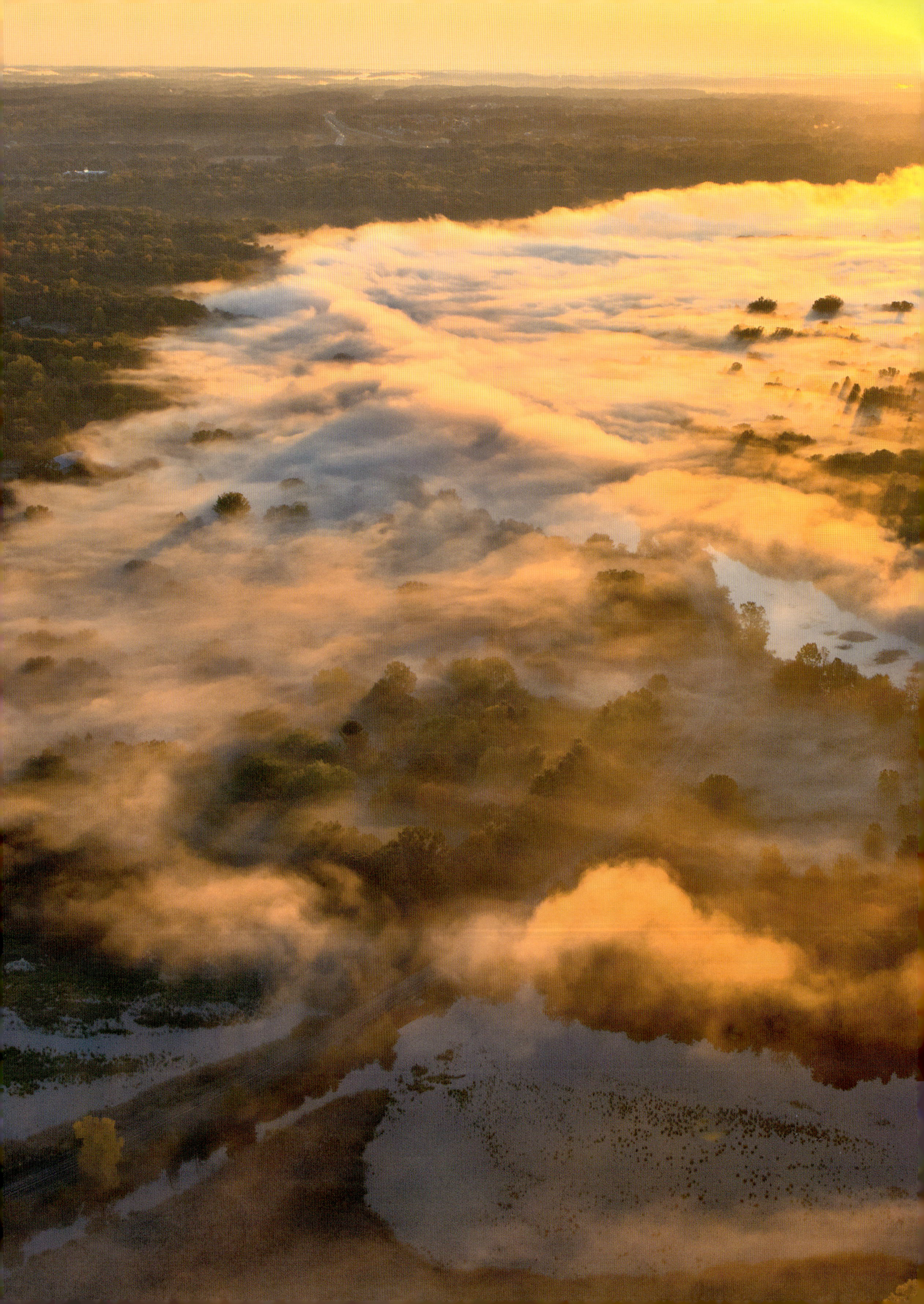

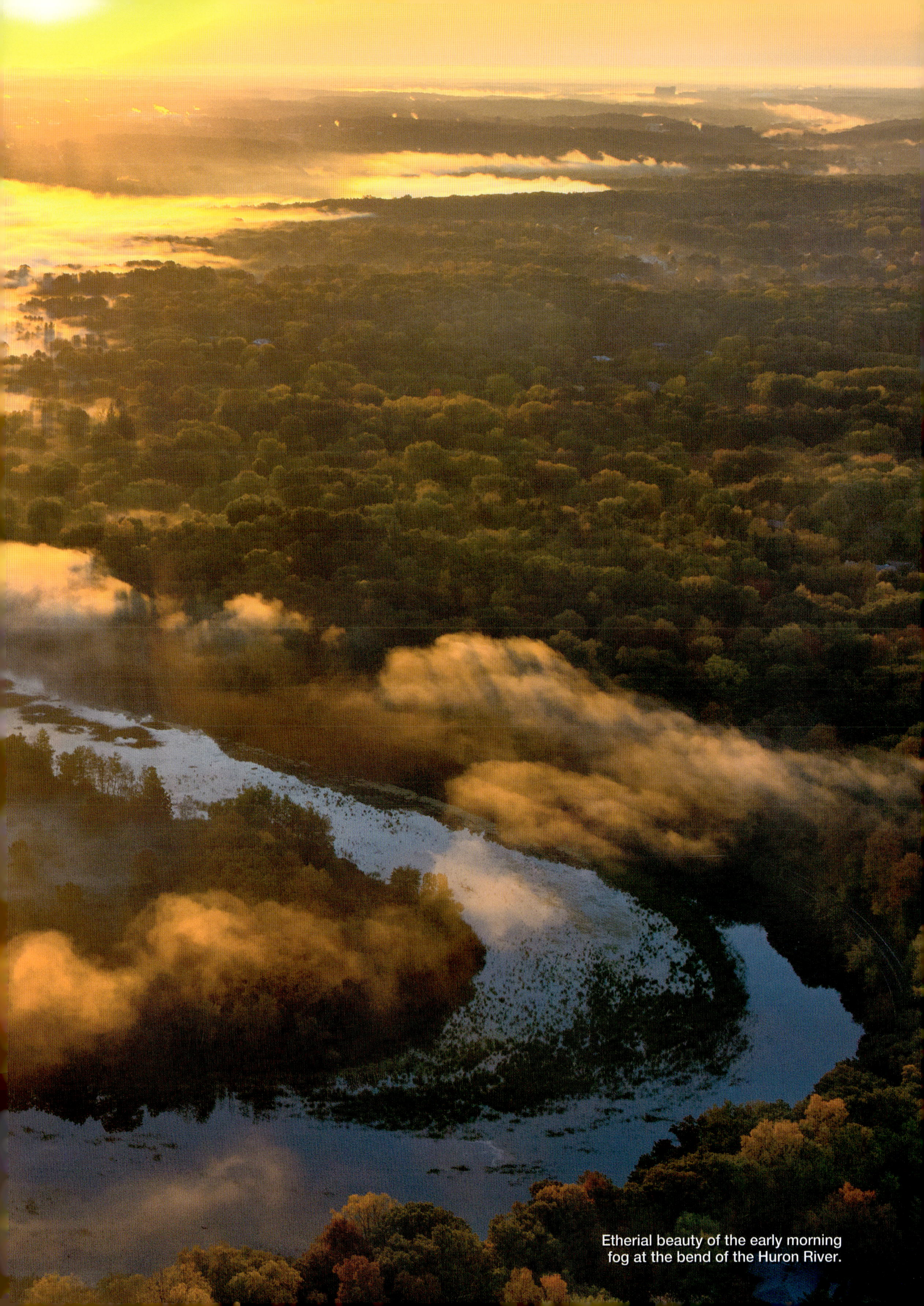

Etherial beauty of the early morning fog at the bend of the Huron River.

Alro Steel

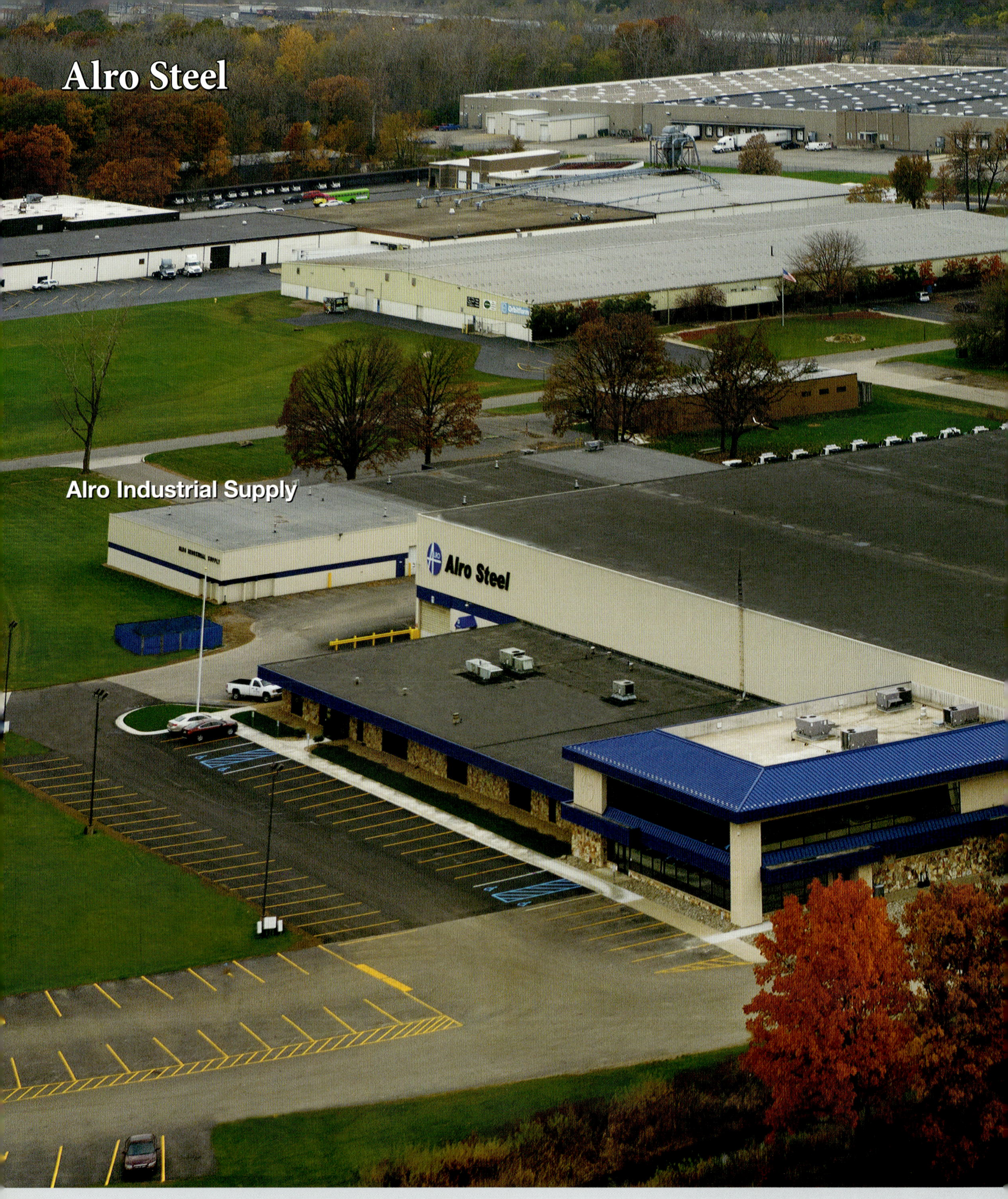

In 1916, Louis Glick and his family arrived in Michigan and started a scrap metal business, Glick Iron & Metal. Louis instilled in his family the ideals of supporting the local business community and helping those less fortunate.

Brothers Al and Robert Glick founded Alro Steel in 1948 in Jackson, Michigan. The company name is a combination of the brothers' first names. An industry leader, Alro is a distributor of metals, industrial supplies, and engineering plastics.

Alro's focus is its offering of cut-to-size metals and plastics with next day delivery to over 25,000 customers in North America. The company has grown to over 70 locations in 12 states and remains committed to its founding principles: integrity, loyalty and honesty.

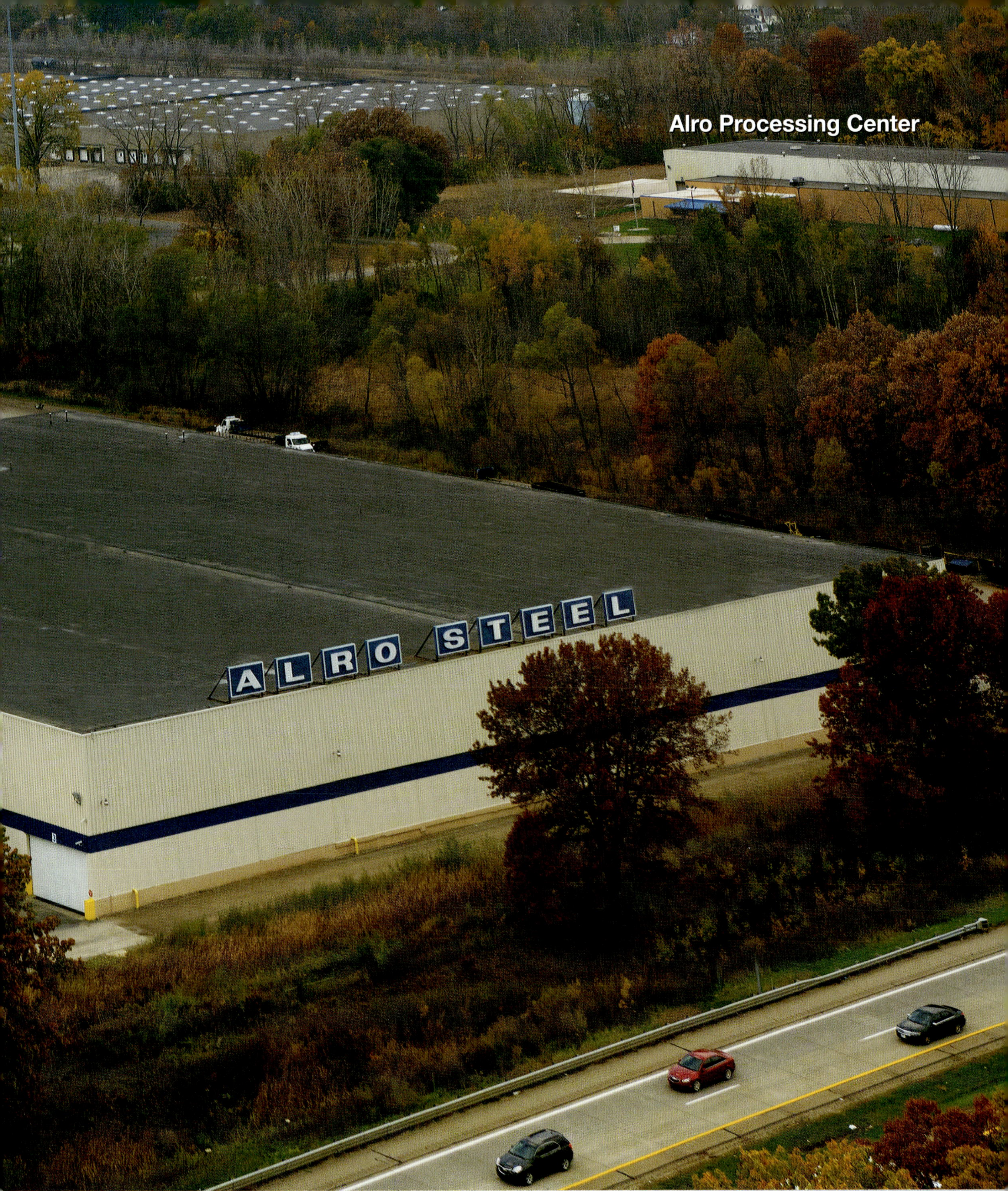

More than 100 years later, his legacy continues through son Al Glick, co-founder of Alro Steel, and the Glick family. The Glick's support non-profit organizations, local businesses, youth education, youth sports, and manufacturing job training. They have been generous with Michigan Medicine, Mott Children's Hospital, and the University of Michigan.

In 2009, the Al Glick Field House at the University of Michigan was completed and dedicated. The 104,000 square foot state-of-the-art building is U-M's Indoor Football Practice Facility and rivals elite practice structures used in college and professional football nationwide.

ALRO STEEL
Corporate Headquarters
3100 E. High St.
Jackson, MI
517-787-5500

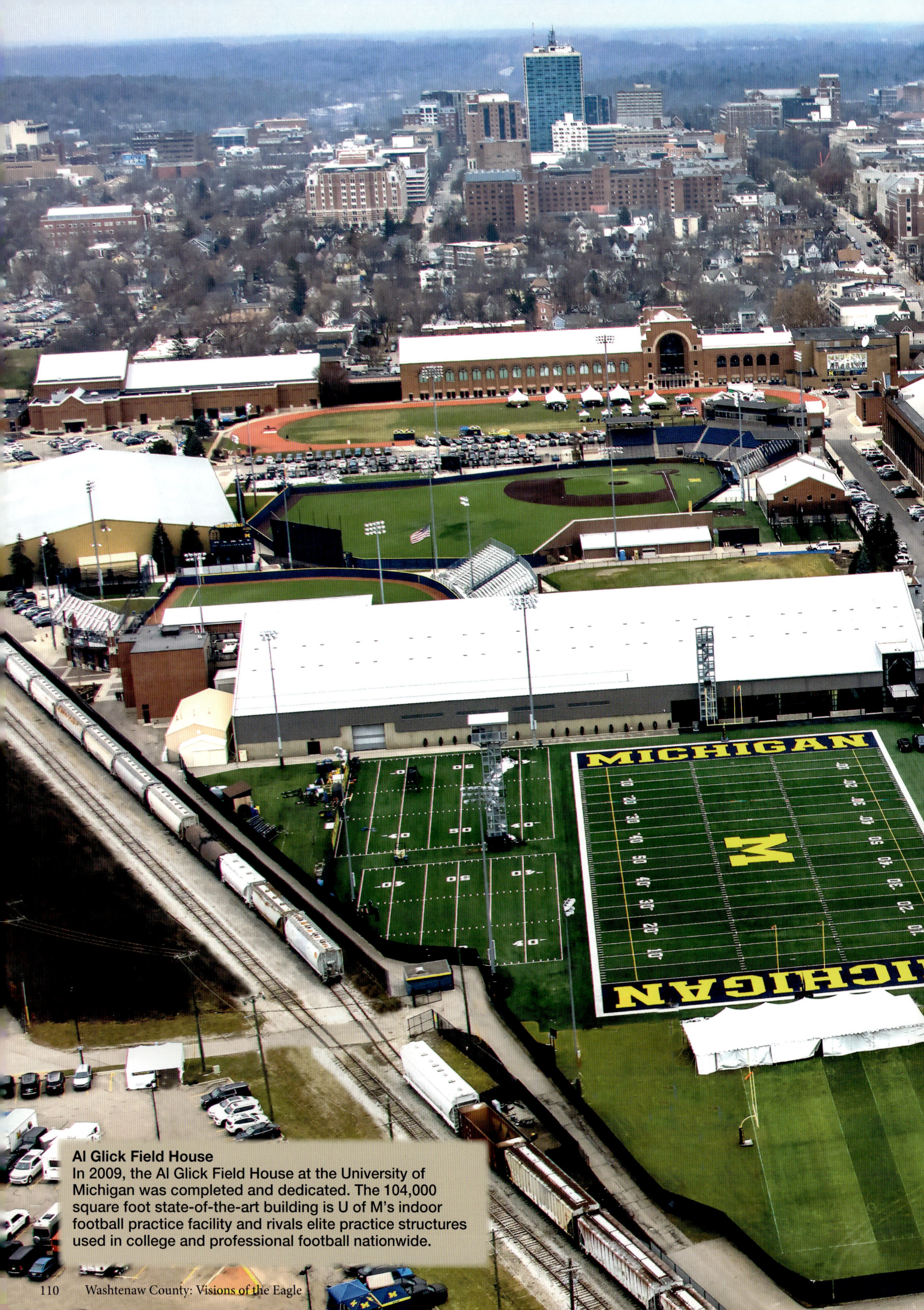

Al Glick Field House
In 2009, the Al Glick Field House at the University of Michigan was completed and dedicated. The 104,000 square foot state-of-the-art building is U of M's indoor football practice facility and rivals elite practice structures used in college and professional football nationwide.

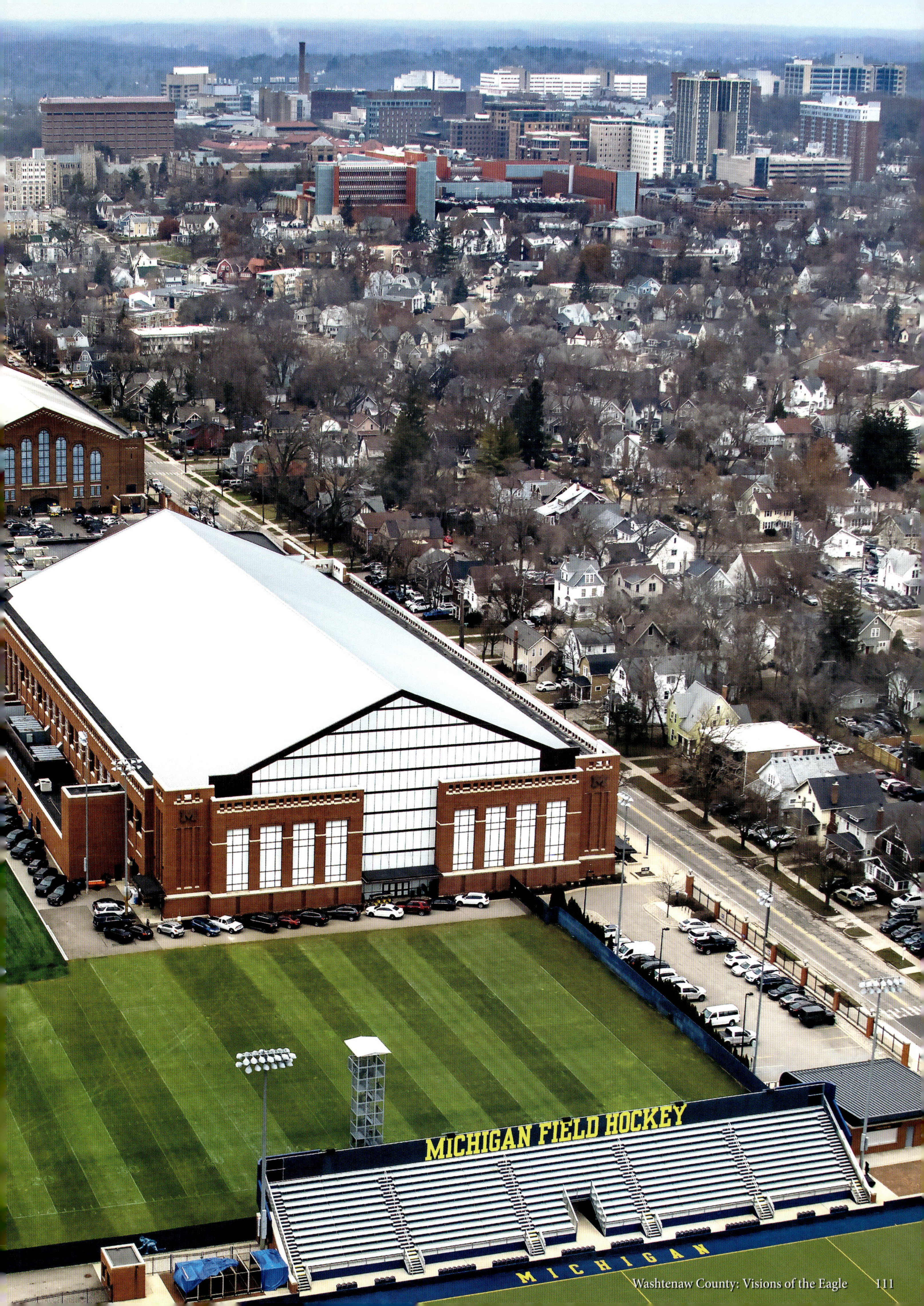
MICHIGAN FIELD HOCKEY
MICHIGAN

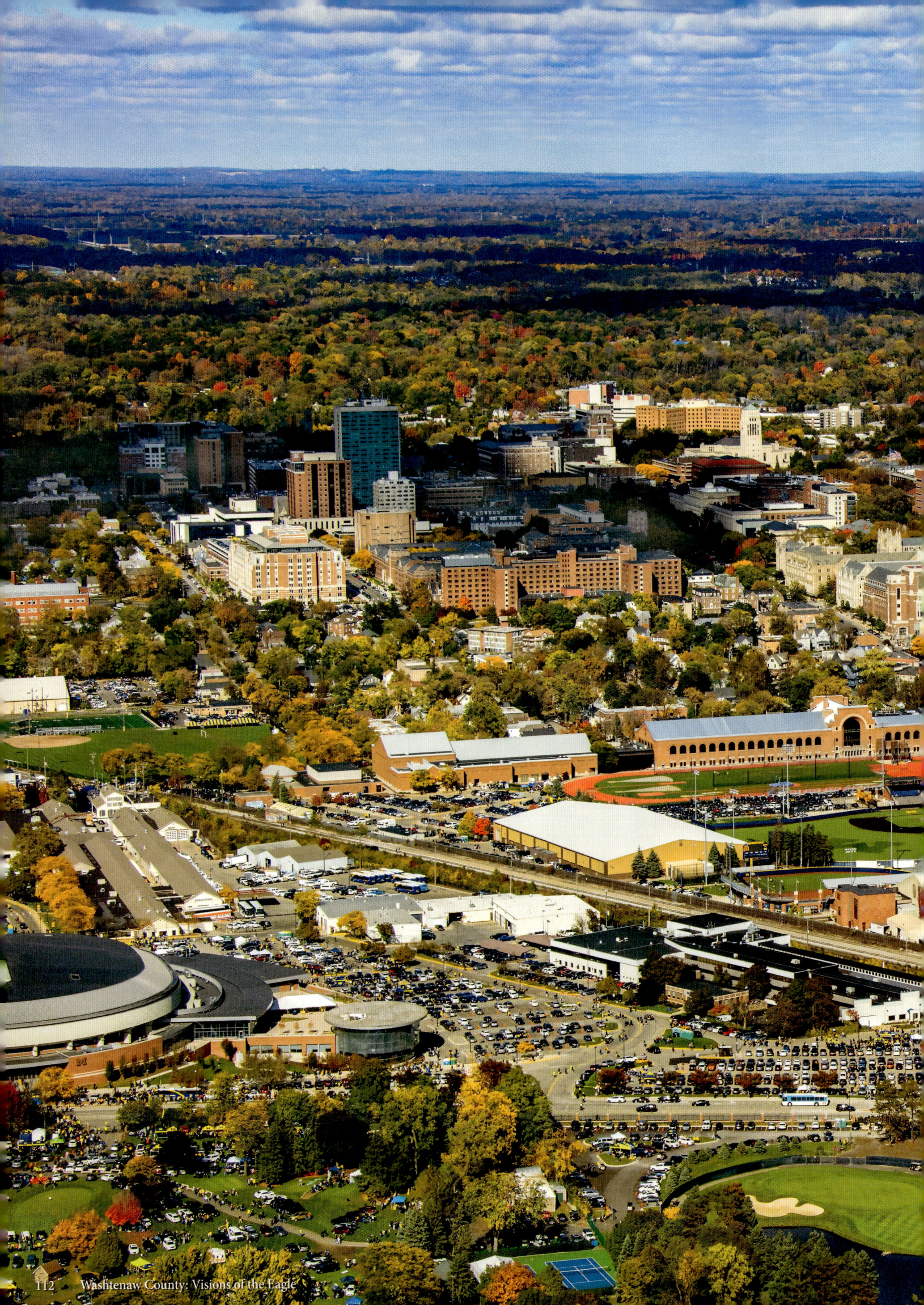

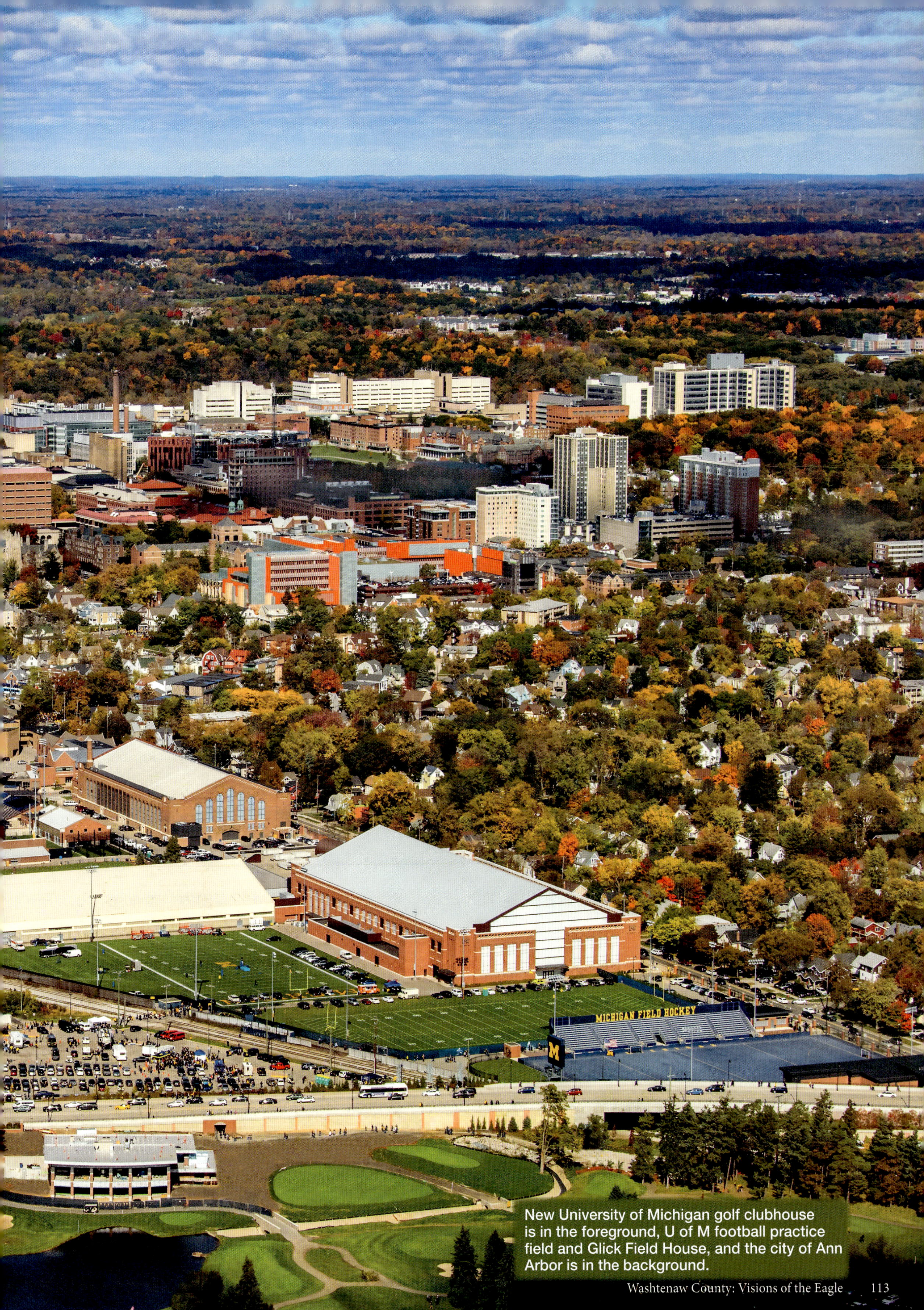

New University of Michigan golf clubhouse is in the foreground, U of M football practice field and Glick Field House, and the city of Ann Arbor is in the background.

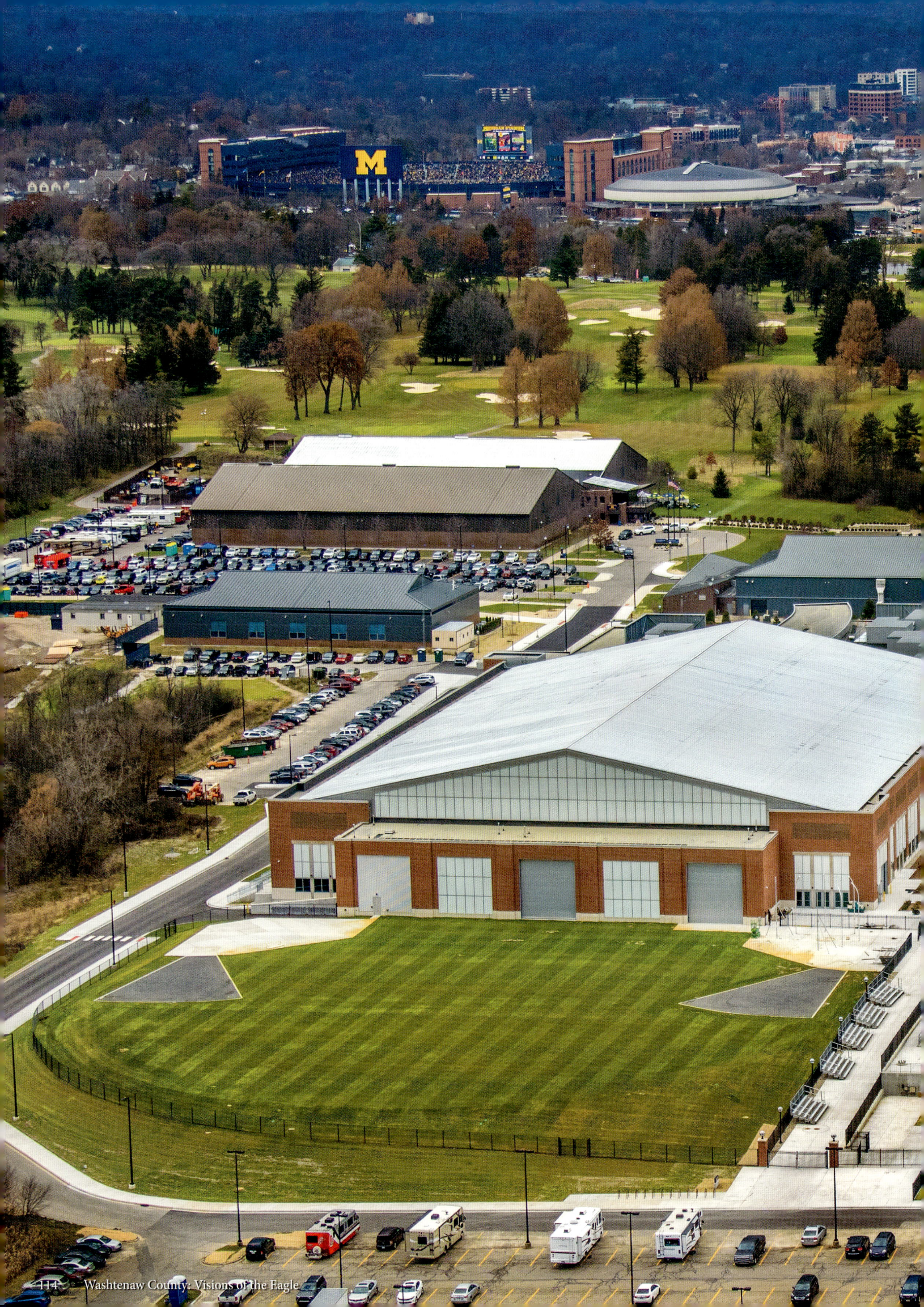
M

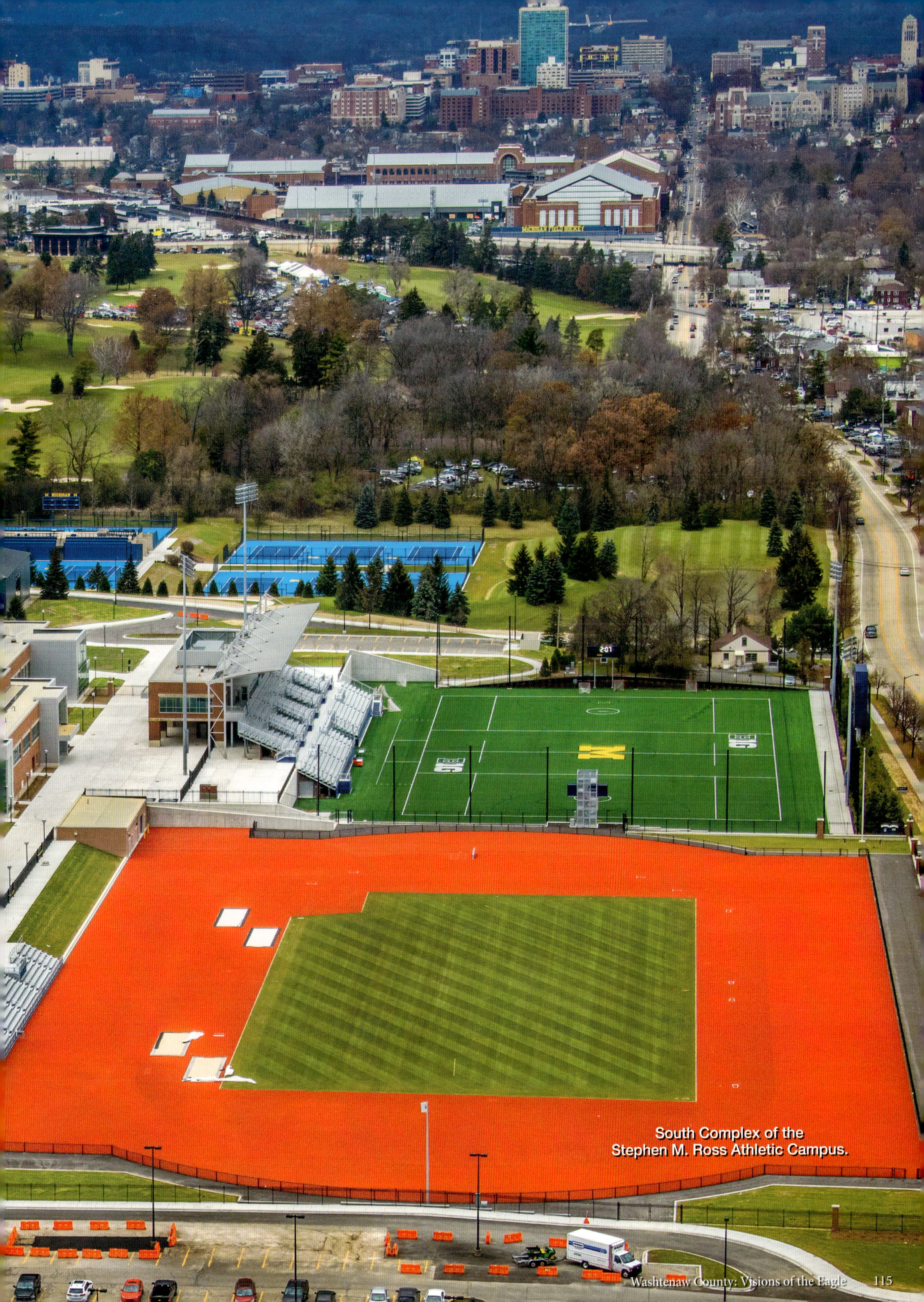

South Complex of the
Stephen M. Ross Athletic Campus.

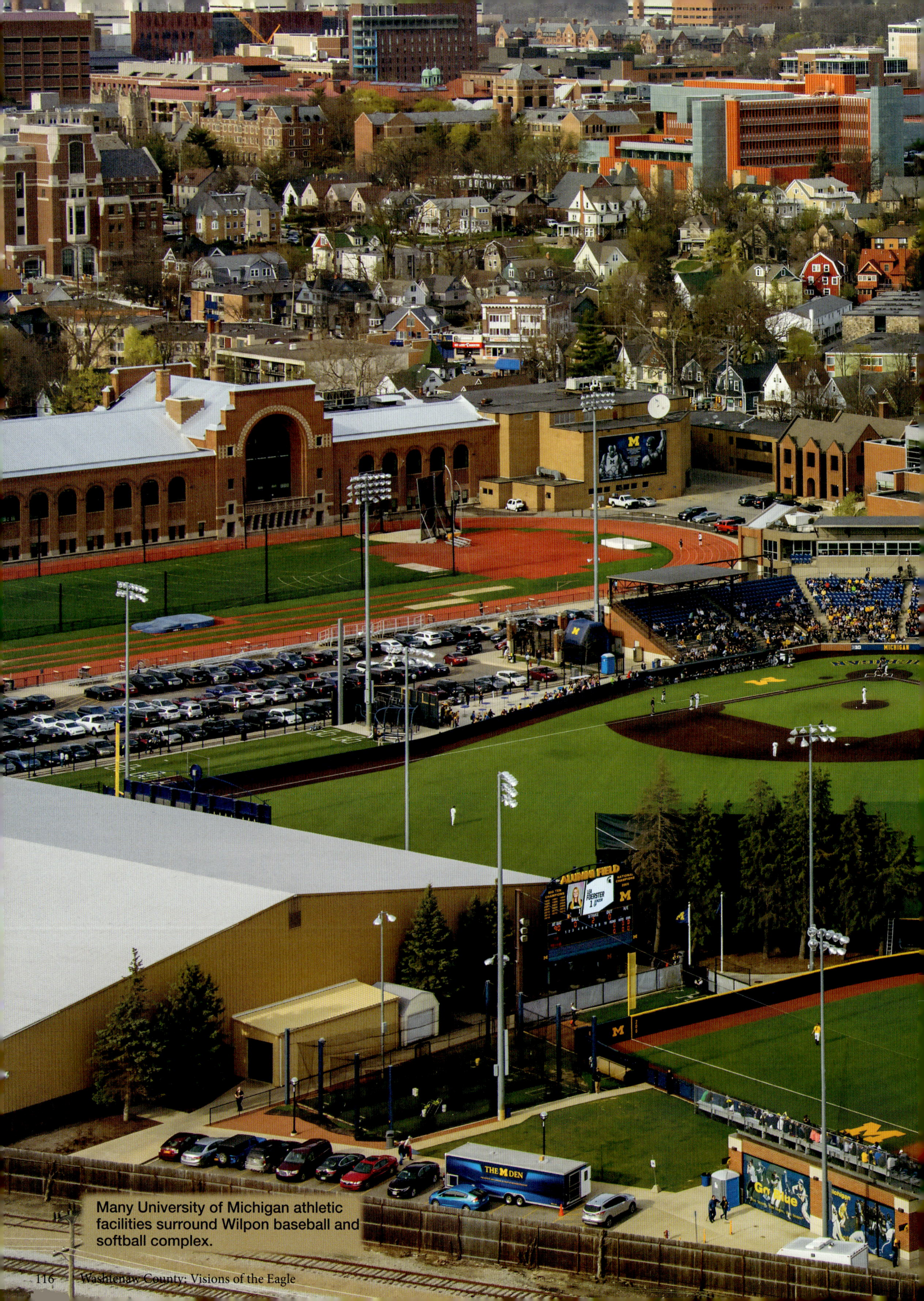

Many University of Michigan athletic facilities surround Wilpon baseball and softball complex.

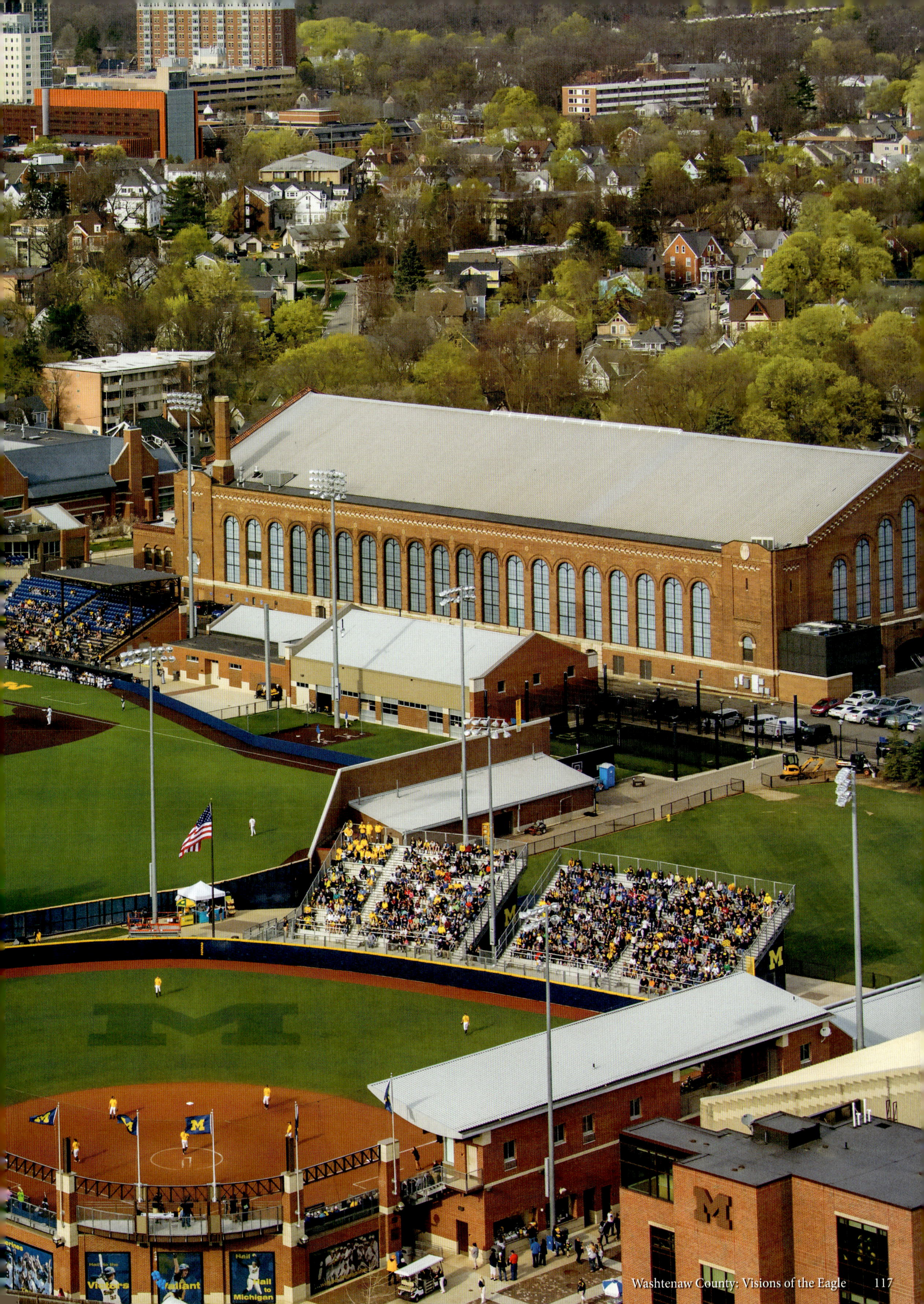
Hail to the
Victors
Hail
Hail to Michigan

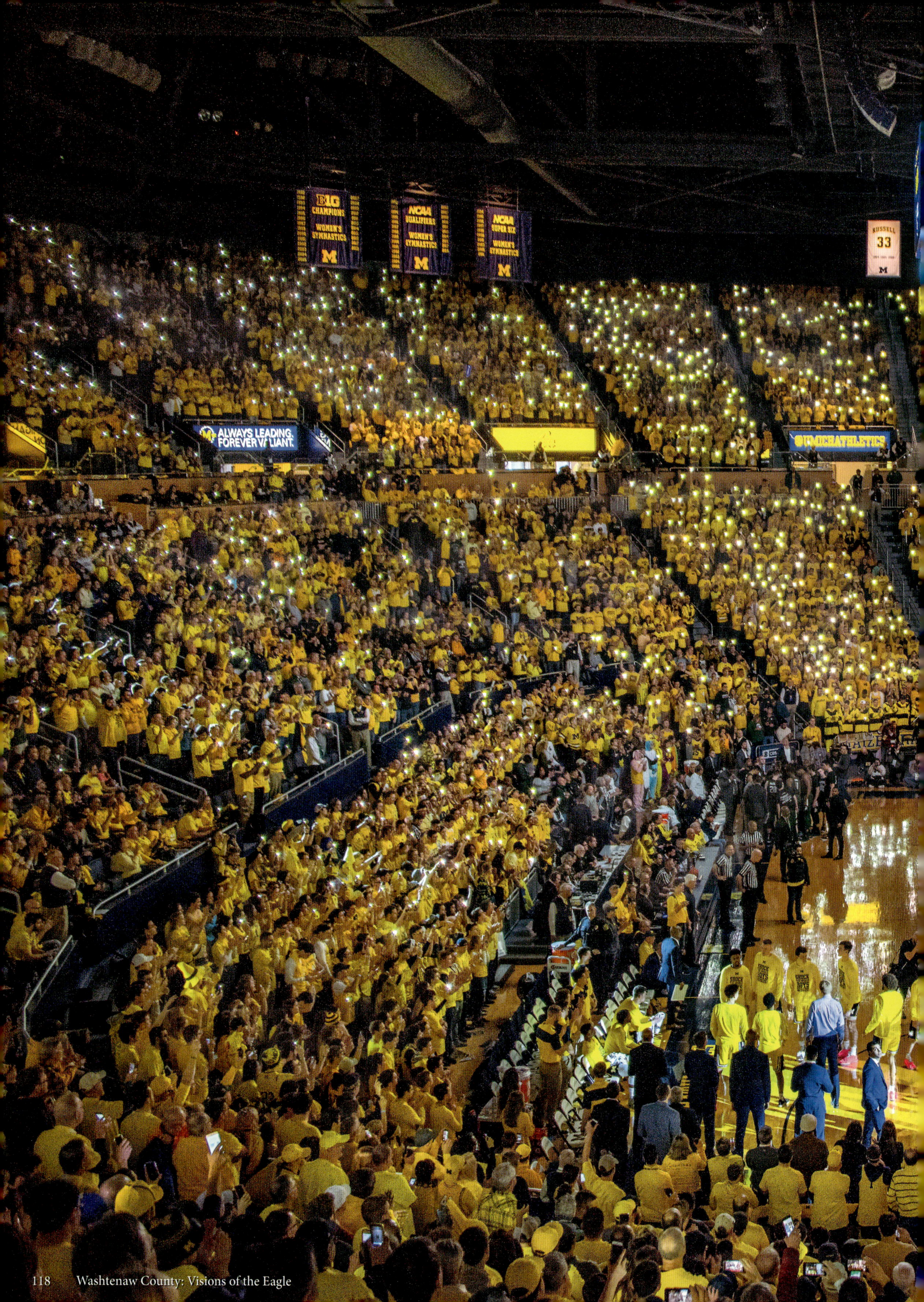
B1G CHAMPIONS WOMEN'S GYMNASTICS
NCAA QUALIFIERS WOMEN'S GYMNASTICS
NCAA SUPER SIX WOMEN'S GYMNASTICS
RUSSELL
33
ALWAYS LEADING. FOREVER VALIANT.
@UMICHATHLETICS

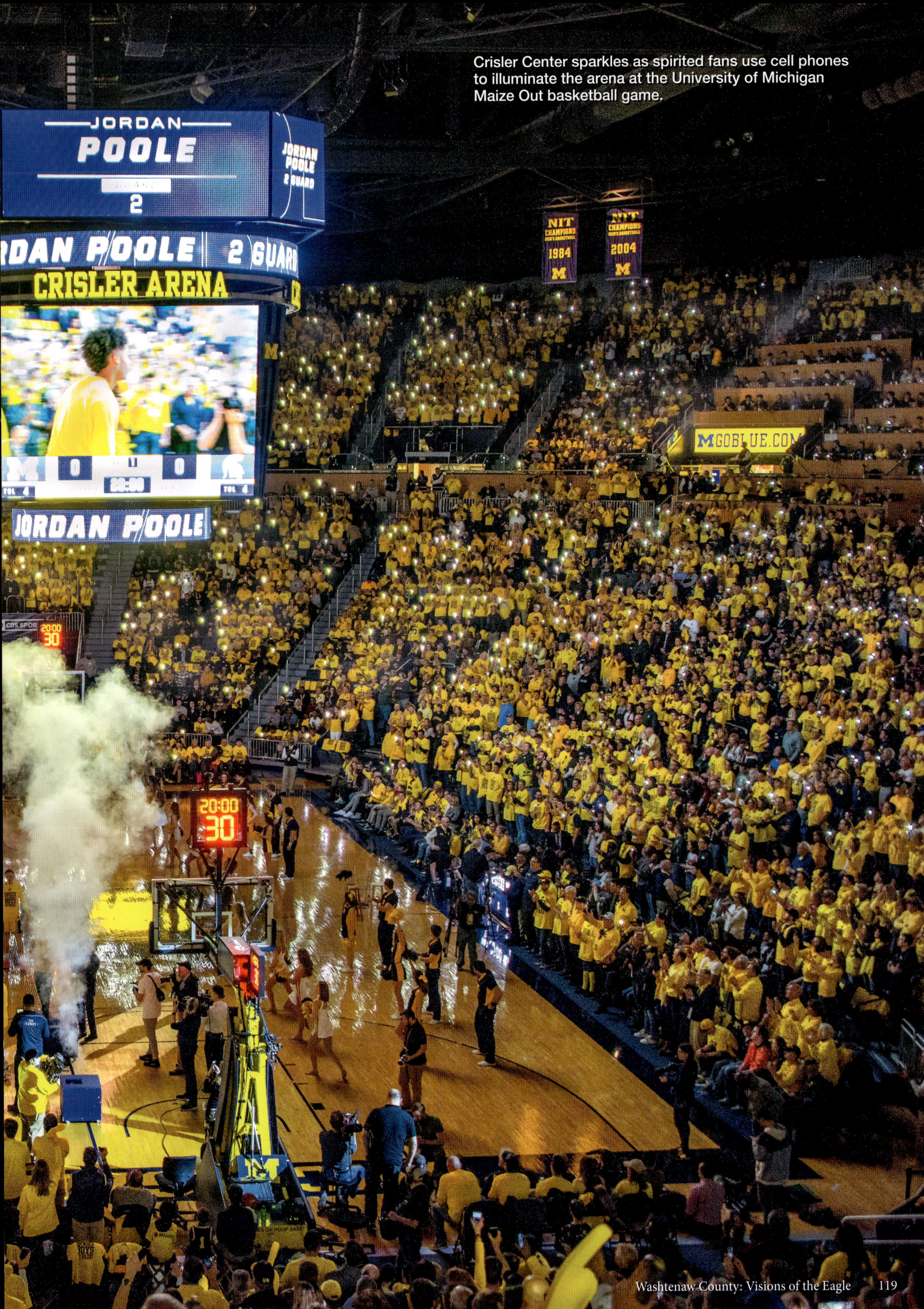

Crisler Center sparkles as spirited fans use cell phones to illuminate the arena at the University of Michigan Maize Out basketball game.

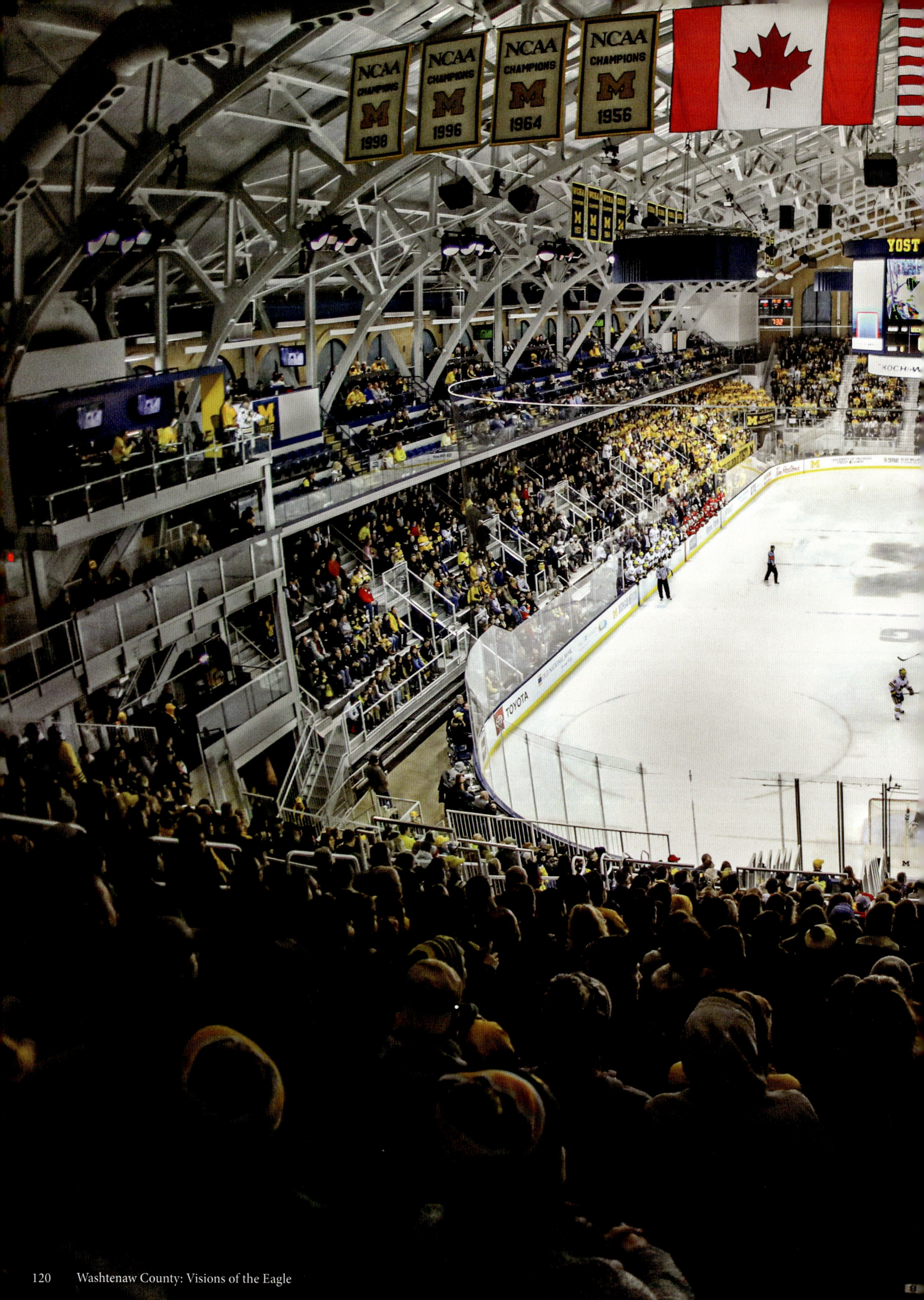
NCAA CHAMPIONS M 1998
NCAA CHAMPIONS M 1996
NCAA CHAMPIONS M 1964
NCAA CHAMPIONS M 1956
YOST
TOYOTA

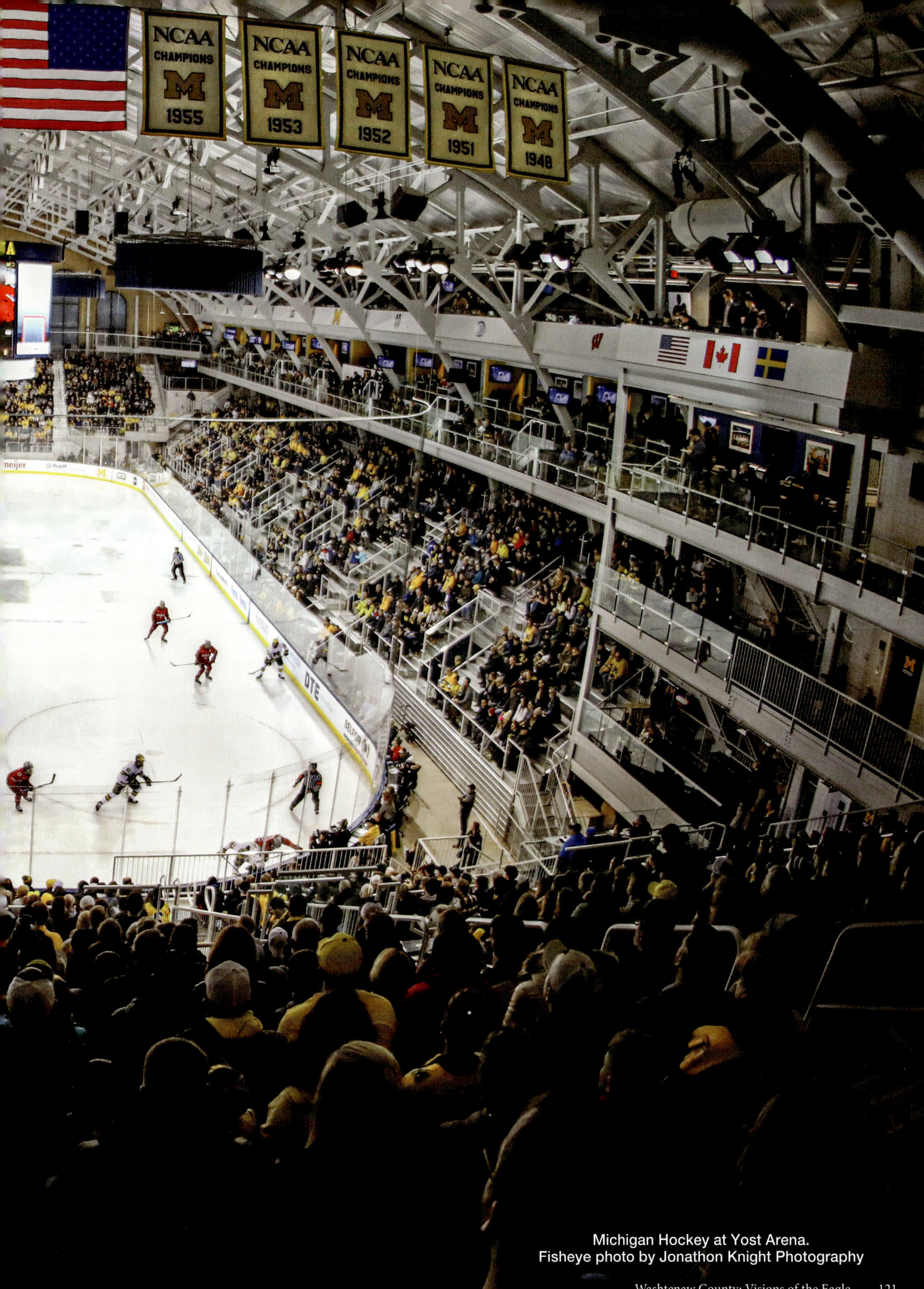

Michigan Hockey at Yost Arena.
Fisheye photo by Jonathon Knight Photography

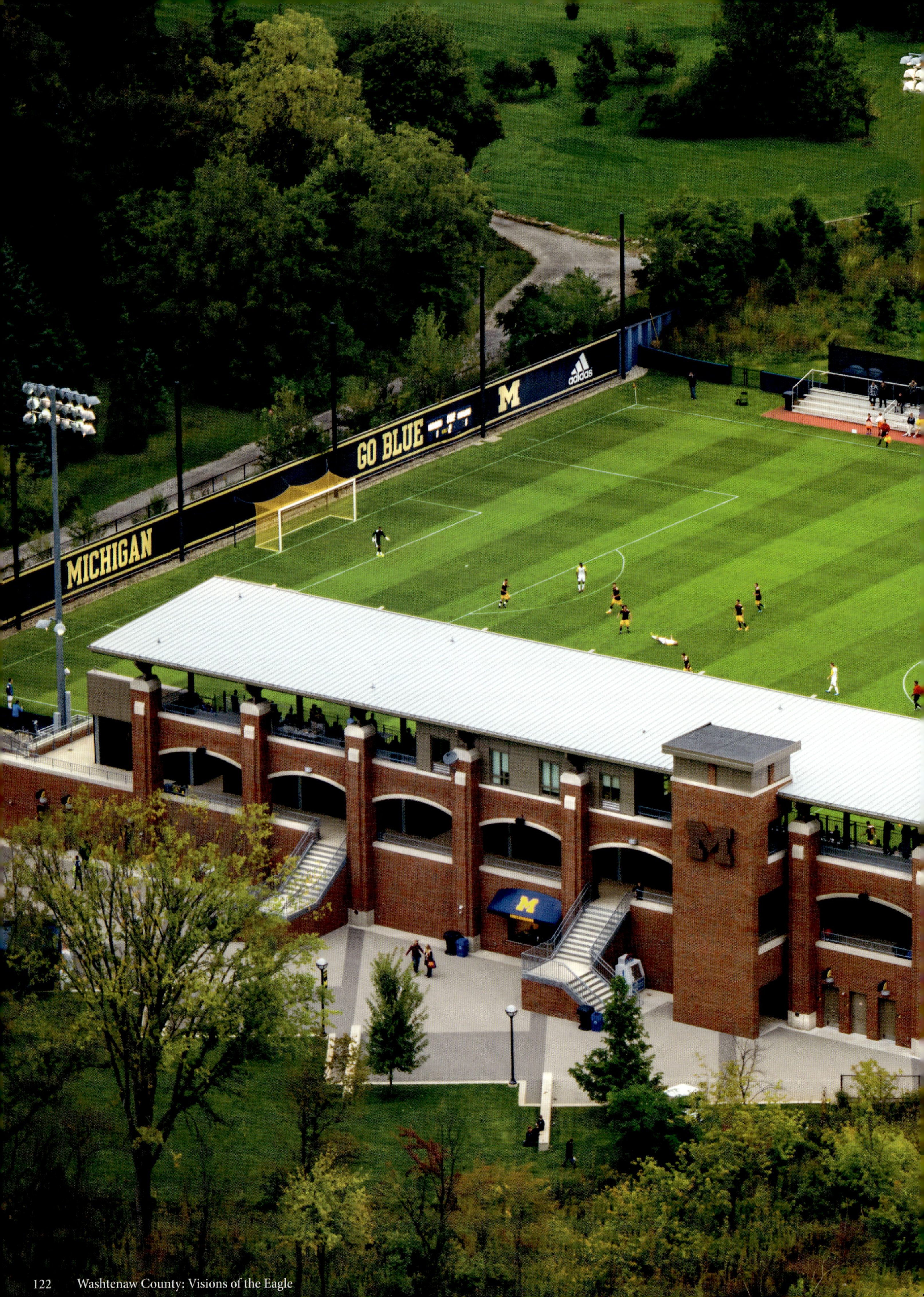
MICHIGAN
GO BLUE
M
adidas

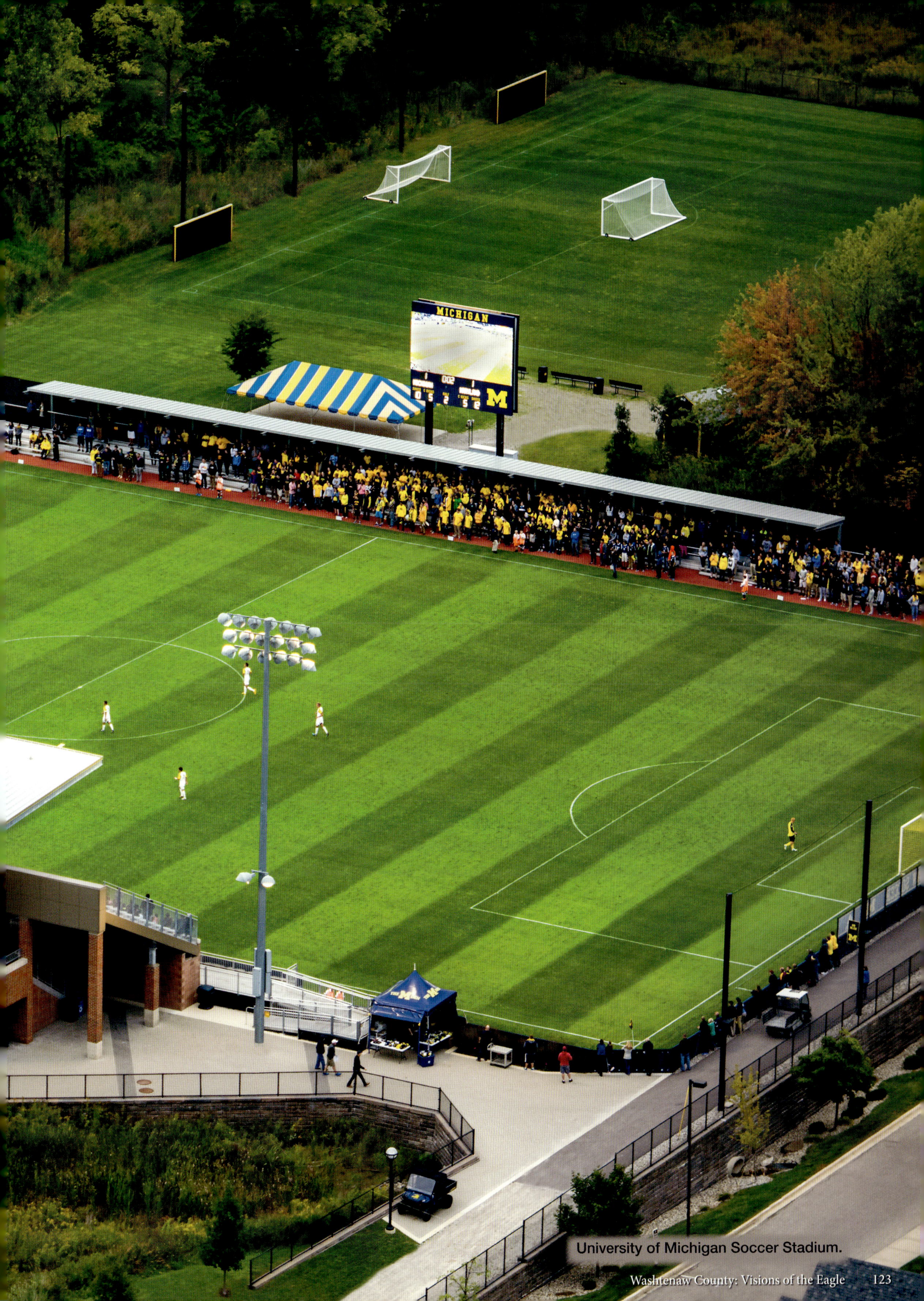

University of Michigan Soccer Stadium.

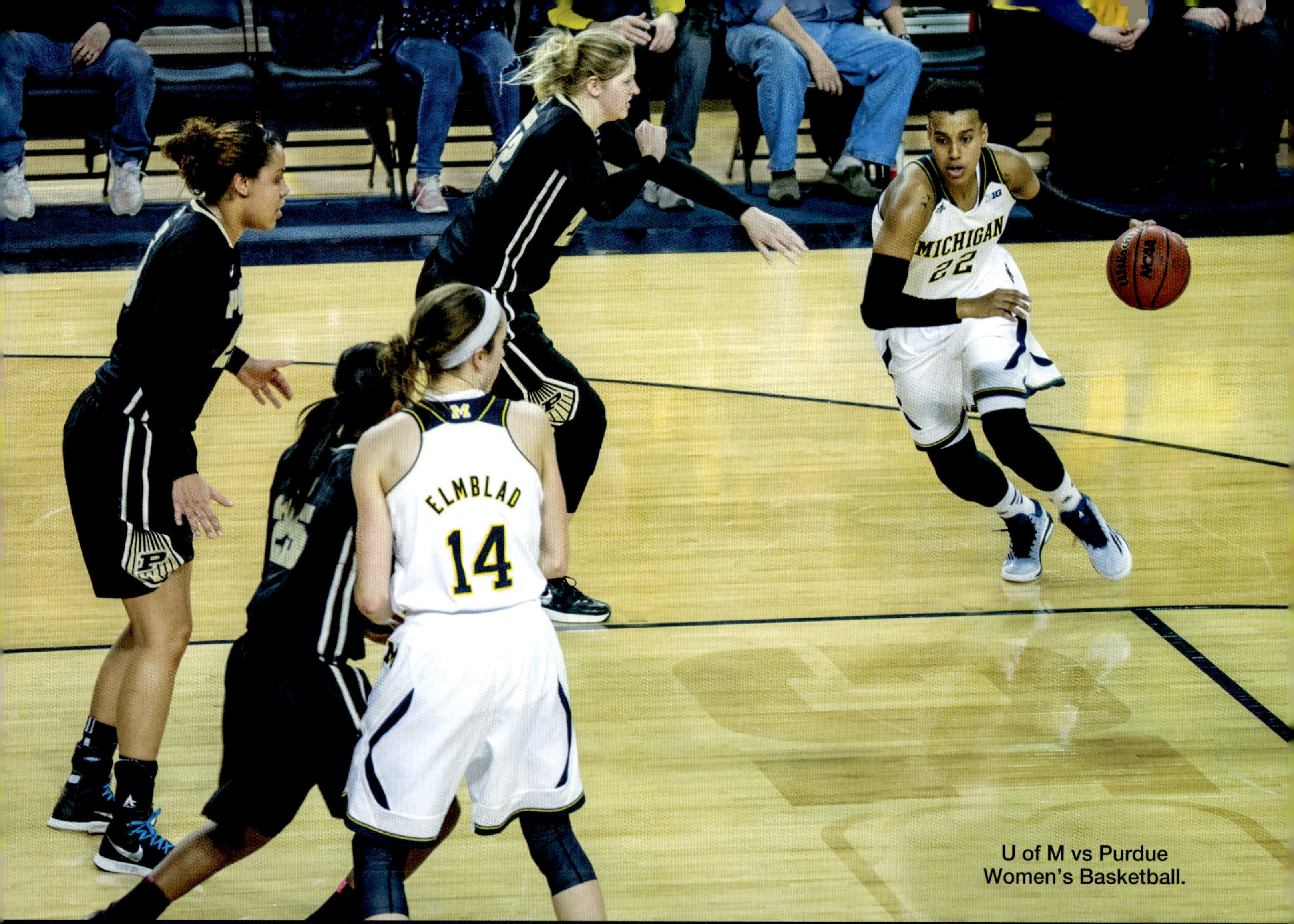

U of M vs Purdue
Women's Basketball.

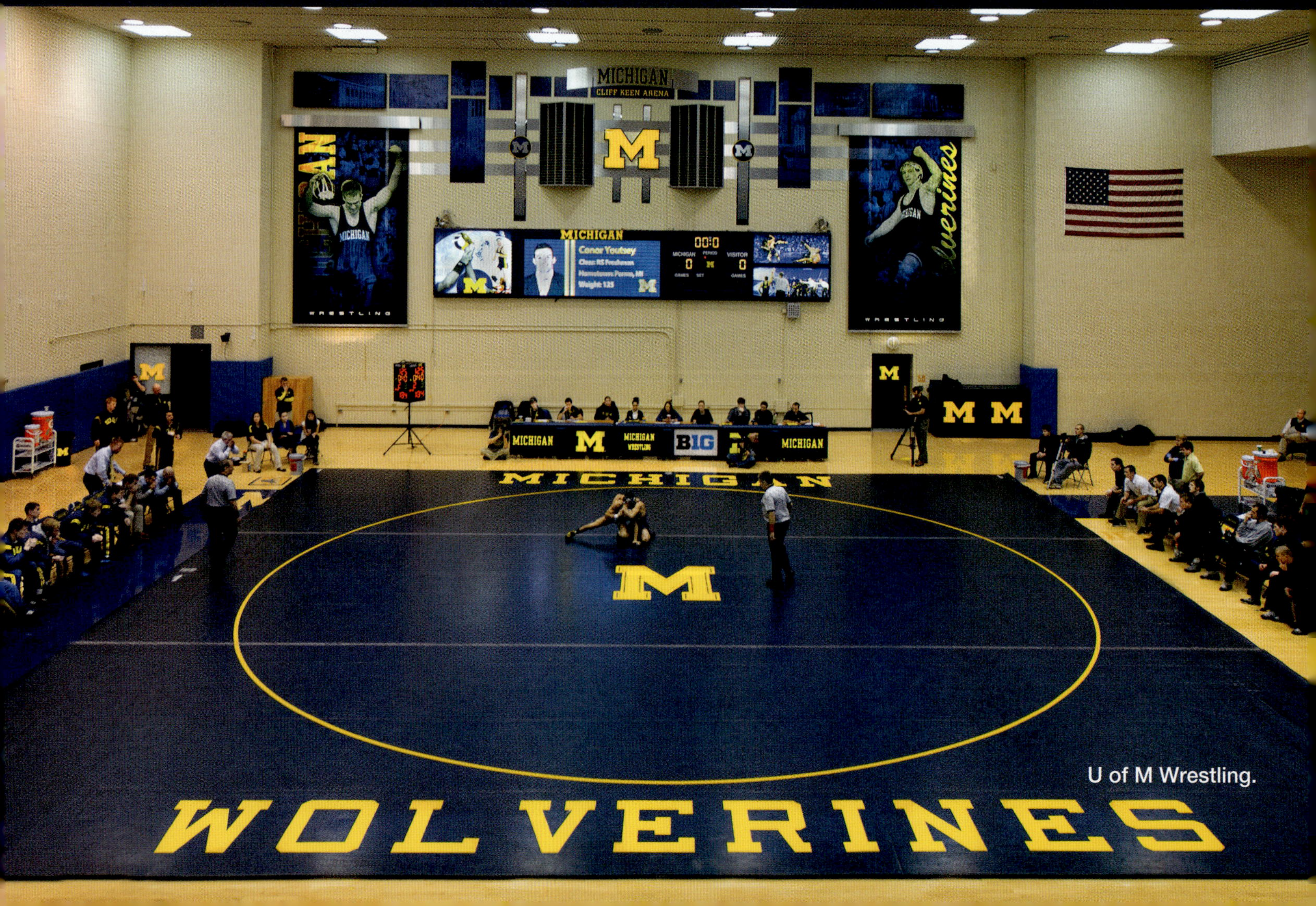

U of M Wrestling.

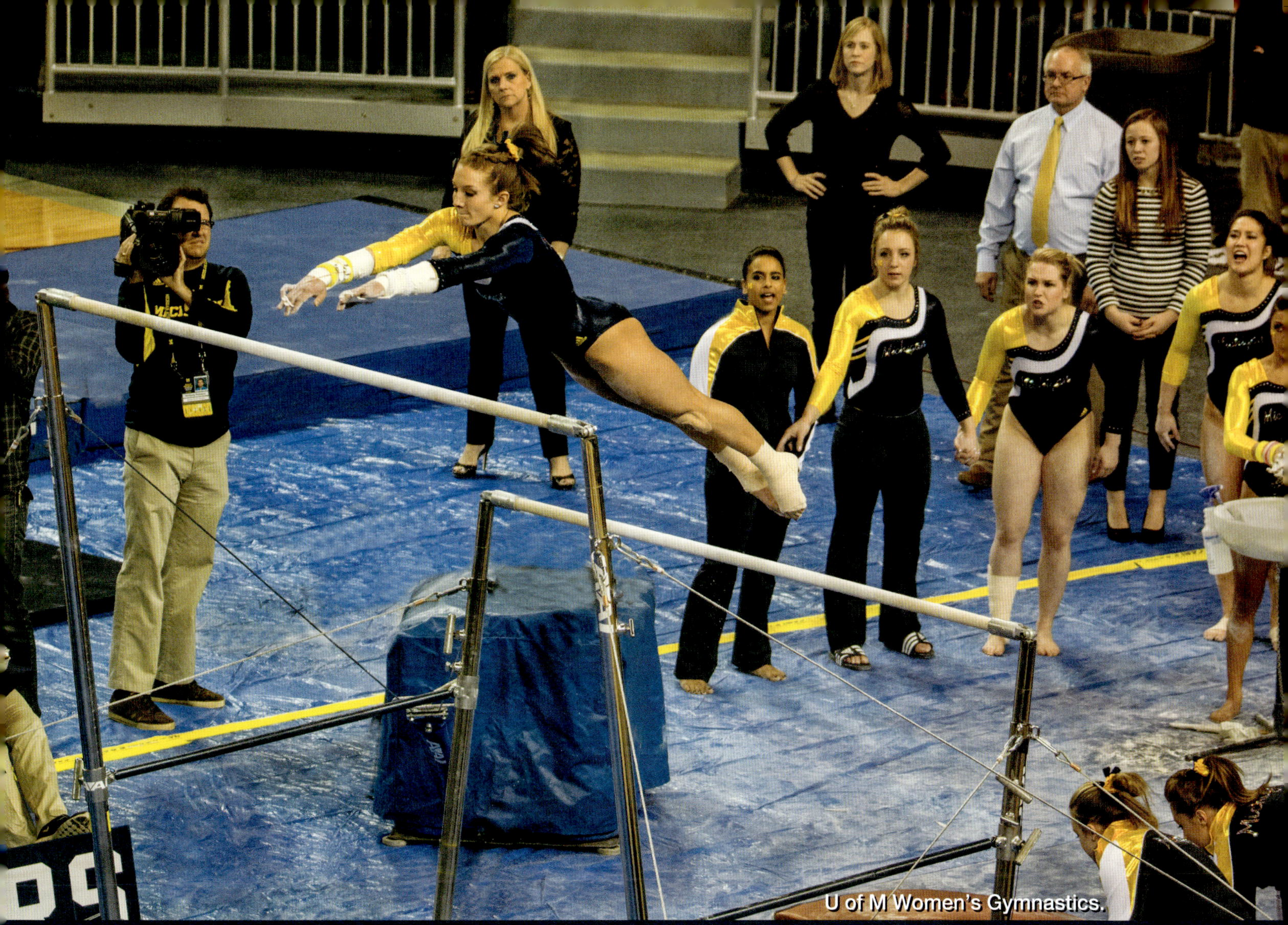

U of M Women's Gymnastics.

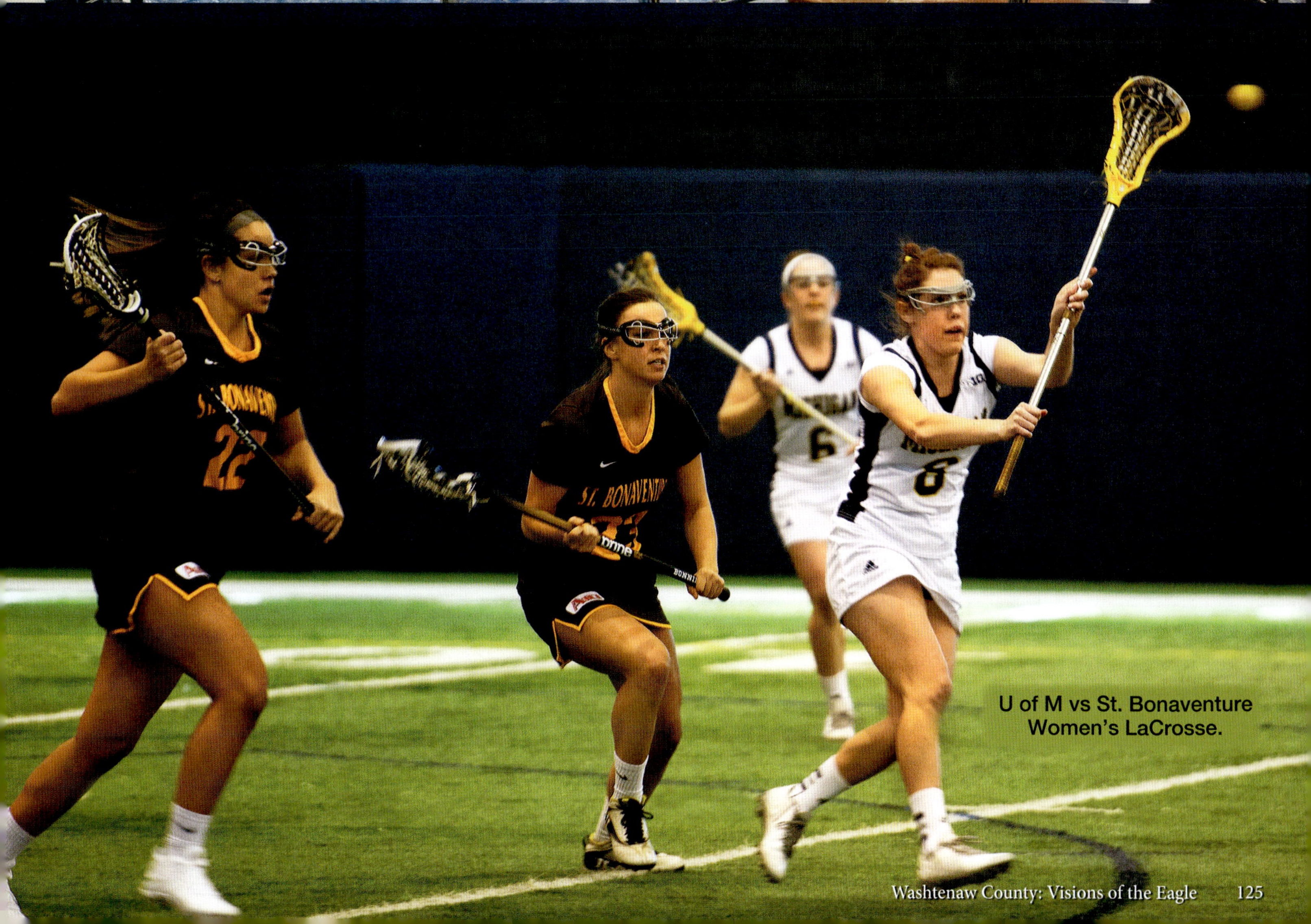

U of M vs St. Bonaventure
Women's LaCrosse.

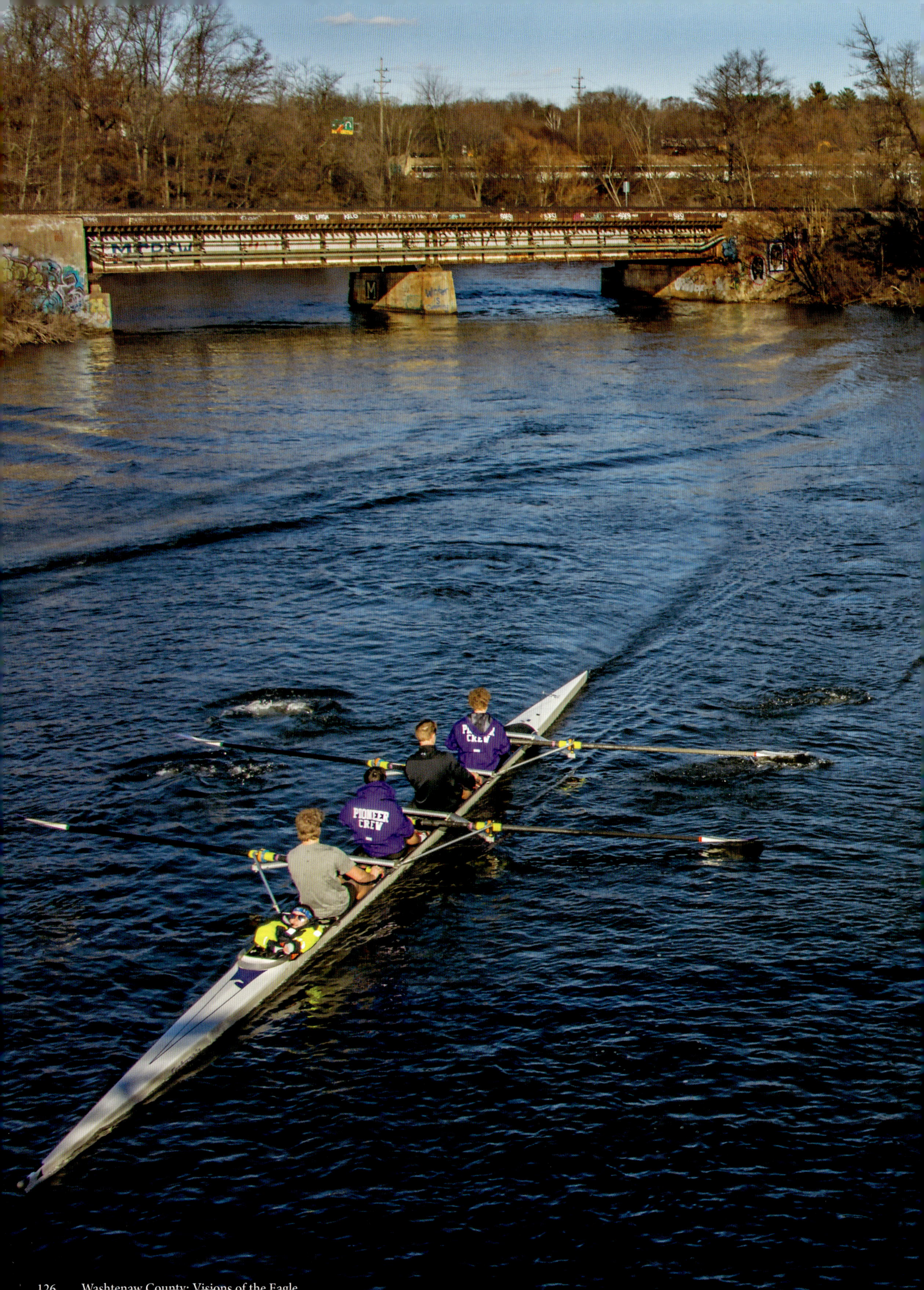
PIONEER
CREW

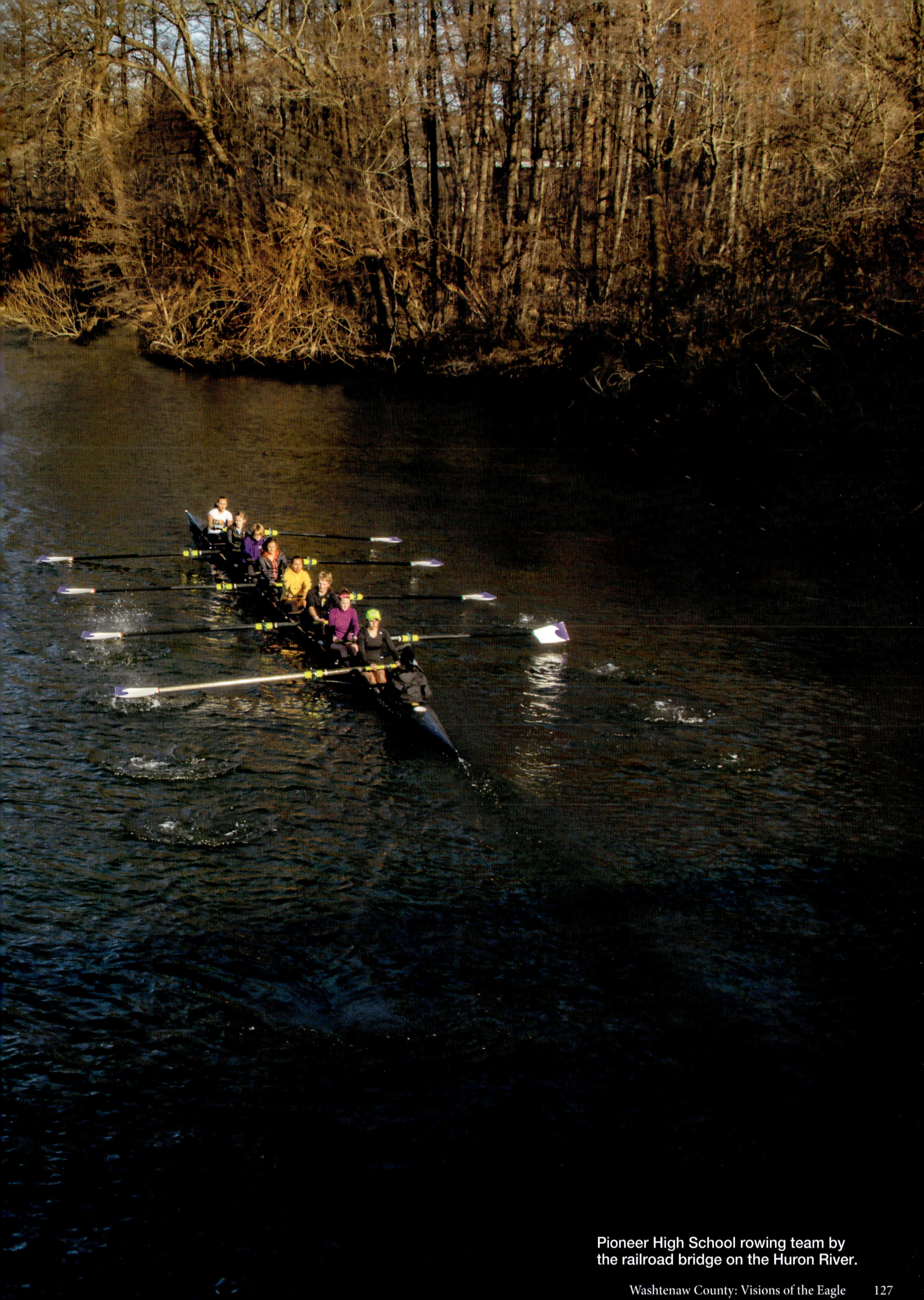

Pioneer High School rowing team by the railroad bridge on the Huron River.

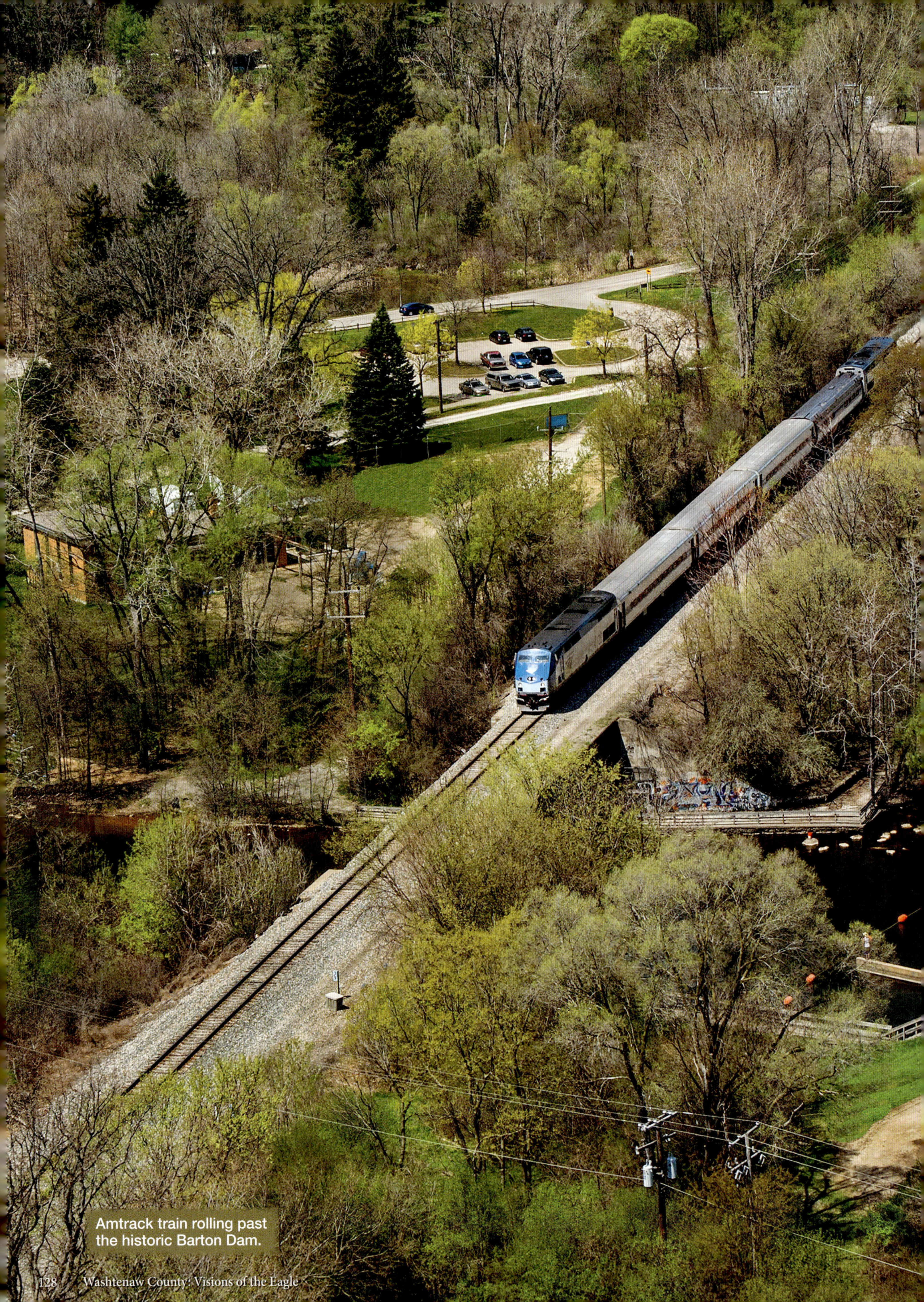
Amtrack train rolling past the historic Barton Dam.

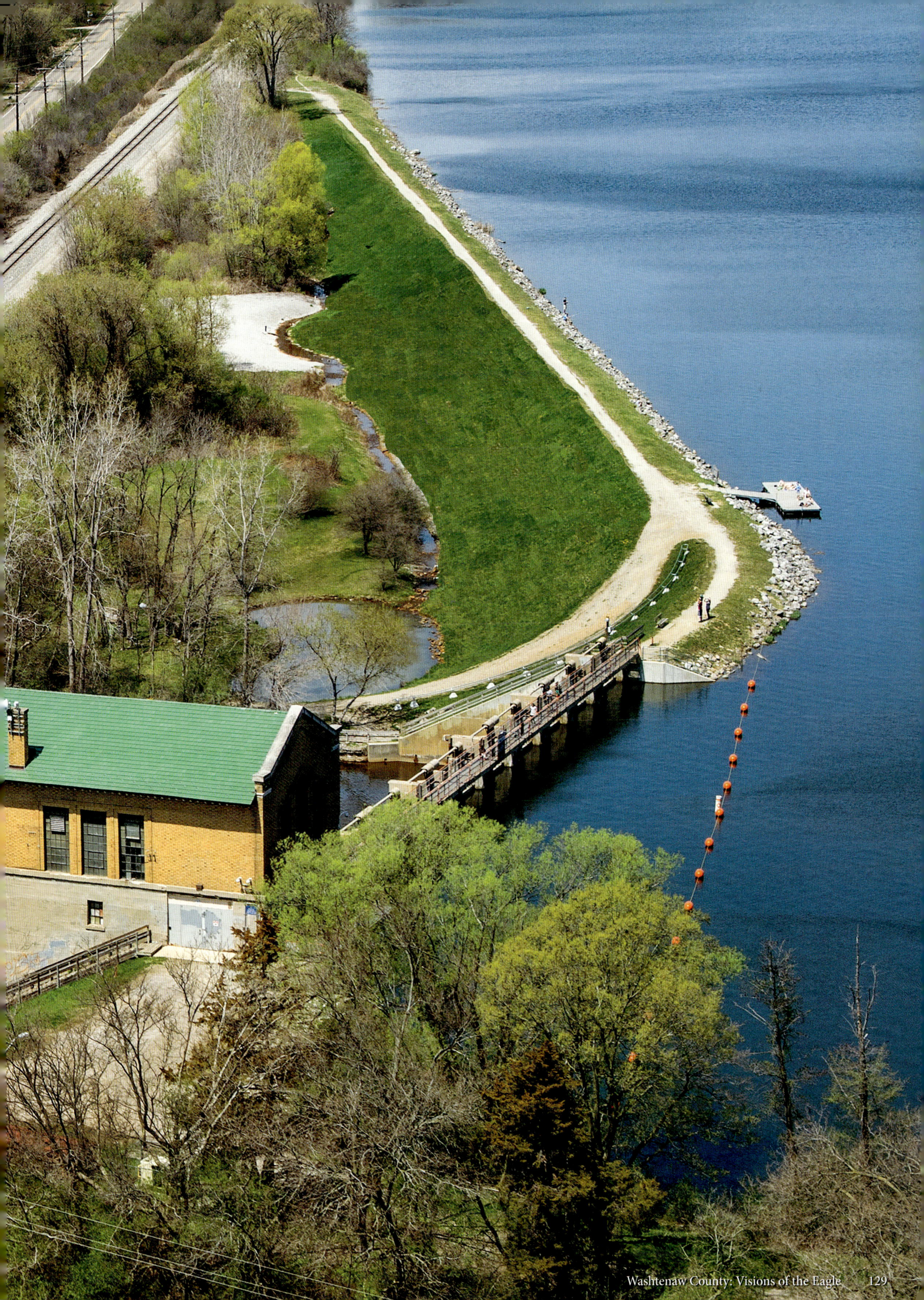

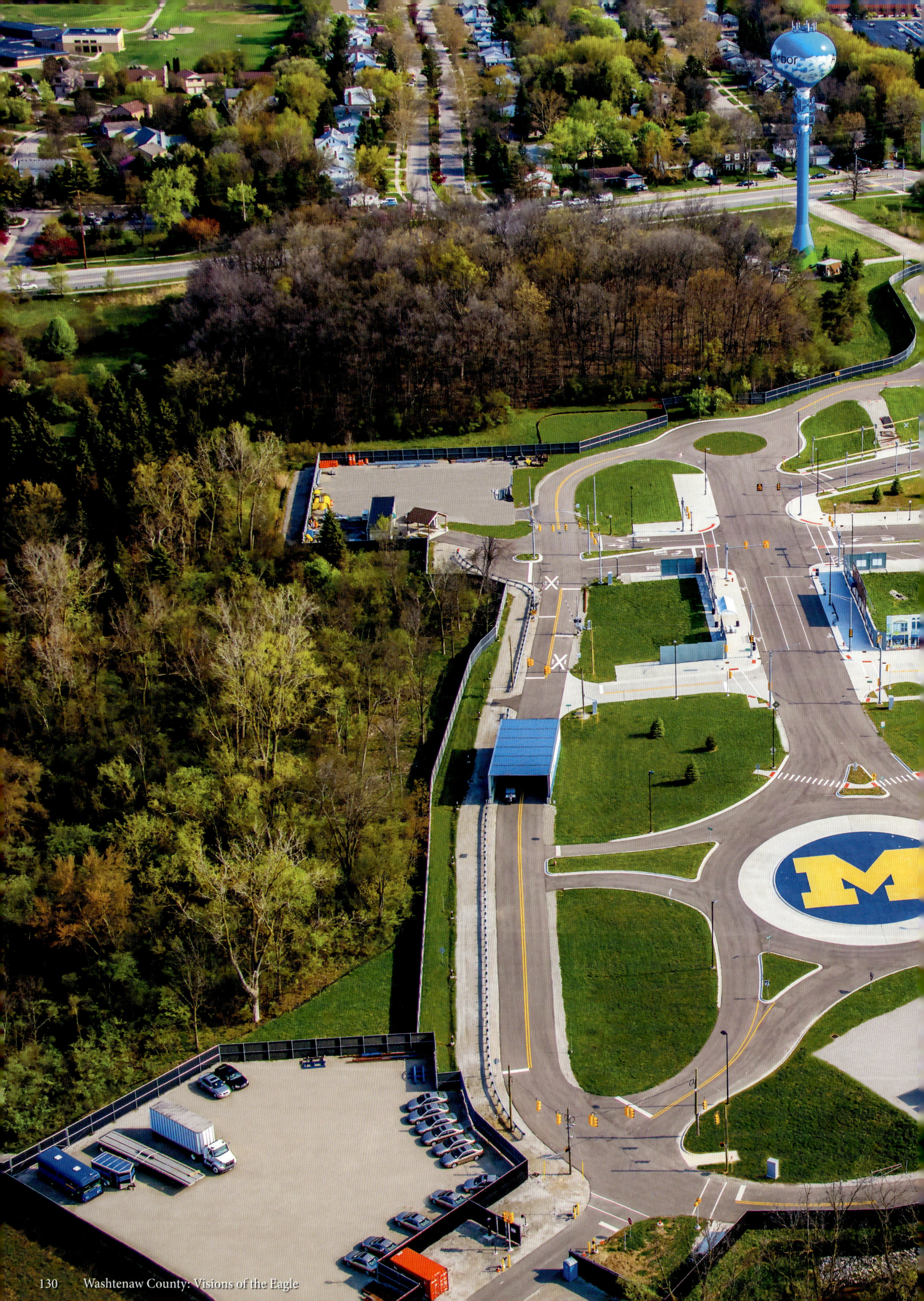

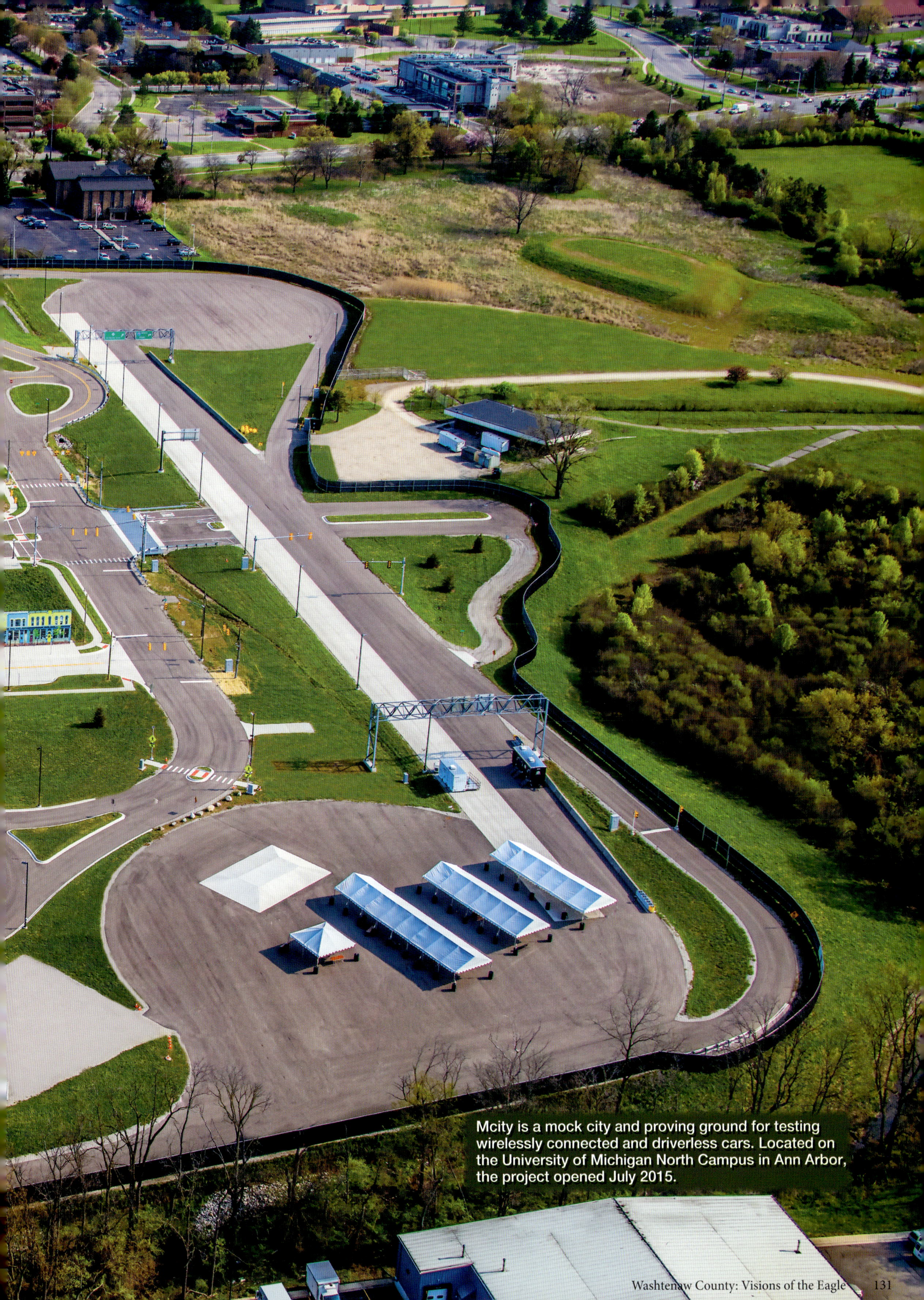

Mcity is a mock city and proving ground for testing wirelessly connected and driverless cars. Located on the University of Michigan North Campus in Ann Arbor, the project opened July 2015.

Bricklayers & Allied Craftworkers Local 2, Michigan

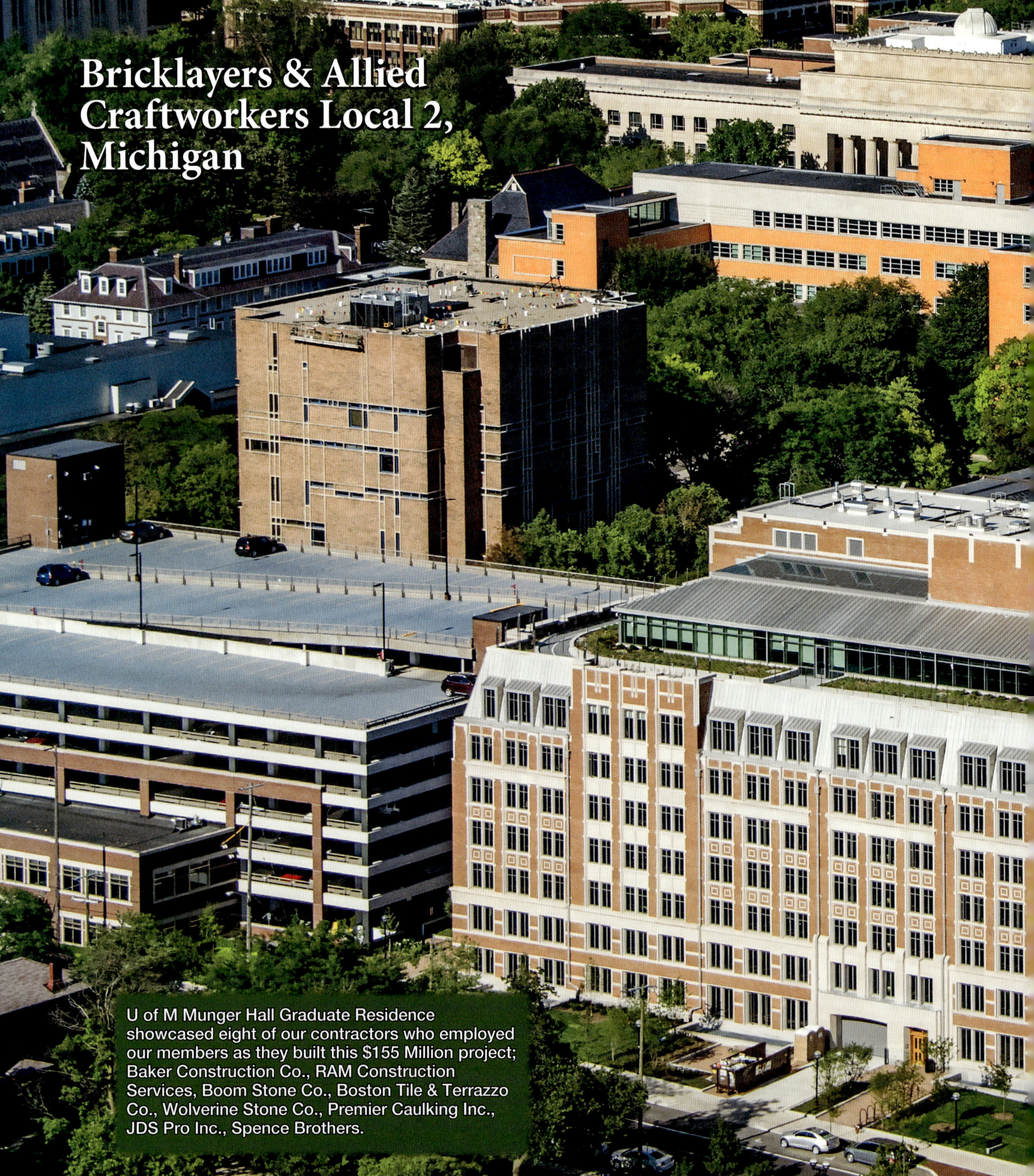

U of M Munger Hall Graduate Residence showcased eight of our contractors who employed our members as they built this $155 Million project; Baker Construction Co., RAM Construction Services, Boom Stone Co., Boston Tile & Terrazzo Co., Wolverine Stone Co., Premier Caulking Inc., JDS Pro Inc., Spence Brothers.

The International Union of Bricklayers and Allied Craftworkers (BAC) is the oldest continuously operating Building Trades Union in the United States. Out of the earth's elements, stone, granite, marble, sand, clay, brick and block, our craftworkers build with creativity, confidence and artisanship. We are part of a tradition as ancient as mankind's first buildings, yet as modern as an architect's dream.

This Union has been serving our members in Michigan since our Grand Rapids Local was chartered October 1, 1884. Now, BAC Local 2, MI represents nearly 4,000 members across the state in all facets of the trowel trades industry, including bricklayers, cement masons, tile, marble & terrazzo workers, pointer, cleaner, caulkers (restoration), plasterers, refractory craftworkers and stone masons.

Local 2 members benefit from above average hourly base wages, health insurance, reliable defined benefit pensions

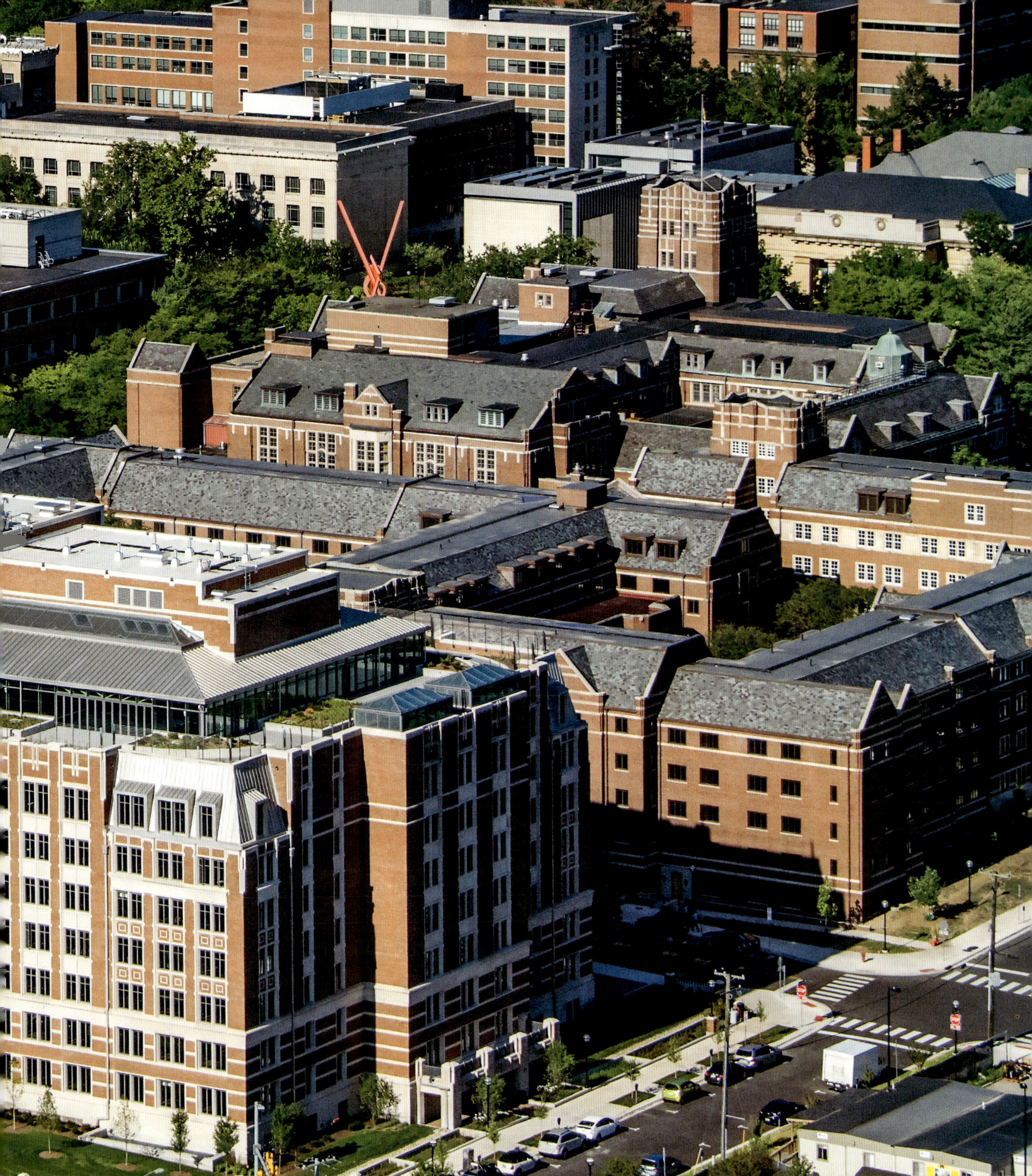

and educational scholarships for their children. The Union's International Masonry Institute Training Centers, located in Warren, Lansing and the Upper Peninsula, offer free training to those interested in entering our Union for a career in our trade. Union Contractors receive services including legislative representation, construction safety services and industry research and development.

We are proud to carry on a tradition of excellence by training and employing our members in the construction and restoration of projects throughout the state. The work of our members is timeless, and the projects they create will endure beyond their lifetime!

BRICKLAYERS & ALLIED CRAFTWORKERS LOCAL 2, MICHIGAN

21031 Ryan Rd.
Warren, MI
586-754-0888

3321 Remy Dr.
Lansing, MI
517-886-9781

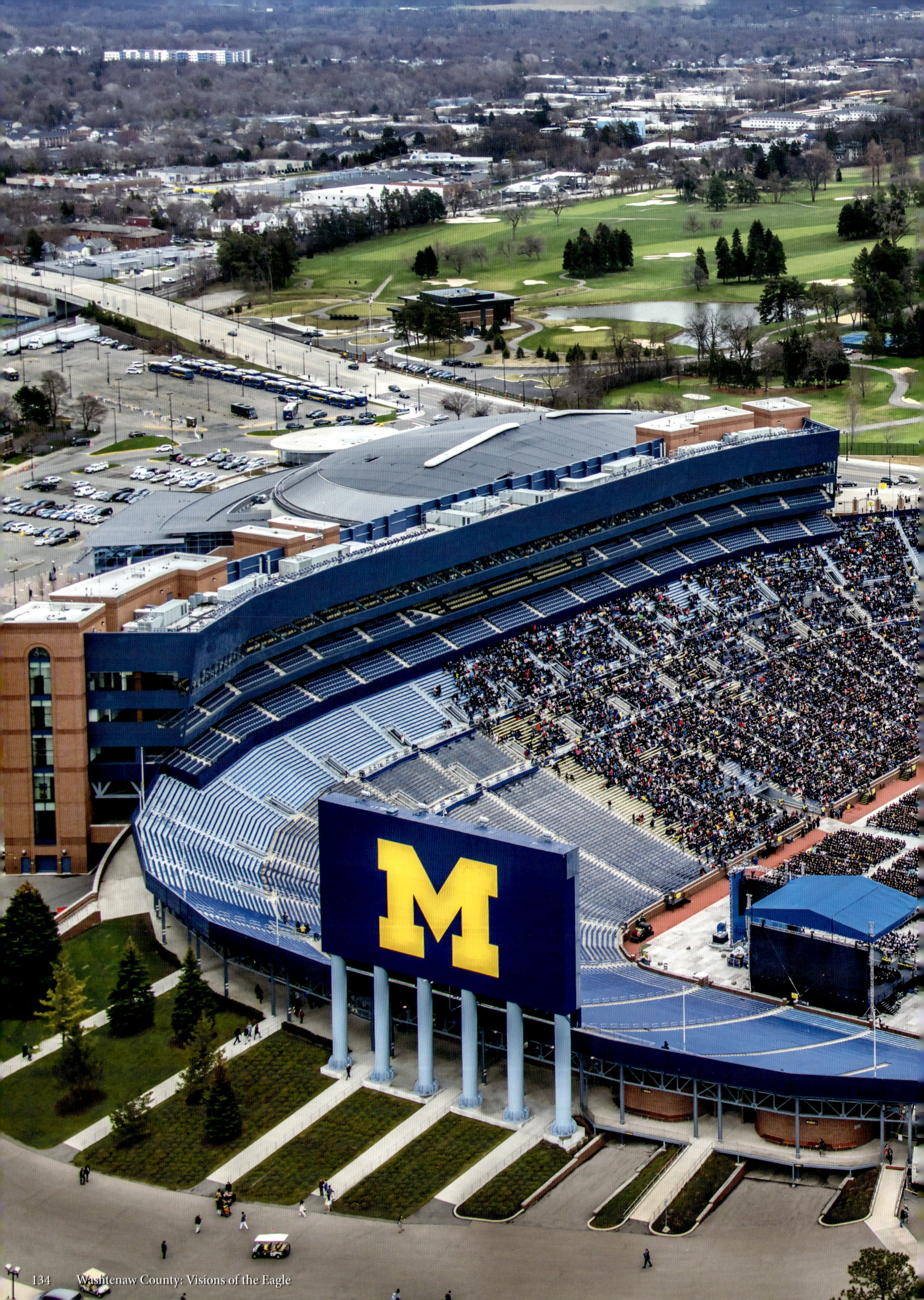
M

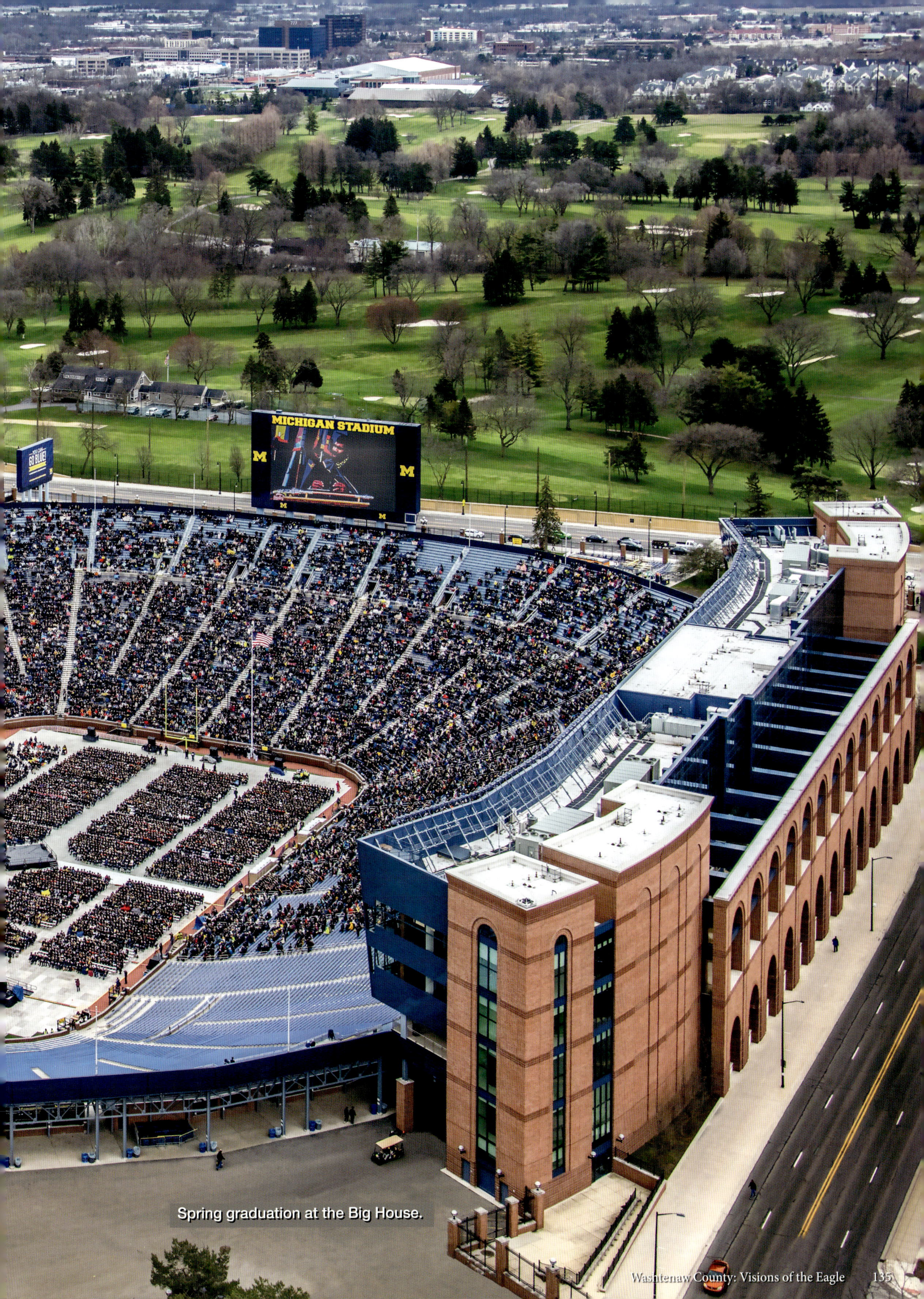

Spring graduation at the Big House.

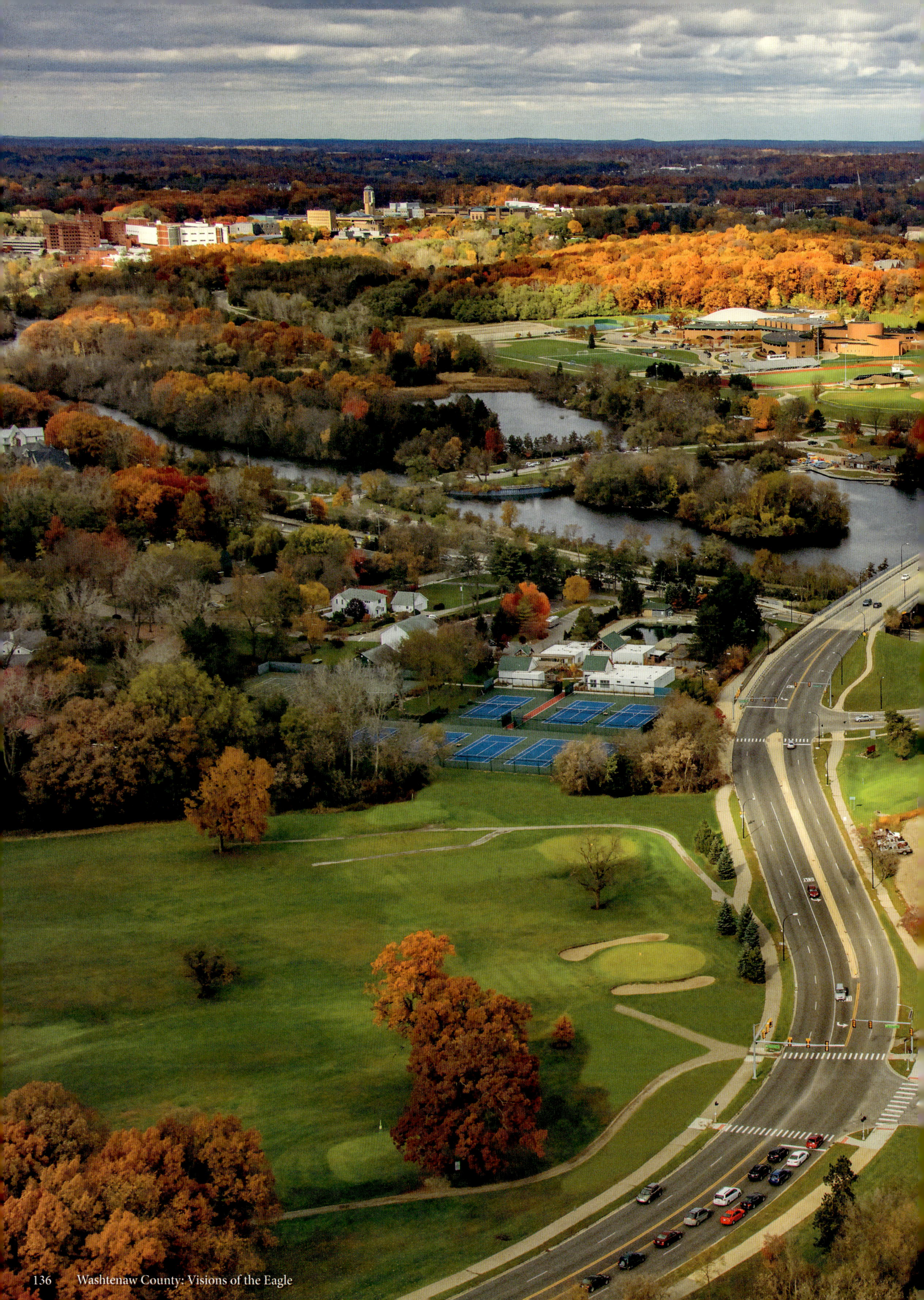

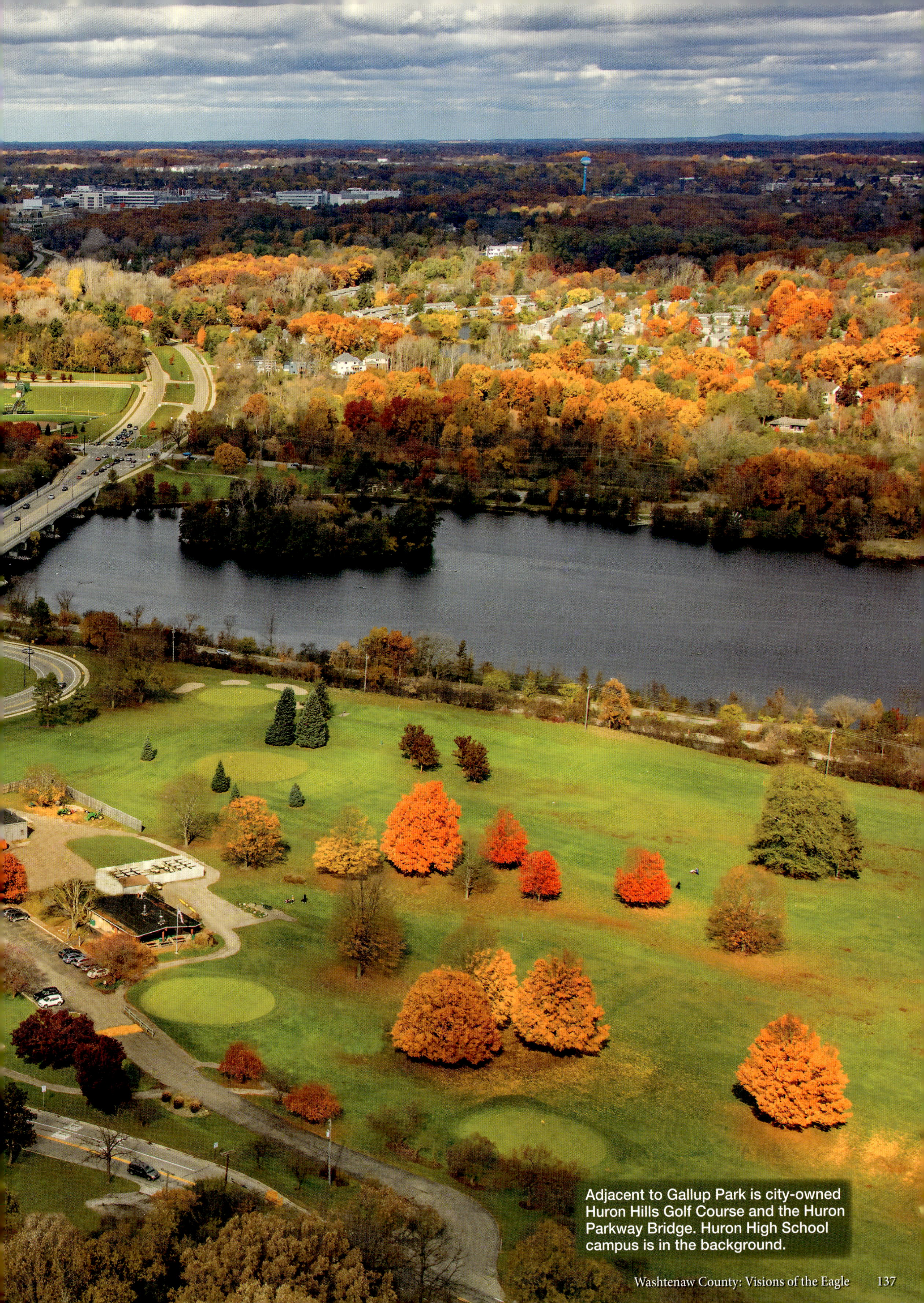

Adjacent to Gallup Park is city-owned Huron Hills Golf Course and the Huron Parkway Bridge. Huron High School campus is in the background.

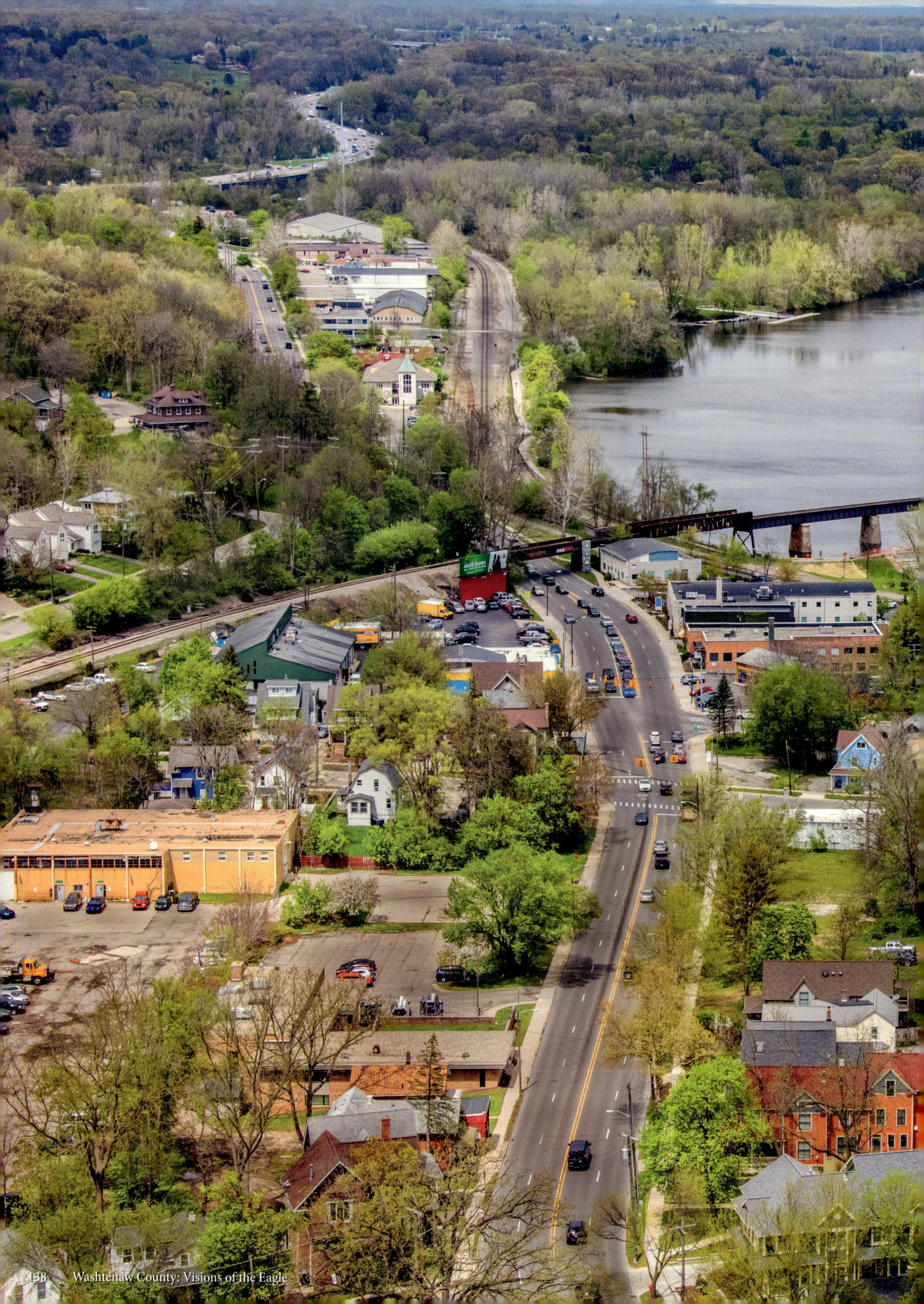

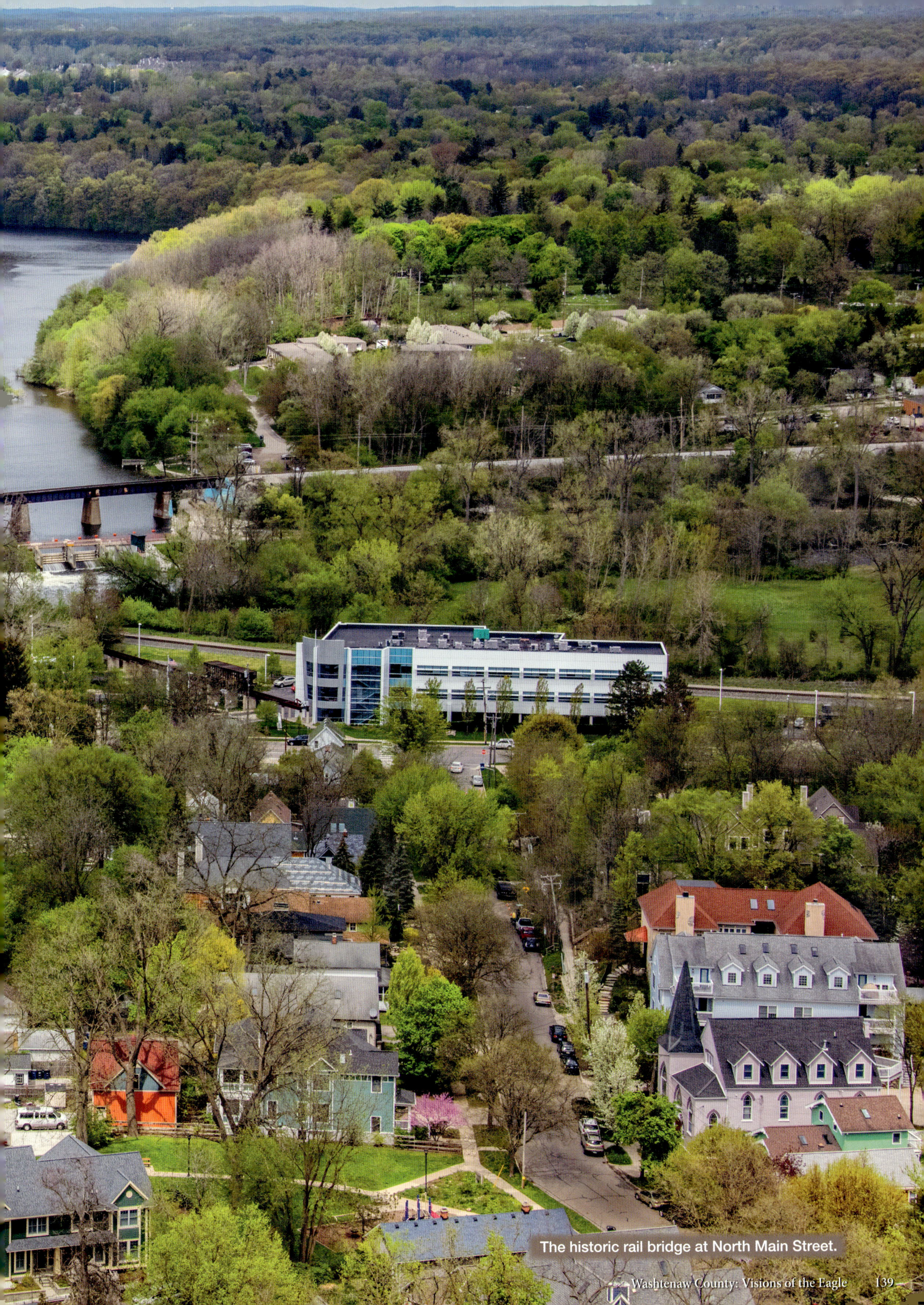

The historic rail bridge at North Main Street.

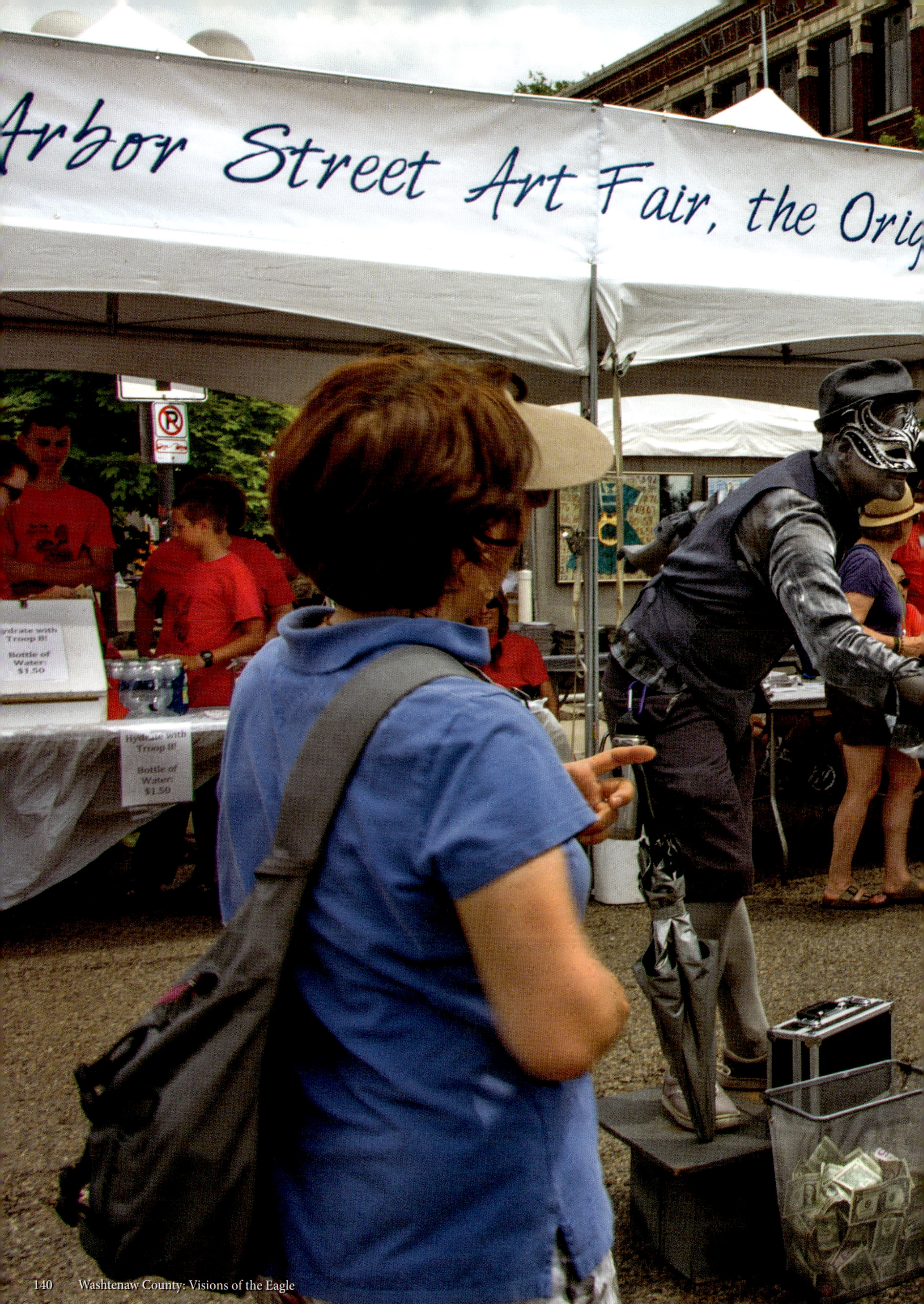
Arbor Street Art Fair, the
Hydrate with Troop 8!
Bottle of Water: $1.50

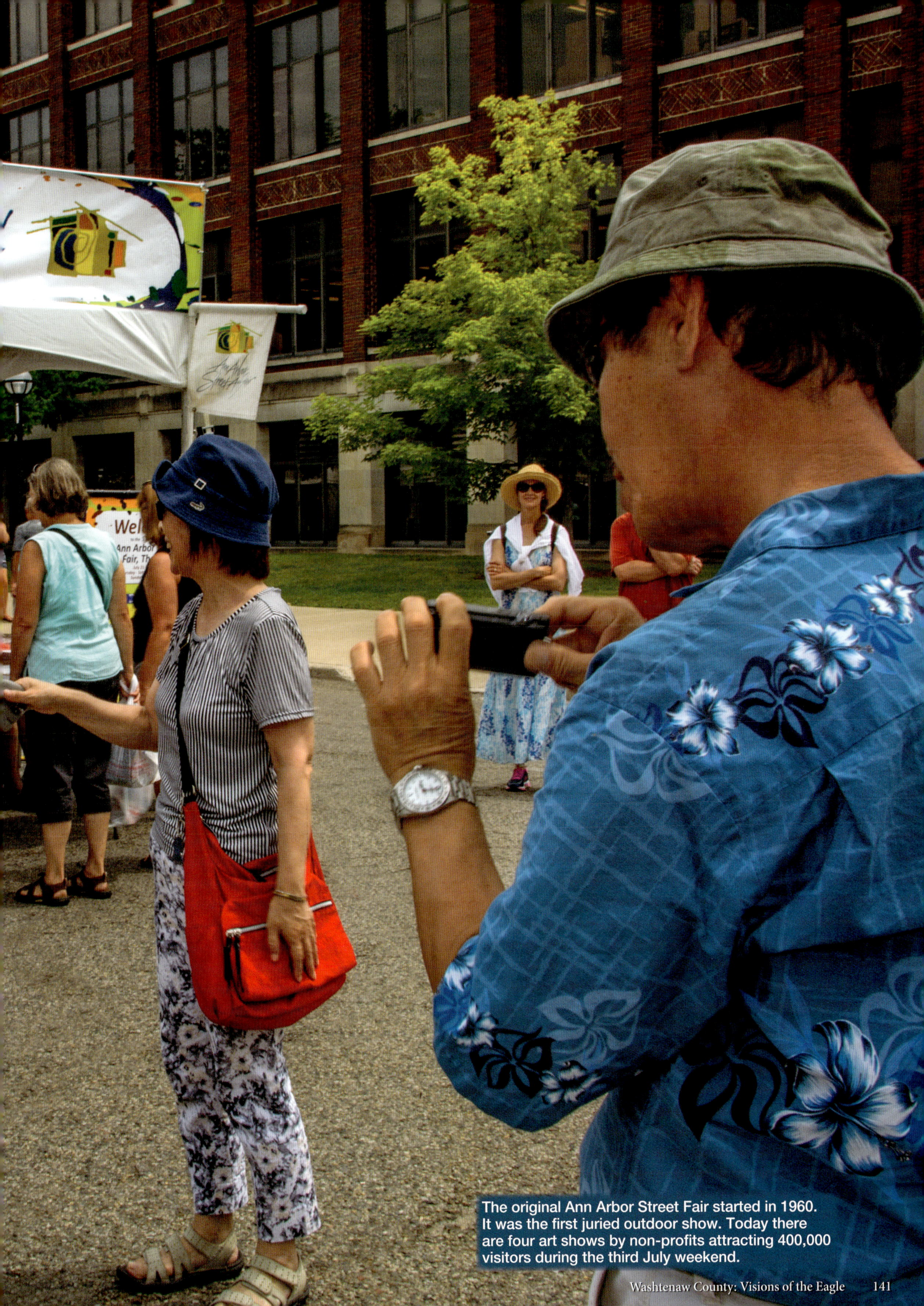

The original Ann Arbor Street Fair started in 1960. It was the first juried outdoor show. Today there are four art shows by non-profits attracting 400,000 visitors during the third July weekend.

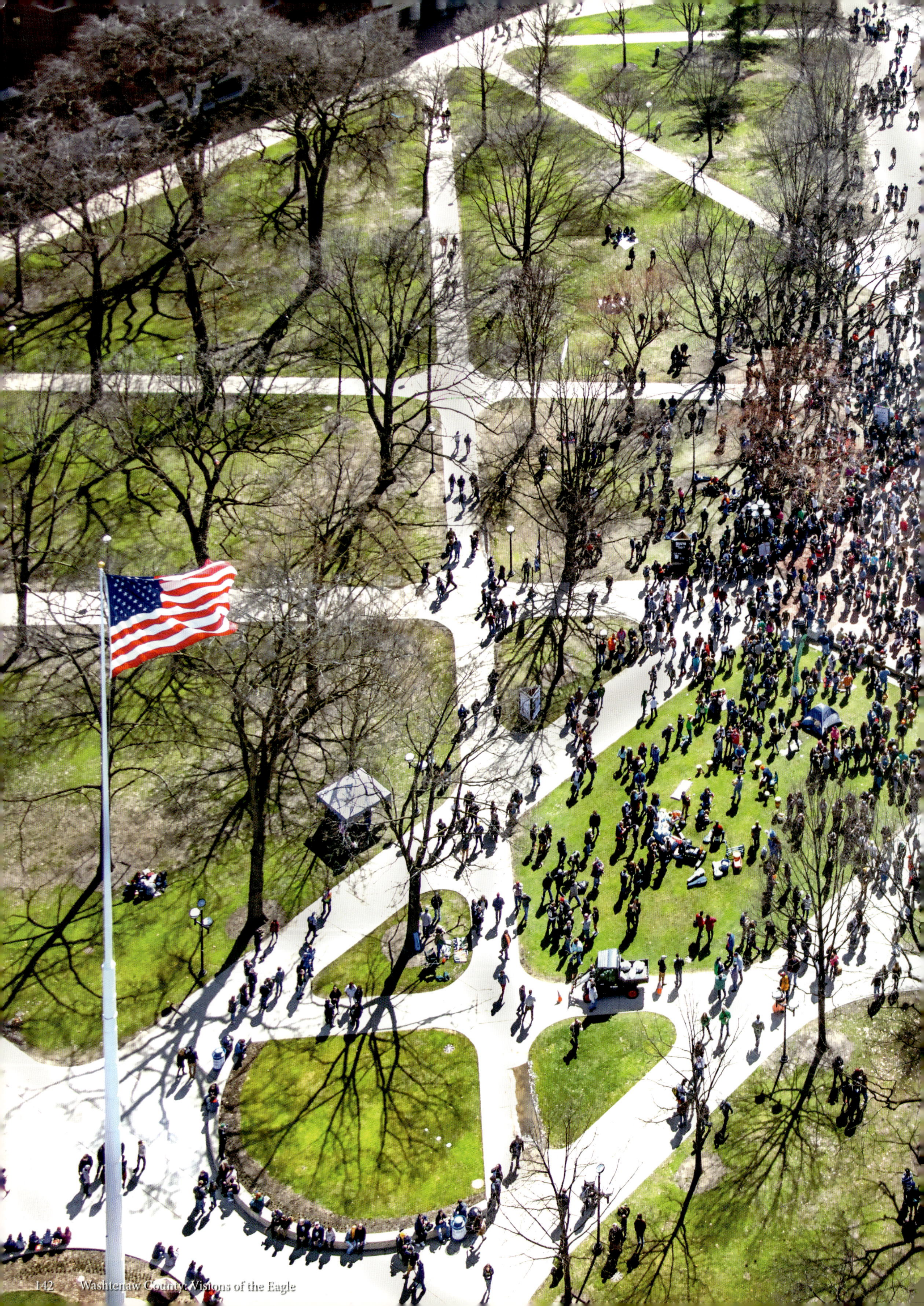

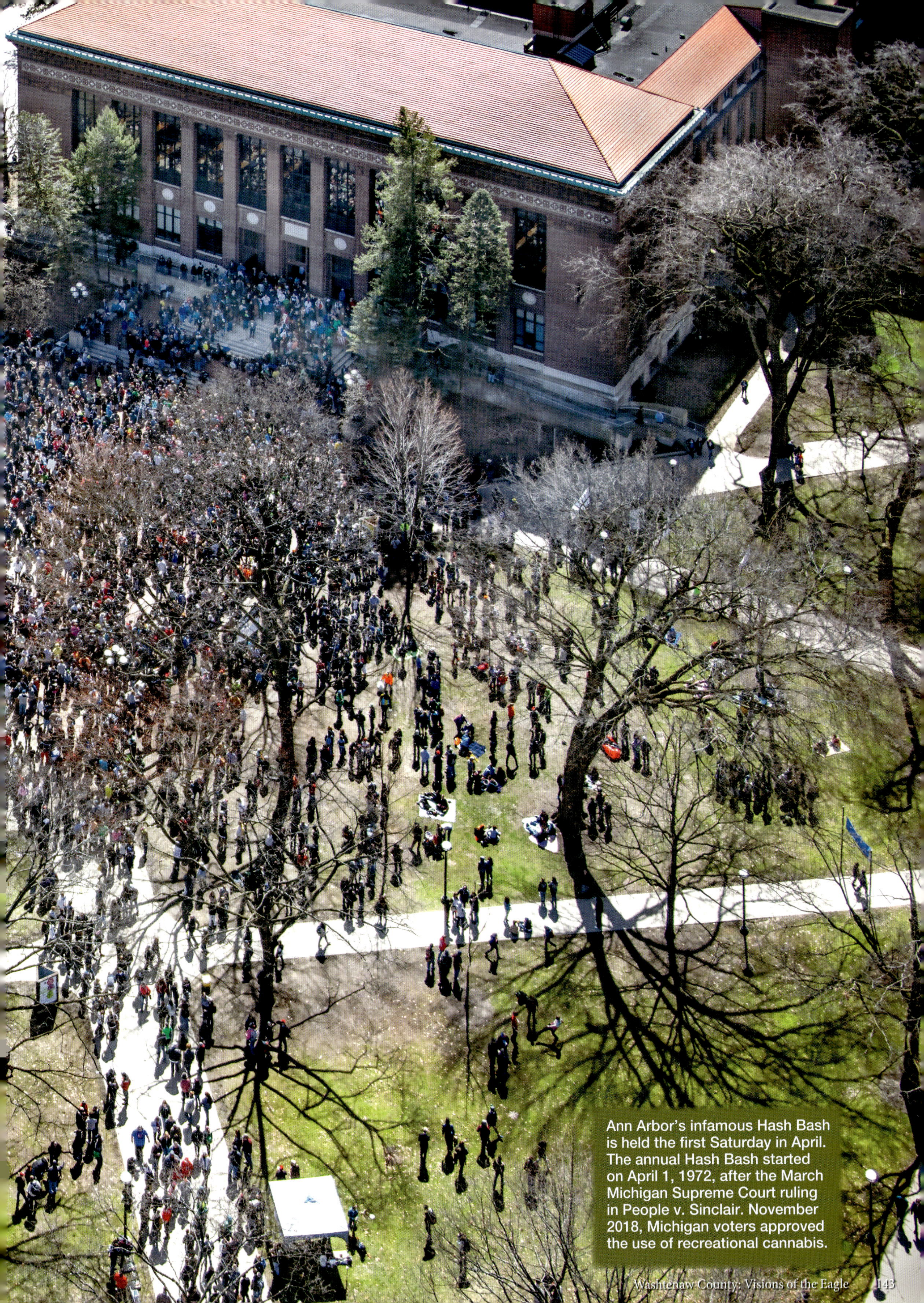

Ann Arbor's infamous Hash Bash is held the first Saturday in April. The annual Hash Bash started on April 1, 1972, after the March Michigan Supreme Court ruling in People v. Sinclair. November 2018, Michigan voters approved the use of recreational cannabis.

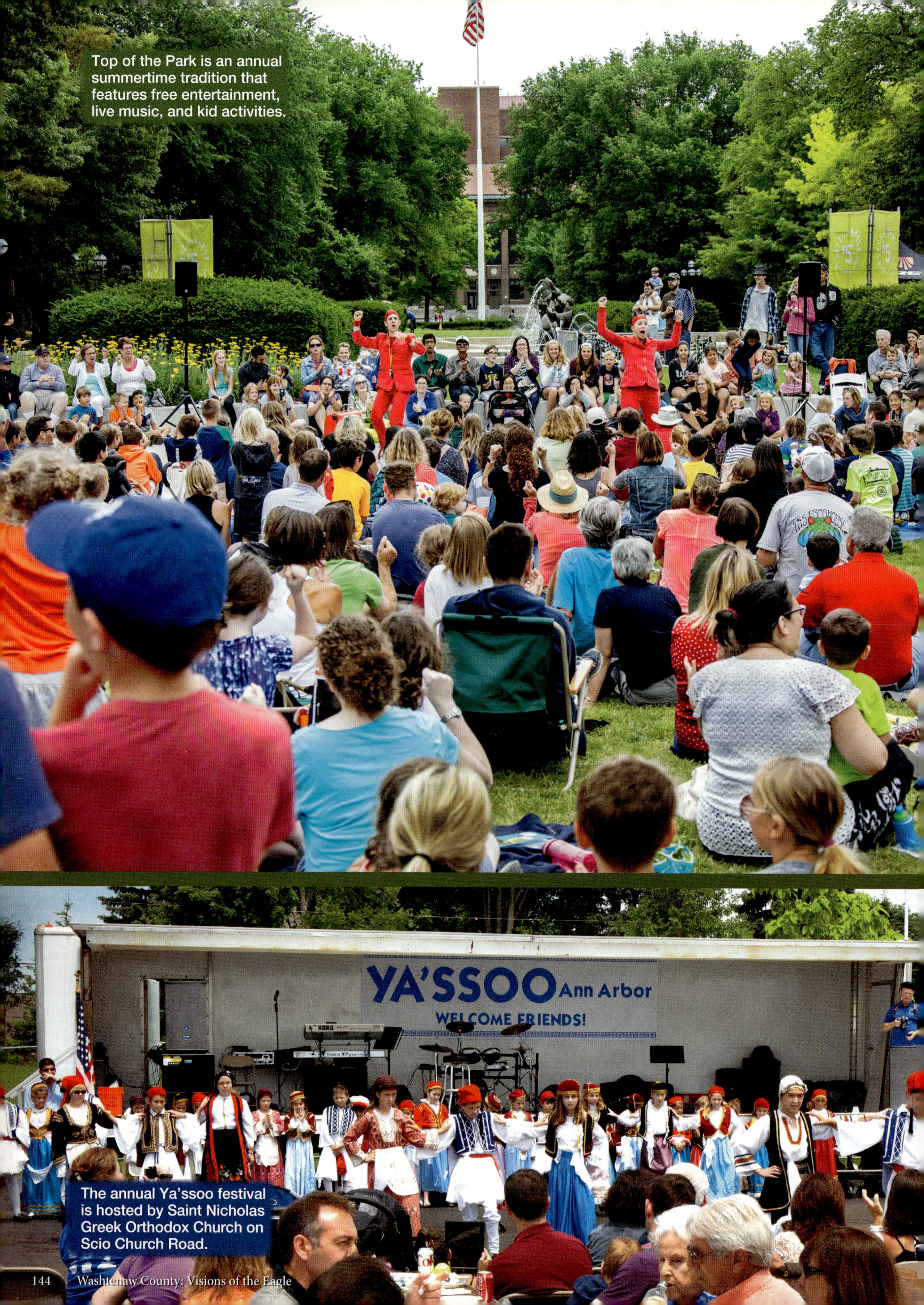

Top of the Park is an annual summertime tradition that features free entertainment, live music, and kid activities.

The annual Ya'ssoo festival is hosted by Saint Nicholas Greek Orthodox Church on Scio Church Road.

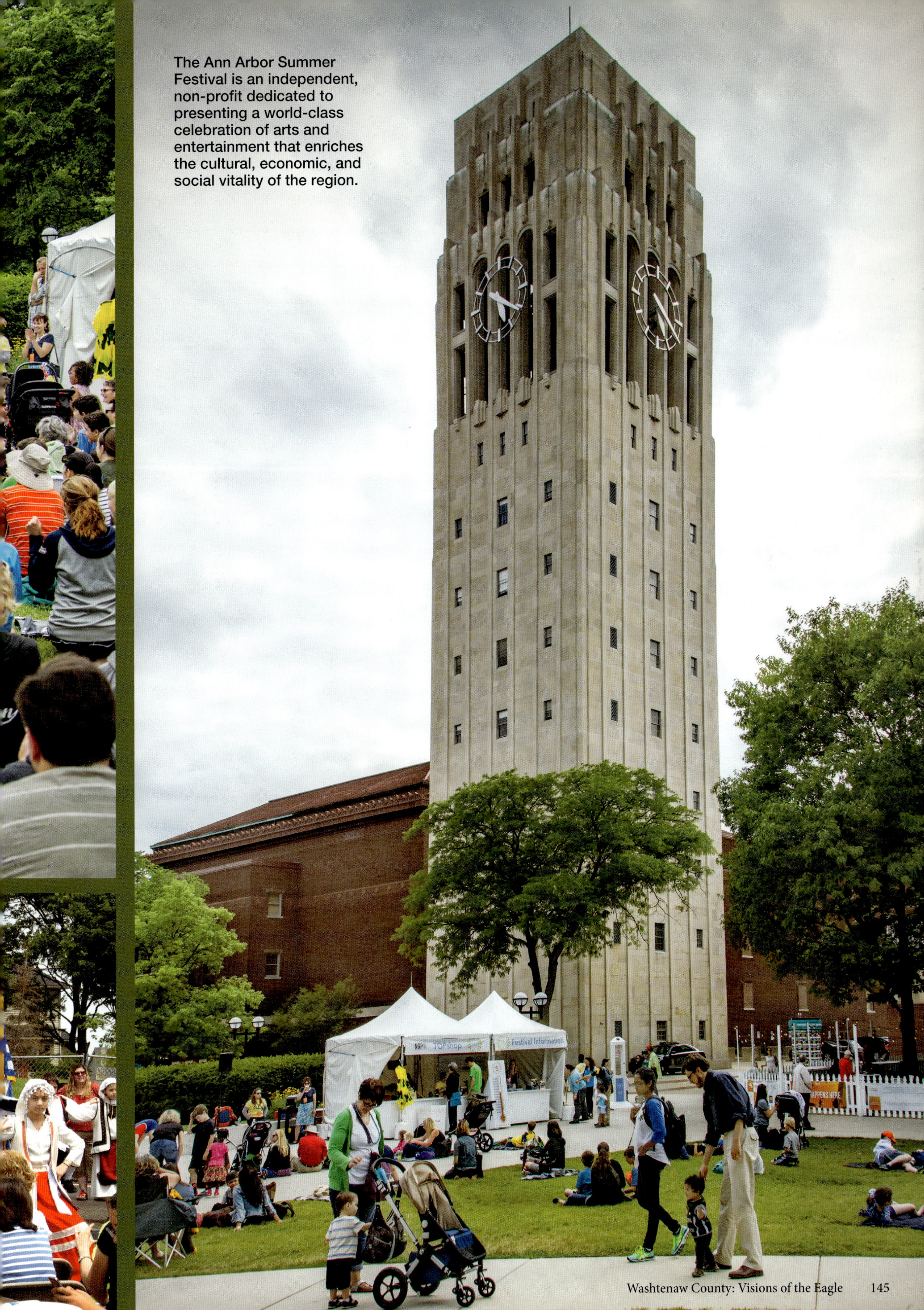

The Ann Arbor Summer Festival is an independent, non-profit dedicated to presenting a world-class celebration of arts and entertainment that enriches the cultural, economic, and social vitality of the region.

Ronald McDonald House Charities - Ann Arbor

Giving Children What They Need Most – Their Families

The Ronald McDonald House Charities Ann Arbor (RMHCAA) has been built around one simple idea – nothing else should matter when a family is focused on the healing of their ill child. Since opening the doors 35 years ago, the RMHCAA has impacted thousands of children and families during their greatest time of need. Soft beds, warm showers and home-cooked meals are just a few of the ways RMHCAA alleviates stress and anxiety for families, so their main focus remains on the health and well-being of their child. Over the course of a year, over 1,100 families stay in the Houses, and nearly 2,000 are served by the Hospitality Carte Program in the hospital. All services are provided at no cost to families, regardless of length of stay.

Families come from all over the United States as well as from around the world to access medical care at C.S. Mott Children's Hospital. Often, they have no arrangements for a place to stay, and no expectation of how long they will be away from home and family. In addition to the stress of being far from home, they may have to leave their jobs to be near their sick child, so there is added financial stress. Because RMHCAA is right across the street from the hospital, and families do not have to pay to stay, they can focus on what is most important – the healing of their child.

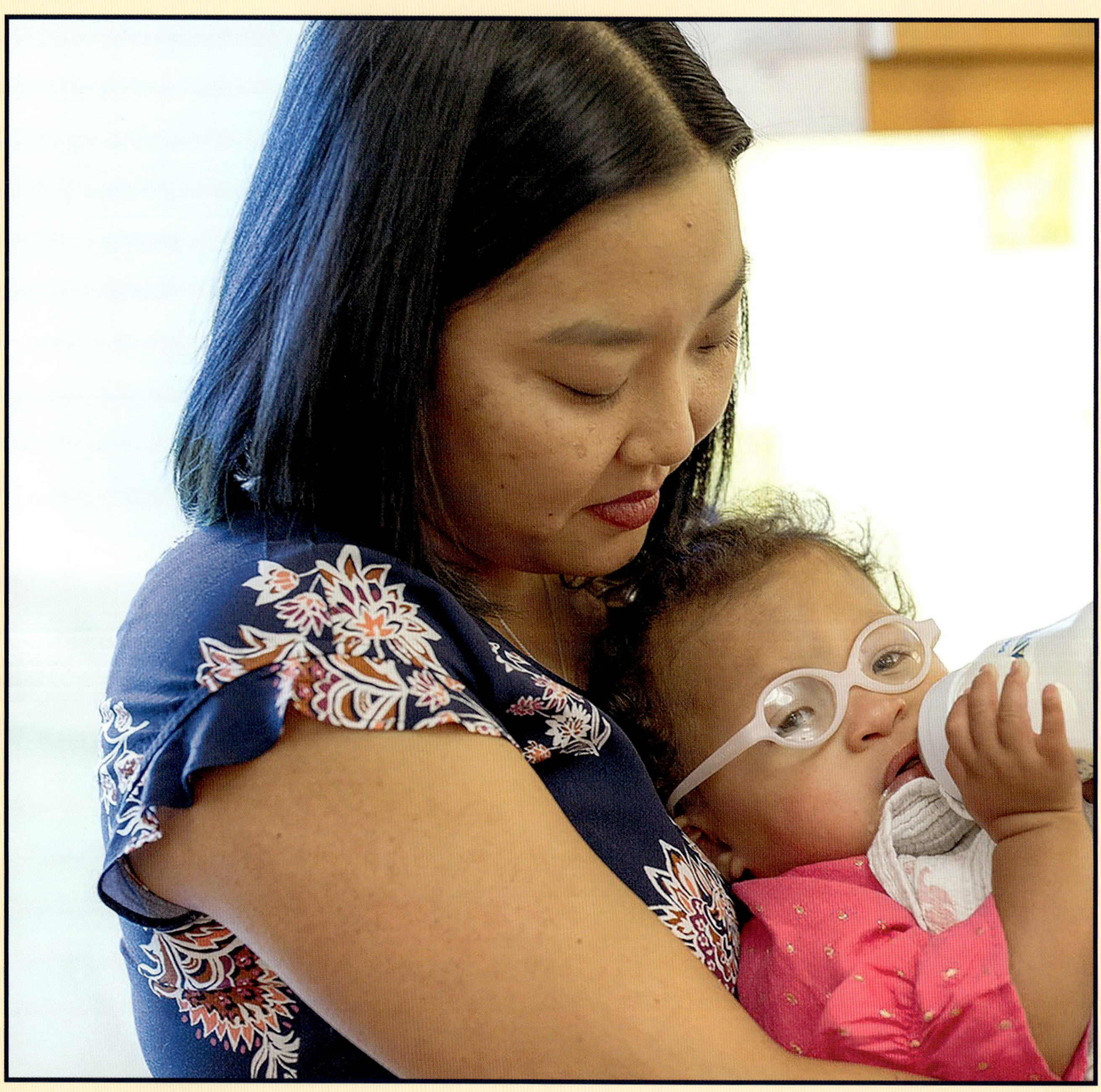

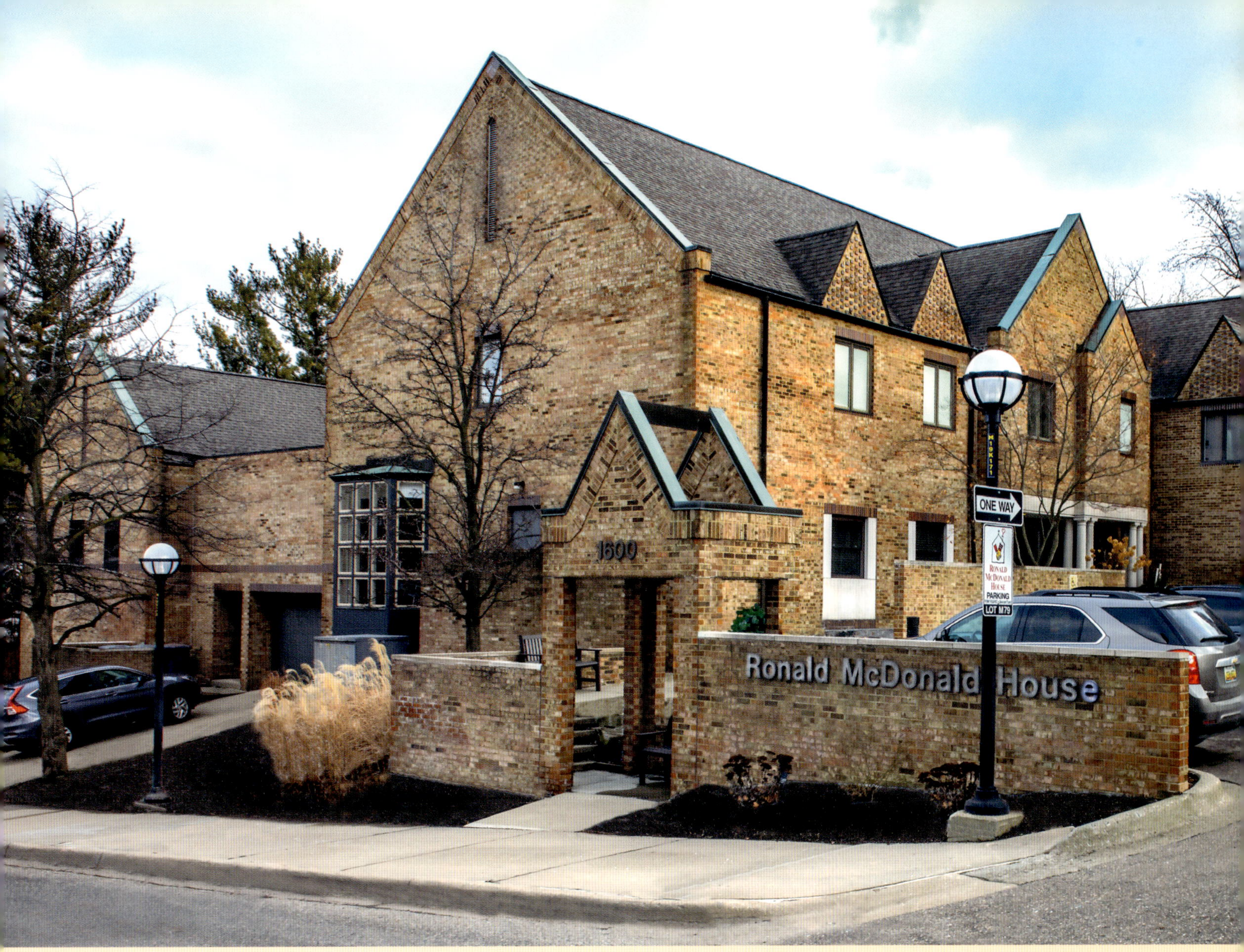

"I don't even know how to begin to thank you! My family was blessed enough to stay at the Ronald McDonald House during our son's stay in the NICU. He was born at 25 weeks and was in the NICU for over 70 days. Thanks to your generous support I was able to stay here with him. We live over four hours away and without the RMHCAA we would have only been able to come on weekends. He is our first child and we were so scared. I will always remember the kindness received when we checked in, how grateful I was to have a warm meal that I didn't have to prepare (and take time away from our son) and a comfortable bed away from hospital noises. Thank you so much!"

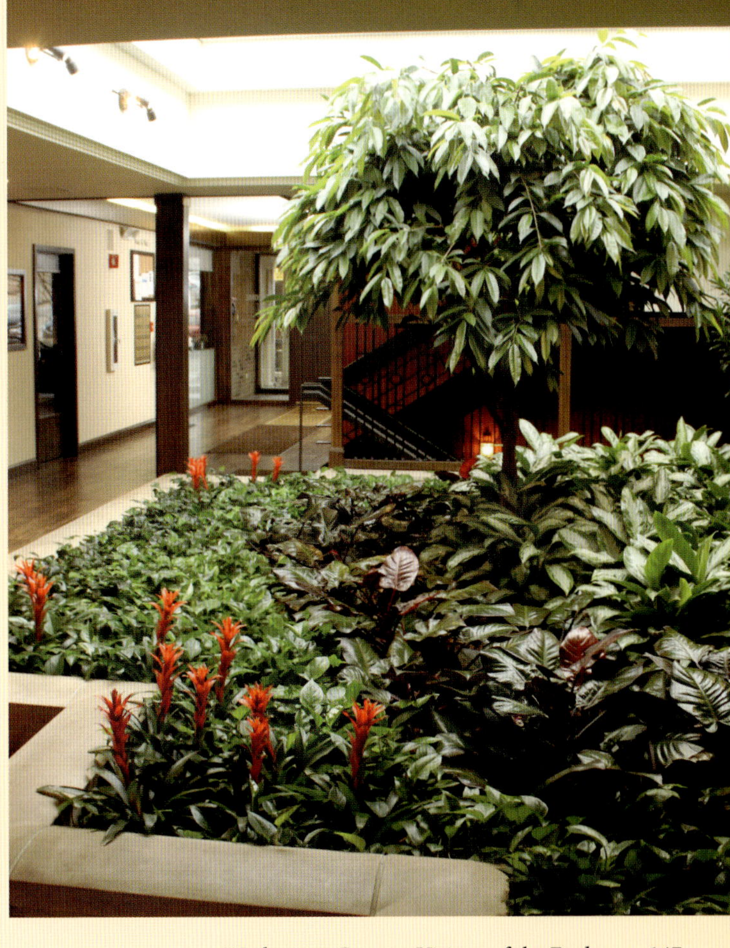

Ronald McDonald House Charities Ann Arbor

1600 Washington Heights ~ Ann Arbor, MI 48104
734-994-4442 ~ www.rmhcannarbor.org

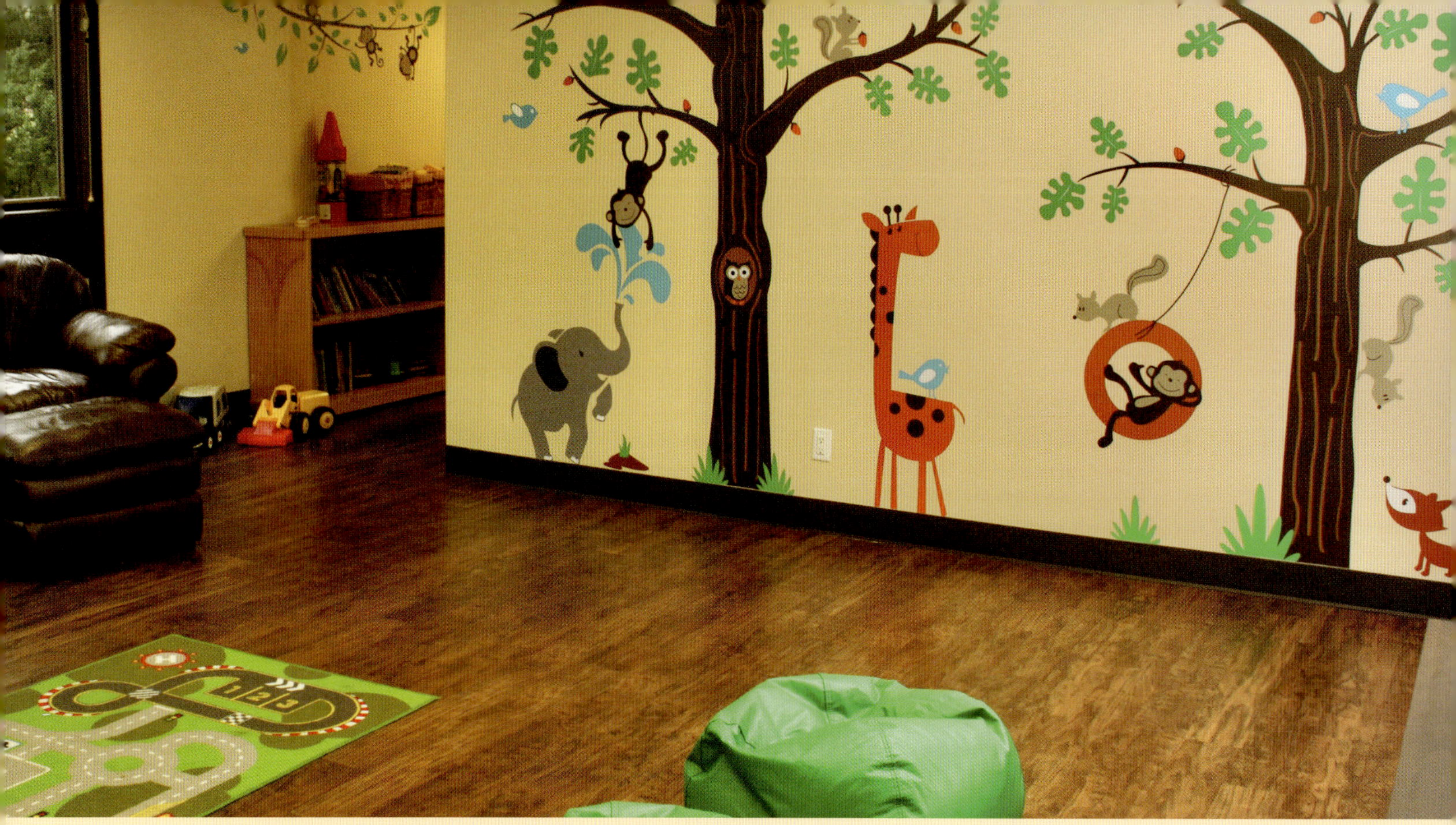

The Playroom is stocked with toys, games, and a playhouse for siblings who are staying at RMHCAA.

A Place To Call "Home"

The Main House

RMHCAA has served over 29,000 families since its opening in 1985. Located on the campus of the University of Michigan, across the street from Michigan Medicine's C.S. Mott Children's Hospital, families find the comforts of home with 31 private bedrooms and bathrooms, a large kitchen, laundry facilities, several living rooms for relaxation, and indoor and outdoor play areas for children. Families stay for two weeks to several months, and sometimes even more than a year, the House is always full.

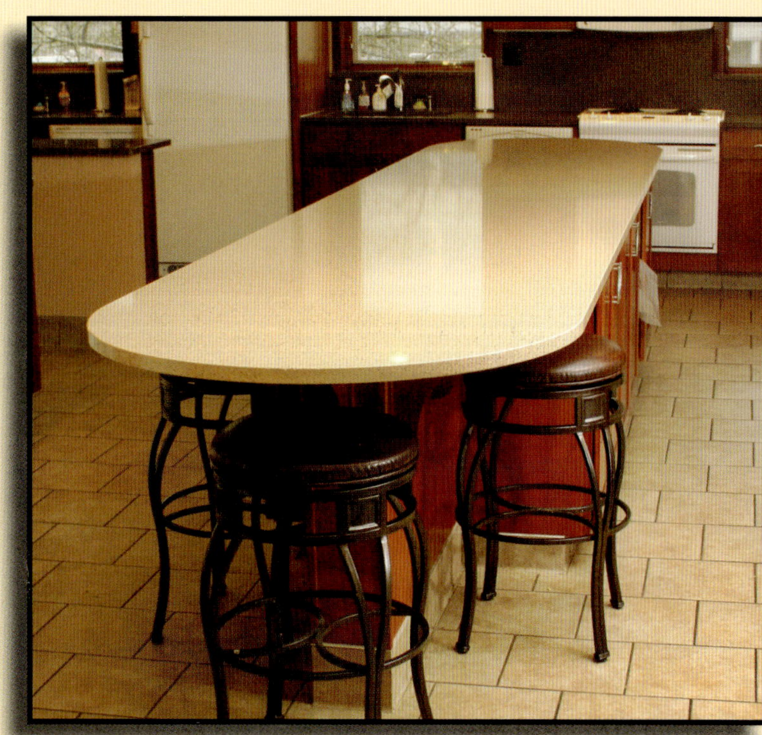

Meals are prepared by volunteers nightly in our Kitchen, so families have a hot meal waiting for them after a long day in the hospital.

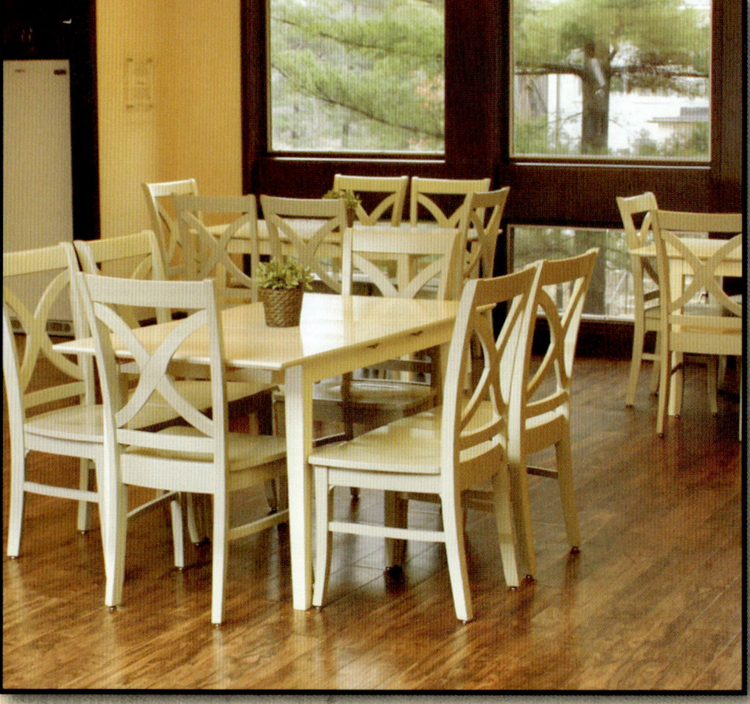

The Dining Room is a gathering place in the evening for families to touch base with each other and enjoy a hot meal.

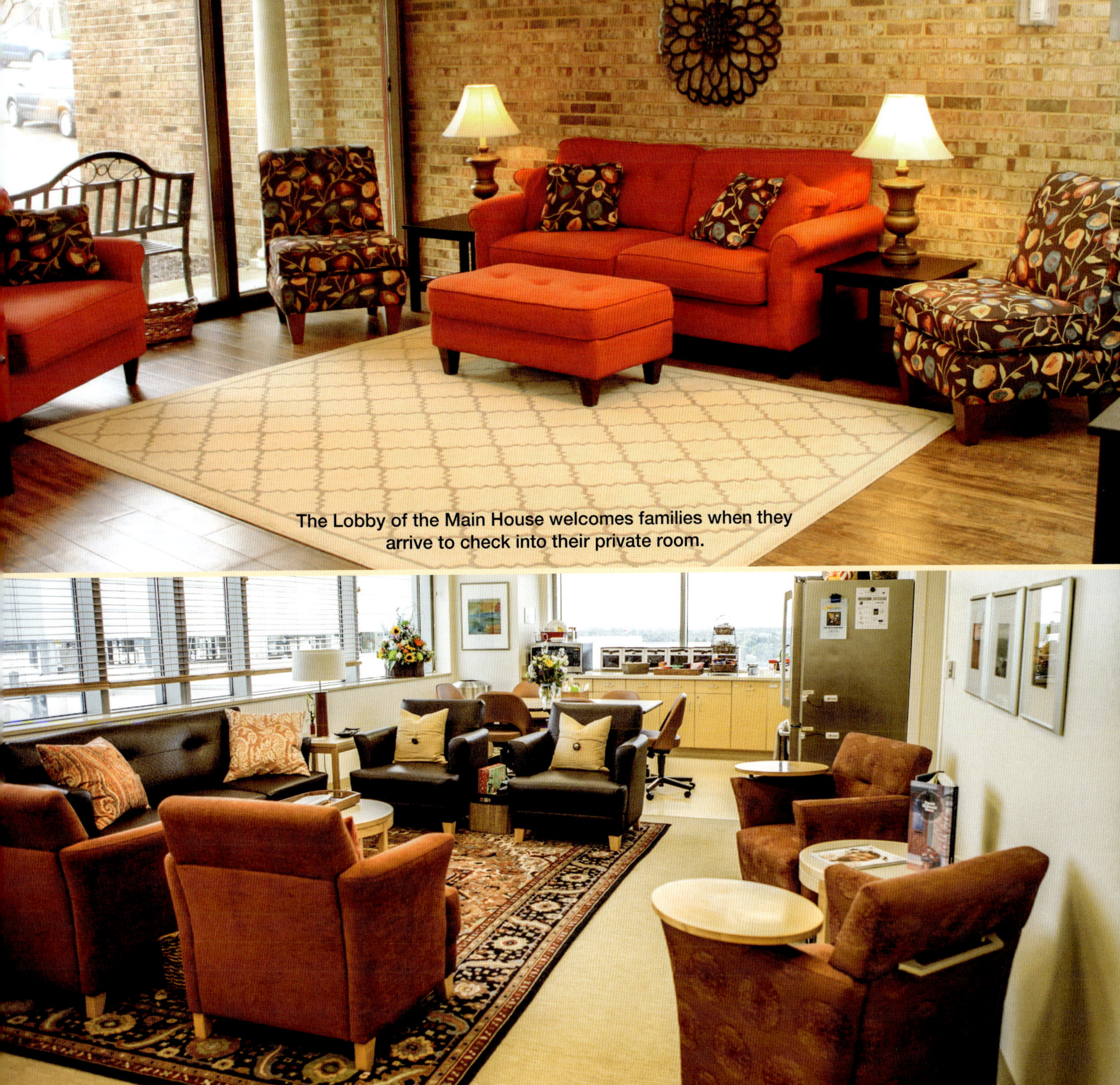

The Lobby of the Main House welcomes families when they arrive to check into their private room.

The Lobby of the Mott House is a place for families to relax and refresh for a moment with a hot cup of coffee and a snack, just steps away from their child.

The Ronald McDonald House within C.S. Mott Children's Hospital

The Ronald McDonald House within C.S. Mott Children's Hospital offers 12 bedrooms that include private rooms and bathrooms and was the 11th of its kind upon opening in 2011. A lounge, kitchenette and eating area offer a place that feels like home, steps away from a child's bedside. The House within the Hospital is reserved for the most medically fragile patient families, since being across the street is just too far.

Hospitality a la Carte Program

The Ronald McDonald Hospitality a la Carte Program provides needed resources and comfort items to families directly in patient rooms and waiting areas. The Carte can be found circulating through the halls, stocked with hygiene and comfort items, a selection of healthy snacks, family-centered activities, games, and craft kits. The Hospitality a la Carte program allows Ronald McDonald House Charities Ann Arbor to serve families who may not be staying at one of the Houses, allowing us to support even more families.

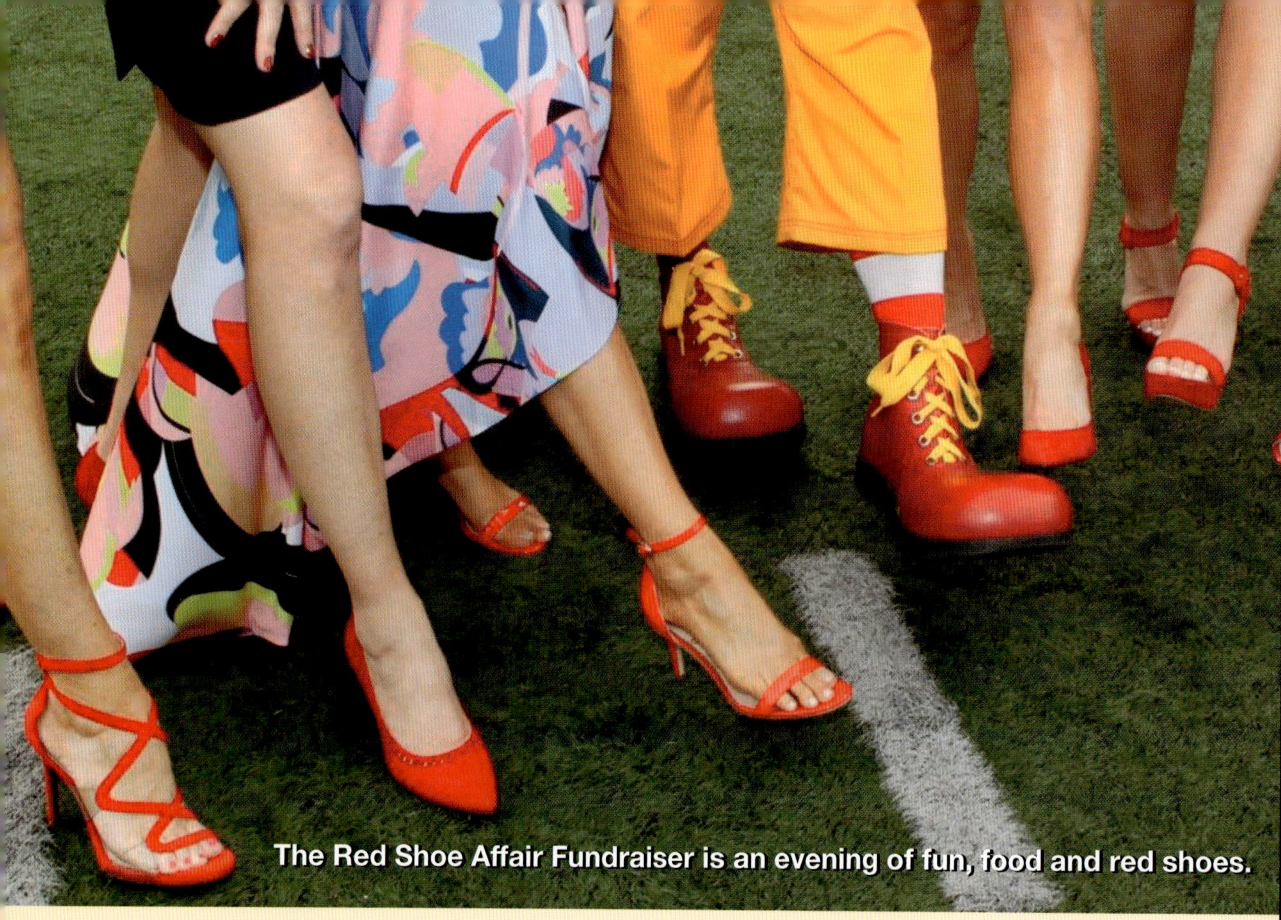

The Red Shoe Affair Fundraiser is an evening of fun, food and red shoes.

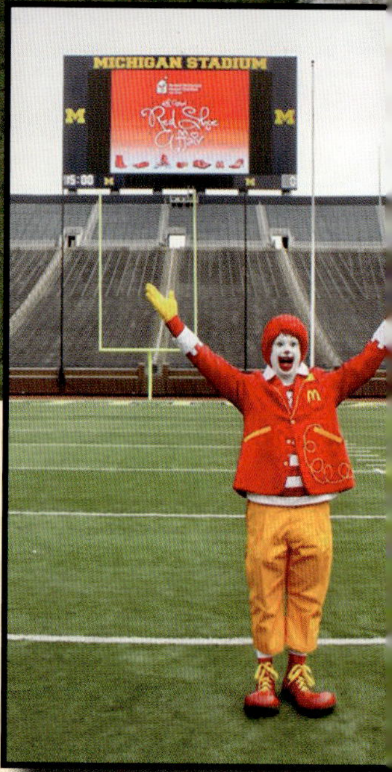

"We cannot express our gratitude and appreciation enough for giving us space to rest and recharge while being steps away from our daughter in the NICU. We are grateful for the wonderful hospitality and kindness we experienced during our stay. Thank you for all that you do to keep families close together!"

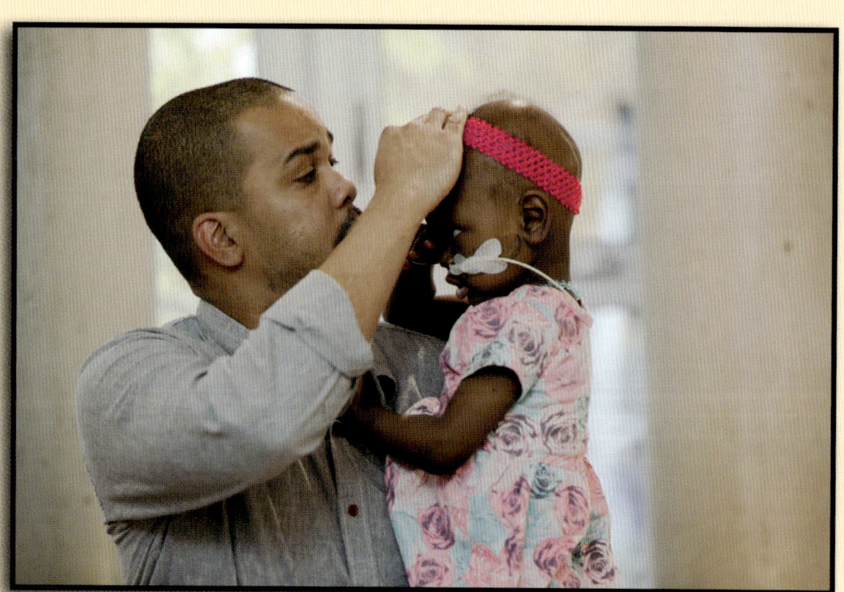

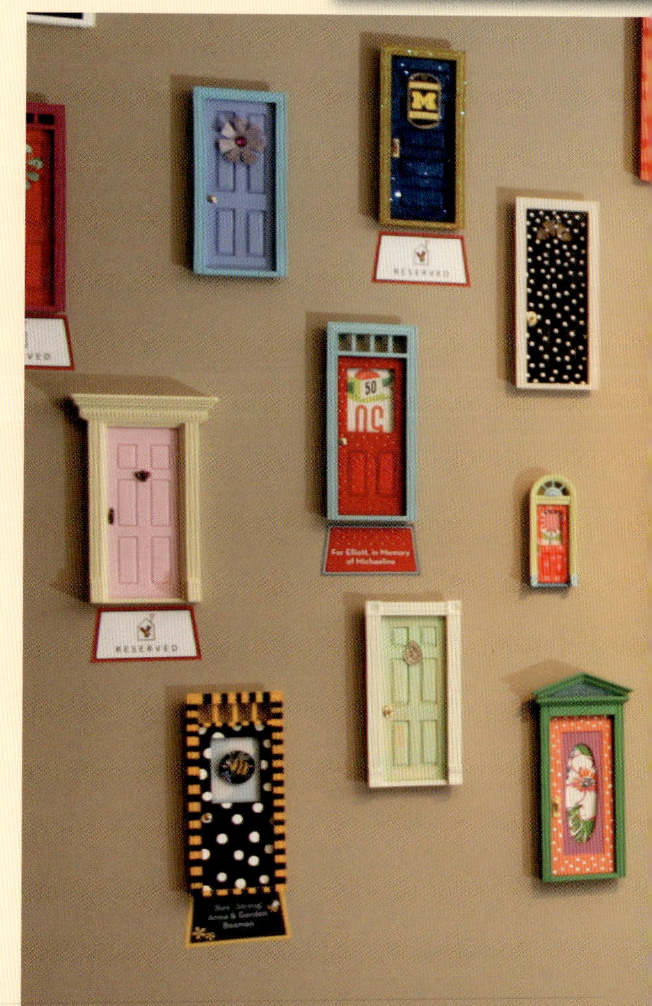

"As a couple that was blindsided eight months into pregnancy with our first child with a heart disorder, we needed some good luck. Thankfully it was provided to us via RMHCAA and the excellent care we received there, across the street from the hospital. Your service is the welcome part in a stormy sea; words do no justice."

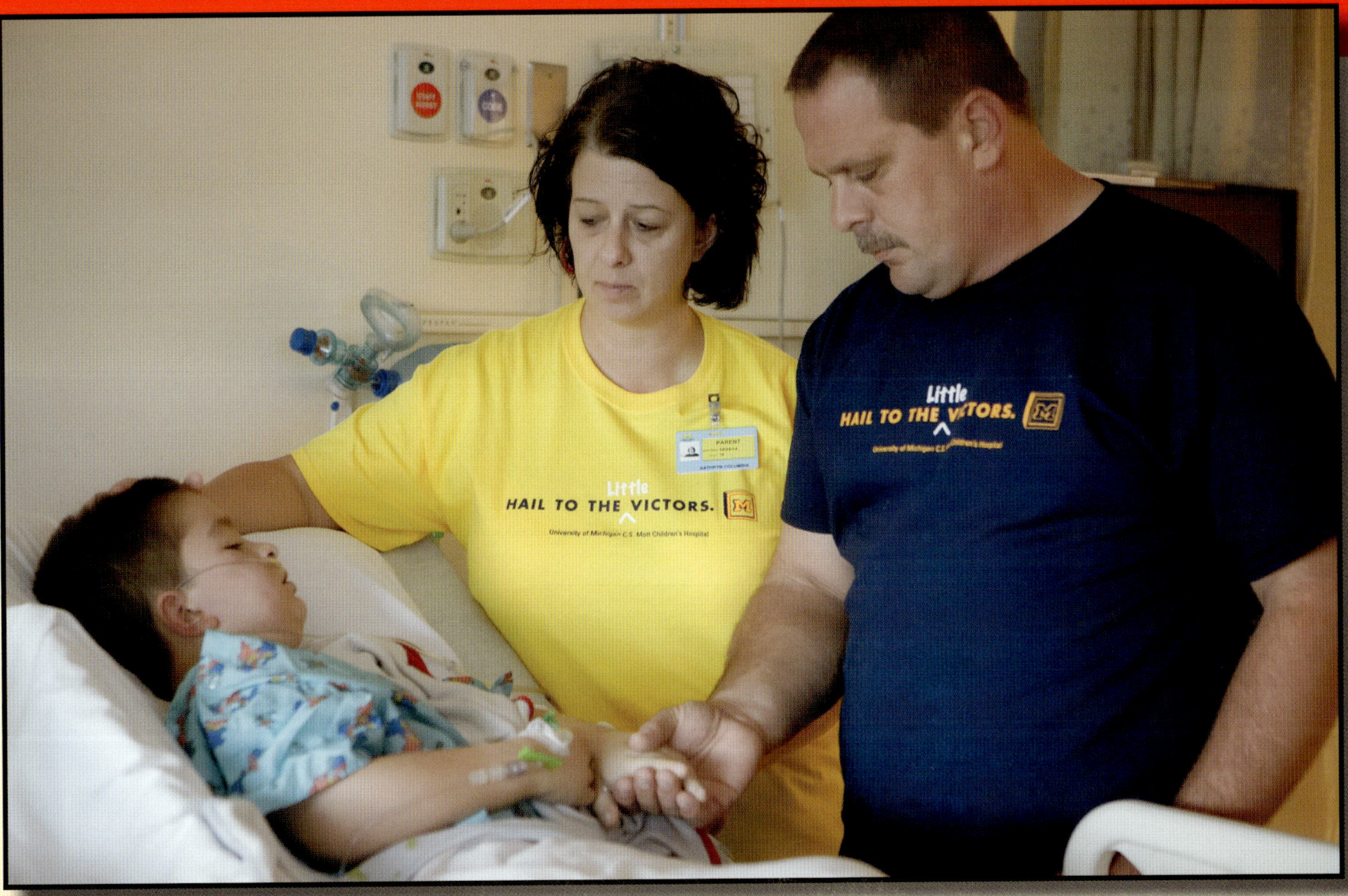

"Thank you for helping us stay close to our son, who had heart surgery. We live in Missouri and when we got to Michigan we didn't know where we were going to stay. The night of the surgery after we knew he had made it through fine, the social worker told us that we could stay in the Ronald McDonald House. It was such an answer to our prayers..."

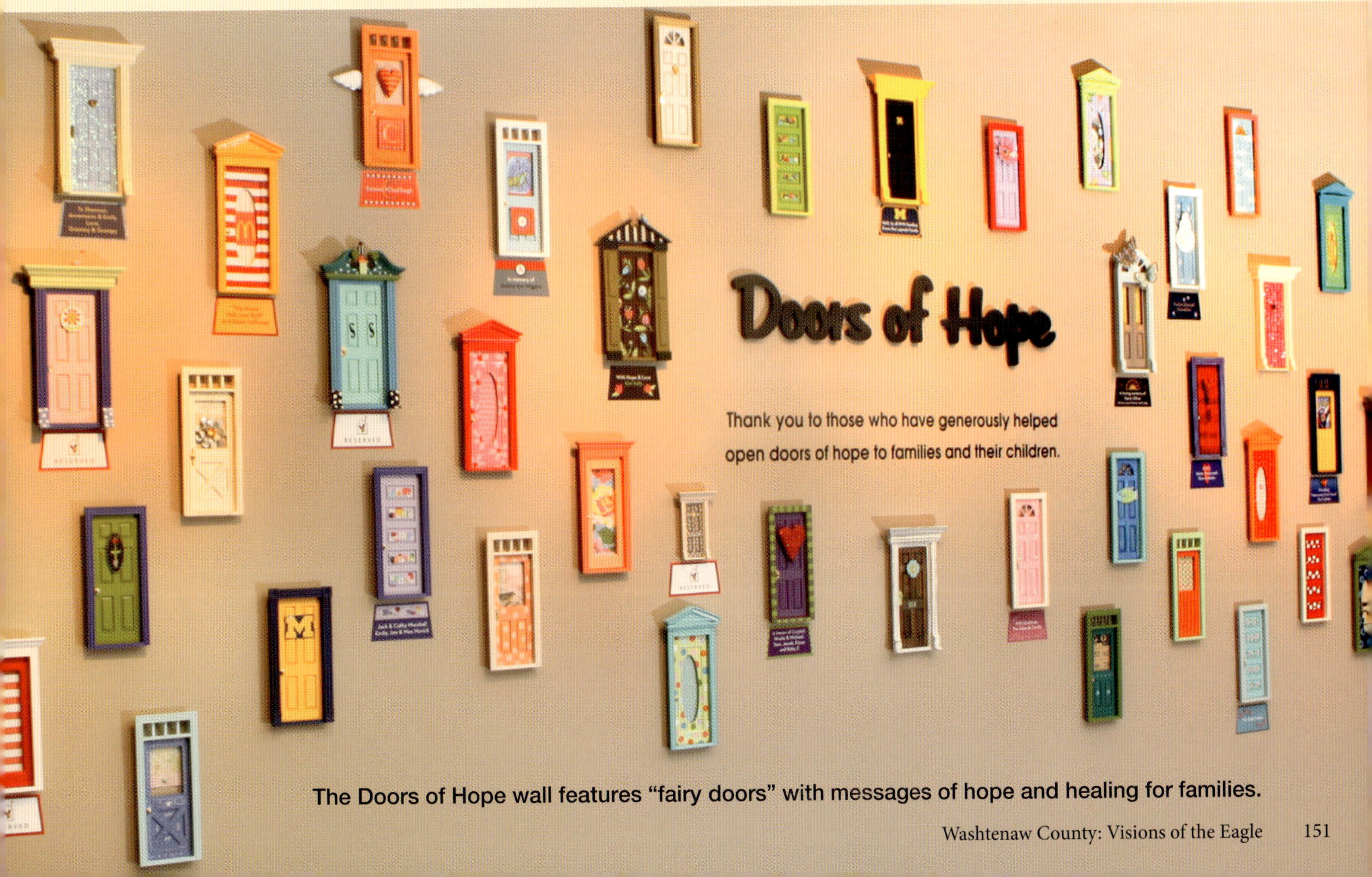

Doors of Hope

Thank you to those who have generously helped open doors of hope to families and their children.

The Doors of Hope wall features "fairy doors" with messages of hope and healing for families.

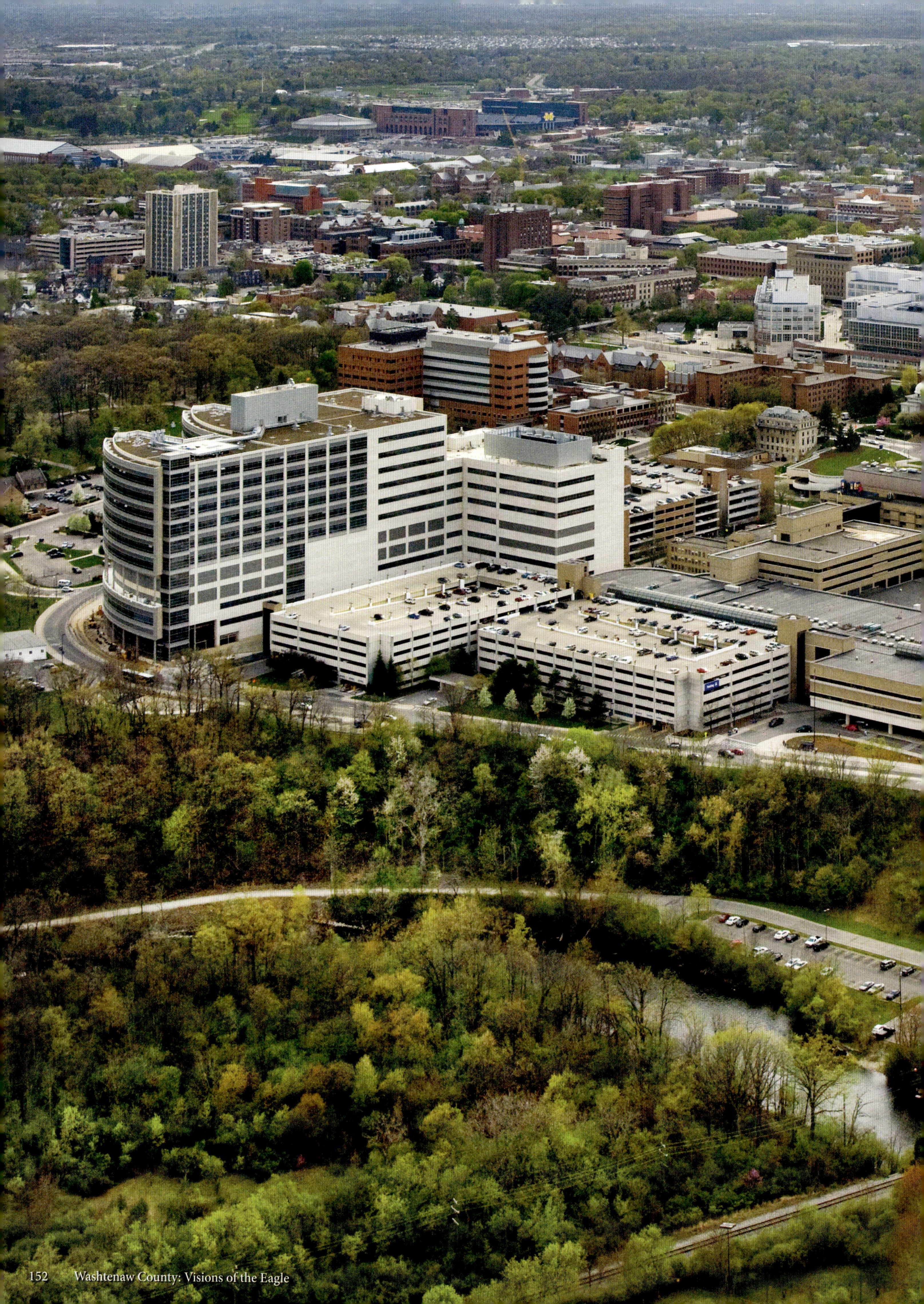

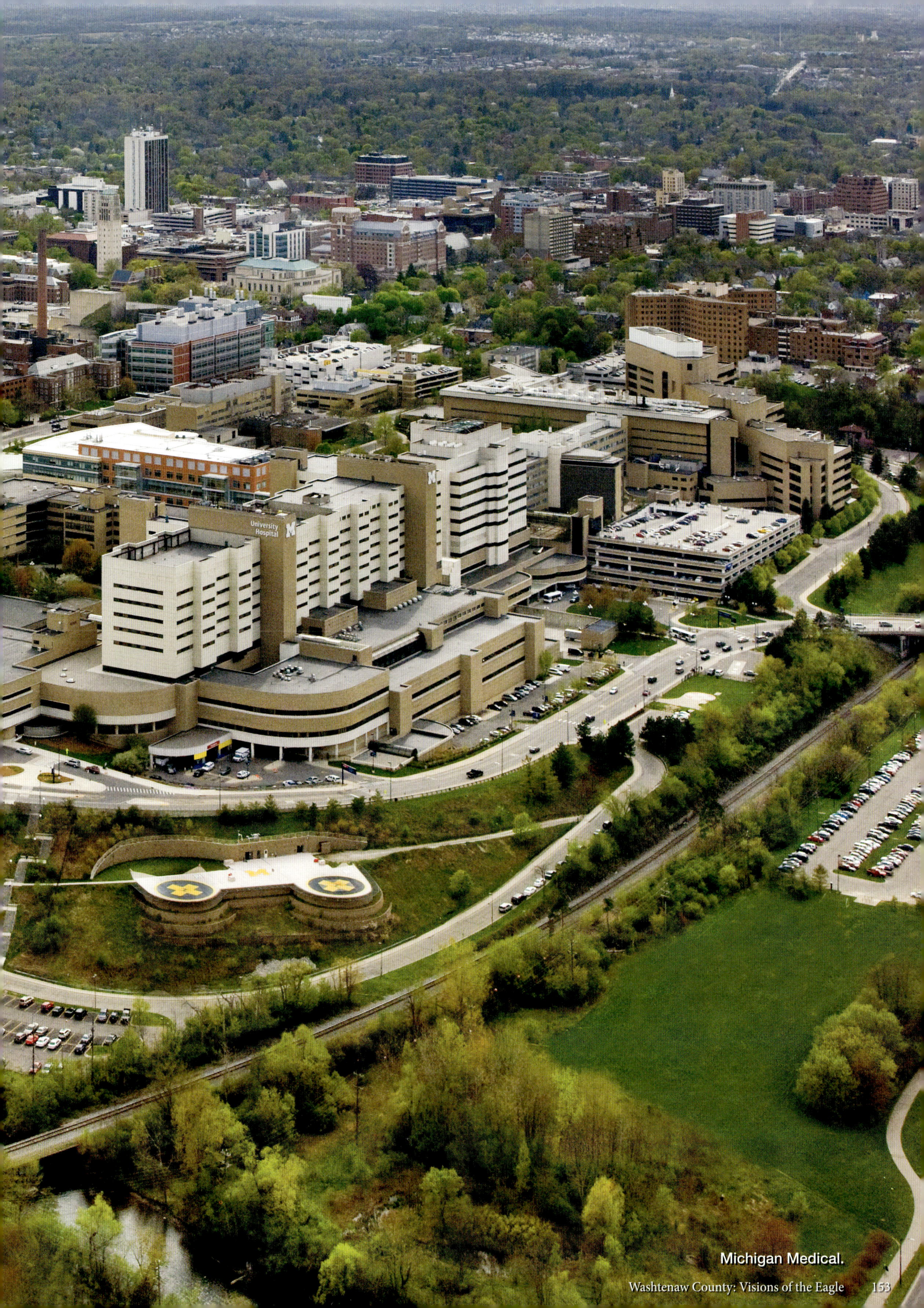

Michigan Medical.

U-M Transplant Center

They were there at the beginning, from the beginning. The first transplant performed at Michigan Medicine was also the first transplant in the state of Michigan. Between that moment in 1964 when the scalpel was raised to remove a kidney from one sister and transplant it into her twin, all the way to the present moment, their curiosity, determination and ever-growing experience have sparked the hope of a new life for thousands of patients.

The U-M Transplant Center at Michigan Medicine brings together specialists in adult and pediatric heart, kidney, pancreas, liver and lung transplantation. Additional transplantation services are available through the Kellogg Eye Center, Comprehensive Cancer Center and C.S. Mott Children's Hospital.

Survival Flight operates 24 hours a day, 365 days a year and is at the ready to transport donor organs at a moment's notice. More than 200 people participate as providers in the transplant care continuum exclusively, which makes them one of the largest centers in the country. Their experience in taking on complex cases gives families a place to turn when their loved ones are at their most vulnerable, and each patient benefits from highly individualized specialty care. Their research is leading to treatment options that can delay or even eliminate the need for a transplant, while also advancing the medications and technologies that make safe, effective transplants possible. Their programs train tomorrow's transplant leaders with mentors who are passionate about education. Patients and their families find comfort in the boundless support provided by expert caregivers, peers, and a myriad of activities and events tailored to the transplant community.

Since 1964, U-M Transplant Center at Michigan Medicine has been there and they will continue to be there for patients and families for years to come.

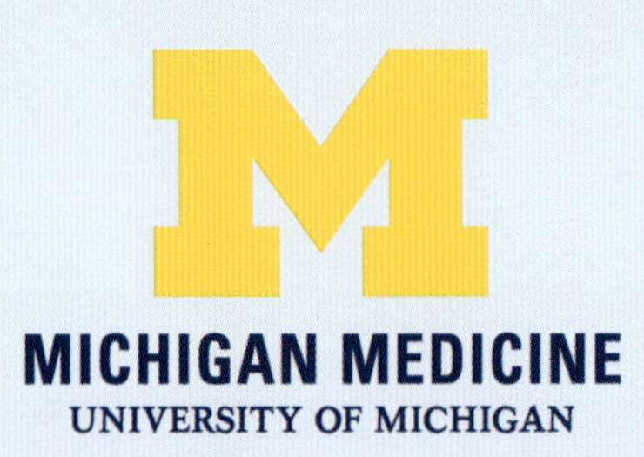

To give to the Transplant Center and learn about events supporting our mission:
www.umtransplantevents.org

For patients and families and to learn about our care and services:
www.uofmhealth.org/transplant

For more information on upcoming events:
www.umtransplantevents.org

1-800-333-9013

John R. Charpie, M.D., PhD. is Division Director and Amnon Rosenthal Professor of Pediatric Cardiology at C.S. Mott Children's Hospital. His clinical focus is on cardiac intensive care for infants, children, and young adults with congenital and acquired heart disease. Dr. Charpie enjoys mentoring and teaching junior colleagues and trainees, and he is actively involved in multiple research projects aimed at improving outcomes for patients and their families.

John is also an organ donor who, at the age of 18, donated a kidney to his brother David at Massachusetts General Hospital. As a high school student, David suddenly and inexplicably developed acute renal failure requiring hemodialysis.

The gift of a kidney from his brother John gave him a second chance thanks to his transplant. David and his wife Joanne now live in the suburbs outside of Boston. They are blessed with four healthy children and several grandchildren who are their absolute pride and joy.

David is eternally grateful for the opportunity to enjoy a full and healthy life for the last 35 years, thanks to organ transplantation.

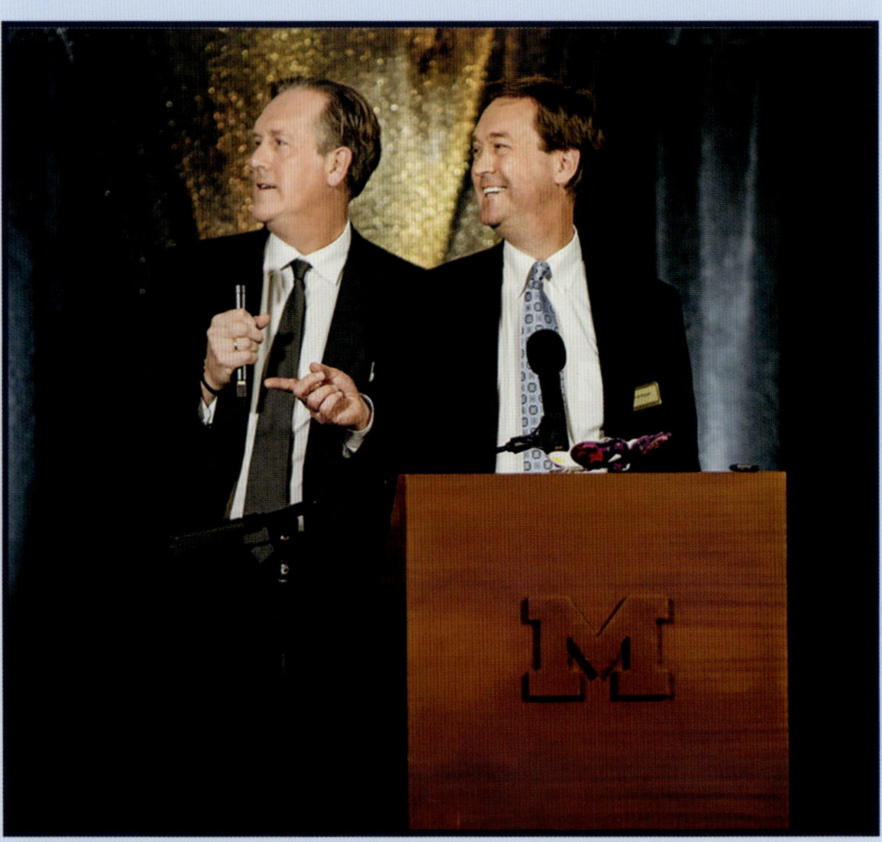

John R. Charpie (L) with brother David Charpie (R) at the 2018 University of Michigan Transplant Center Vita Redita ("Life Restored") Gala at Michigan Stadium. The brothers told their inspirational story of donation and transplantation at the event.

Steven Dye

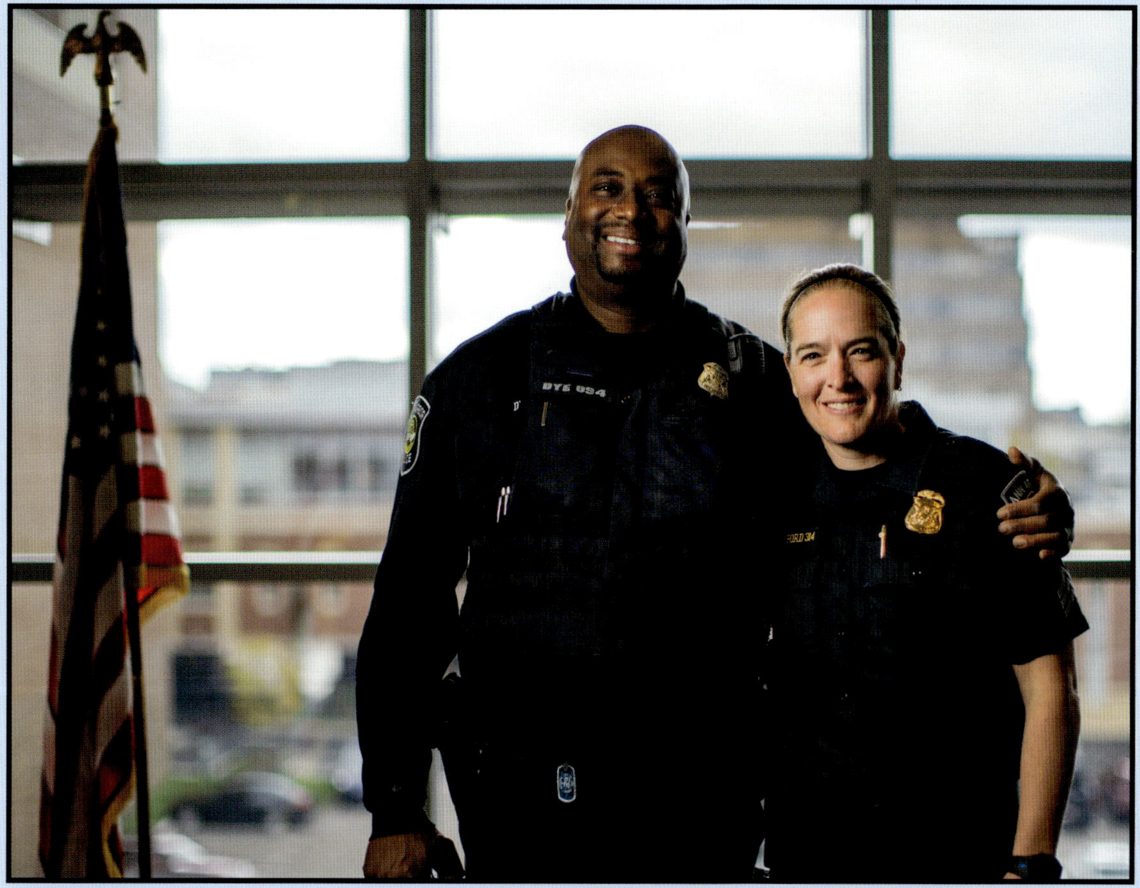

Officer Steven Dye (L), kidney transplant recipient with Sergeant Jamie Crawford (R) living kidney donor. Photo Credit: Bryan McCullough

Ann Arbor Police Sergeant Jamie Crawford says it's in a police officer's nature to help others. That is why she offered to be evaluated as a living kidney donor after she learned fellow officer Steven Dye had late-stage kidney disease. "I was caught off guard by her offer," says Dye. "She asked if she could help and that meant a lot."

Bev Cherwinski

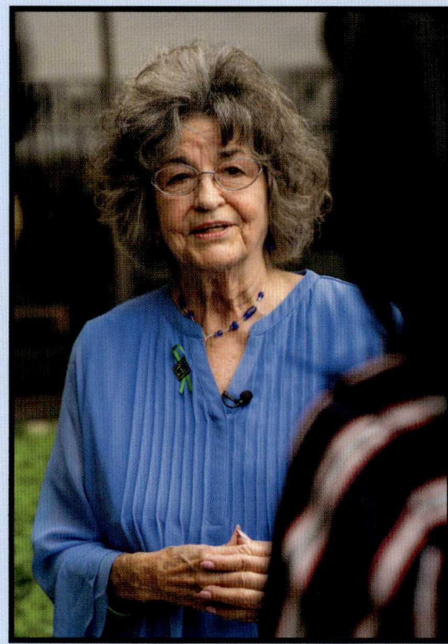

Bev Cherwinski
Photo Credit: Cherwinski family

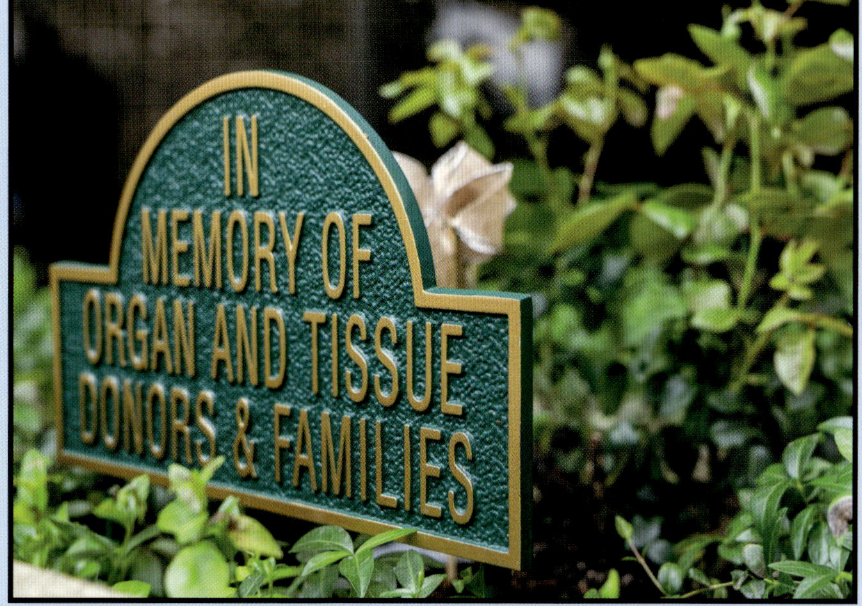

The memorial plaque and rose bush at Michigan Medicine, located outside the entrance to the Taubman Center, is fittingly near the Survival Flight memorial sculpture. Photo Credit: Camren Clouthier

For 20 years, Bev Cherwinski, lung transplant recipient, has said "thank you" with roses. "After I recovered from the procedure, I went from existing to living again," she says. "I had a spring in my step and wanted to give back to the process that helped me get to where I am today." Since then, Bev has given back to organizations that helped her gain new life by organizing rose bush planting ceremonies with Gift of Life Michigan.

Devin O'Halloran

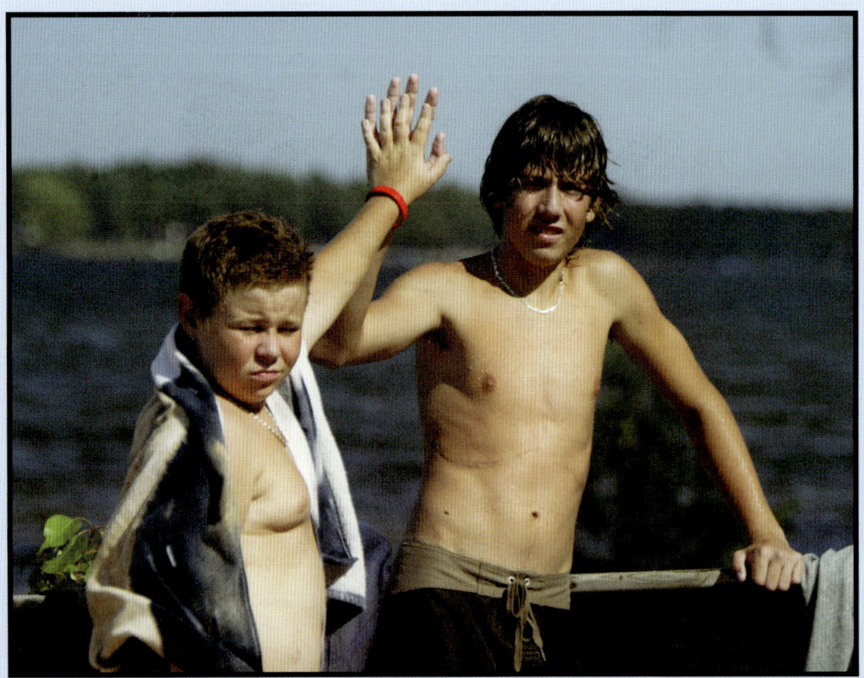

Devin at age 15 with a fellow camper at Michitanki.
Photo credit: Marilyn Indahl

Devin O'Halloran remembers very little of life at age 5, when he received a life-saving liver transplant. Devin often talks of his best memory of that day-his Dad telling him on the way into surgery: "I love you."

Devin recovered quickly and was invited at age 6 to join other Michigan liver transplant kids to attend Camp Chihopi in West Virginia. When the U-M Transplant Center announced in 2003 that it would be hosting its own transplant camp, Devin's parents immediately began to organize a benefit golf event so more children could go. The Camp Michitanki Golf Classic presented by Victory Honda remains a vibrant and successful annual event.

Devin's father Dan is a seasoned NHL referee, yet he found time to help transplant kids by organizing the golf event. While Dan's work sees him crisscrossing the U.S. and Canada every week, he continues his dedicated work on the Camp Michitanki Golf Classic.

Today, Devin is 29 years old and lives north of Ann Arbor with his wife Brie and their son Connor, who was born in 2018. Devin is the Assistant Golf Professional at Oak Pointe Country Club in Brighton, MI.

Devin and his son Connor presenting prizes to winning golf teams at the 2019 Michitanki Golf Classic.

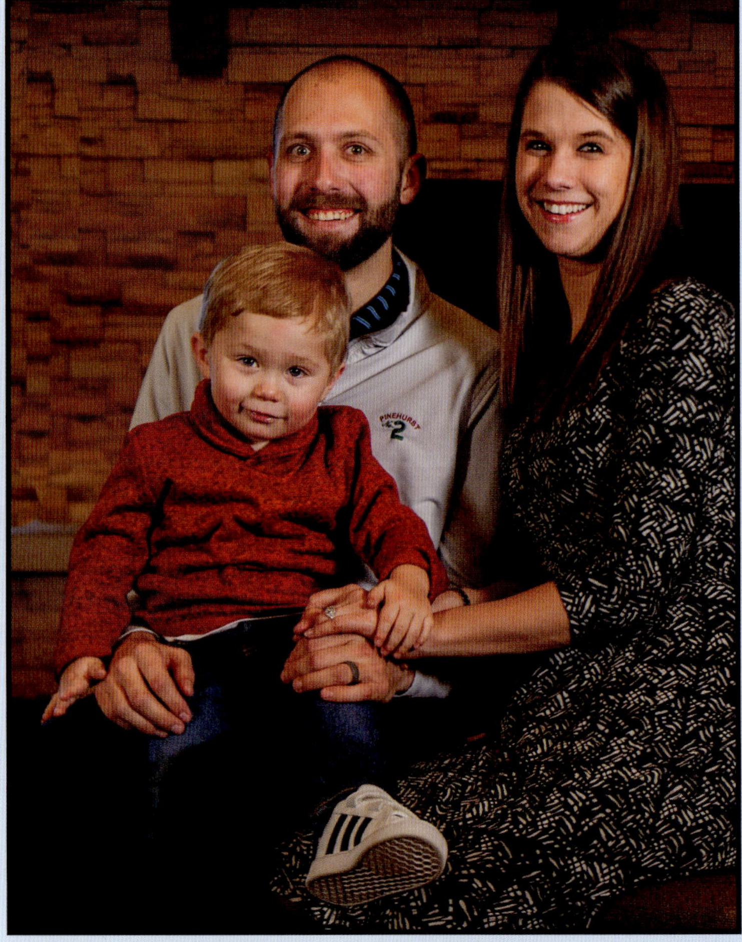

Transplant recipient, Devin O'Halloran, with wife Brie and son Connor.
Photo credit: Bob Garypie

Tommy Schomaker

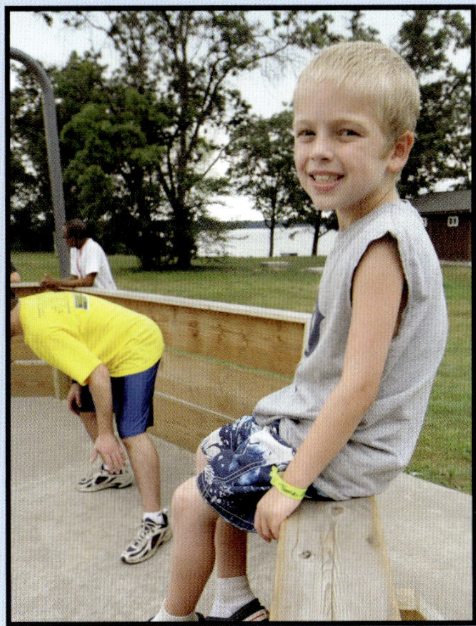

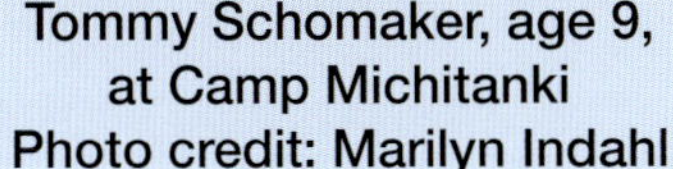

Tommy Schomaker, age 9,
at Camp Michitanki
Photo credit: Marilyn Indahl

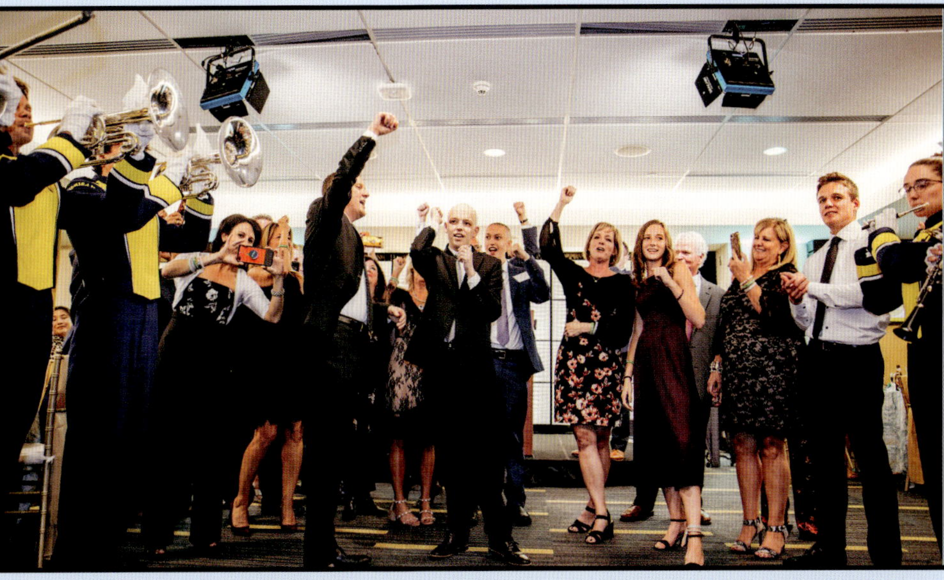

Tommy Schomaker (center) surrounded by family at the 2019 Vita Redita gala as the University of Michigan Marching Band plays the Michigan State University fight song for Tommy, who is enrolled as a freshman at MSU.

Tommy Schomaker was born December 10, 2000 at C.S. Mott Children's Hospital with a severe congenital heart defect called Hypoplastic Left Heart Syndrome. He endured five open heart surgeries by age five and then went into heart failure.

At seven, Tommy was placed on the heart transplant waiting list. A year later, he and his family received the call that a new heart was available. Tommy received his miracle and gift of life on June 3, 2009.

Tommy graduated from Lutheran High Northwest in Rochester, Michigan in 2019, planning to attend Michigan State University. His college plans were postponed when he was diagnosed with cancer shortly after his high school graduation.

Tommy fought through rigorous chemotherapy to overcome the cancer, spending many weeks in the same hospital where he was born and where he received his heart transplant.

Despite his physical challenges, Tommy gathered the strength to speak at the 2019 Transplant Center Vita Redita Gala. His story was riveting and videos of his speech have been seen by tens of thousands of people via social media. Tommy again rejoiced in his restored health following successful chemotherapy and looks forward to starting at MSU in the Fall of 2020.

Tommy is forever grateful to his donor family as they made the most selfless decision in their darkest hours to donate life. Tommy and his family have stayed in touch with his donor family, and his heart donor's mother attended Tommy's high school graduation in 2019.

Camp Michitanki has always held a very special place in Tommy's heart. He attended camp for nine straight years from the age of nine until 2018 and plans to return as a volunteer.

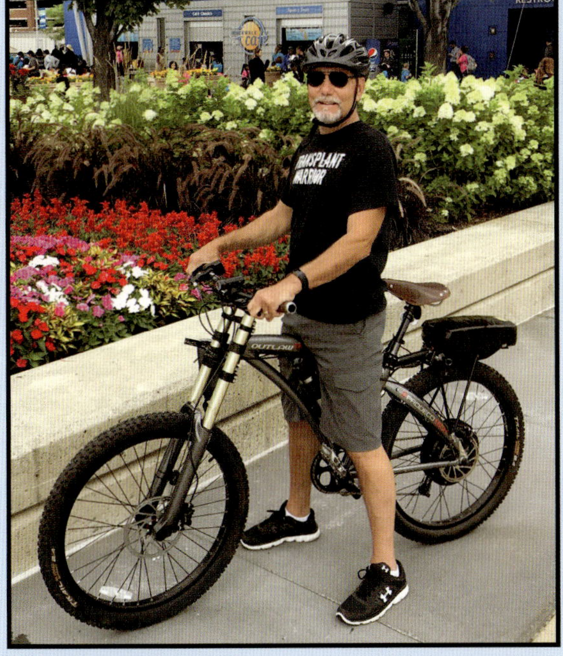

Paul DeWyse

For nearly 20 years, Paul DeWyse fought a losing battle against a rare lung disease which caused his lungs to slowly die. At age 55, he escalated his fight against the disease with the boldest treatment medicine can offer: a double lung transplant.

"I am seriously just so happy to be alive and have a second chance at life," he says.

Paul DeWyse after making a full recovery from his lung transplant.
Photo Credit: DeWyse family

Camp Michitanki

Camp Michitanki (Michigan Transplant Kids) is a summer camp experience originally created by the University of Michigan Transplant Center in 2003. The camp is for children 7-15 years of age who have had an organ transplant. Campers spend six days each summer participating in a variety of activities and they have the opportunity to develop life skills in a fun residential camp setting.

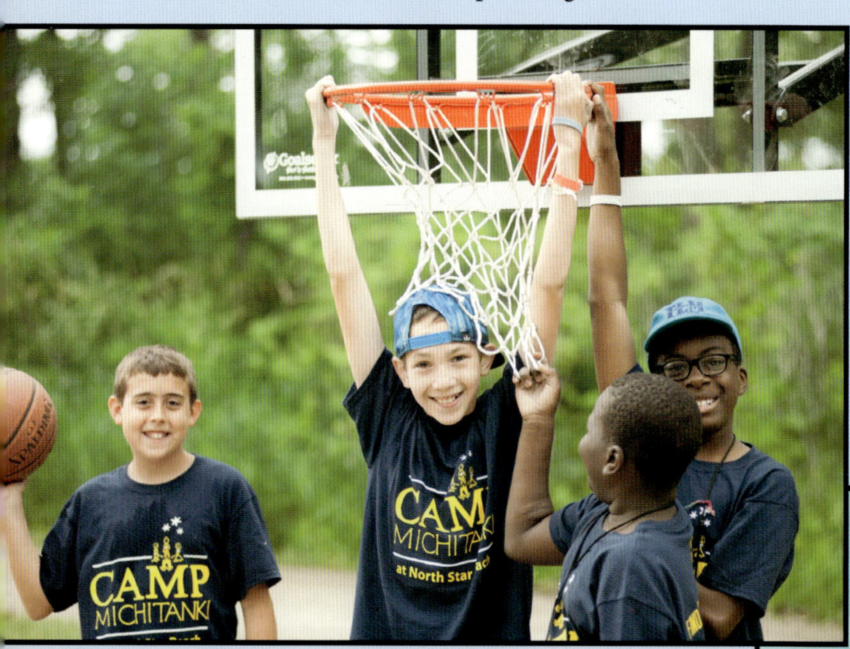

Transplant nurses, physicians, social workers and other community volunteers work with camp staff to provide a "normal" and medically supervised camping experience. Children are divided by age and gender and assigned into cabin groups for the week. Camp Michitanki began as a project of the U-M Transplant Center when it was staged at YMCA camps in Michigan. Today, Camp Michitanki is settled in its forever home – North Star Reach in Pinckney, MI. North Star Reach is a special place, dedicated to providing camp experiences for children with many kinds of medical challenges. One week each summer is Camp Michitanki week – just for transplant kids.

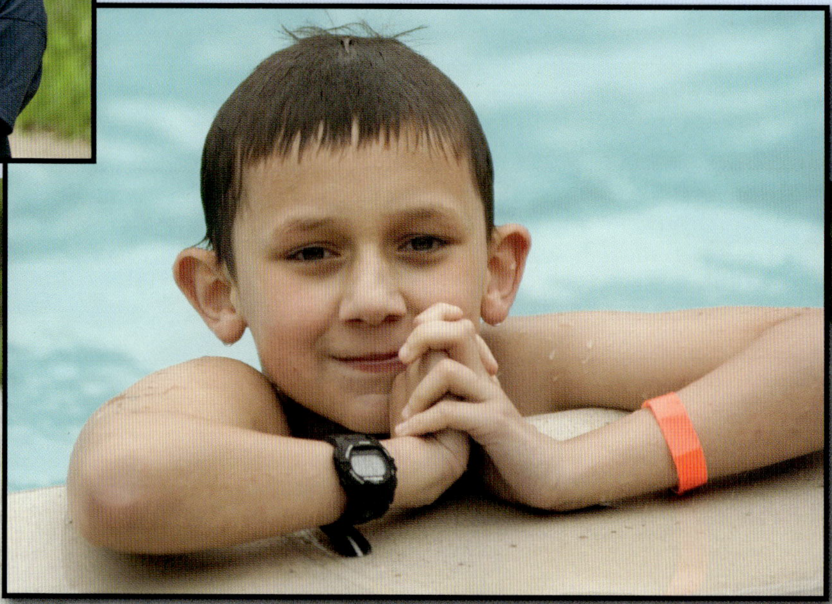

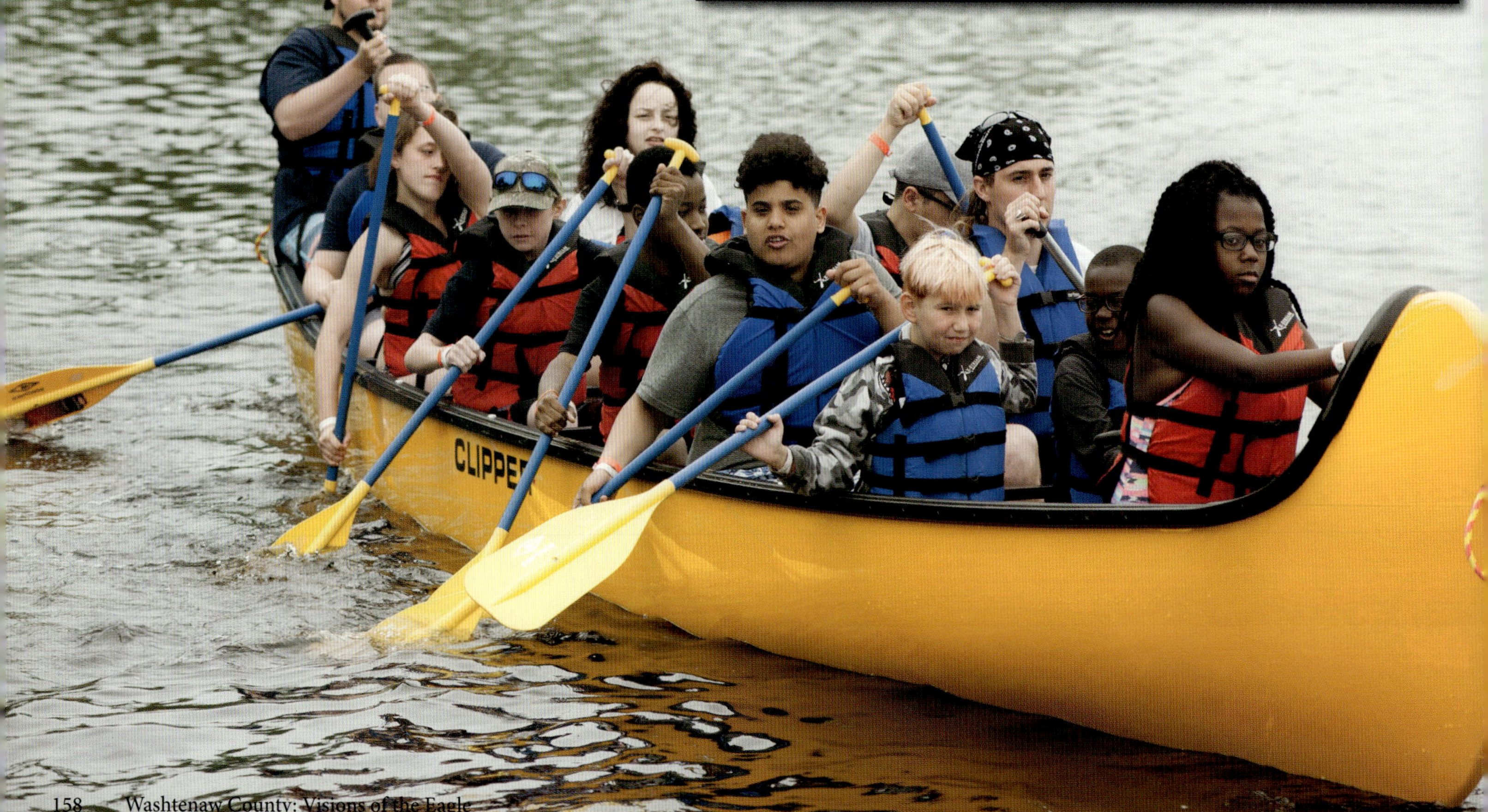

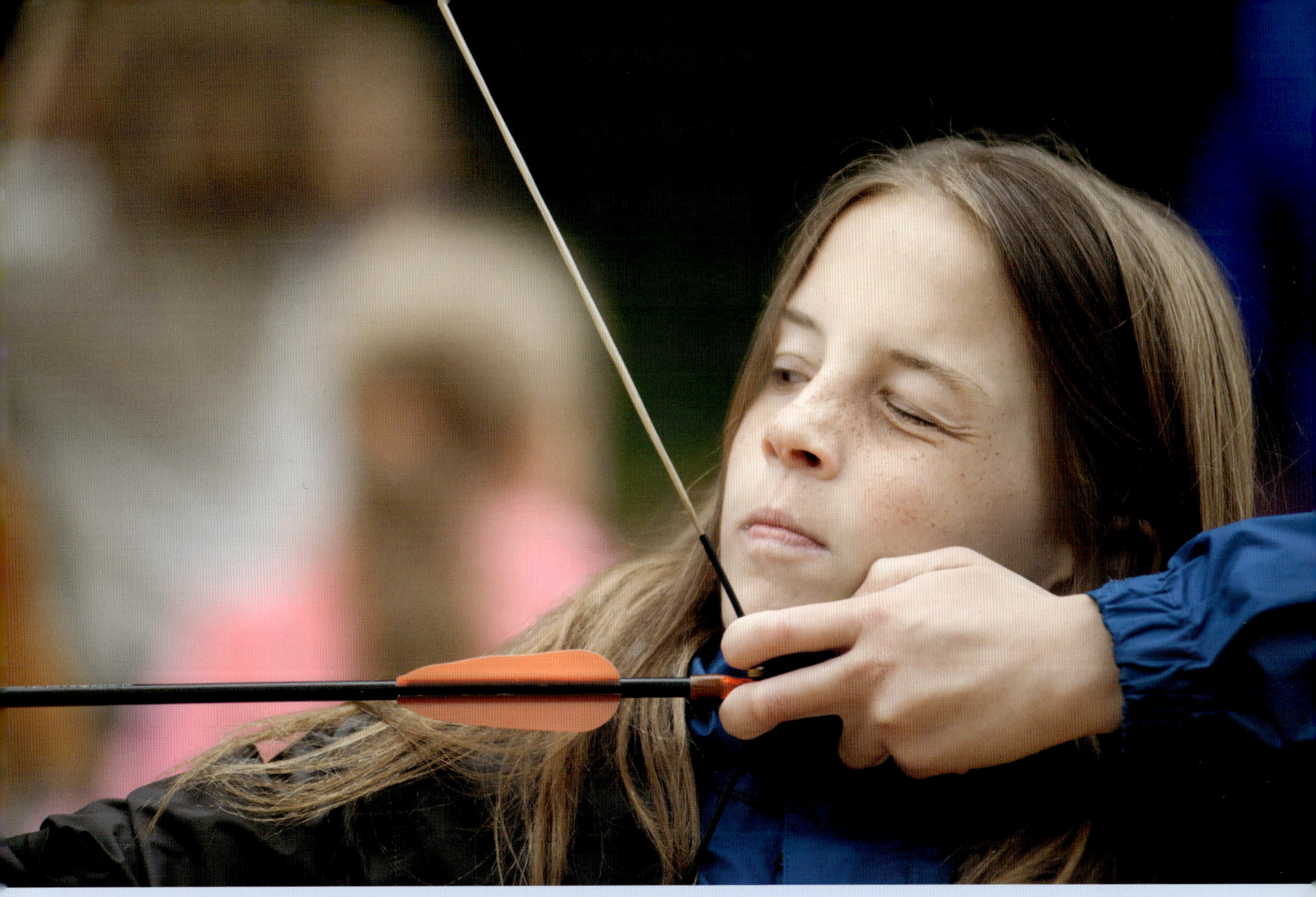

Camp Michitanki is sponsored by the U-M Transplant Center. That support is funded entirely by donations and proceeds from fundraising events. Children who have been very sick and have survived because they received a heart, lung, liver, small bowel or kidney transplant have obstacles that are different than those of other kids. We believe that transplant recipient kids should be exposed to an environment that allows participation in every activity, fosters relationships with kids who have overcome similar medical hurdles, and encourages personal growth through supervised physical and social challenges.

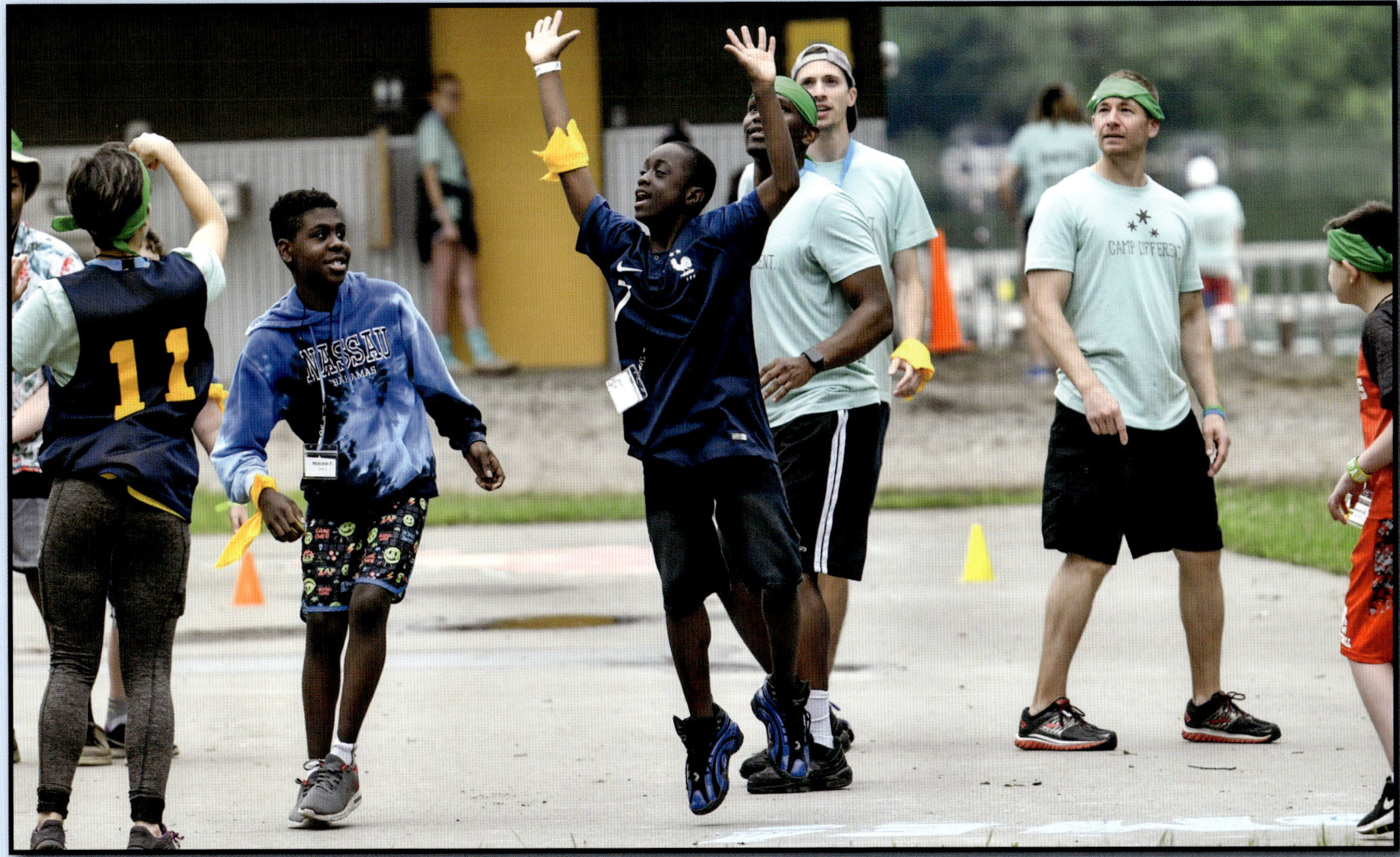

Zion Lutheran

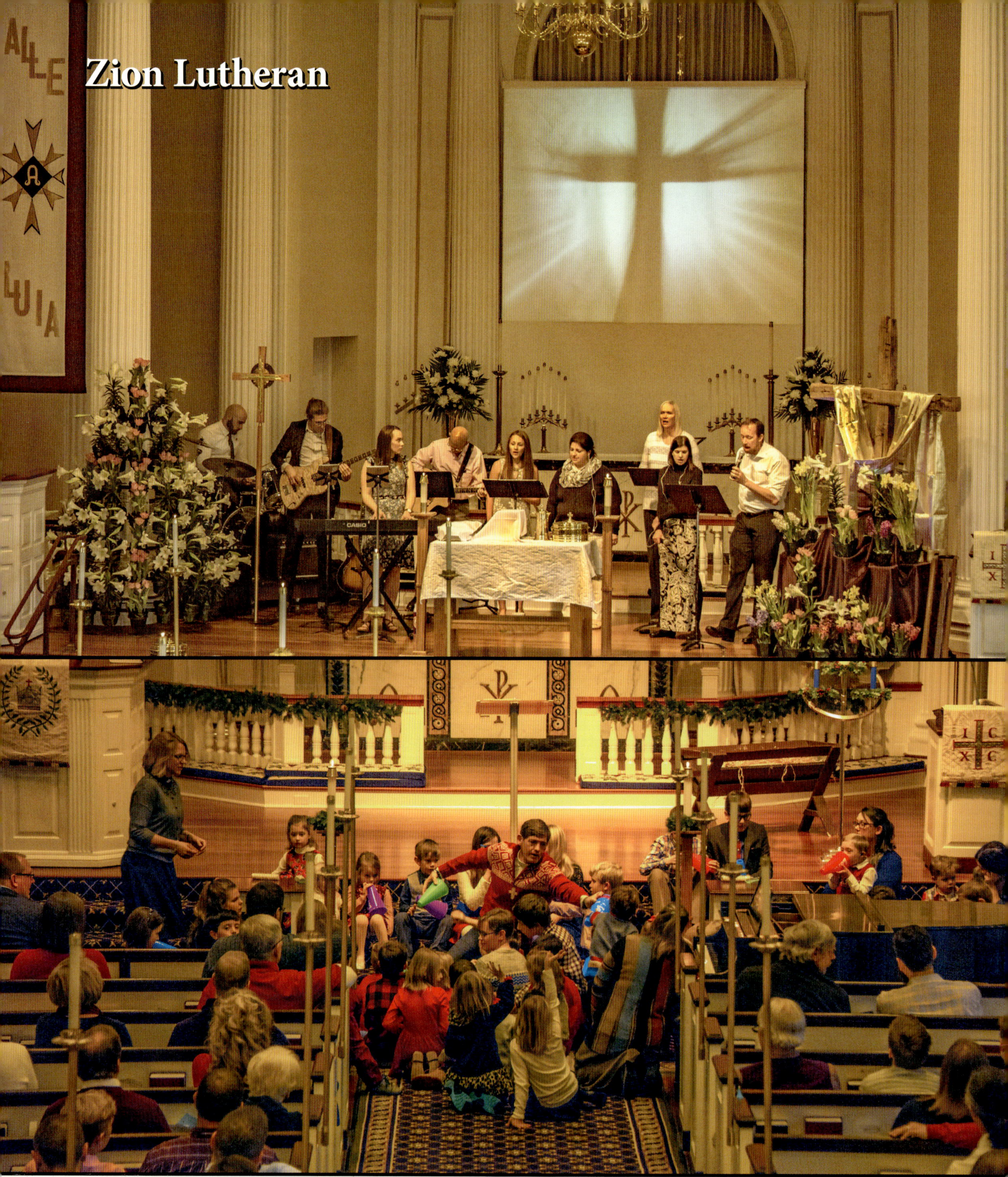

Welcome to Zion! There is a place here for you. We believe that worship is the heart of any community of faith. We are intentional about living out our purpose at Zion Lutheran Church: To Know Christ is to understand God's message of love and forgiveness. To Grow in Christ is to trust God's grace and mercy. We recognize that all people are God's children and are worthy of love and belonging. We are open and affirming as we welcome and accept all. To Make Christ Known is to serve all who are in immediate need of Jesus' caring compassion, locally, nationally and globally. We are committed to feeding the hungry, providing shelter, clothing the needy, comforting the weary and giving hope to all.

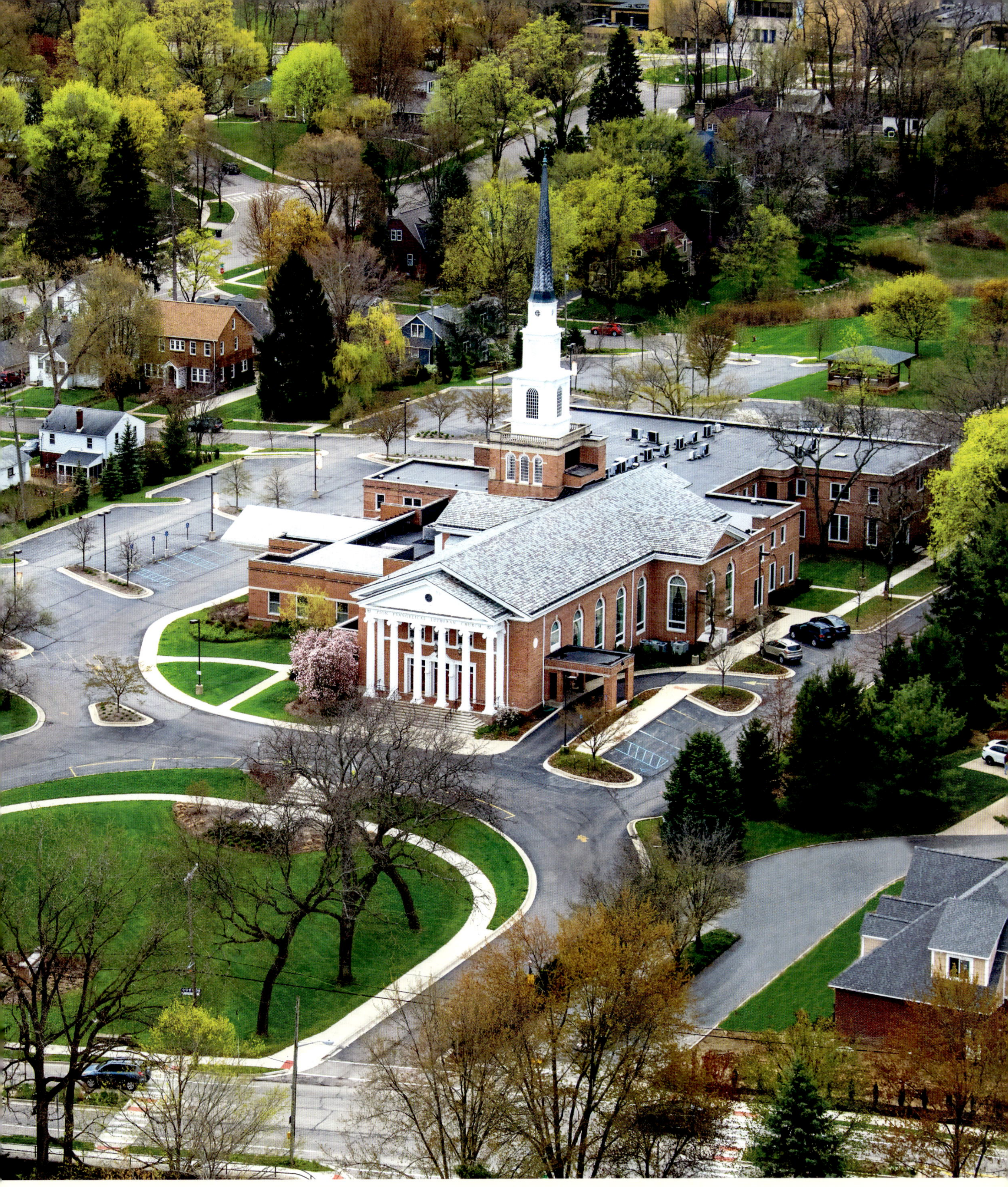

The Colonial-style Zion Evangelical Lutheran Church on West Liberty Street was designed and built by the George Mason Company in 1958 with a major remodel in 2008. An offshoot of the original German church founded in 1833, Zion Church was organized in 1874 by Pastor Friedrich Schmid. Zion outgrew two churches, first the old Congregational Church at the corner of Fifth and Washington Streets, and then a larger building on the same site, before moving to its current home on Ann Arbor's far west side.

Grace upon Grace!
Rev. James Debner, Senior Pastor
Rev. Vicky Lovell, Associate Pastor

ZION LUTHERAN CHURCH OF ANN ARBOR

1501 West Liberty St.
Ann Arbor, MI
734-994-4455

Robert H. Lurie Engineering Center & Lurie Tower

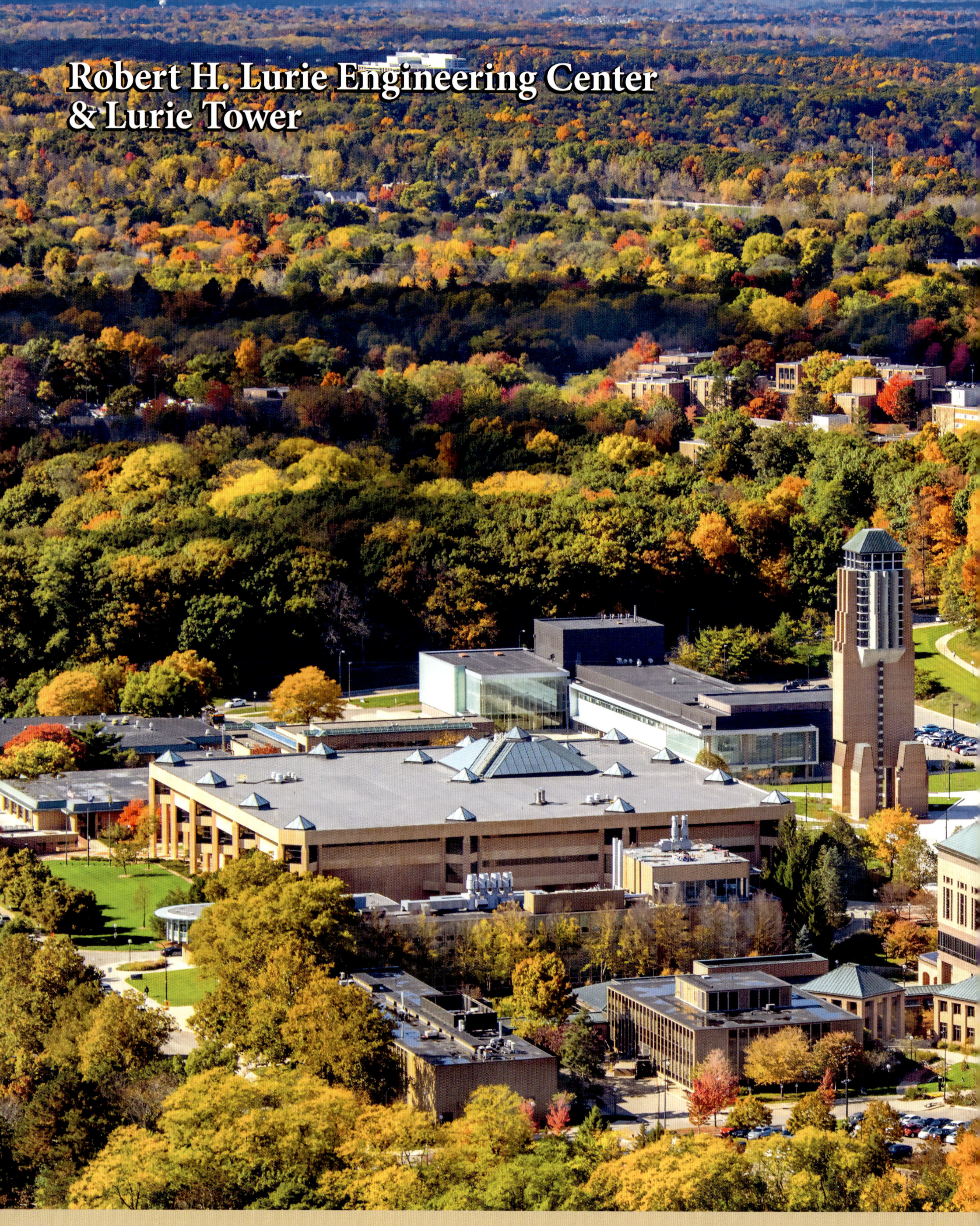

The Robert H. Lurie Engineering Center on the University of Michigan's vibrant North Campus is home to U-M's College of Engineering. The complex, completed in 1996, positions a cluster of smaller-scale buildings around its five-story core to create a welcoming "front door" for students, faculty, and visitors.

Designed as a companion structure and completed the same year, Lurie Tower is a memorial built for Michigan alumnus Robert H. Lurie. A gift to the College of Engineering from the Ann and Robert H. Lurie Foundation, it houses a 60-bell

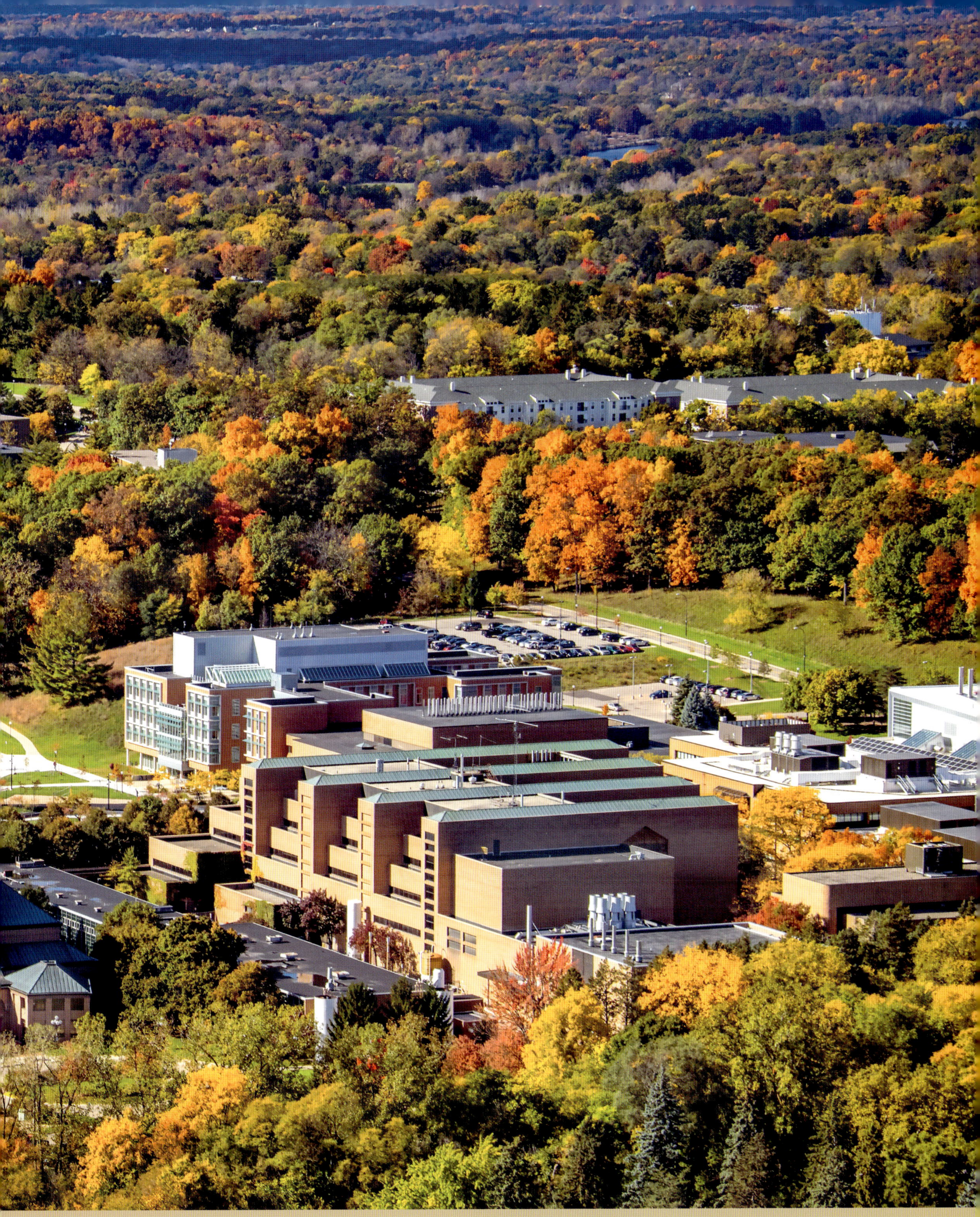

grand carillon, one of only 23 grand carillons in the world. It is recognized as the most significant carillon installation in the U.S. in the past 30 years with bells designed and cast by the renowned Royal Eijsbouts Bell Foundry of Asten, The Netherlands.

The center and tower are the final built works of renowned late architect Charles W. Moore, a graduate of the U-M College of Architecture and Design.

ROBERT H. LURIE ENGINEERING CENTER & LURIE TOWER

1221 Beal Ave.
Ann Arbor, MI

University Commons

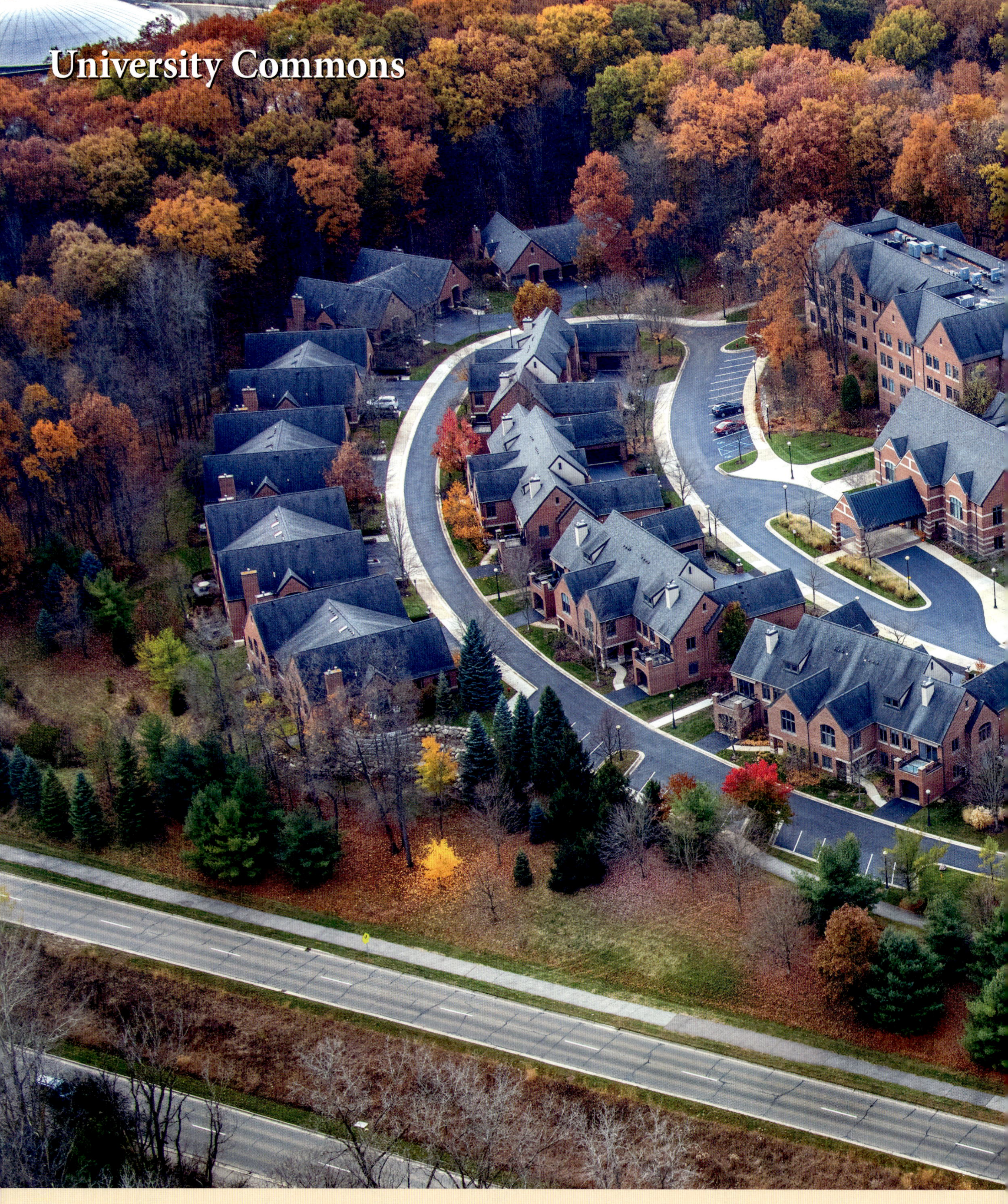

The condominium community of University Commons borders the University of Michigan North Campus. It sits atop a hill on the west side of Huron Parkway, and blends into a beautiful landscape of mature woodlands and natural wetlands. There are 92 independently owned residences, including apartments, townhomes, and villas.

Built on land was purchased from the University of Michigan, University Commons is not associated with U-M; it is an independent condominium association.

University Commons was initially conceived in the 1980s by U-M faculty, who envisioned combining the convenience of condominium living with life-long learning and the intellectually satisfying pursuits enjoyed in academia.

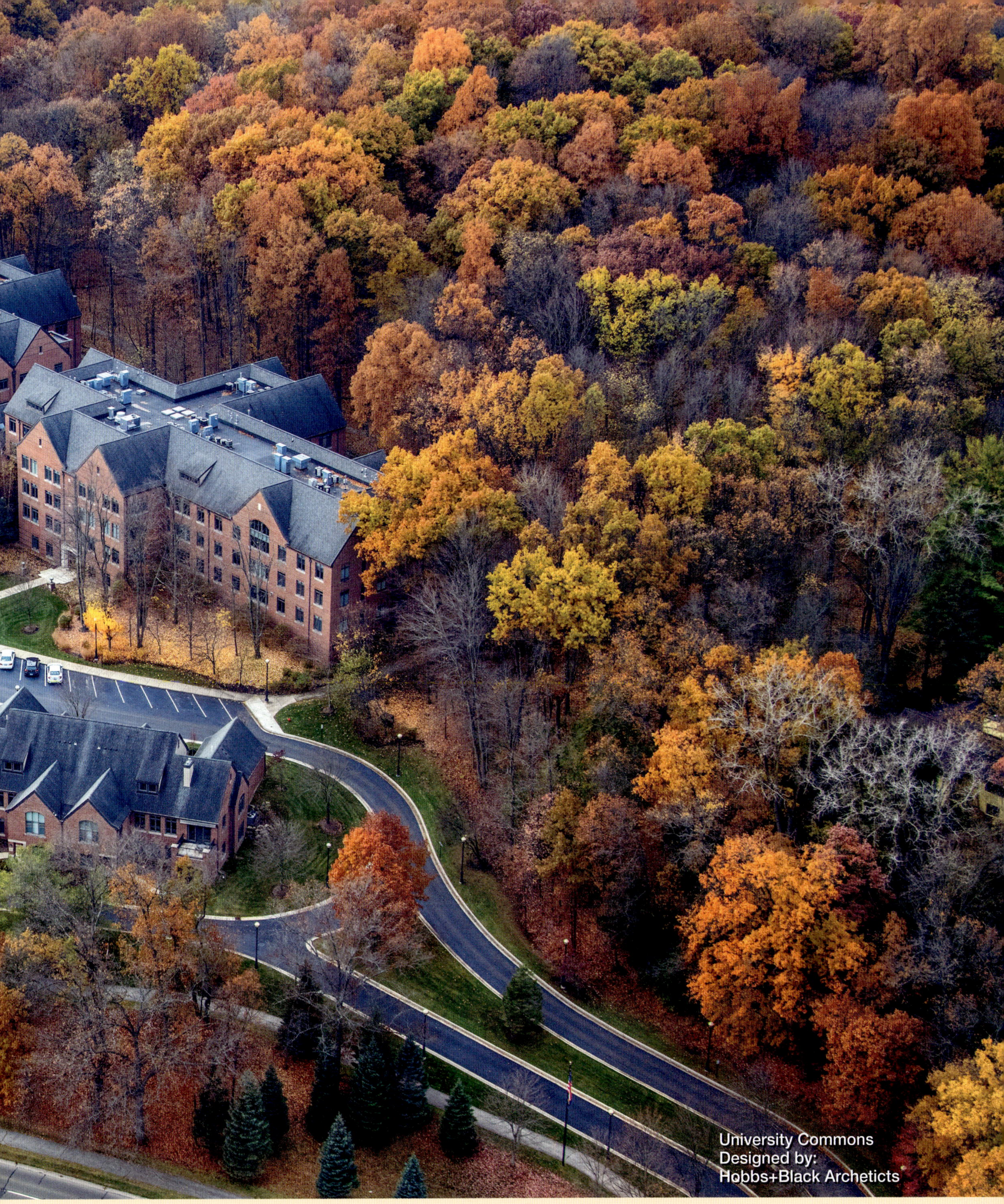

Residents must be at least 55 years old and must hold a bachelor's degree. Many, but not all, have had careers at U-M or other colleges or universities.

Common areas include class and meeting rooms, a fitness center, a dining area, and shared outdoor spaces. Speakers conduct lectures and musicians give concerts in the spacious recital hall. The community is a hub of learning and cultural experiences with an active network of committees, clubs and interest groups to keep minds and bodies active.

UNIVERSITY COMMONS

817 Asa Gray Dr.
Ann Arbor, MI
734-332-1221

Pittsfield Township

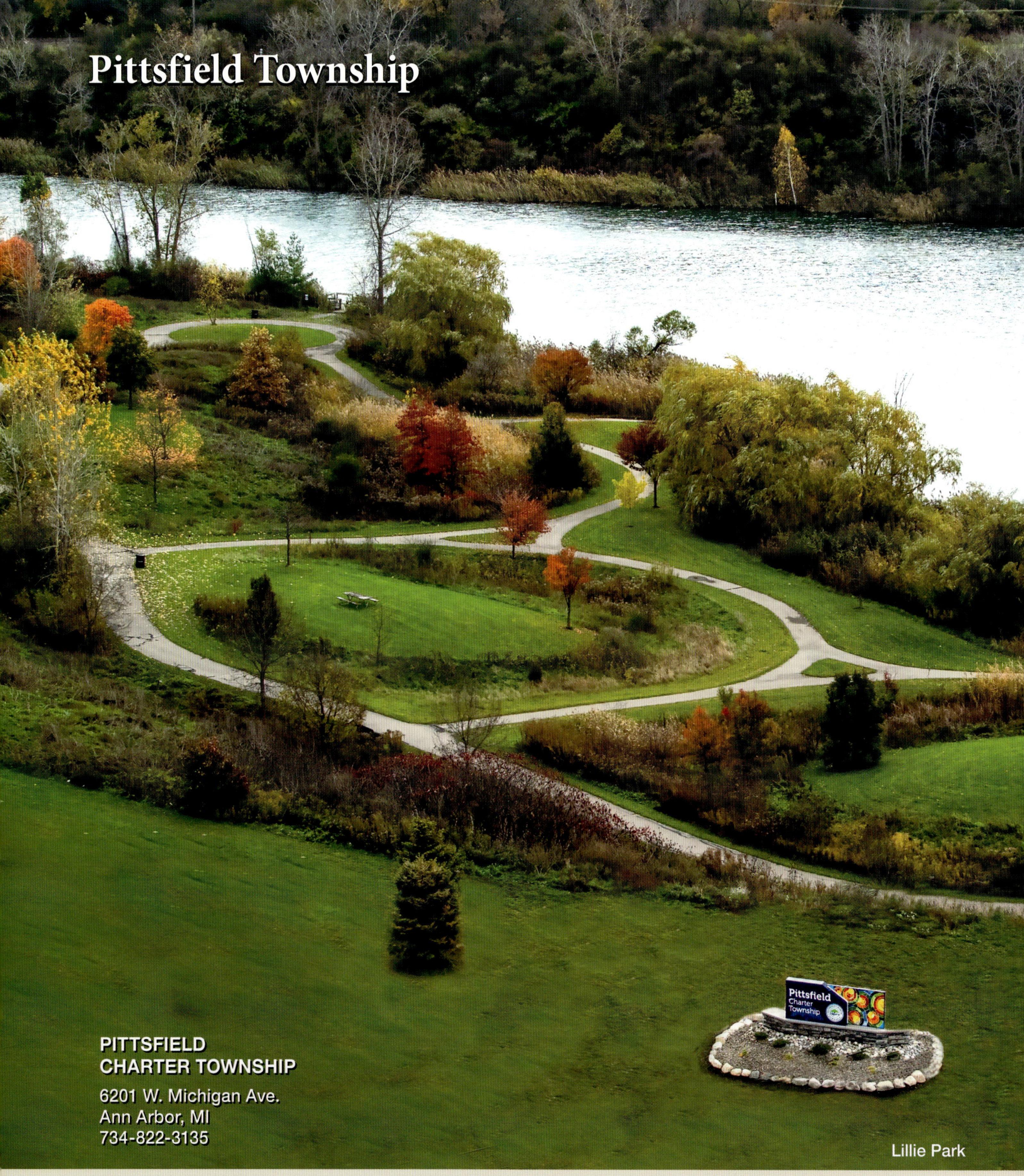

PITTSFIELD CHARTER TOWNSHIP

6201 W. Michigan Ave.
Ann Arbor, MI
734-822-3135

Lillie Park

Pittsfield Township has, over the past decade, come to be recognized as a premier destination to live, work, and recreate in. Consistently named one of the best suburbs and most diverse places in the State of Michigan, we provide for an outstanding spectrum of housing, education, talent, businesses, and a vibrant quality of life for all, which is supported by the second largest tax base in Washtenaw County.

Striking a balance between green/recreational spaces and commercial/retail destinations, which are inter-connected by a robust multi-modal transportation network, Pittsfield Township has leveraged its geographic advantage of being in the center of Washtenaw County to welcome residents and businesses looking to live, work and recreate in a community that is truly inclusive and respectful to all.

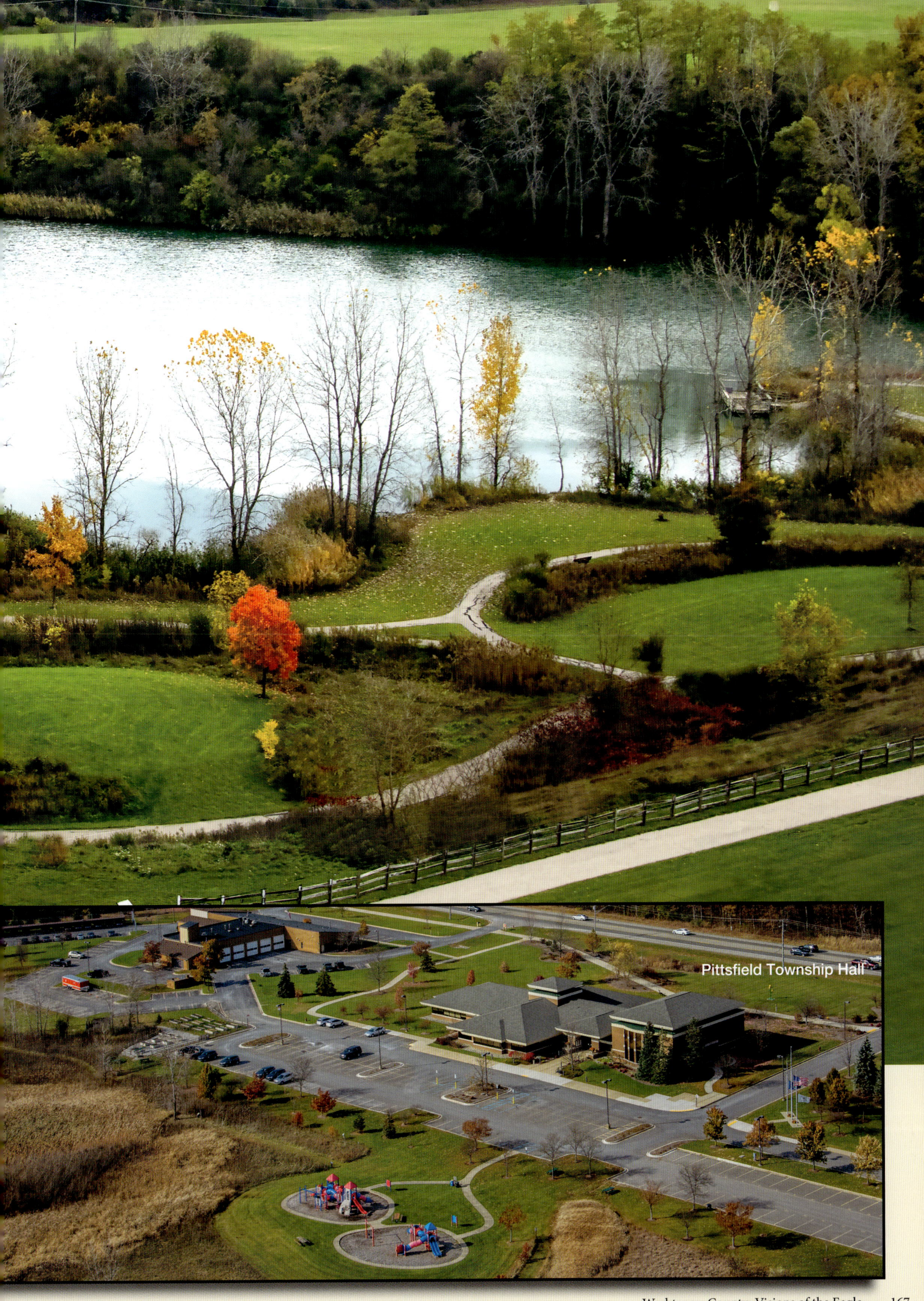
Pittsfield Township Hall

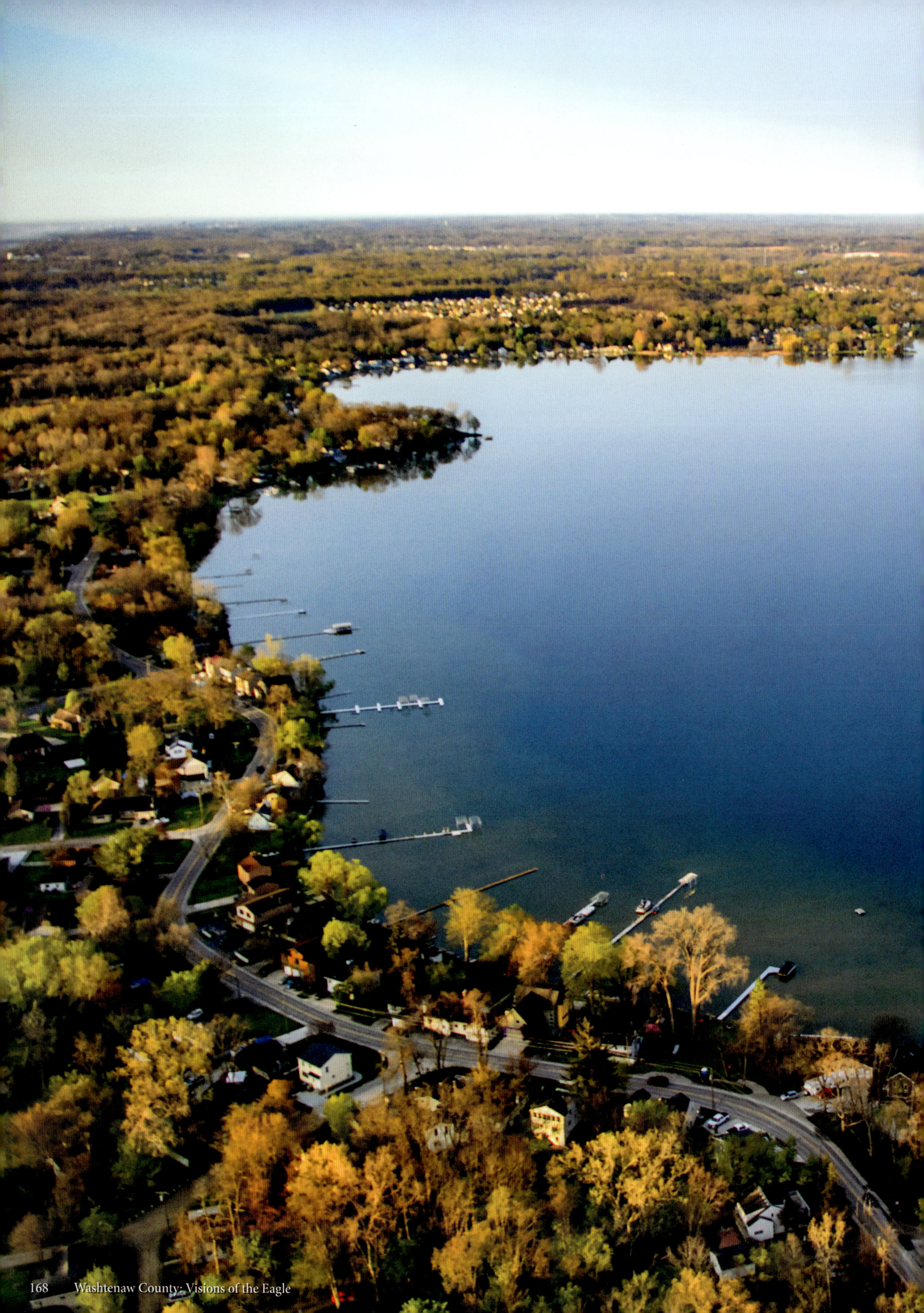

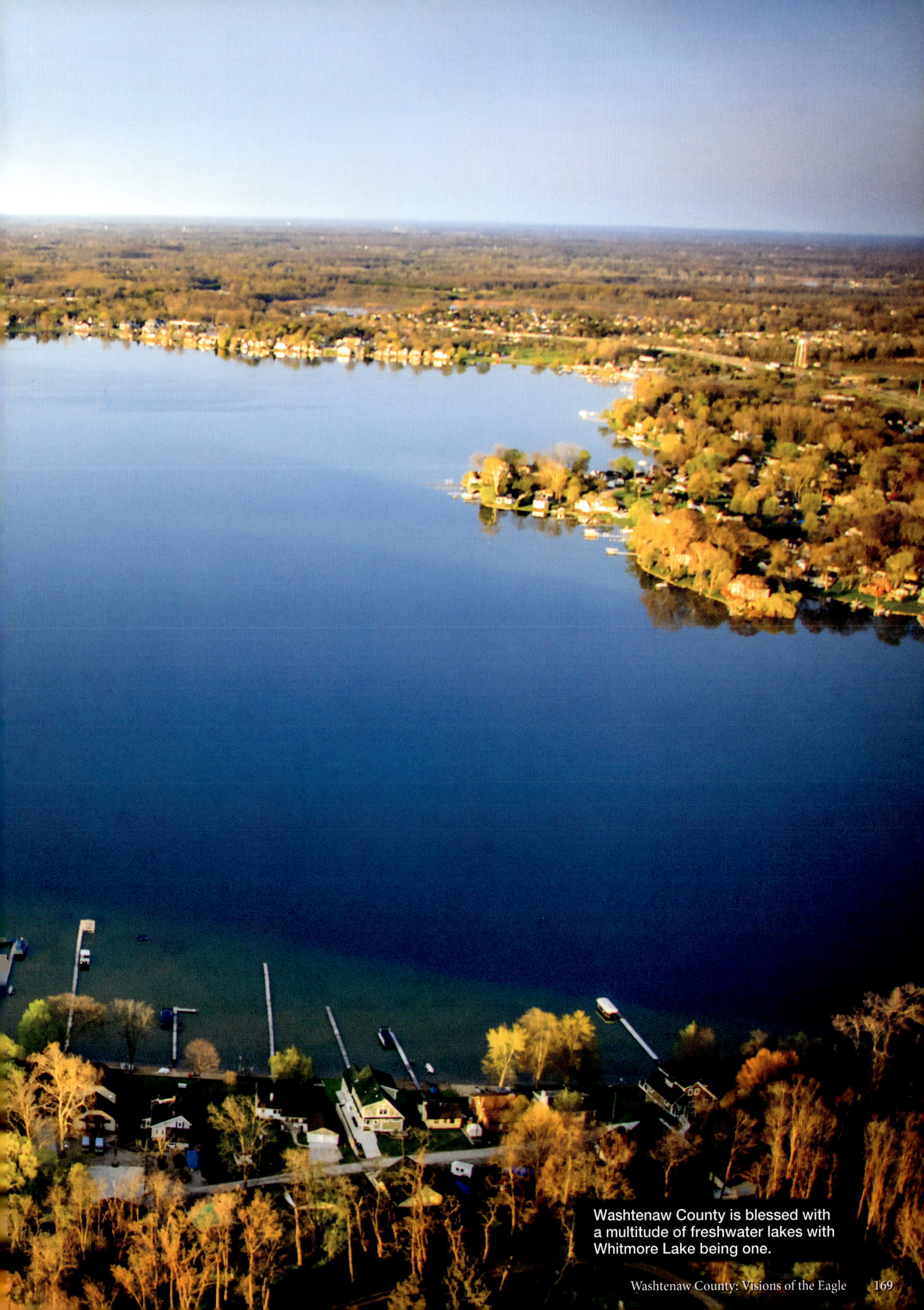

Washtenaw County is blessed with a multitude of freshwater lakes with Whitmore Lake being one.

CHELSEA

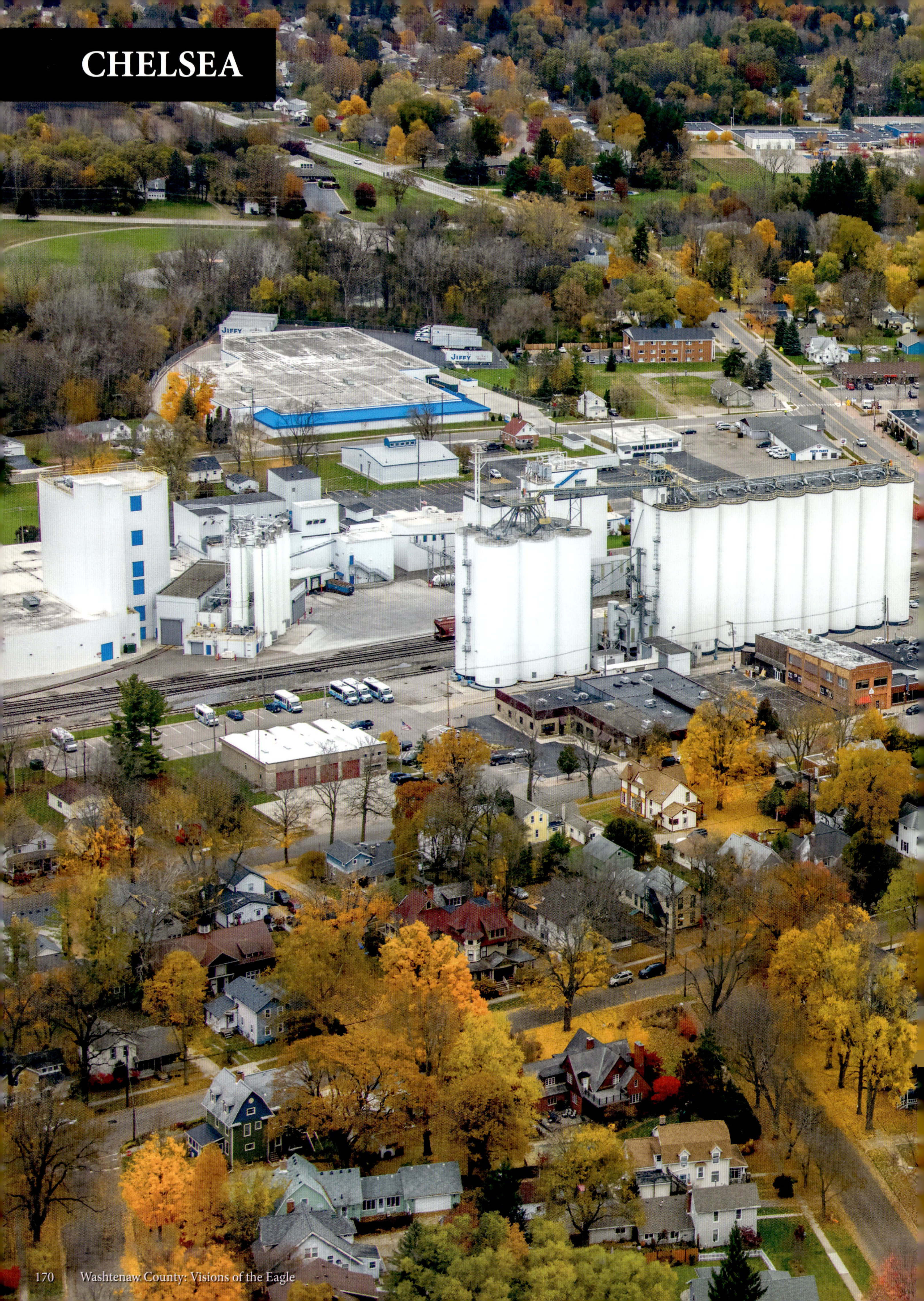

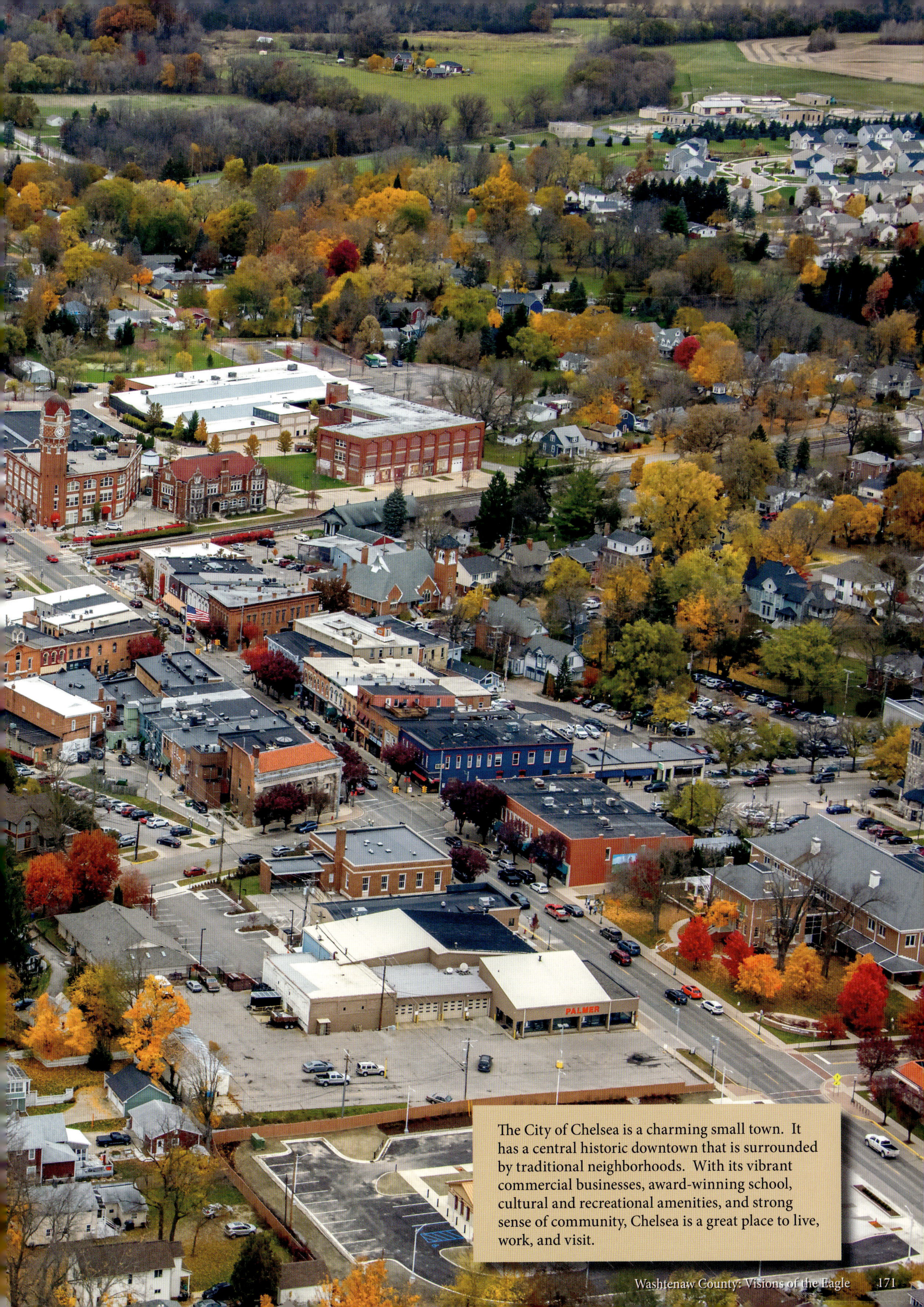

The City of Chelsea is a charming small town. It has a central historic downtown that is surrounded by traditional neighborhoods. With its vibrant commercial businesses, award-winning school, cultural and recreational amenities, and strong sense of community, Chelsea is a great place to live, work, and visit.

Chelsea Milling

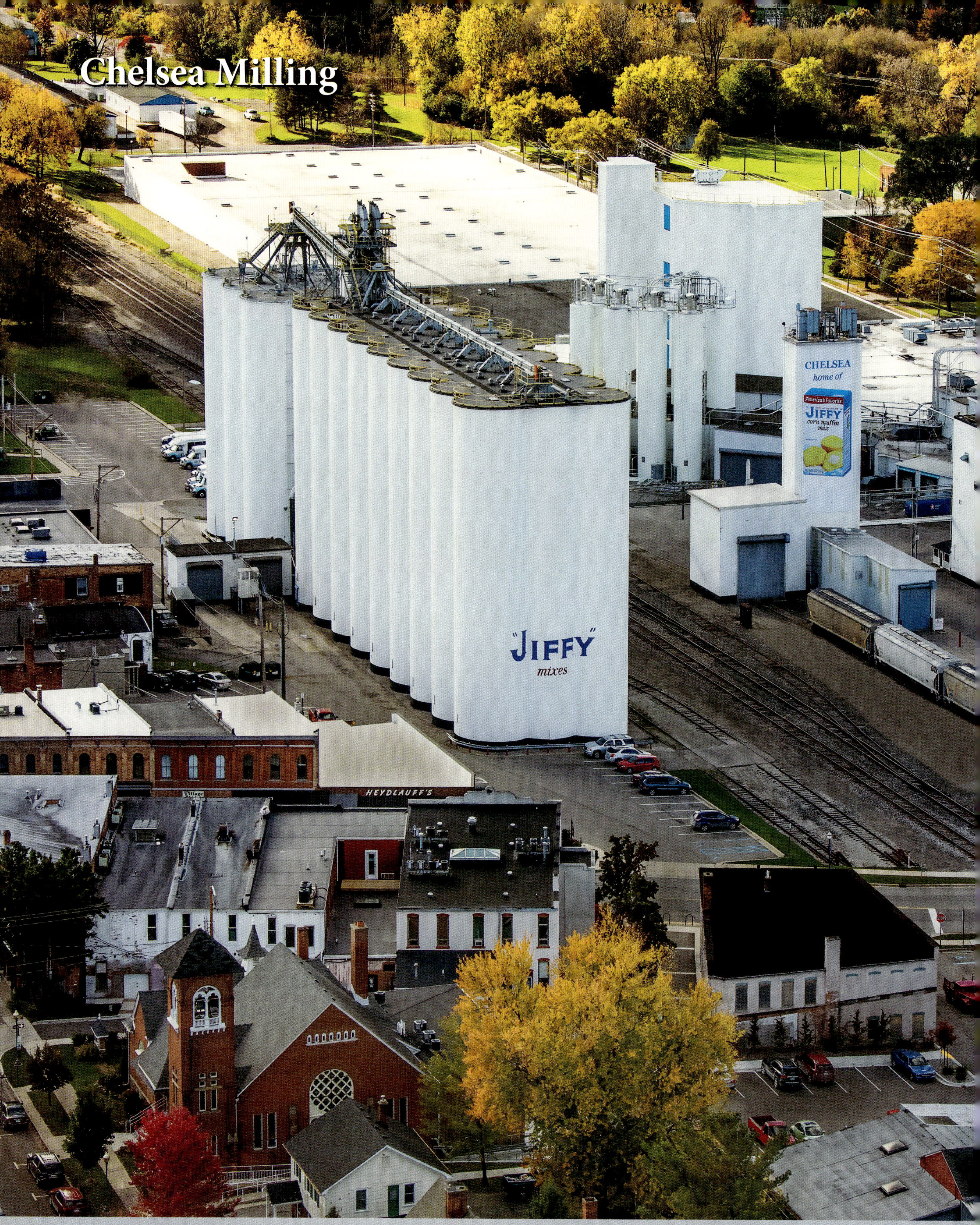

Chelsea Milling Company, home of "JIFFY" Mix, was established in 1887 as a flour mill. Mabel White Holmes invented and introduced the first retail prepared baking mix product ever in 1930: "JIFFY" All-Purpose Baking Mix. Today, "JIFFY" Mix is the leader in dry baking mixes and produces products for commercial and non-commercial foodservice customers.

CHELSEA MILLING COMPANY
201 W. North St.
Chelsea, MI
734-475-1361

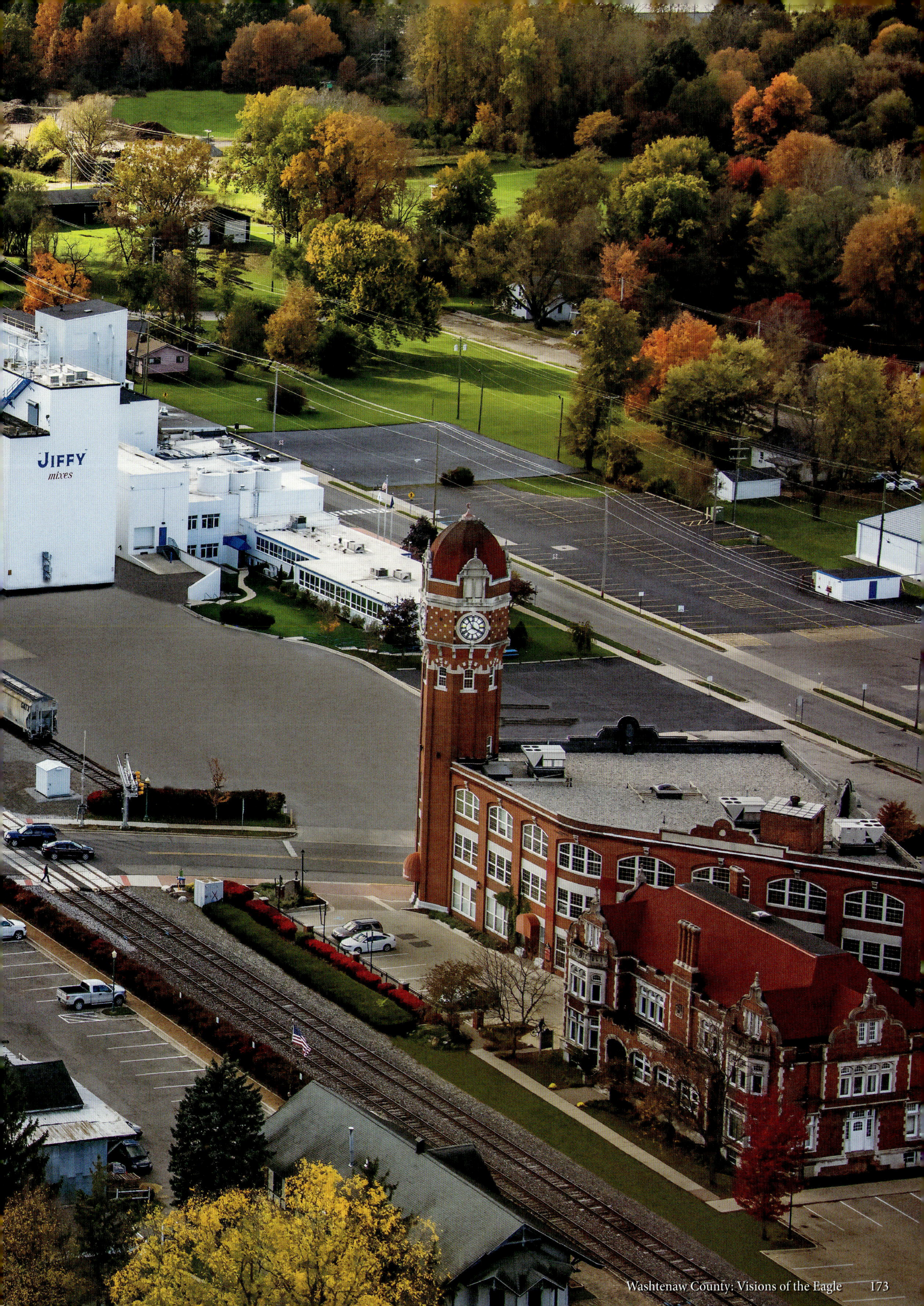
JIFFY
mixes

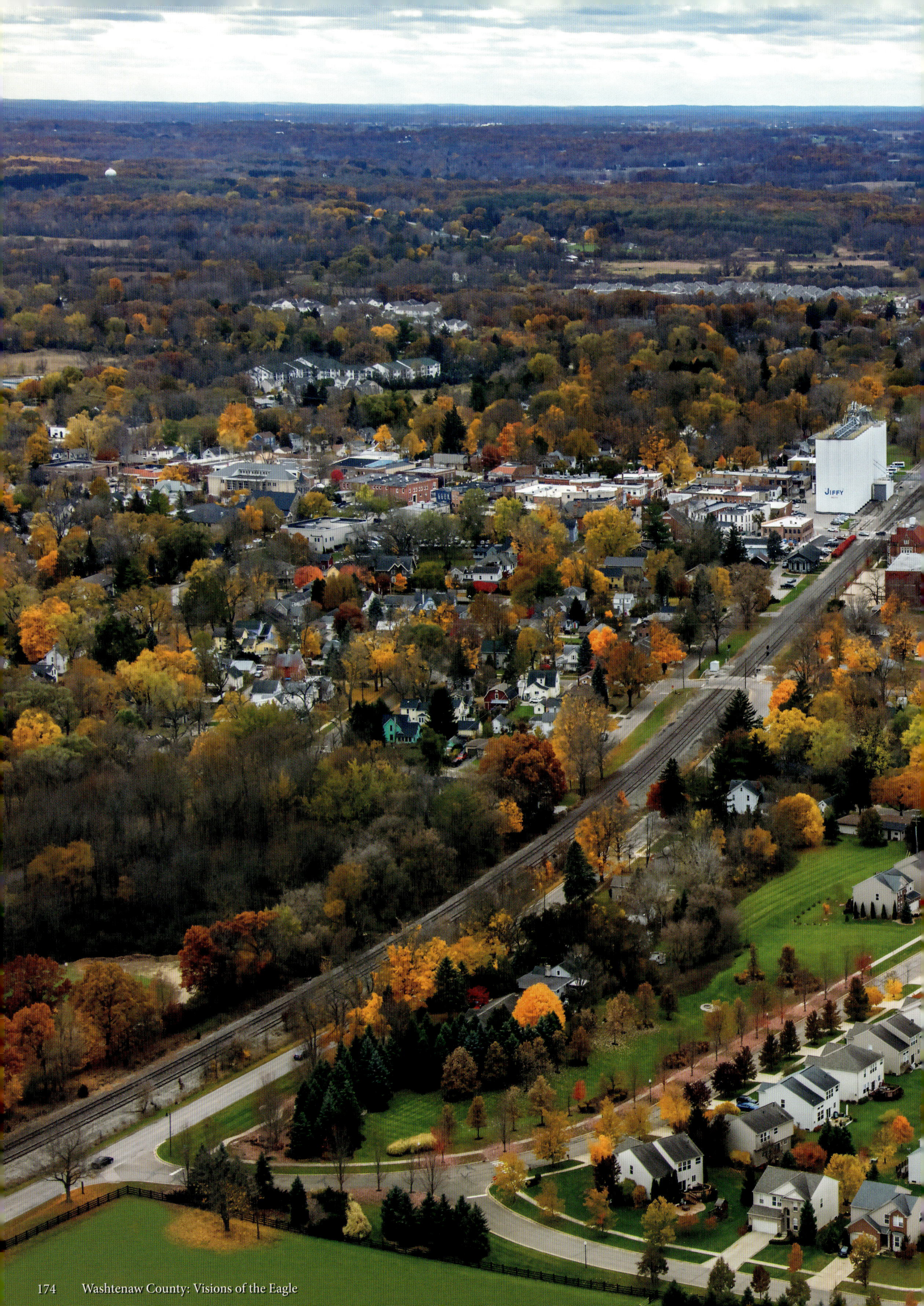
JIFFY

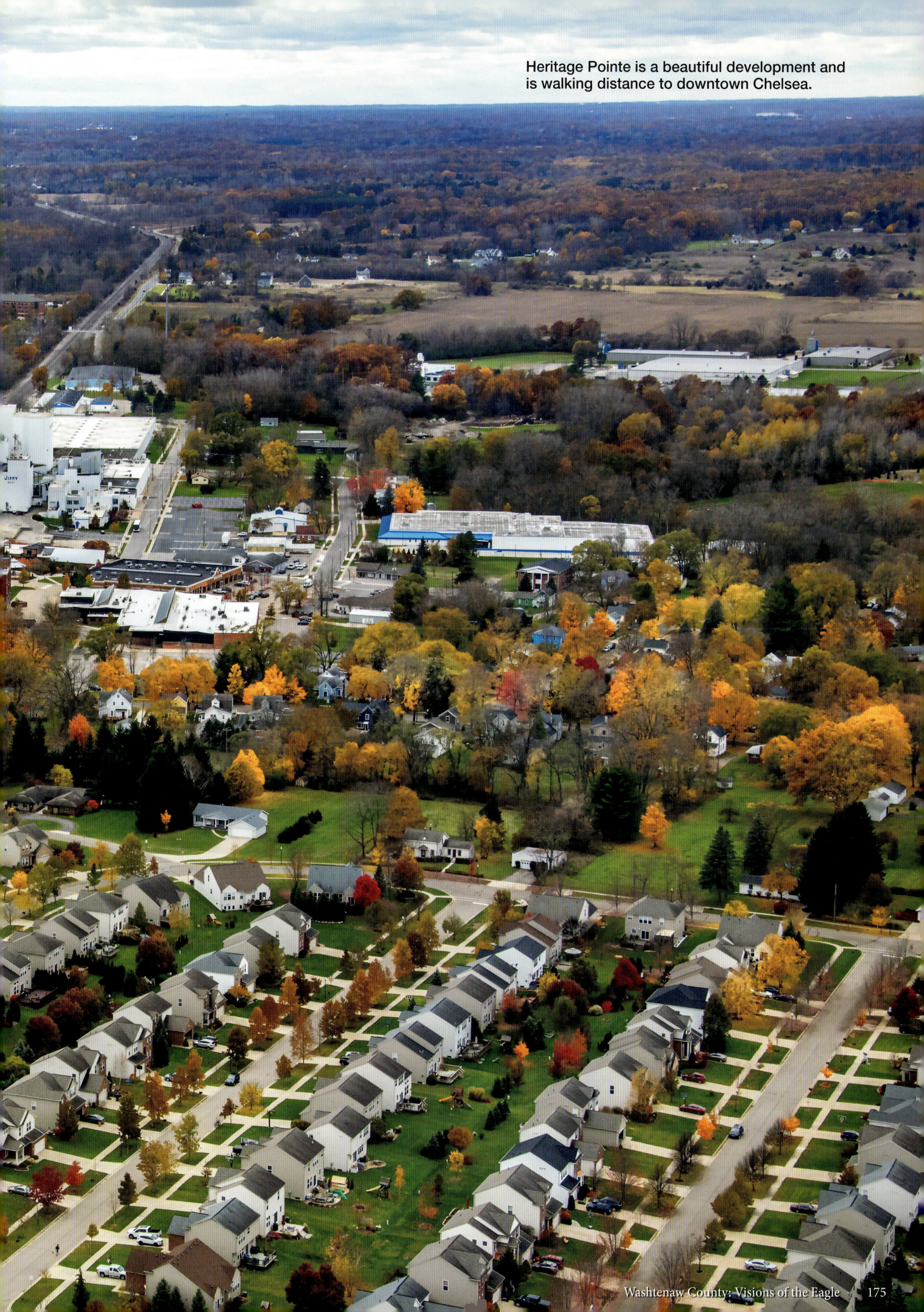

Heritage Pointe is a beautiful development and is walking distance to downtown Chelsea.

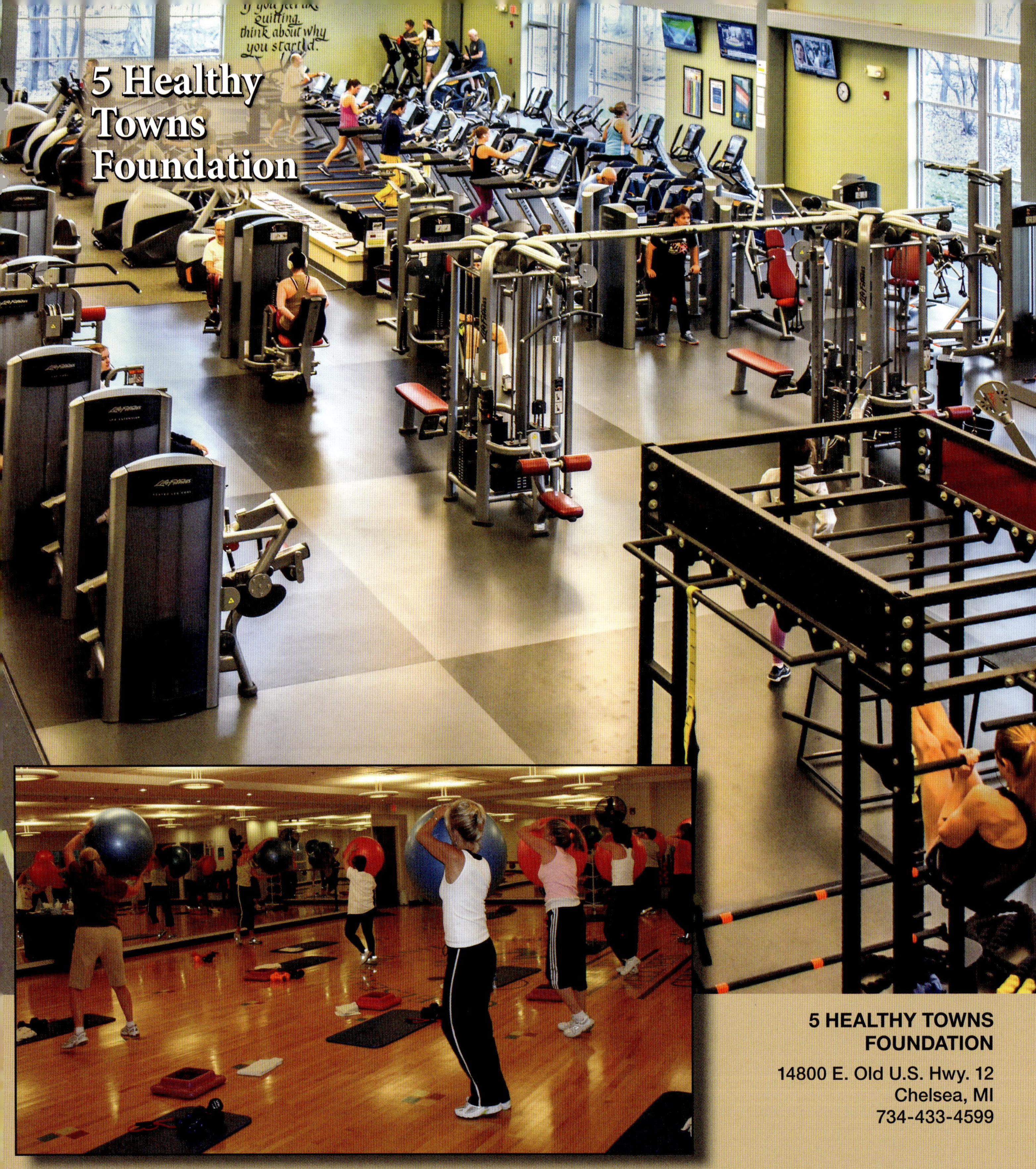

5 Healthy Towns Foundation

5 HEALTHY TOWNS FOUNDATION

14800 E. Old U.S. Hwy. 12
Chelsea, MI
734-433-4599

The 5 Healthy Towns Foundation (5HF) service area encompasses the cities of Chelsea, Dexter, Grass Lake, Manchester, and Stockbridge. Its goal is to encourage residents in these rural communities to eat better, move more, avoid unhealthy substances, and connect with others in healthy ways. 5HF owns and operates Wellness Centers in three of these communities.

The Chelsea Wellness Center (CWC) opened in 2001 and was the first medically integrated wellness center in Michigan. The center is a gathering place for the community and offers support and expert guidance on how to live a healthy lifestyle, including programs for those transitioning from or managing a medical condition. The family-oriented facility provides prevention and wellness programs to individuals and in group settings.

With over 50,000 square feet, CWC includes an indoor track, extensive fitness equipment, lap and therapy pools, wellness education and coaching, nutrition counseling, and childcare. This one-stop wellness resource provides the means to improve your health, prevent illness and injury, and live your healthiest life.

St. Joseph Mercy Chelsea

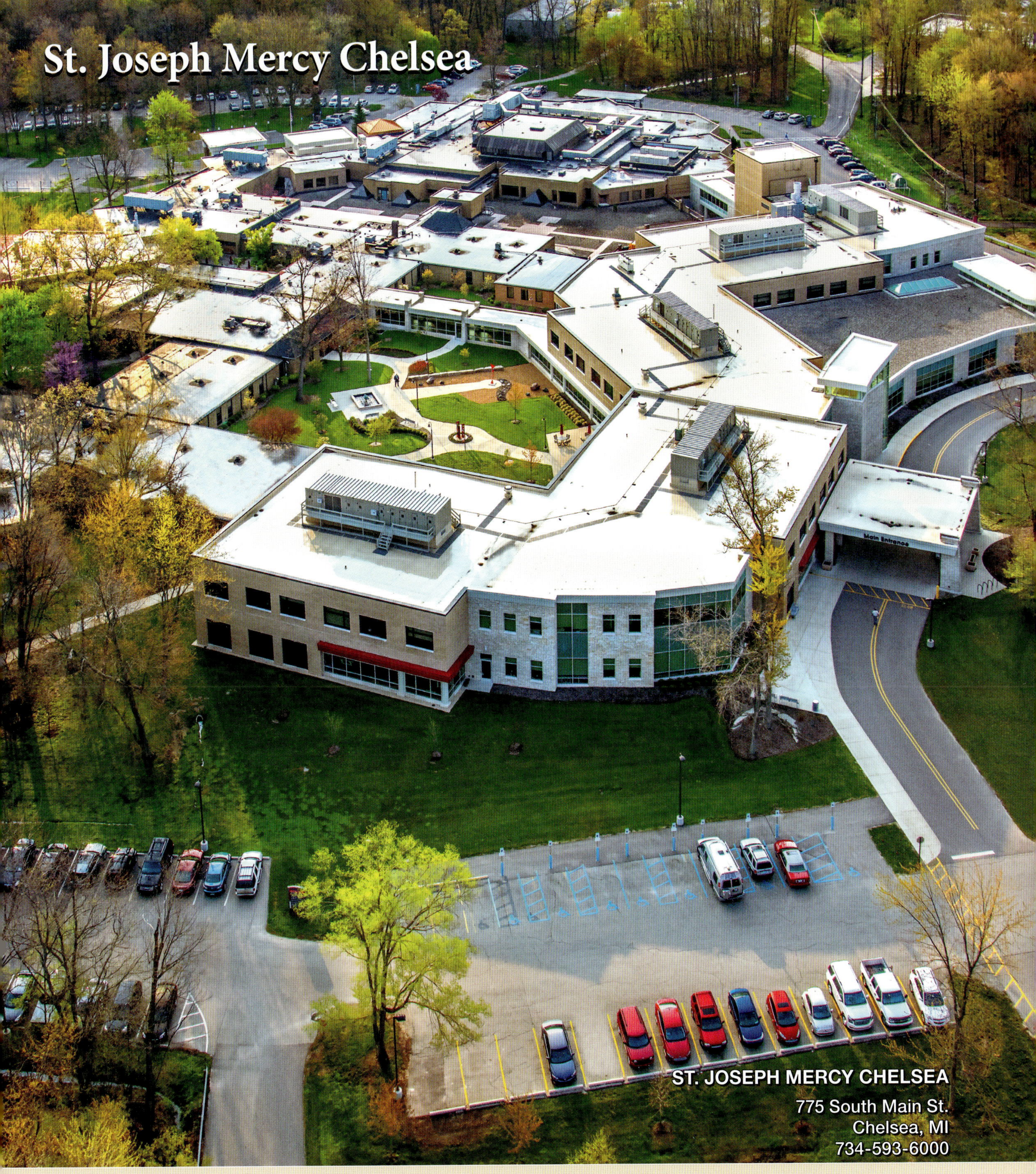

St. Joseph Mercy Chelsea is an award-winning joint-venture hospital between Saint Joseph Mercy Health System and University of Michigan Health.

St. Joe's prides itself on providing top-notch patient care using leading-edge technology. It is known for its peaceful setting, high patient safety and satisfaction, and compassionate care. Services include women's health, routine care, rehabilitation, behavioral health, emergency medicine, and imaging to orthopedics, plus educational classes and events.

To improve the health and well-being of the communities served, St. Joe's invests in initiatives to promote healthier living. These include supporting local community partners, diabetes education, ensuring access to fresh fruit and vegetables, and addressing issues that negatively impact overall health. In 2020, St. Joseph Mercy Chelsea has proudly served Chelsea and surrounding communities for 50 years.

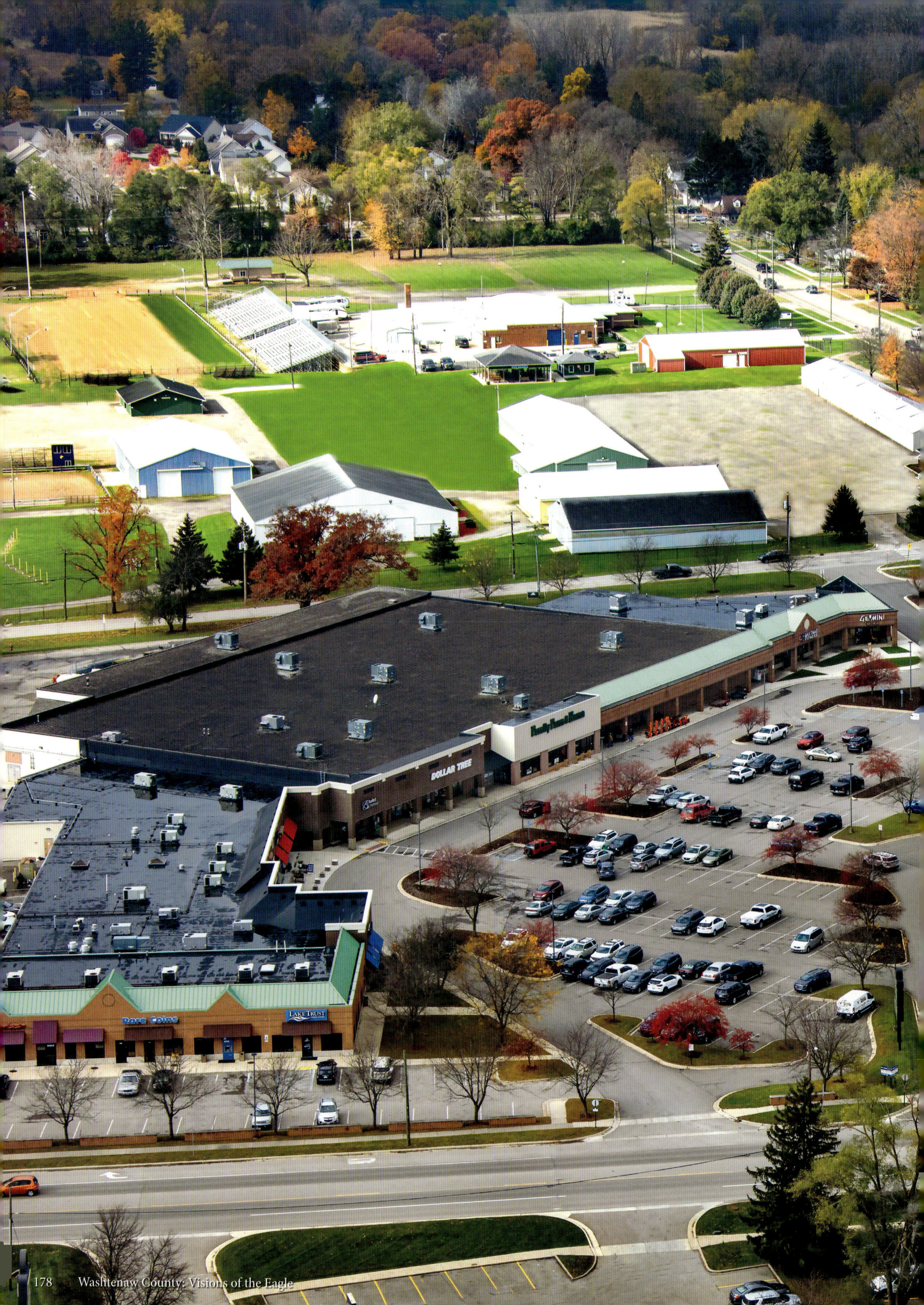
DOLLAR TREE
Family Farm & Home
ANYTIME FITNESS
GEMINI
Rare Coins
LAKE TRUST

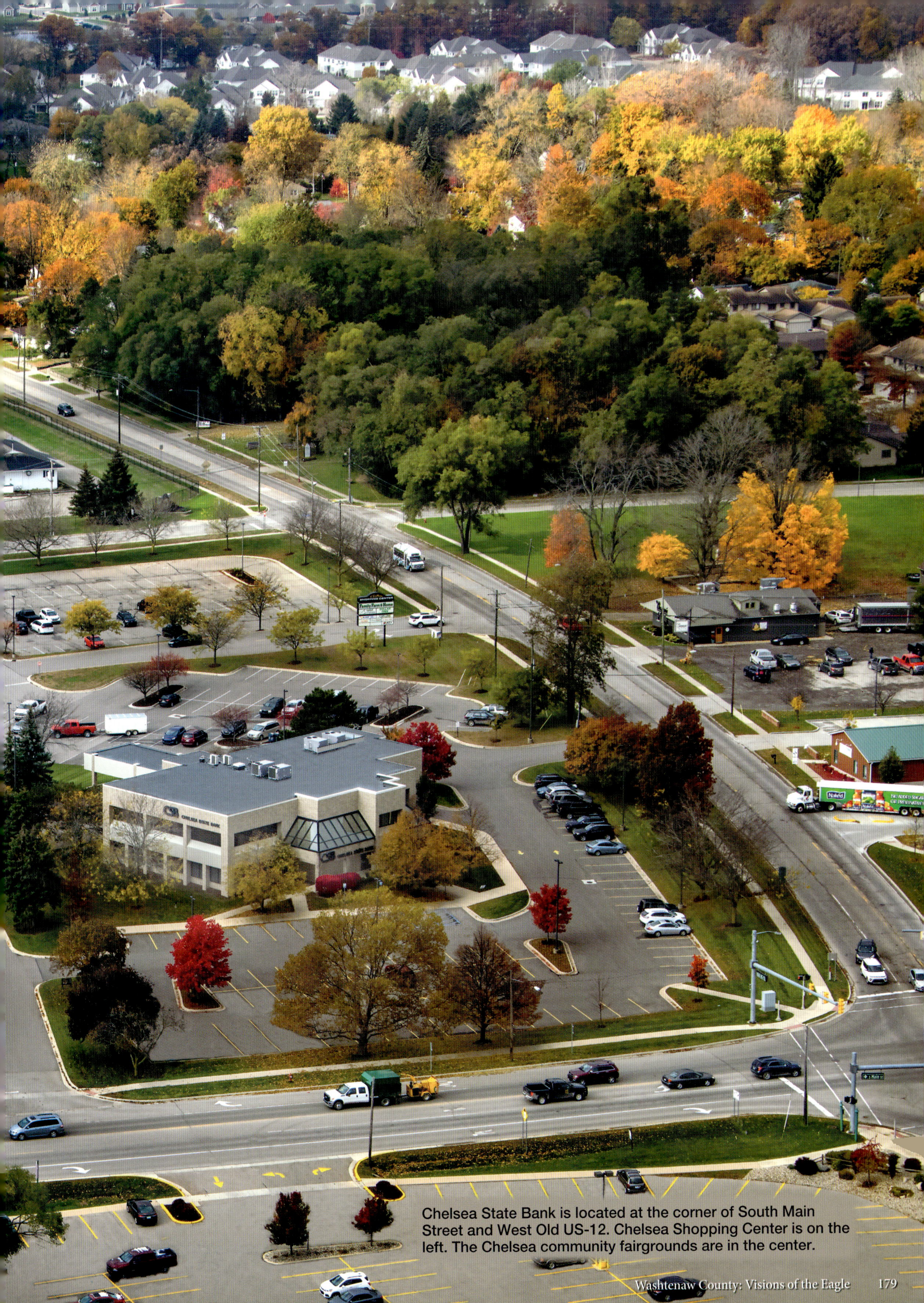

Chelsea State Bank is located at the corner of South Main Street and West Old US-12. Chelsea Shopping Center is on the left. The Chelsea community fairgrounds are in the center.

Chelsea State Bank

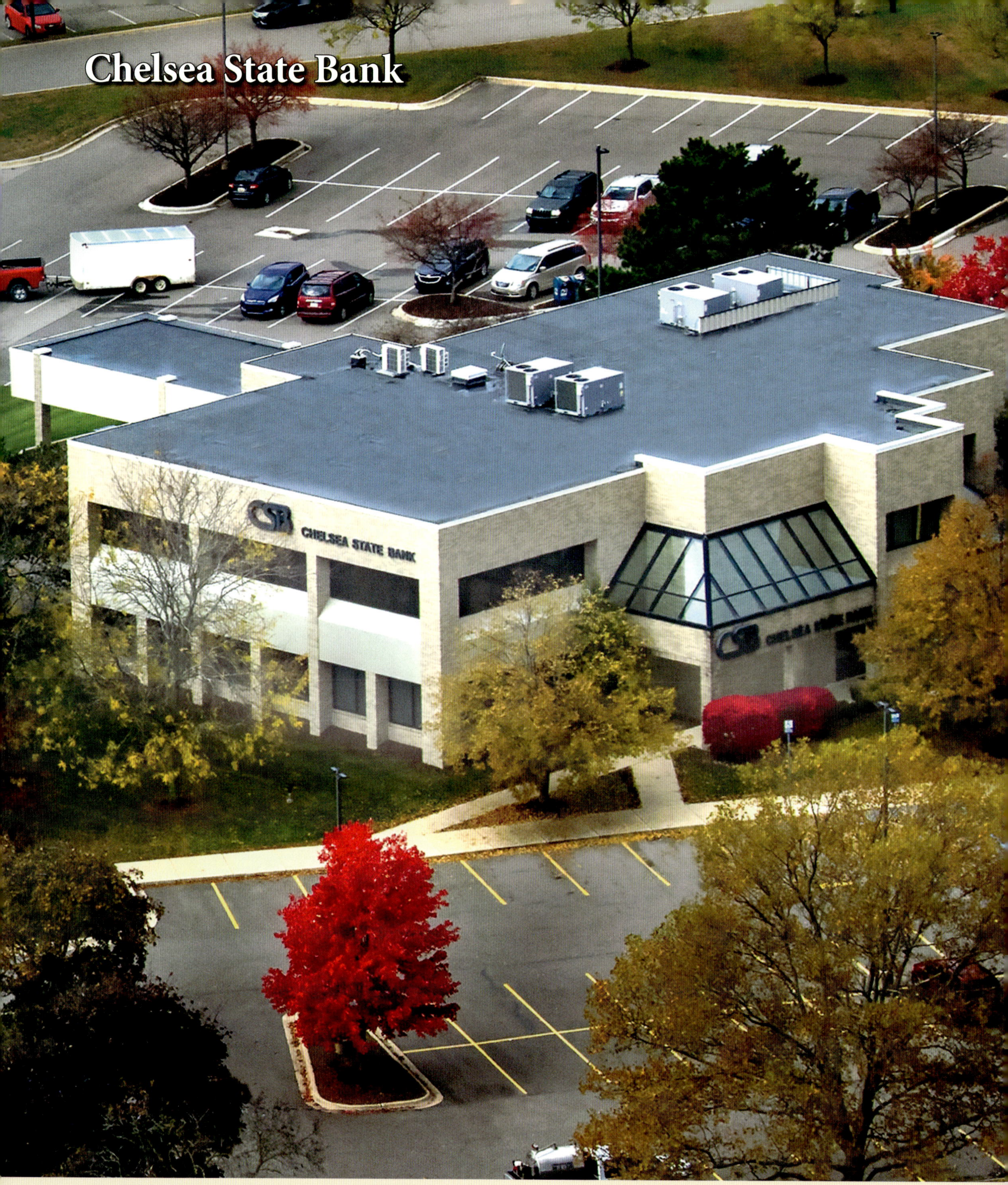

For over 100 years, Chelsea State Bank has been one of the most trusted financial institutions serving Washtenaw and Jackson Counties. The bank's strong and deep local ties have been the foundation of its comprehensive offering of banking and financial services since 1897.

The story of Chelsea State Bank is the story of our community. As a community bank, the people of Chelsea State Bank will be here building relationships with residents and businesses, and providing them with stability, progressive financial services, and a commitment to their success.

CHELSEA STATE BANK
1010 S. Main St.
Chelsea, MI
734-475-1355

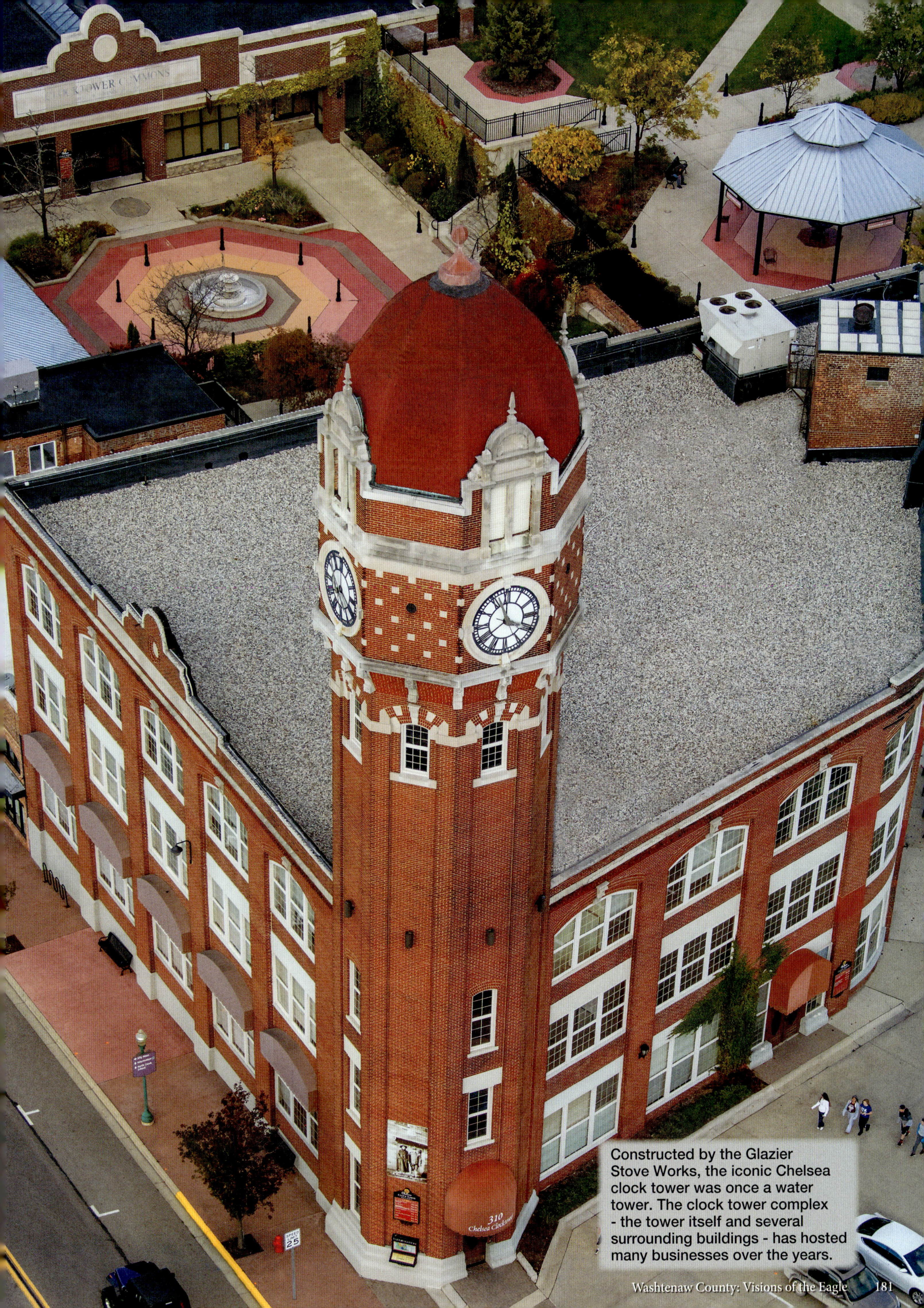

Constructed by the Glazier Stove Works, the iconic Chelsea clock tower was once a water tower. The clock tower complex - the tower itself and several surrounding buildings - has hosted many businesses over the years.

Silver Maples of Chelsea Retirement Neighborhood

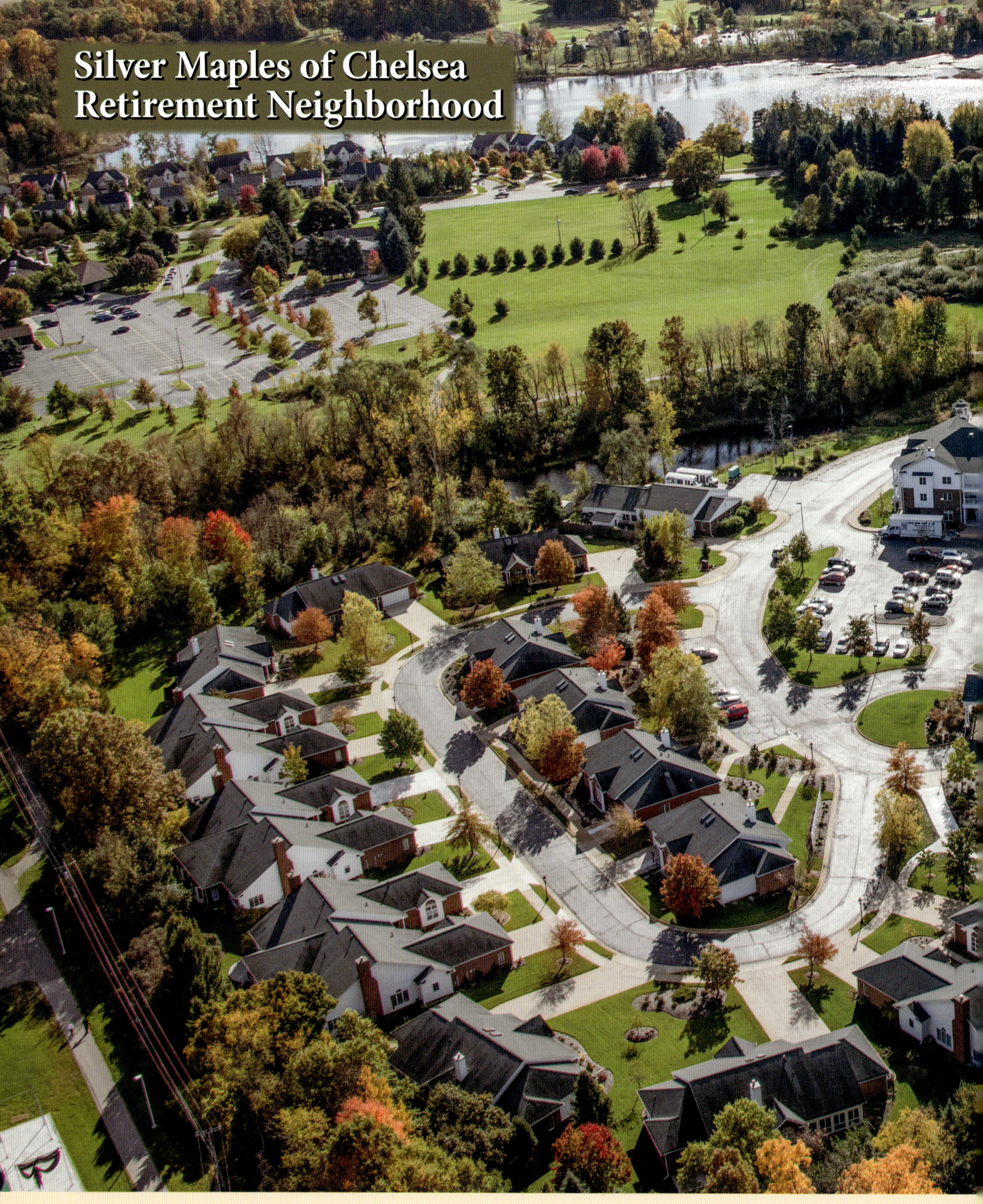

Silver Maples of Chelsea is a vibrant, non-profit Life Plan community that excels at creating and supporting a positive aging experience. This trendy, upscale retirement neighborhood, founded in 1997, offers both independent living and licensed assisted living accommodations for those 62 years and older. Nestled in serene woods on over 17 acres, Silver Maples is just minutes from Chelsea's quaint downtown and only fifteen minutes from Ann Arbor.

Silver Maples is known for its warm sense of community and family, which is fostered by positive, compassionate leadership and embraced by staff and residents alike. Through enriching experiences, residents develop meaningful

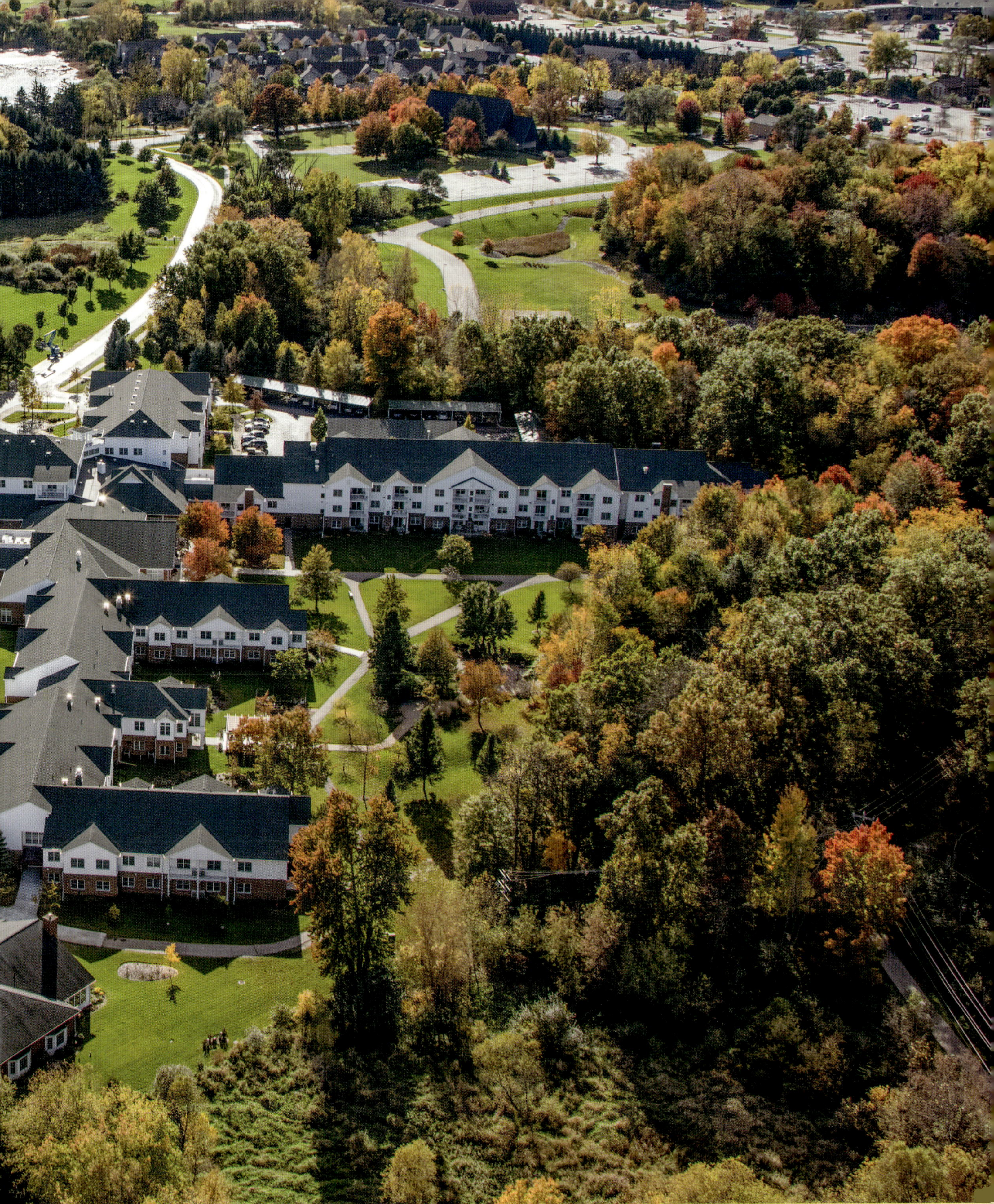

relationships among friends, family, and the greater community. Silver Maples is committed to providing a healthy, secure, and supportive place for older adults to call home.

Silver Maples is a locally owned non-profit organization that is jointly sponsored by the 5 Healthy Towns Foundation and United Methodist Retirement Communities, Inc. Learn more at www.silvermaples.org.

SILVER MAPLES OF CHELSEA RETIREMENT NEIGHBORHOOD

100 Silver Maples Drive
Chelsea, MI
734-475-4111

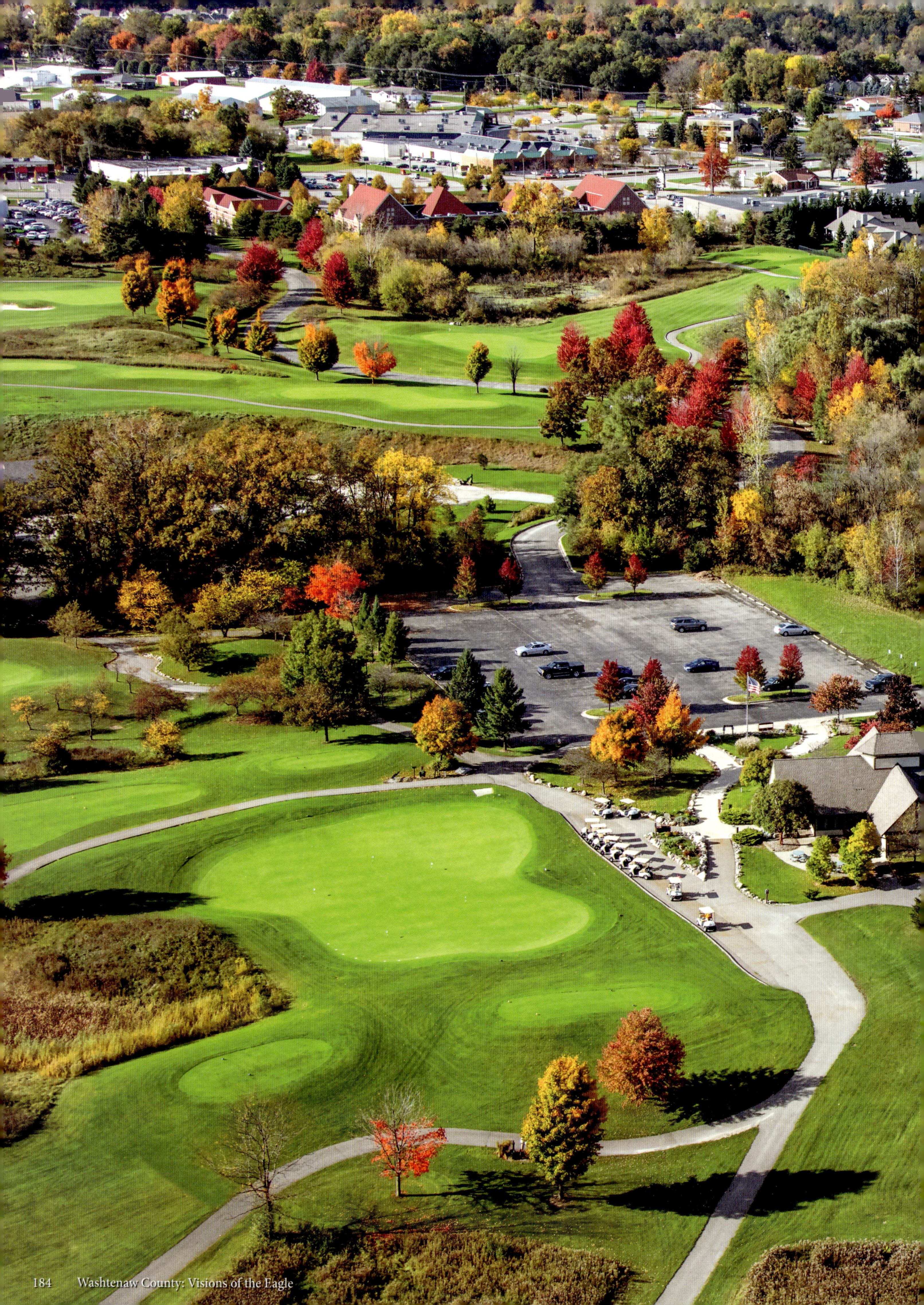

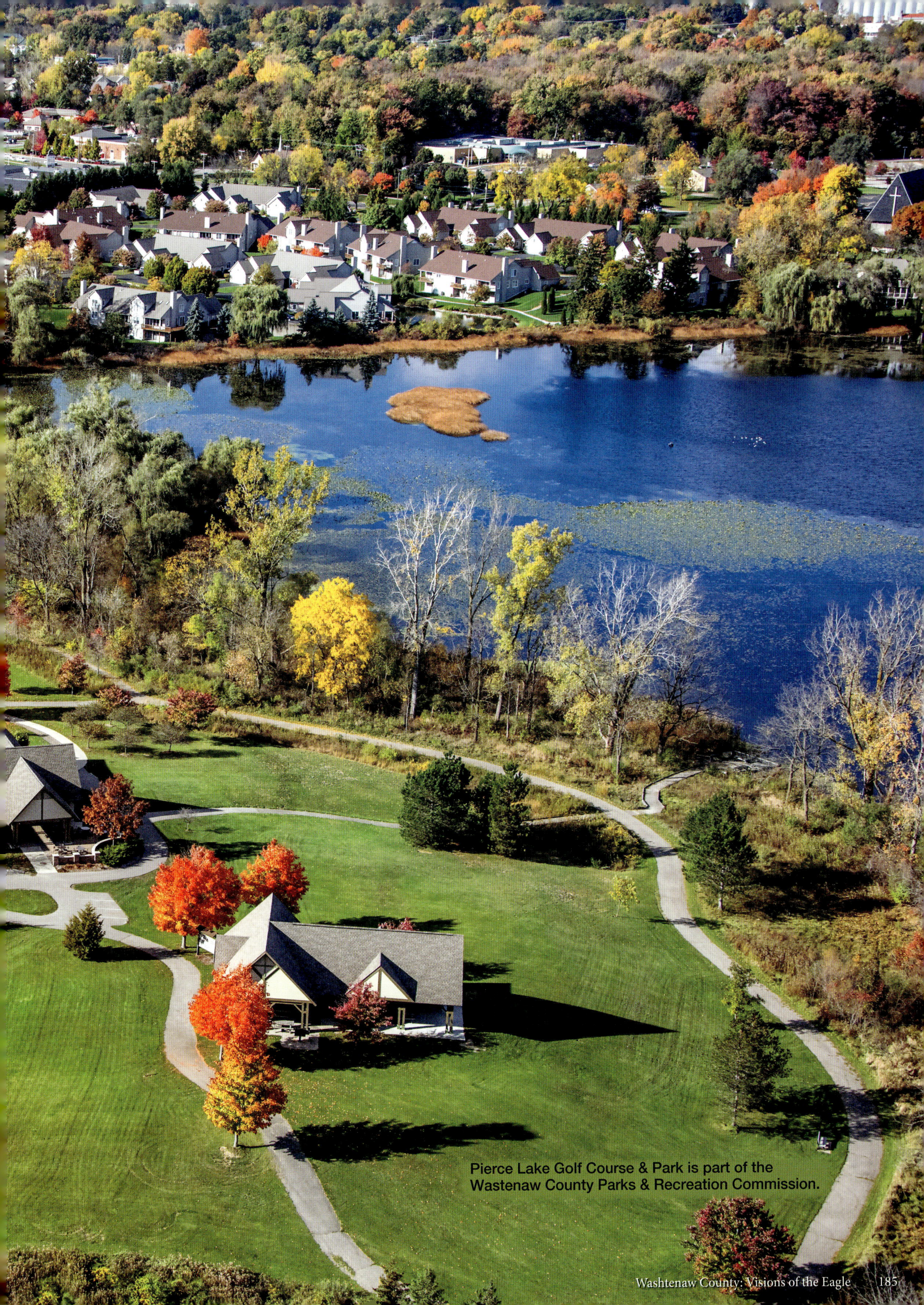

Pierce Lake Golf Course & Park is part of the Wastenaw County Parks & Recreation Commission.

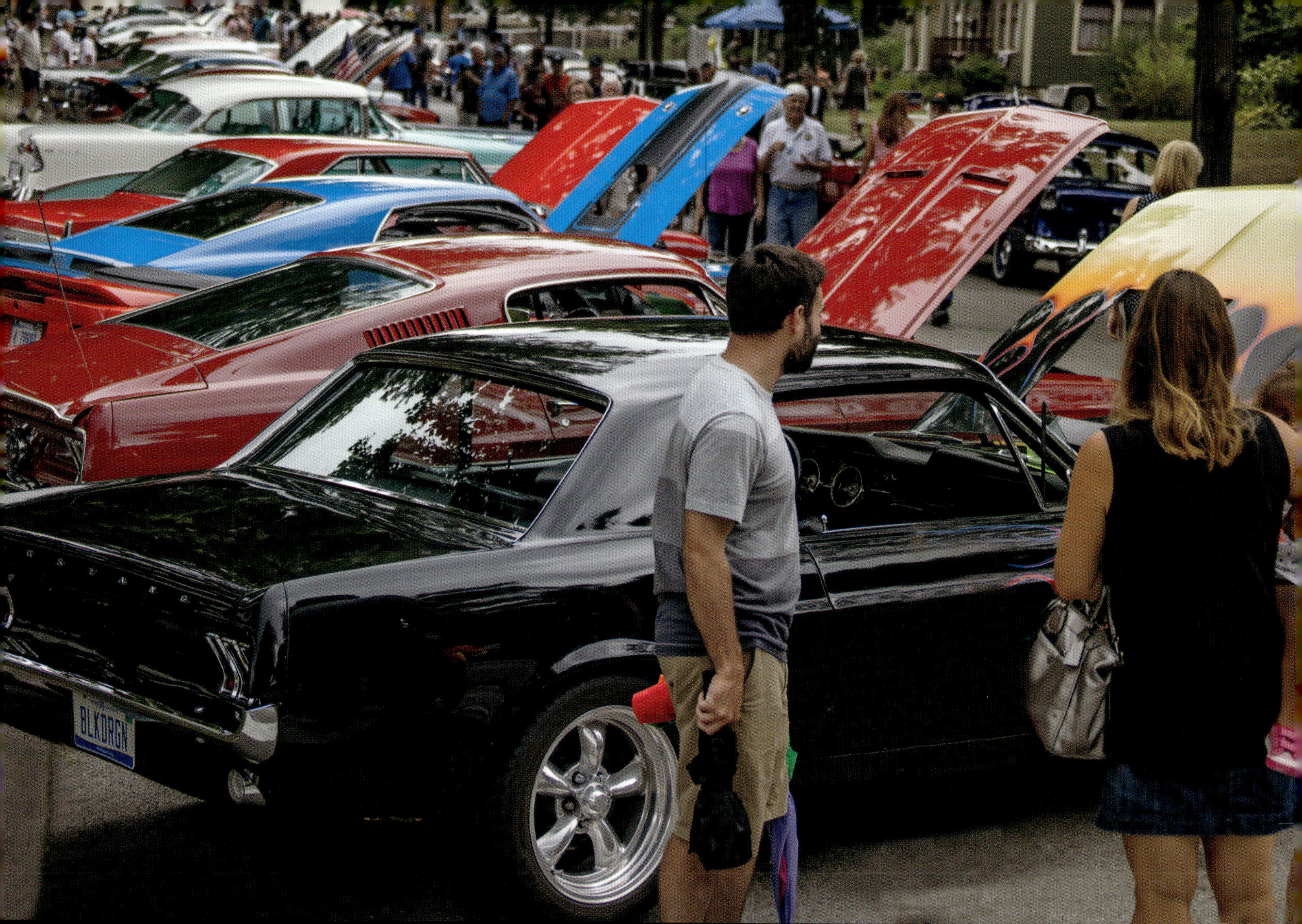

Sounds & Sights Festival is an event packed weekend.
The Art Market offers judged options, and the Car Show goes for blocks.

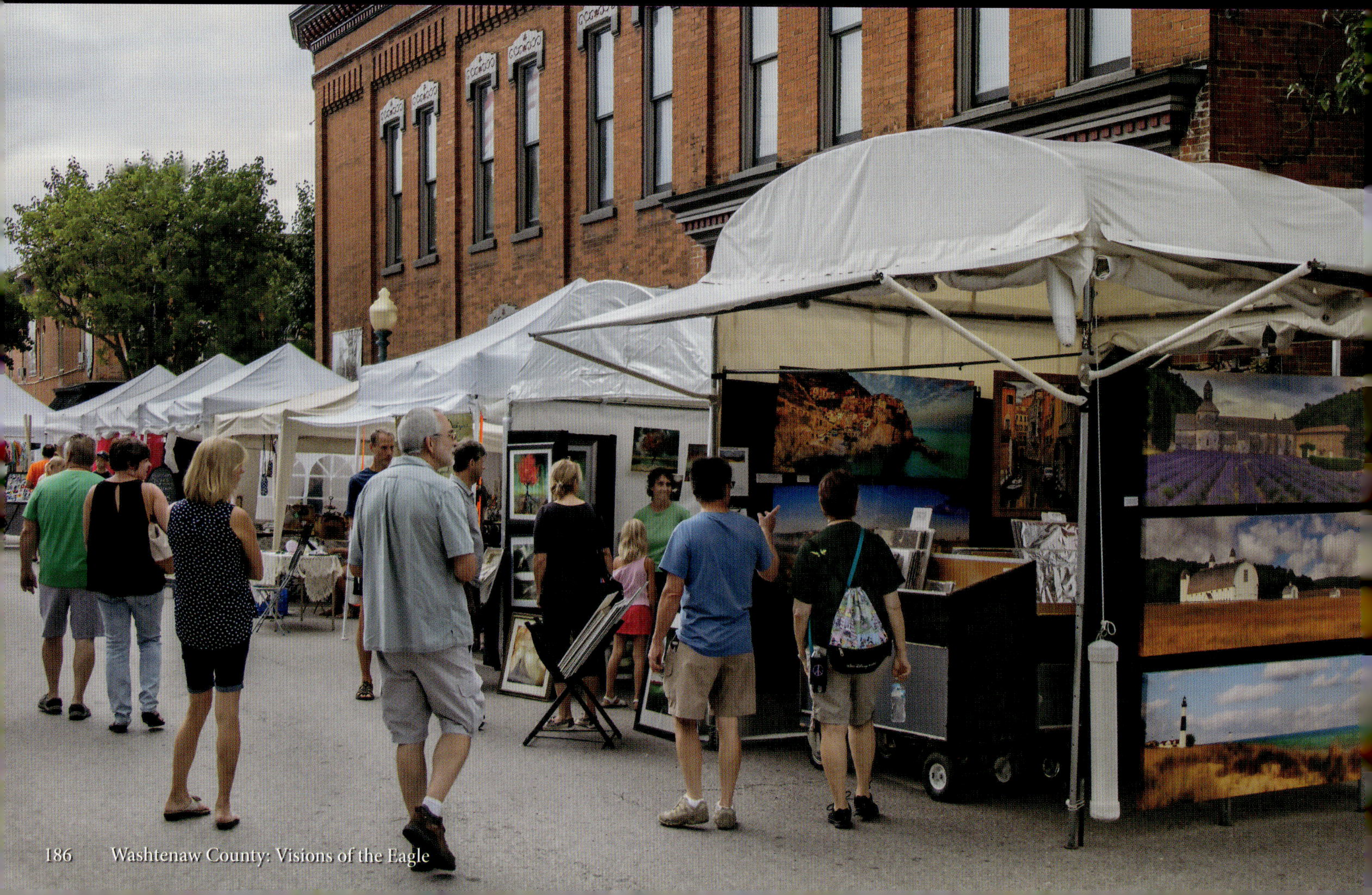

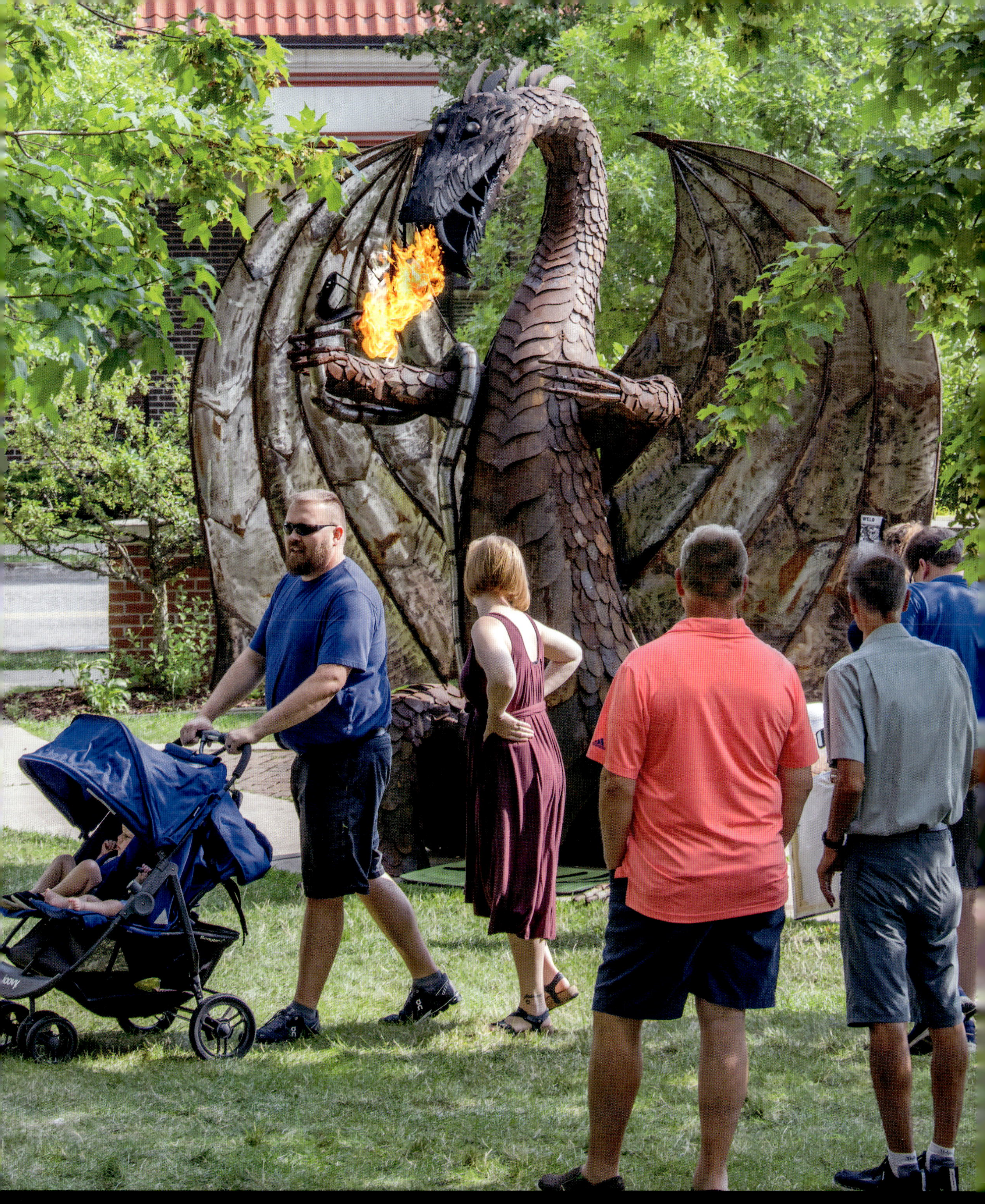

The Dragon - Metal Artist, Keith Coleman

The Dragon is created from 30 hot water tanks and the snake is made from car parts.
Created outdoors, the sculpture has 3000 hand cut pieces and stands 12 feet tall and 20 feet long.
It took 800 hours to complete and contains 15,000 welds.

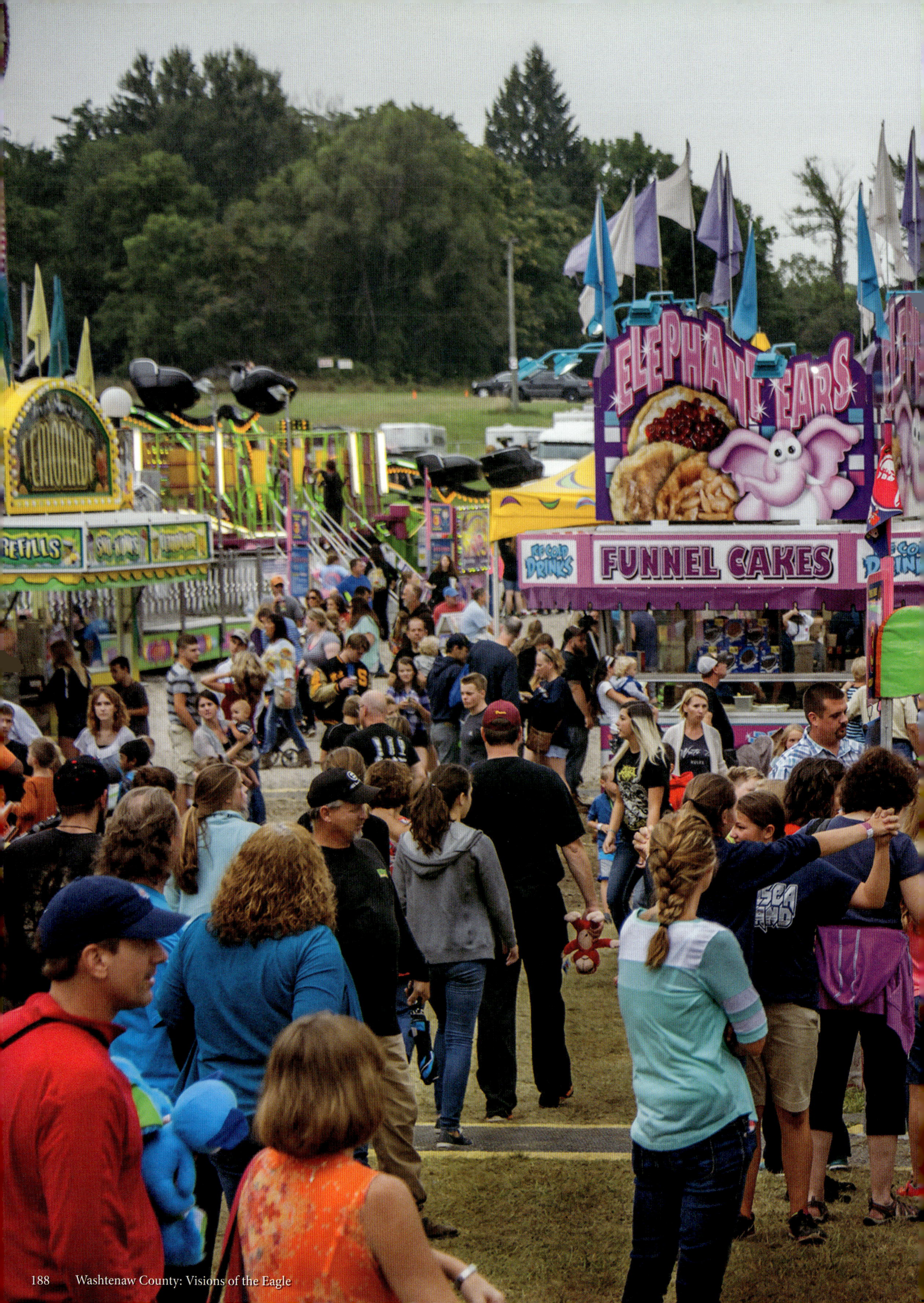
LEMONADE
REFILLS
ELEPHANT EARS
FUNNEL CAKES

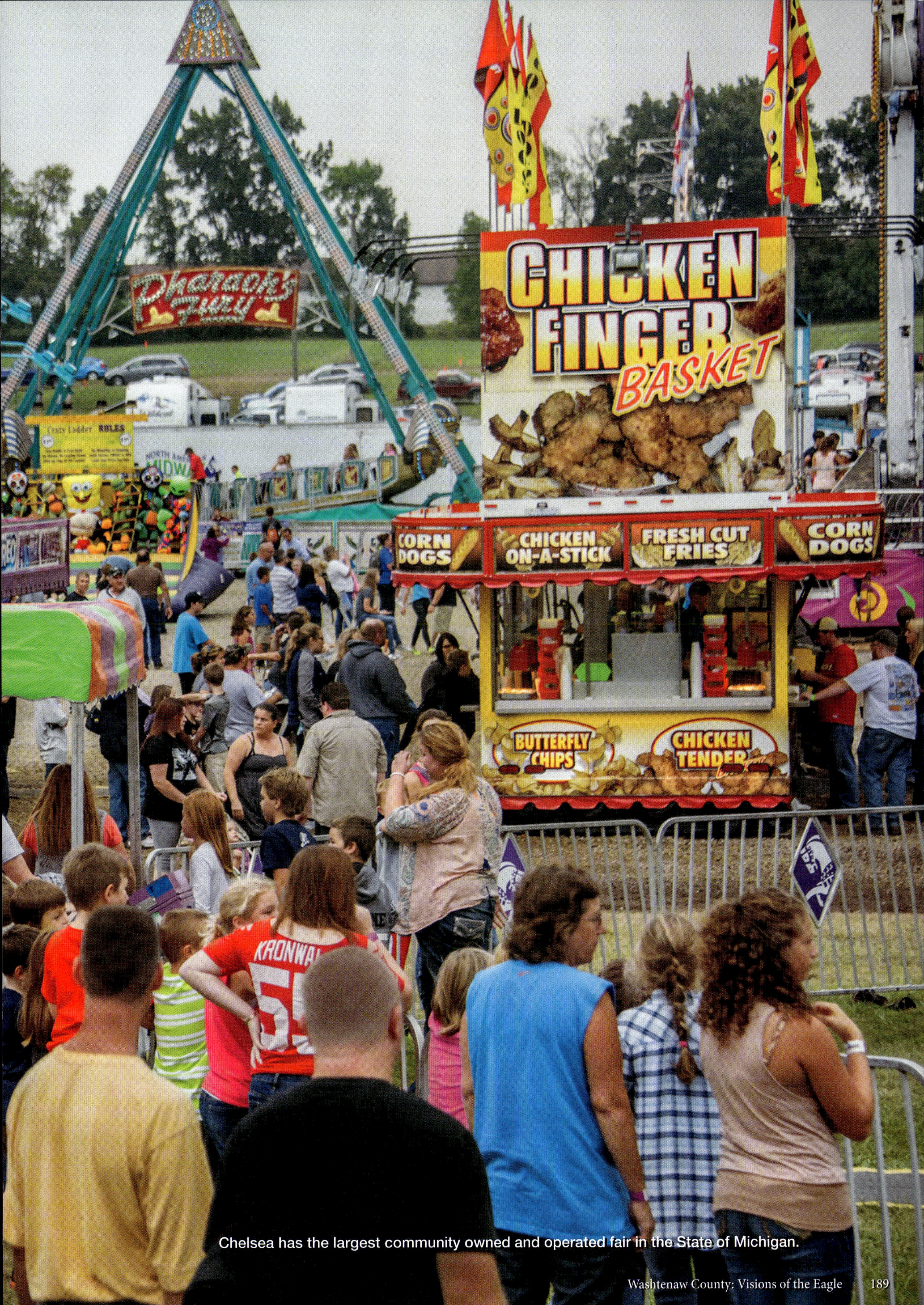

Chelsea has the largest community owned and operated fair in the State of Michigan.

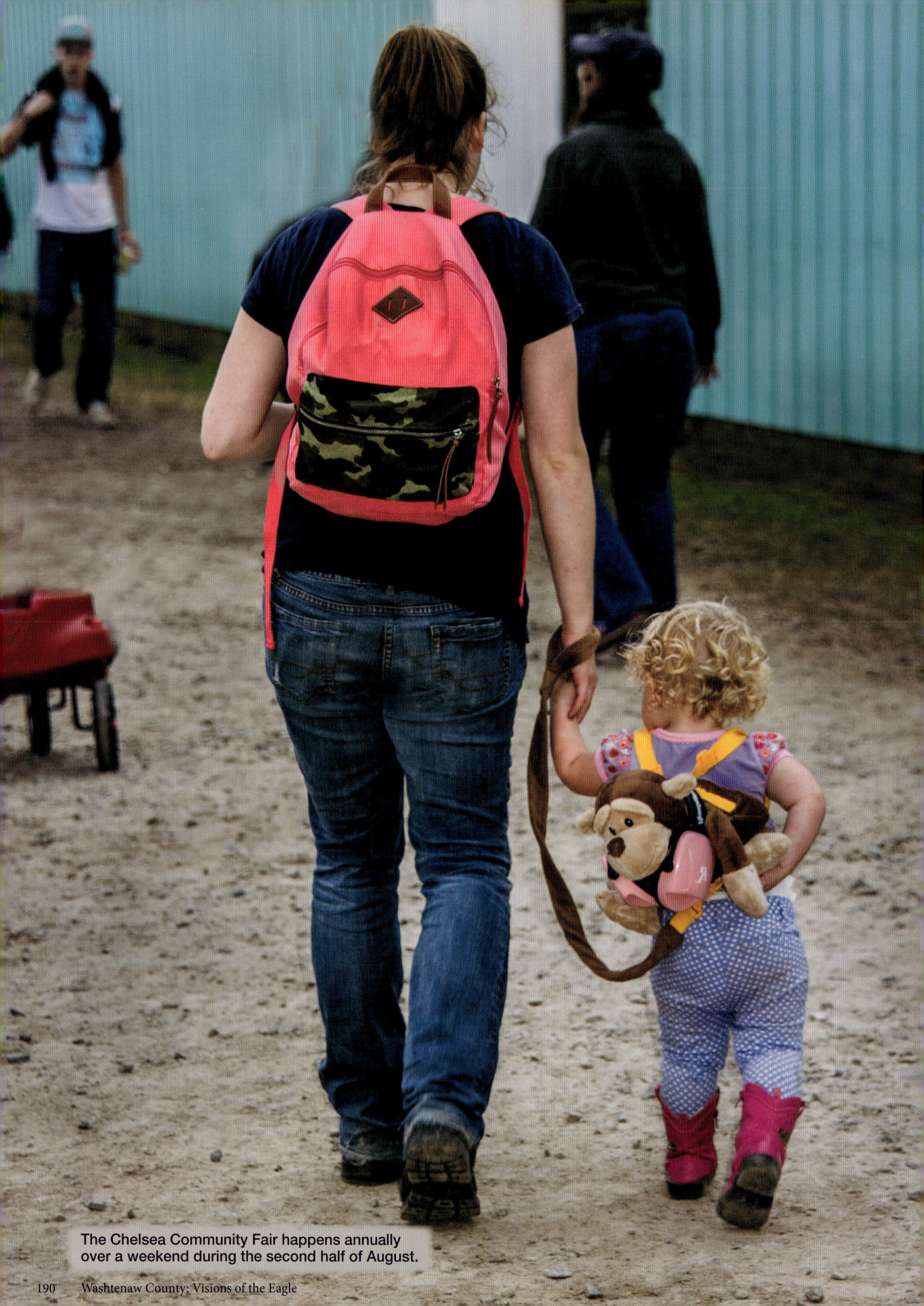

The Chelsea Community Fair happens annually over a weekend during the second half of August.

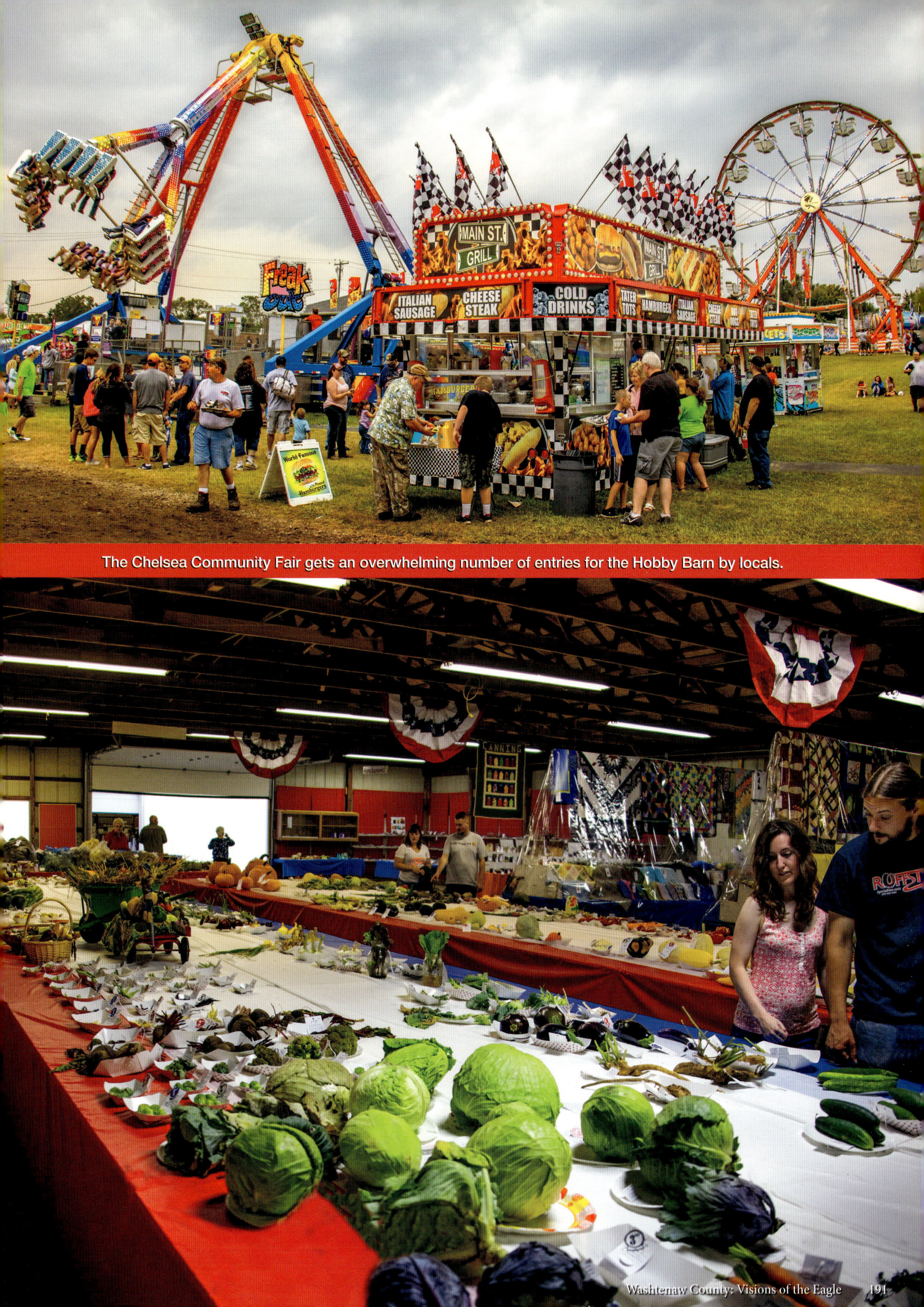

The Chelsea Community Fair gets an overwhelming number of entries for the Hobby Barn by locals.

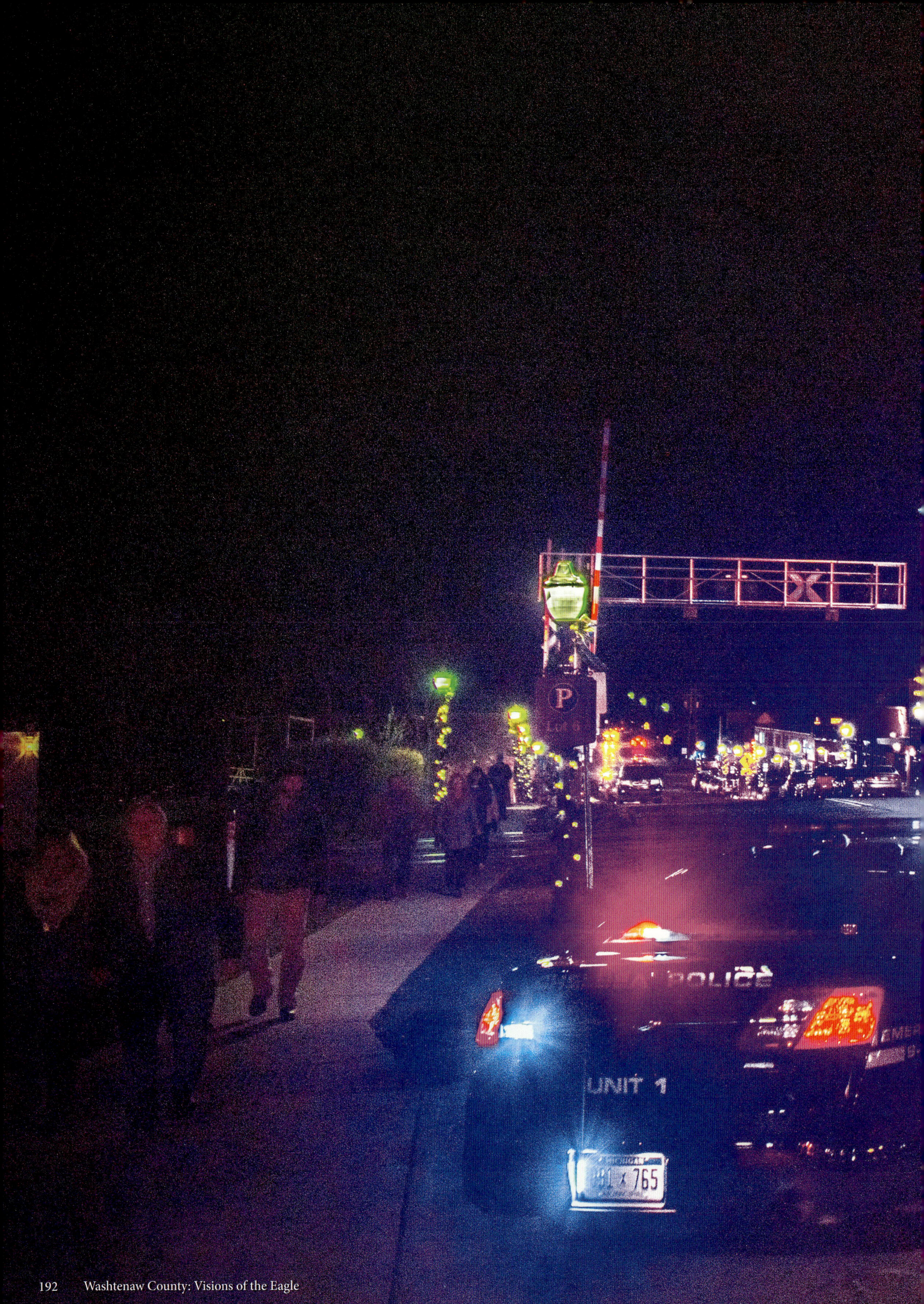
P
POLICE
UNIT 1

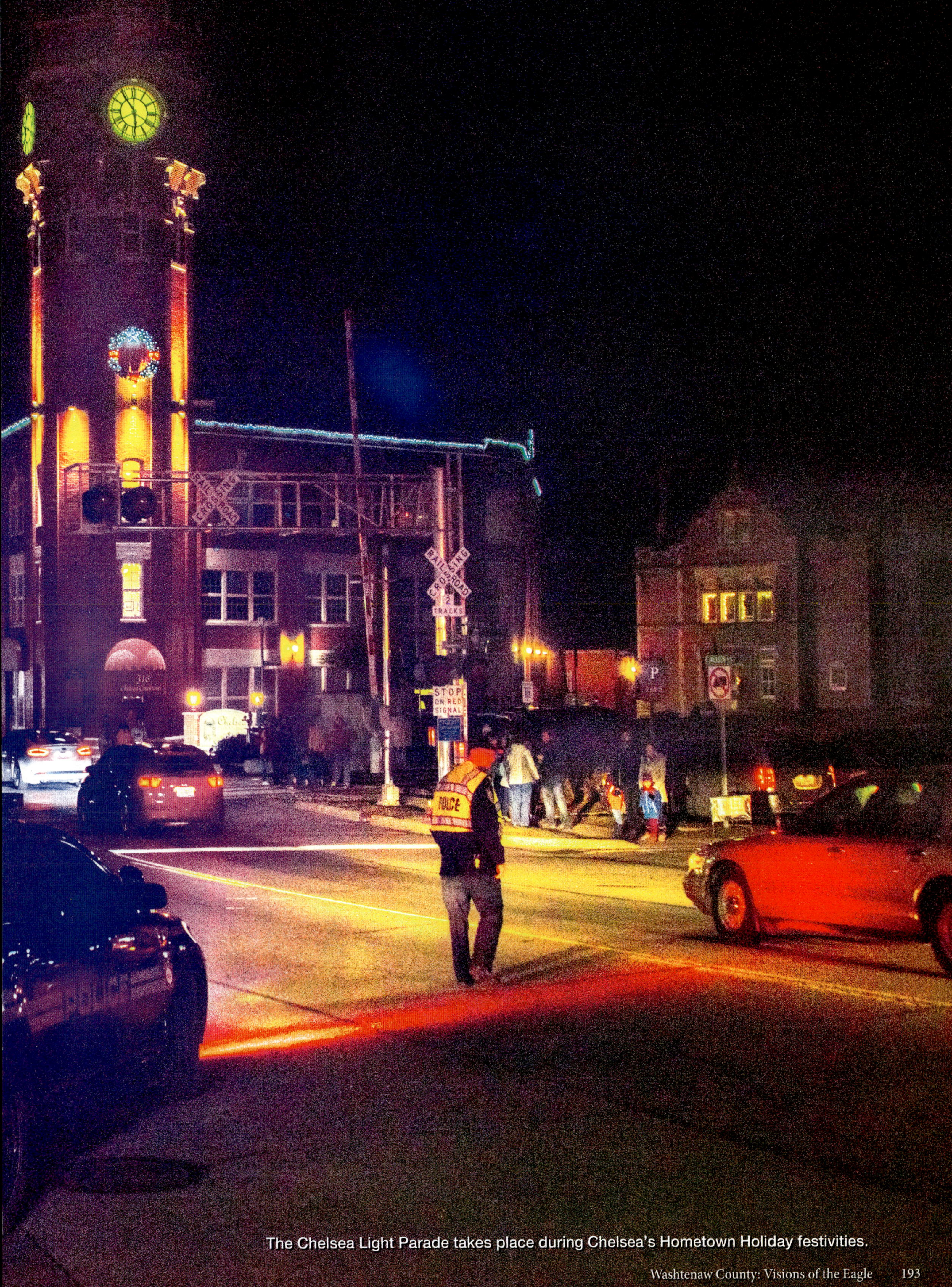

The Chelsea Light Parade takes place during Chelsea's Hometown Holiday festivities.

DEXTER

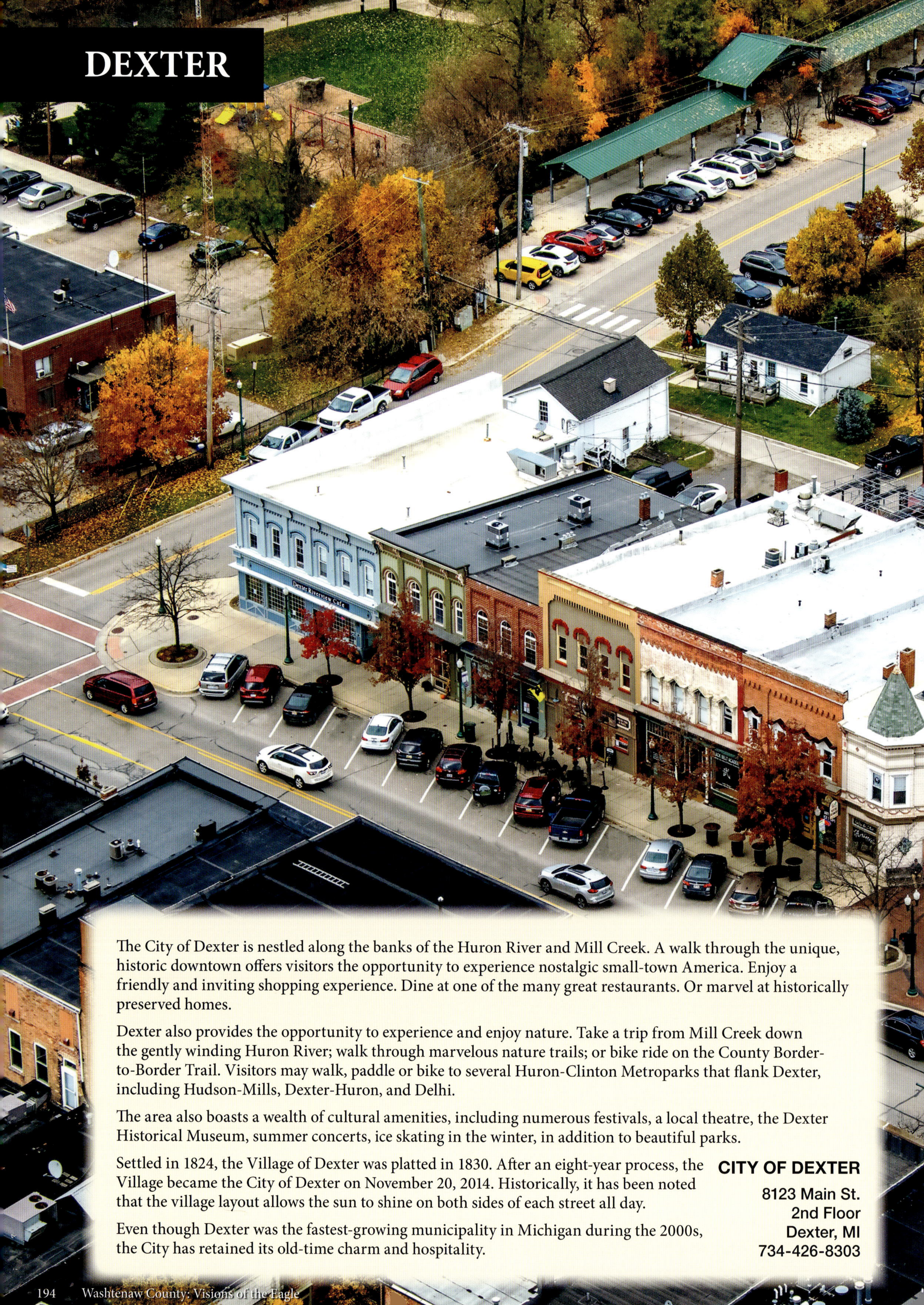

The City of Dexter is nestled along the banks of the Huron River and Mill Creek. A walk through the unique, historic downtown offers visitors the opportunity to experience nostalgic small-town America. Enjoy a friendly and inviting shopping experience. Dine at one of the many great restaurants. Or marvel at historically preserved homes.

Dexter also provides the opportunity to experience and enjoy nature. Take a trip from Mill Creek down the gently winding Huron River; walk through marvelous nature trails; or bike ride on the County Border-to-Border Trail. Visitors may walk, paddle or bike to several Huron-Clinton Metroparks that flank Dexter, including Hudson-Mills, Dexter-Huron, and Delhi.

The area also boasts a wealth of cultural amenities, including numerous festivals, a local theatre, the Dexter Historical Museum, summer concerts, ice skating in the winter, in addition to beautiful parks.

Settled in 1824, the Village of Dexter was platted in 1830. After an eight-year process, the Village became the City of Dexter on November 20, 2014. Historically, it has been noted that the village layout allows the sun to shine on both sides of each street all day.

Even though Dexter was the fastest-growing municipality in Michigan during the 2000s, the City has retained its old-time charm and hospitality.

CITY OF DEXTER
8123 Main St.
2nd Floor
Dexter, MI
734-426-8303

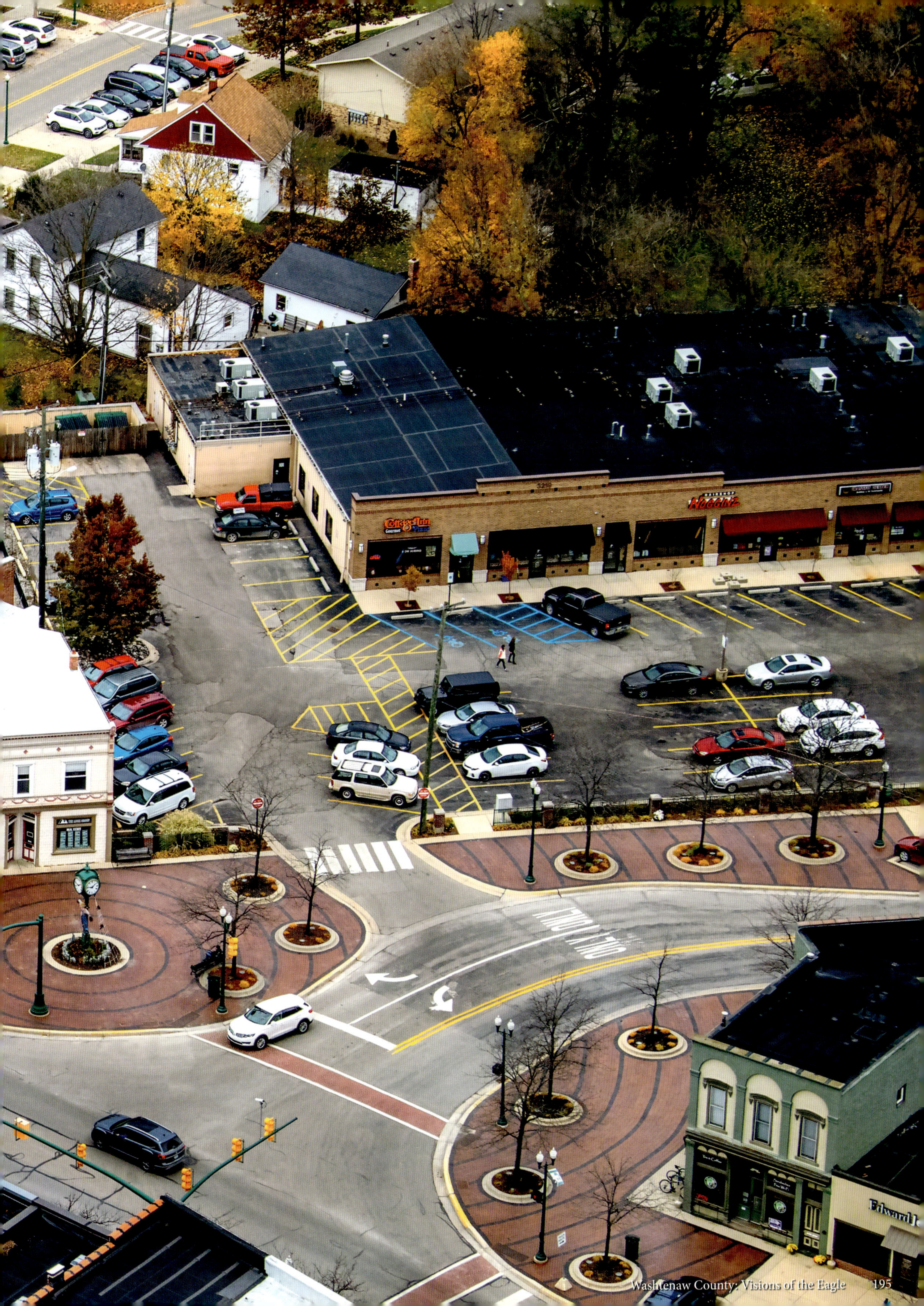
Cottage Inn

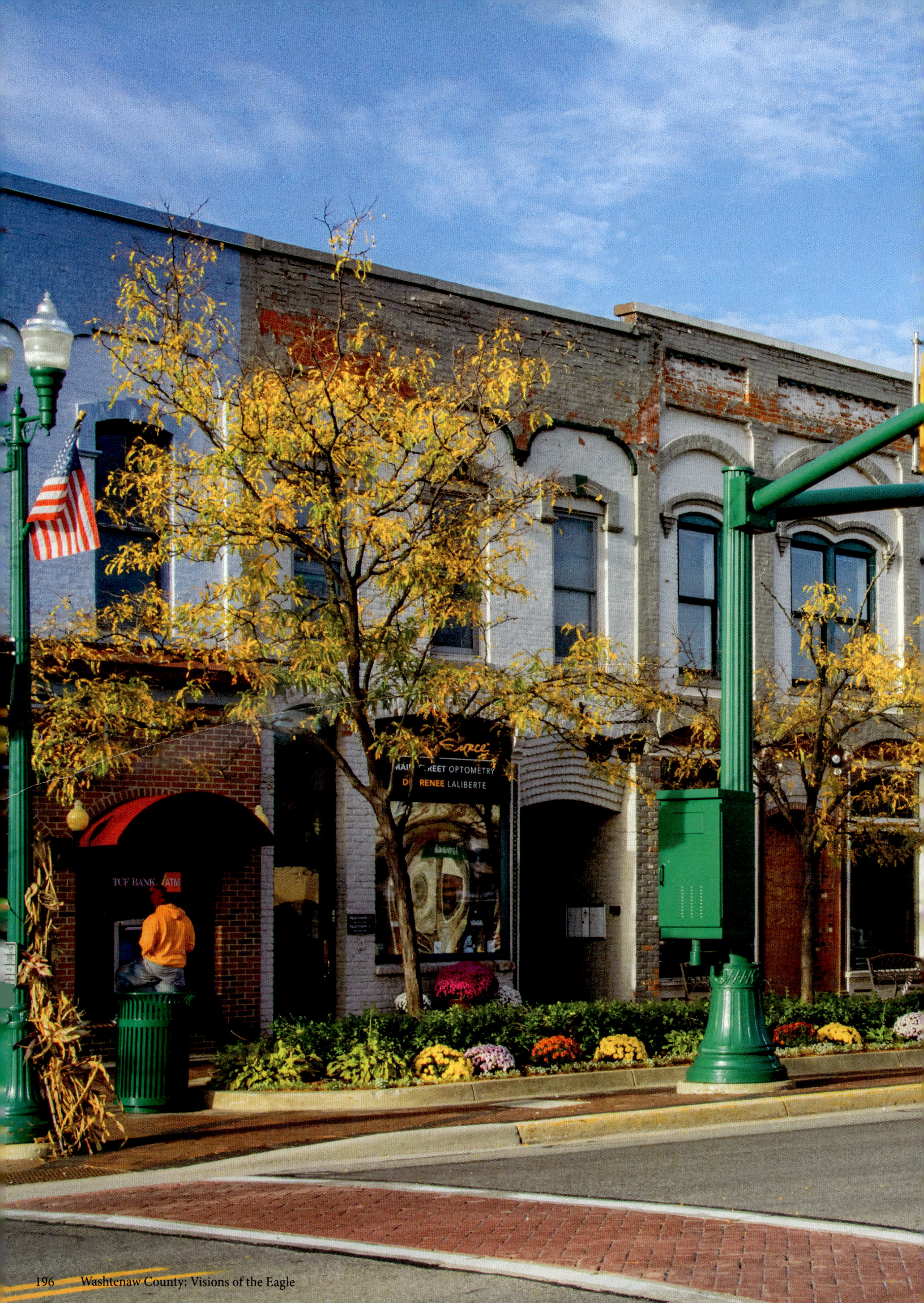
OPTOMETRY
RENEE LALIBERTE
TCF BANK
ATM

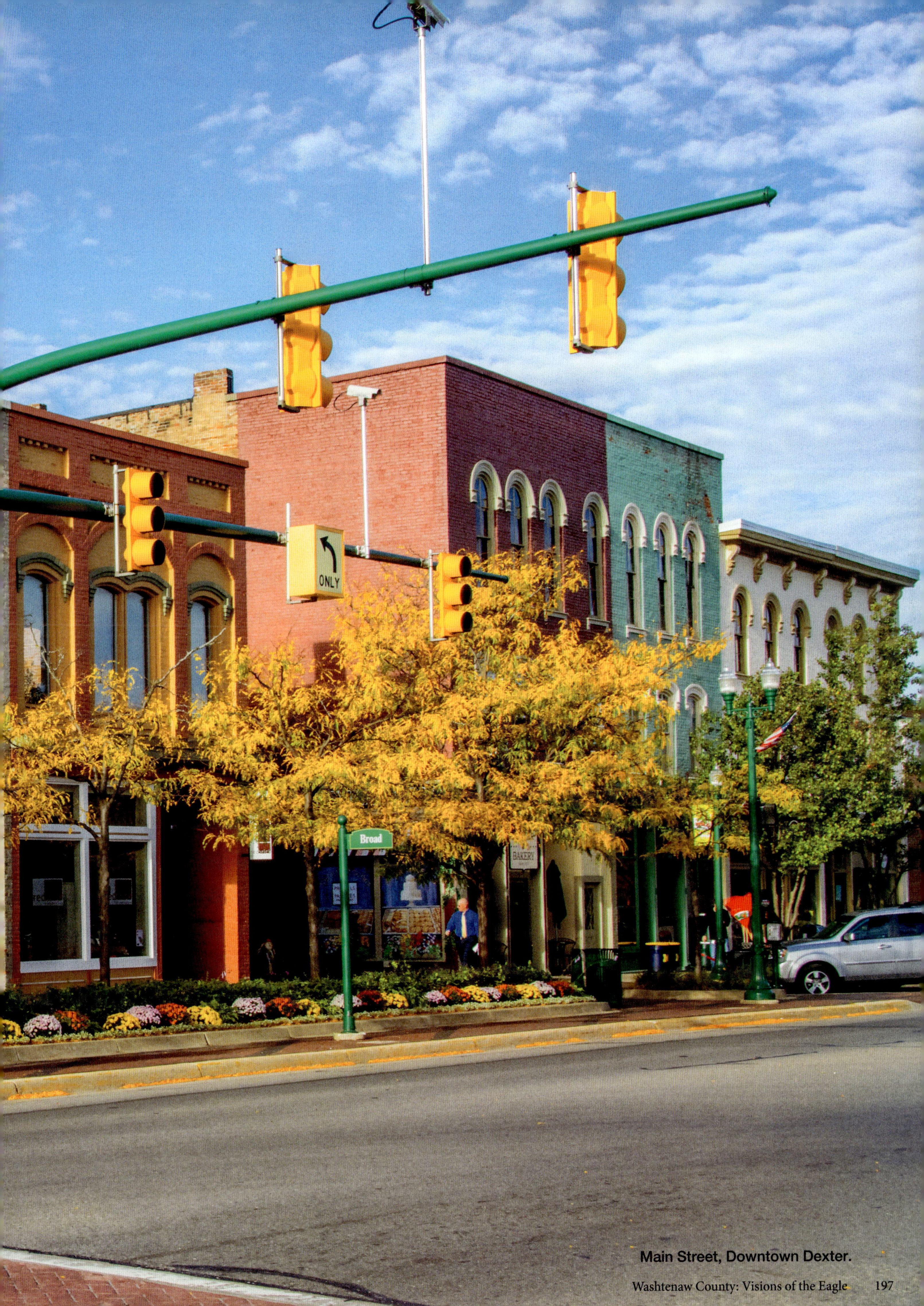

Main Street, Downtown Dexter.

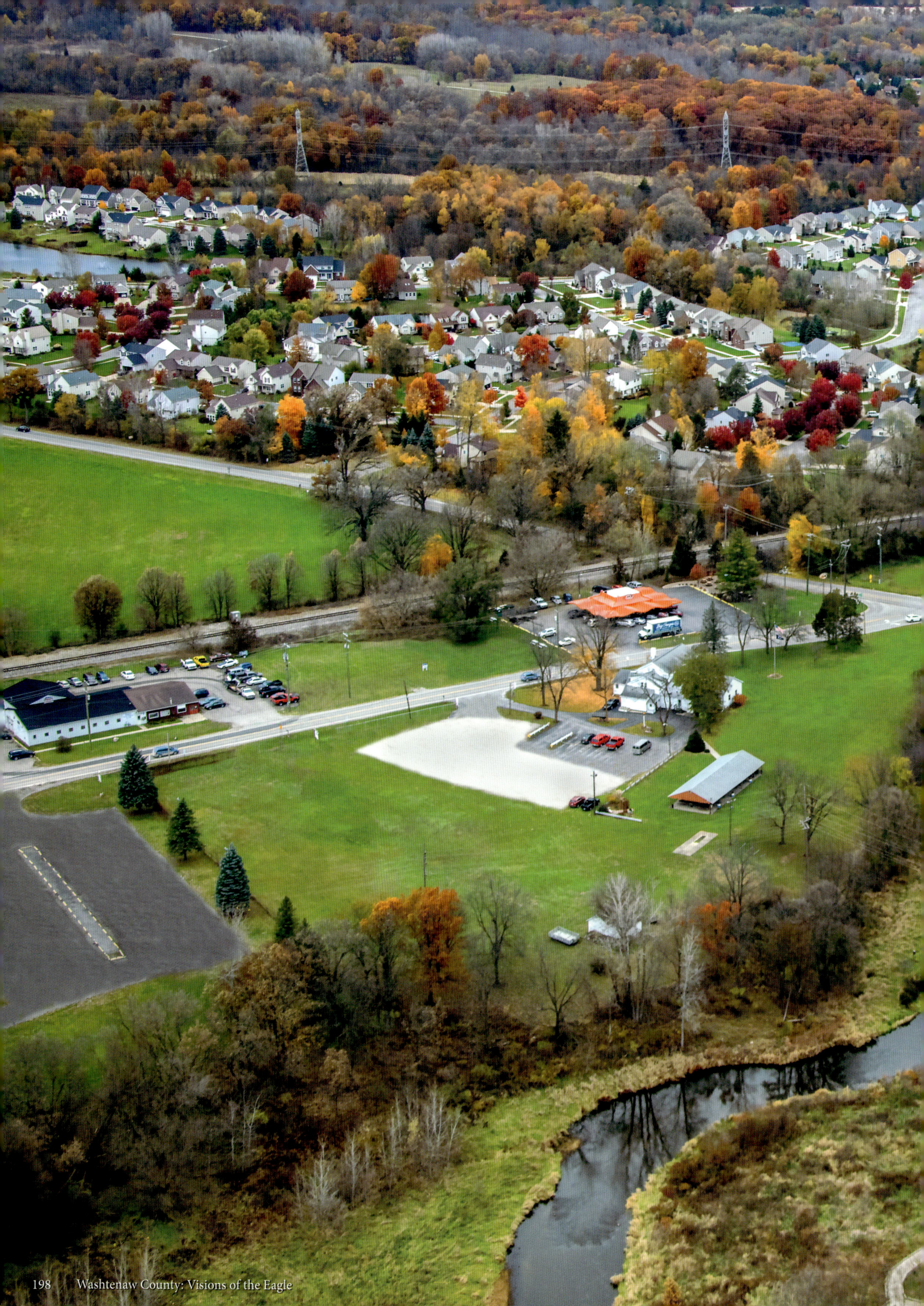

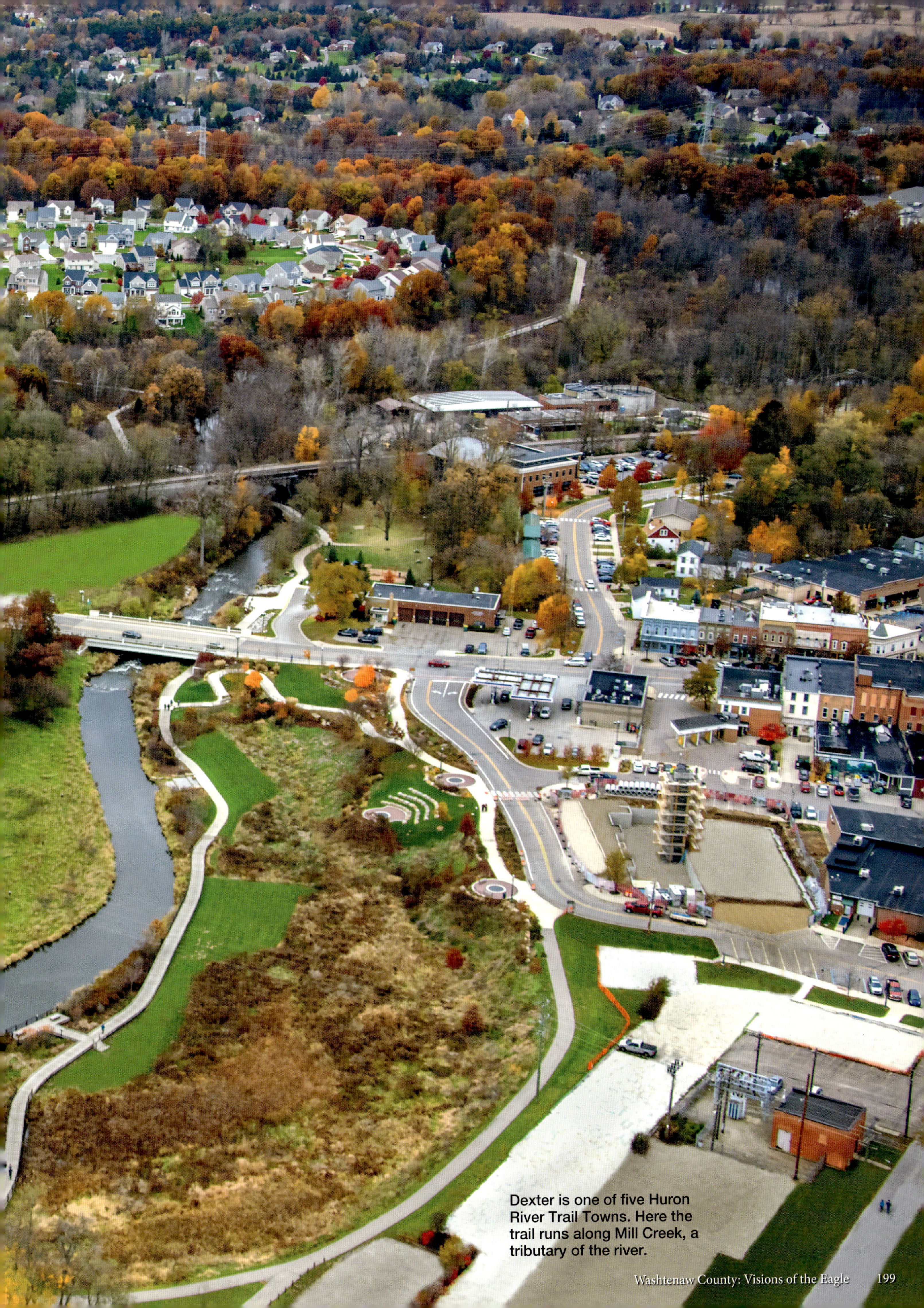

Dexter is one of five Huron River Trail Towns. Here the trail runs along Mill Creek, a tributary of the river.

Guenther Building Company

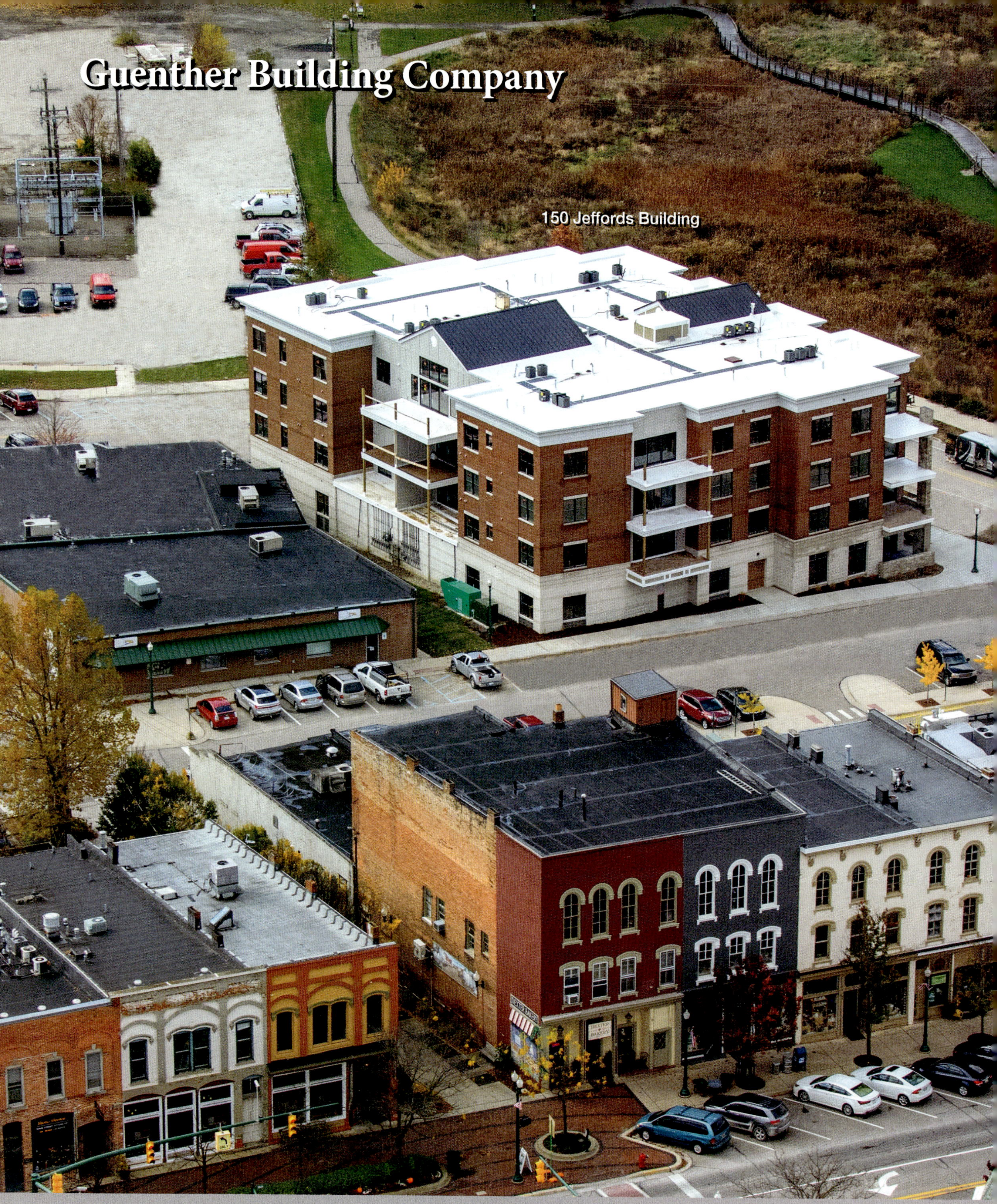

Guenther Building Company has built more than 30 housing communities nestled among lakes, parks, and woodlands in Washtenaw County since it was founded in 1946 by Rueben Guenther. His son, Bob Guenther, took over the Ann Arbor-based business in 1963 and grew the company into one of the leading homebuilders in Southeast Michigan.

Bob's children Natalie Ceccolini and Rob Guenther carry on the tradition of fine homebuilding along with the fourth generation, Jessica and Nick Ceccolini.

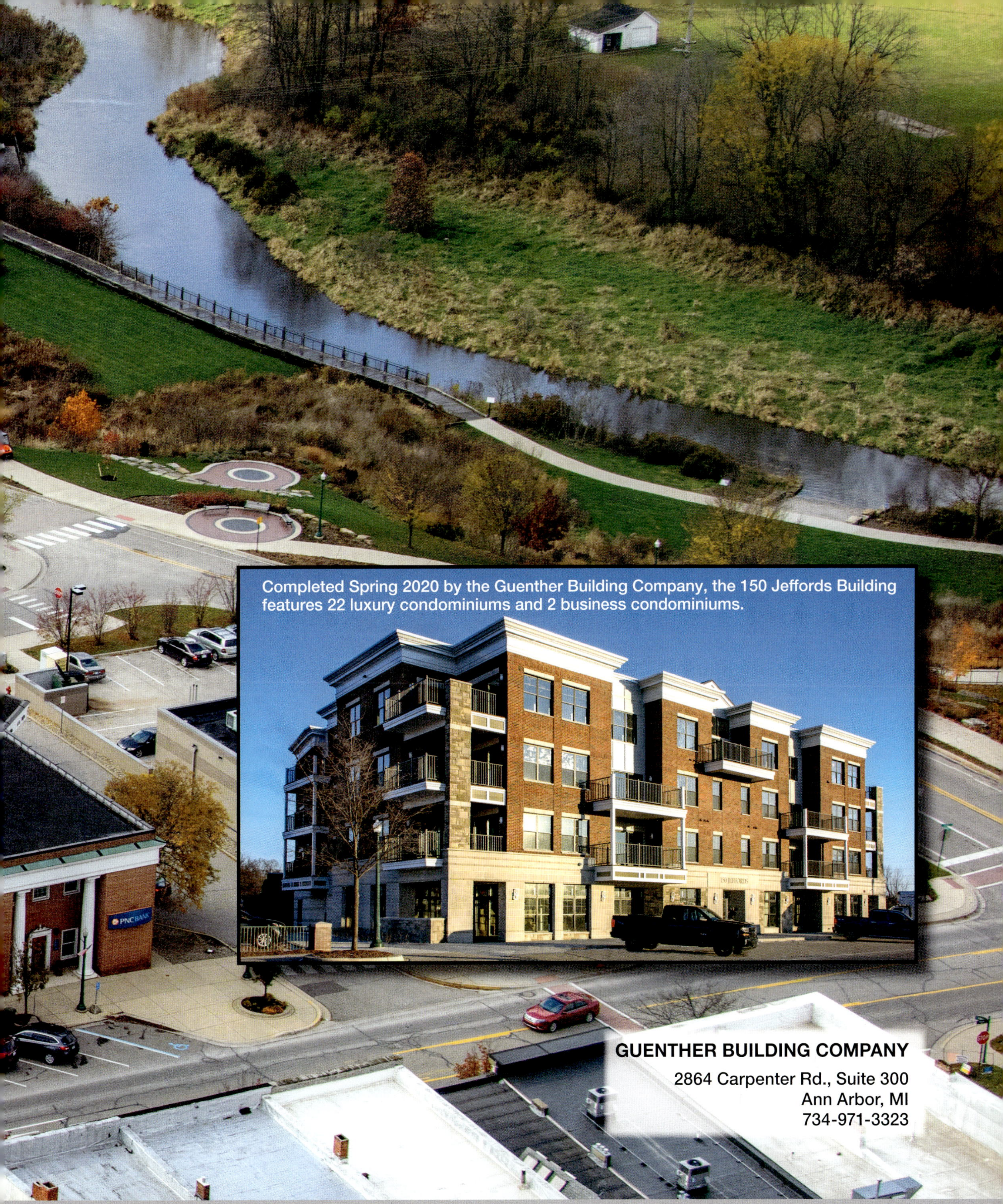

Completed Spring 2020 by the Guenther Building Company, the 150 Jeffords Building features 22 luxury condominiums and 2 business condominiums.

GUENTHER BUILDING COMPANY

2864 Carpenter Rd., Suite 300
Ann Arbor, MI
734-971-3323

"I grew up in Ann Arbor, and the people and land of Washtenaw County are an inspiration for the company we built. I learned from my father," Bob Guenther said. "My son and daughter have learned from me the meaning of building something that will last for years to come. I am lucky to see my grandchildren take on that same commitment."

Guenther Building Company has sponsored numerous community sporting teams and has contributed to hospitals and organizations that promote health and wellbeing. Bob has been instrumental in the Ann Arbor Student Building Industry Program, supporting students interested in the construction industry.

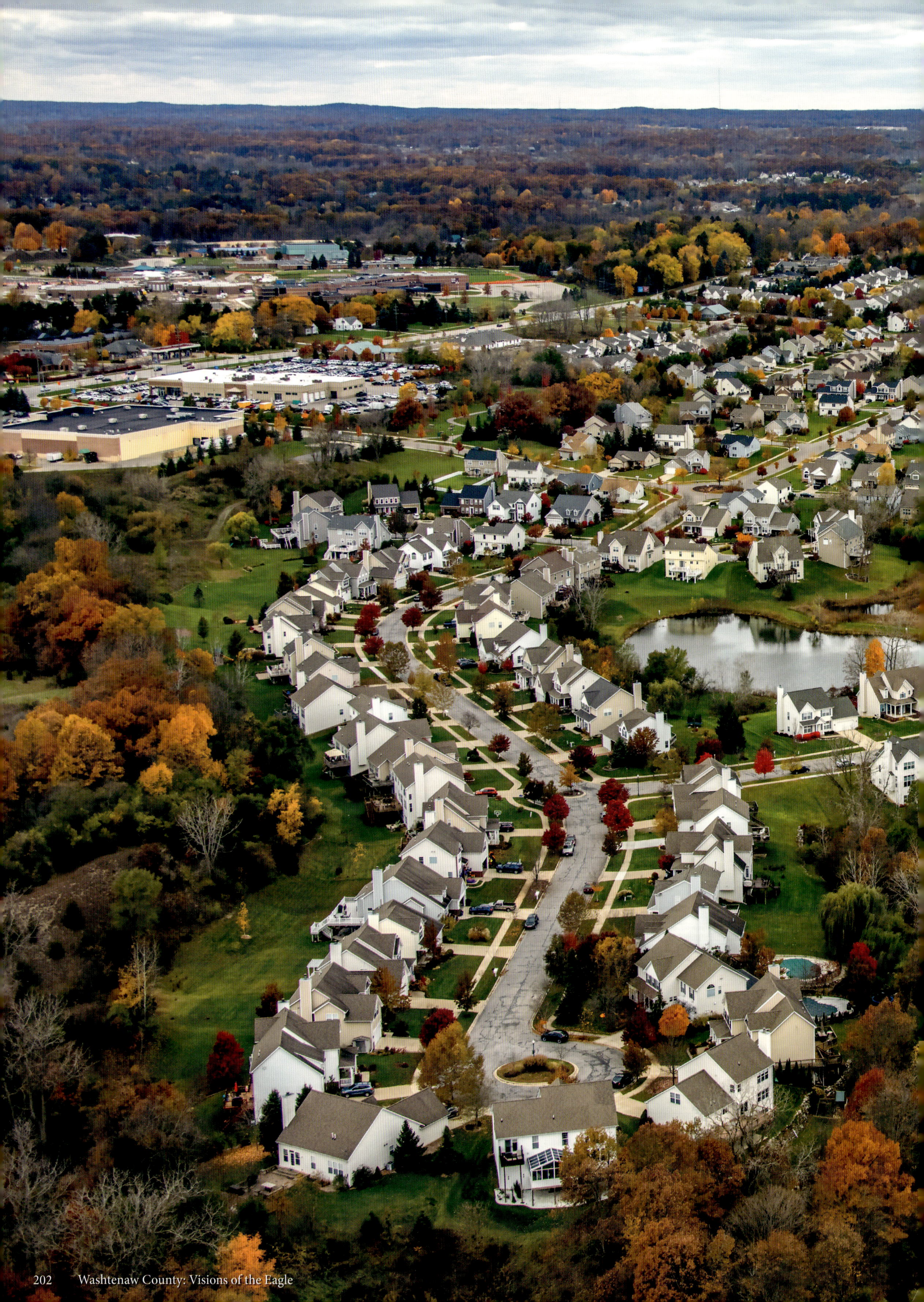

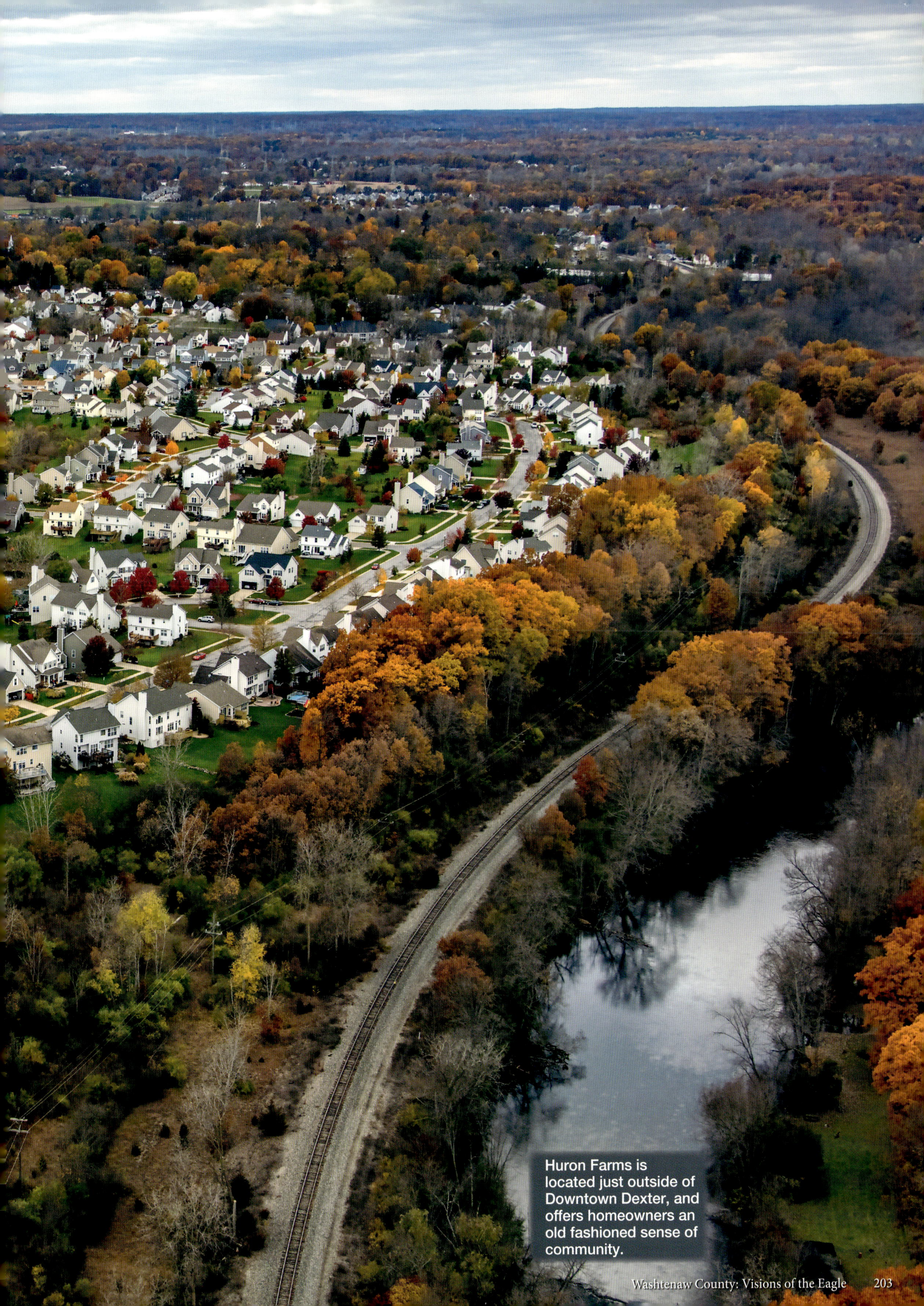

Huron Farms is located just outside of Downtown Dexter, and offers homeowners an old fashioned sense of community.

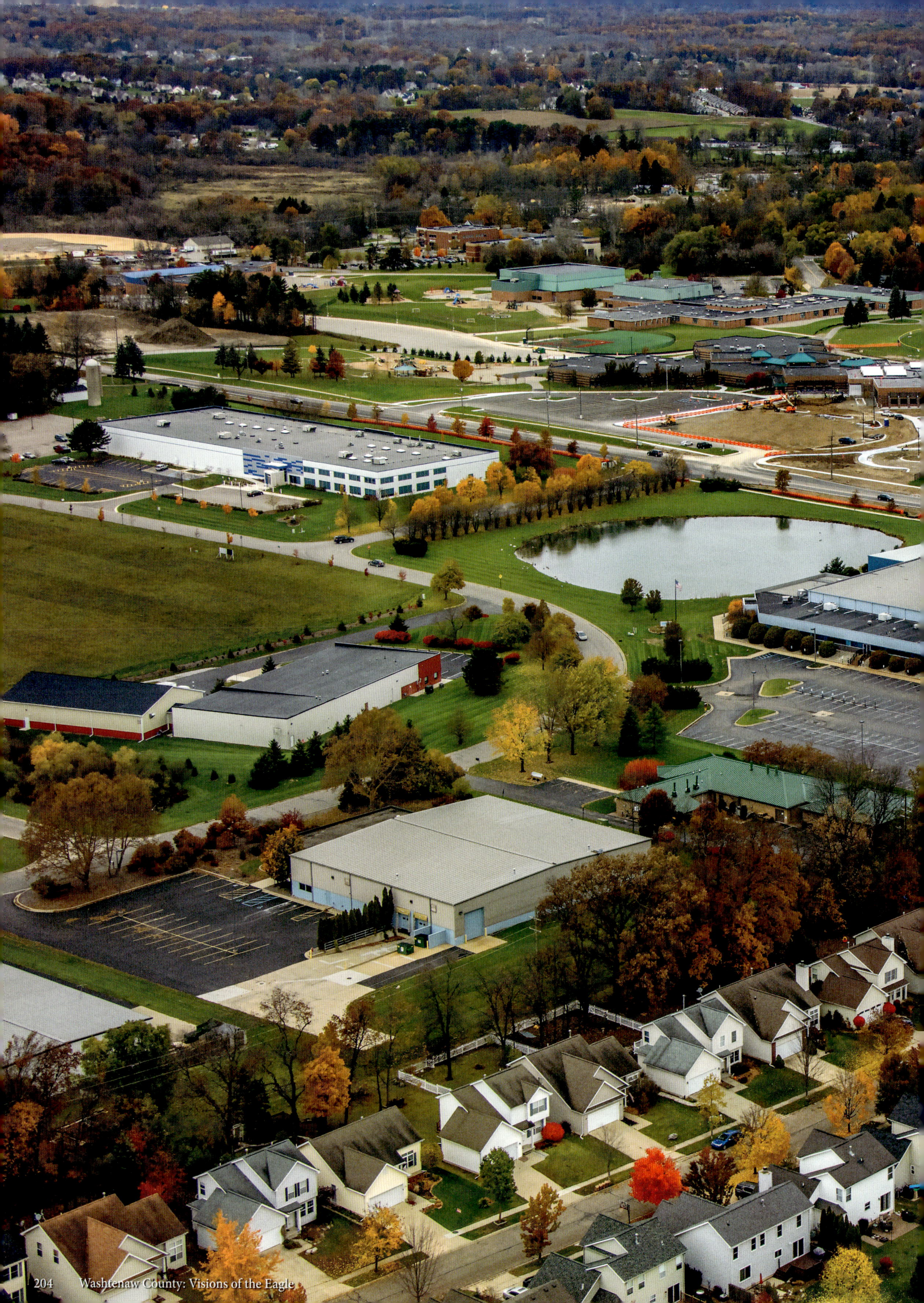

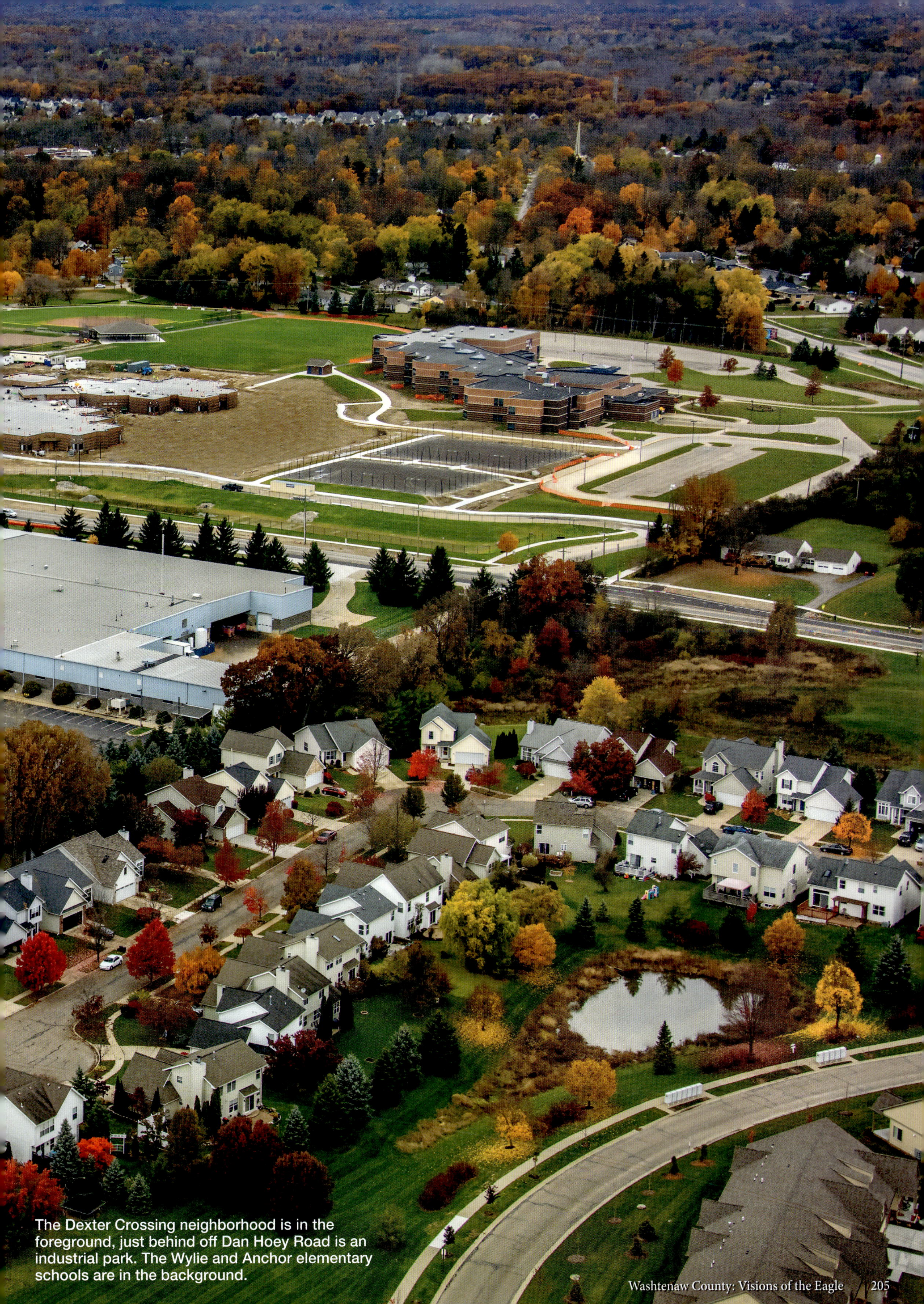

The Dexter Crossing neighborhood is in the foreground, just behind off Dan Hoey Road is an industrial park. The Wylie and Anchor elementary schools are in the background.

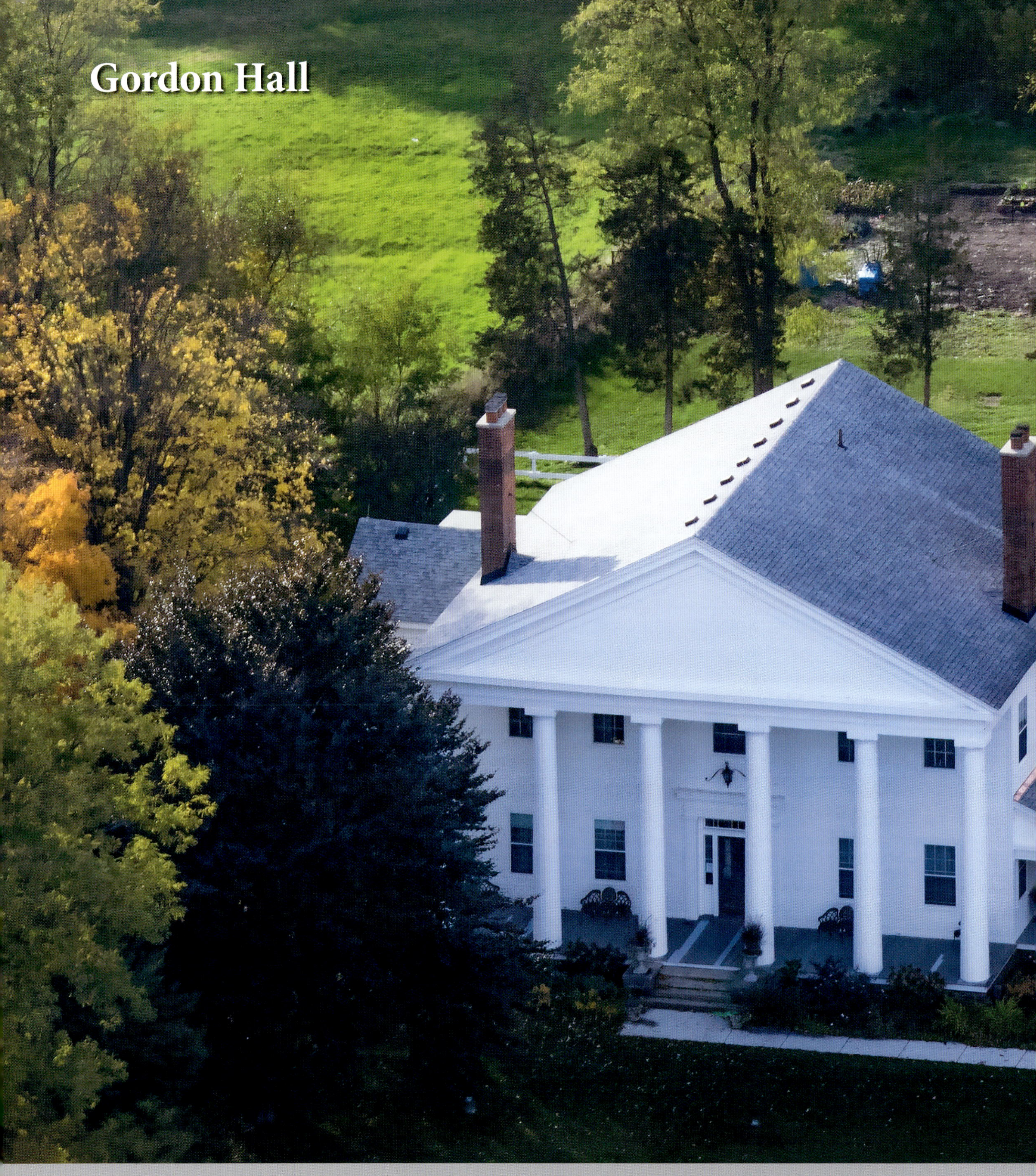

Gordon Hall

Judge Samuel W. Dexter, the founder of the village of Dexter, began building his home known as Gordon Hall in 1841 on a low hill on his farm west of the village. It was named after his mother's family. Calvin Fillmore, brother of President Millard Fillmore, was one of the designers and builders of Gordon Hall.

The 9,000 square-foot Greek revival home built with hand-hewn white oak timber originally had 22 rooms and nine fireplaces. Two pieces of lumber in the attic each run 50 feet long without a knot. The floorboards are yellow poplar. A single hallway ran from the front to back doors, and a walnut staircase reached the second floor in a single flight. The home included quarters for the many servants needed to run the house.

Judge Dexter died in 1863. His third wife, Millicent Bond Dexter, lived in the mansion until her death in 1899. It was then sold and rented and eventually fell into disrepair.

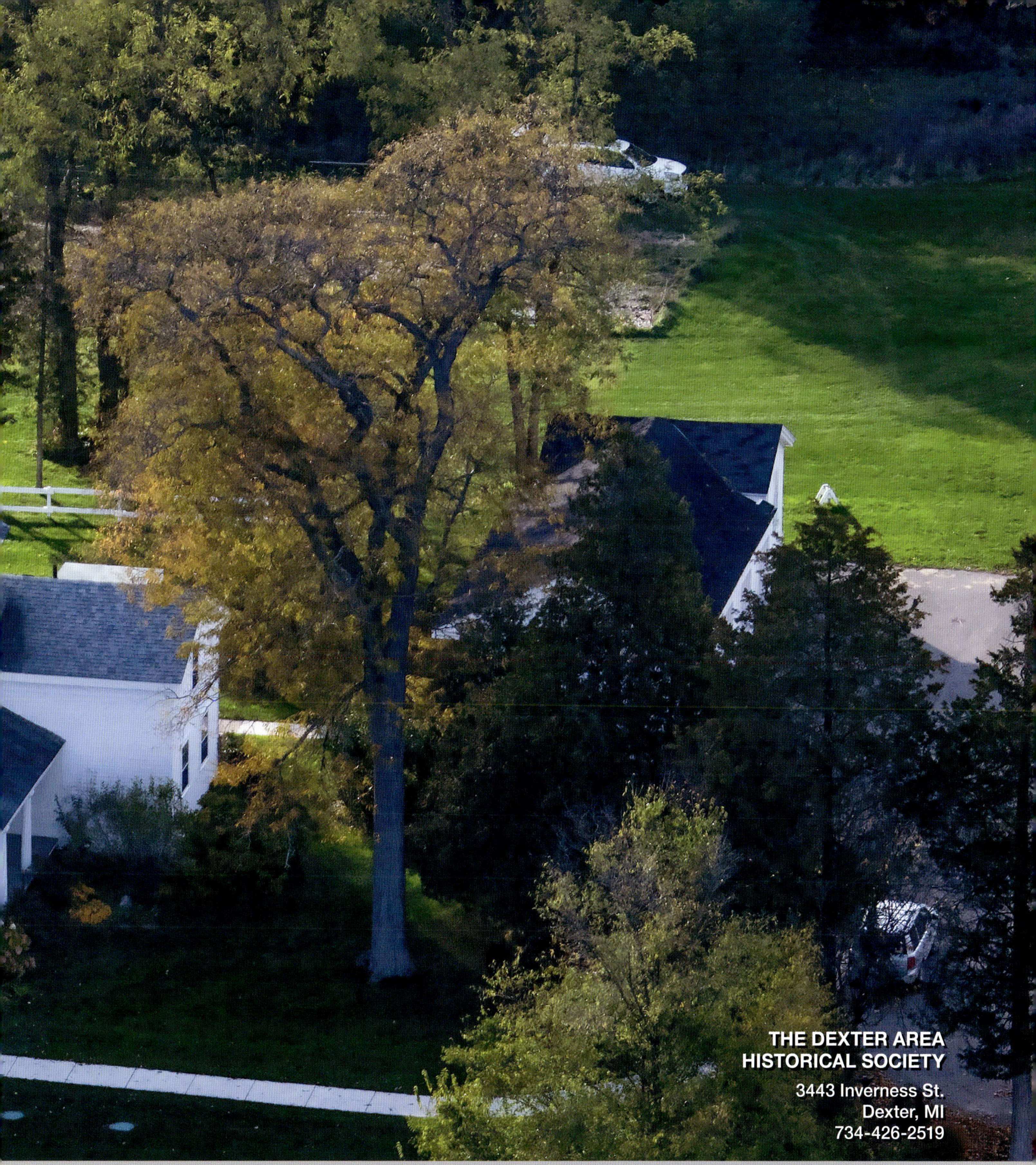

THE DEXTER AREA HISTORICAL SOCIETY

3443 Inverness St.
Dexter, MI
734-426-2519

In 1934, the U.S. Department of the Interior identified Gordon Hall as one of the most historic Greek revival homes in Michigan. Five years later, Judge Dexter's granddaughter, Katharine Dexter McCormick, philanthropist and heir to the McCormick fortune, purchased the estate.

Restoration began in the 1940s under Professor Emeritus Emil Lorch of the University of Michigan School of Architecture. In 1950, McCormick donated the property to the University of Michigan. Most of the interior was removed, including the staircase and five fireplaces, to create four apartments.

The mansion was placed on the National Register of Historic Places in 1972. In 2001, the Washtenaw County Board of Commissioners designated it a Historic Site. The Dexter Area Historical Society purchased the mansion and its 67 remaining acres in 2005 to protect and preserve this vital part of Dexter's heritage. Rehabilitation on the house continues and it is available to rent for special events.

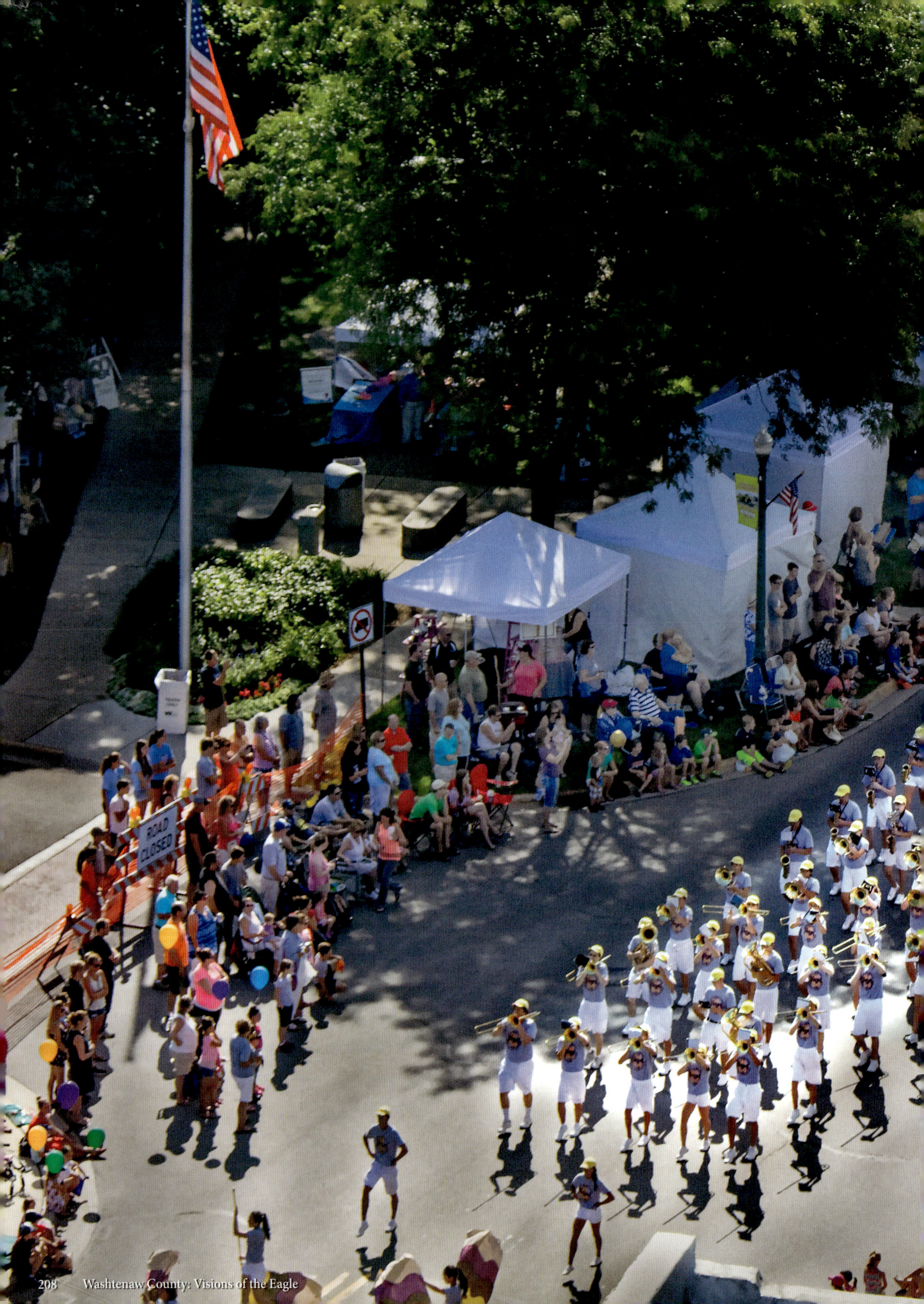
ROAD
CLOSED

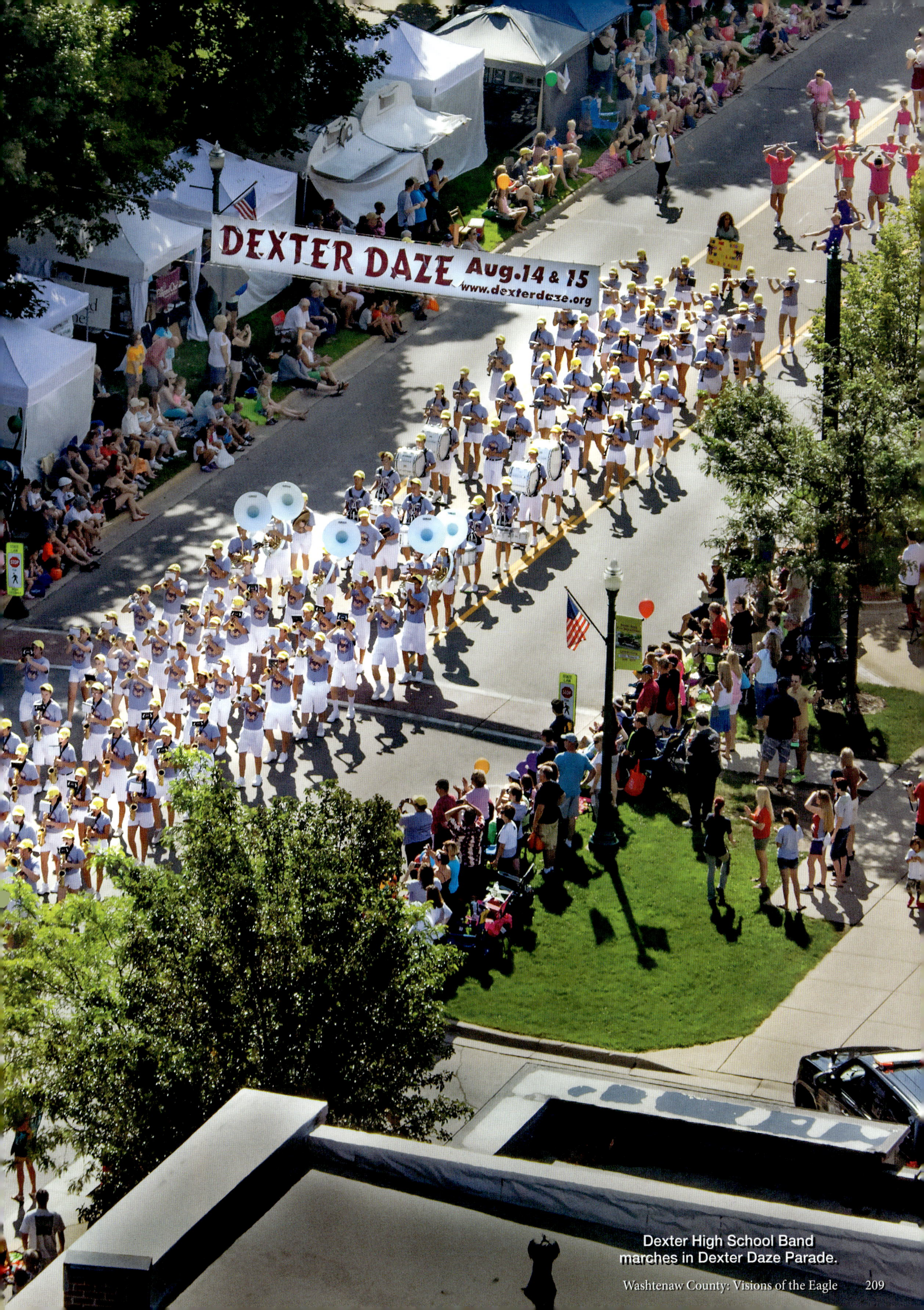

Dexter High School Band marches in Dexter Daze Parade.

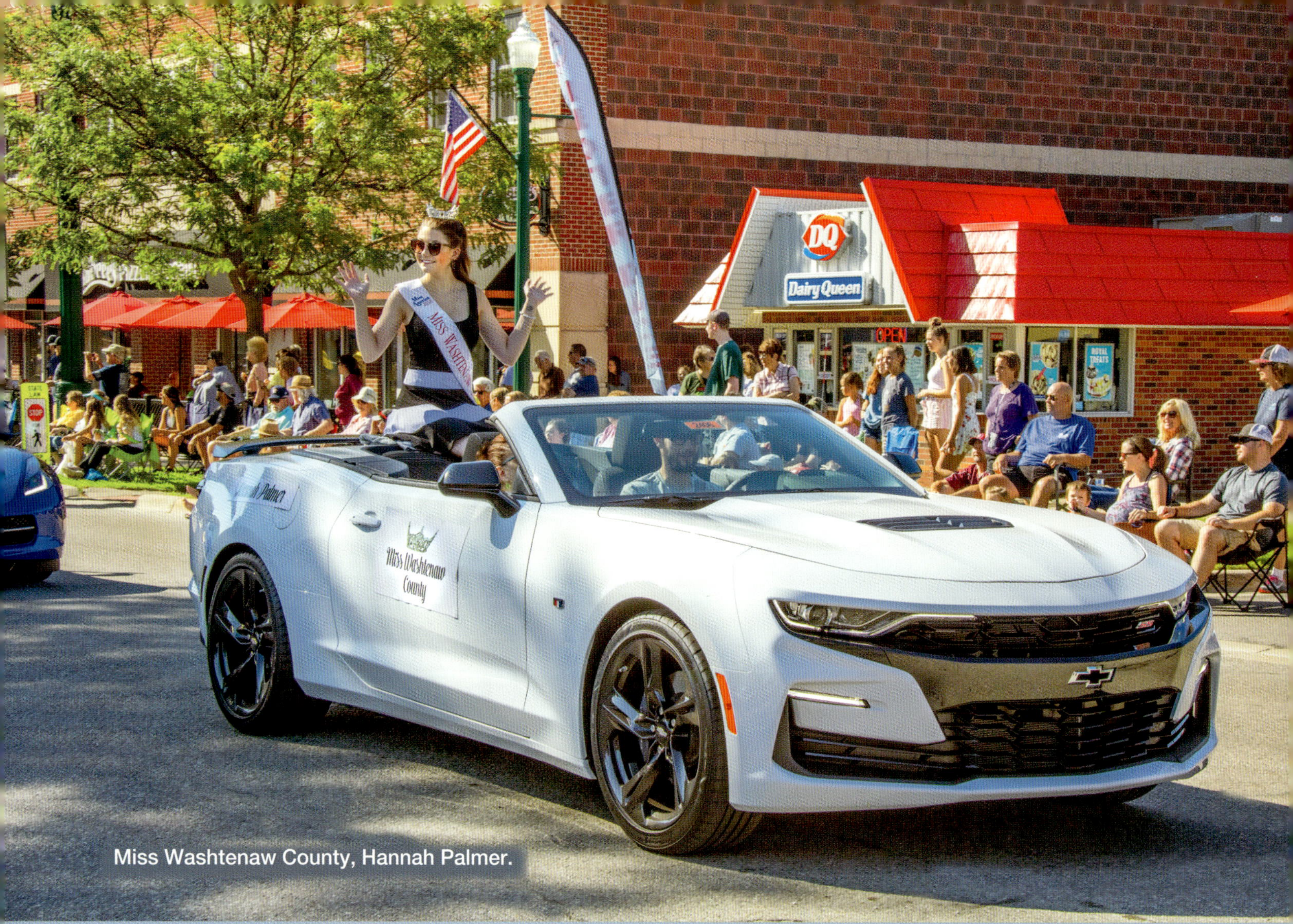

Miss Washtenaw County, Hannah Palmer.

Master Lockman's Black Belt Academy.

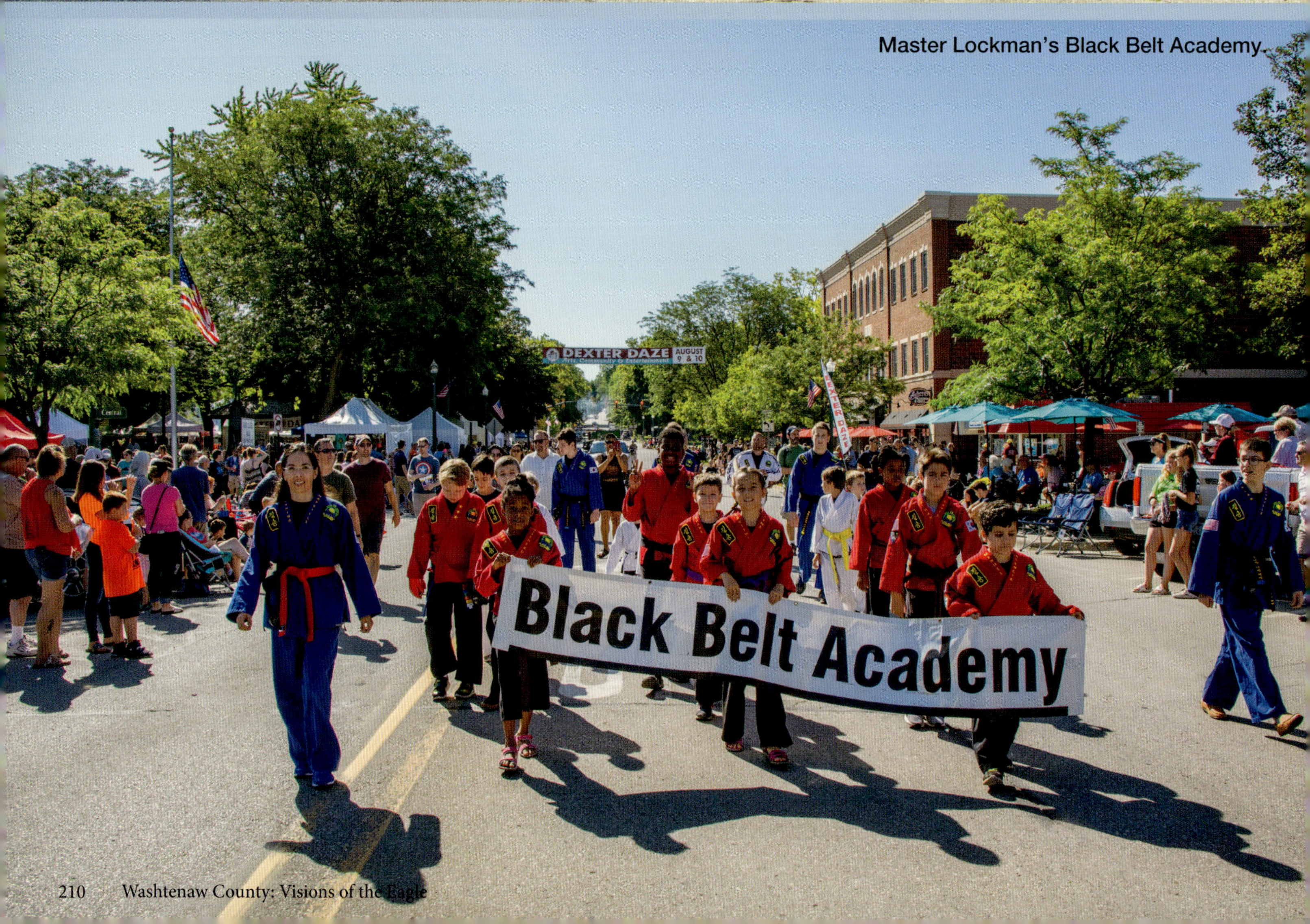

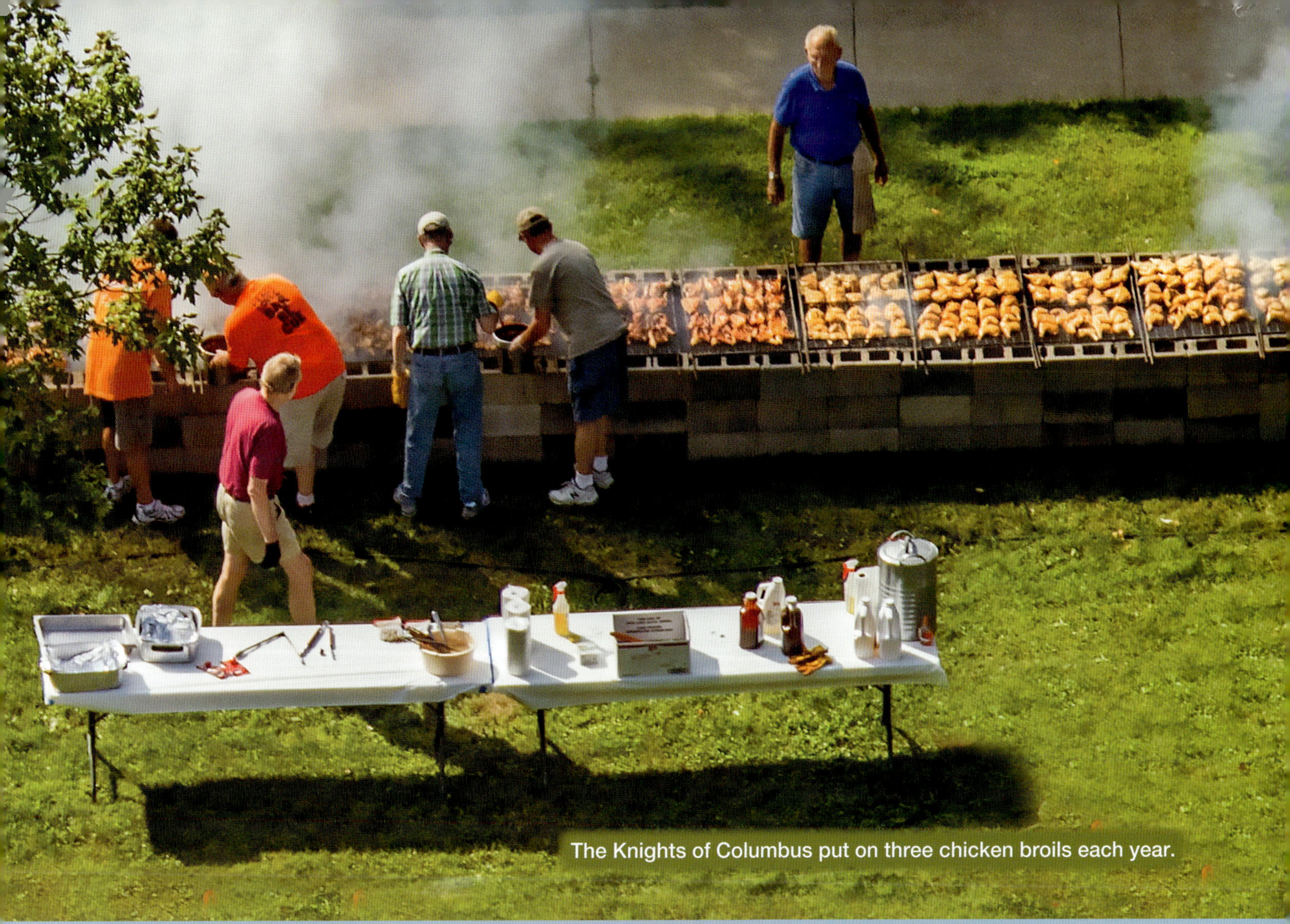

The Knights of Columbus put on three chicken broils each year.

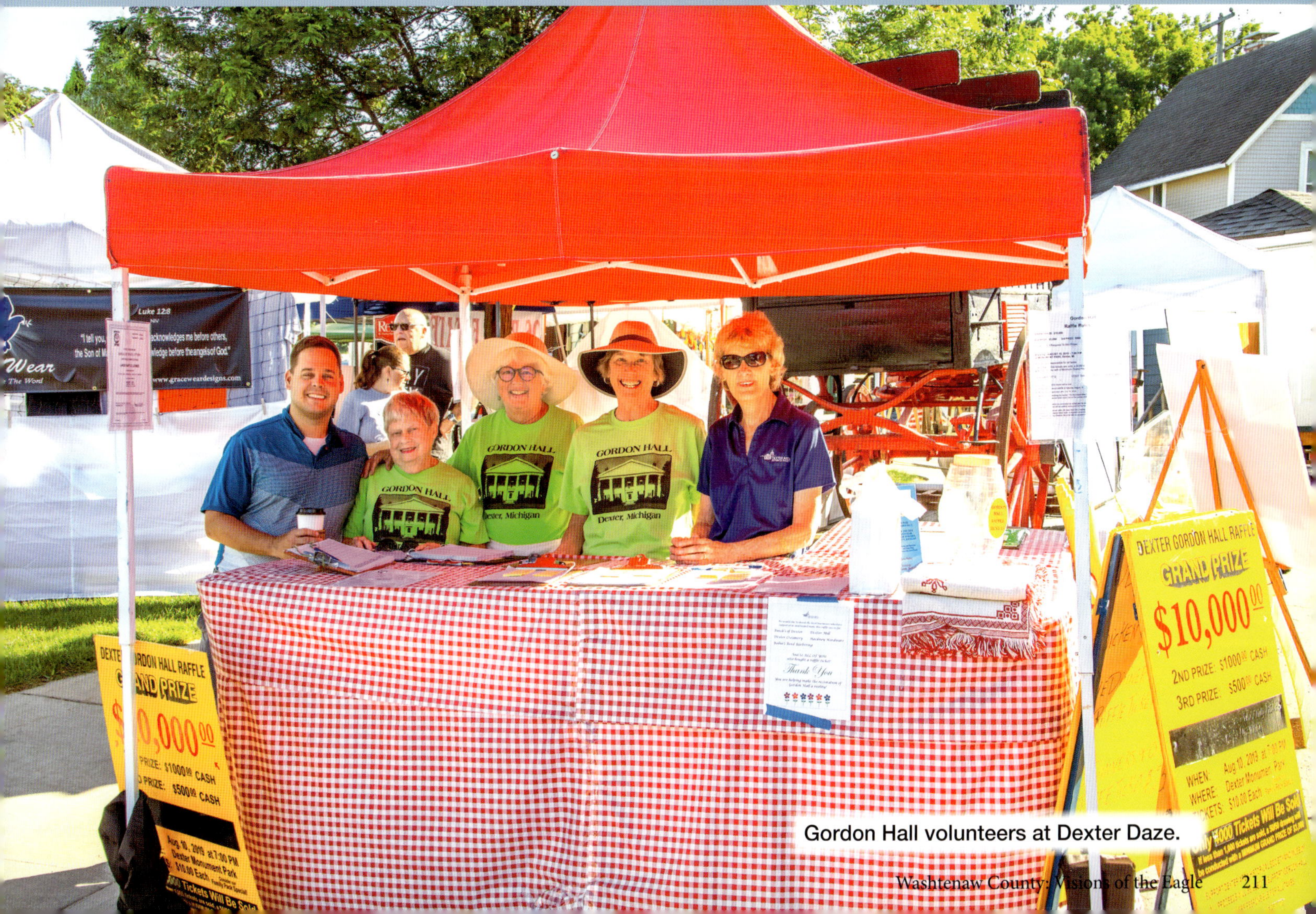

Gordon Hall volunteers at Dexter Daze.

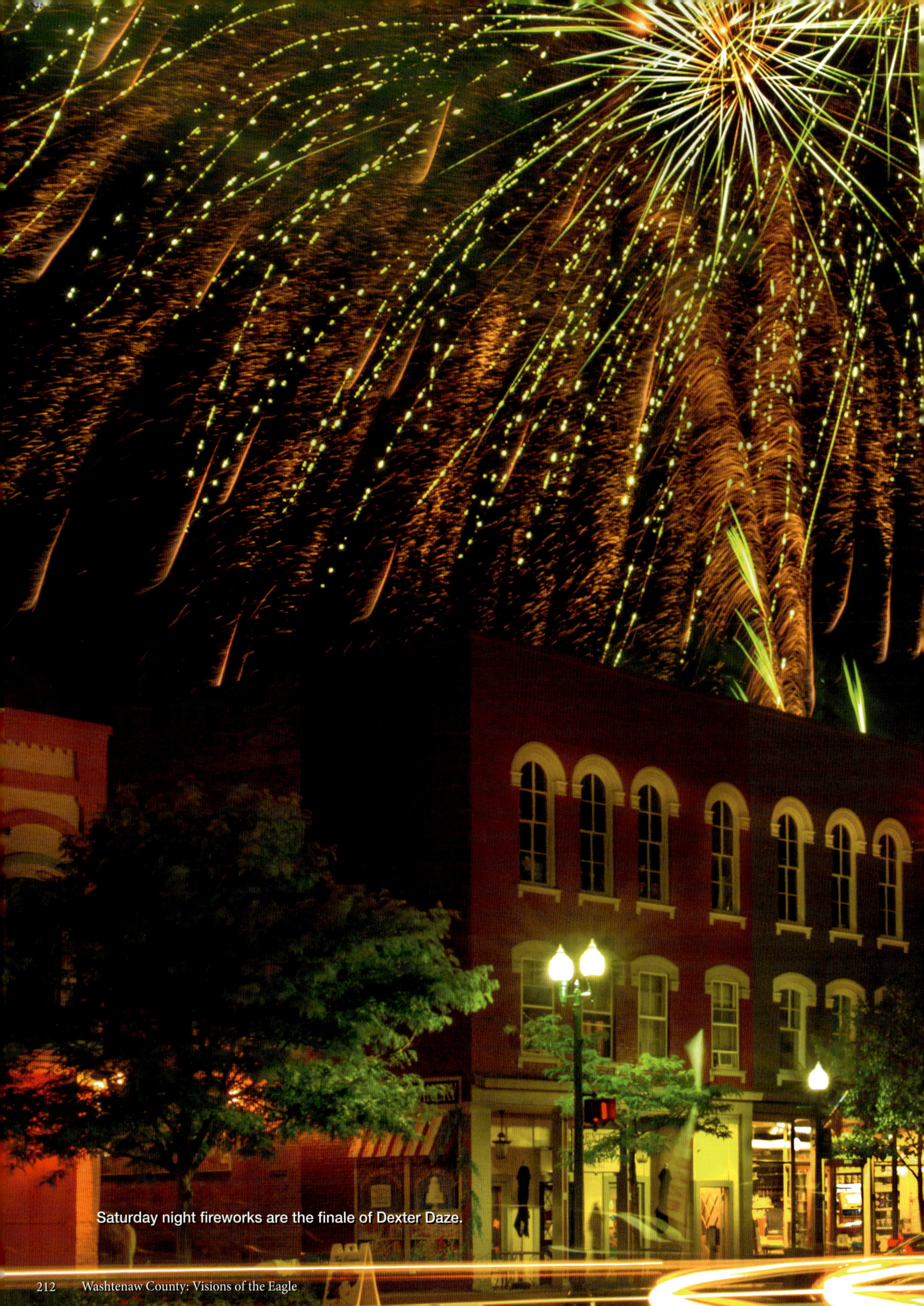
Saturday night fireworks are the finale of Dexter Daze.

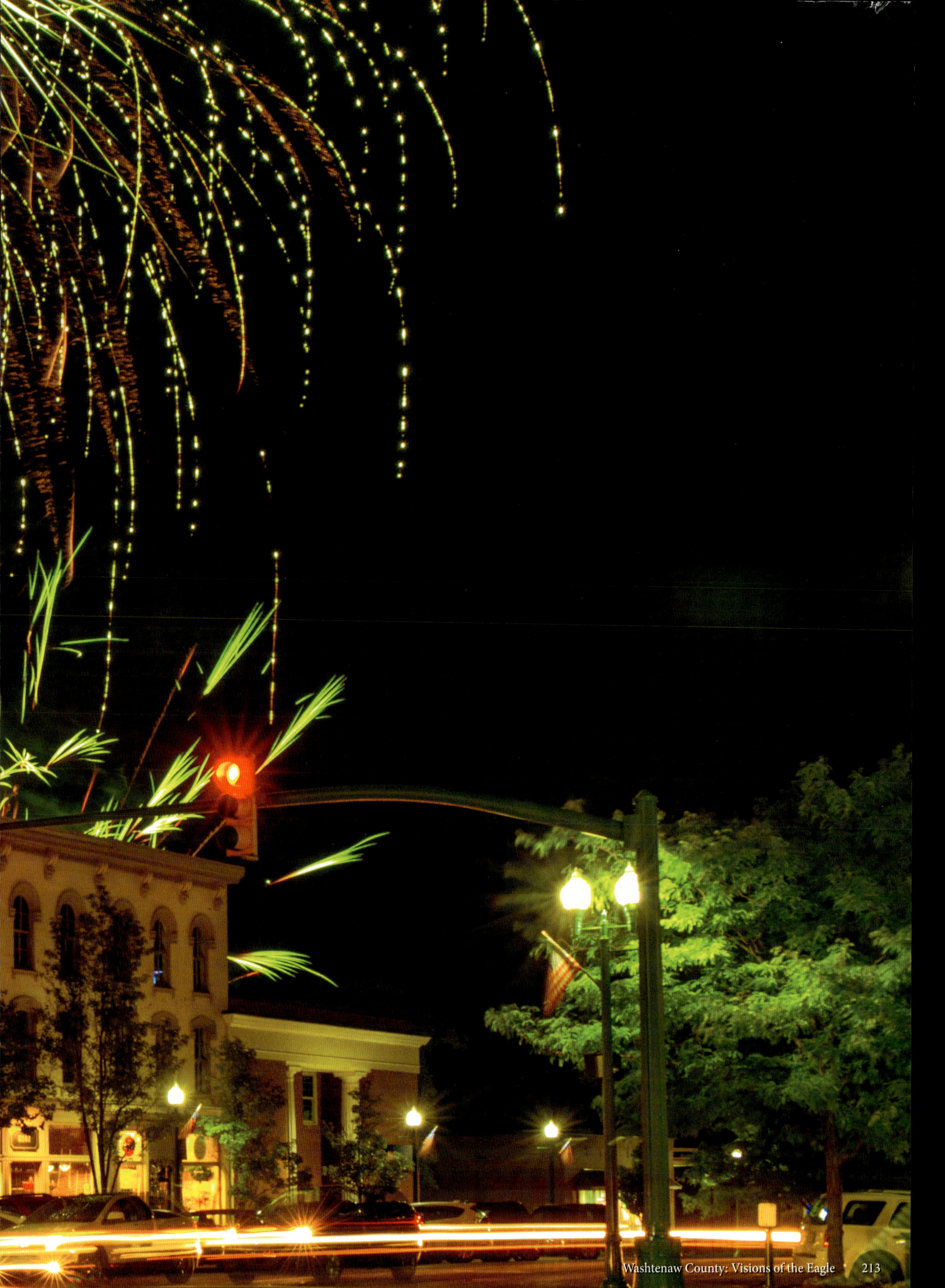

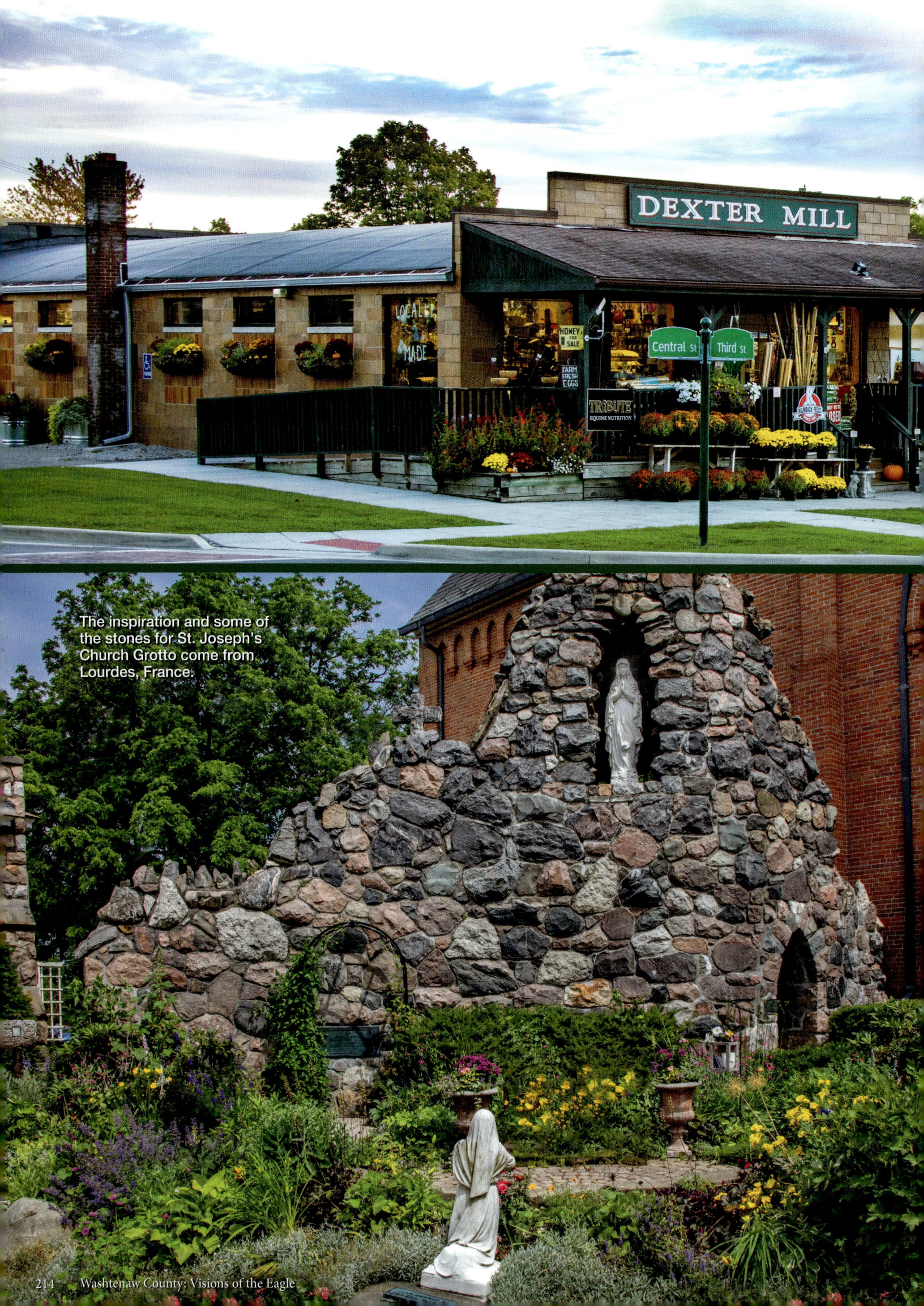

The inspiration and some of the stones for St. Joseph's Church Grotto come from Lourdes, France.

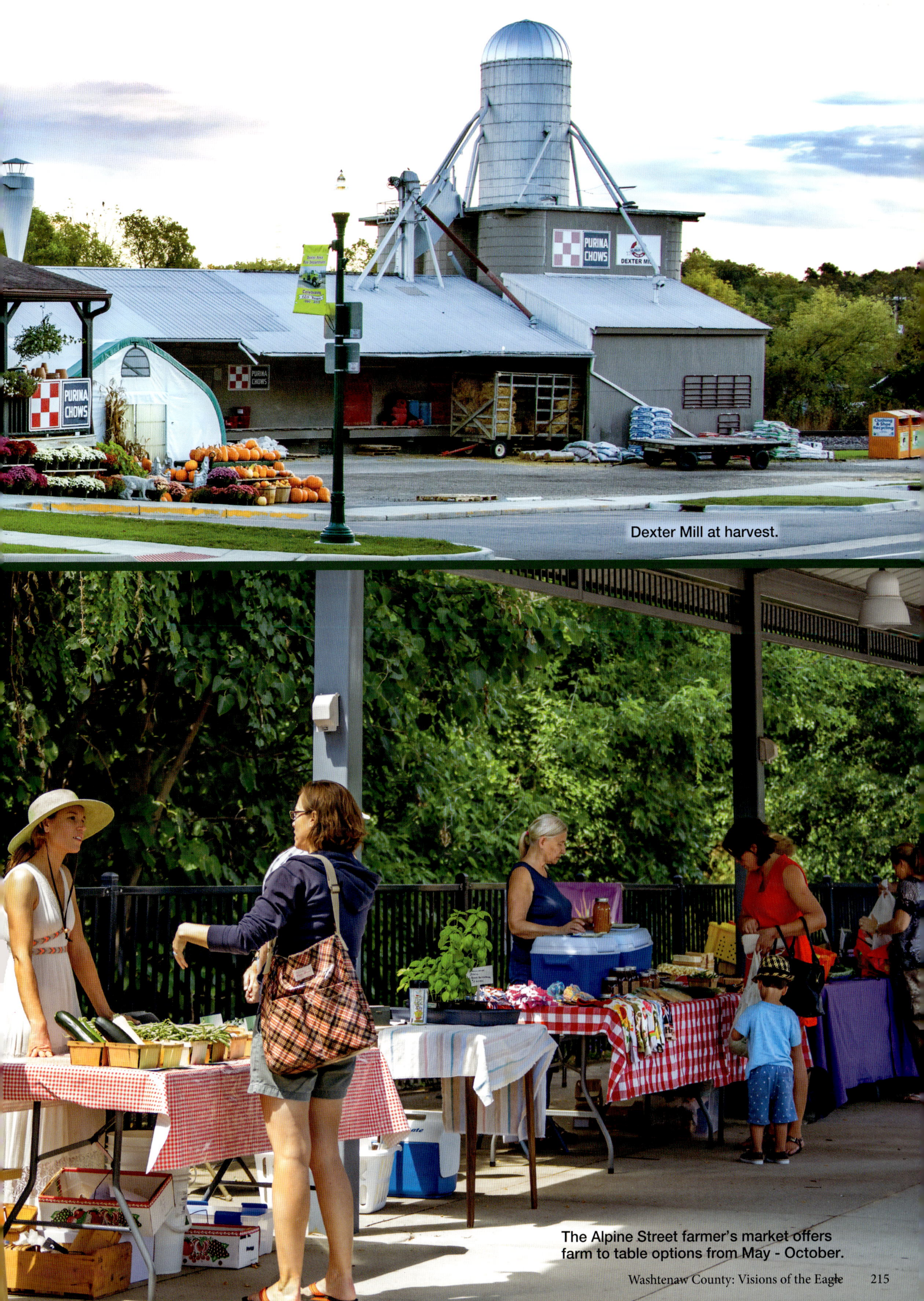

Dexter Mill at harvest.

The Alpine Street farmer's market offers farm to table options from May - October.

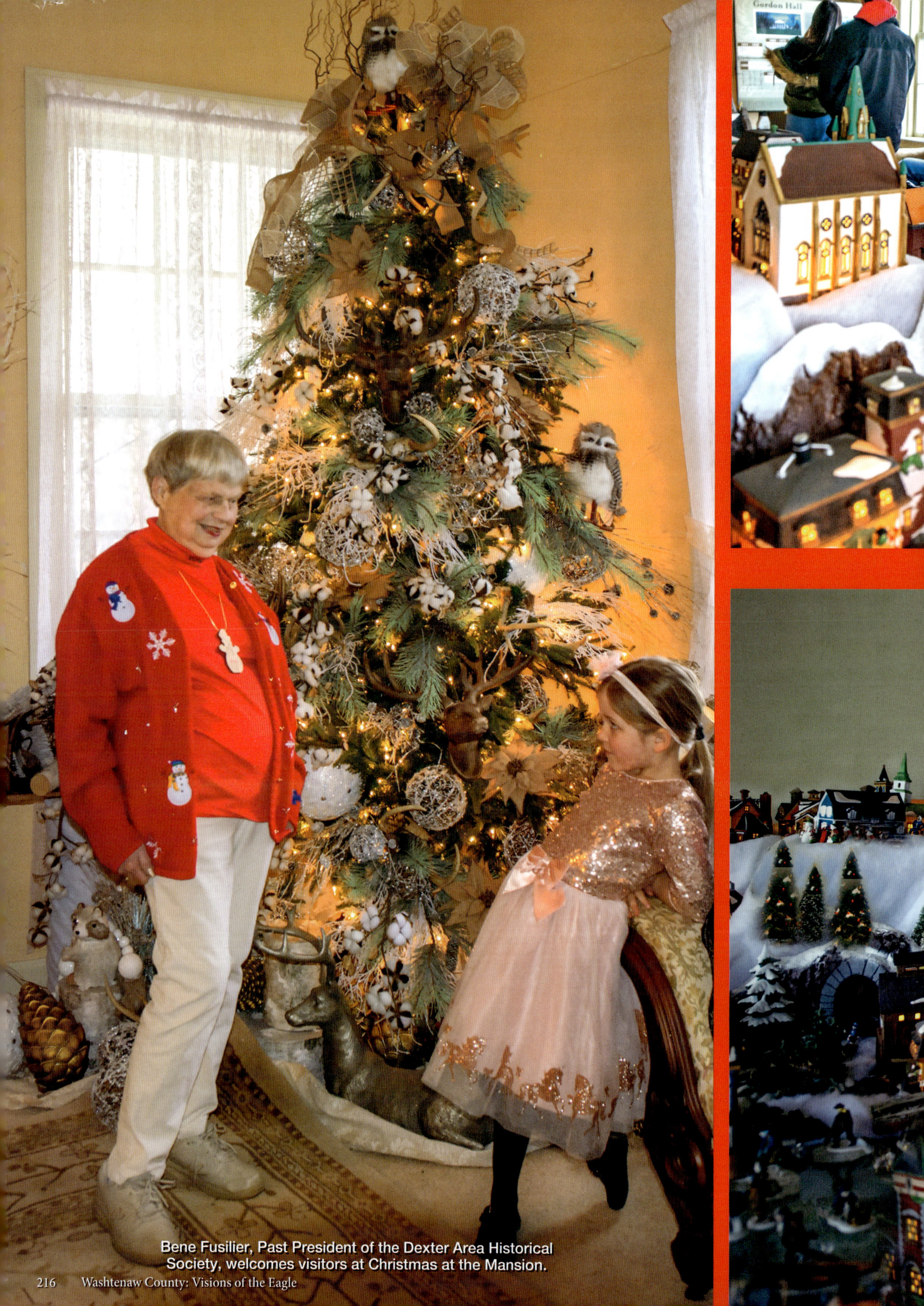

Bene Fusilier, Past President of the Dexter Area Historical Society, welcomes visitors at Christmas at the Mansion.

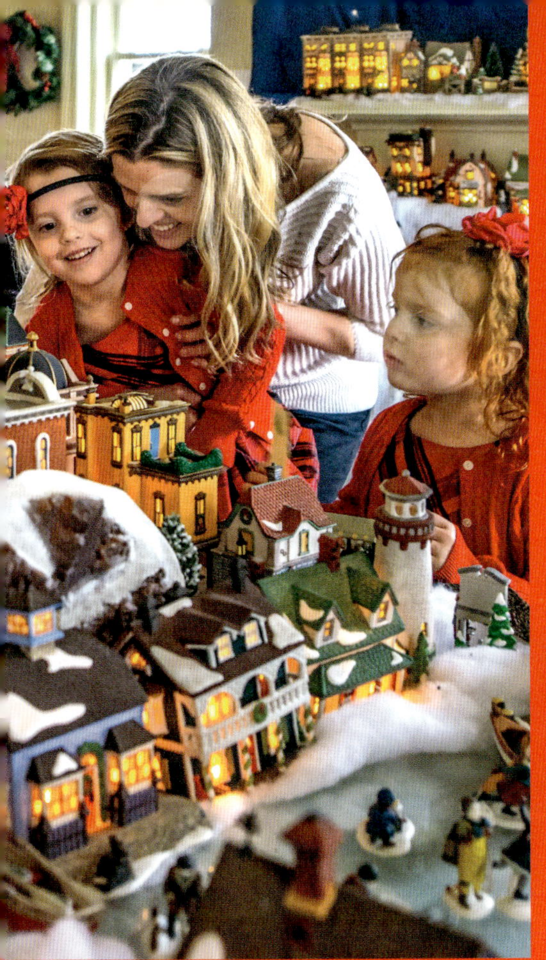

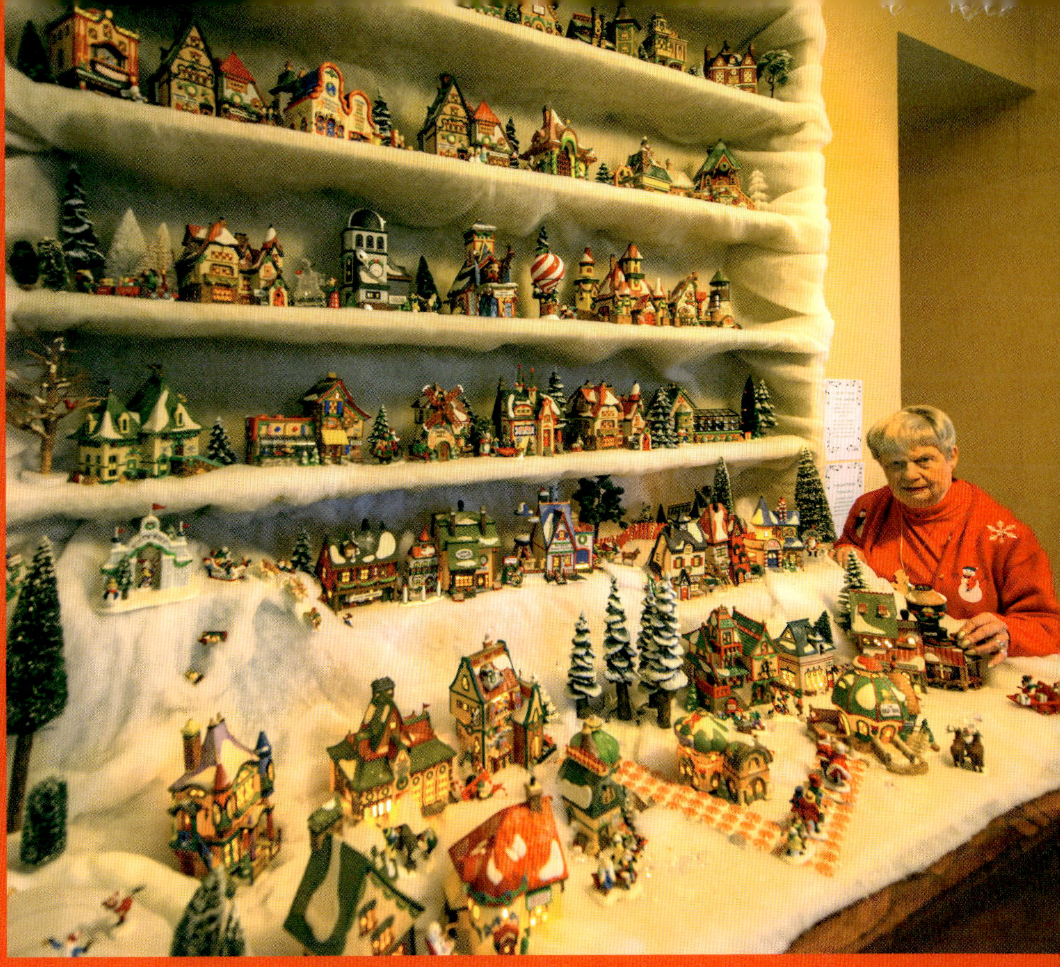

Christmas at Gordon Hall features many Christmas decorations and an extensive Christmas village collection.

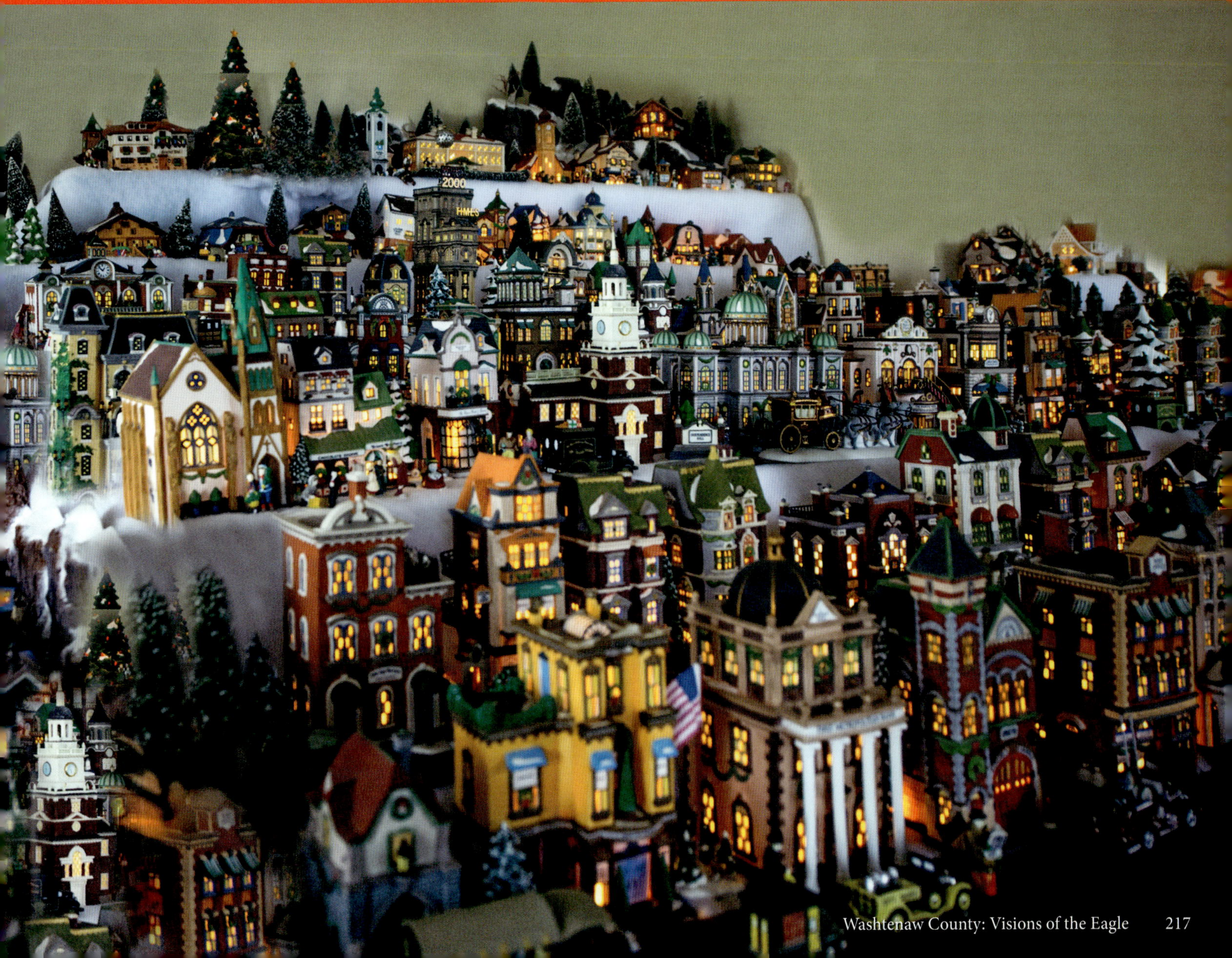

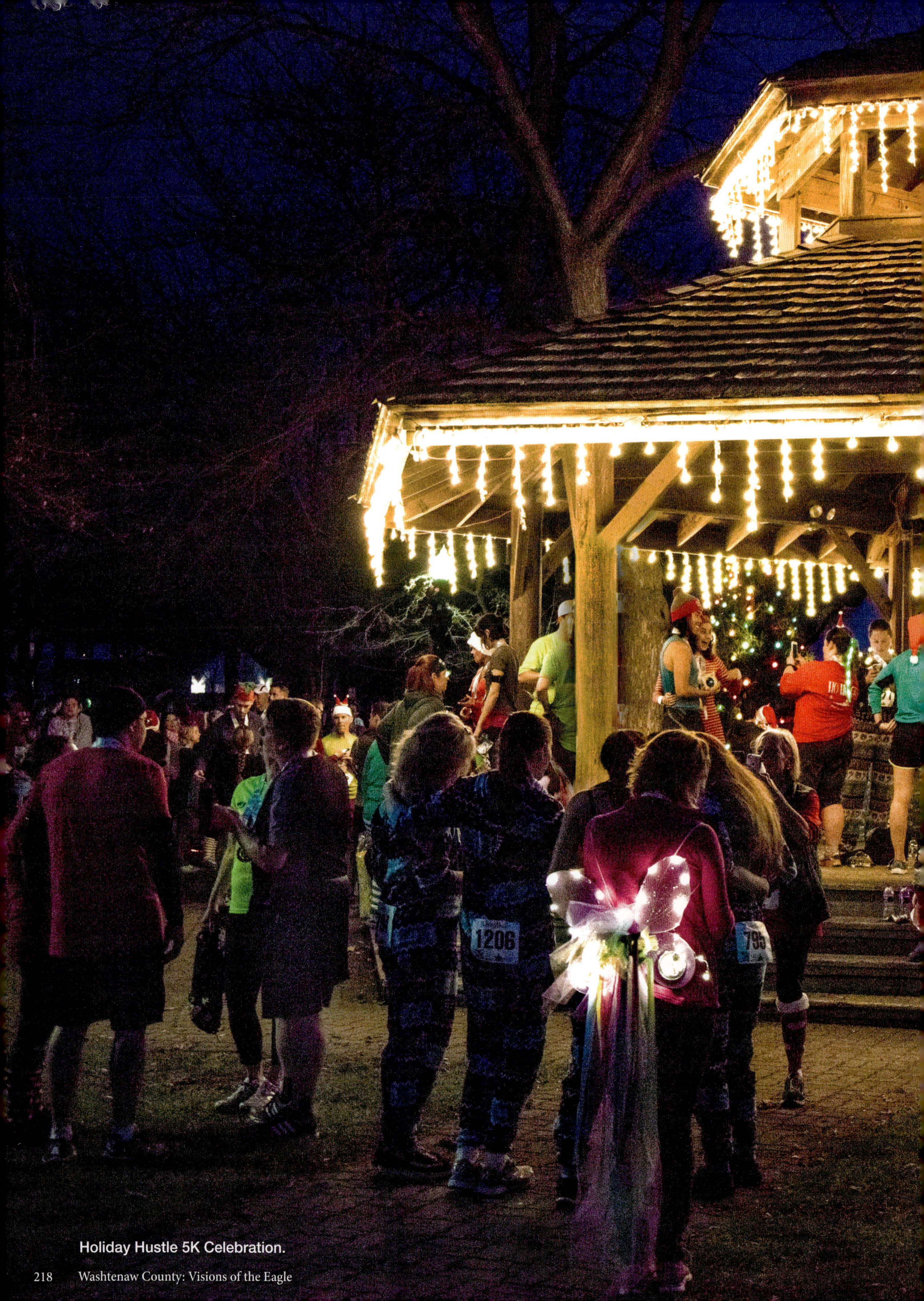

Holiday Hustle 5K Celebration.

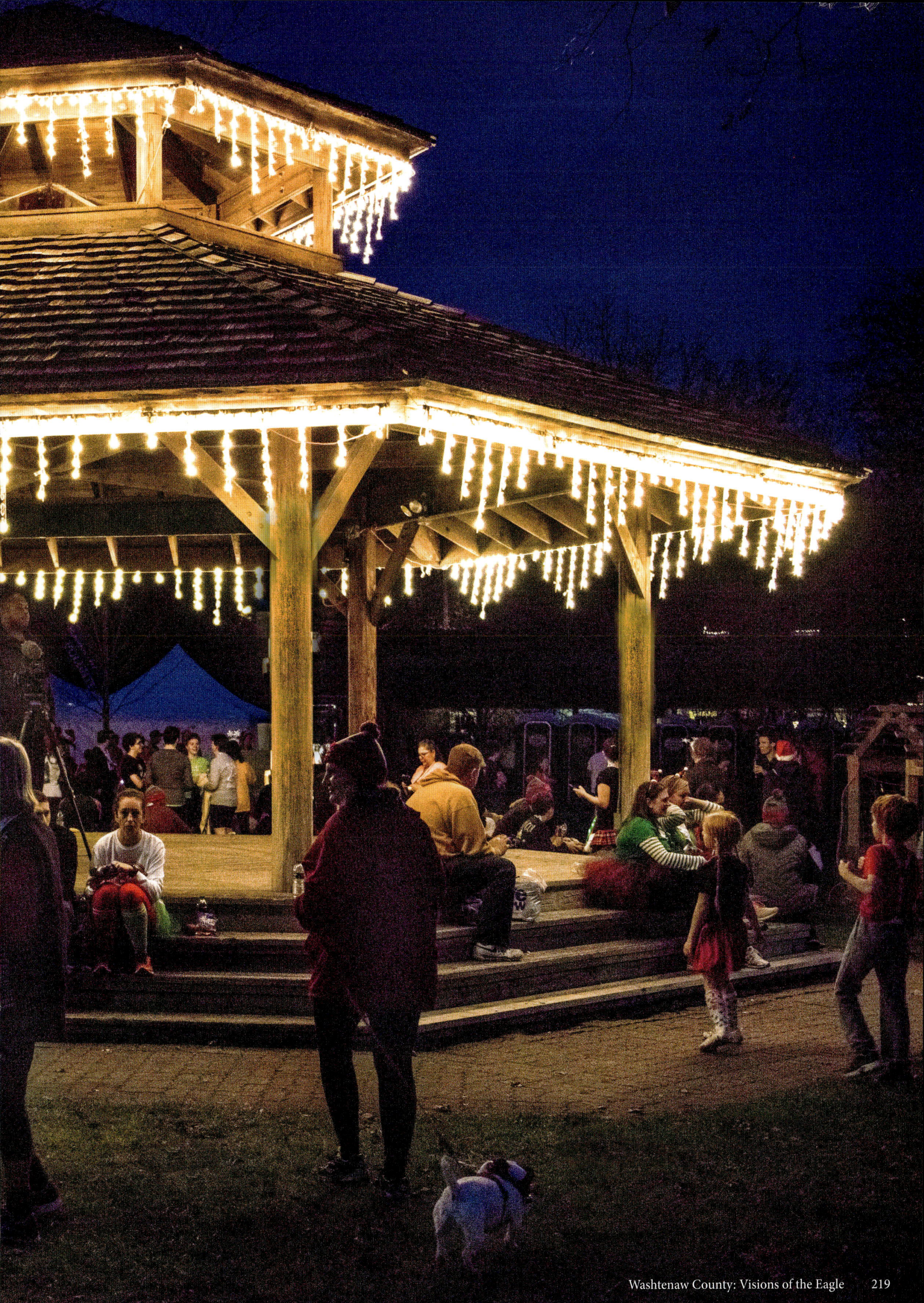

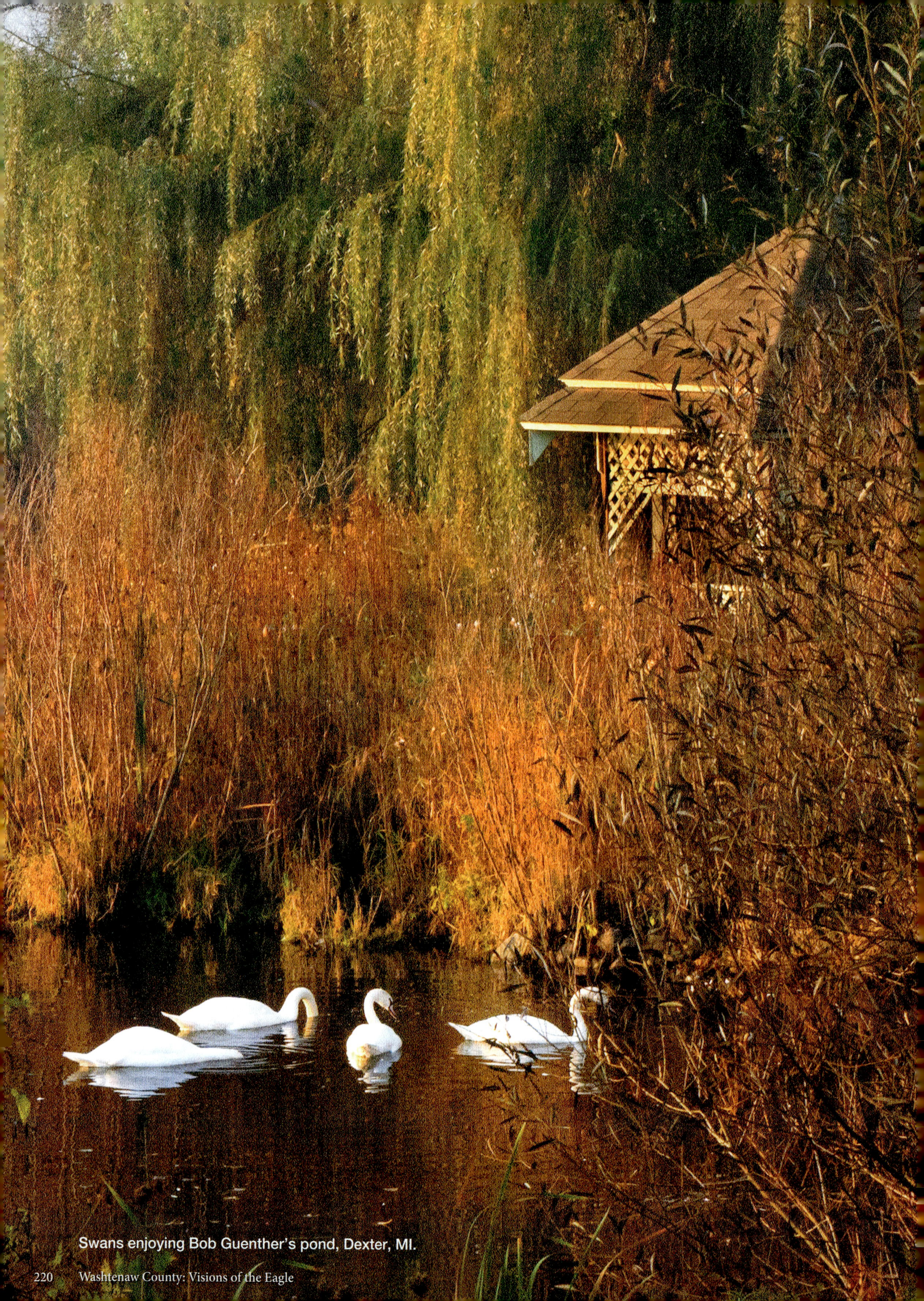

Swans enjoying Bob Guenther's pond, Dexter, MI.

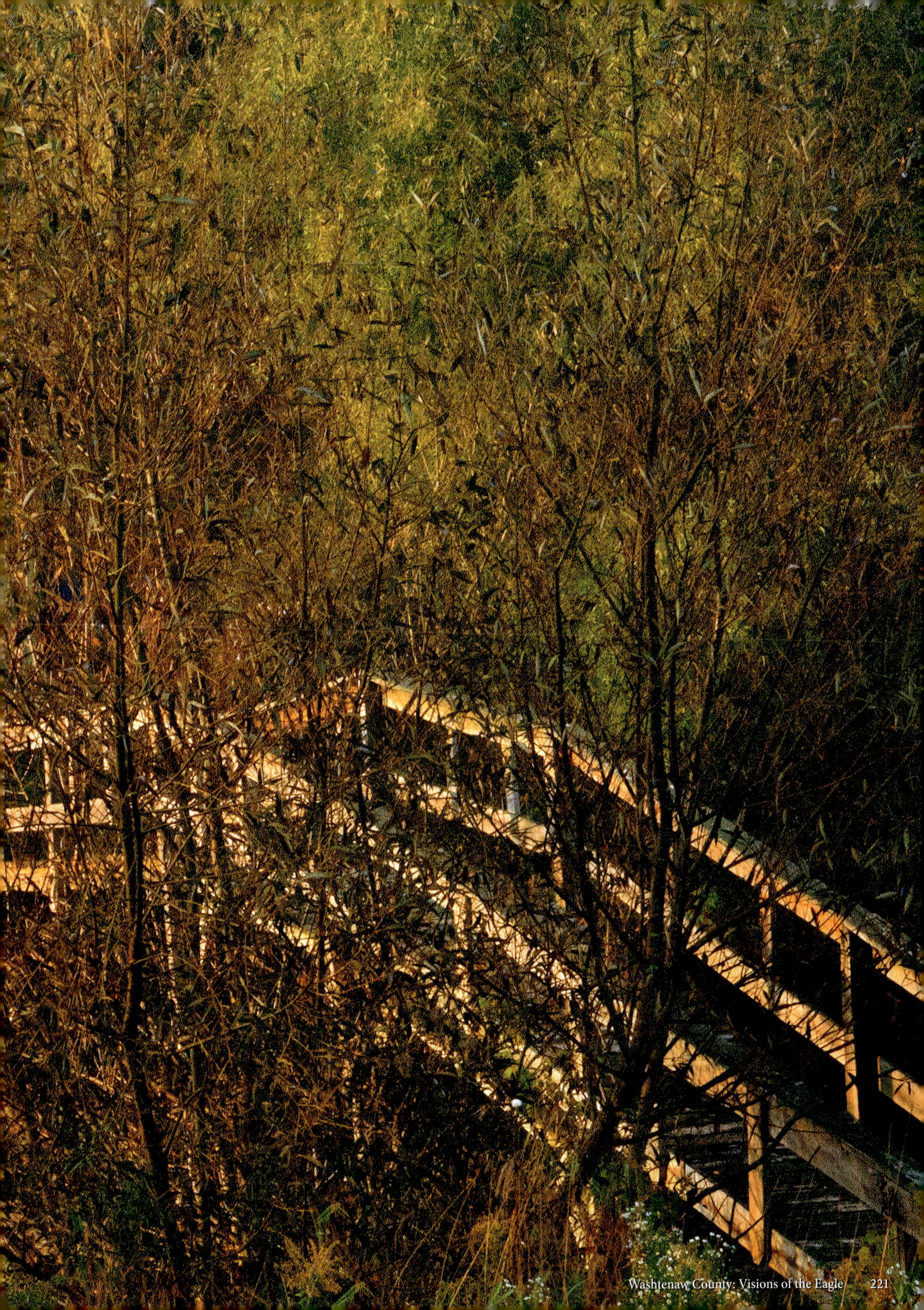

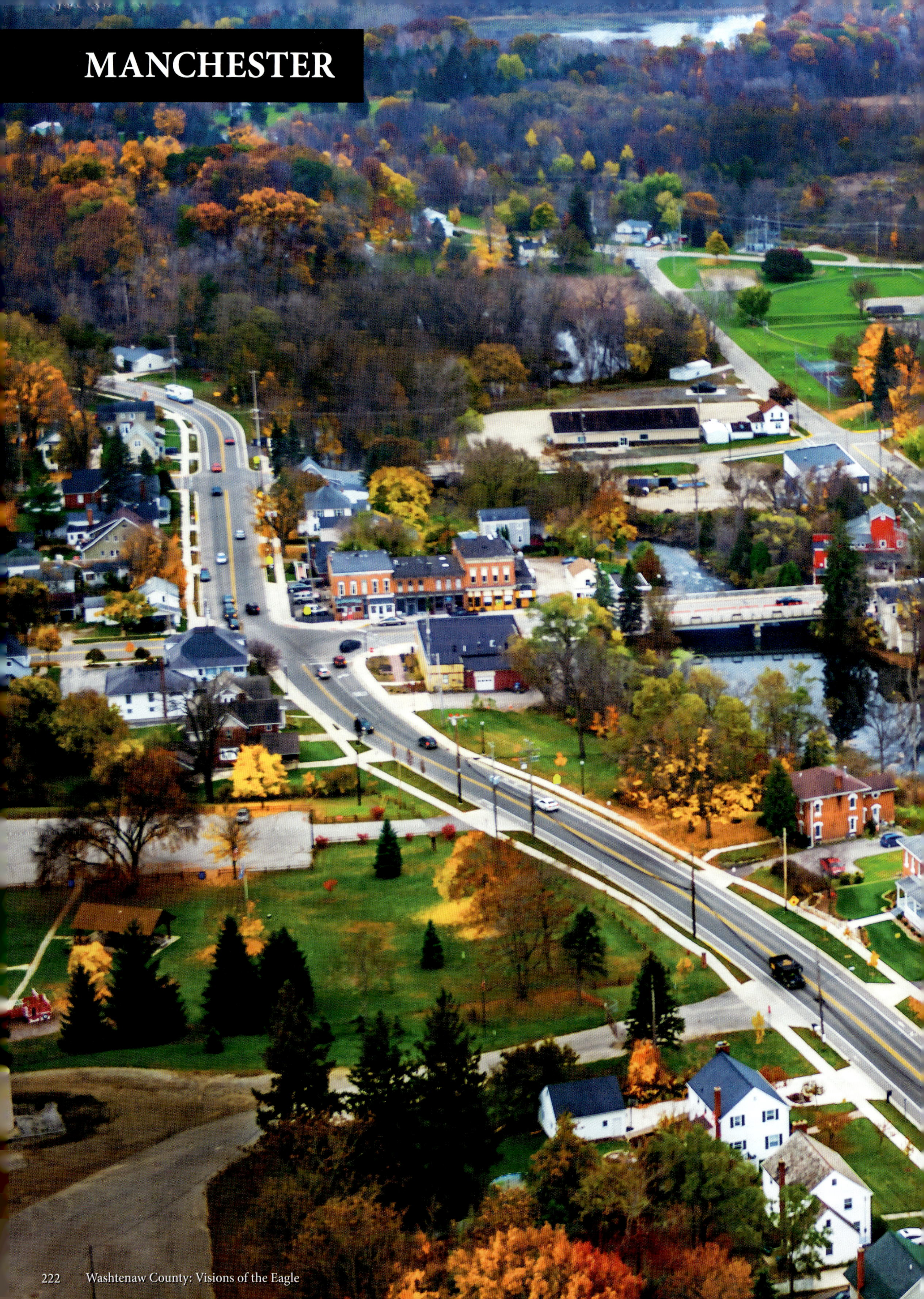

MANCHESTER

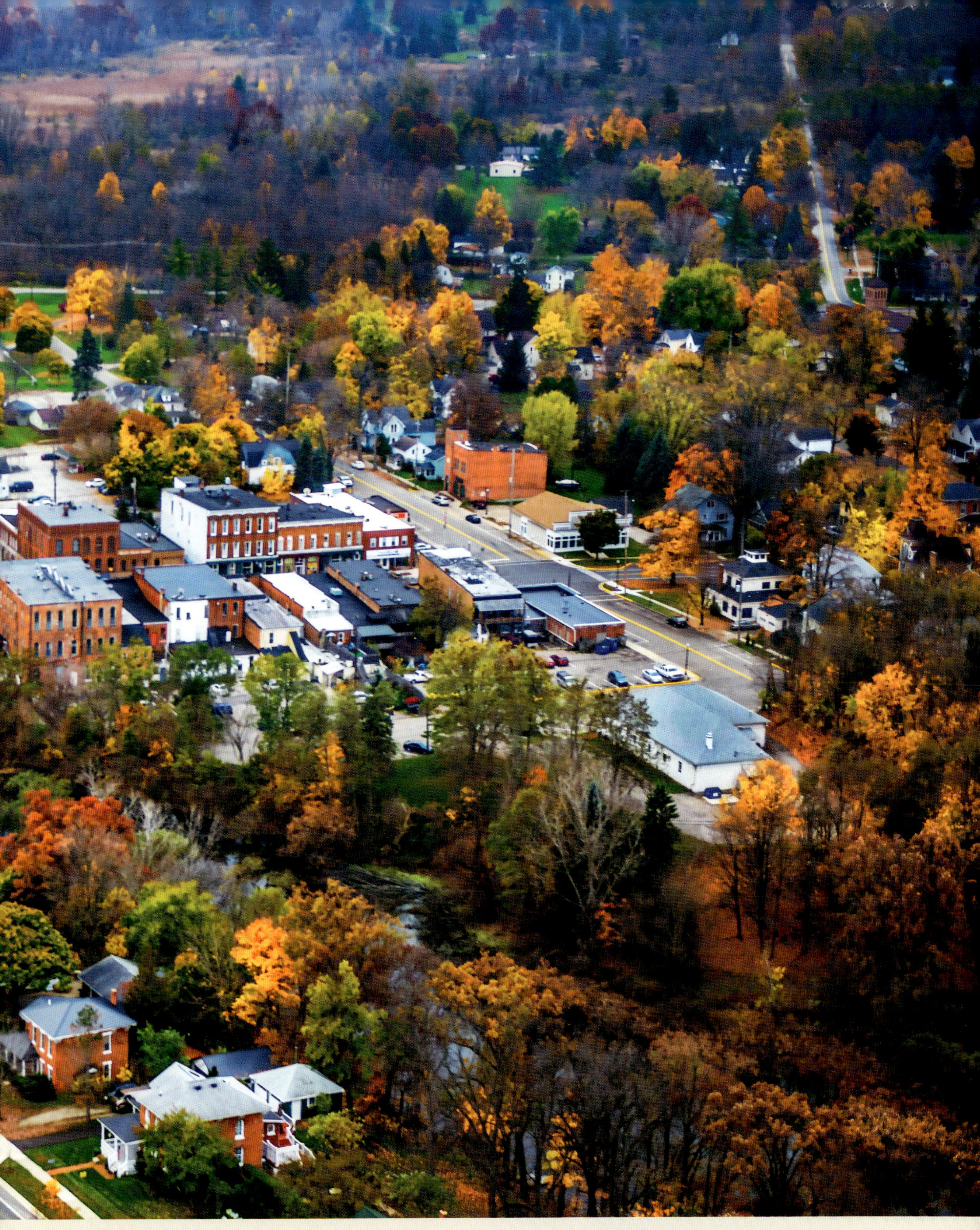

Manchester Village is a small, closely-knit community, which provides opportunities for leisure-time involvement in organizations, churches, and schools. It provides cultural resources for residents of the adjacent rural townships. Its geographical position has thus far saved it from the pressures of rapid urbanization and encourages self-sufficiency even in recreational pursuits. However, the Village is within driving distance of a variety of cultural events in Ann Arbor, Ypsilanti, Adrian, Jackson, and of programs at two universities and several colleges.

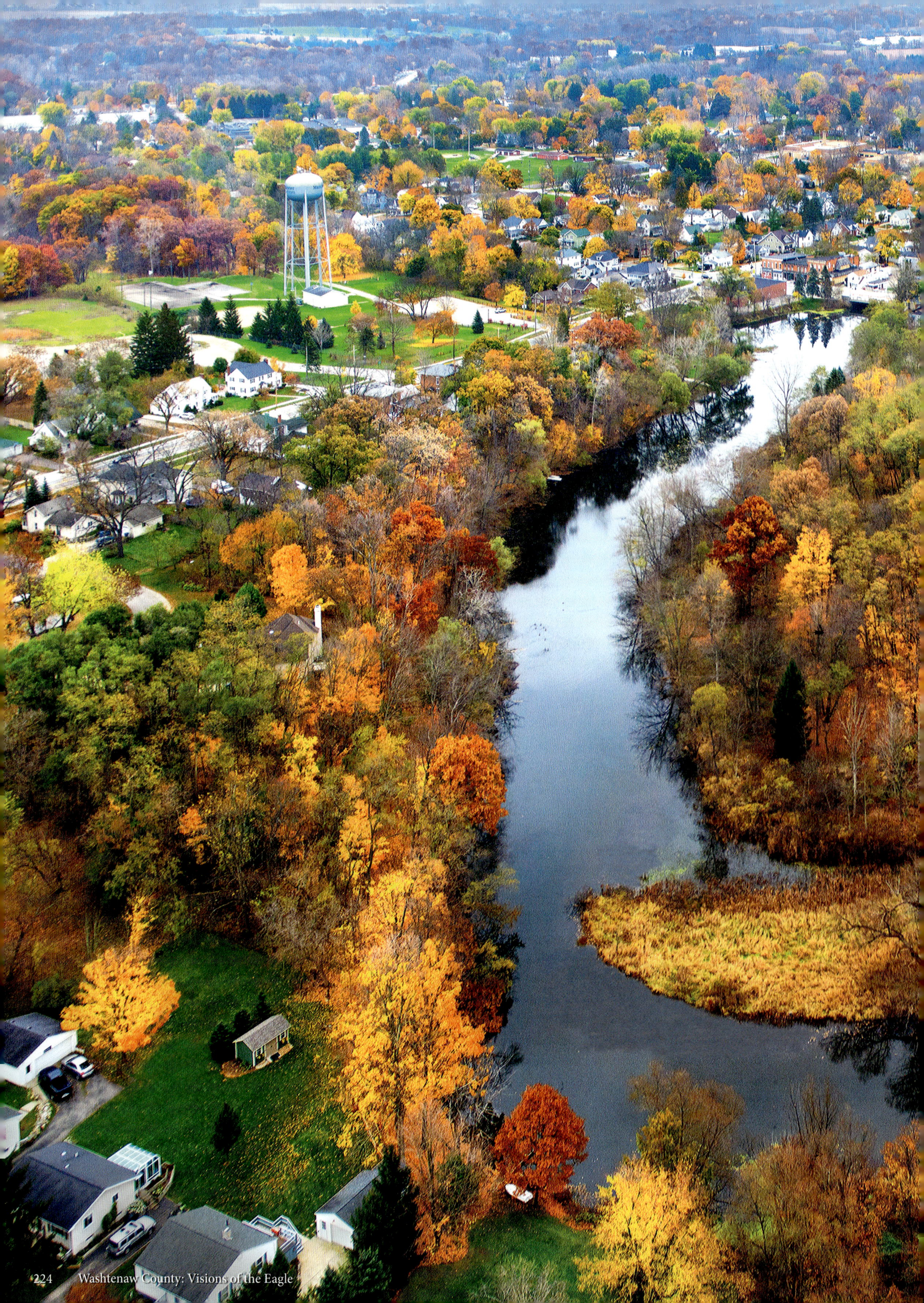

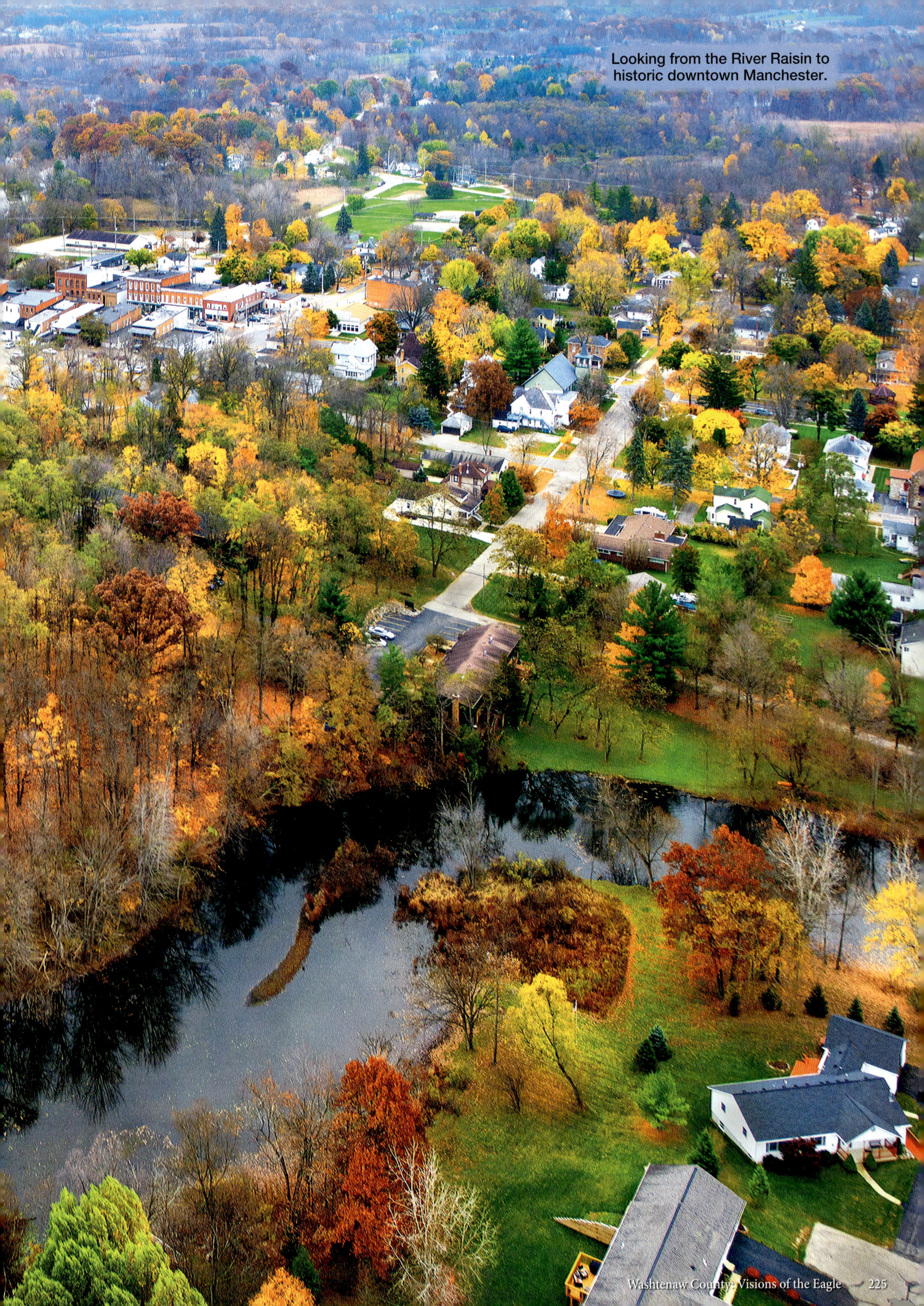
Looking from the River Raisin to historic downtown Manchester.

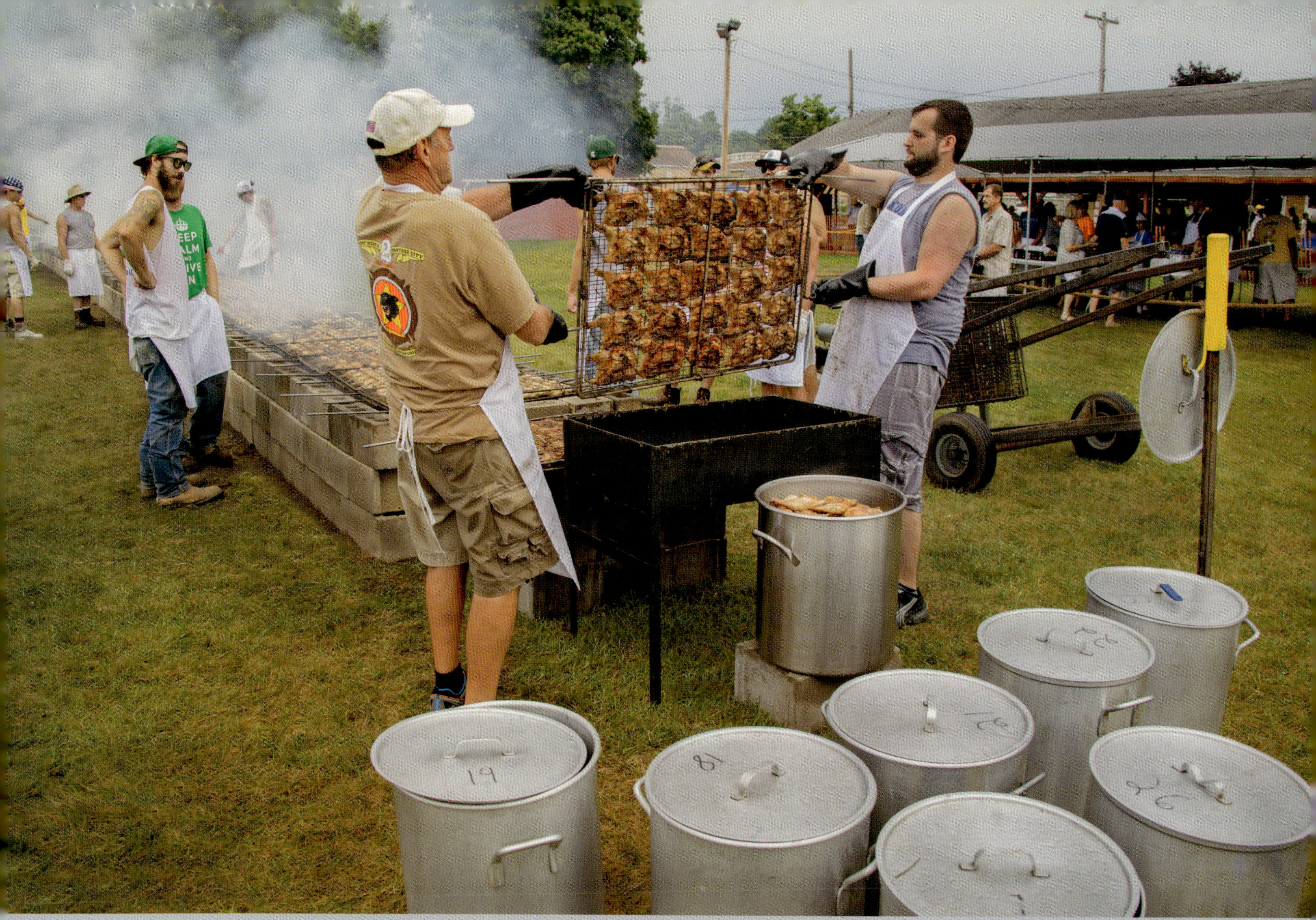

Since 1953, the third Thursday in July is the famed Manchester Chicken Broil. The continued success for this annual event is due to the dedication of community organizations and businesses providing volunteers and sponsorships.

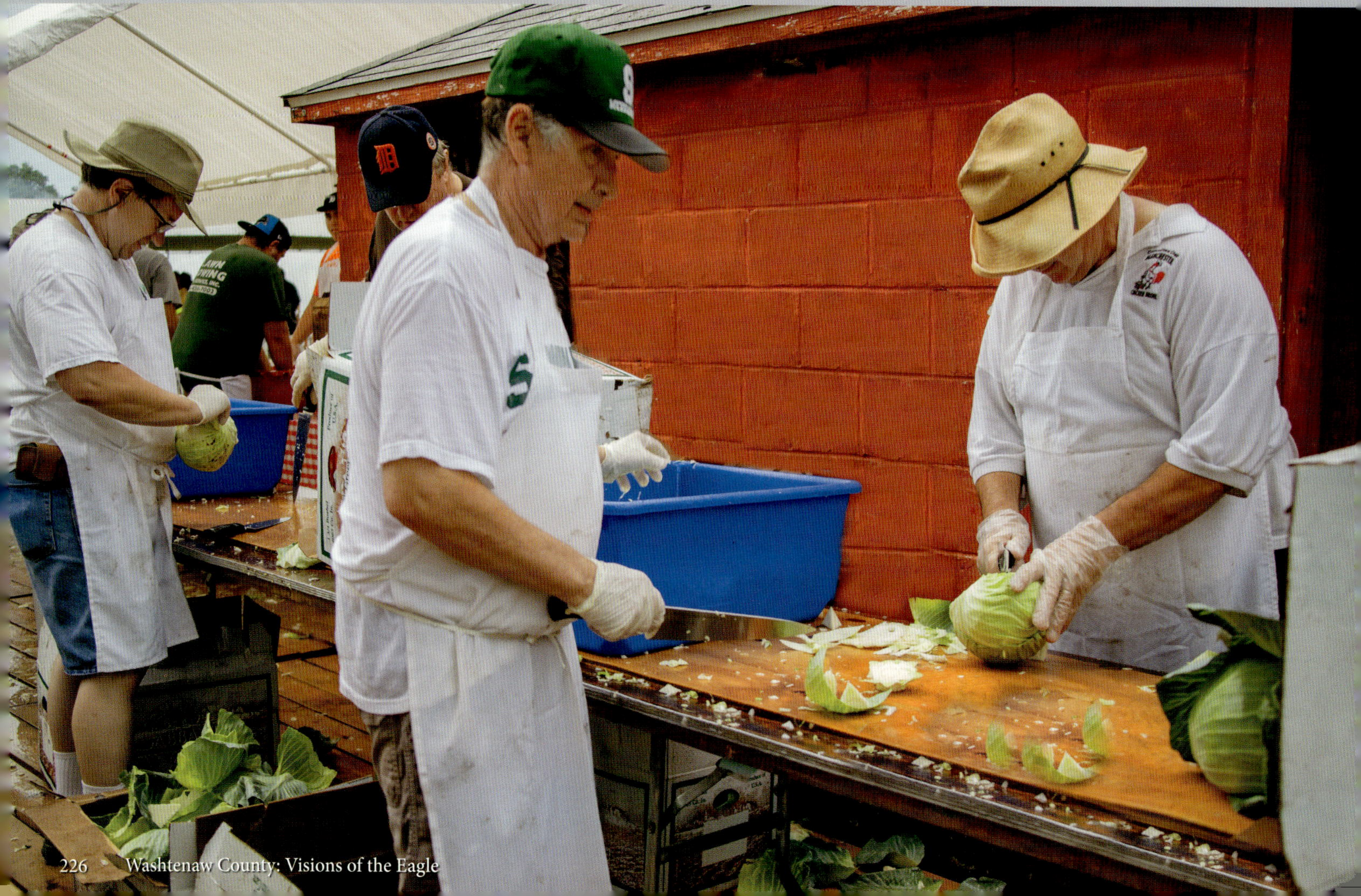

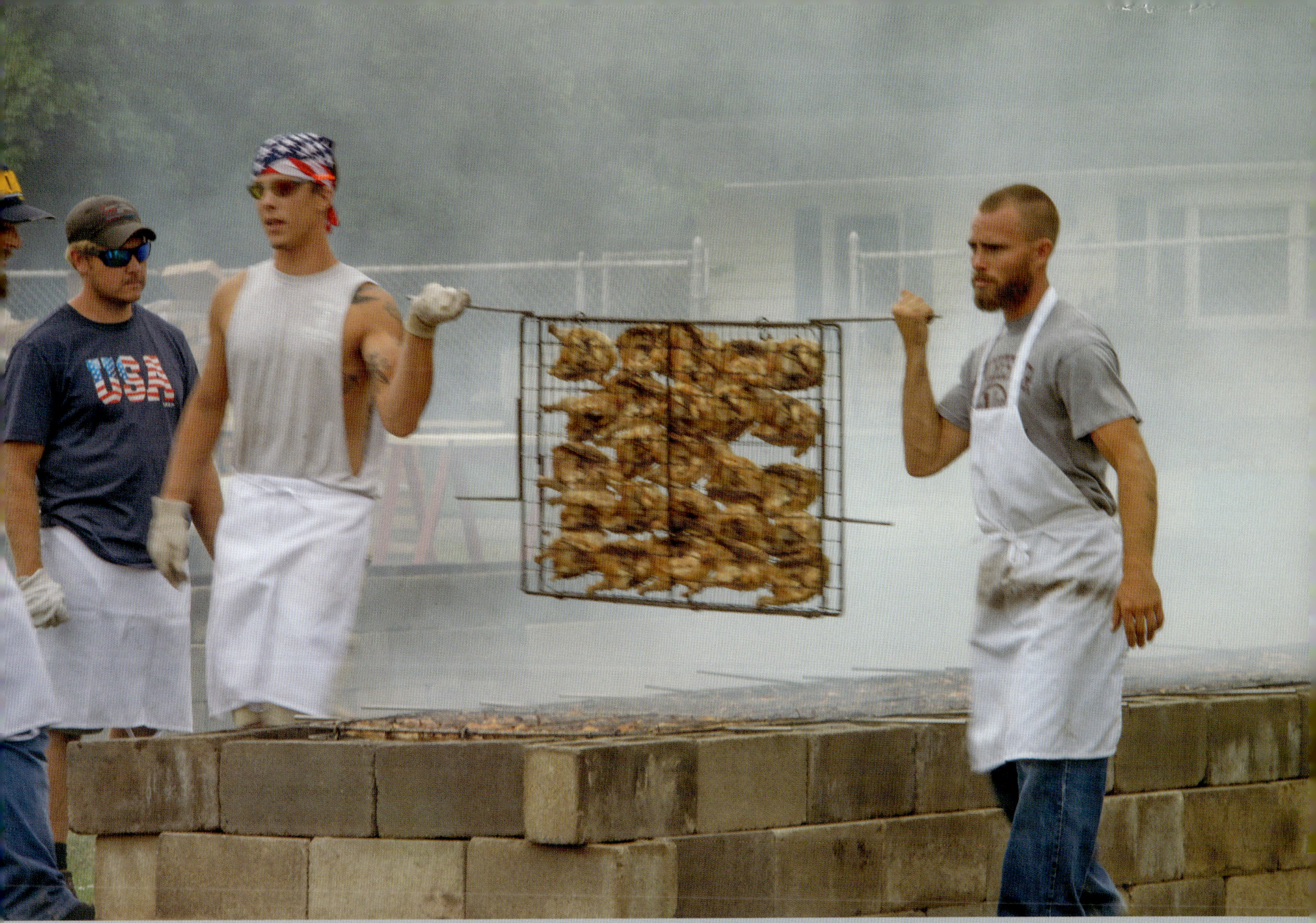

The Manchester Chicken Broil serves more than 4,000 dinners annually.
Community projects benefit from the proceeds.

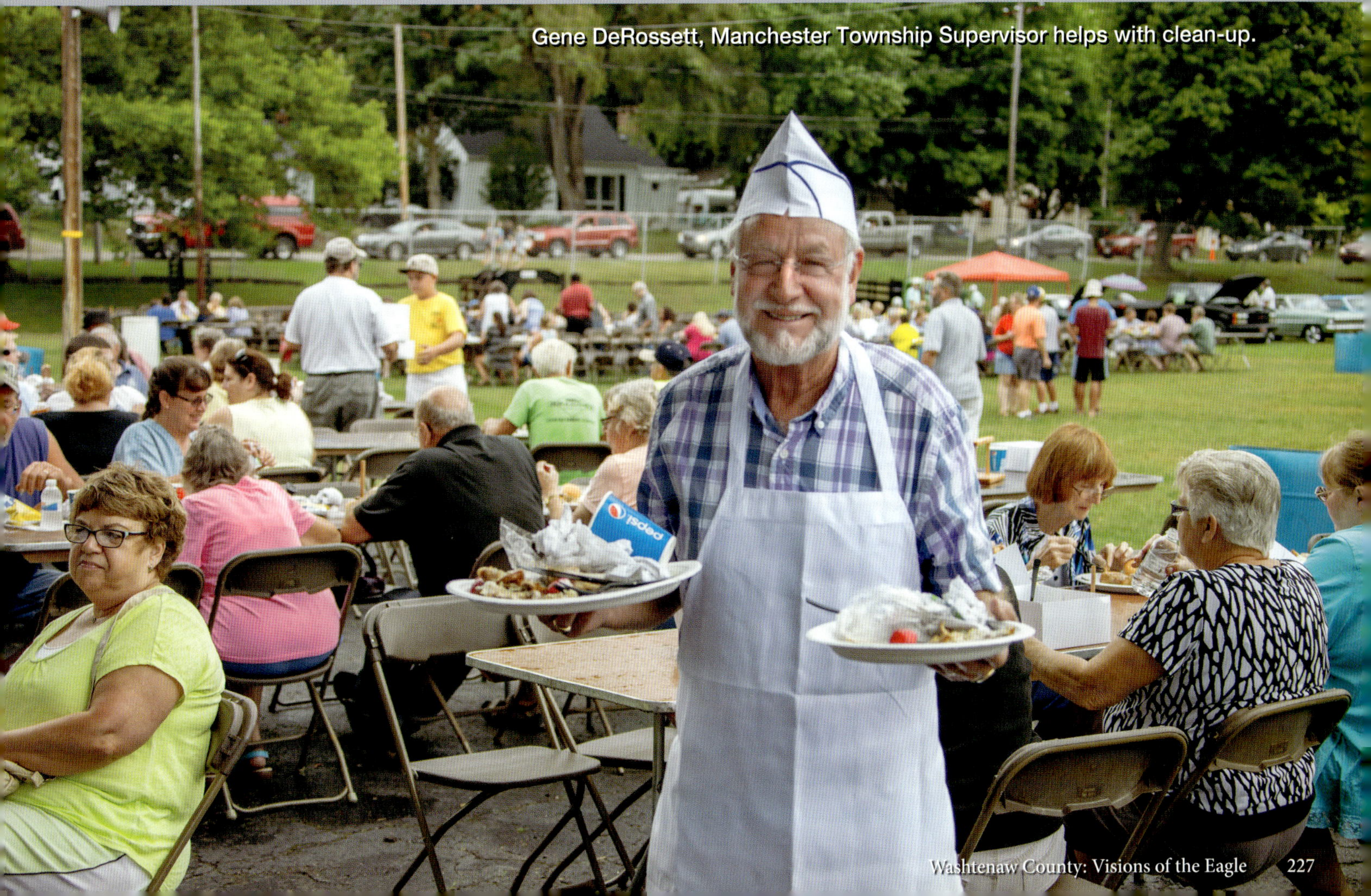

Gene DeRossett, Manchester Township Supervisor helps with clean-up.

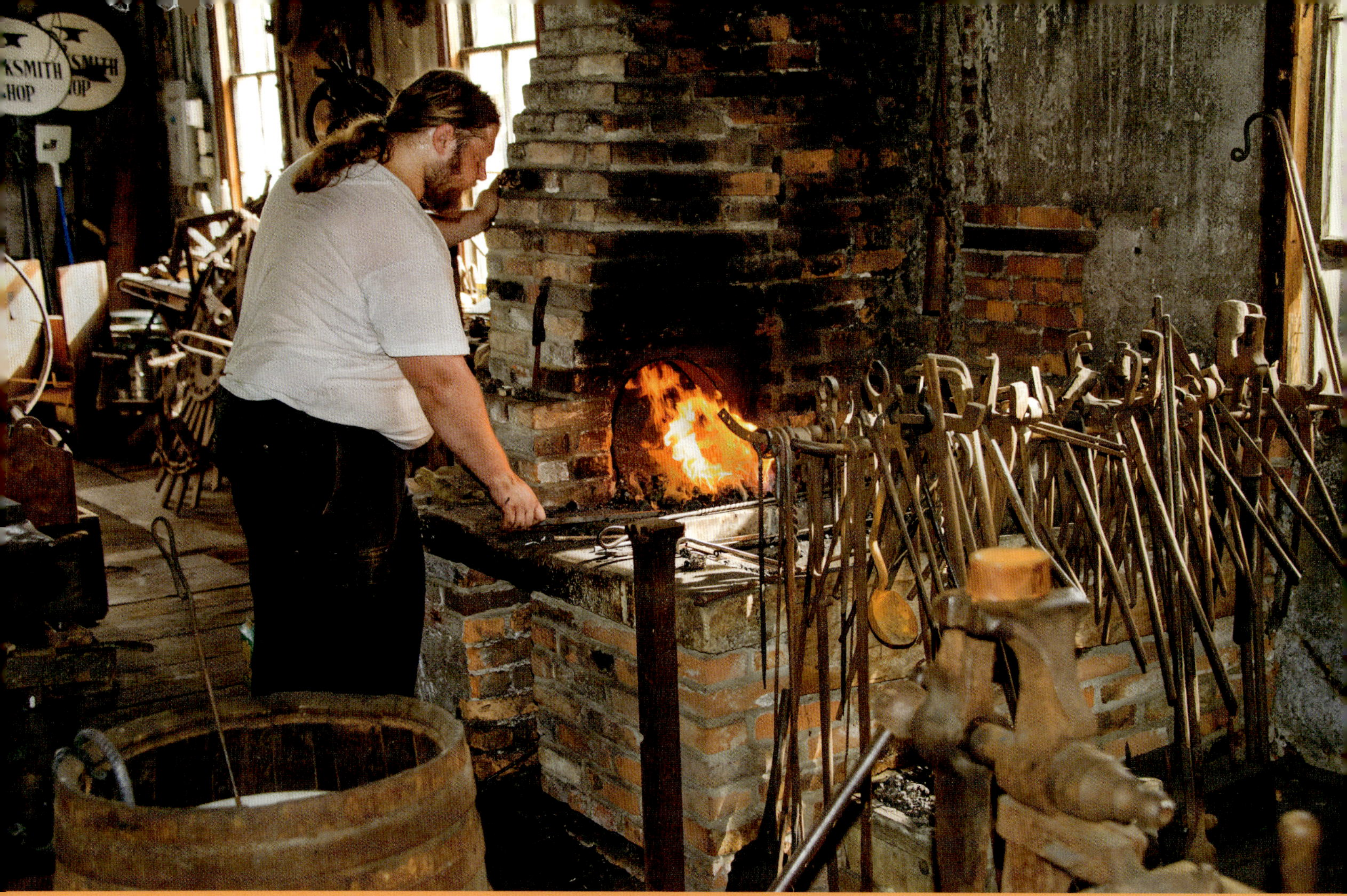

The Manchester Area Historical Society has spearheaded State and National Historic Register recognitions. The blacksmith shop opened in 1877 by Mr. Neebling as a carriage factory. Demonstrations are held Sunday afternoons.

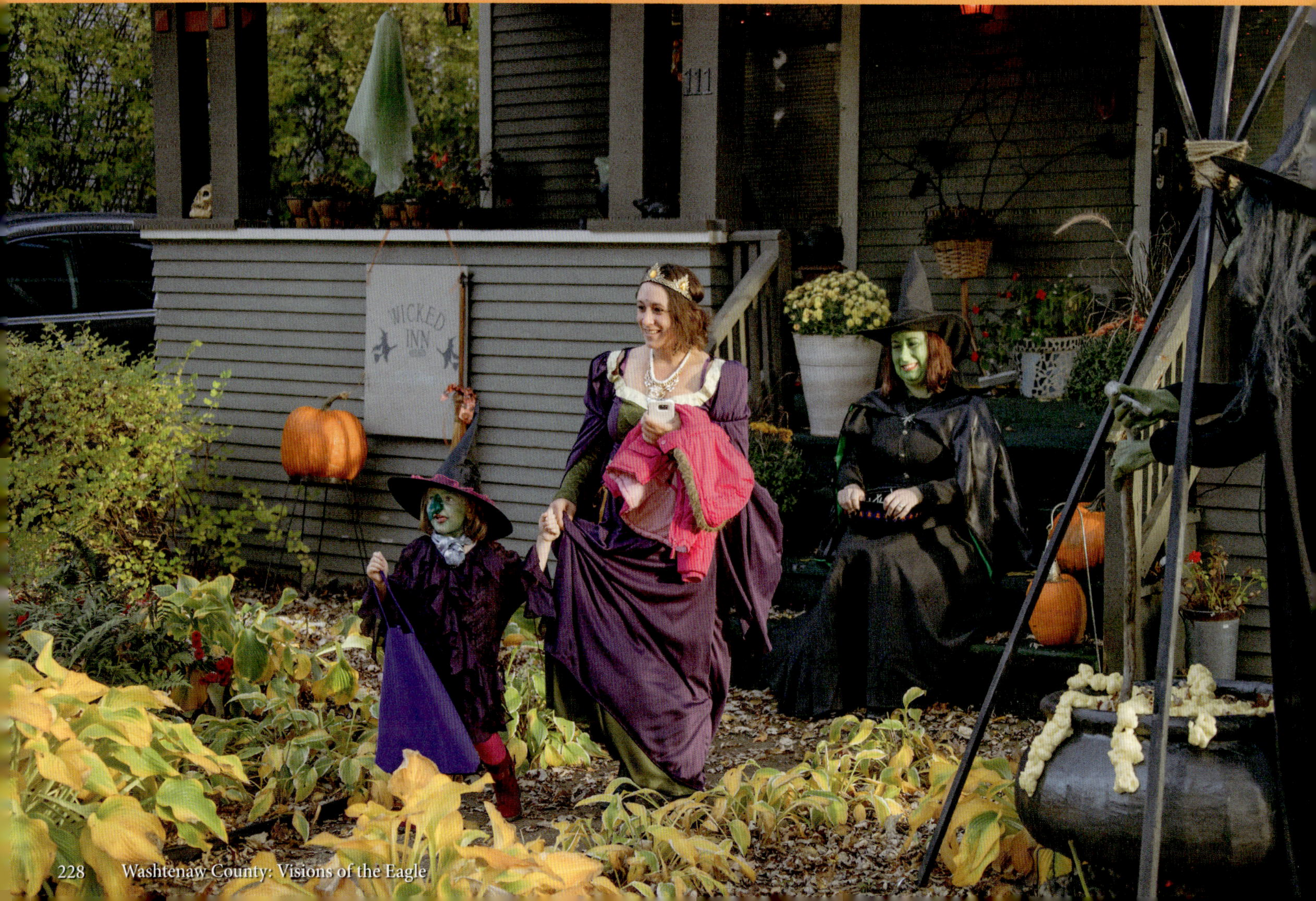

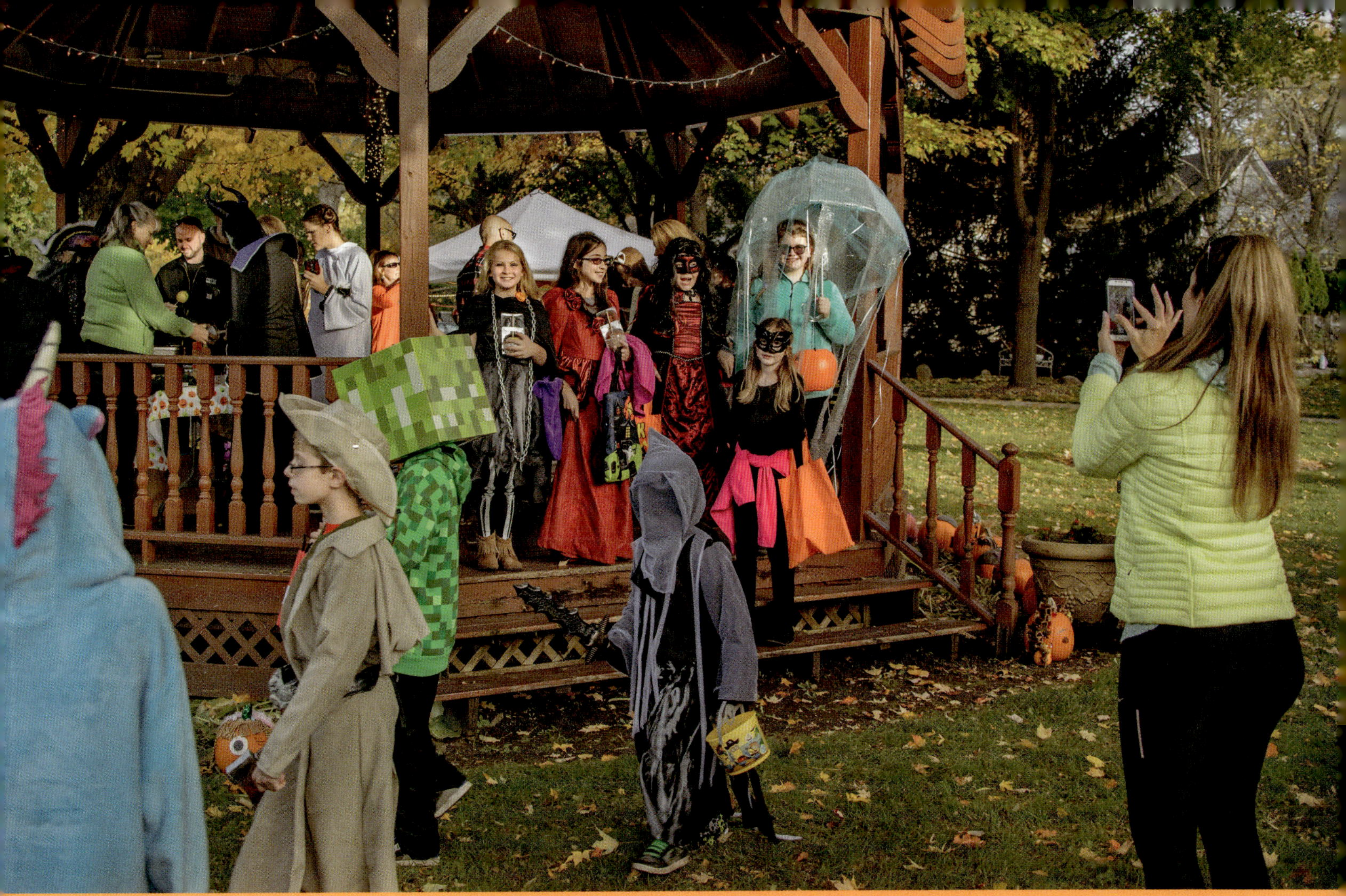

From Trick-or-Treat to sponsored activities and fresh caramel apples, the community enjoys Halloween festivities.

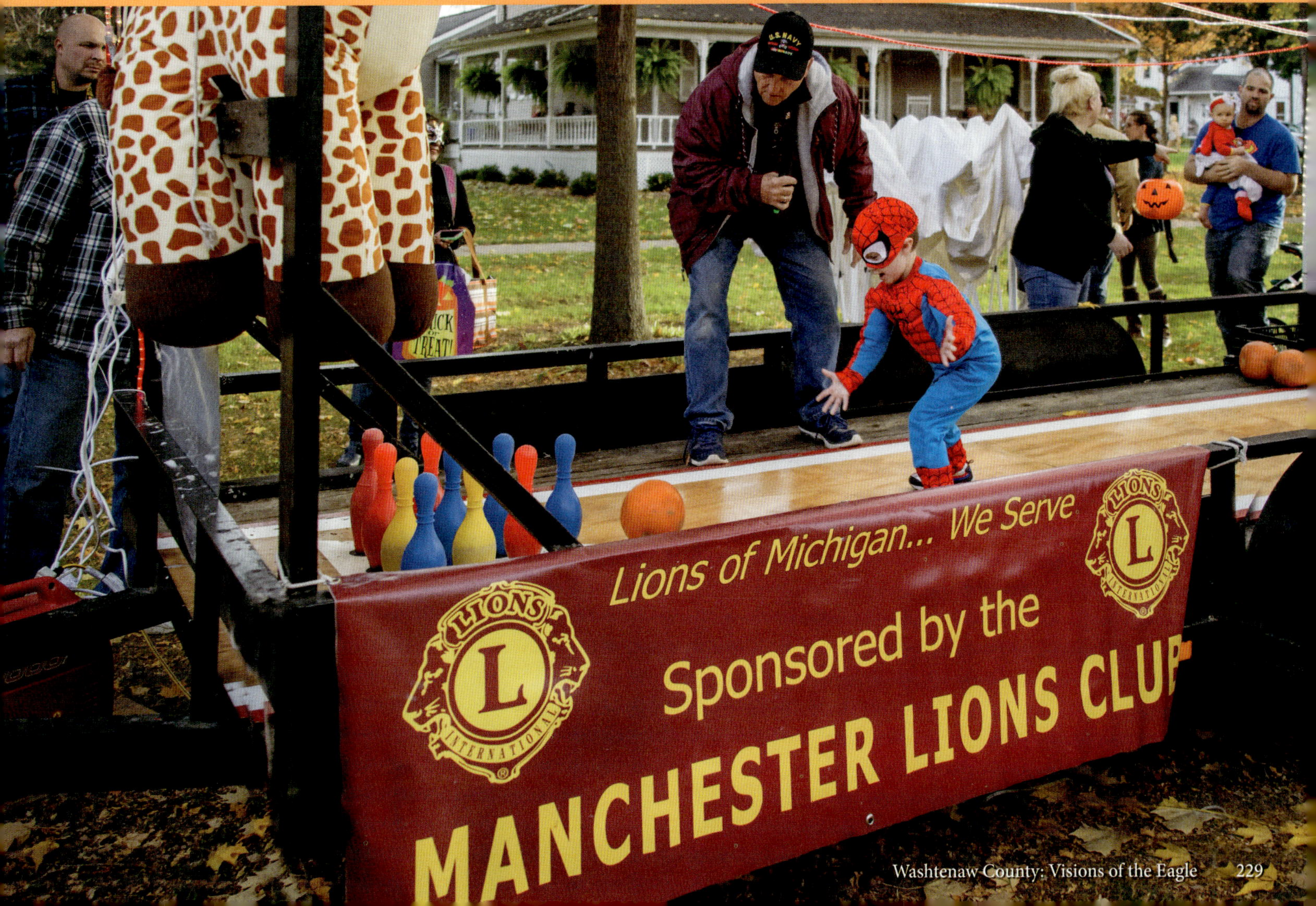

MILAN

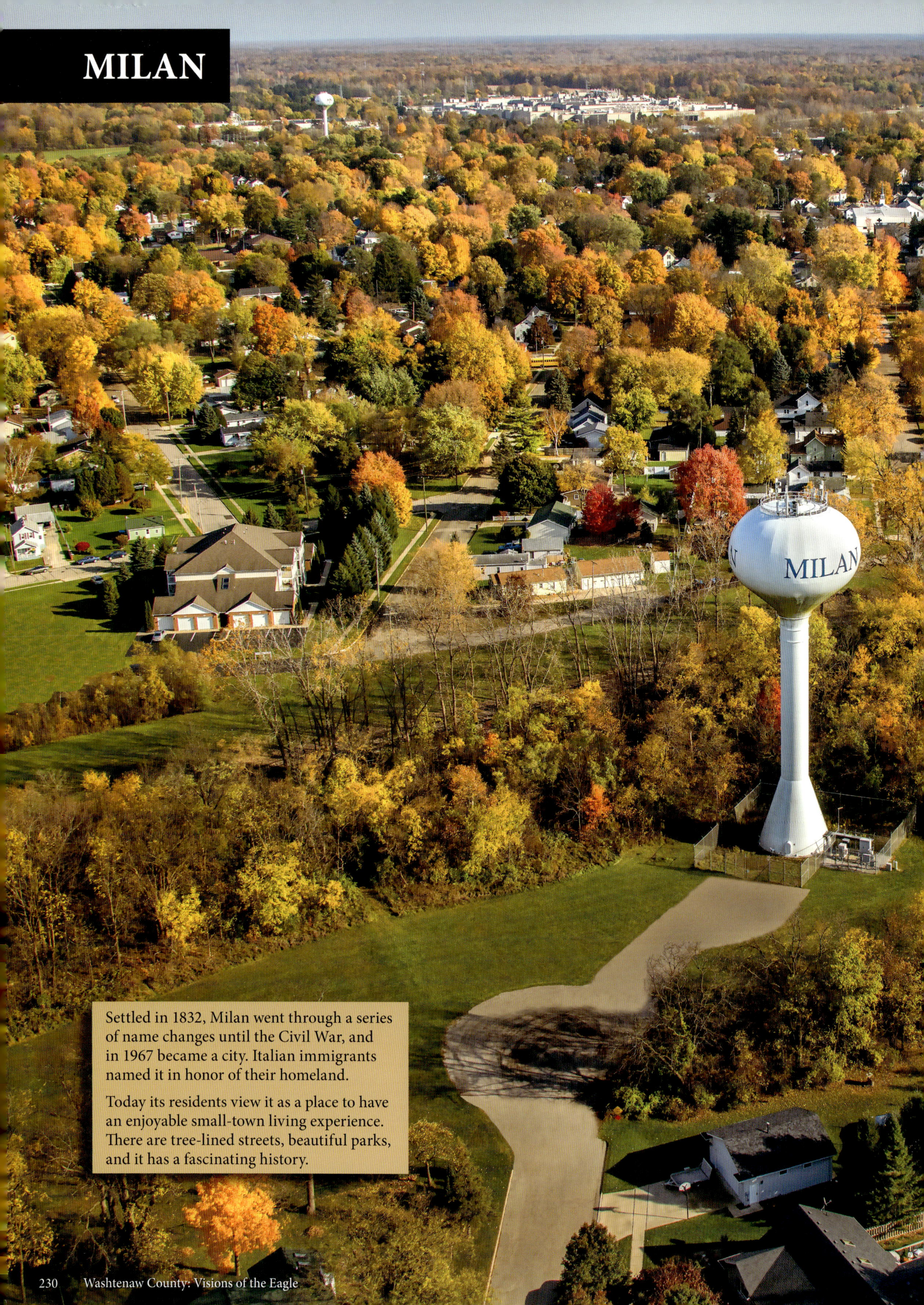

Settled in 1832, Milan went through a series of name changes until the Civil War, and in 1967 became a city. Italian immigrants named it in honor of their homeland.

Today its residents view it as a place to have an enjoyable small-town living experience. There are tree-lined streets, beautiful parks, and it has a fascinating history.

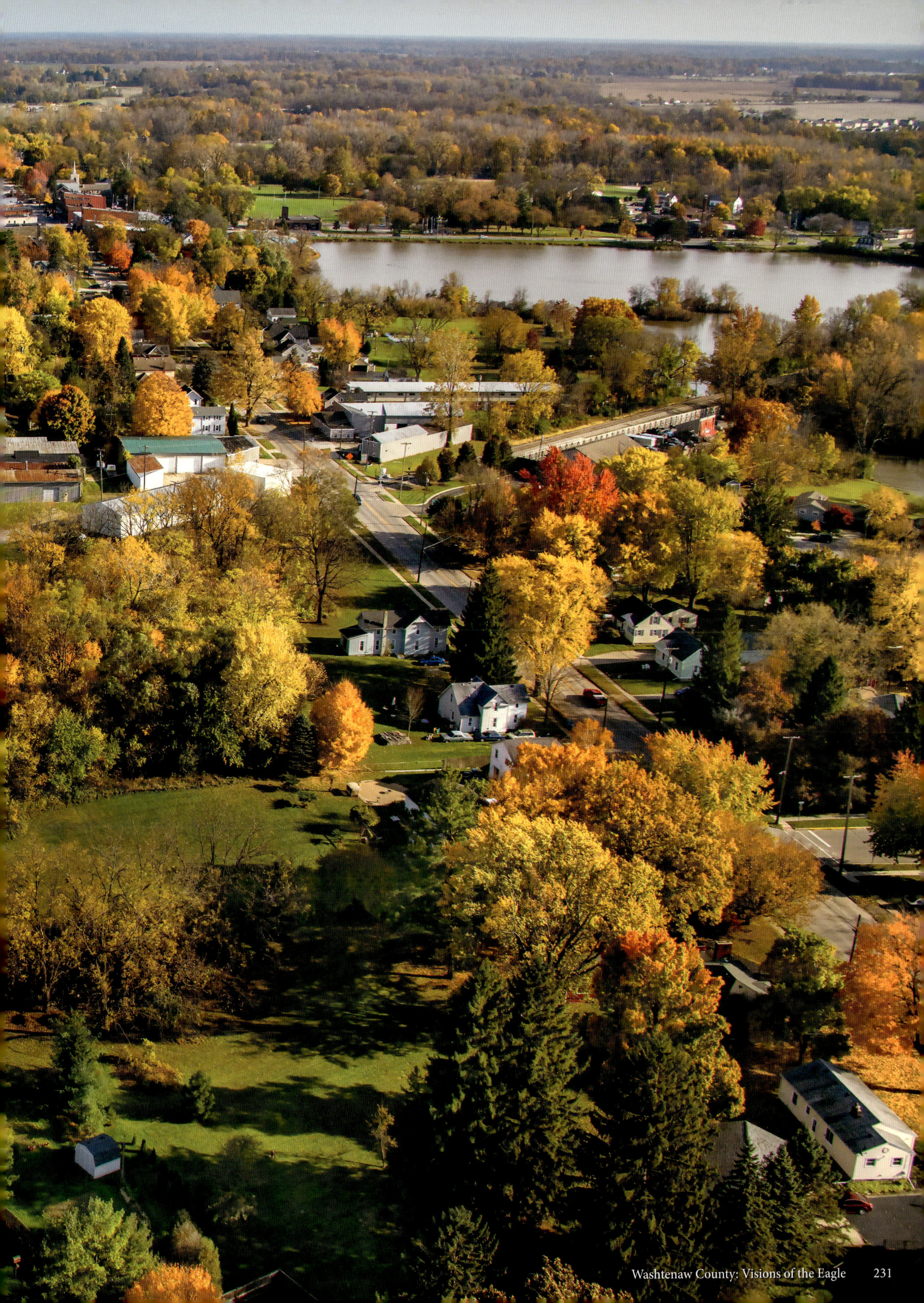

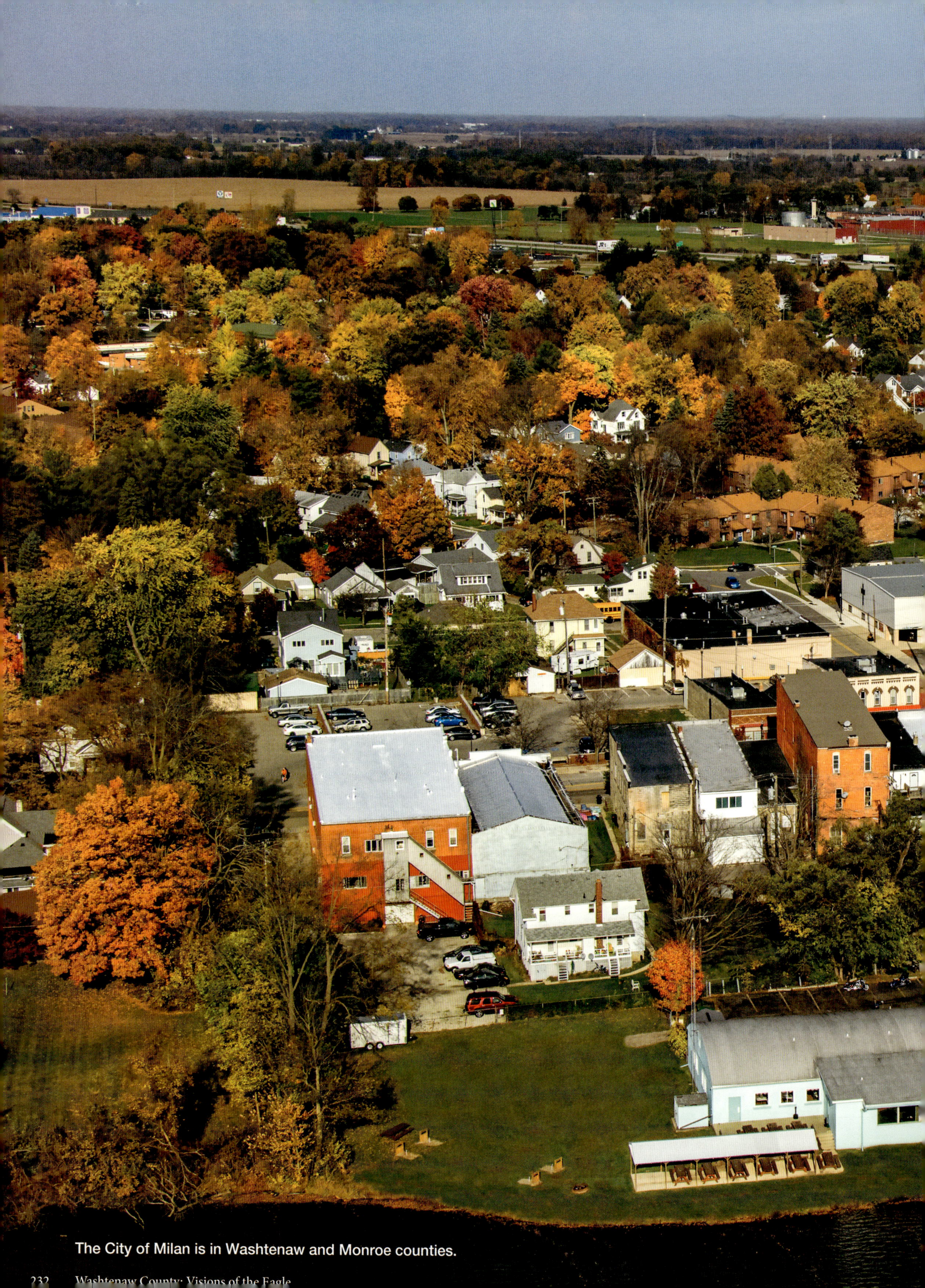

The City of Milan is in Washtenaw and Monroe counties.

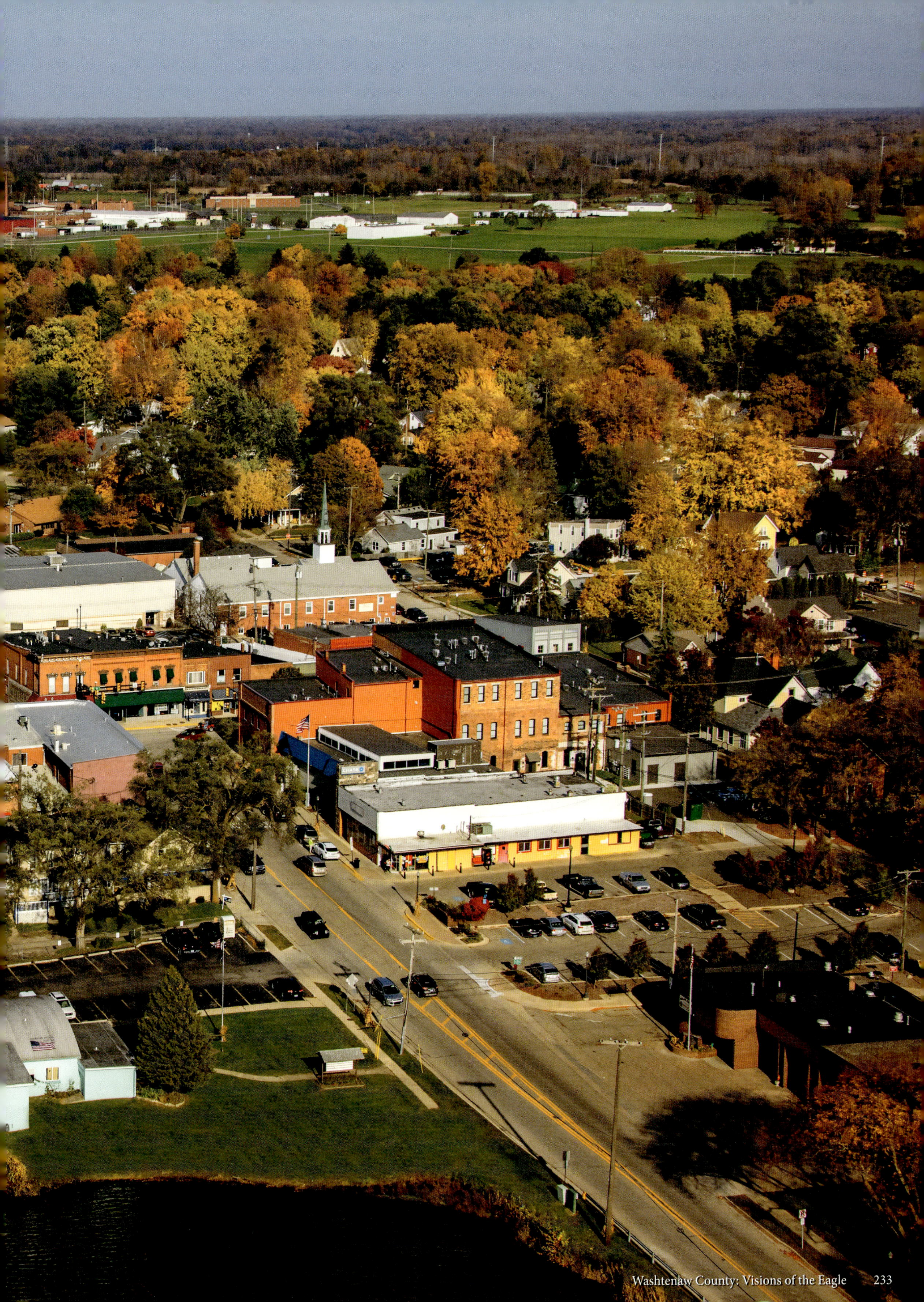
CHASE

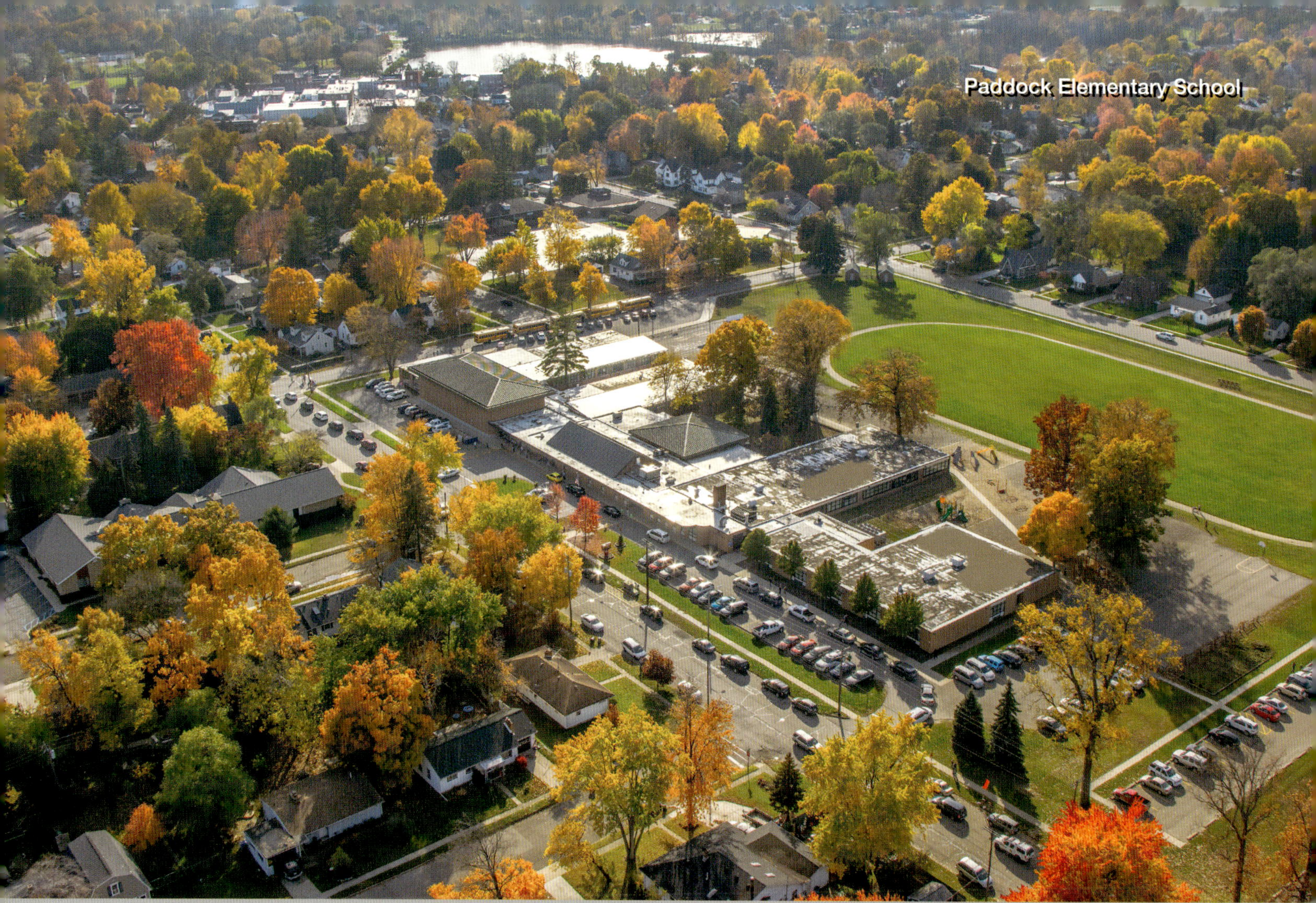

Paddock Elementary School

Fall on the farm with a pumpkin patch.

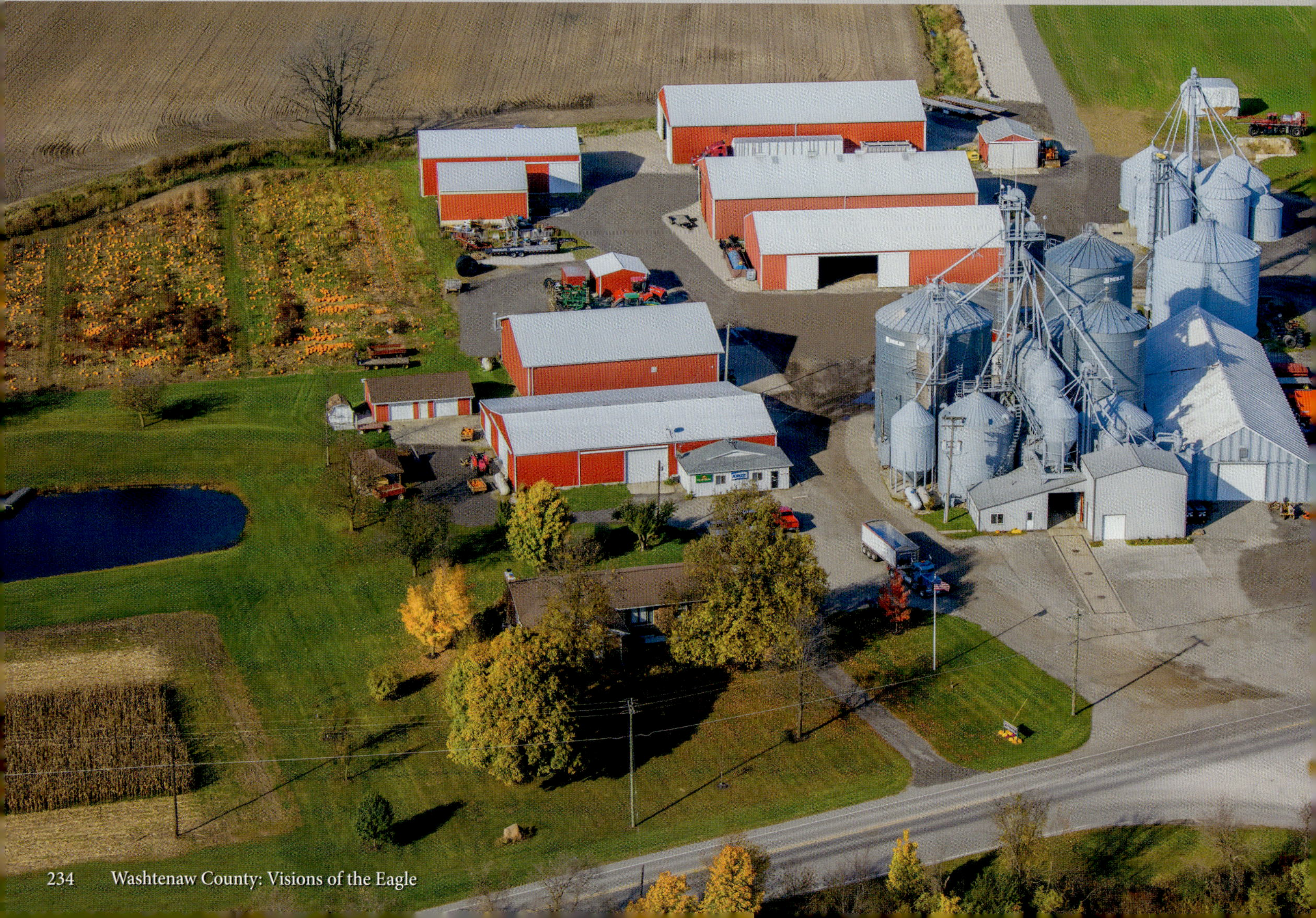

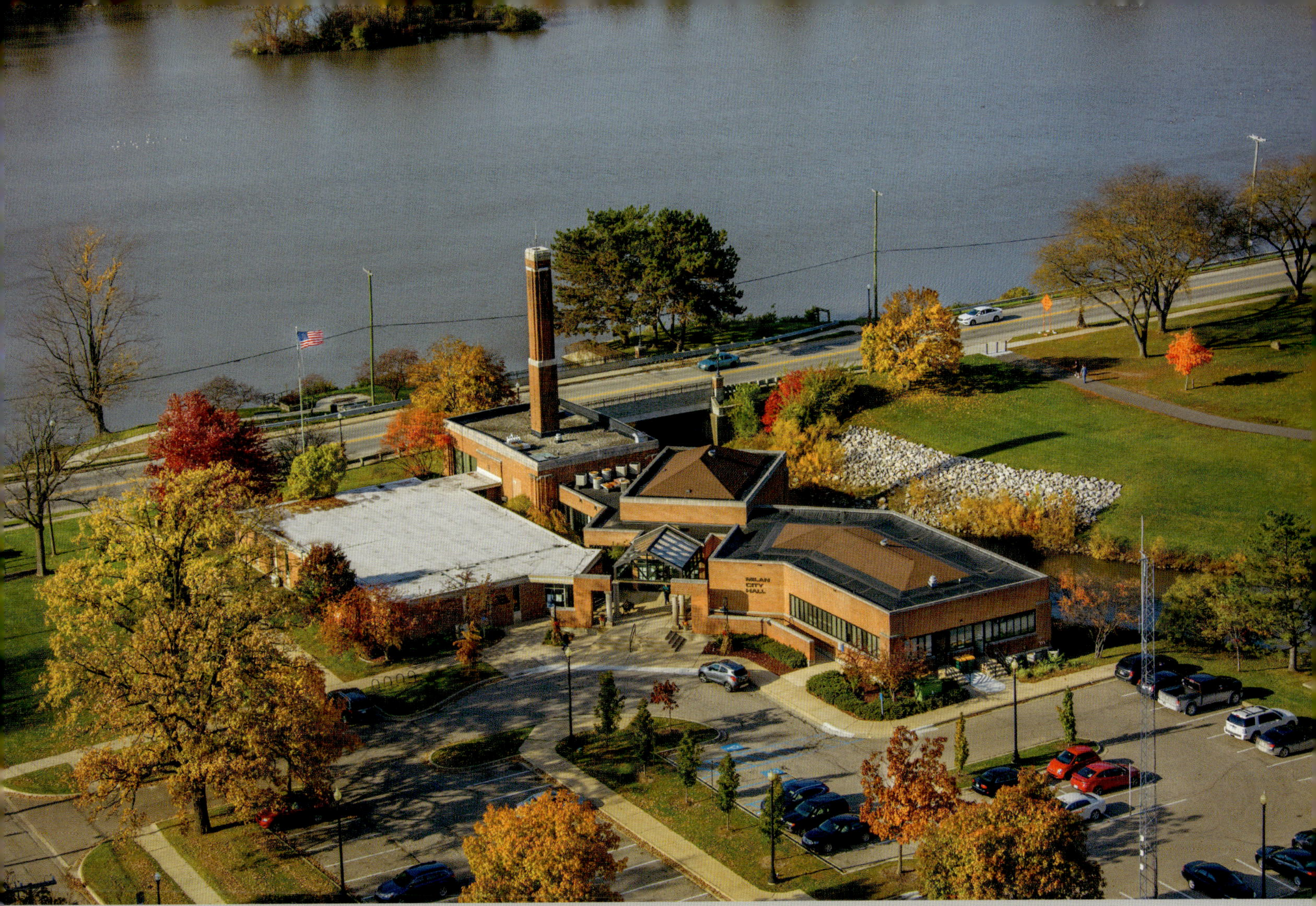

Milan City Hall.

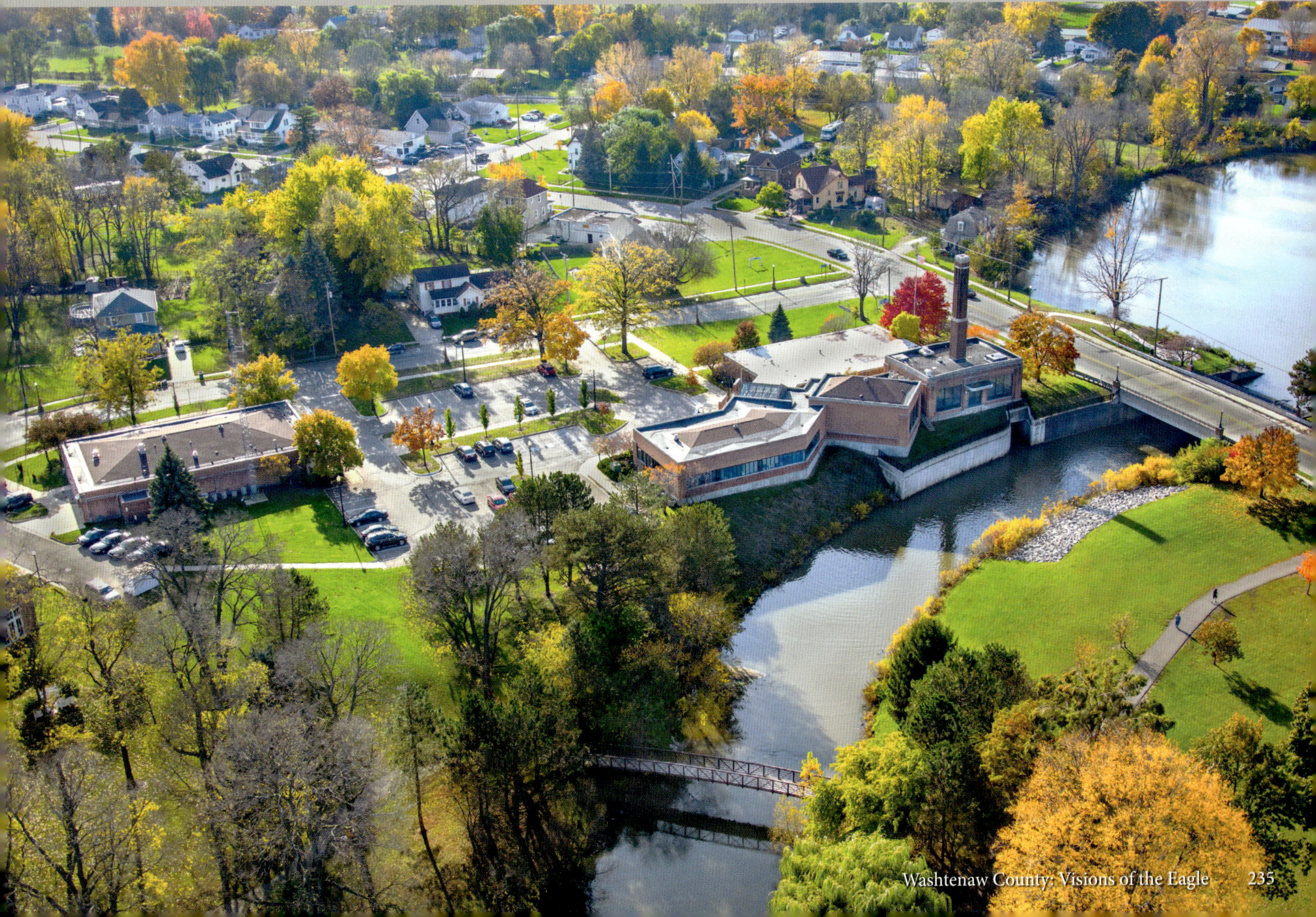

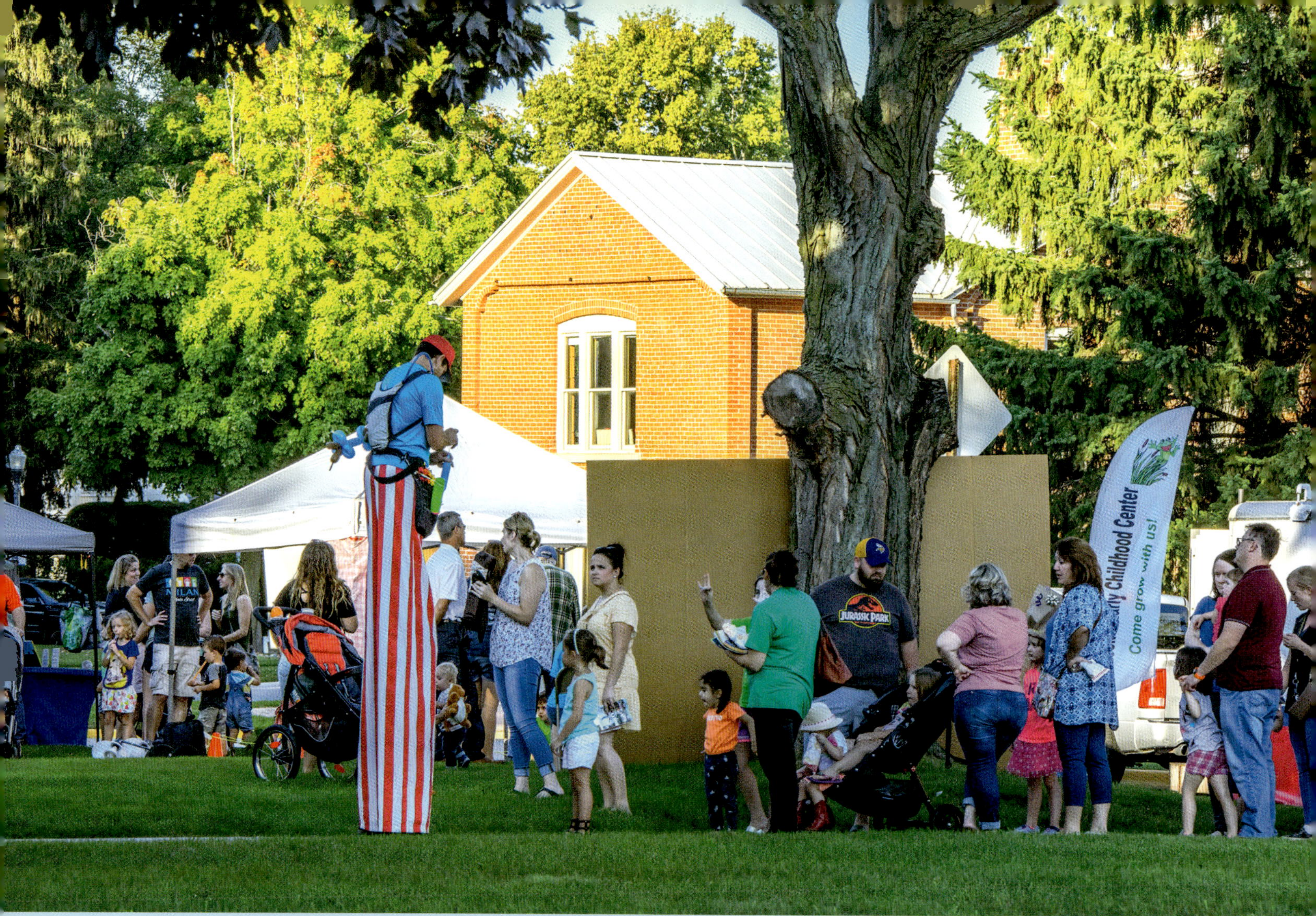

Officers Austin Bryant (left) and Christopher Kish (right) riding the Commando model from Recon Power Bikes. A grant from Norfolk Southern Railroad helped revitalized the bicycle patrol program.

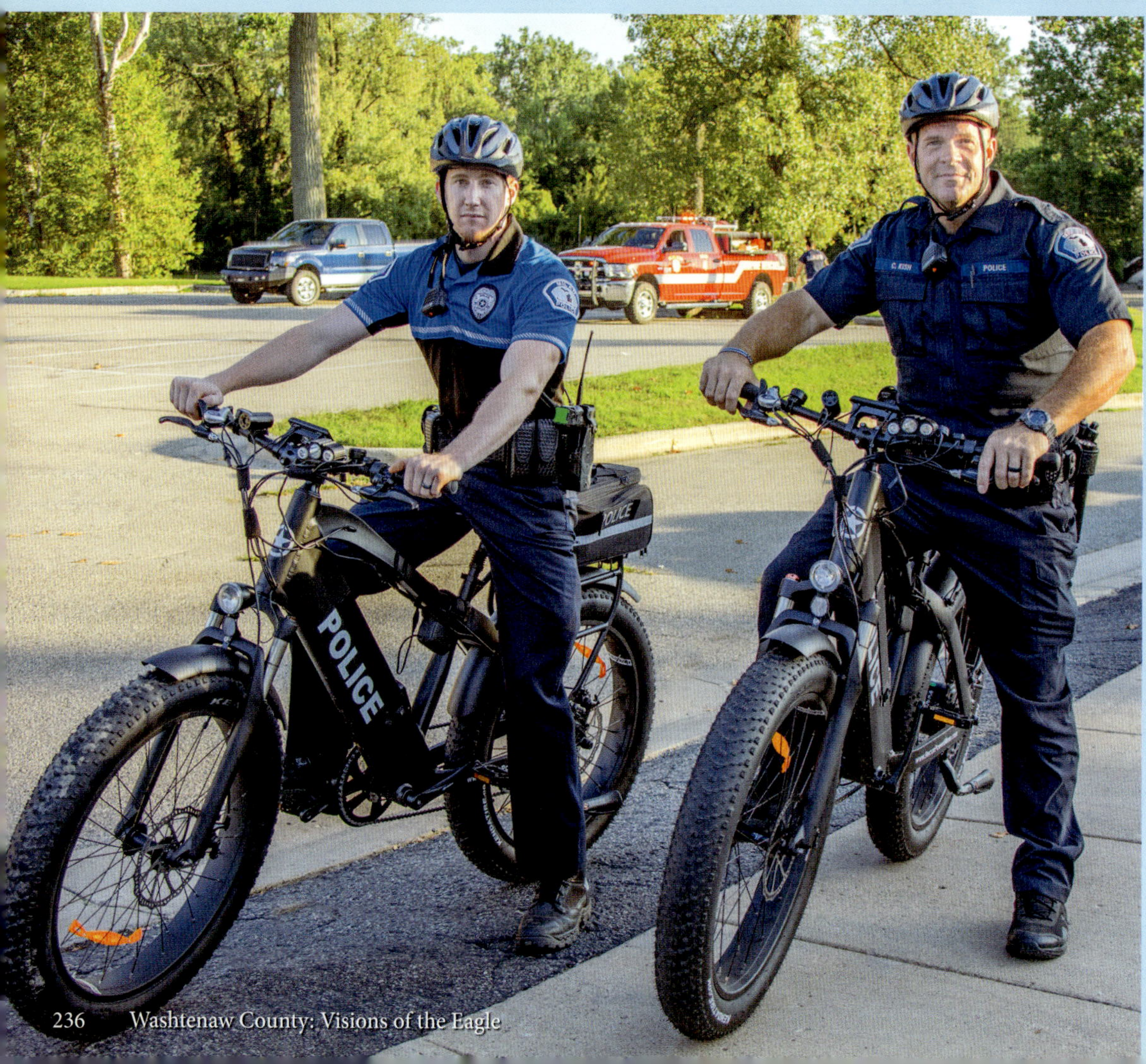

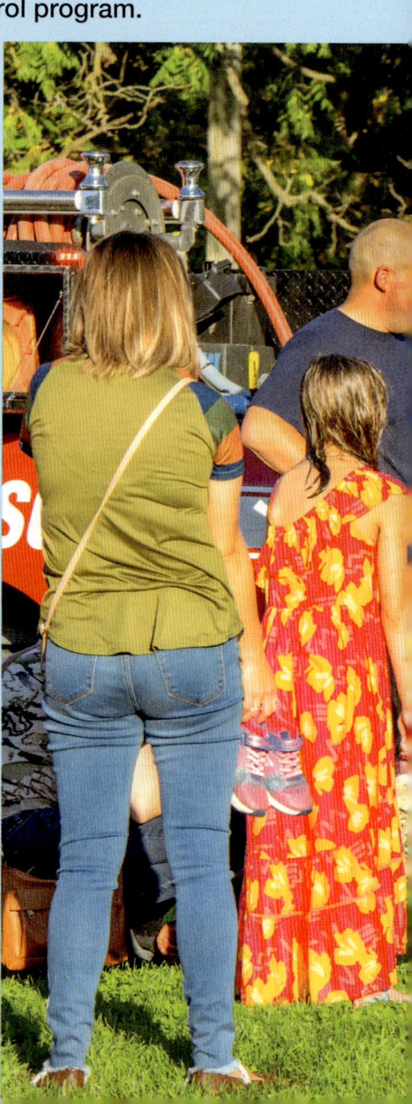

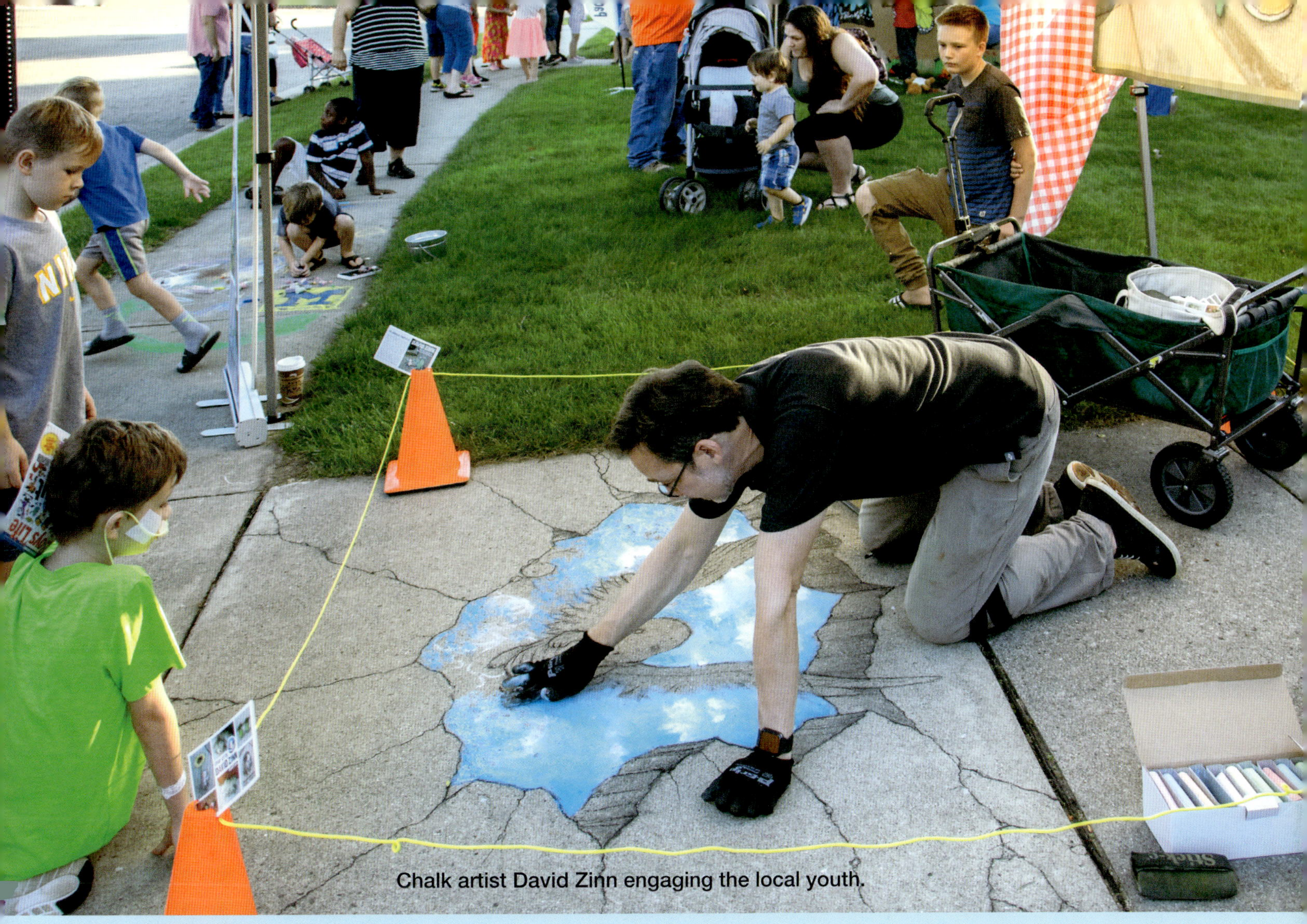

Chalk artist David Zinn engaging the local youth.

Designed to engage the community with a variety of activities, entertainment, and shopping options, Milan Main Street presents 3rd Thursdays from June - October.

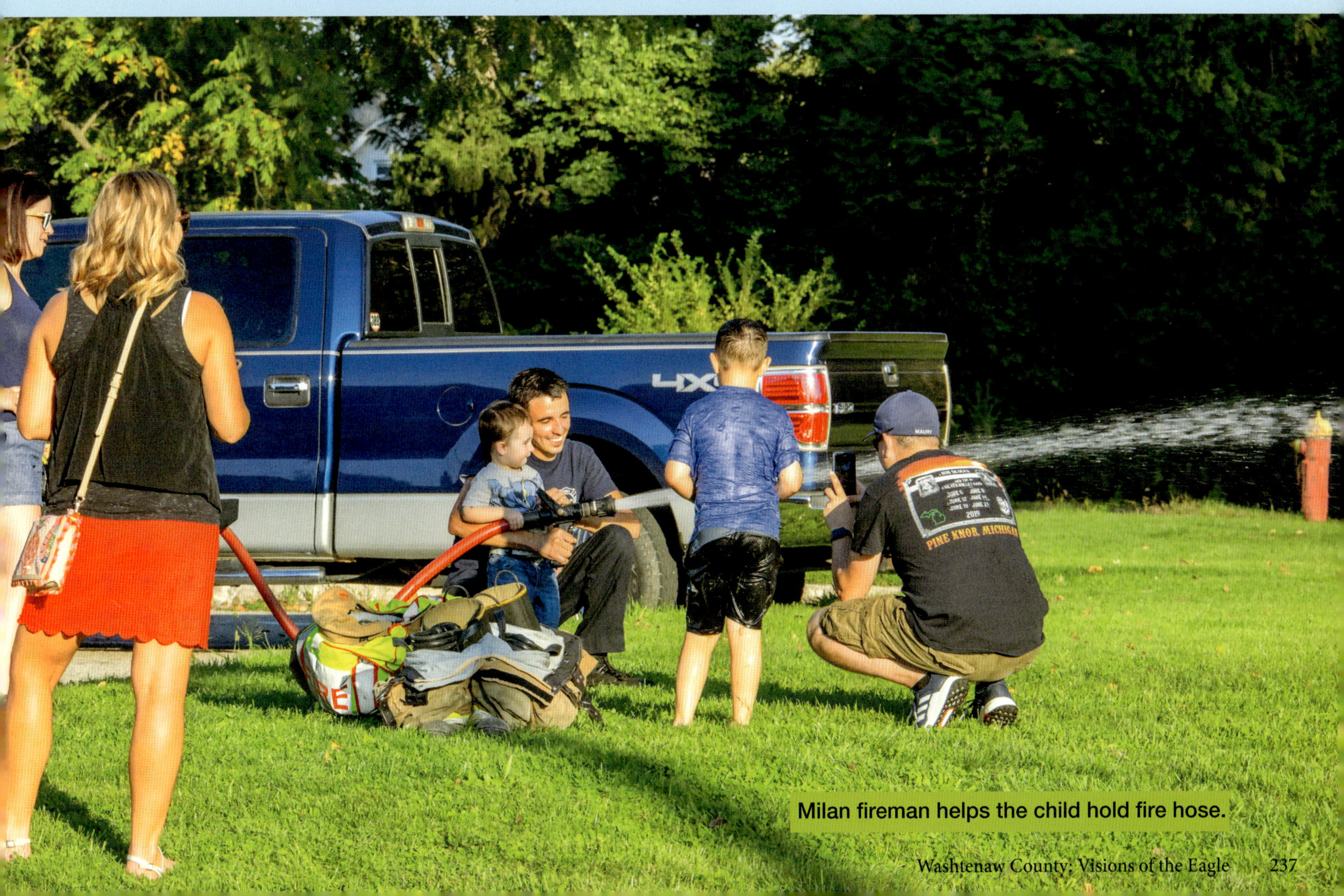

Milan fireman helps the child hold fire hose.

SALINE

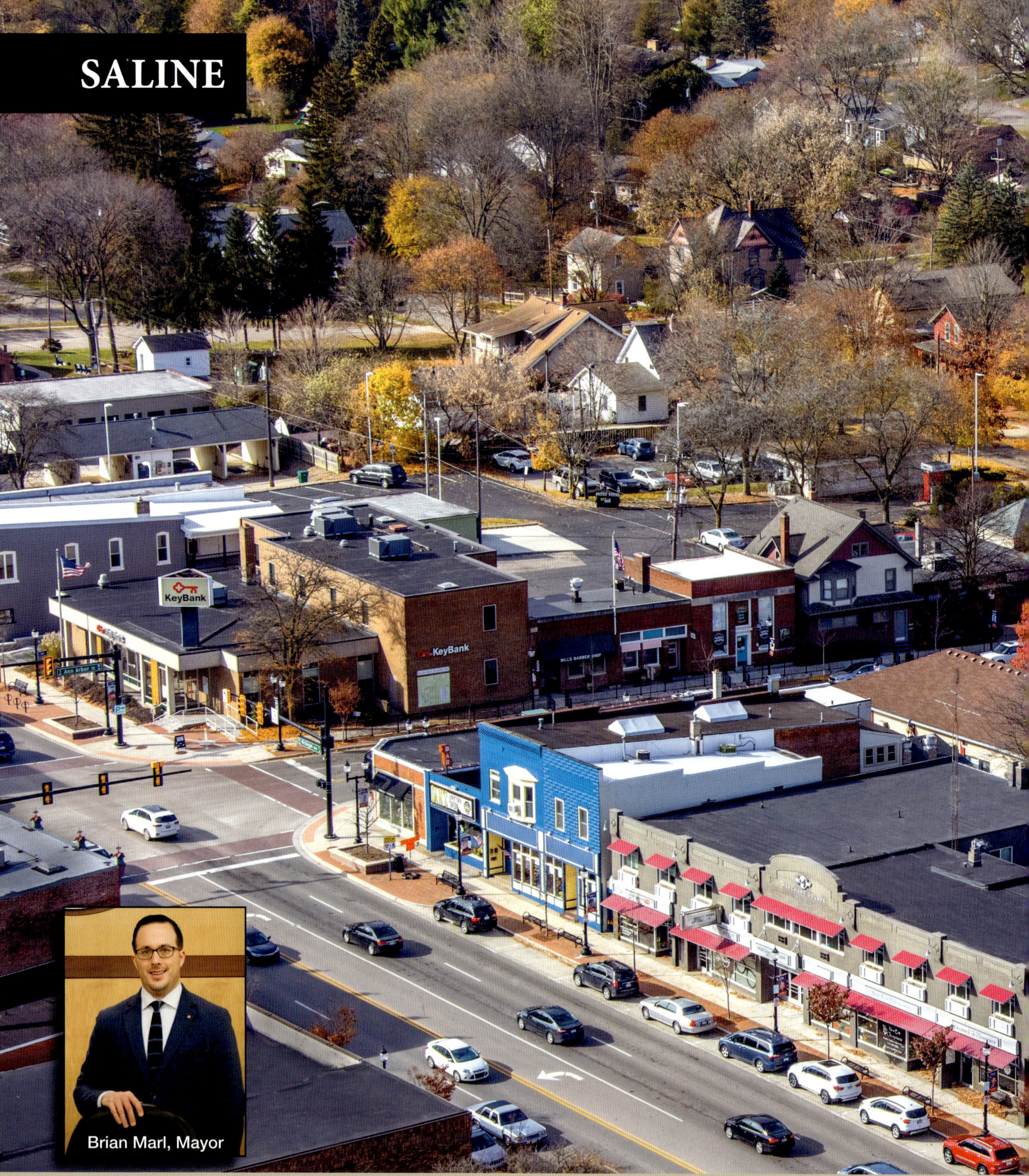

Brian Marl, Mayor

The City of Saline, a quintessential American small town, was incorporated in 1866 and celebrated its sesquicentennial in 2016. The lively community keeps its history alive through the Saline Area Historical Society, Rentschler Farm Museum, and the Saline History & Depot Museum.

Ranked one of the most desirable small towns to live in the U.S., Saline includes a vibrant and walkable downtown with eclectic restaurants, boutiques, and services. Just 20 minutes from Ann Arbor, Saline has retained its rural flavor and friendly, family-oriented community. Carefully tended parks, biking and walking paths offer outdoor recreation. Saline's excellent schools, historic and new homes, and access to Washtenaw County's abundant resources make it an ideal place to call home.

CITY OF SALINE

100 N. Harris St.
Saline, MI
734-429-4907

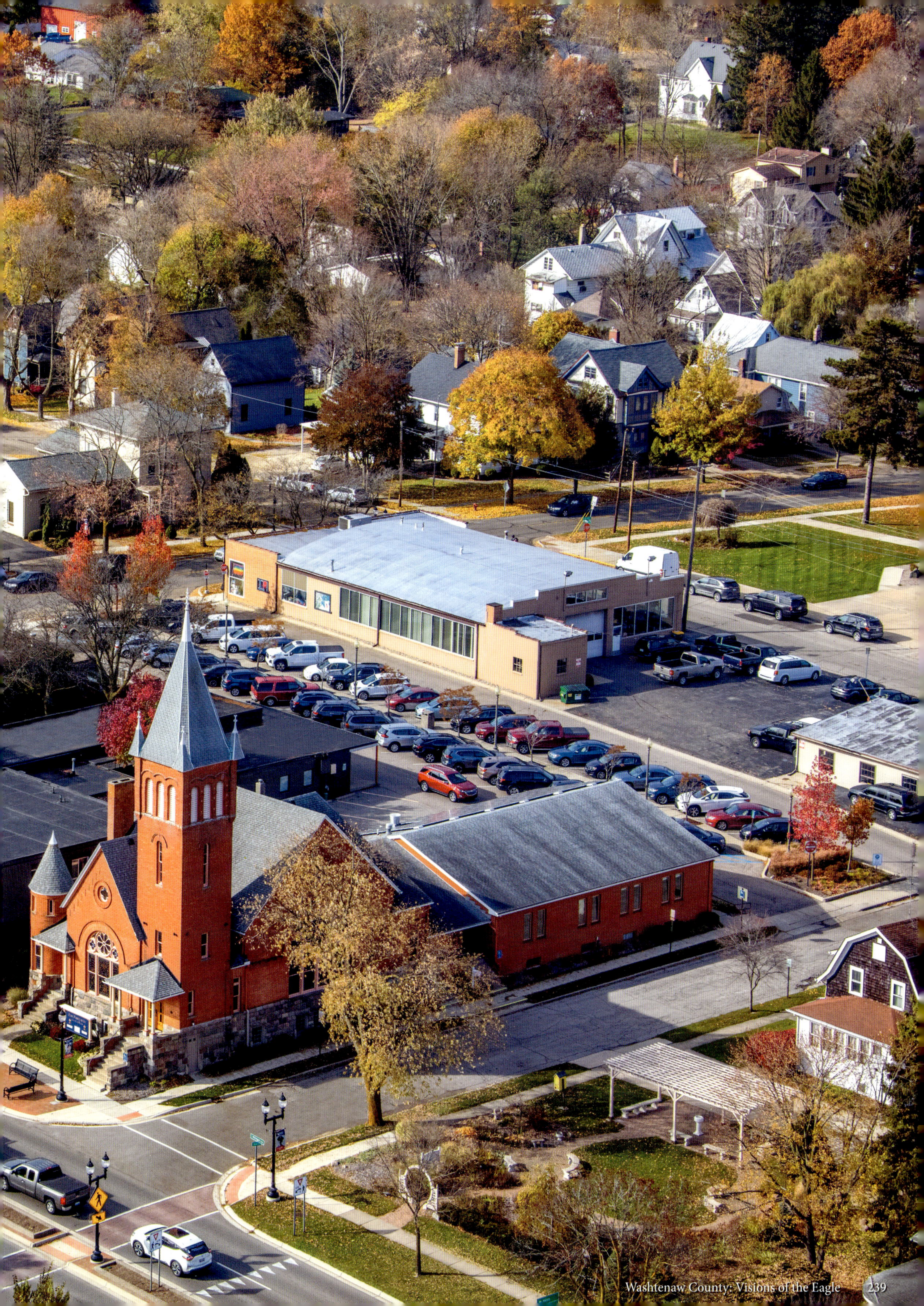

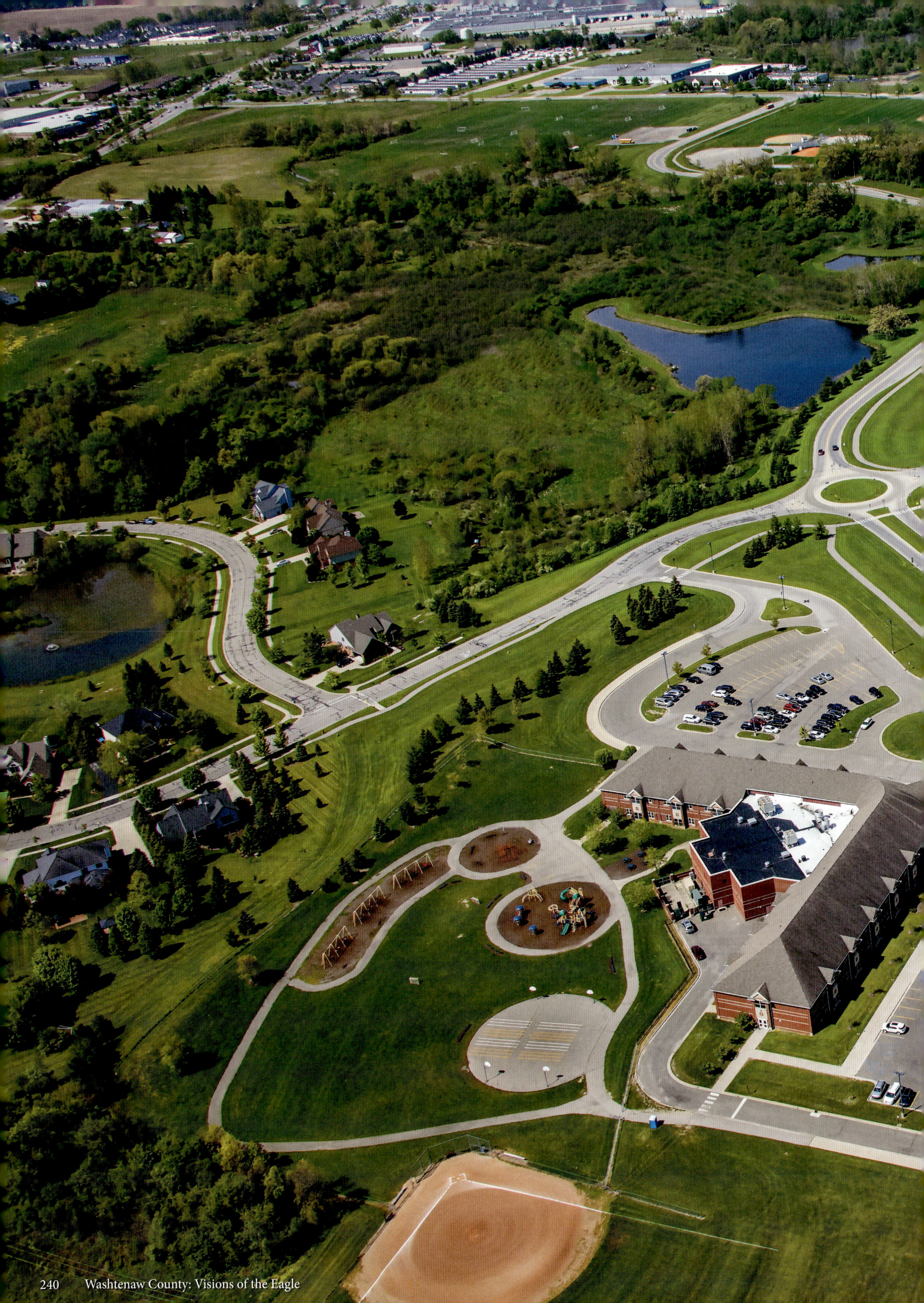

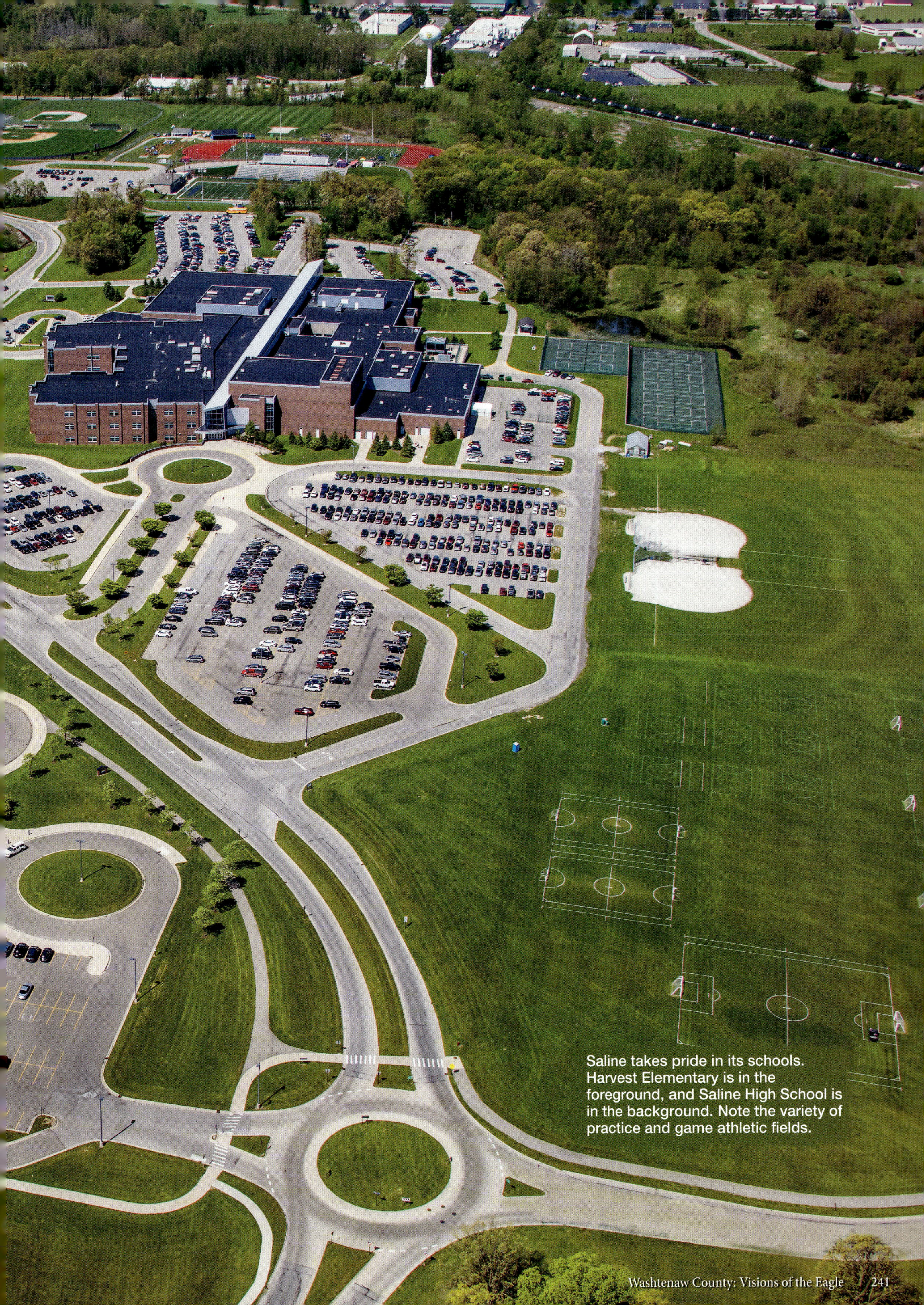

Saline takes pride in its schools. Harvest Elementary is in the foreground, and Saline High School is in the background. Note the variety of practice and game athletic fields.

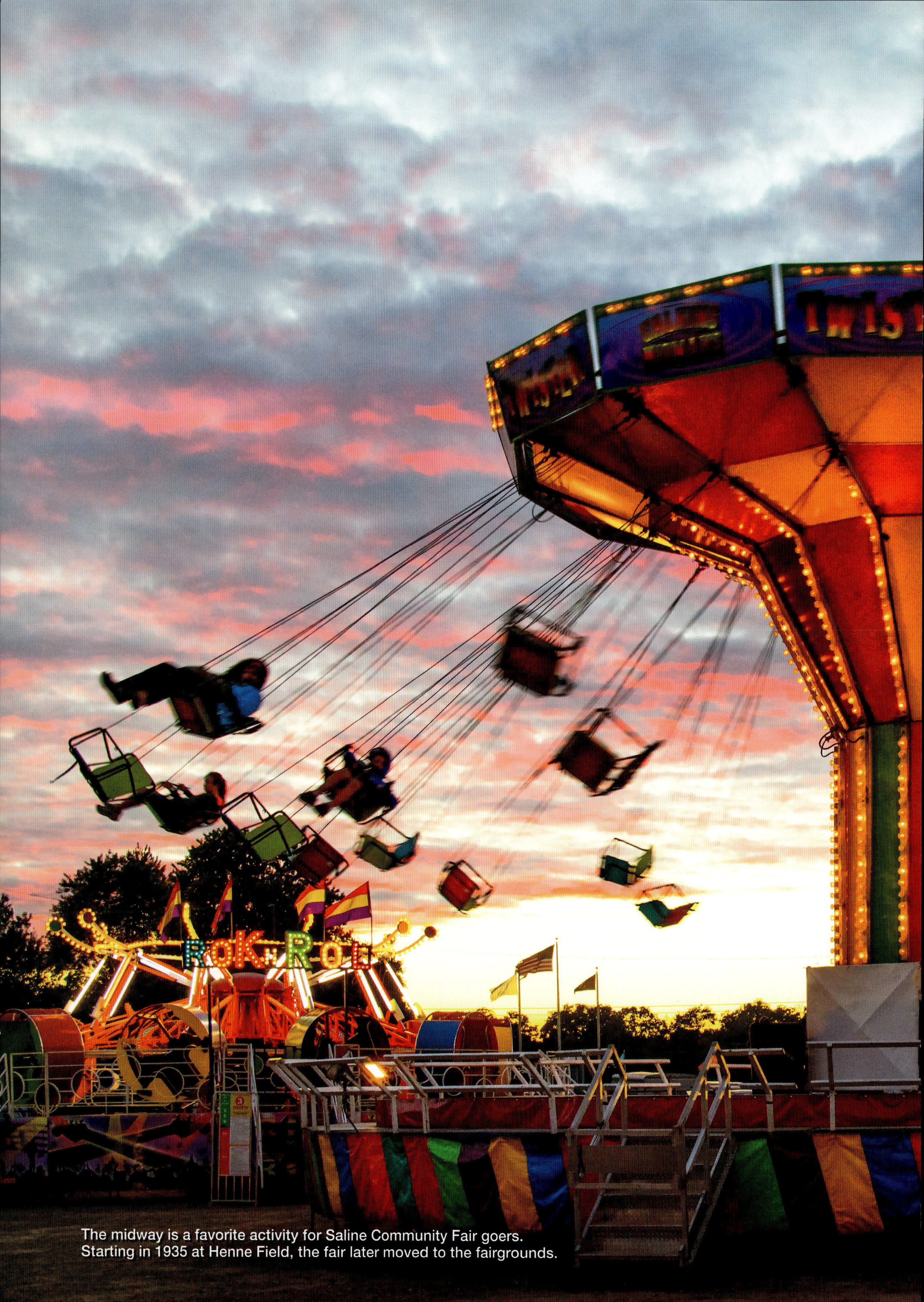

The midway is a favorite activity for Saline Community Fair goers.
Starting in 1935 at Henne Field, the fair later moved to the fairgrounds.

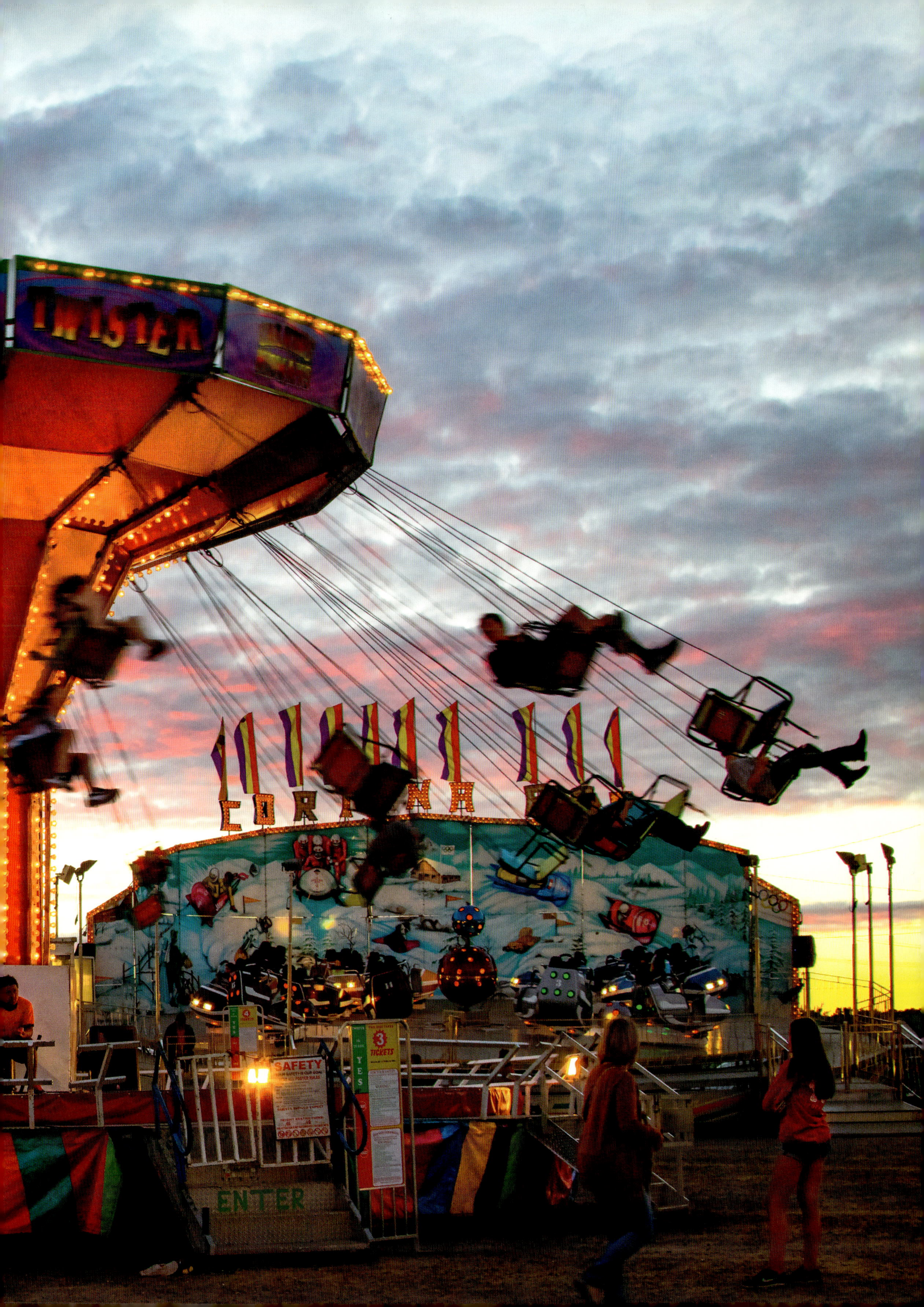
TWISTER
SAFETY
3 TICKETS
YES
ENTER

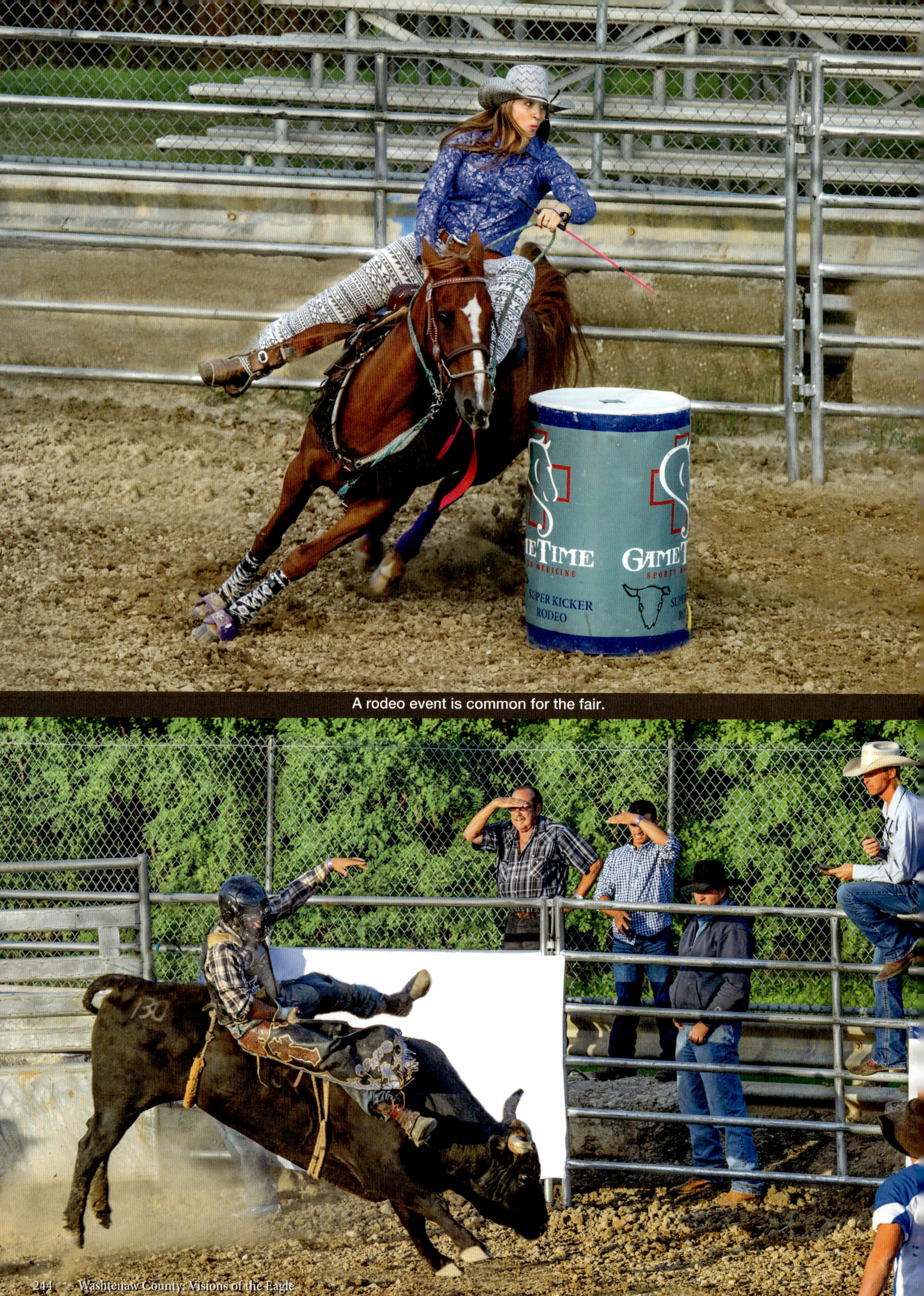

A rodeo event is common for the fair.

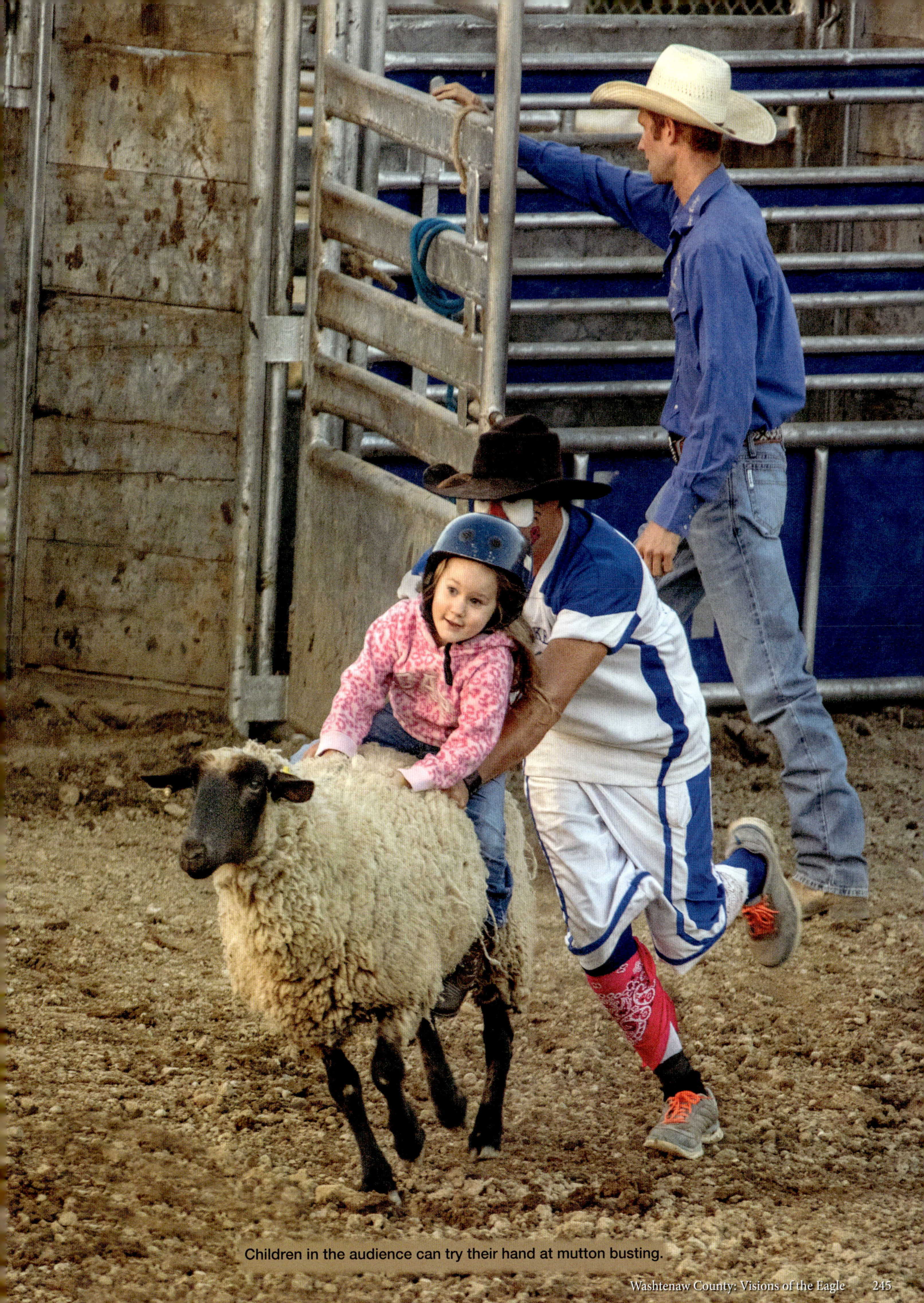

Children in the audience can try their hand at mutton busting.

Emagine Saline

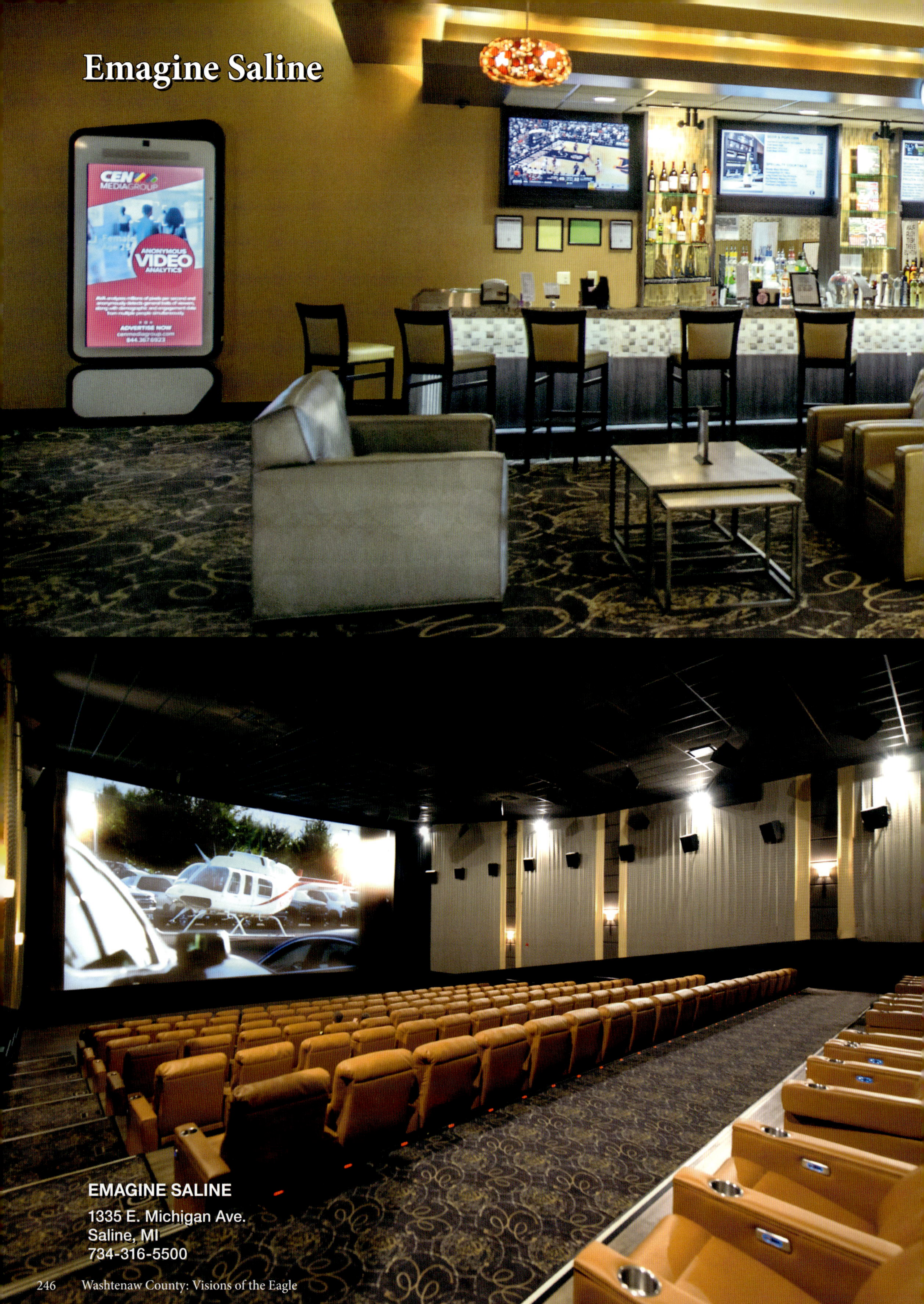

EMAGINE SALINE

1335 E. Michigan Ave.
Saline, MI
734-316-5500

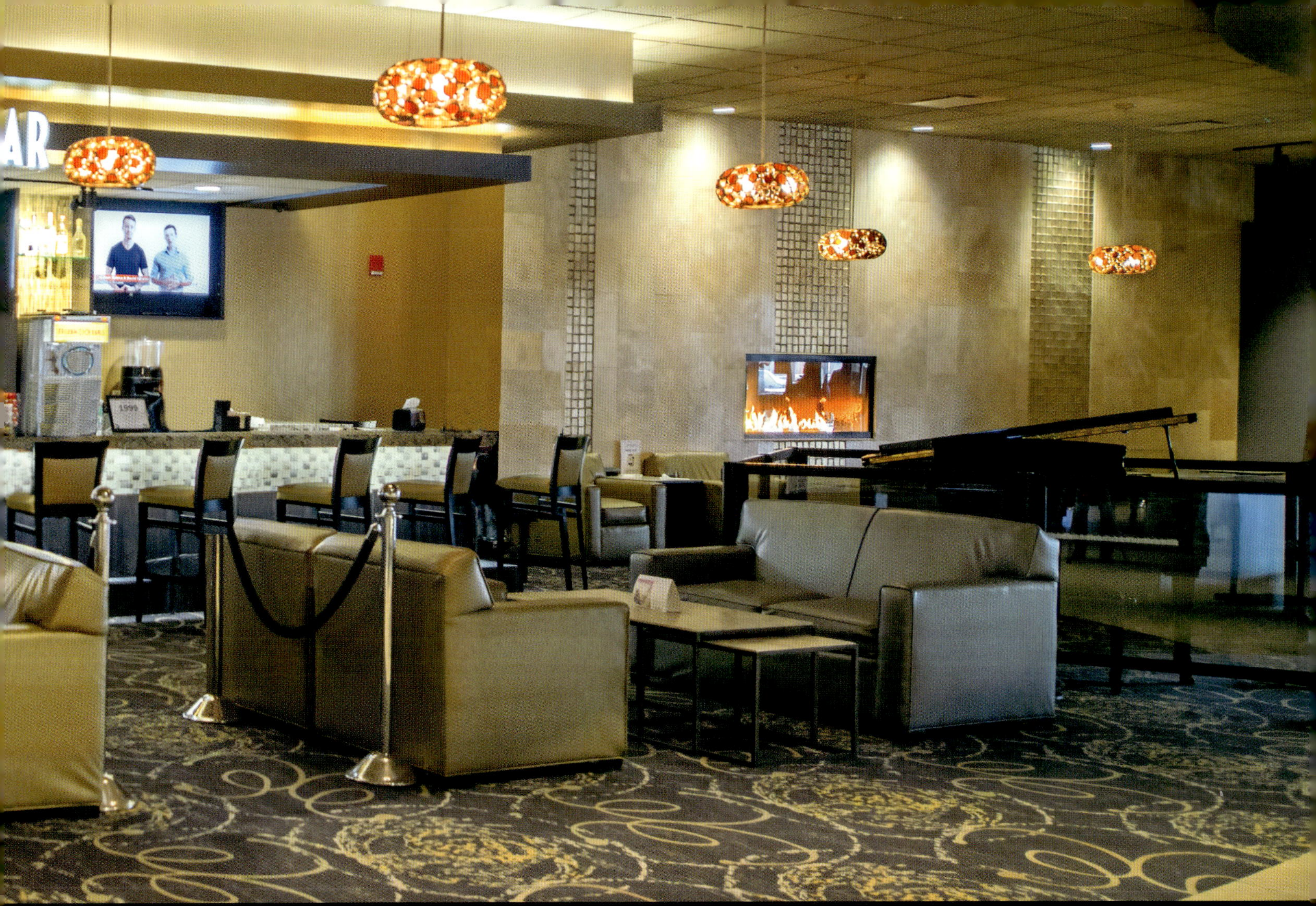

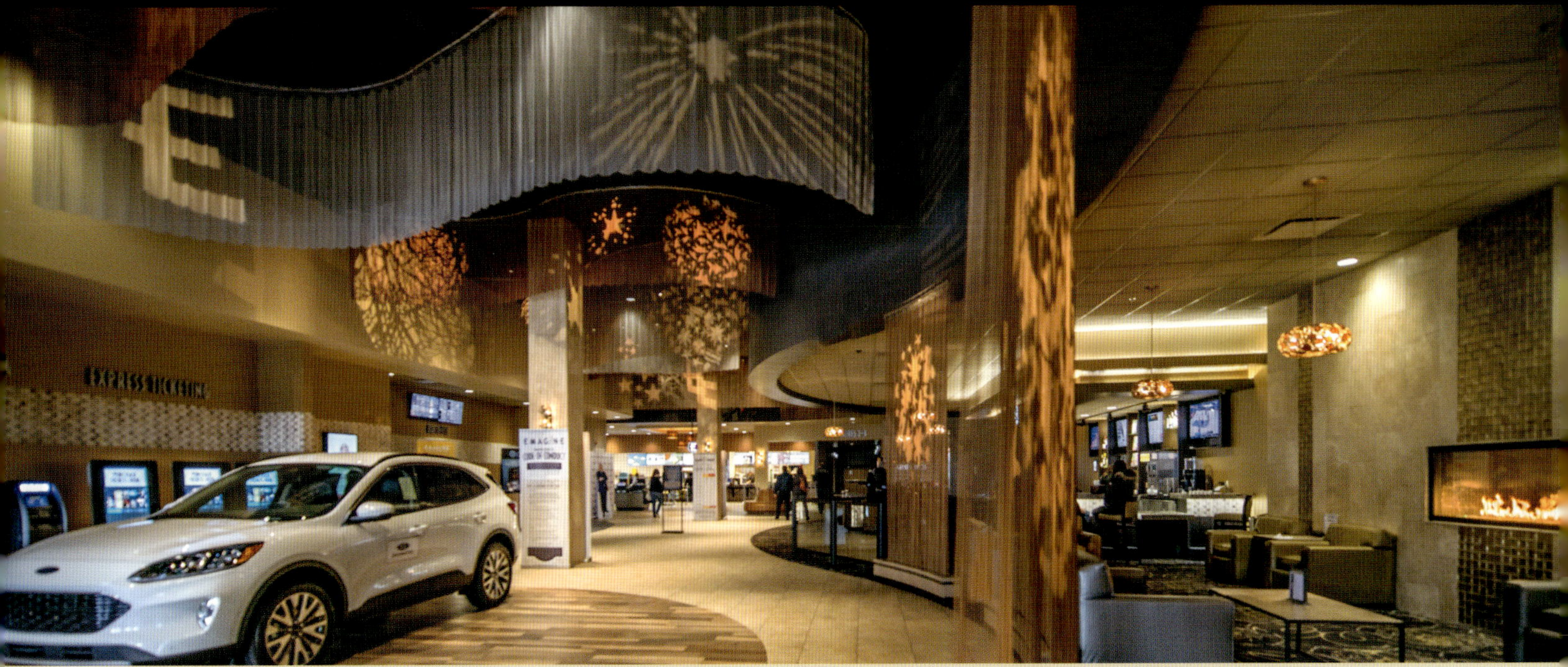

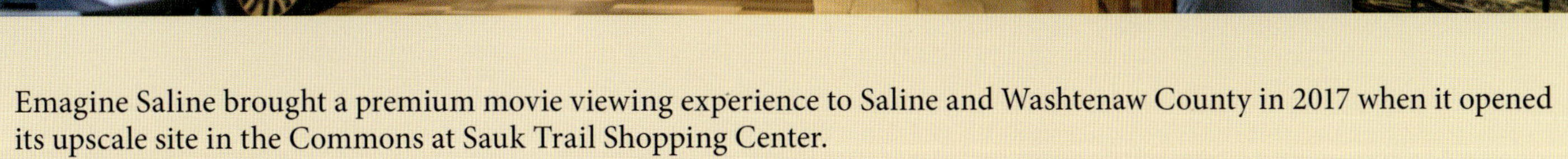

Emagine Saline brought a premium movie viewing experience to Saline and Washtenaw County in 2017 when it opened its upscale site in the Commons at Sauk Trail Shopping Center.

Going to the movies has never been more convenient with advanced ticket purchase and seat reservations online or via Emagine's mobile app.

Emagine has reimagined the entire movie theatre experience. Come early and lounge near the fireplace in the lobby or sit at the bar where local craft beers and hand-made cocktails await. Order a handcrafted pizza prepared in a brick oven or choose from an assortment of deliciously prepared snacks, and of course, popcorn! With 1,000 powered reclining chairs in 9 state-of-the-art luxury auditoriums, including an EMAX Theatre, Emagine invites moviegoers to put their feet up and enjoy the show.

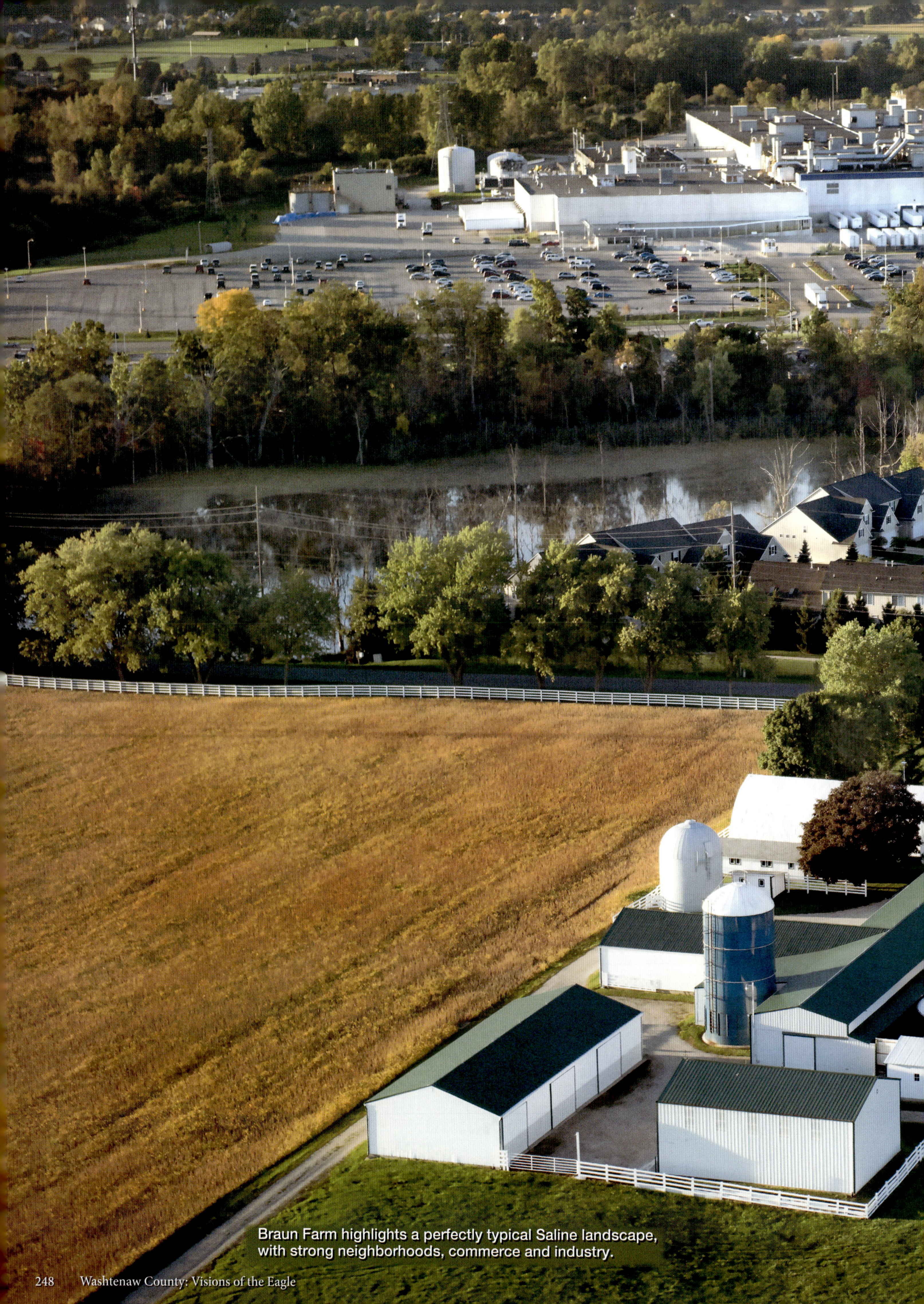

Braun Farm highlights a perfectly typical Saline landscape, with strong neighborhoods, commerce and industry.

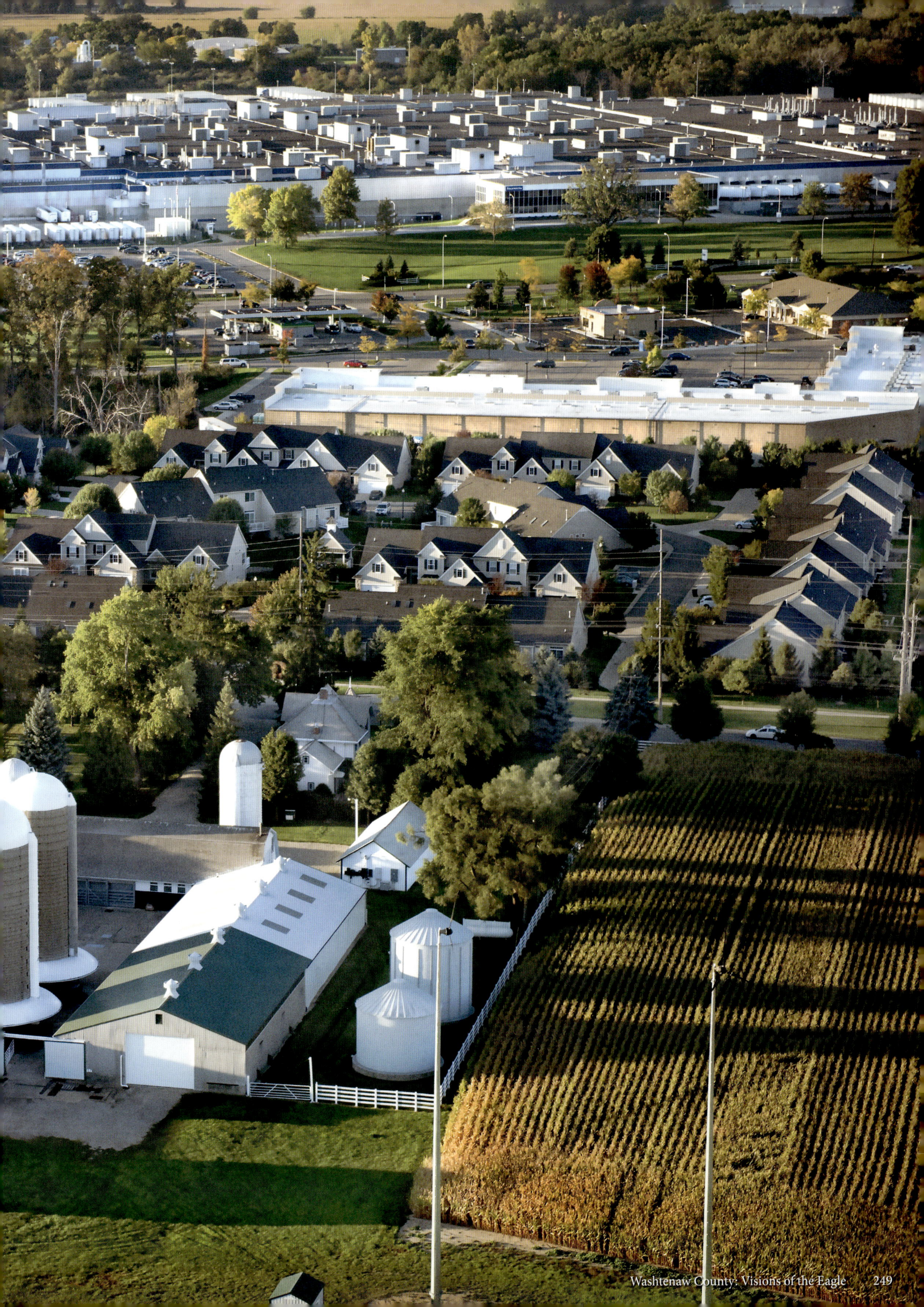

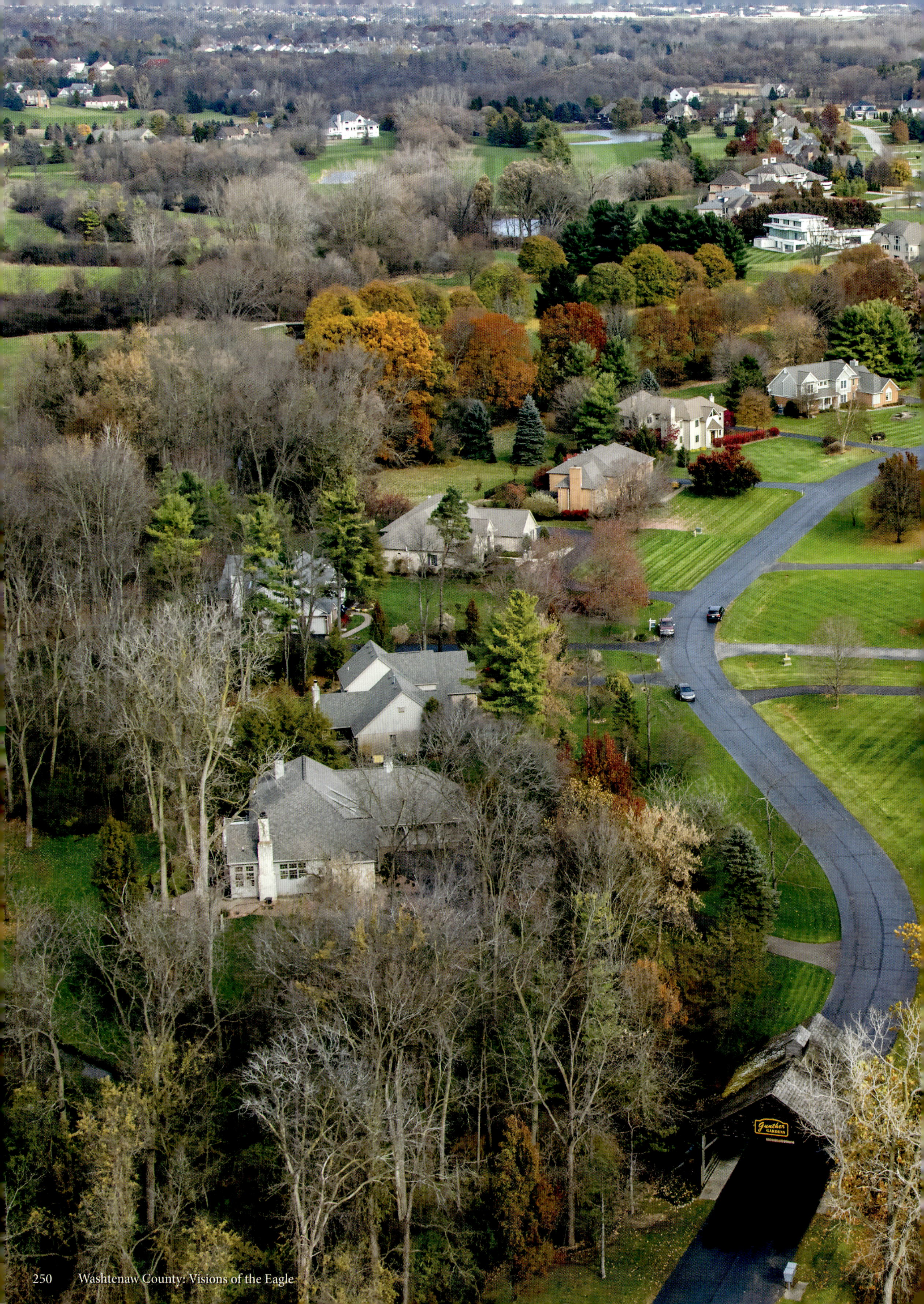
Gunther
GARDENS

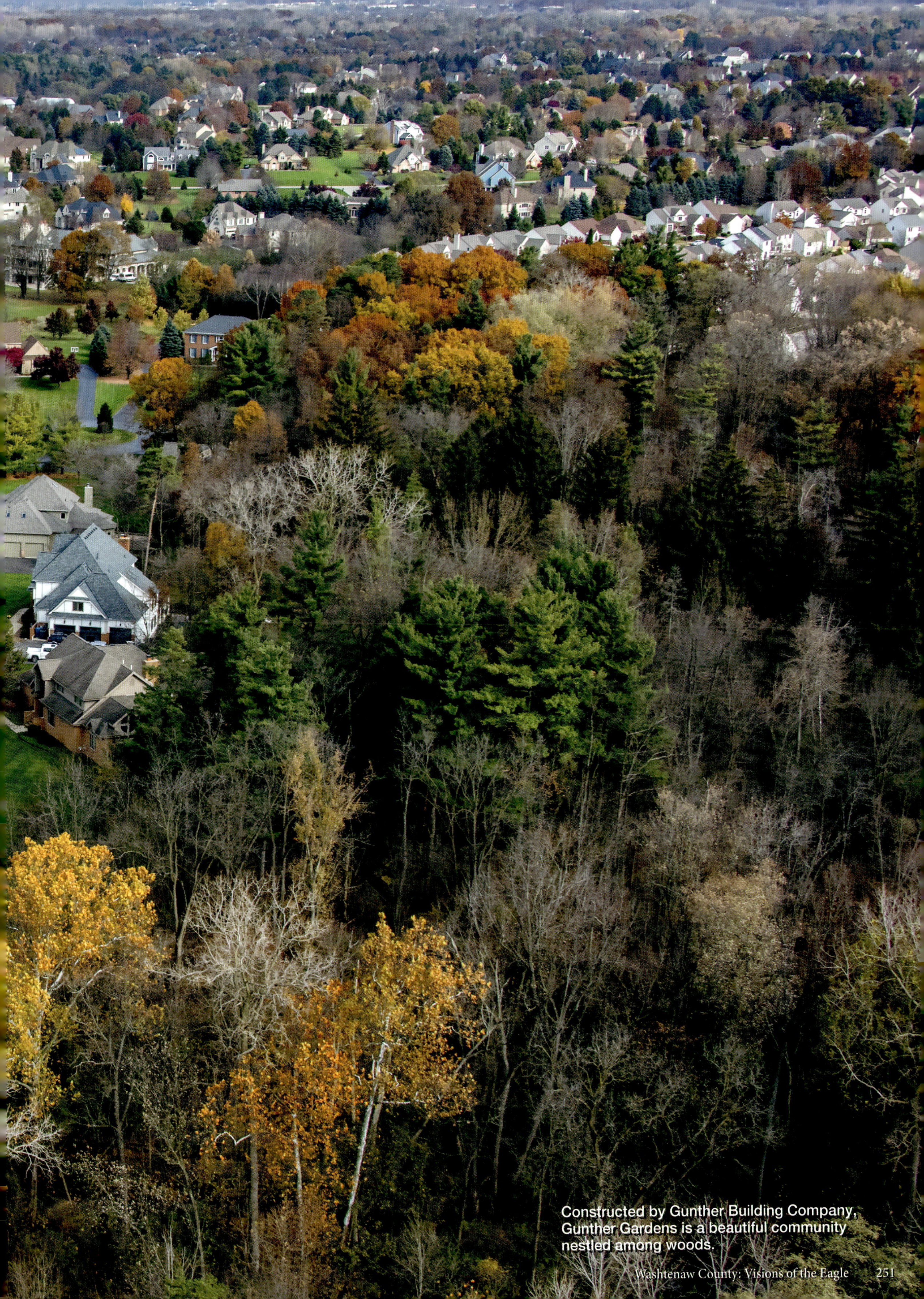

Constructed by Gunther Building Company, Gunther Gardens is a beautiful community nestled among woods.

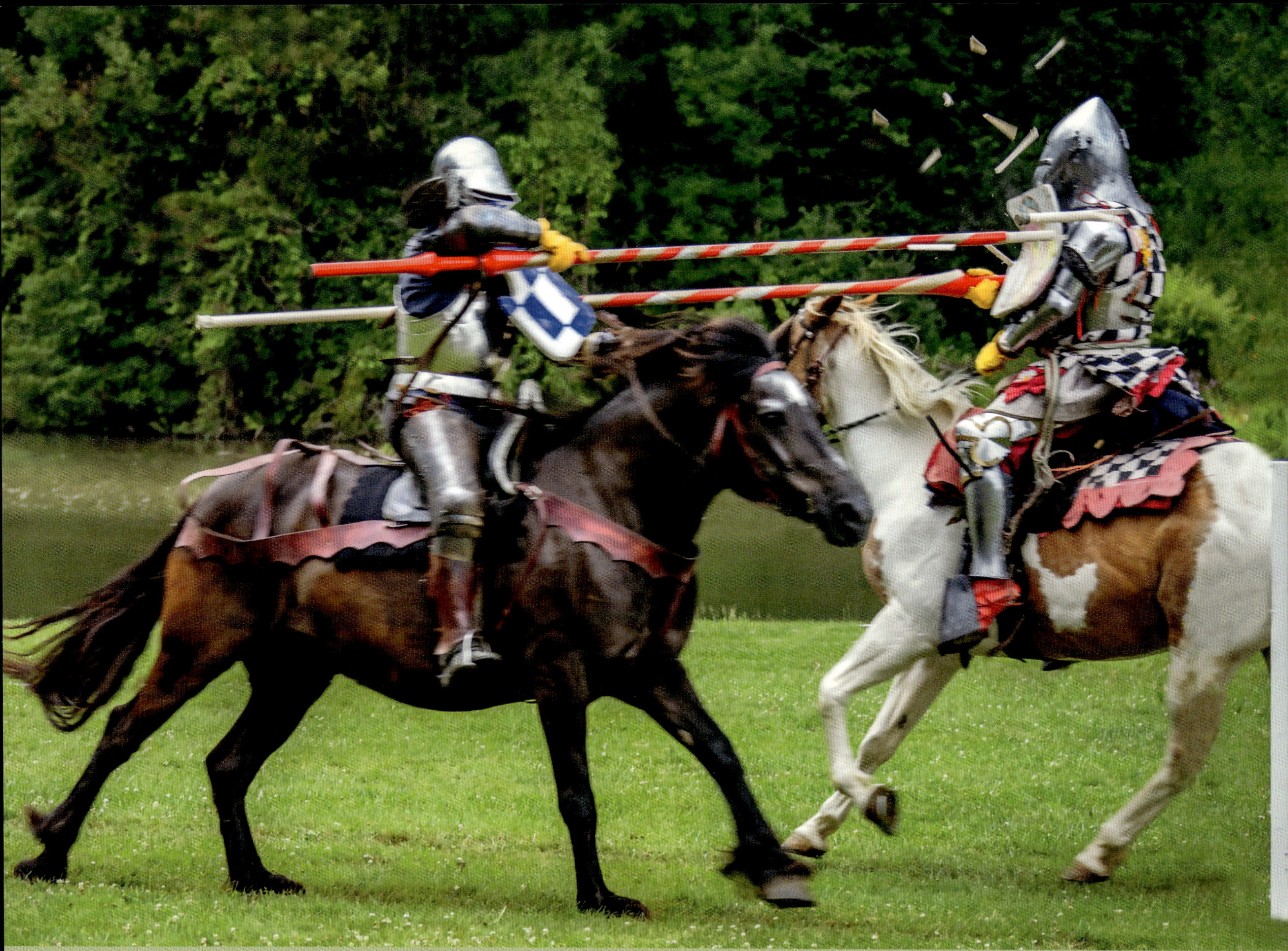

Clans participate in Highland games during the Celtic Festival.

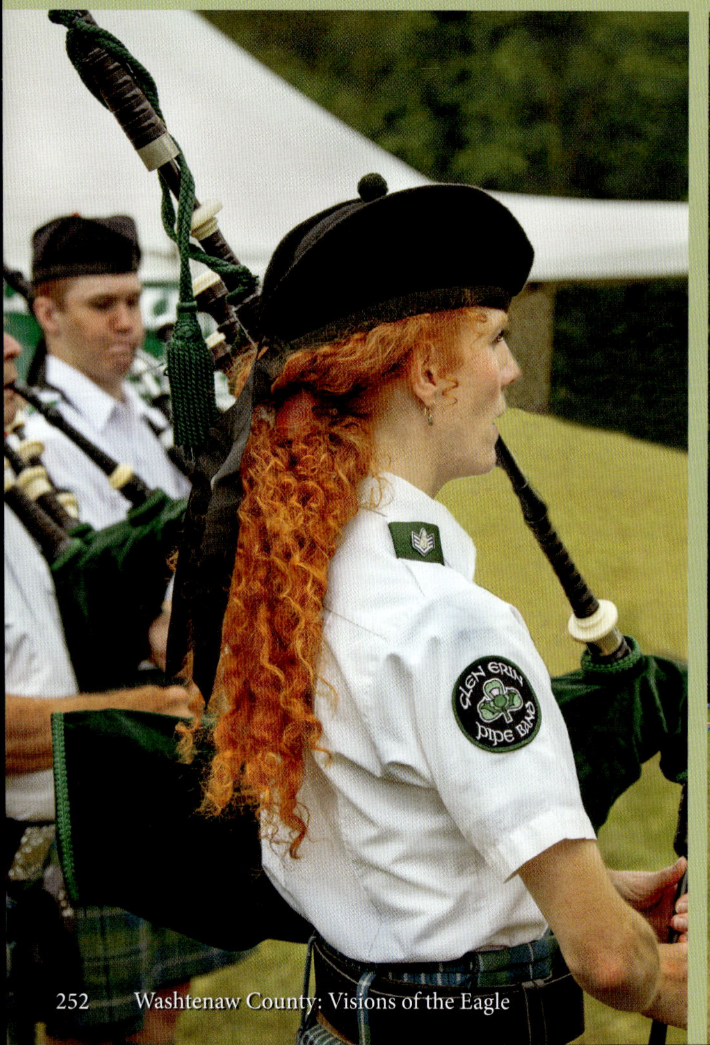

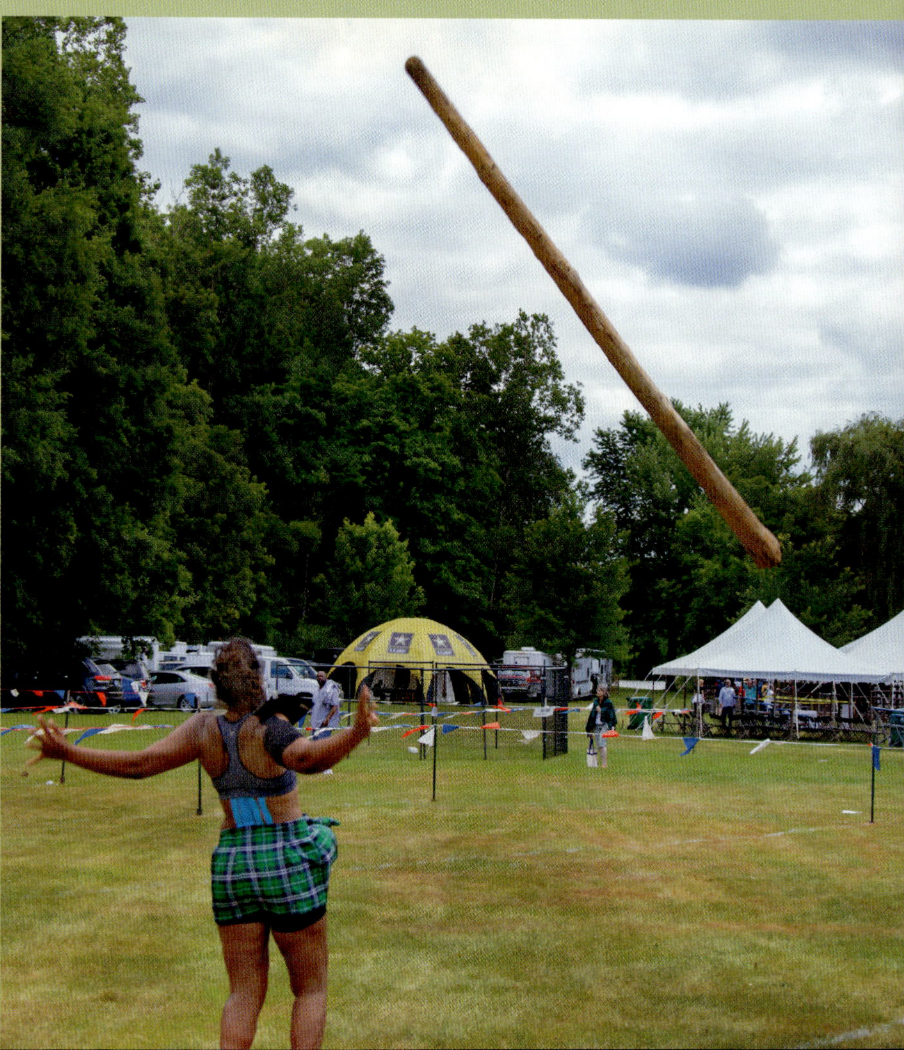

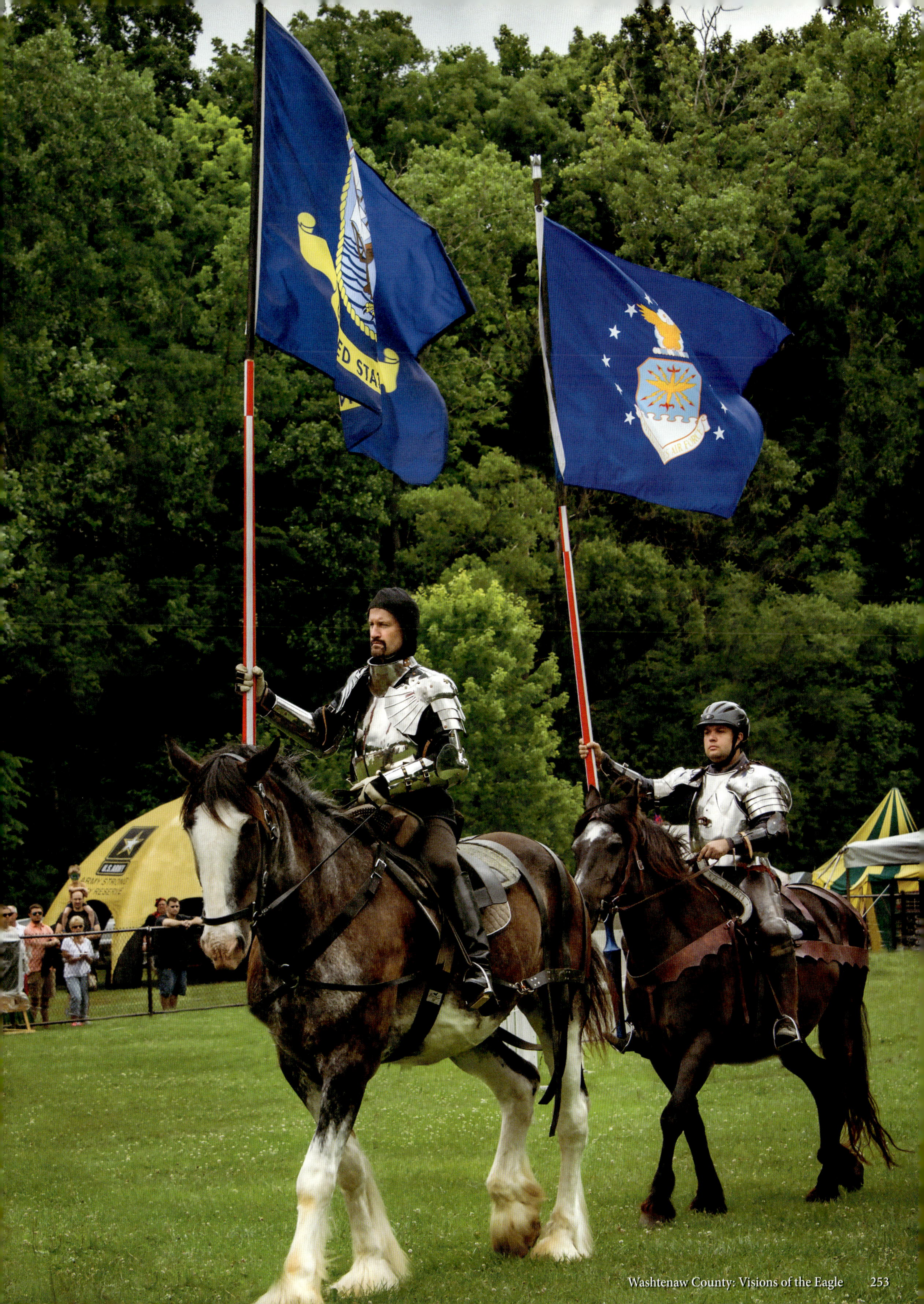

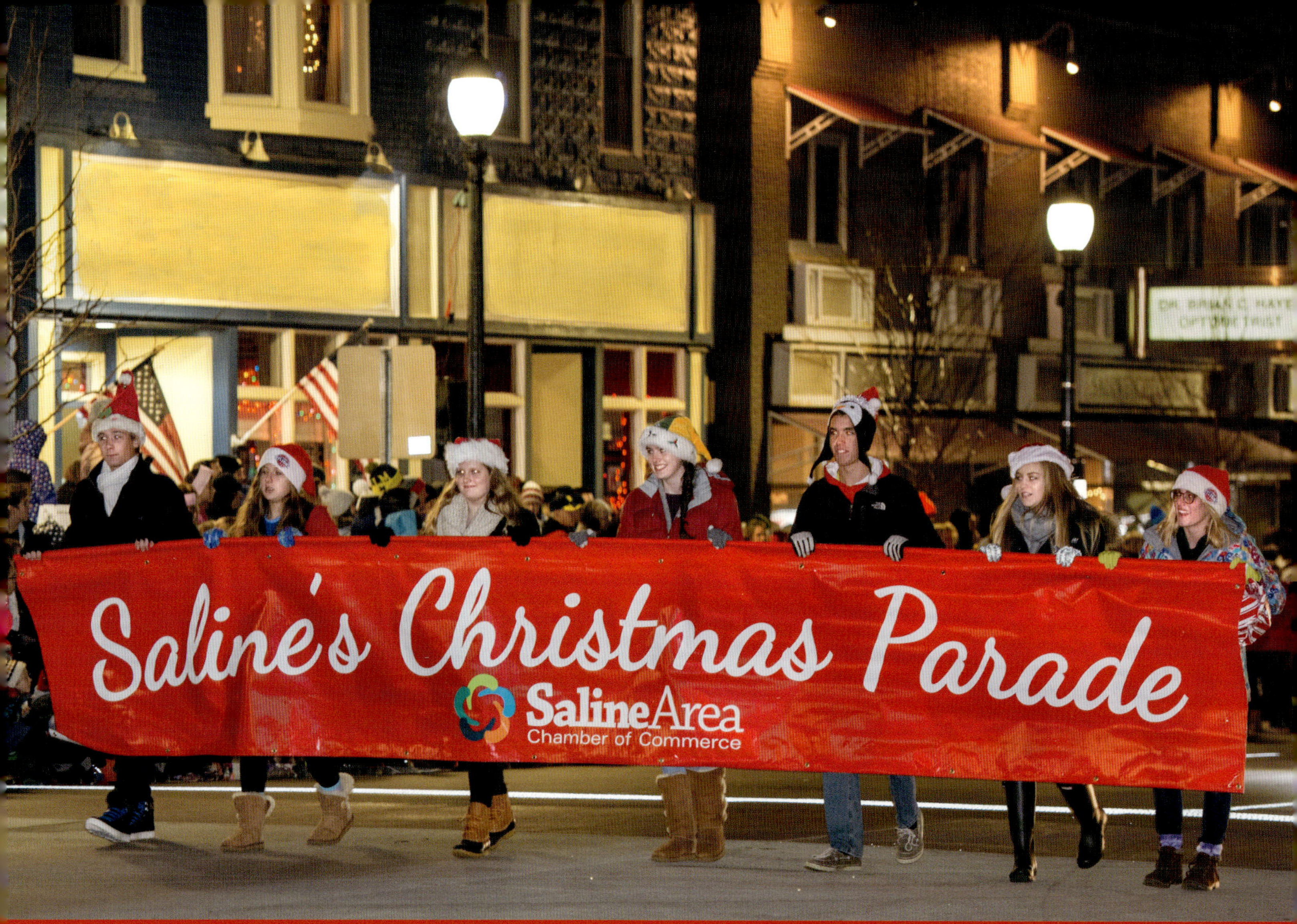

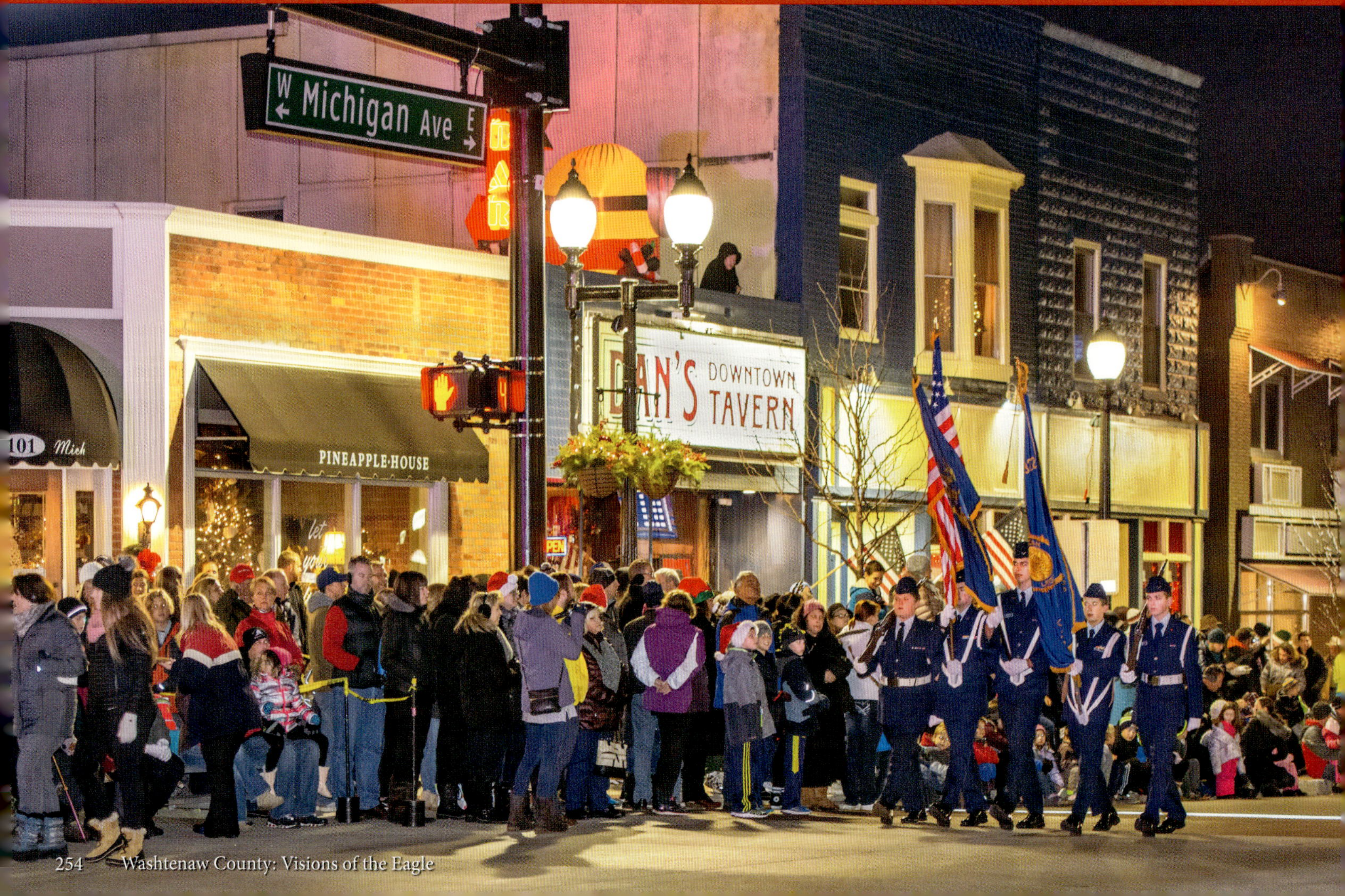

Kevin Adams Civil Air Patrol Memorial Squadron from Ann Arbor.

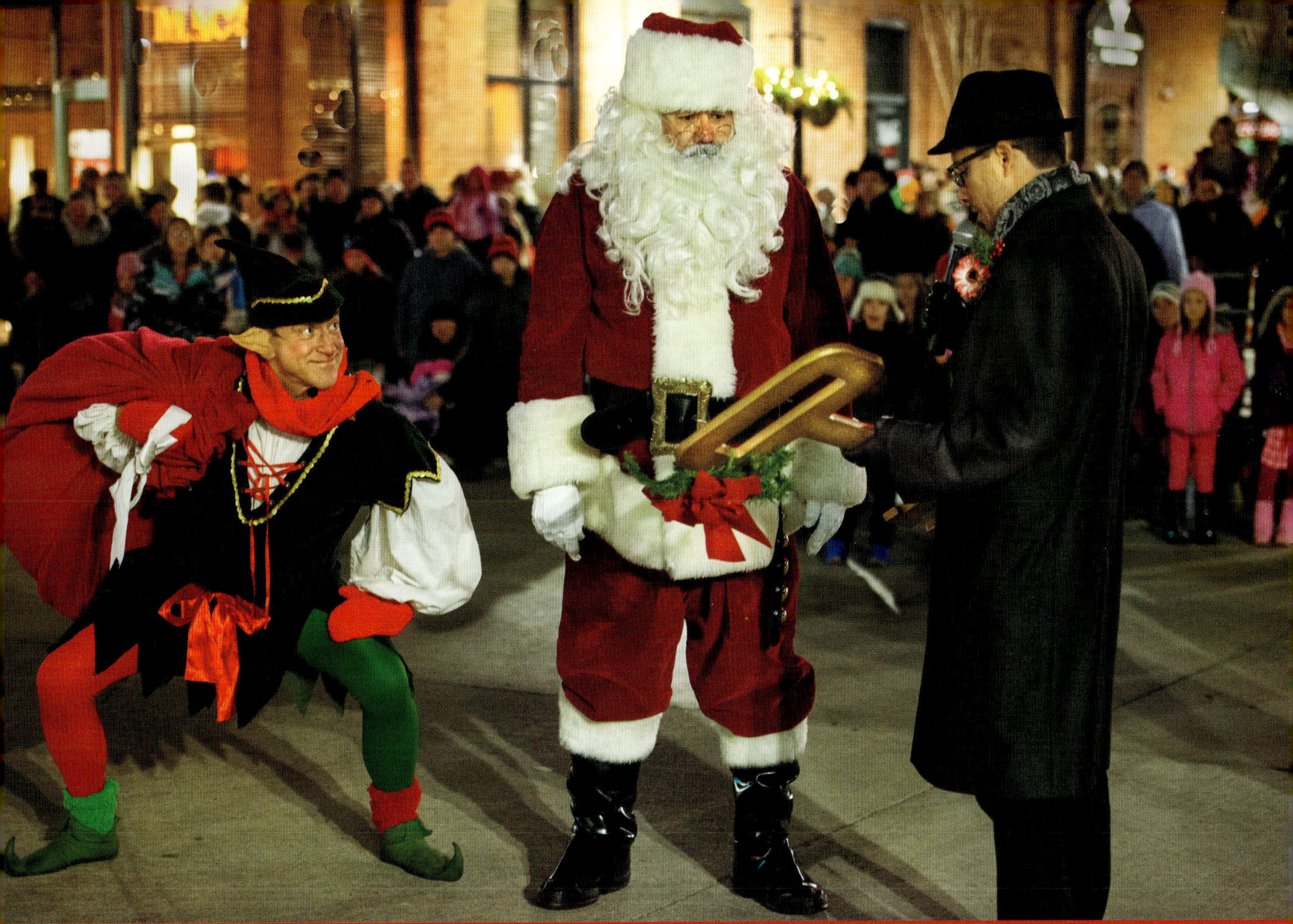

Mayor Marl presents Santa with a key to Saline.

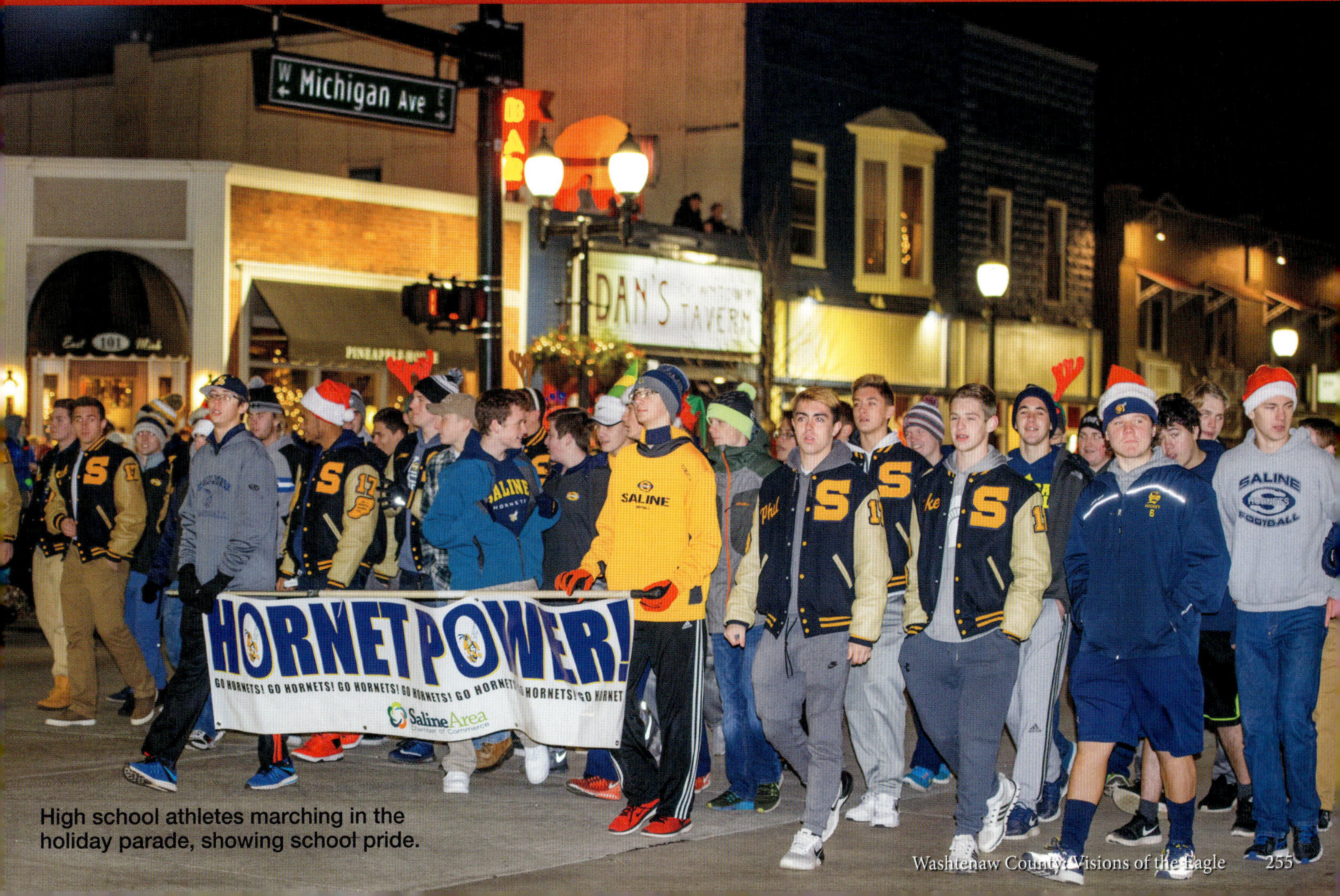

High school athletes marching in the holiday parade, showing school pride.

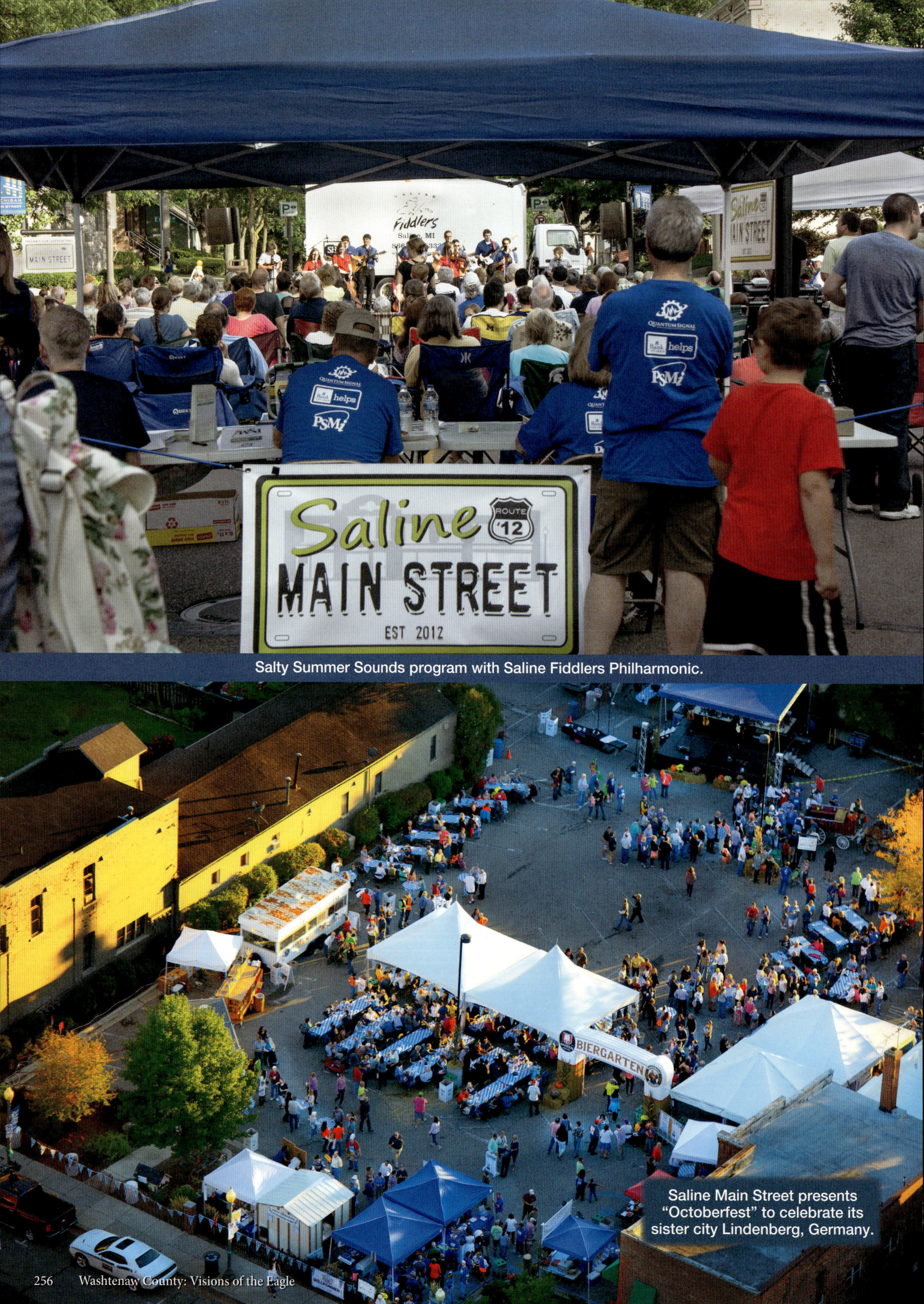

Salty Summer Sounds program with Saline Fiddlers Philharmonic.

Saline Main Street presents "Octoberfest" to celebrate its sister city Lindenberg, Germany.

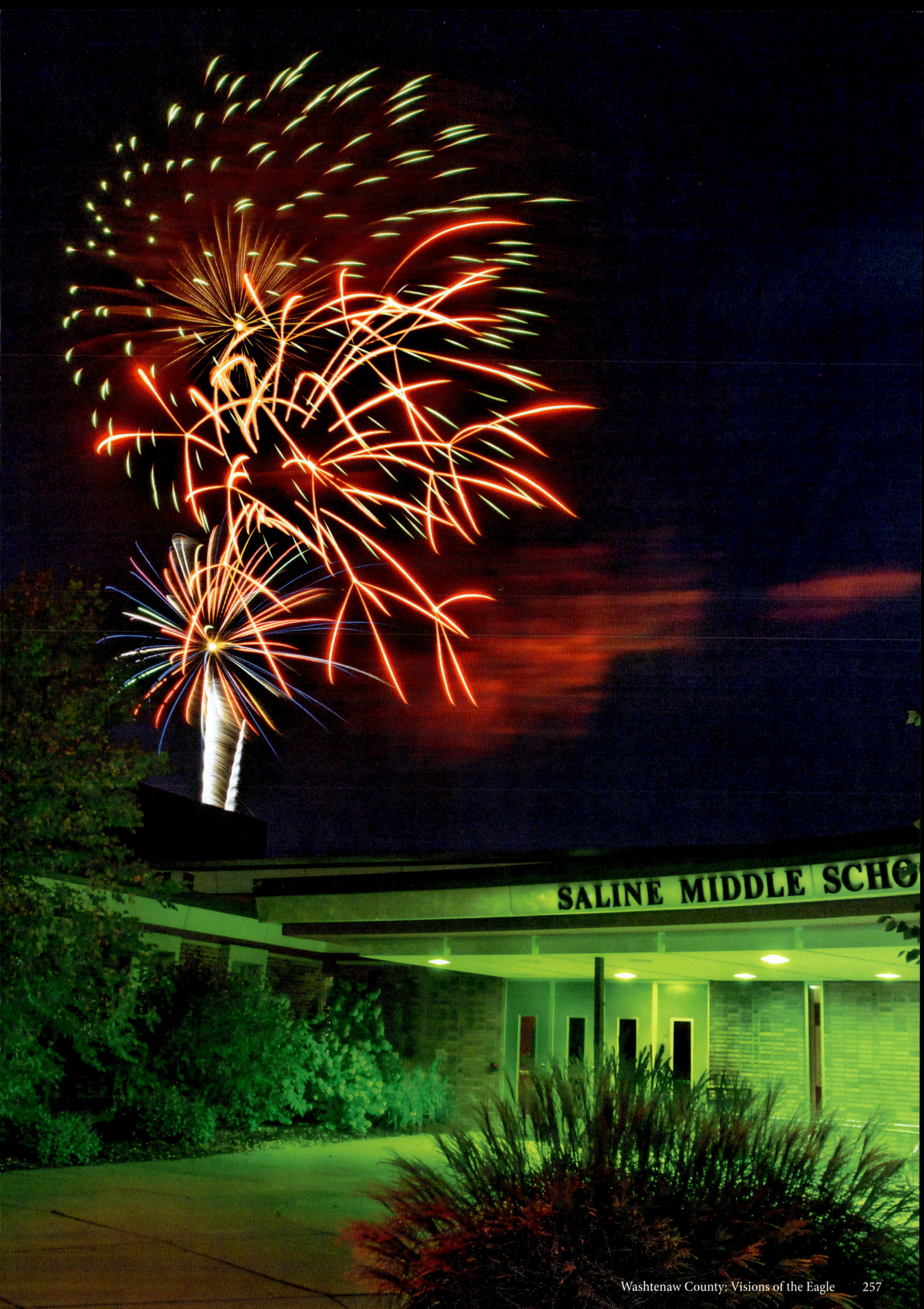
SALINE MIDDLE SCHO

YPSILANTI

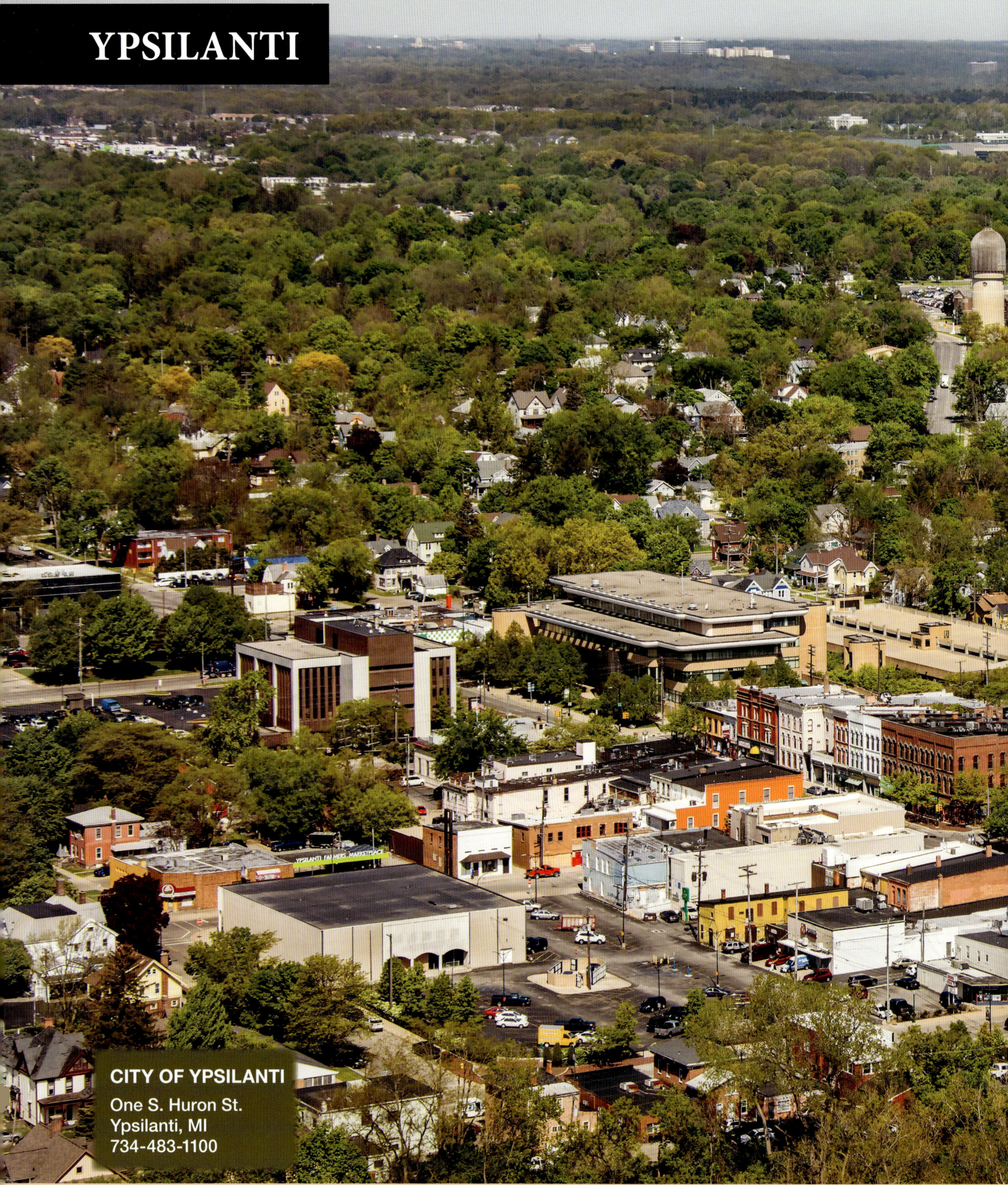

CITY OF YPSILANTI
One S. Huron St.
Ypsilanti, MI
734-483-1100

The City of Ypsilanti, a quirky, creative midwestern college town, is home to Eastern Michigan University. The city's iconic water tower says you have arrived. EMU opened in 1853 as Michigan State Normal School. In 1899, it became the Michigan State Normal College, the first teacher-training school to offer a four-year degree program.

Downtown Ypsilanti has an impressive selection of restaurants and bars and shops ranging from vintage to contemporary. East of downtown, Depot Town is a destination and a neighborhood with a hip vibe, a popular place to get a bite and peruse boutiques for local art.

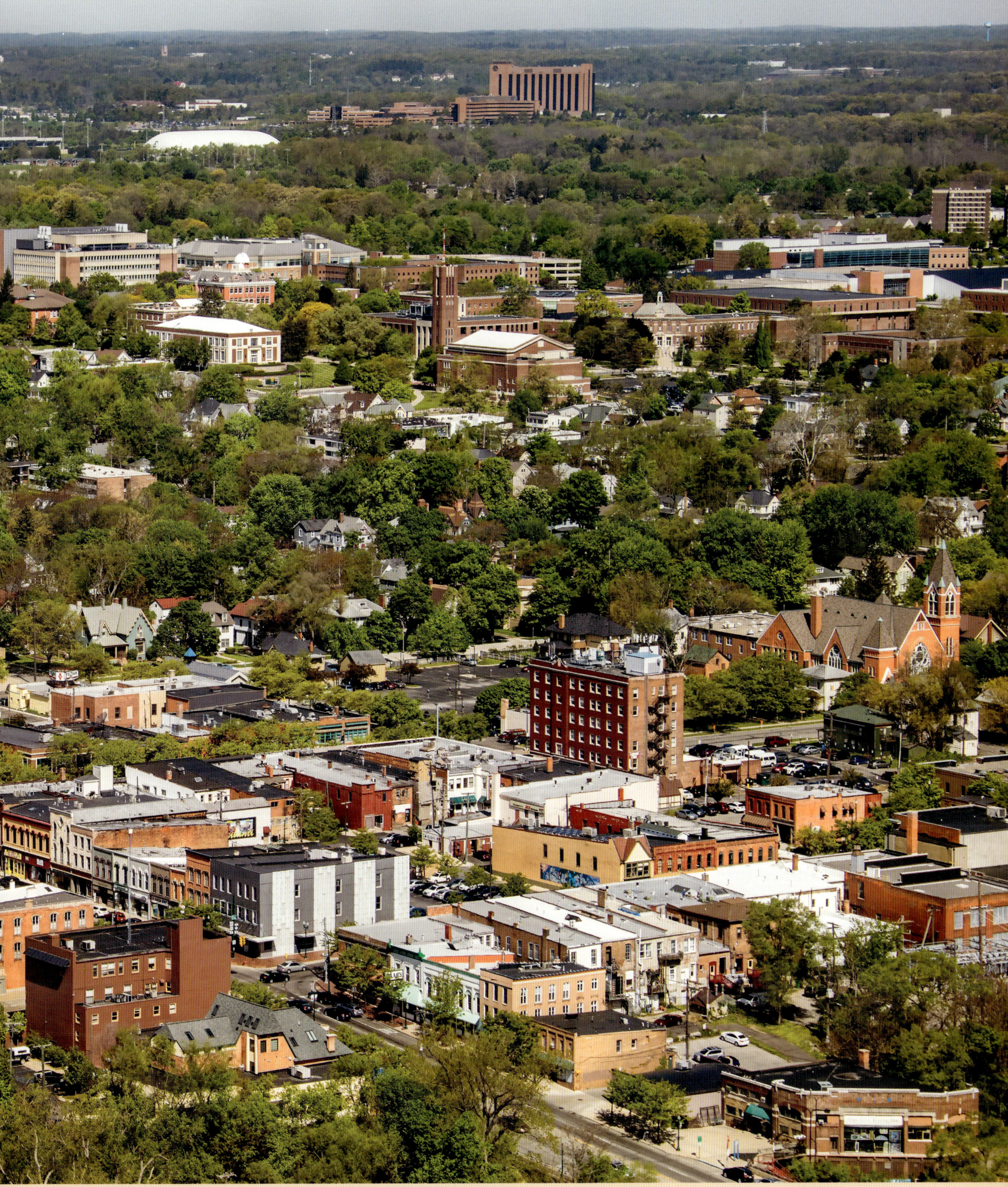

Ypsilanti has a rich history. The area was home to Native American tribes, including the People of the Three Fires, Odawa, Potawatomi, Anishinaabe, and others before the first white settlement (Woodruffs Grove) in 1823. Michigan Avenue, which runs through the city, was the Sauk Trail, one of several trails that crossed the Nottawaseppi, or Huron River.

Ypsilanti was at one time home to the state's largest black community. Frederick Douglass visited the city, and residents assisted runaway slaves via the Underground Railroad. Its residents fought for equality and continue to do so, embracing the progressive values Ypsi is known for. It's a community committed to pride, diversity, and heritage and hosts endless events in support of those values.

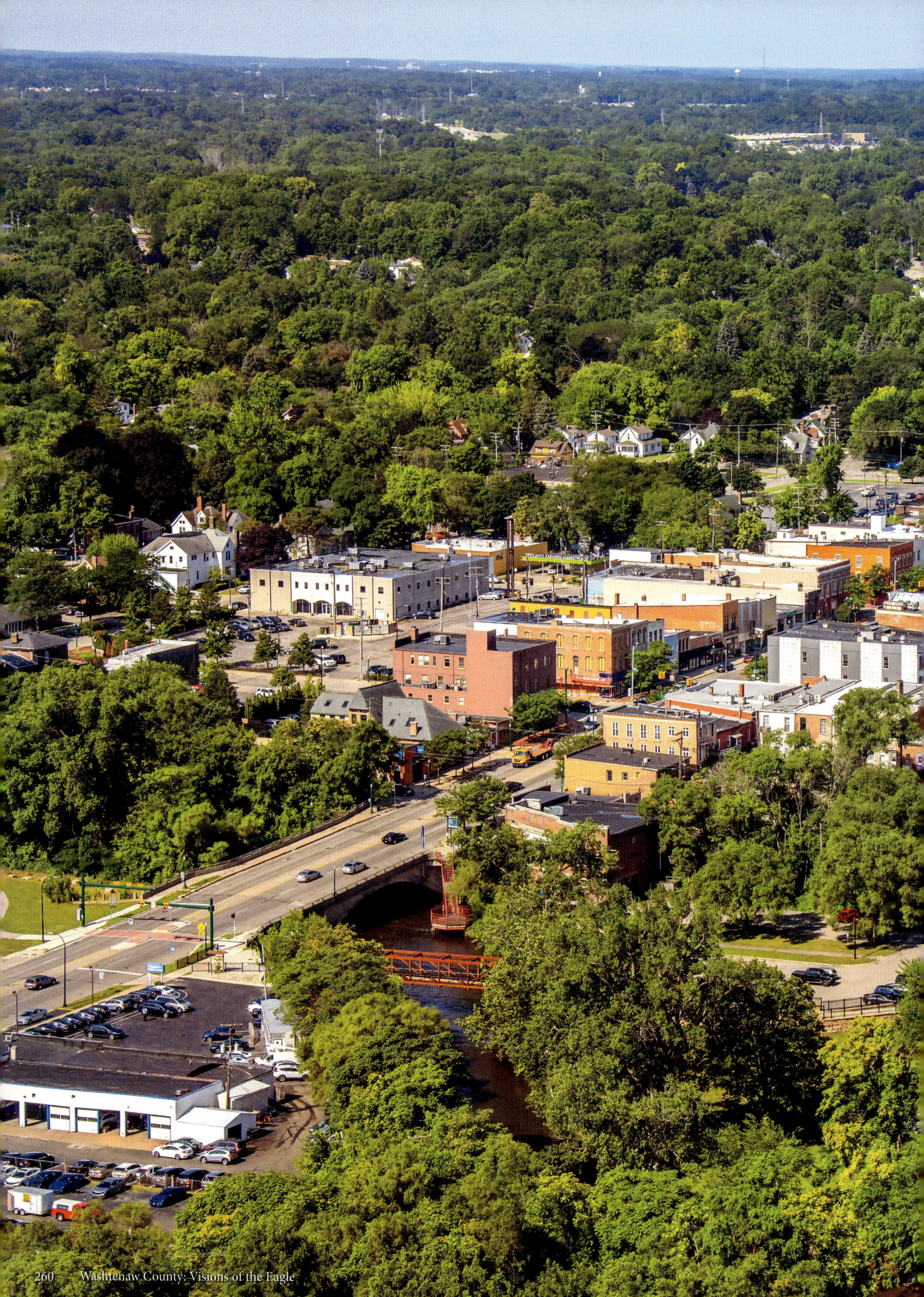

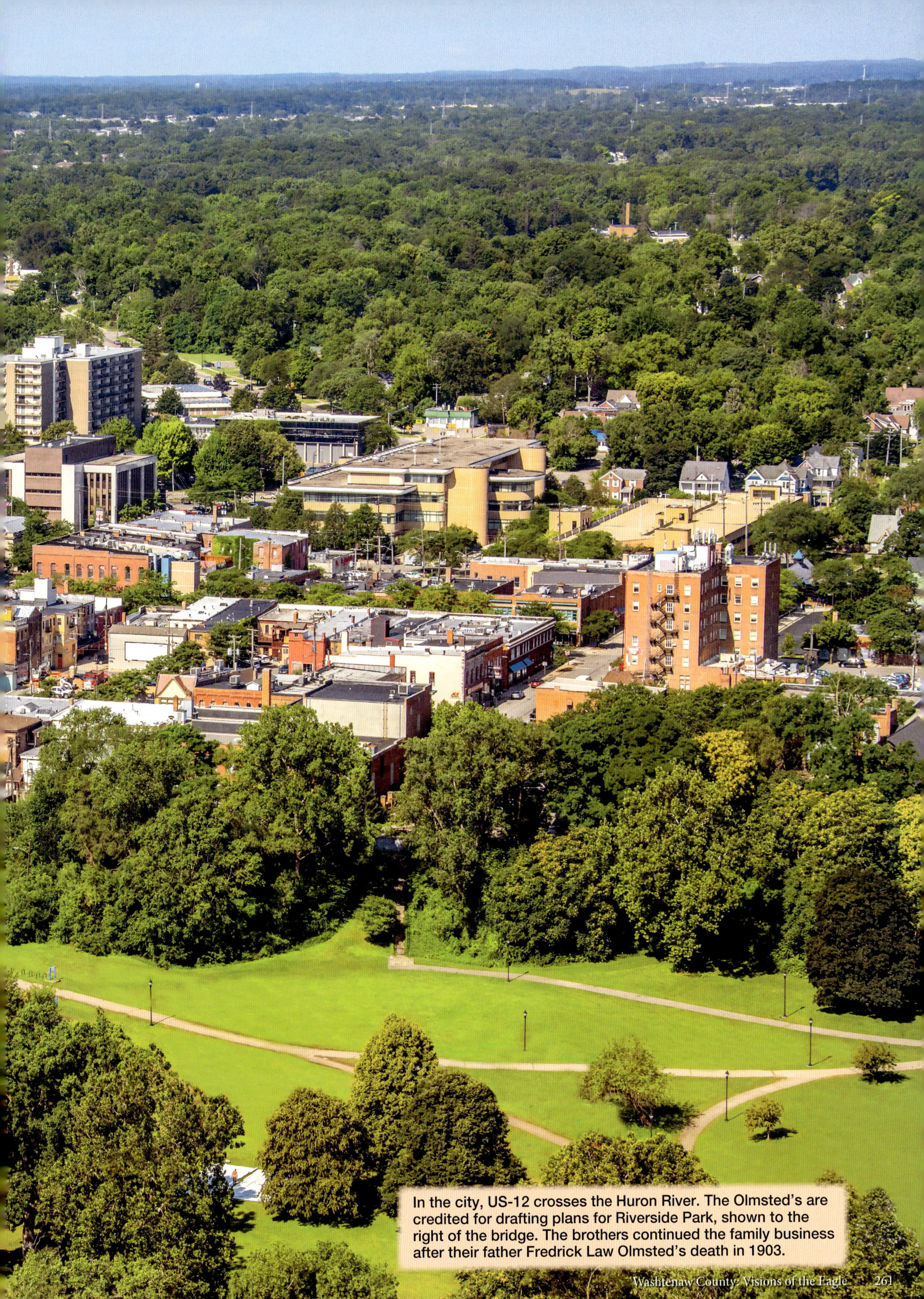

In the city, US-12 crosses the Huron River. The Olmsted's are credited for drafting plans for Riverside Park, shown to the right of the bridge. The brothers continued the family business after their father Fredrick Law Olmsted's death in 1903.

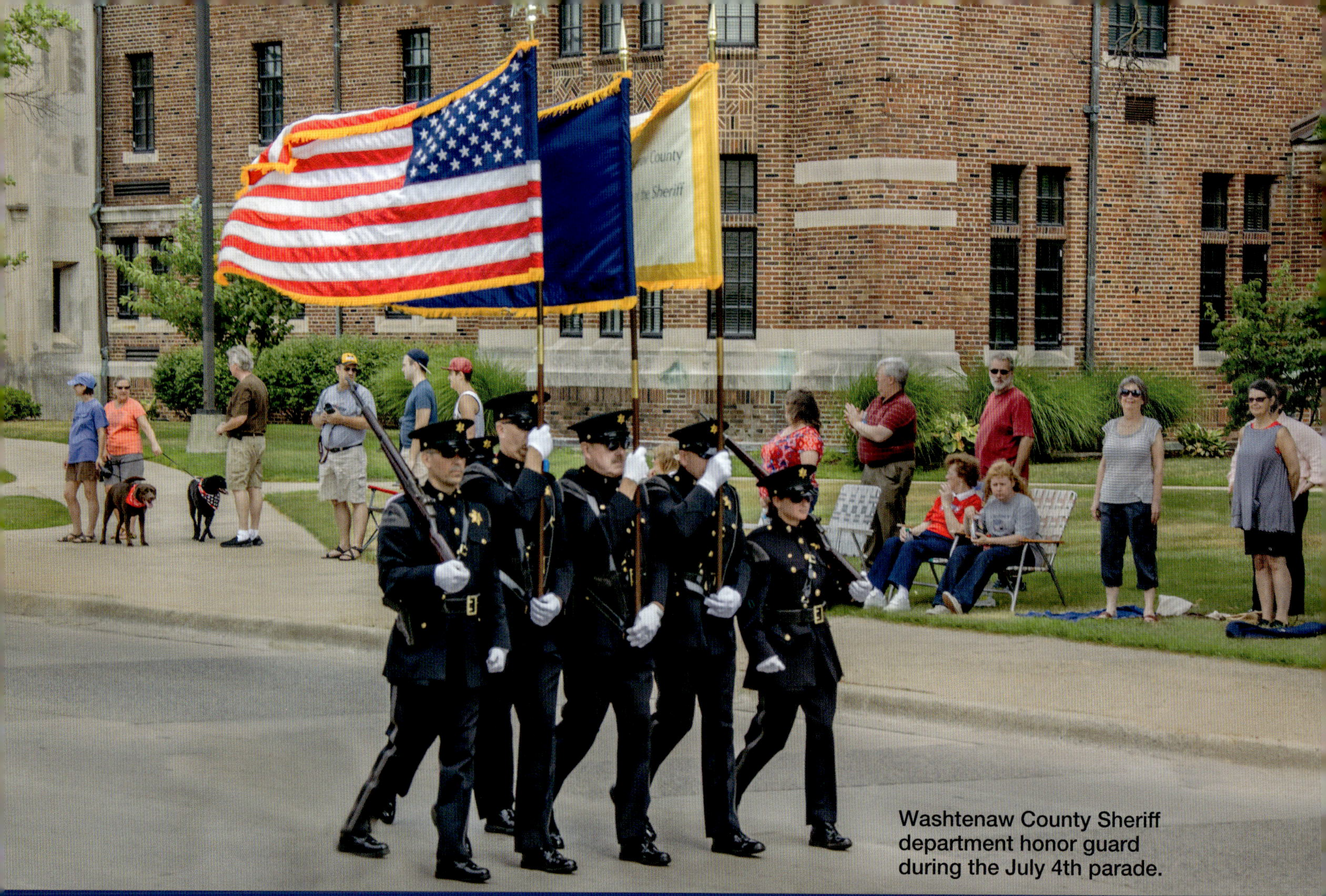

Washtenaw County Sheriff department honor guard during the July 4th parade.

Ypsilanti July 4th Parade

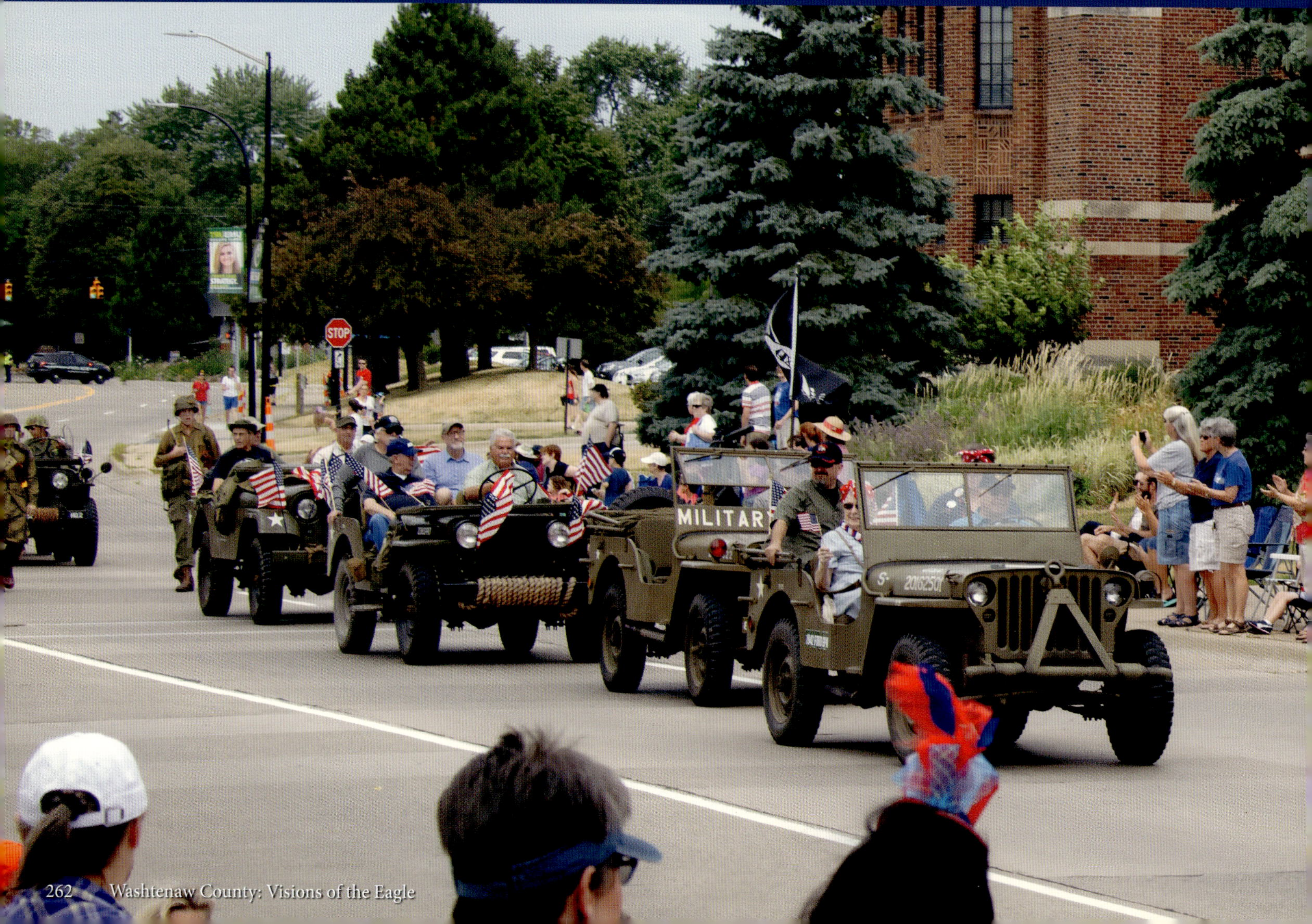

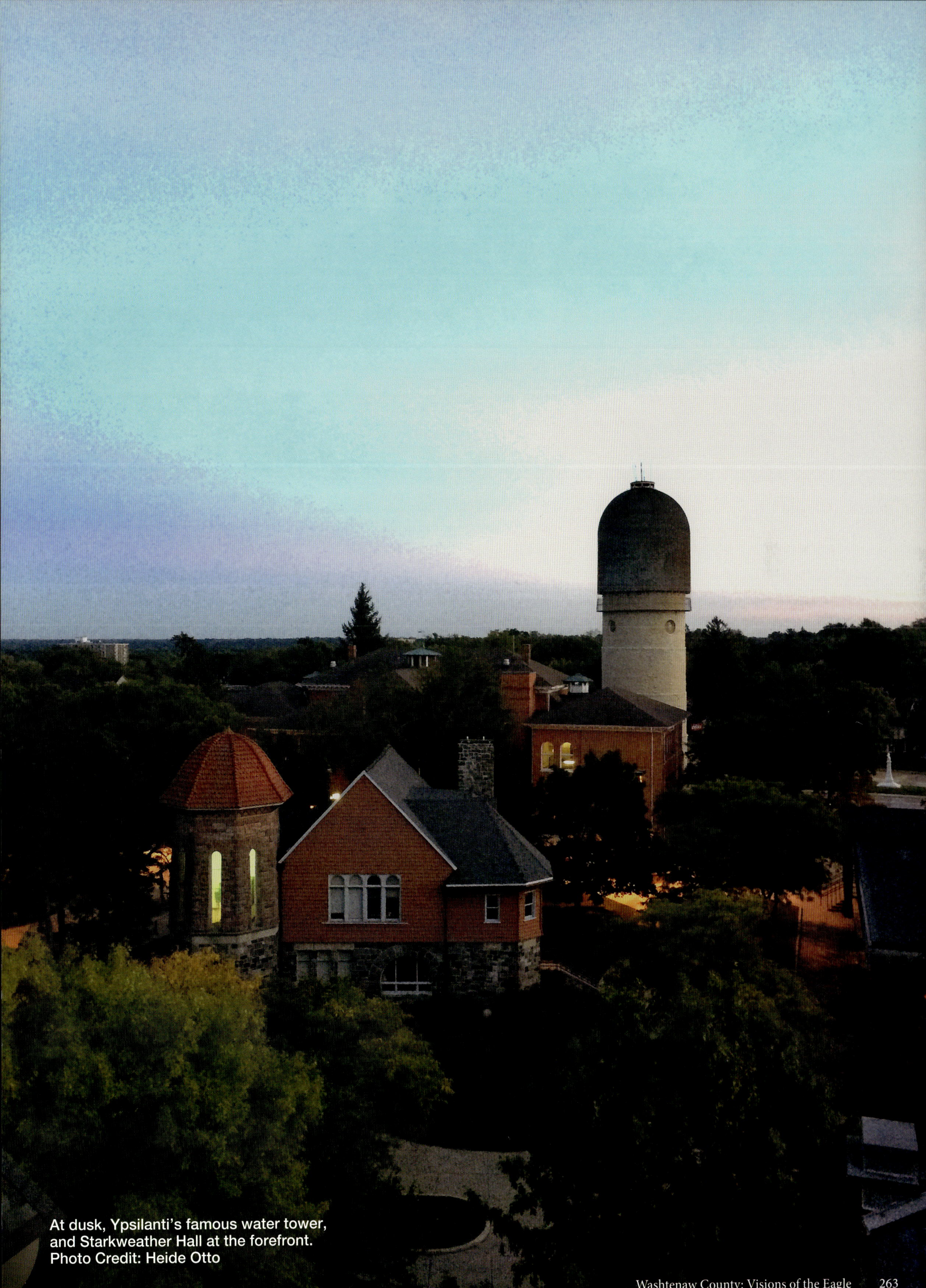

At dusk, Ypsilanti's famous water tower, and Starkweather Hall at the forefront.
Photo Credit: Heide Otto

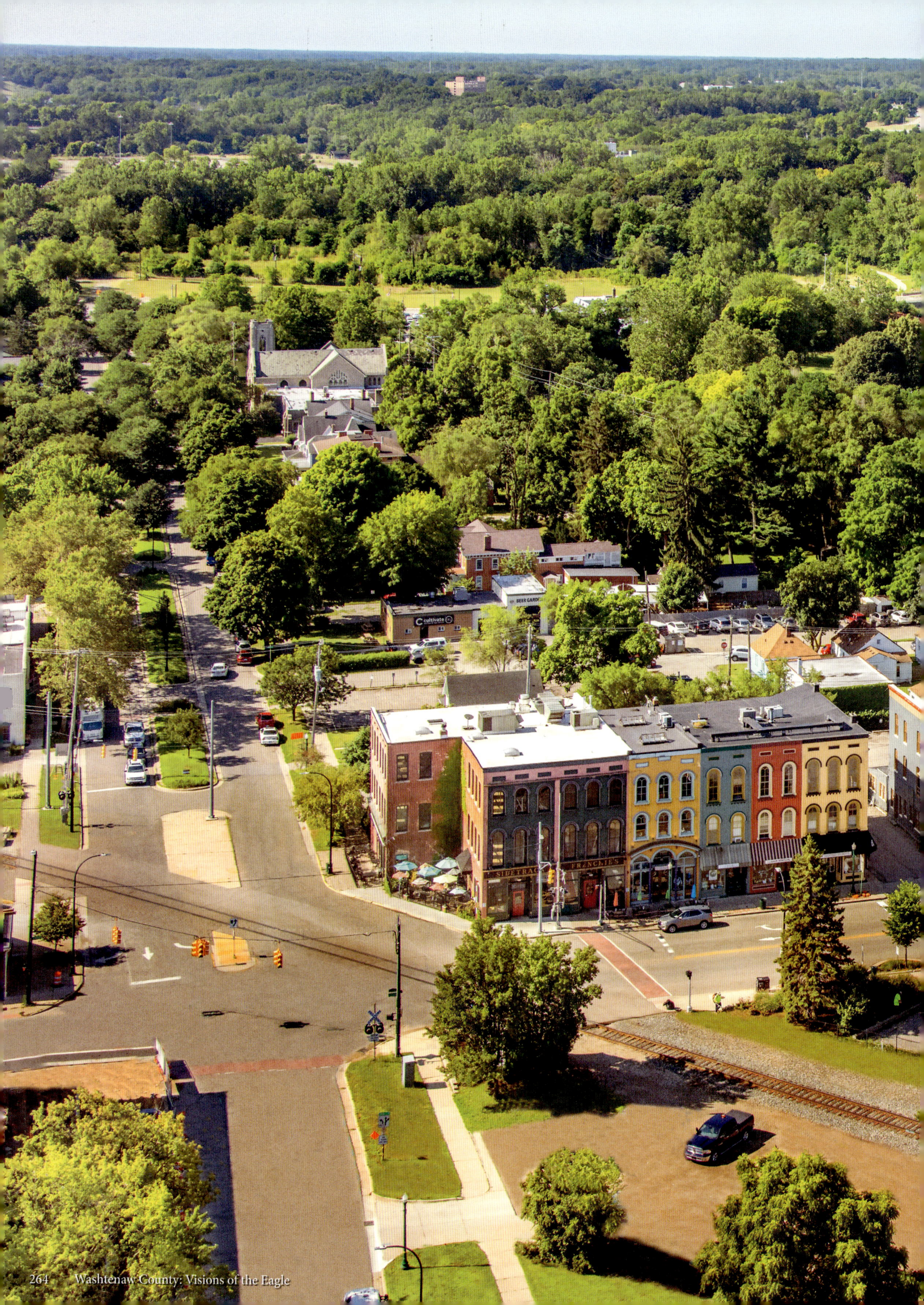
cultivate

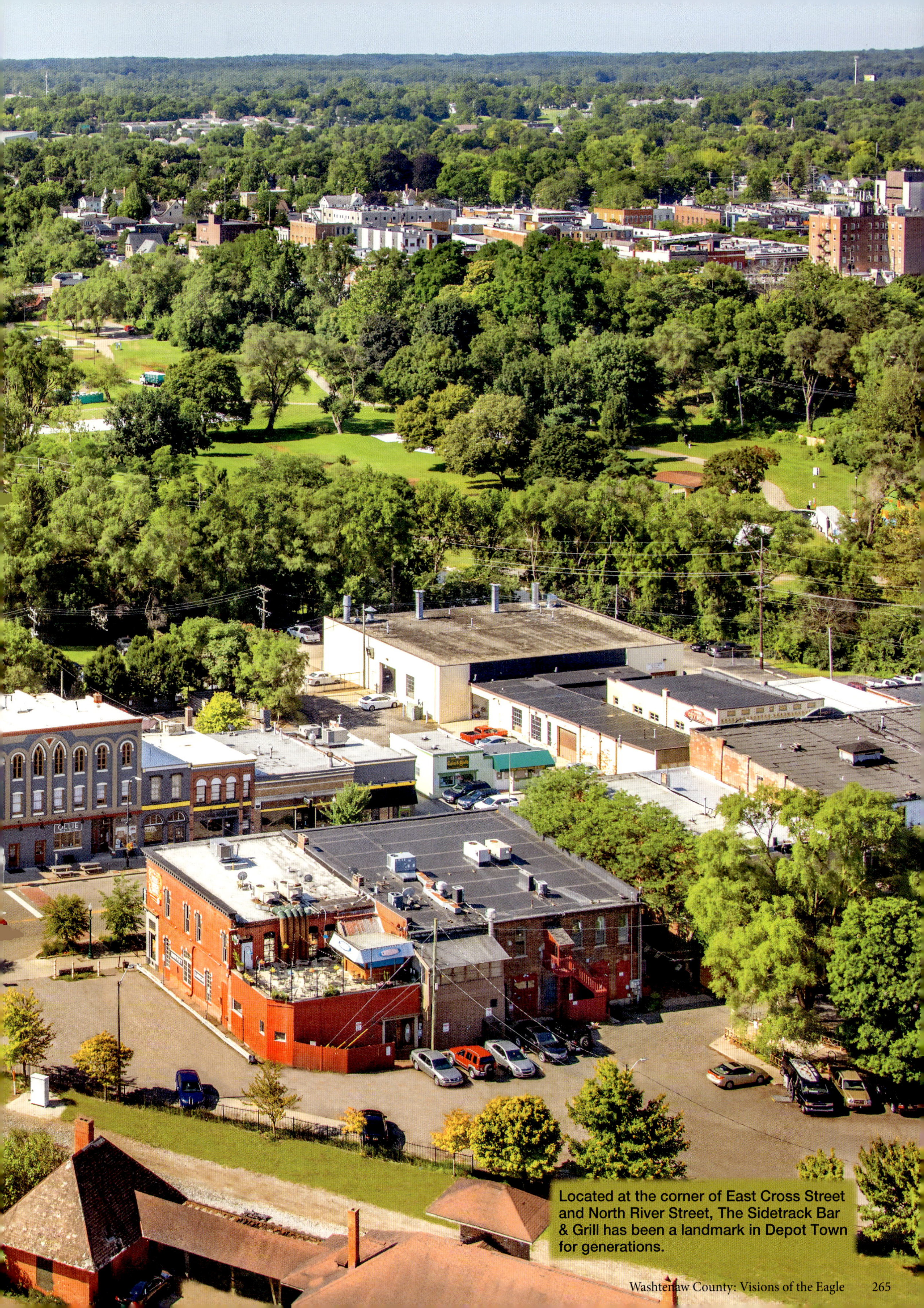

Located at the corner of East Cross Street and North River Street, The Sidetrack Bar & Grill has been a landmark in Depot Town for generations.

The Sidetrack Bar & Grill

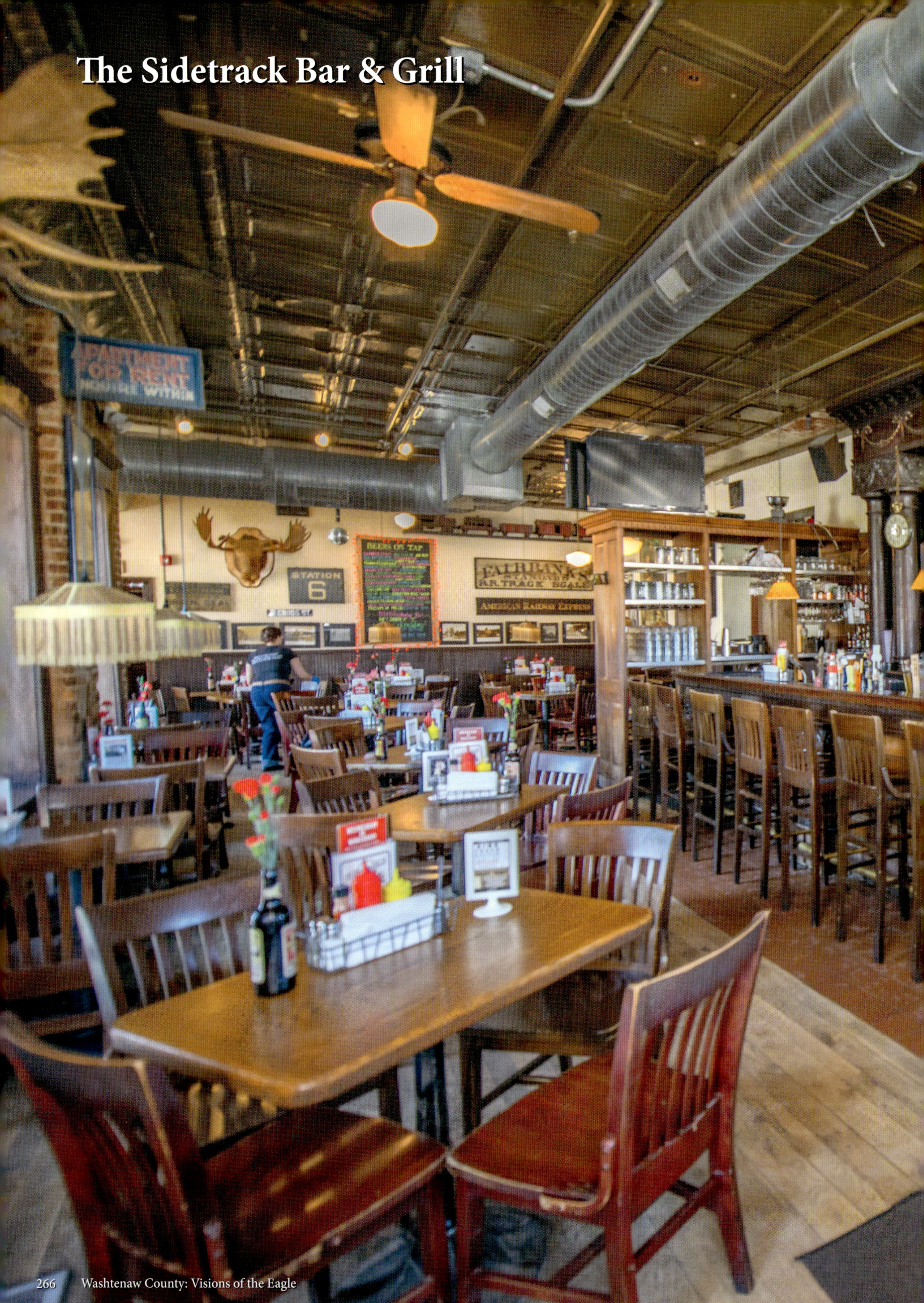

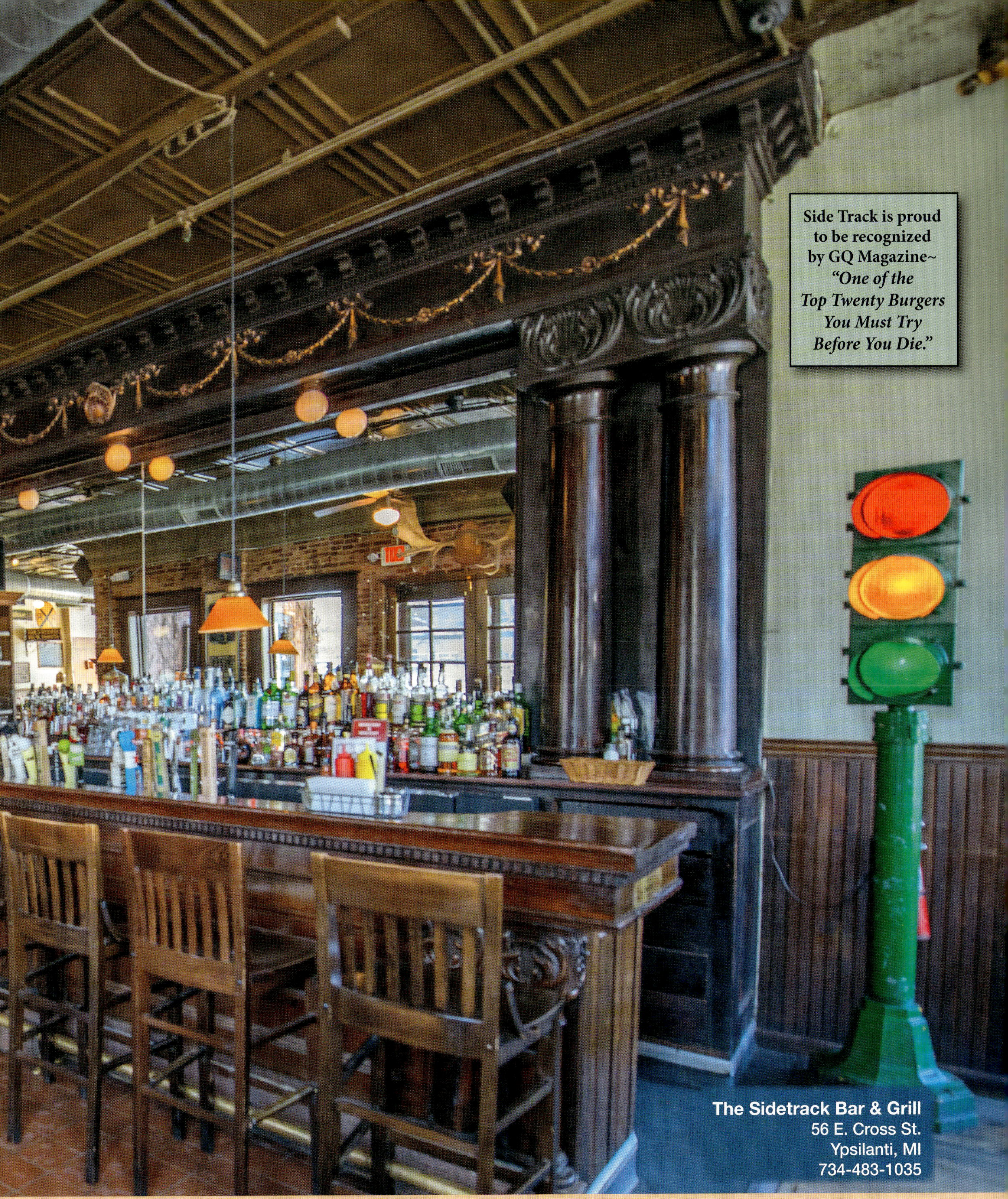

The Sidetrack Bar & Grill
56 E. Cross St.
Ypsilanti, MI
734-483-1035

The 19th-century Sidetrack building has, under different names and owners, served as a bar since the 1850s. Only during Prohibition did that change, and it became a soft drink and sandwich shop.

In the early 1900s, the adjoining buildings that have since combined to make up The Sidetrack included what was an off-track betting parlour called the Lewis Horse Exchange, and upstairs - Ma Bush and Her Girls of Ill Repute. In 1929, the building took on a dramatic new look when a passing freight train derailed and crashed into the corner of the building. Today, that corner is one of three outdoor patios.

Shown is the 19th-century mahogany back bar, original to the building, and a view of The Sidetrack's main dining area.

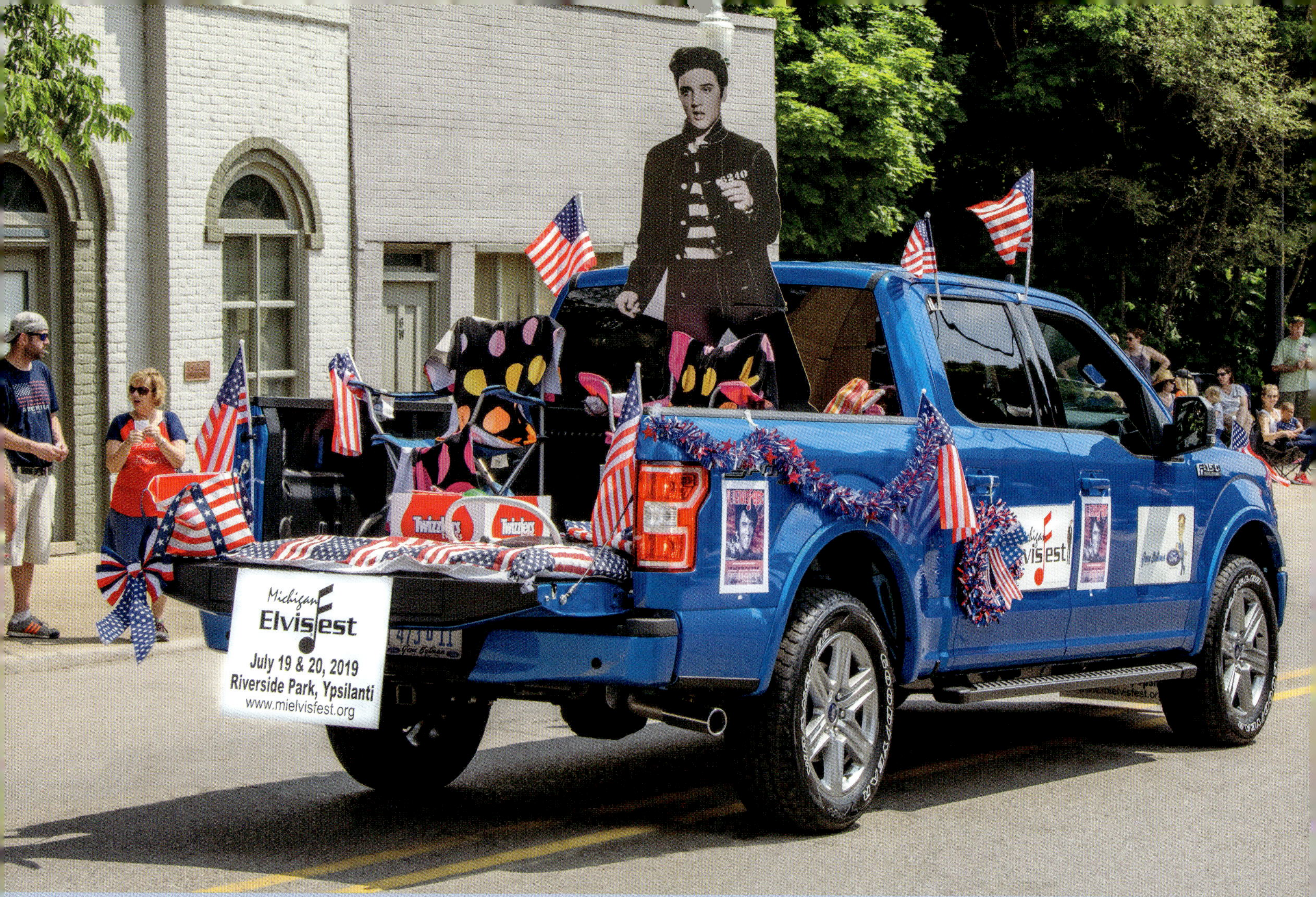

Car enthusiasts during the Michigan Elvisfest, a car show hosted by America's Most Wanted Car Club.

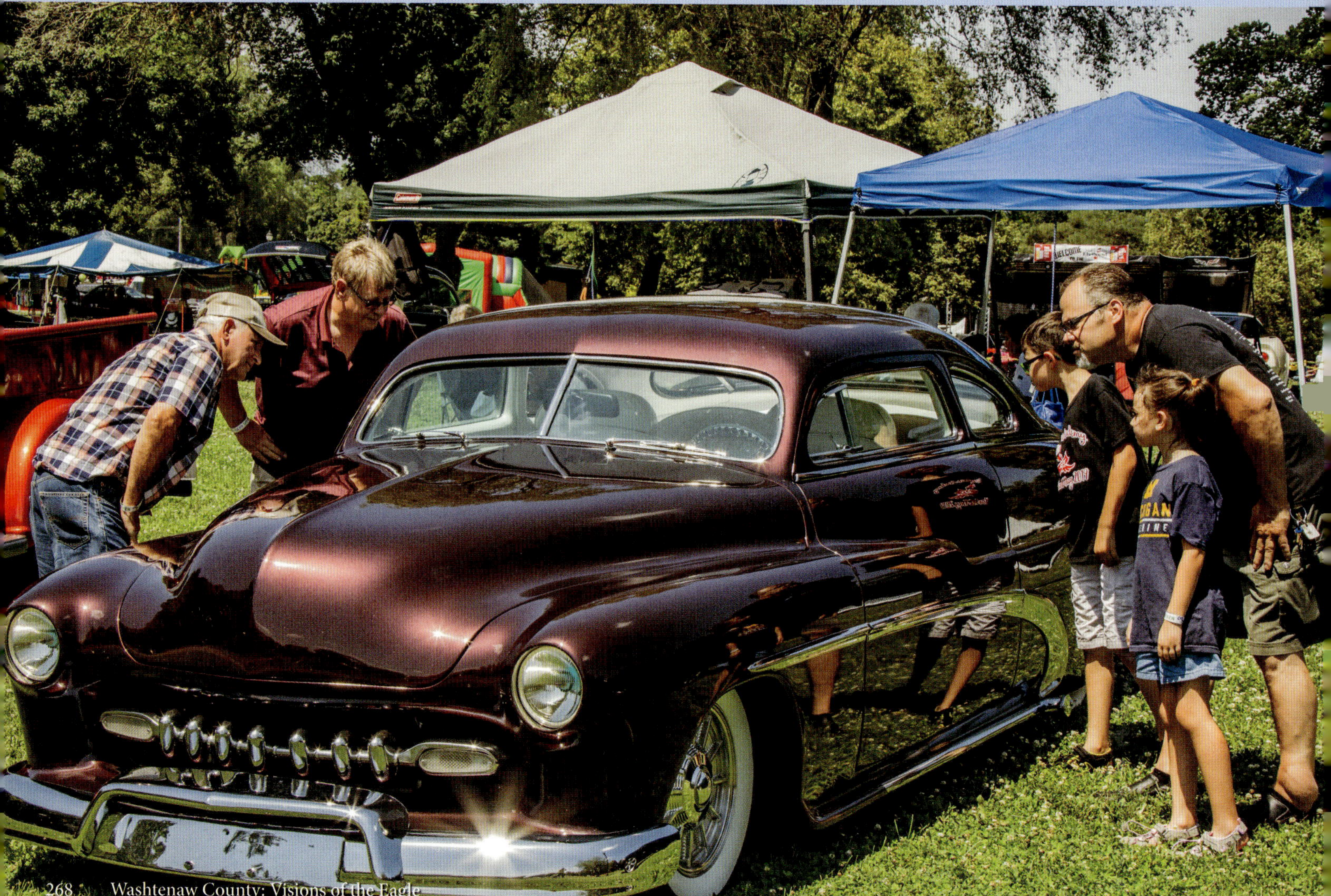

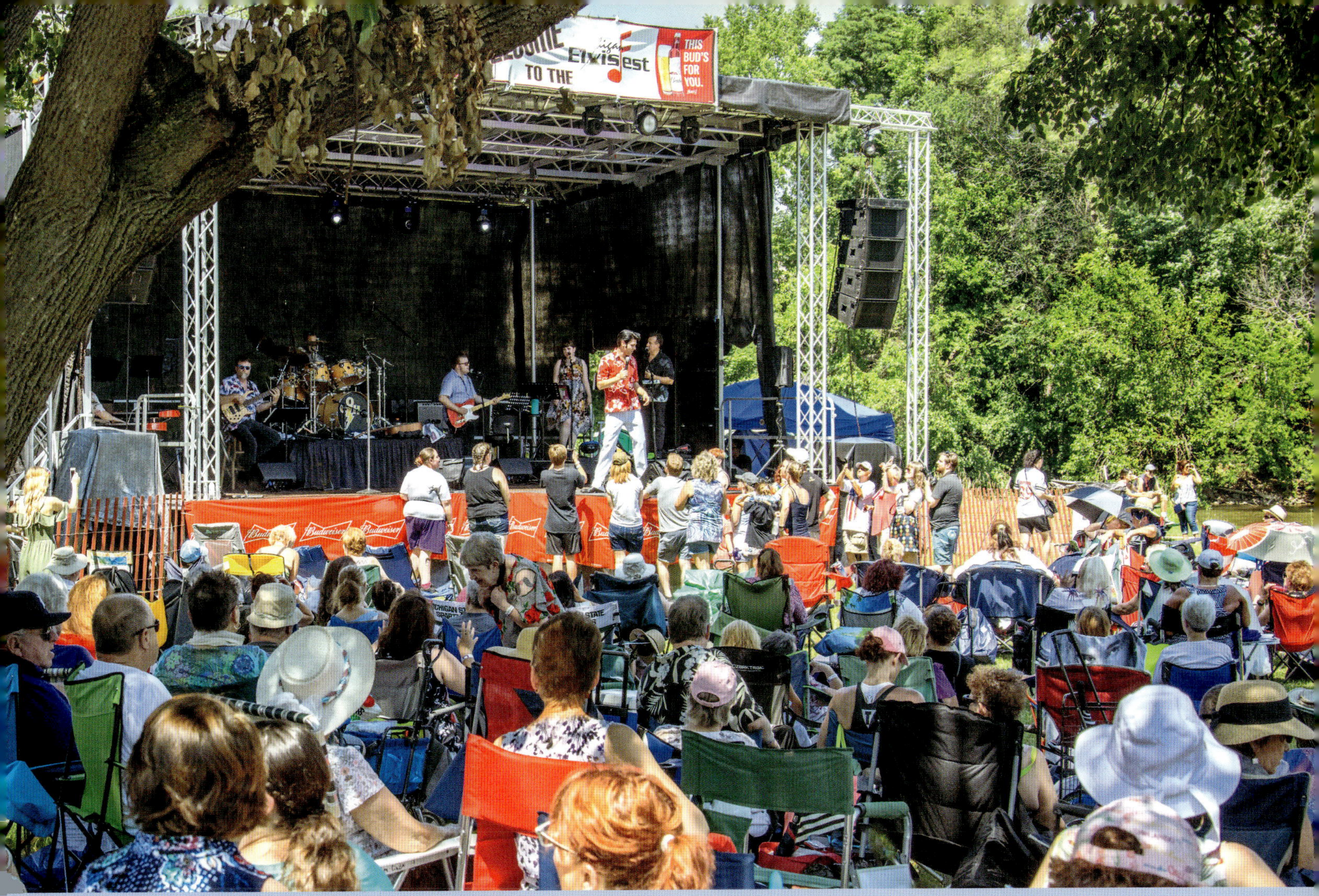

The Michigan Elvisfest patrons enjoying the shade at Riverside Park.

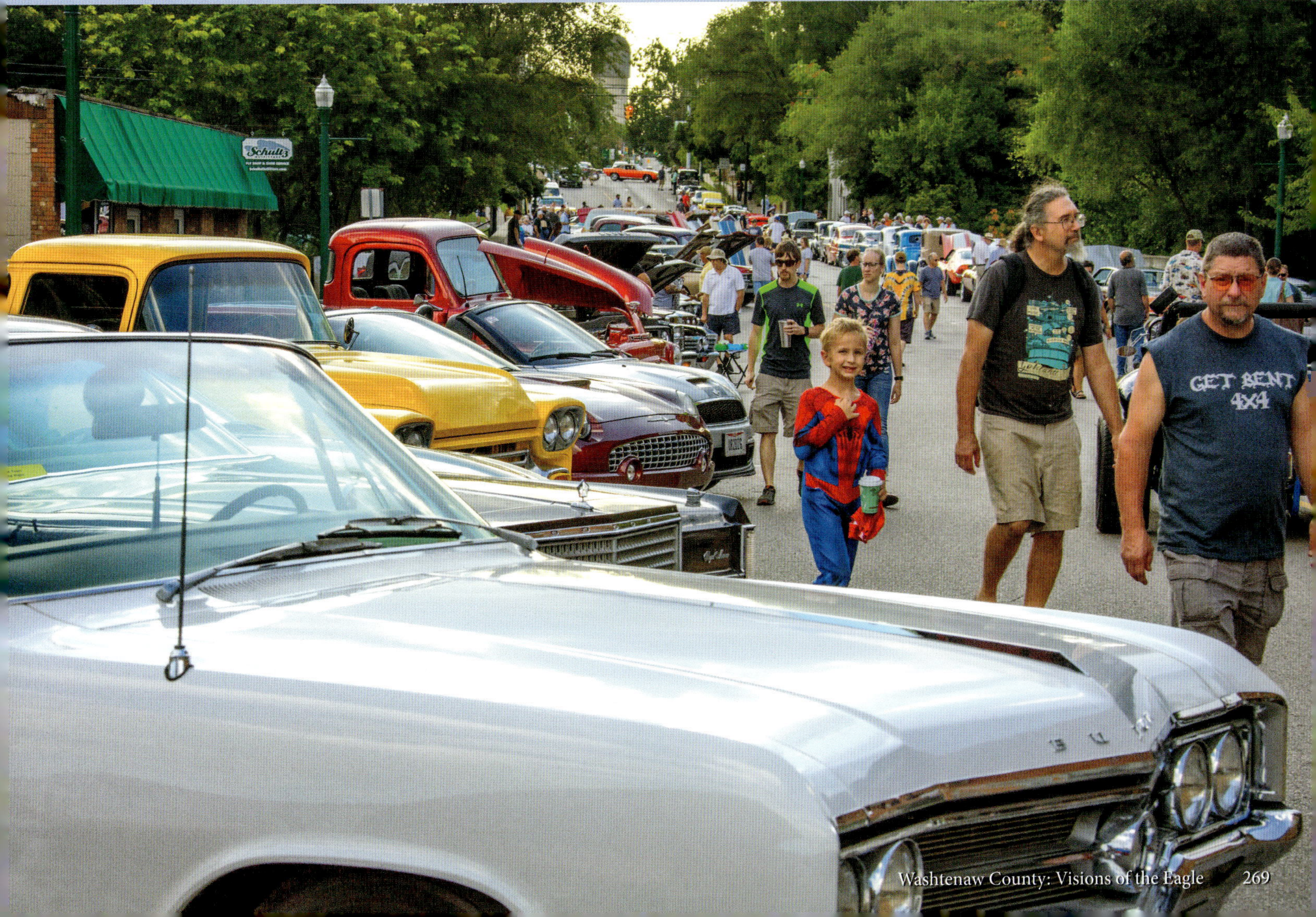

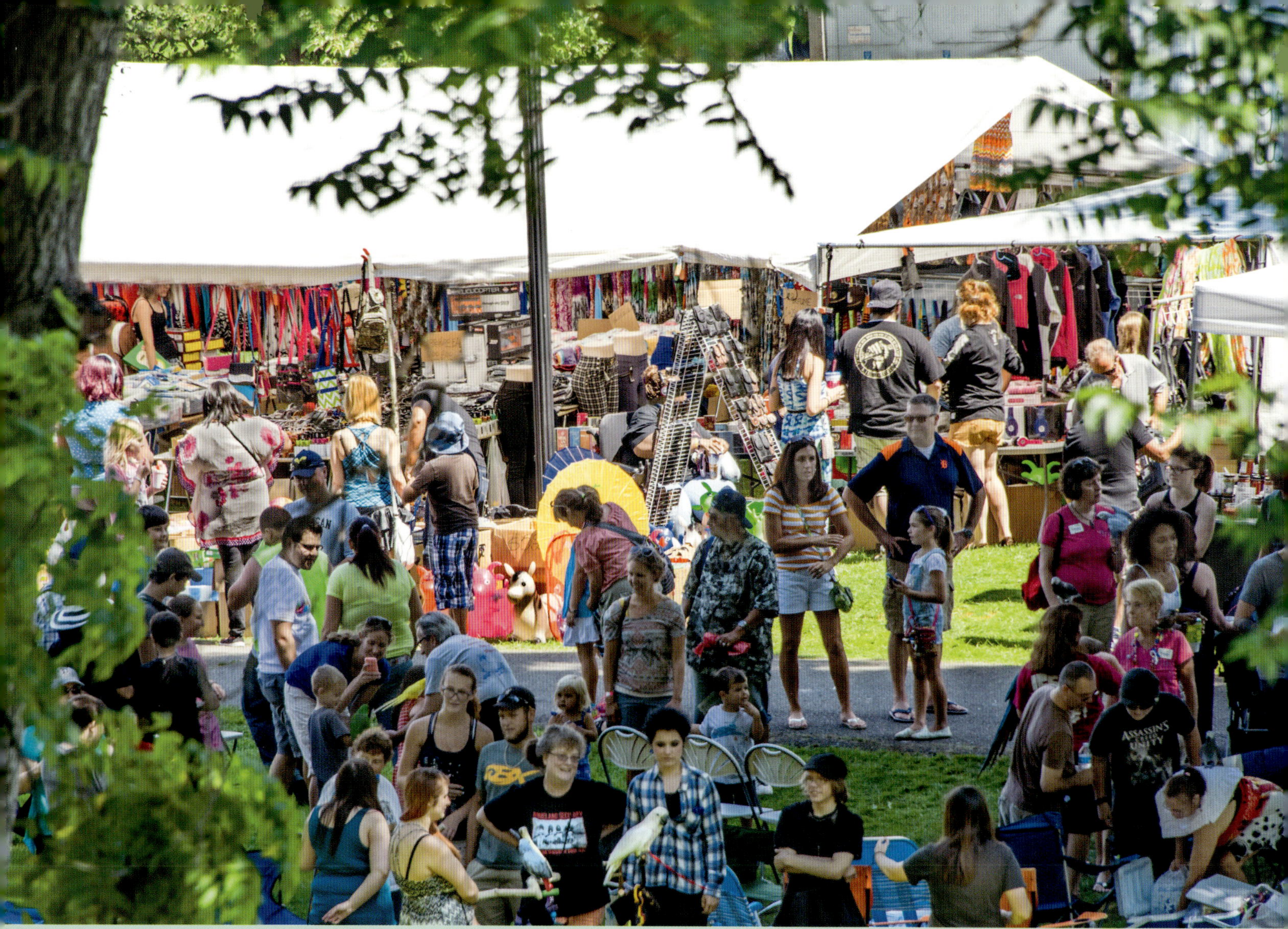

Heritage Festival sprawls across Frog Island Park, Riverside Park, Depot Town, and downtown Ypsilanti.

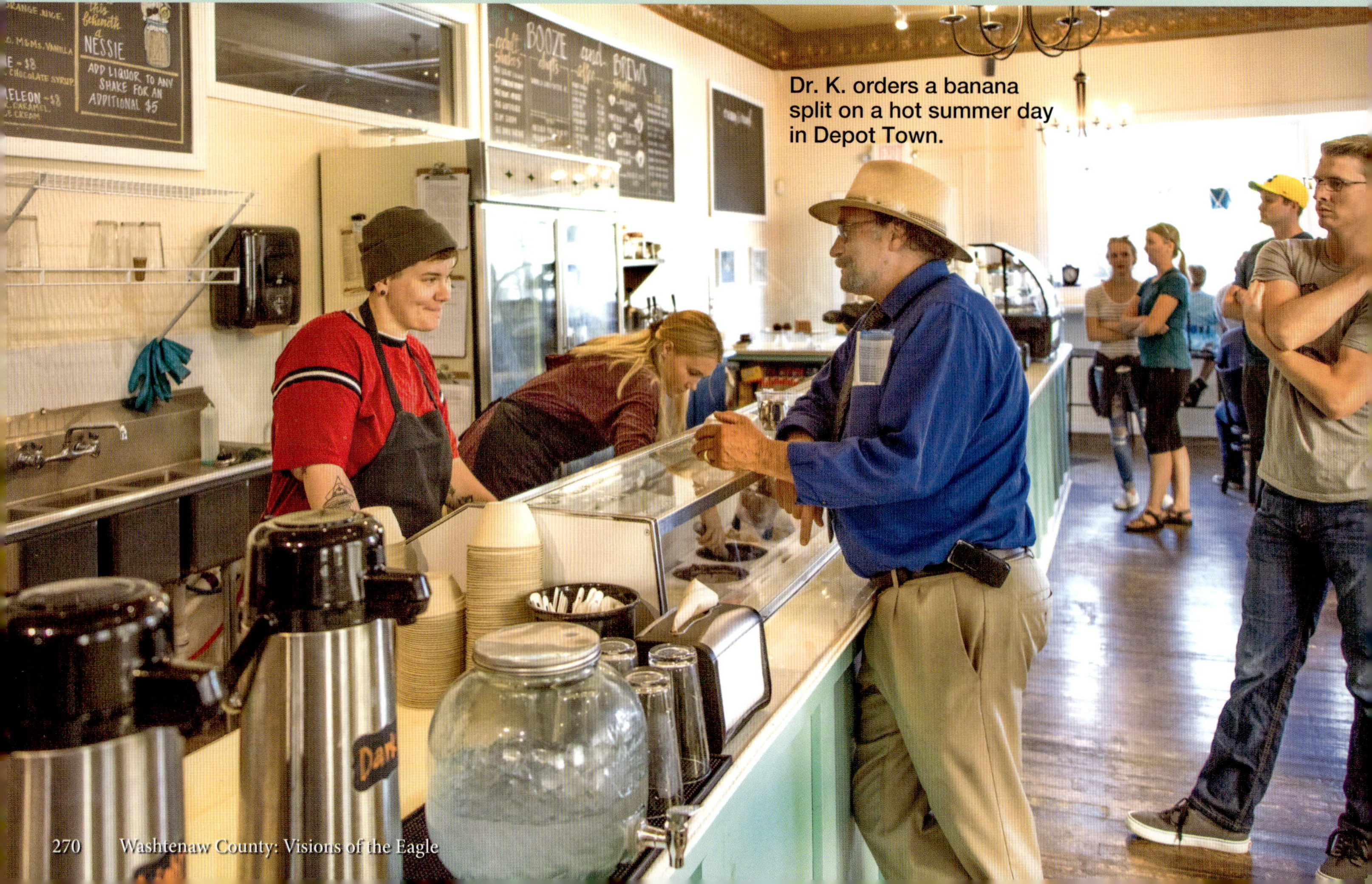

Dr. K. orders a banana split on a hot summer day in Depot Town.

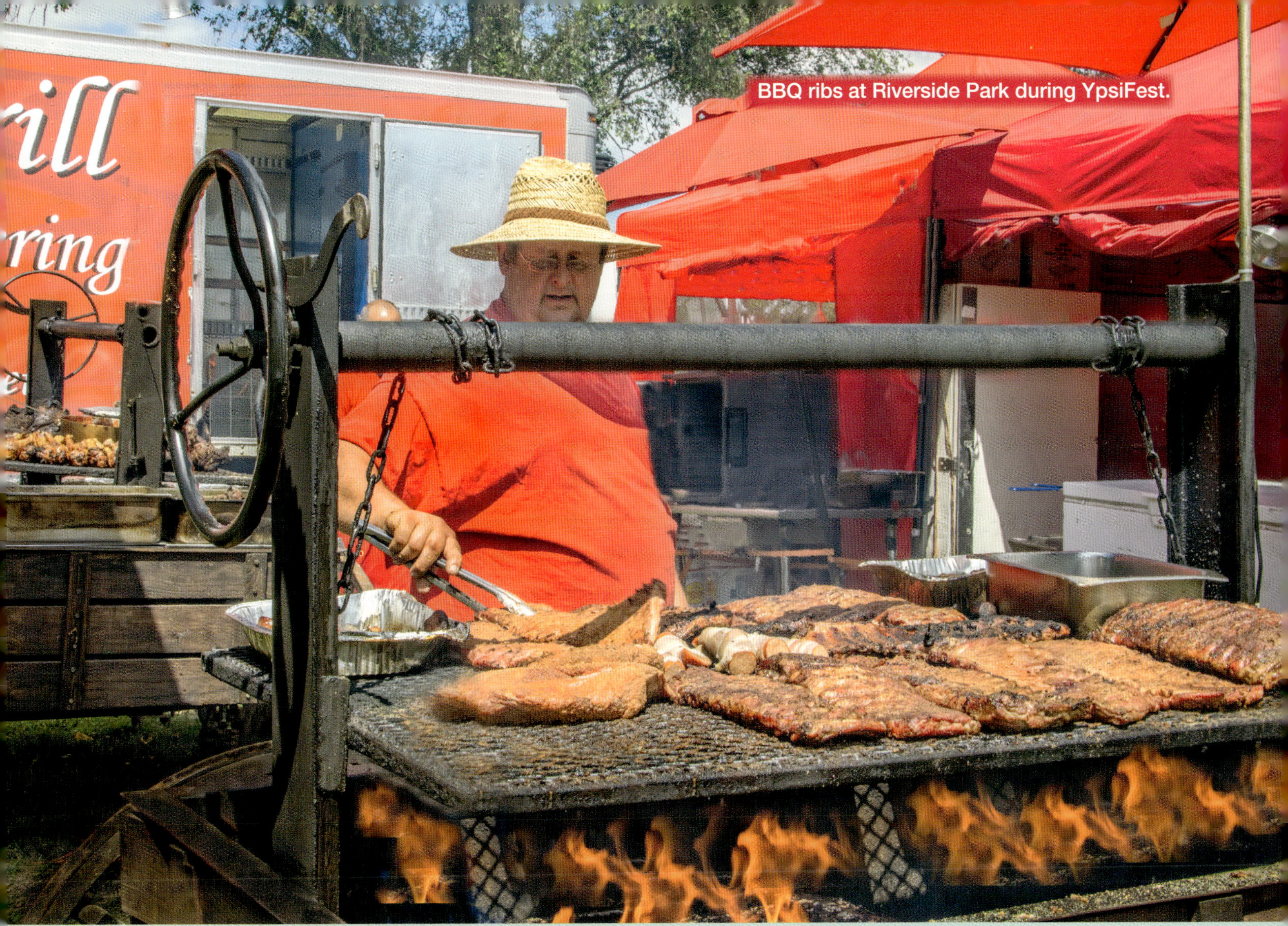

BBQ ribs at Riverside Park during YpsiFest.

Depot Town is host to Thursday night car cruises during the summer.
Children get into the swing with a hula hoop contest.

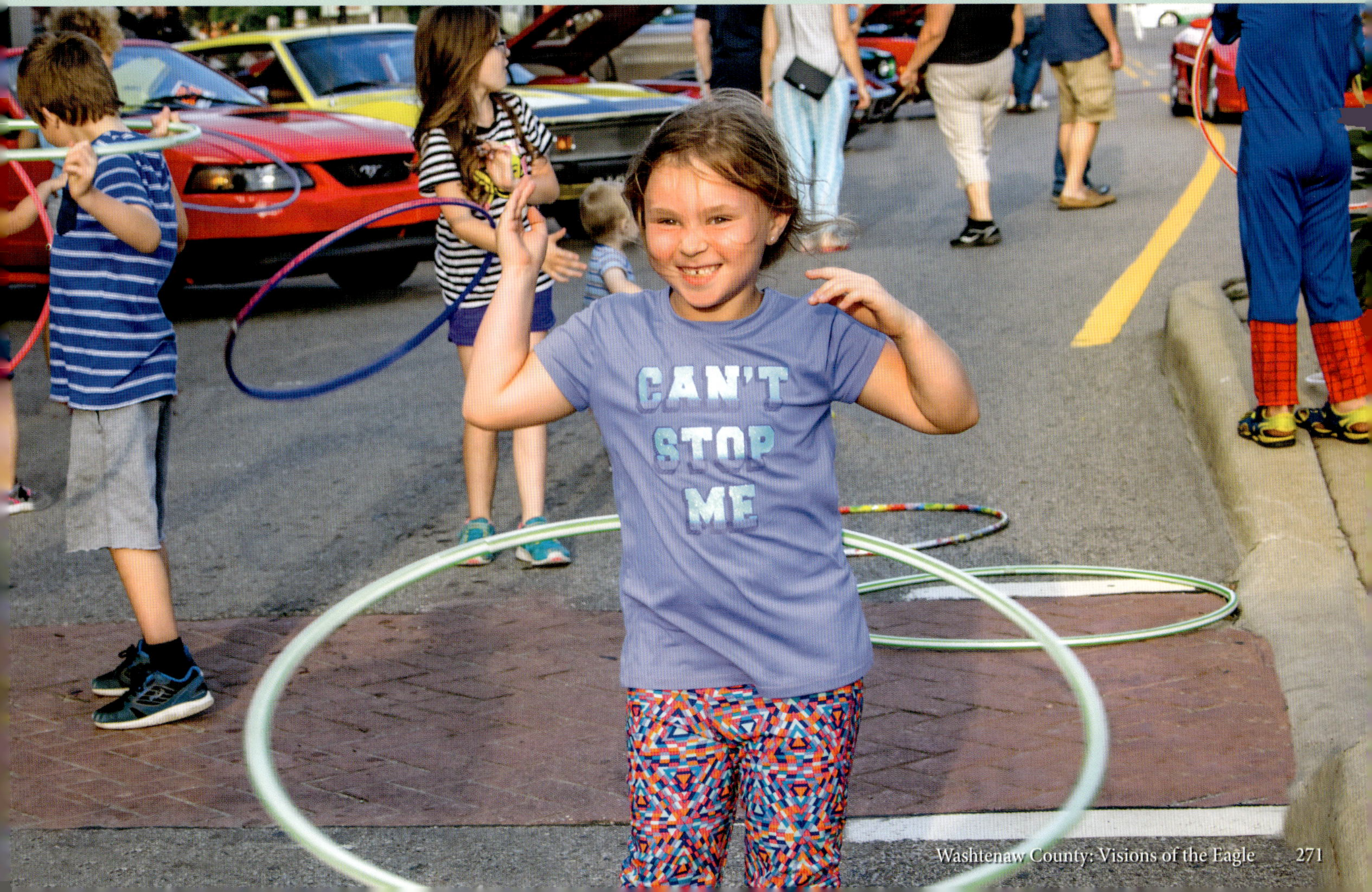

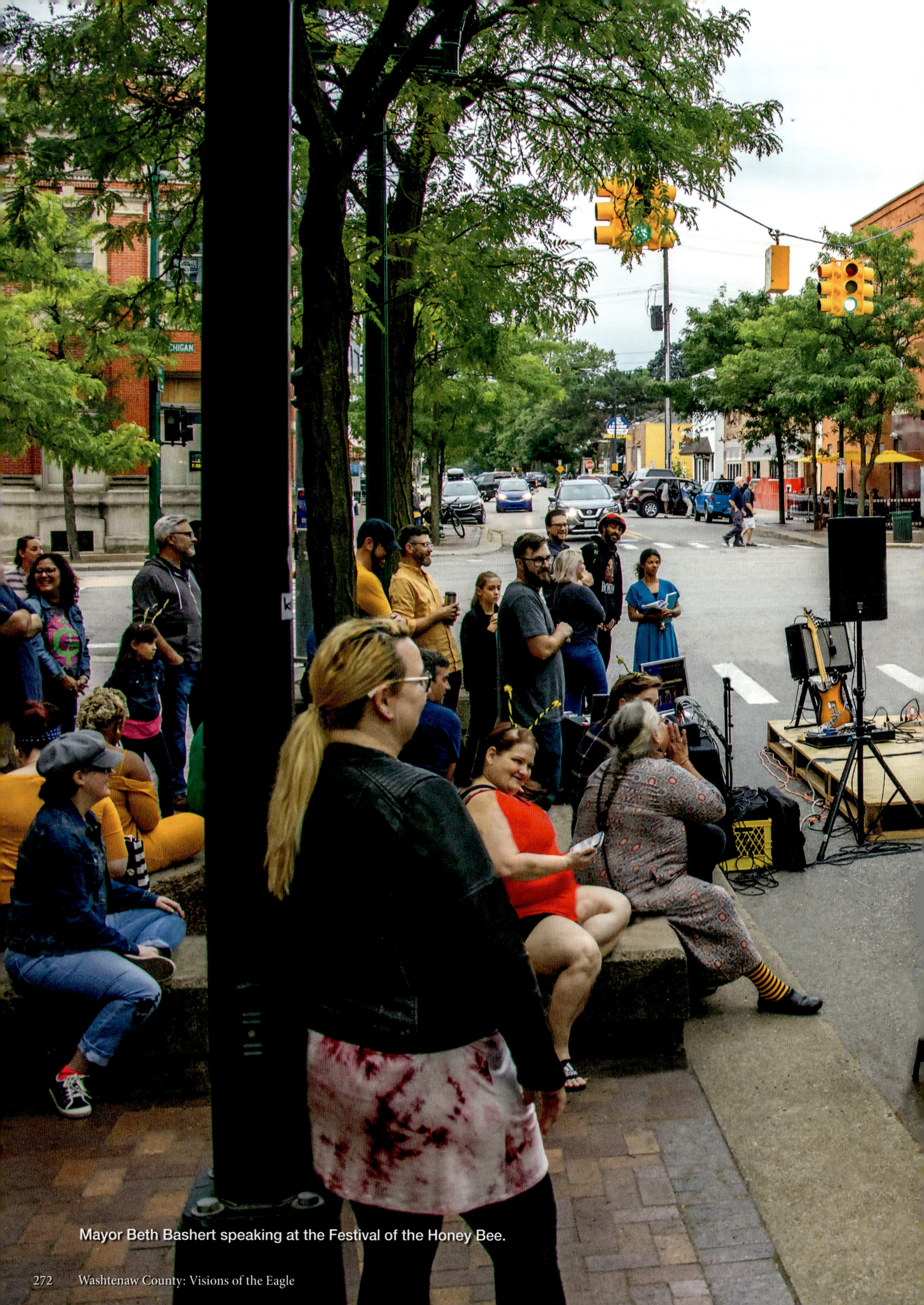

Mayor Beth Bashert speaking at the Festival of the Honey Bee.

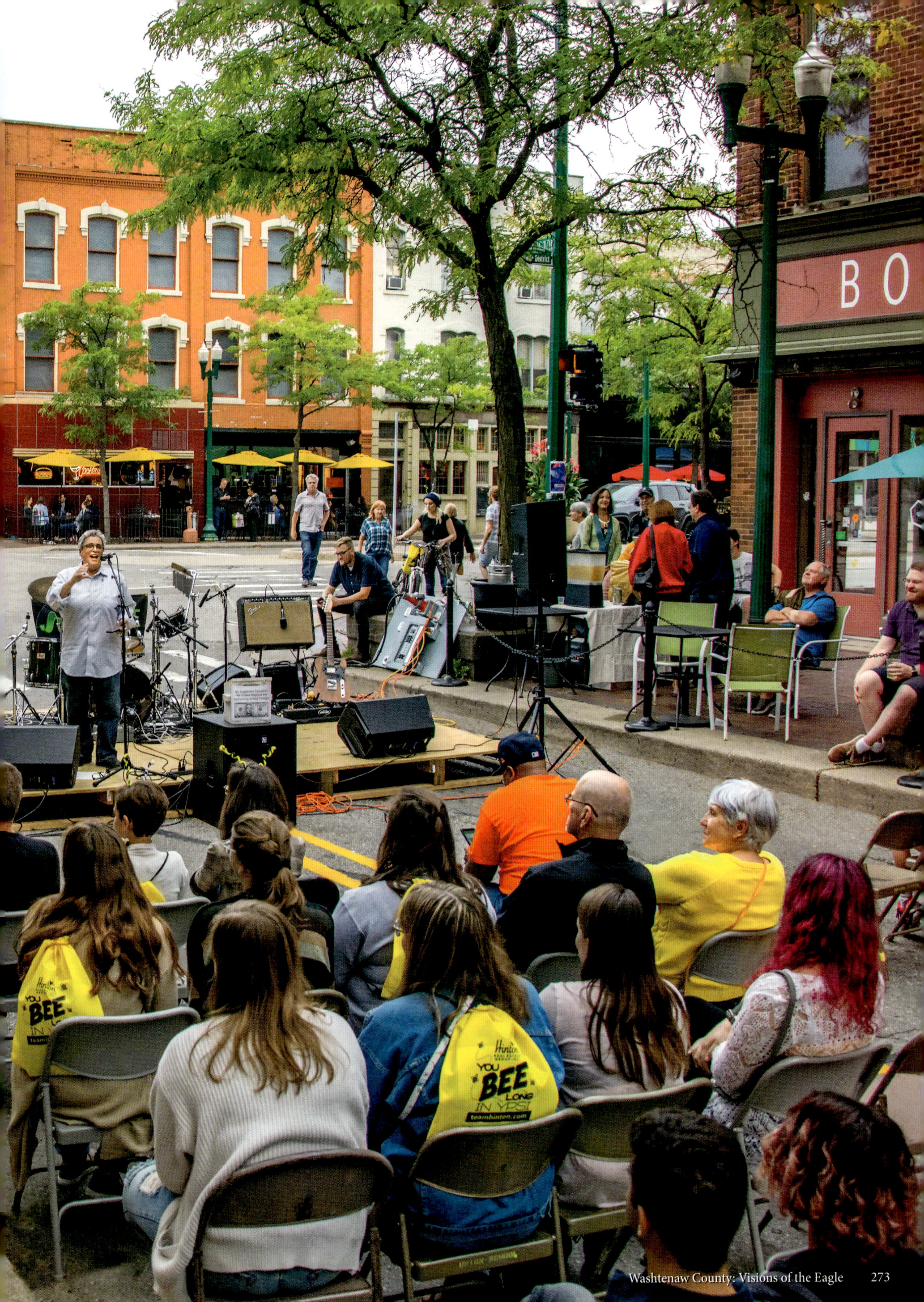
BO
Hinton
YOU BEE LONG IN YPSI
teamhinton.com

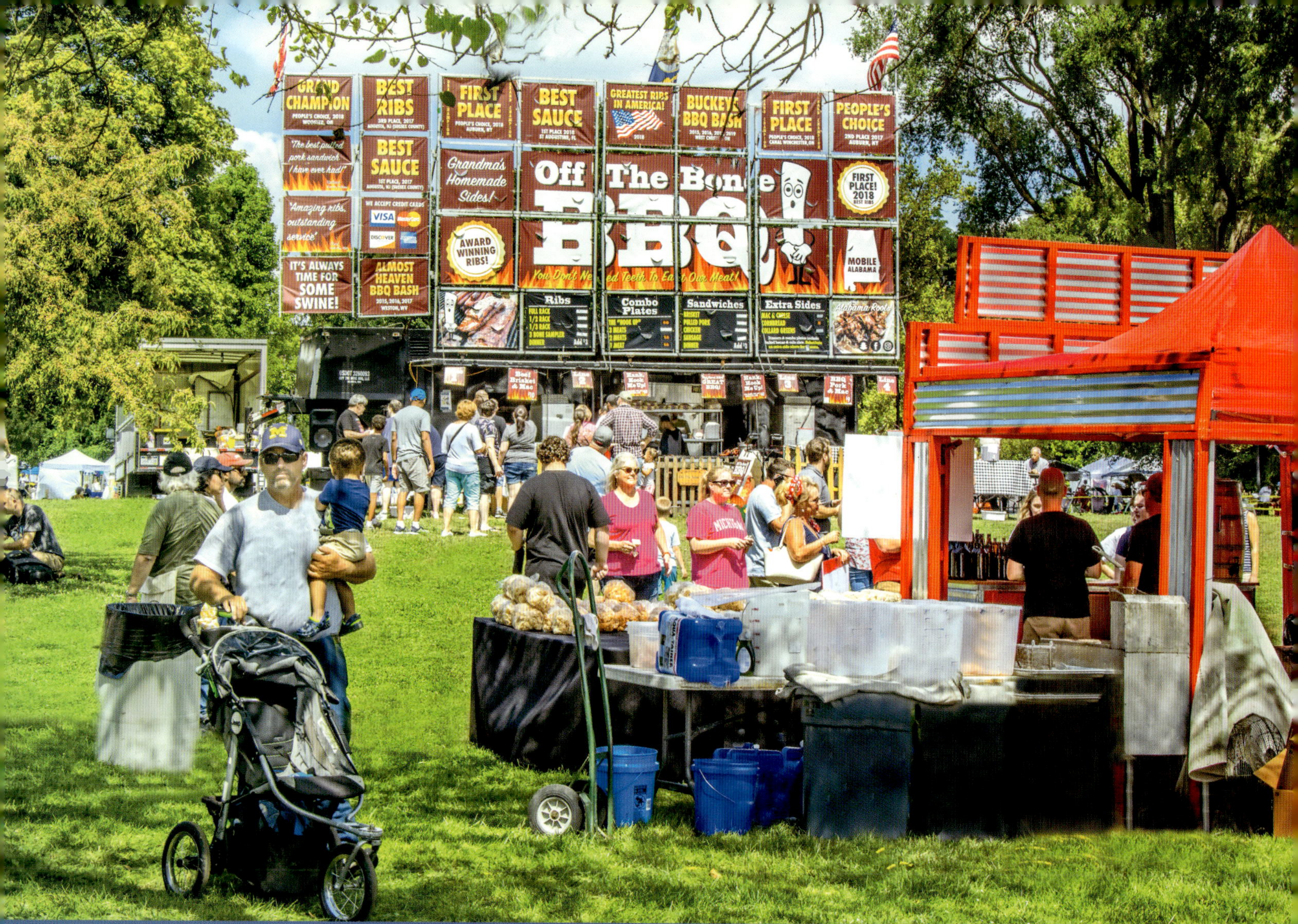

Ypsi BBQ Fest included prizes for Director's choice, Co-directors choice, and People's choice, at Riverside Park.

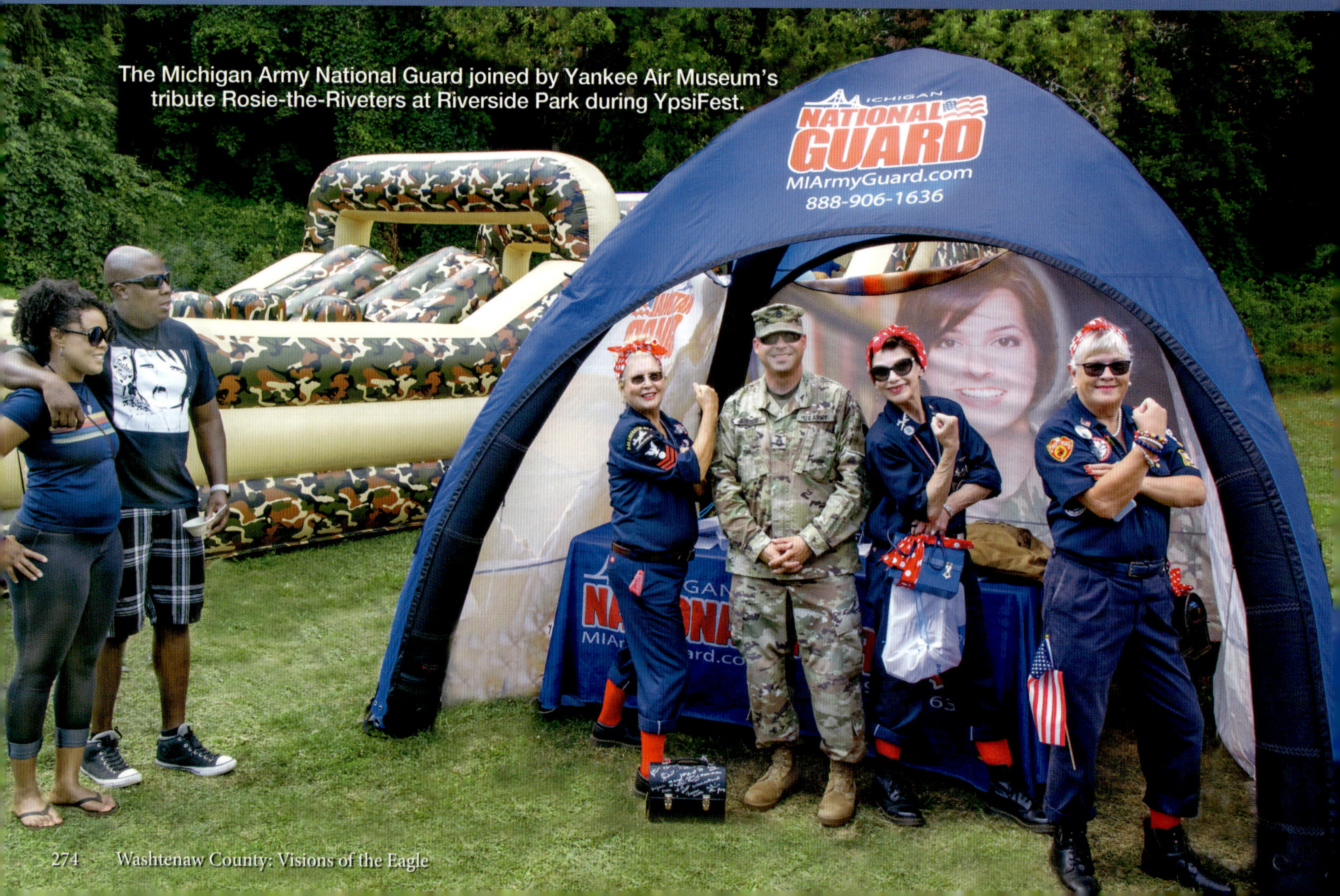

The Michigan Army National Guard joined by Yankee Air Museum's tribute Rosie-the-Riveters at Riverside Park during YpsiFest.

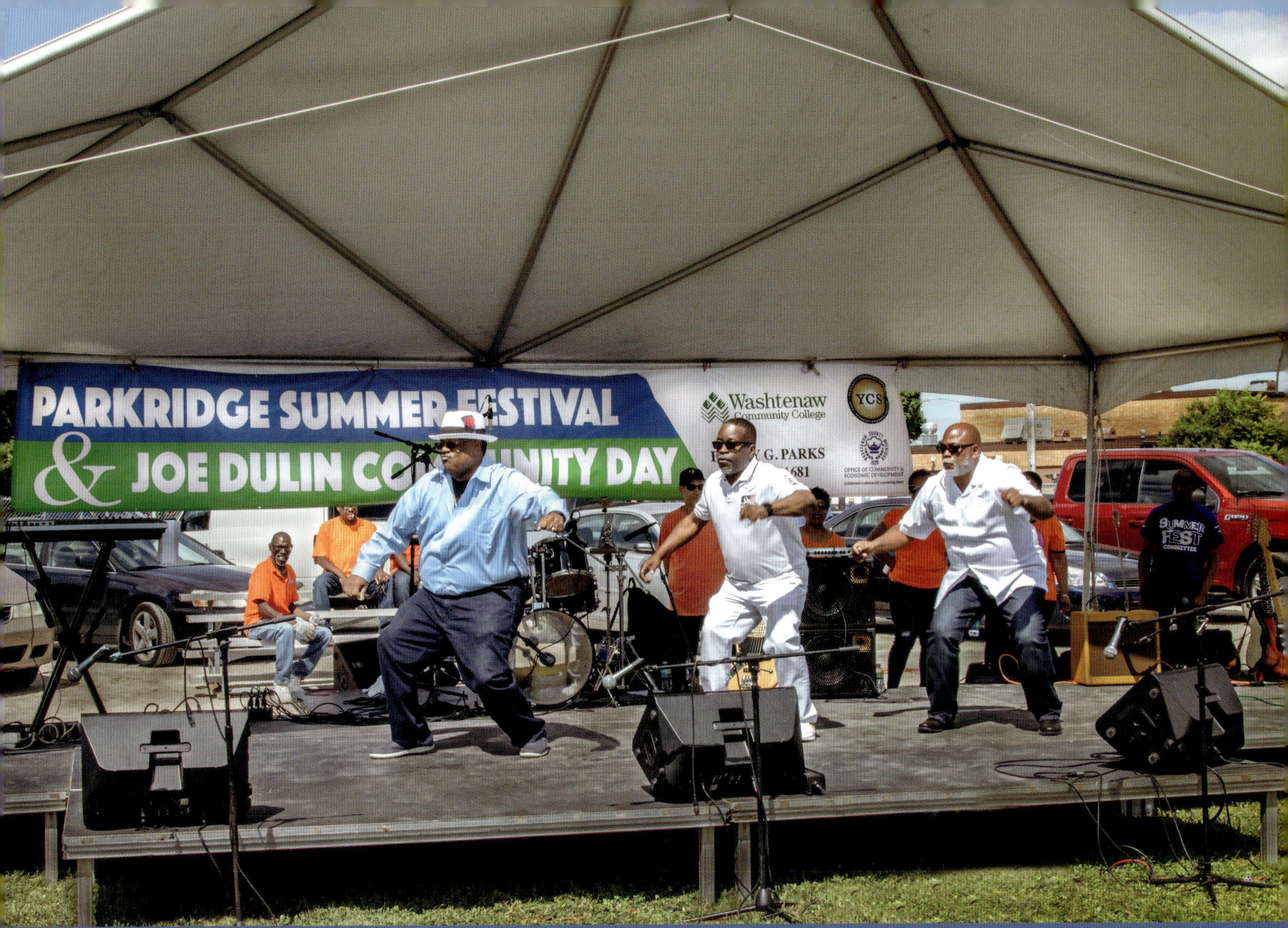

The Funkateers reunion at the Parkridge Summer Festival & Joe Dulin Community Day.

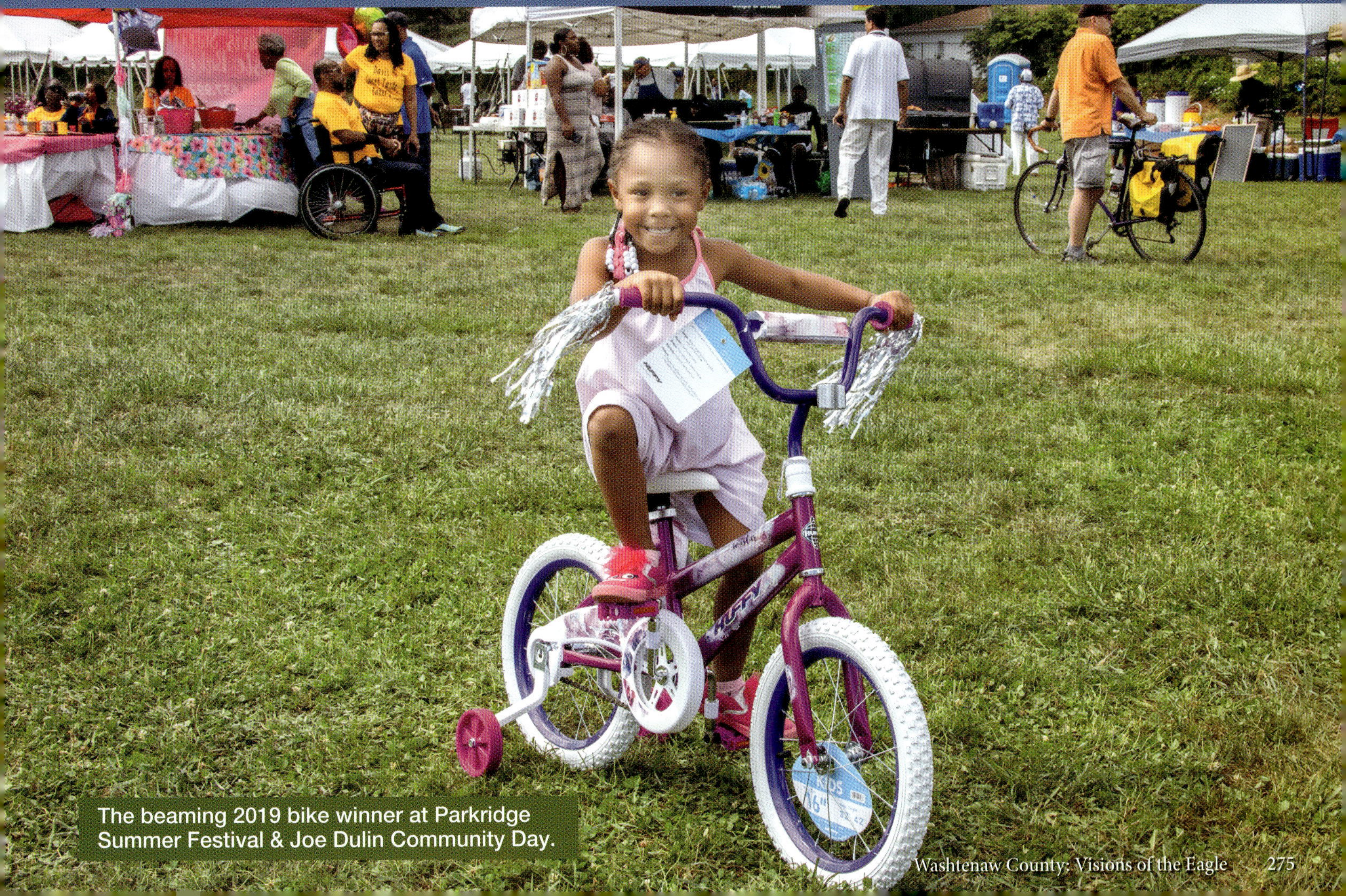

The beaming 2019 bike winner at Parkridge Summer Festival & Joe Dulin Community Day.

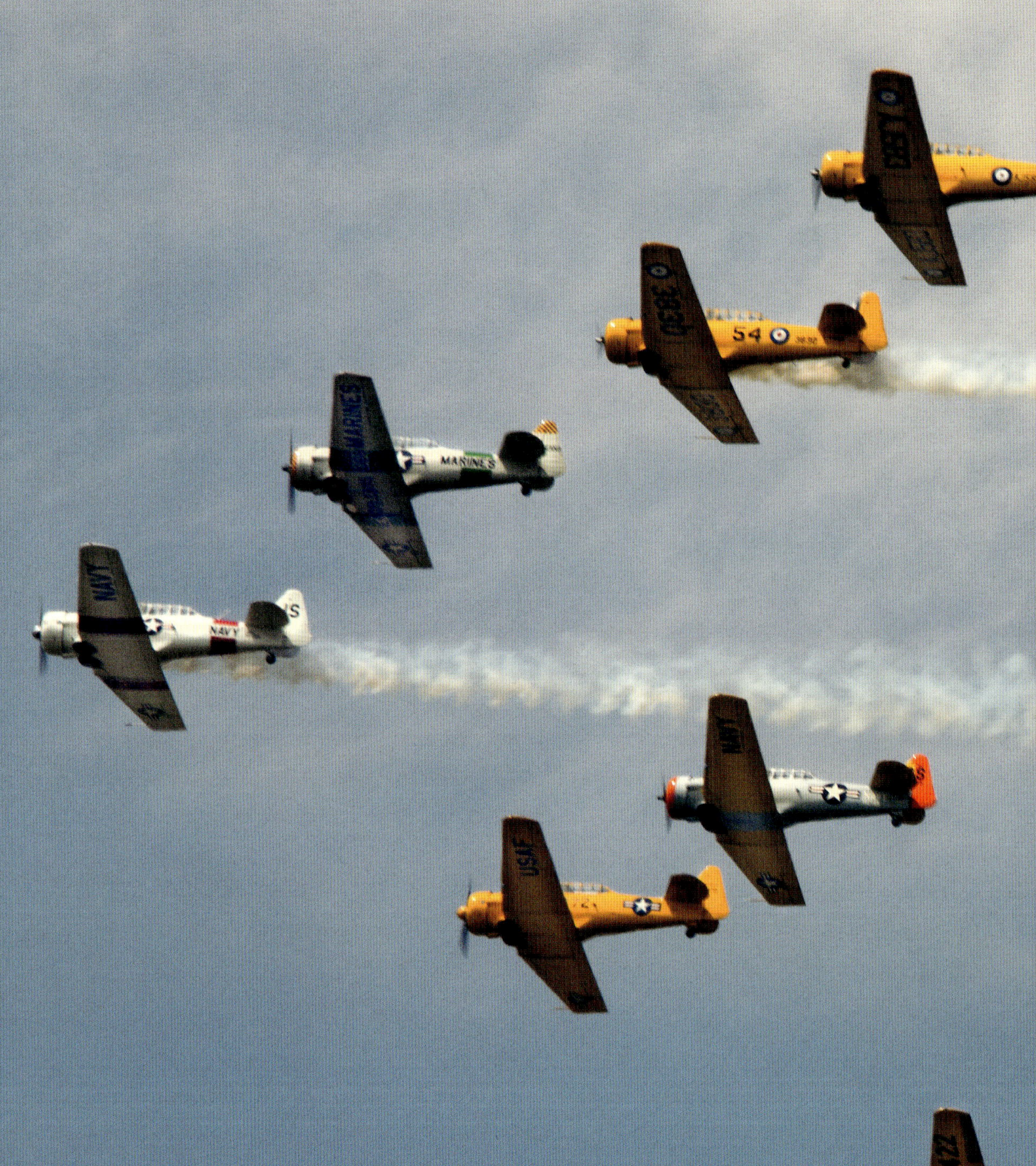

A-6 Texan trainer planes at Historic Willow Run Airport during Thunder Over Michigan Airshow.

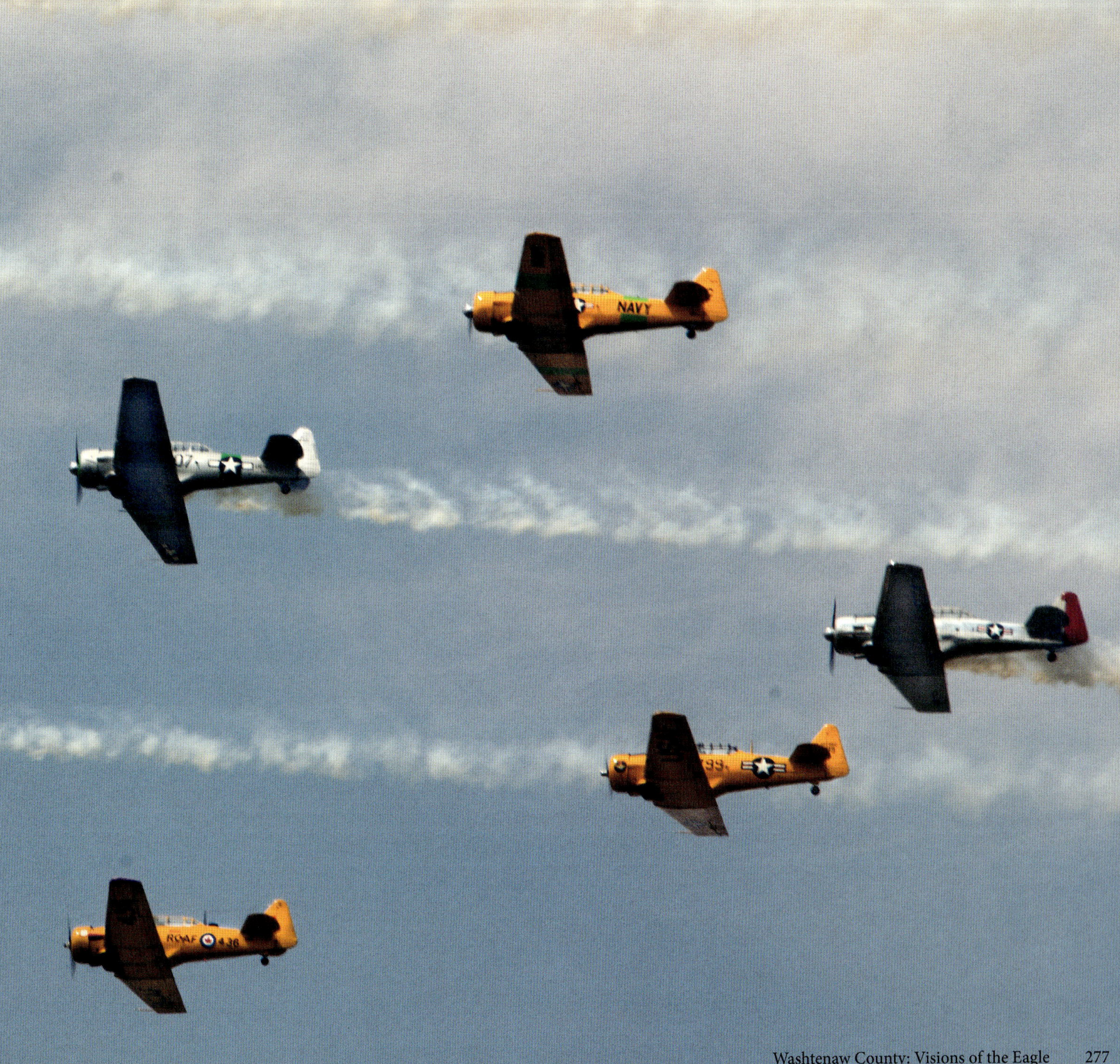
NAVY

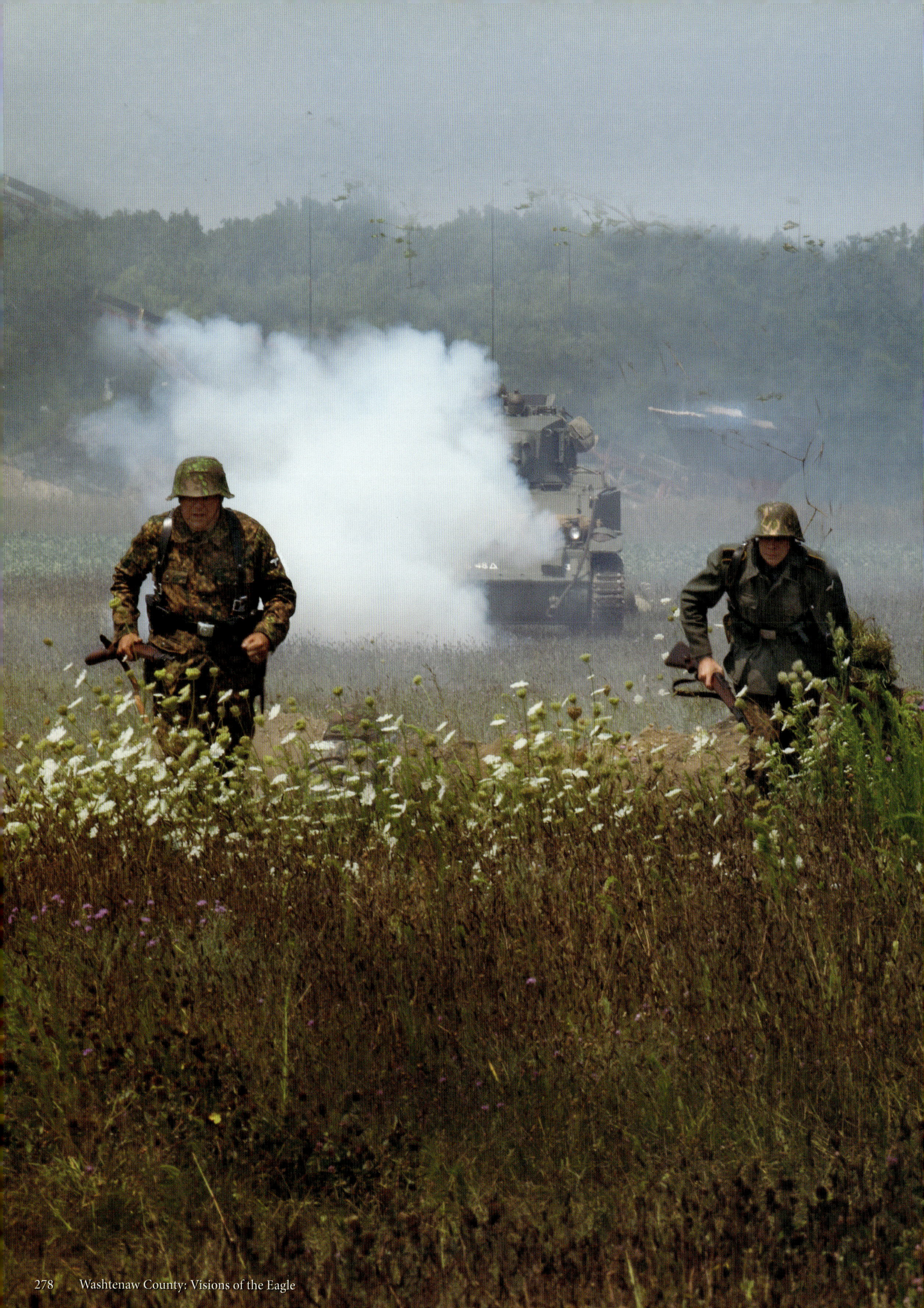

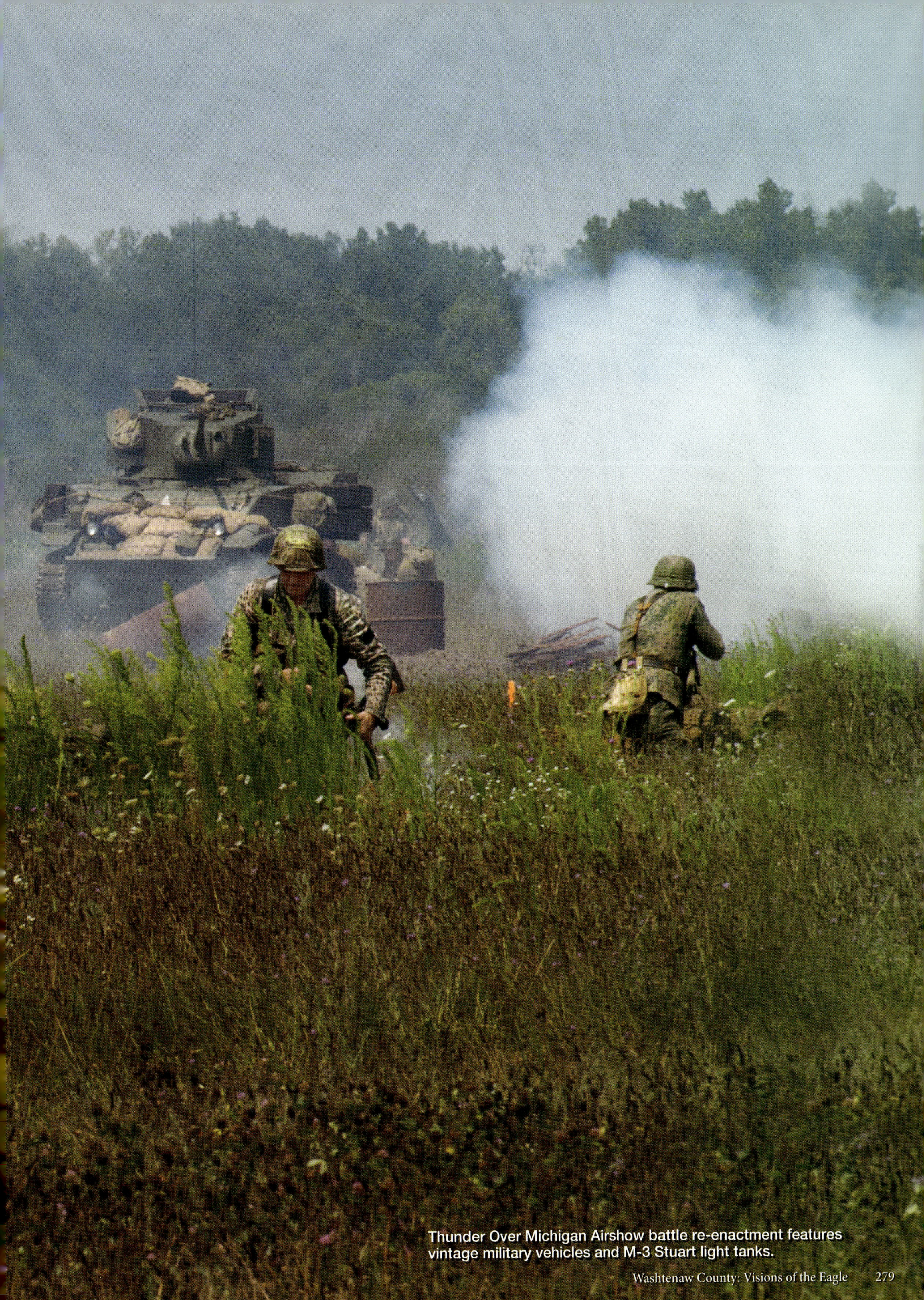

Thunder Over Michigan Airshow battle re-enactment features vintage military vehicles and M-3 Stuart light tanks.

Ypsilanti Charter Township

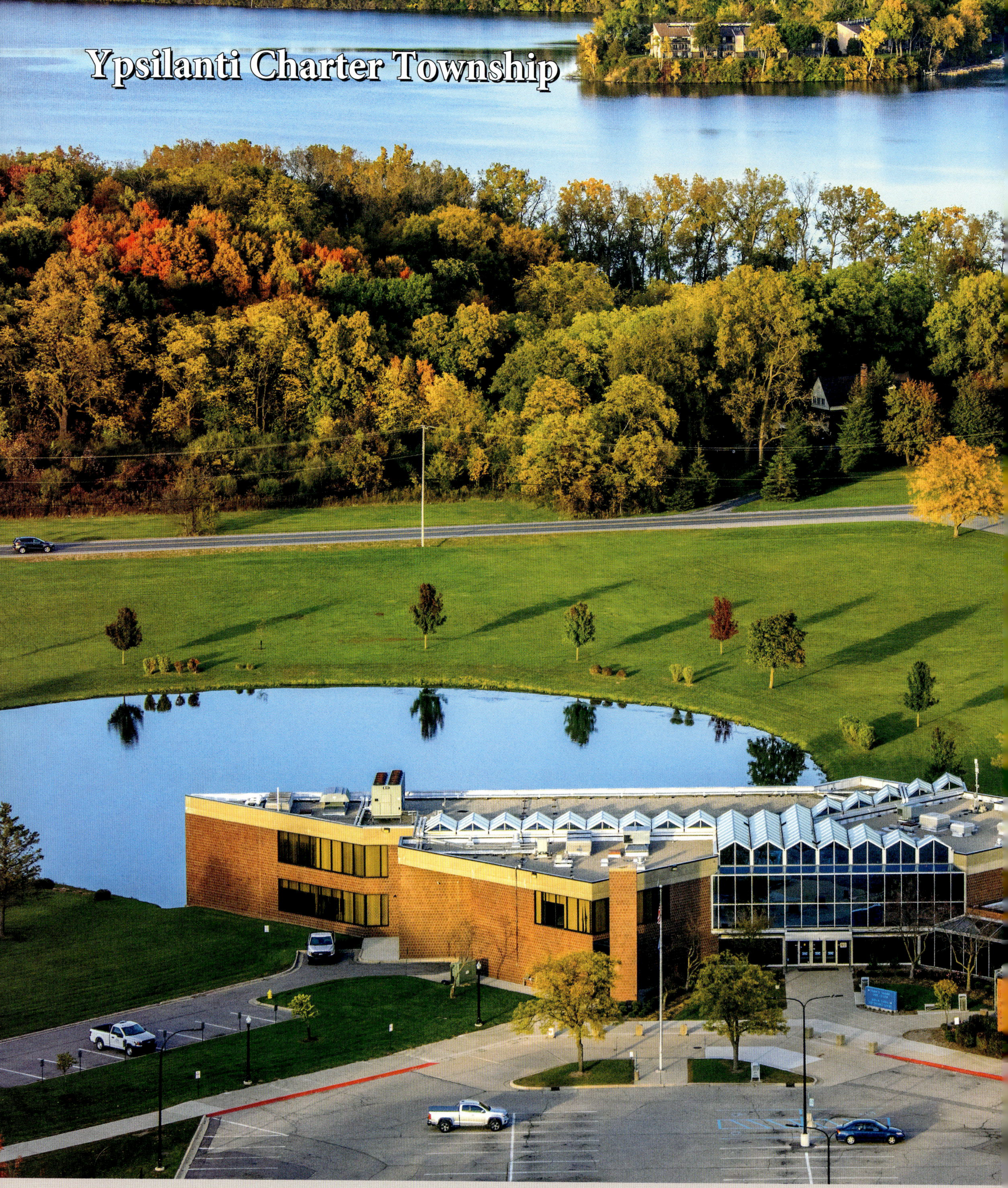

Located on the eastern edge of Washtenaw County just east of Ann Arbor, Ypsilanti Township is the largest township in Washtenaw County and the seventh largest in the State of Michigan. Fondly referred to as YTown, it is home to more than 55,000 residents.

Ypsilanti Township covers 32 square miles and is only a short drive from Detroit Metro Airport. Its proximity to I-94, US-23, Willow Run Airport, and Detroit Metropolitan Airport combined with the serenity of recreational areas, Ford Lake, and a diverse selection of residential neighborhoods make the township attractive to residents and employers. Blending the vibrant and bustling downtown of Ann Arbor with their great arts and culture and the historical treasures of the City of Ypsilanti, YTown enjoys the benefits of both.

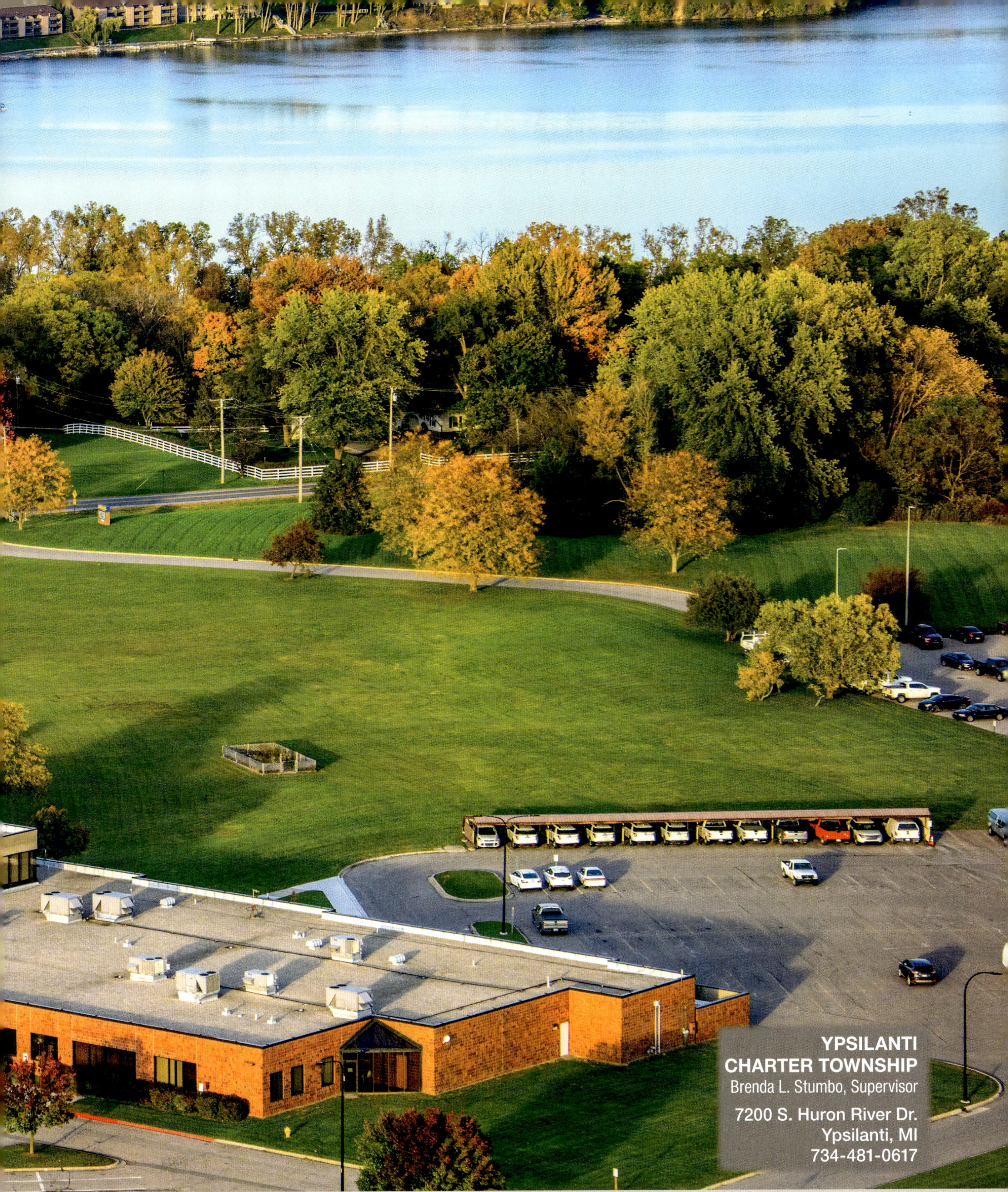

YPSILANTI CHARTER TOWNSHIP
Brenda L. Stumbo, Supervisor

7200 S. Huron River Dr.
Ypsilanti, MI
734-481-0617

Ypsilanti Township was chartered in 1974 and was originally a farming community. The area still bears the influences of Henry Ford, who created Ford Lake to harness hydropower for the automotive industry.

The Ford Motor Company built a manufacturing complex at Willow Run to produce aircraft, especially the B-24 Liberator, during World War II. Half of the B-24 planes used in the war came from Willow Run. Today, the Yankee Air Museum keeps that legacy alive.

Ford drew people from across the nation with his pledge of equal opportunity regardless of race or gender. His innovative and progressive ideas imbue the fiber of the community today.

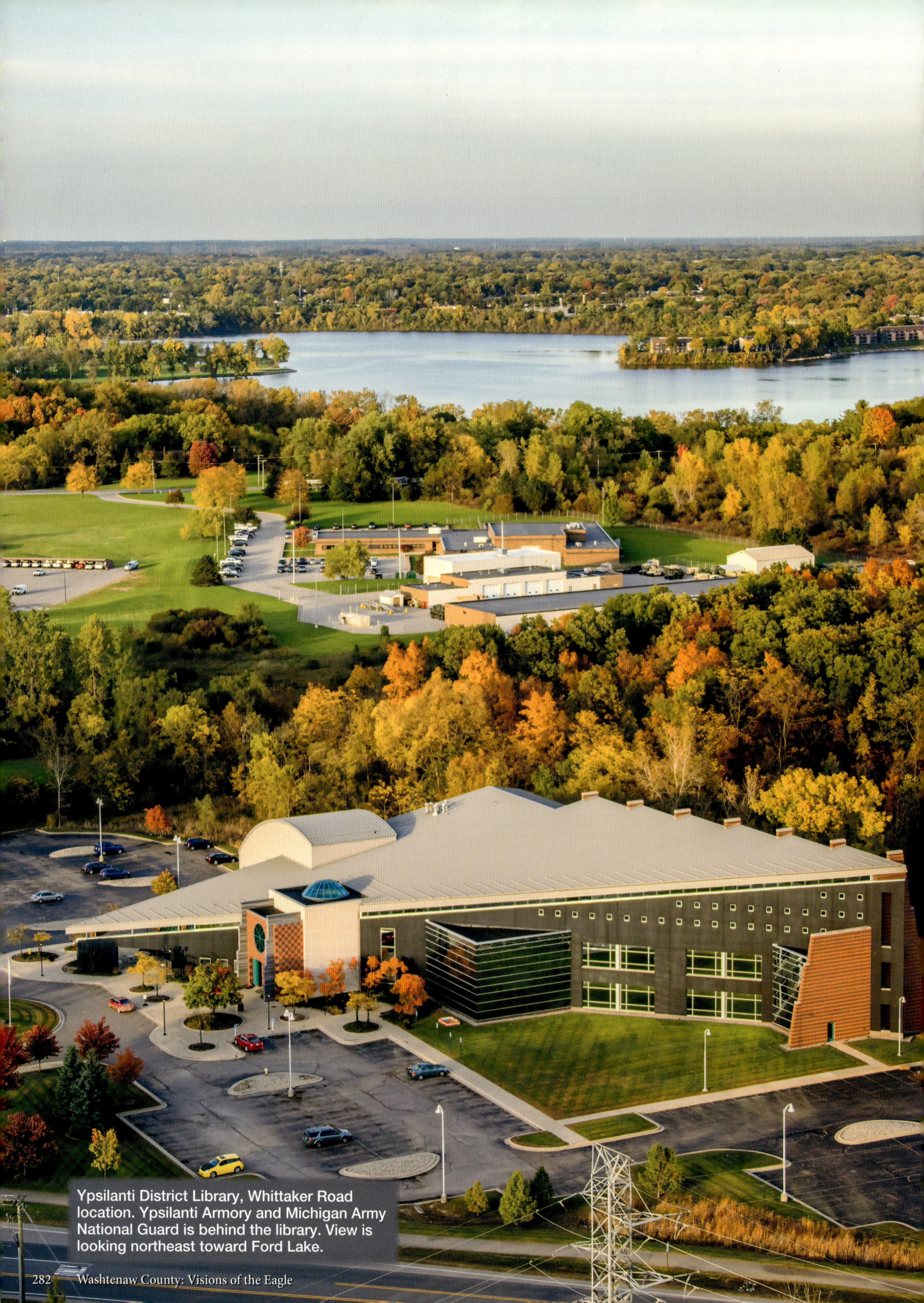

Ypsilanti District Library, Whittaker Road location. Ypsilanti Armory and Michigan Army National Guard is behind the library. View is looking northeast toward Ford Lake.

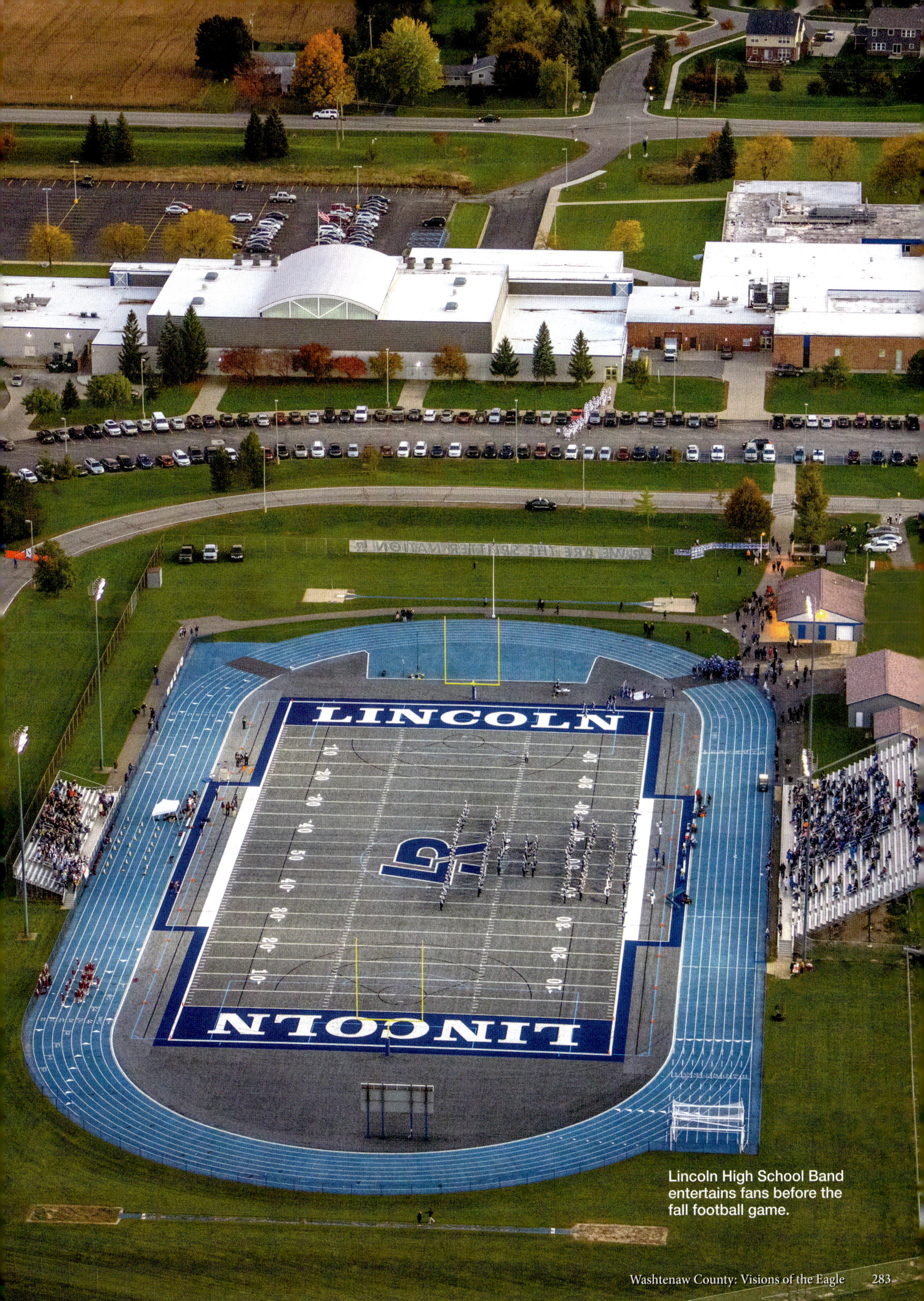

Lincoln High School Band entertains fans before the fall football game.

Lincoln Consolidated Schools

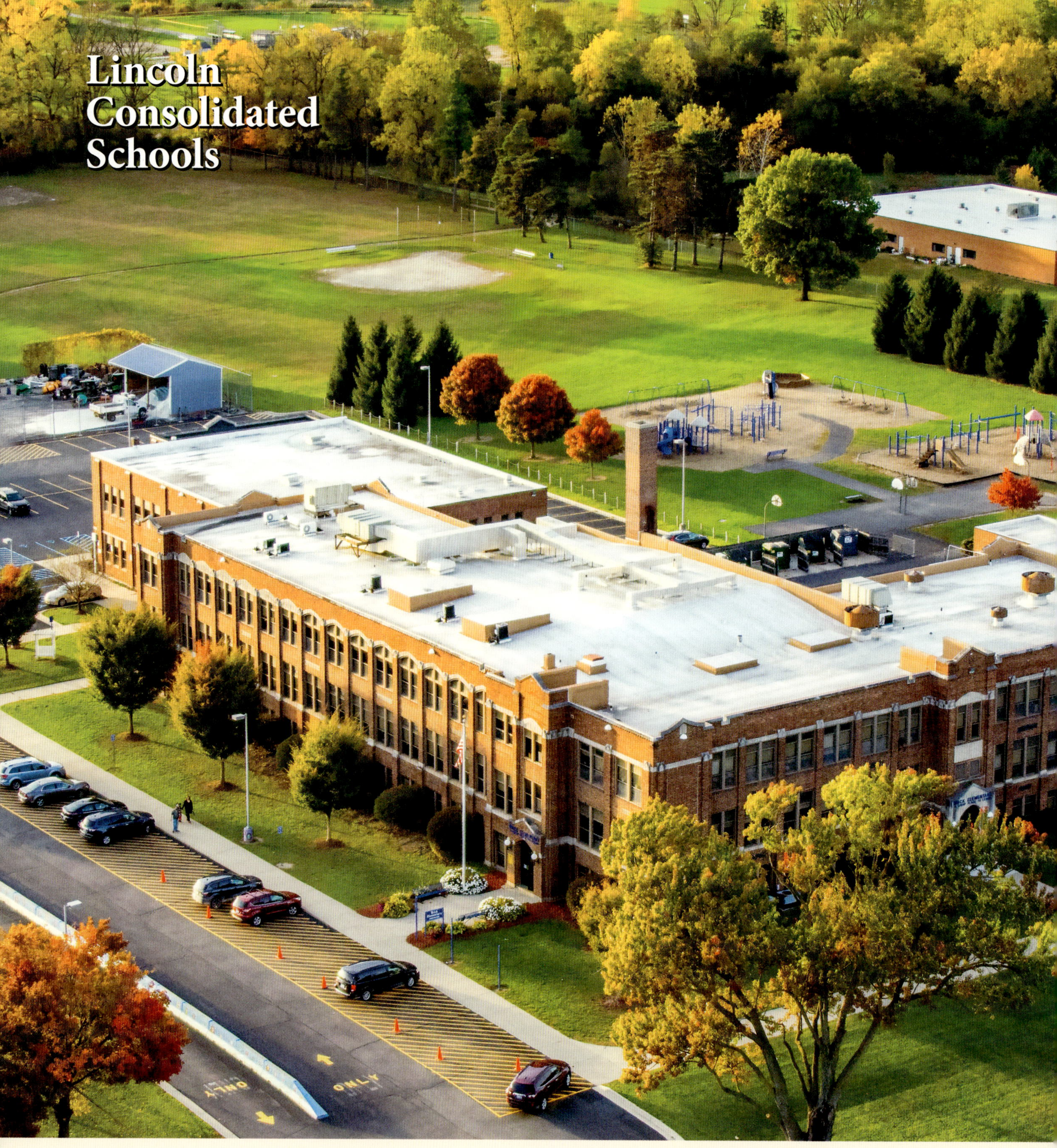

In 1924, Lincoln Consolidated Schools opened its doors to 500 students, combining 13 one-room schoolhouses into the first multi-township school in Michigan. Lincoln was the earliest rural consolidated school in the country to be affiliated with a teacher training college, Michigan Normal College, now Eastern Michigan University.

Today, Lincoln Consolidated Schools encompasses four elementary schools to suit each child's needs. Lincoln Early Childhood Center at Model Elementary provides children from birth to five the best educational start in life.

Bishop Elementary offers a multi-age learning environment where students of different ages share classrooms that are divided by grade level. Bishop is home to Lincoln's Spanish Immersion program, unique in Washtenaw County, in which students use an identical curriculum but in Spanish, providing the opportunity to be fluent in two languages.

Brick Elementary is a Washtenaw County Historic Landmark, and once housed Lincoln's entire student body. Today, Brick elementary students focus on Science, Technology, Engineering, and Math (STEM) curriculum.

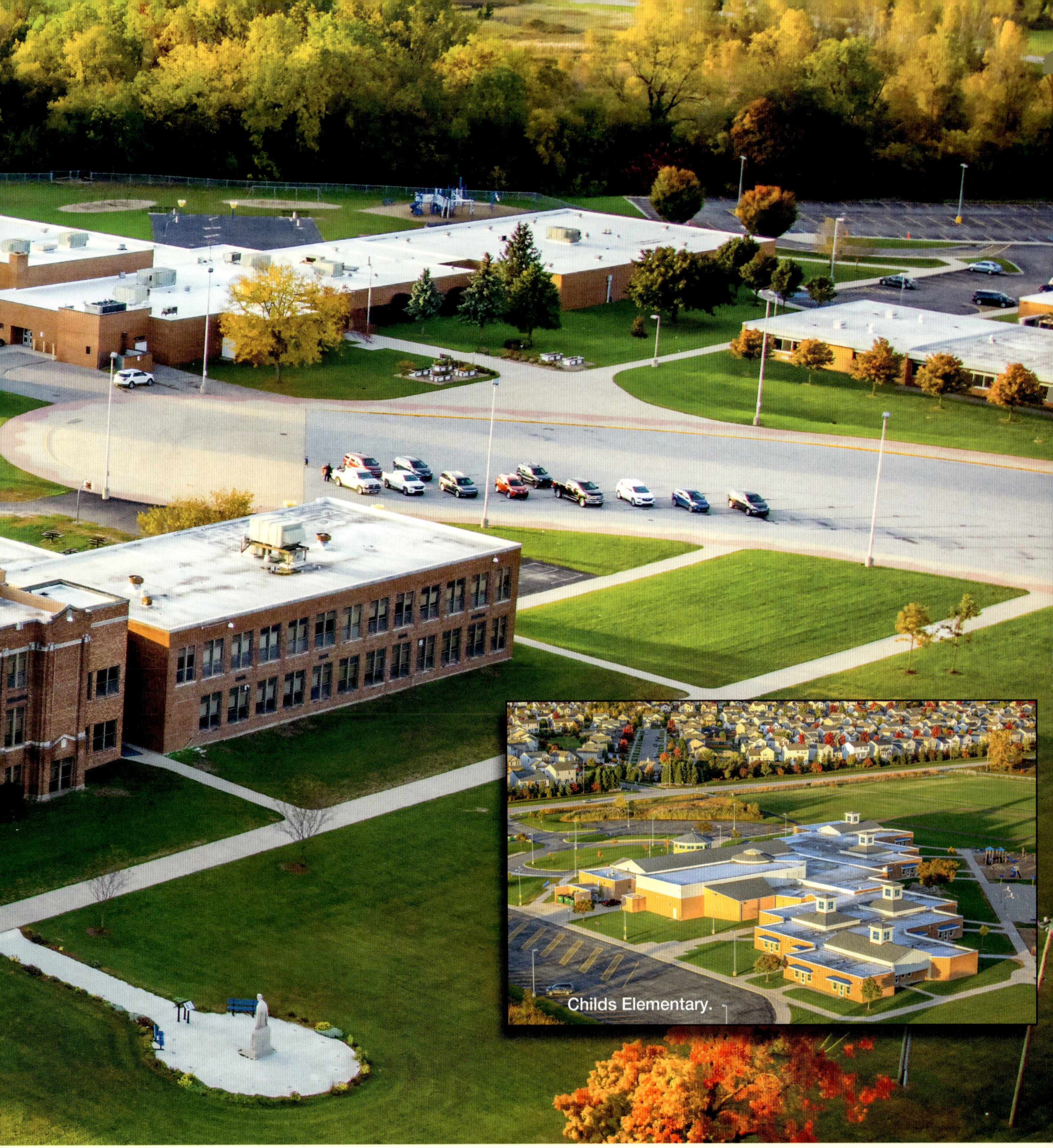
Childs Elementary.

Childs Elementary follows a community-inclusive approach with a collaborative teaching style, active parent organization, and even building design to foster its goals.

Lincoln Middle School ensures student success through teaching done in small, grade-level teams, with close attention to social and emotional development as well.

The academically rigorous Lincoln High School offers AP, Dual Enrollment, Career Teach, Early College, and International Baccalaureate opportunities, allowing each student to achieve their goals.

Steeped in history and tradition, Lincoln Consolidated Schools is the community center with strong community education and active senior citizen programs, promoting lifelong learning and preparing students to be high achieving, compassionate, and inspired to make a difference.

LINCOLN CONSOLIDATED SCHOOLS

7425 Willis Rd.
Ypsilanti, MI
734-484-7000

Lincoln High School sophomore, 2019 Gatorade Player of the Year and 2-time ESPN ranked #1 high school basketball player regardless of class, Emoni Bates (#21), drives the ball past his opponent with help from his teammate, DeCorion Temple (#15). During his record-breaking freshman season, Bates led the Splitter Nation men's basketball program to the district's first Division 1 State Championship. The 2019 State Championship was also the first state championship, in any sport, in school history.

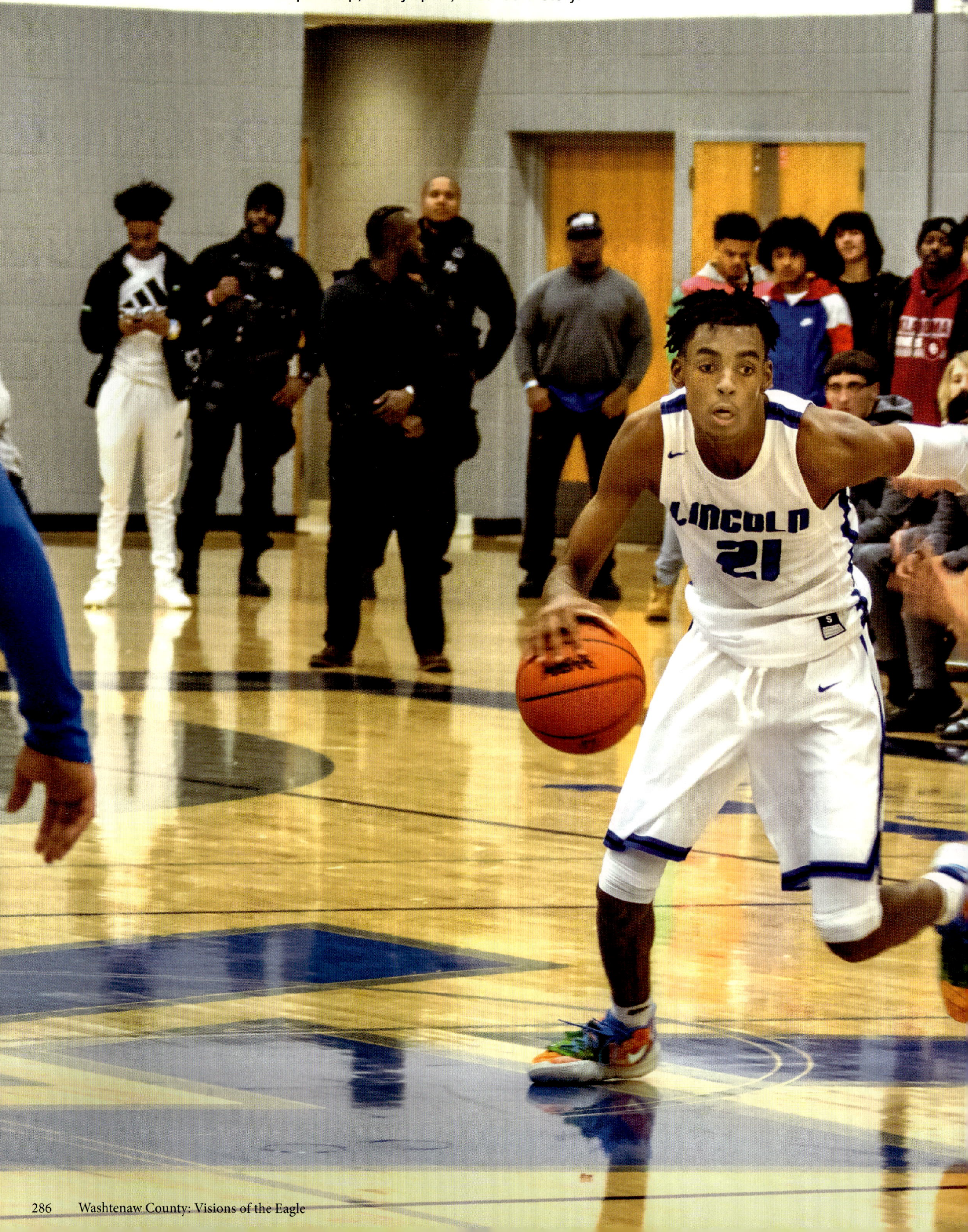

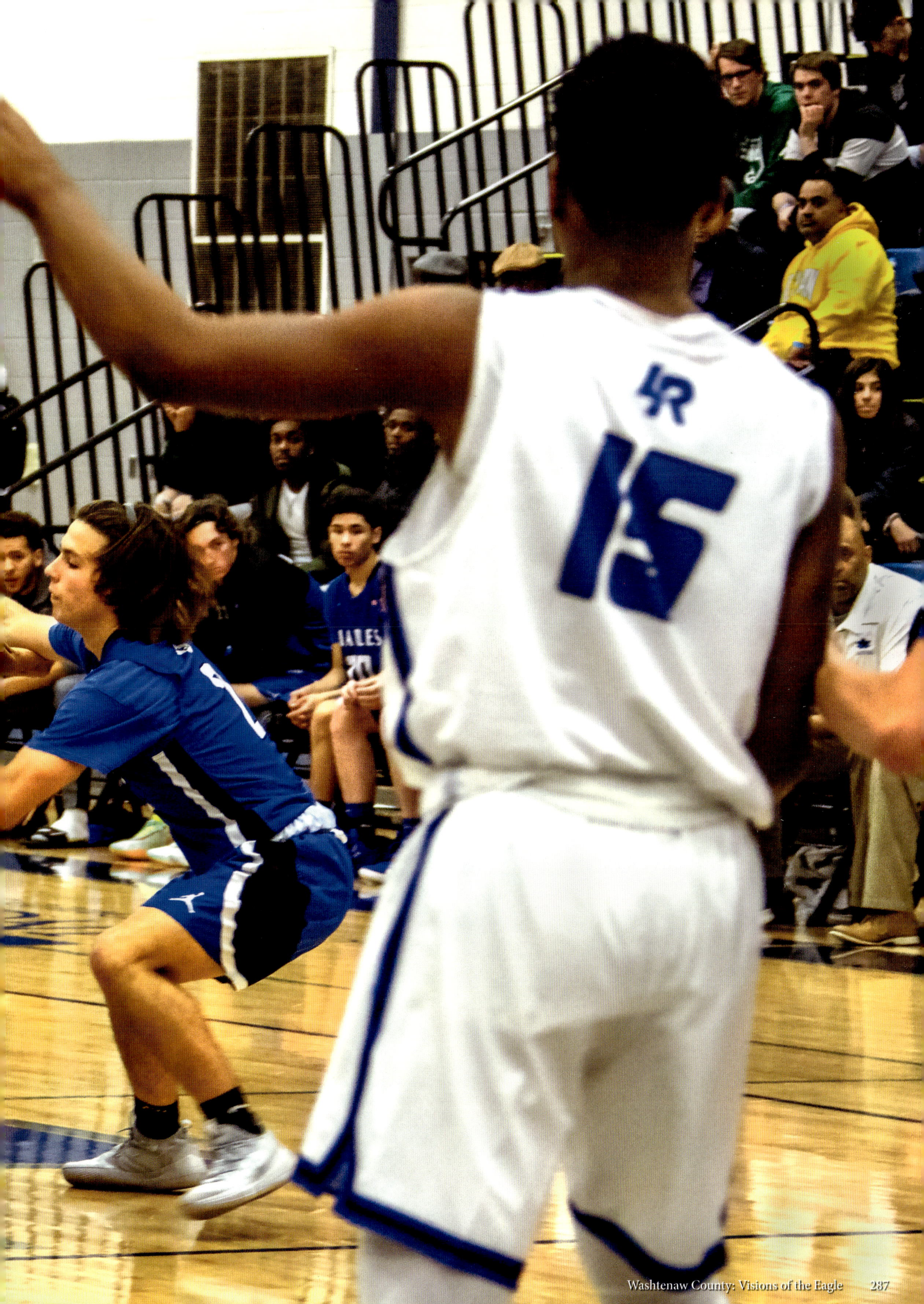
LR
15

Washtenaw County: Visions of the Eagle Sponsors

Thank you to these sponsors, without whom, this book would not have been possible.

Alro Steel
3100 E. High St.
Jackson, MI 49204
517-787-5500
www.alro.com

Ann Arbor/Ypsilanti Regional Chamber
2010 Hogback Rd., Suite 4
Ann Arbor, MI 48105
734-665-4433
www.a2ychamber.org

Bethlehem United Church of Christ
423 South 4th Ave.
Ann Arbor, MI 48104
734-665-6149
www.bethlehe-ucc.org

The Bouma Group Realtors
564 S. Main St., Suite 100
Ann Arbor, MI 48104
734-761-3060
www.bouma.com

Bricklayers & Allied Craftworkers Local 2, Michigan
21031 Ryan Rd.
Warren, MI 48091
586-754-0888
www.bricklayers.org

Chelsea Milling Company
201 W. North St., P.O. Box 460
Chelsea, MI 48118
734-475-1361
www.jiffymix.com

Chelsea State Bank
1010 S. Main St.
Chelsea, MI 48118
734-475-1355
www.chelseastate.bank

Dale Fisher Galleries
1916 Norvell Rd.
Grass Lake, MI 49240
517-522-3505
www.dalefishergalleries.com

Destination Ann Arbor
315 W. Huron St,. Suite 340
Ann Arbor, MI 48103
734-995-7281
www.annarbor.org

Dexter, City
8123 Main St., 2nd Floor
Dexter, MI 48130
734-426-8303
www.dextermi.gov

Emagine Saline
1335 E. Michigan Ave.
Saline, MI 48176
734-316-5500
www.emagine-entertainment.com

5 Healthy Towns Foundation
14800 E. Old U.S. Hwy. 12
Chelsea, MI 48118
734-433-4599
www.5healthytowns.org

Bene Fusilier
Dexter, MI

Guenther Building Co.
2864 Carpenter Rd., Suite 300
Ann Arbor, MI 48108
734-971-3323
www.guentherhomes.com

Hobbs+Black Architects
100 N State St.
Ann Arbor, MI 48104
734-663-4189
www.hobbs-black.com

IBEW
7920 Jackson Rd., Suite A
Ann Arbor, MI 48103
734-424-0978
www.ibew252.org

IHA
24 Frank Lloyd Wright Dr.
Lobby J2000
Ann Arbor, MI 48105
844.IHA.DOCS
IHAcares.com

IMRA America, Inc.
Headquarters and Manufacturing
1044 Woodridge Ave.
Ann Arbor, MI 48105
734-930-2560
www.irma.com

Lewis Jewelers
300 S. Maple Rd.
Ann Arbor, MI 48103
734-994-5111
www.lewisjewelers.com

Level One Bank
Formerly Ann Arbor State Bank
125 West William St.
Ann Arbor, MI 48104
734-761-1475
www.levelonebank.com

Lincoln Consolidated Schools
7425 Willis Rd.
Ypsilanti, MI 48197
734-484-7000
www.lincolnk12.org

The M Den
315 S. Main St.
Ann Arbor, MI 48104
734-761-1030
www.mden.com

Pittsfield Charter Township
6201 W. Michigan Ave.
Ann Arbor, MI 48108
734-822-3135
www.pittsfield-mi.gov

Pizza House
618 Church St.
Ann Arbor, MI 48104
734-995-5095
www.pizzahouse.com

Saline, City
100 N. Harris St.
Saline, MI 48176
734-429-4907
www.cityofsaline.org

The Sidetrack Bar & Grill
56 E. Cross St.
Ypsilanti, MI 48197
734-483-1035
www.sidetrackbarandgrill.com

Silver Maples of Chelsea Retirement Neighborhood
100 Silver Maples Dr.
Chelsea, MI 48118
734-475-4111
www.silvermaples.org

St. Joseph Mercy Ann Arbor
5301 E. Huron River Dr.
Ann Arbor, MI 48106
800-676-0437
www.stjoeshealth.org

St. Joseph Mercy Chelsea
775 South Main St.
Chelsea, MI 48118
734-593-6000
www.stjoeshealth.org

UA Local 190-Plumbers, Pipefitters, Gas Distribution & HVAC
7920 Jackson Rd., Suite B
Ann Arbor MI, 48103
734-424-0962
www.ua190.org

Varsity Ford
3480 Jackson Rd.
Ann Arbor, MI 48103
734-996-2300
www.varsityford.com

Washtenaw Community College
4800 E. Huron River Dr.
Ann Arbor, MI 48105
734-973-3300
www.wccnet.edu

WISD- Washtenaw Intermediate School District
1819 S. Wagner Rd., P.O. Box 1406
Ann Arbor, MI 48106-1406
(734) 994-8100
www.washtenawisd.org

Ypsilanti, City
One S. Huron St.
Ypsilanti, MI 48197
734-483-1100
www.cityofypsilanti.com

Ypsilanti Charter Township
7200 S. Huron River Dr.
Ypsilanti, MI 48197
734-481-0617
www.ytown.org

Zion Lutheran Church
1501 West Liberty St.
Ann Arbor, MI 48103
734-994-4455
www.zlc-aa.org